# The Genetic and Basis for Differences in Form and Behavior

As elucidated by studies of contrasted pure-line dog breeds and their hybrids

Charles R. Stockard

Alpha Editions

This edition published in 2020

ISBN : 9789354014475

Design and Setting By
**Alpha Editions**
email - alphaedis@gmail.com

As per information held with us this book is in Public Domain. This book is a reproduction of an important historical work. Alpha Editions uses the best technology to reproduce historical work in the same manner it was first published to preserve its original nature. Any marks or number seen are left intentionally to preserve its true form.

THE AMERICAN ANATOMICAL MEMOIRS
NUMBER 19

# THE GENETIC AND ENDOCRINIC BASIS FOR DIFFERENCES IN FORM AND BEHAVIOR

AS ELUCIDATED BY STUDIES OF CONTRASTED
PURE LINE DOG BREEDS AND THEIR HYBRIDS

*by*

CHARLES R. STOCKARD

and

collaborators

WITH SPECIAL CONTRIBUTIONS ON BEHAVIOR

*by*

O. D. ANDERSON AND W. T. JAMES

DEPARTMENT OF ANATOMY, CORNELL UNIVERSITY MEDICAL COLLEGE,
NEW YORK, N. Y.

One hundred twenty-eight text figures, one hundred thirteen plates,
and frontispiece

*Published by*
THE WISTAR INSTITUTE OF ANATOMY AND BIOLOGY
PHILADELPHIA      OCTOBER 1941

## FOREWORD

It is not often that a man's calling is both his vocation and his avocation; not often that the interests and inclinations of his youth, much as he may want them to, are permitted to shape and determine his career. More often than not, those youthful enthusiasms turn out to be nothing more than passing fancies or end in wishful thinking. Charles Rupert Stockard was the exception. Nor was this due to chance or circumstances, for if circumstances make the man — then Doctor Stockard was determined to make his circumstances, and determined to fashion them to his purpose. Beginning with his boyhood interests, it was apparent that his enthusiasm was along zoological and biological lines; this with his love of nature and all living creatures, and his natural curiosity marked him as destined to be a scientist in the field of research and experimentation.

The spirit that animated his teaching, the philosophy that guided him in his relations with students, graduate students and colleagues, and influenced his attitude toward his profession is best illustrated by Doctor Stockard's own words, quoted from a lecture given at the dedication of the Theobald Smith Laboratory at the Albany Medical College in 1937. He believed that a laboratory should be "invaded by that shy and intangible spirit which inspires enthusiasm and creates devotion to research, a free dwelling for students of nature conscious of and charitable to the faults and virtues of all that surround them."

Doctor Stockard was a true lover of animals. Anyone who visited the Cornell Dog Farm at Shrub Oak must have been impressed with the fondness of the Doctor for his animals and their affection for him. He kept them in the best of health and their living quarters and conditions were far better than those of thousands of pet household dogs we see daily in our cities. In response to my sending him a copy of "Jock of the Bushveld" during his last illness he wrote: "I have read it and it just hits my 'tender' spot. If this book appeals so strongly to you, then your heart and mine are tuned with the same strings. The style it is written in is wonderful and one must have come from the woodlands to appreciate it fully!"

Just as the doctor must work with human material dead and alive to gain knowledge for the better understanding of man in health and disease, so also he realized that man must work with animals dead and alive to understand better the processes which are in control of man and animals in health and in the fight against disease. Both groups benefitted from his researches. In all his work with animals, and I may add with men, he treated them with kindness and consideration.

The most cursory glance at Doctor Stockard's career reveals two striking characteristics: the magnitude of his successes and the extended front along which they were achieved, the conquest of any one of which might be the life ambition of a less skilled, less daring explorer in research. Doctor Stockard possessed a charm of manner which was at once compelling and contagious. He did not need to make claims for himself; he won high honors because he was a man of ability who had succeeded.

It is regrettable indeed that Doctor Stockard could not have lived to complete his work. The manuscript presented is as he left it -- unfinished.

WILLIAM SARGENT LADD<br>For the Committee

When Doctor Stockard conceived the idea of using the dog to test experimentally his views on the endocrine basis of constitution, he was not fully aware of the difficulties and vastness of the undertaking. In order to avoid loss of valuable time until proper arrangements for experimental work could be made, he began collecting material from seemingly pure-bred dogs of various breeds destroyed at the city pound. However, it was soon obvious to him that most of the animals thus obtained were either diseased or too old to be of value for histological studies on the endocrines.

The experimental study of the problem was made possible through the generosity of the Rockefeller Foundation. In 1926 a farm was purchased at Shrub Oak, near Peekskill, N. Y., and pure-bred dogs were obtained. However, unforeseen difficulties began to arise. Parasitic infections, distemper and unsuspected dietary deficiencies interfered with the experiment from the beginning. It was necessary first to overcome these difficulties, a task that took several years and during which Doctor Stockard freely applied the trial and error method in view of the scarcity of data on the subject. This explains to some extent the slowness with which the scientific data began to accumulate, and the consequent delay in writing up the results of the experiment. Moreover, it was found that certain characteristics supposedly dependent on the endocrine constitution of the breeds employed were actually inherited in a Mendelian fashion, a situation that required further breeding experiments in order to ascertain the ratios in the offspring. The aims and organization of the Cornell Anatomy Farm, as it was called, and the methods followed were described by Doctor Stockard some time ago.*

In the preparation of the histological material, covering a period of many years, Doctor Stockard was ably assisted by Miss Emilia Vicari and Miss Eugenia Berry, among others. Dr. A. LeRoy Johnson made observations on the dentition of the different breeds and worked out the indices of the skull. The differences in behavior of the diverse breeds and the possibility of studying their inheritance by means of the conditioned reflex method widened the scope of the work at the farm. The results of these experiments, carried out by

* An experimental dog farm for the study of form and type. The Collecting Net, Woods Hole, vol. 6, pp. 257–264, 1931.

Dr. William T. James, are reported by him in the present monograph. Dr. O. D. Anderson, who studied the rôle of the endocrines in the production of behavioral types, contributes the last chapter.

During the last two years of his life, Doctor Stockard spent much of his time organizing and digesting the large mass of data which had been slowly accumulating. In the winter of 1938 he began the redaction of the present monograph on which he worked continuously during the summer of that same year at his home in Woods Hole. At the time of his death in the following spring, the manuscript was taken over by a committee formed of Drs. Alan Gregg, Herbert S. Gasser, Joseph C. Hinsey, A. LeRoy Johnson, Oscar D. Anderson, William T. James, José F. Nonidez, and William S. Ladd, Chairman.

A reading of the manuscript by the committee disclosed the fact that it was in a form finished enough for publication. Undoubtedly, Doctor Stockard would have made changes in the manuscript after a few more readings. The policy of the committee, however, has been to do a minimum of editing, and the style and phraseology have been left untouched. It is a matter of regret that the chapter on the histology of the endocrines was left unfinished; only introductory remarks on the cross of the St. Bernard and great Dane were found. It is still more regrettable that Doctor Stockard was unable to offer a discussion of the relation of the endocrines to type, probably the most important chapter of the whole monograph.

For the preparation of the manuscript and illustrations the committee is much indebted to Mrs. Ellen P. Schoenborn, who also undertook the tedious task of reading the proofs.

José F. Nonidez
*For the Committee*

By action of the Trustees of Cornell University, the Stockard collection of material on genetics at Cornell University Medical College has been presented to The Wistar Institute of Anatomy and Biology at Philadelphia. After the material has been assembled and placed on exhibition it will be made available at The Wistar Institute for continued study by anyone interested in the subject.

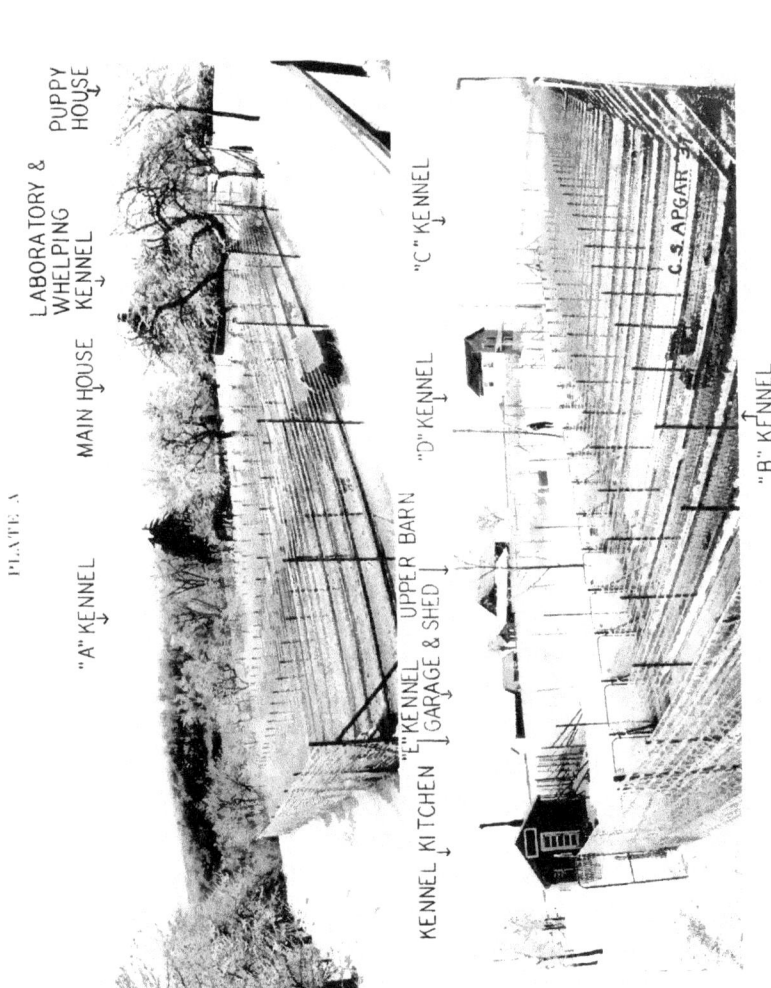

Two views of the Cornell Anatomy Farm at Shrub Oak, near Peekskill, N. Y.

# CONTENTS

## SECTION I

CHARLES R. STOCKARD

| | PAGE |
|---|---|
| Introduction | 3 |
| Statement of the problem | 3 |
| Varieties of form among the dog breeds | 9 |
| Resemblances of growth deviations in man to the modified forms in dog breeds | 12 |
| Modified types among other domestic animals | 19 |
| Divergent forms among the vertebrate species | 22 |
| Genetic mutations in dogs and the evolution of structurally modified species | 24 |
| The primitive or wild ancestral dog type | 28 |
| Hybridization for new combinations and recombinations of modified glands and type tendencies | 37 |
| The pure breeds selected for hybridizing and their strongly contrasted characters | 38 |

## SECTION II

CHARLES R. STOCKARD

| | |
|---|---|
| Achondroplasia of the extremities; a definitely localized and highly altered growth reaction | 45 |
| The genetics of limb achondroplasia in the bassethound | 47 |
| Bassethound-shepherd hybrids | 47 |
| The $F_1$ bassethound-shepherd backcrossed with the shepherd parent stock | 57 |
| The $F_1$ bassethound-shepherd backcrossed with the bassethound | 61 |
| The enhanced effects from two allelomorphs for achondroplasia as compared with the effects from only one such gene | 64 |
| Bassethound-Saluki hybrids | 69 |
| The $F_1$ bassethound-Saluki hybrids | 72 |
| The $F_2$ bassethound-Saluki hybrids | 74 |
| The $F_1$ bassethound-Saluki backcrossed with the Saluki | 81 |
| The $F_1$ bassethound-Saluki backcrossed with the bassethound | 84 |

## CONTENTS

| | PAGE |
|---|---|
| The bassethound and English bulldog hybrids in connection with dwarf leg growth | 90 |
| Test for absence of achondroplasia in the legs of the bulldog | 91 |
| Leg growth in the bassethound-bulldog $F_1$ hybrids | 94 |
| Leg growth in the bassethound-bulldog $F_2$ hybrids | 95 |
| The $F_1$ bassethound-bulldog backcrossed with each of the parent stocks | 101 |
| The effects of different breed constitutions on the fundamental growth pattern of the limb skeleton as responses to a single gene or to a homozygous allelic pair | 103 |
| Leg skeletons of the $F_2$ bassethound-shepherd | 111 |
| Leg skeletons of the $F_2$ bassethound-Saluki | 113 |
| Leg skeletons of the $F_2$ bassethound-bulldog | 118 |
| Localized achondroplasia in the extremities of the dachshund and the Pekingese | 124 |
| The extremities in the dachshund-Boston terrier cross | 125 |
| Leg skeletons of the dachshund-Boston terrier hybrids | 130 |
| Dachshund-French bulldog cross for extremity types | 134 |
| Dachshund-Brussels griffon cross for extremity types | 135 |
| The extremities in the hybrids between the Pekingese and Saluki | 137 |
| Testing the location of the gene which induces achondroplasia of the extremities by crossing the dachshund with the bassethound and with the Pekingese | 140 |

# SECTION III

### Charles R. Stockard and A. L. Johnson

| | |
|---|---|
| The contrasted patterns and modifications of head types and forms in the pure breeds of dogs and their hybrids as the results of genetic and endocrine reactions | 149 |
| The problems involved in the study of head types among dogs | 149 |
| The normal or standard dog skull | 152 |
| Comparisons of linear measurements made on a group of seventy adult dog skulls including various breeds from the large St. Bernards and great Danes to the small Pekingese and toy dogs | 156 |
| Zygomatic widths compared with other skull widths | 156 |
| A comparison of widths at different cranial regions | 163 |
| A comparison of cranial height and width measurements among different breeds | 167 |

## CONTENTS

| | PAGE |
|---|---|
| The least frontal width of the cranium as related to length of total skull base | 169 |
| Comparisons of the lengths of various facial parts and regions of the skull | 171 |
| Does the length of jaw directly determine tooth size? | 177 |
| Comparisons of mandibular length with other mandibular dimensions | 180 |
| The relation of the bony palate to the skull base and to the size of the palatal process of the palate bone | 182 |
| Comparison of measurements from the orifice of the auditory meatus to several definite points | 186 |
| Comparison of the same skull dimensions arranged in another sequence | 193 |
| Comparisons of measurements between given points along the mid dorsal line of the skull | 199 |
| Length of skull base in relation to anteroposterior length of premolar tooth crowns | 203 |
| Resumé of deductions from linear measurements made on different skull types | 205 |
| Determination and comparison of skull indices among various dog breeds | 207 |
| Graphic comparisons of measurements and indices among similar and contrasted skull types | 211 |
| Crosses between dog breeds with highly contrasted types of skulls | 224 |
| The genetics and expression of skull characteristics in hybrids between the Boston terrier and the dachshund | 226 |
| The backcrosses of the $F_1$ hybrid Boston terrier-dachshund on the two pure stocks | 244 |
| The expression of individual features in the skulls of Boston terrier-dachshund hybrids | 249 |
| The behavior of skull characteristics in the French bulldog-dachshund hybrids | 259 |
| The bulldog achondroplasic skull; its modified growth and development | 272 |
| The contrasted skulls of the English bulldog and the German shepherd | 288 |
| Genetic constitution and endocrine abnormality as factors in the growth and structural modifications of the English bulldog-bassethound hybrids | 295 |
| The head and skull features in English bulldog-bassethound hybrids; new types from new constitutional complexes | 298 |
| Indices and proportions in individual skulls from the bassethound-bulldog cross | 304 |
| Both giant and dwarf reactions for body size among $F_2$ bassethound-bulldog hybrids | 322 |

xvi    CONTENTS

|  | PAGE |
|---|---|
| Excessive skin area and other disharmonies of growth in hybrids from breeds with bulldog deformities | 328 |
| The bulldog modification in comparison with other short muzzled and round headed distortions in non related breeds | 335 |
| The head features in Brussels griffon-dachshund hybrids | 337 |
| The head features in dachshund-Pekingese hybrids | 343 |
| The $F_1$ dachshund-Pekingese hybrids | 344 |
| The variety of head characters in the second generation dachshund-Pekingese hybrids | 349 |
| The cross between the Pekingese and the Saluki | 358 |
| Structural disharmony and functional maladjustment between the upper and lower jaws in breed hybrids | 367 |
| The question of premanence and age of establishment for dental occlusion | 372 |
| Relation of dental occlusion to skull indices | 376 |

## SECTION IV

CHARLES R. STOCKARD

| | |
|---|---|
| A crucial test of genetic constitution as against endocrine distortion in determining the type of structural formation; the "screw-tail" in bulldog hybrids | 387 |

## SECTION V

CHARLES R. STOCKARD AND E. M. VICARI

| | |
|---|---|
| Variations in proportional size and modifications in histologic quality of endocrine glands in relation to body types as found among the dog breeds | 399 |
| The relative sizes of thyroid glands in contrasted types of pure dog breeds | 401 |
| The relative sizes of thyroids in hybrids between pure breeds of contrasted types | 409 |
| Gross relative sizes of the pituitary glands in contrasted breed types and their hybrids | 414 |
| Differences in the histologic qualities of thyroid glands from dogs of pure breed | 420 |
| Introductory view | 420 |
| Histologic techniques employed | 422 |
| Survey of histologic modifications in the thyroid | 423 |

| | PAGE |
|---|---|
| The significance of endocrine quality in relation to physical type in Boston terrier-dachshund hybrids | 440 |
| The inheritance of contrasted histologic patterns of the thyroid and their correlation with physical types in Boston terrier-dachshund hybrids | 440 |
| The nature of the pituitary glands in the Boston terrier-dachshund cross and their possible bearing on modifications of the thyroid and gross structural deformity | 447 |
| The histopathology of the pituitary in the $F_1$ generation of Boston terrier-dachshund hybrids | 458 |
| The possible relation of differences in pituitary structure to differences in physical type among the $F_2$ hybrids of the Boston terrier-dachshund cross | 461 |
| The histologic patterns of the pituitary glands in the backcrosses between $F_1$ hybrids and the two parental stocks | 470 |
| Developmental arrests and the quality of differentiation in the parathyroid glands of Boston terrier-dachshund crosses | 475 |
| Summary and deductions | 489 |
| Further tests on the significance of endocrine quality in relation to physical type as supplied by bassethound-bulldog hybrids | 491 |
| The inheritance of contrasted histologic qualities of thyroid glands and their correlation with physical types in bassethound-bulldog hybrids | 492 |
| The histologic quality of the pituitary glands in the bassethound-bulldog hybrids and the possible relations to morphologic distortions and modifications in the histologic quality of the thyroid | 500 |
| The quality of parathyroid glands in the bassethound-bulldog cross and the possible relations to modifications in skeletal growth | 514 |

## SECTION VI

### W. T. JAMES

### MORPHOLOGIC FORM AND ITS RELATION TO BEHAVIOR

| | |
|---|---|
| Introduction | 525 |
| Method | 529 |
| The experimental situation and equipment | 531 |
| Analysis of behavior in the conditioned food taking situation | 535 |
| Characteristics of the lethargic mode of performance, group A | 539 |
| Reactions of the lethargic group to negative signals | 547 |
| Reactions of the lethargic group to intense auditory stimuli | 549 |
| Reactions of the lethargic group to other signals | 549 |
| Summary | 552 |

xviii  CONTENTS

|  | PAGE |
|---|---|
| Characteristics of the active mode of performance, group B | 553 |
| Reactions of the active group to negative signals | 556 |
| Reactions of the active group to other signals | 558 |
| Response of the active group to intense auditory stimuli | 558 |
| Summary | 559 |
| Intermediate groups | 560 |
| Lethargic type A-plus | 560 |
| Active type B-minus | 564 |
| Summary | 568 |
| Discussion | 568 |
| Analysis of behavior in a conditioned avoiding situation | 575 |
| Initial adjustment to the laboratory | 581 |
| Strength of shock necessary to elicit the flexion of the foreleg and the effect of the shock on the dog | 581 |
| Nature and course of the reaction | 583 |
| Reaction time | 584 |
| Behavior during the interval between conditioning signals | 585 |
| Generalization | 587 |
| Excitation inhibition ratio | 588 |
| Intermediate groups A-plus and B-minus | 590 |
| Summary and discussion | 590 |
| Untrainable types | 594 |
| Behavioral type and its relation to physical form | 598 |
| Bassethound-German shepherd $F_1$s | 603 |
| Behavior classification of $F_1$s | 604 |
| Bassethound-shepherd $F_2$s | 606 |
| Behavior classification of bassethound-shepherd $F_2$s | 609 |
| Bassethound-German shepherd $F_1$ backcrossed on bassethound | 611 |
| Five offspring of the two above animals, 709 ♂ and 710 ♀ | 612 |
| General summary of the bassethound and shepherd crosses | 613 |
| Study of dogs showing exaggerated deviations in physical form from the more normal types | 614 |
| English bulldog | 614 |
| Behavior of the English bulldog | 614 |
| Stable types produced by crossing the English bulldog with the normal bassethound | 619 |
| English bulldog-bassethound $F_1$s | 619 |
| Behavior of English bulldog-bassethound $F_1$s | 620 |

| | PAGE |
|---|---|
| Mixed nature of the English bulldog is emphasized in the second generation bulldog-bassethound hybrids | 621 |
| English bulldog-bassethound $F_2s$ | 621 |
| Behavior of English bulldog-bassethound $F_2s$ | 621 |
| Summary | 623 |
| Bassethound-German shepherd $F_1$ by English bulldog-bassethound $F_1$ | 624 |
| The significance of size and its relation to behavioral type | 625 |
| Dachshund | 625 |
| Boston terrier | 626 |
| Dachshund-Boston terrier hybrids | 628 |
| Member of a pure type B with physical abnormalities | 629 |
| Contrast of the behavior of the pure and hybrid dogs under kennel conditions | 630 |
| Summary and discussion of behavior and its relation to physical type | 632 |
| Bassethound-German shepherd $F_1s$ | 634 |
| Bassethound-German shepherd $F_2s$ | 634 |

## SECTION VII

### O. D. ANDERSON

### THE RÔLE OF THE GLANDS OF INTERNAL SECRETION IN THE PRODUCTION OF BEHAVIORAL TYPES IN THE DOG

| | |
|---|---|
| The problem | 647 |
| The method | 649 |
| Behavior during the training or control period | 658 |
| The influence of the thyroid and the parathyroids upon the reflex behavior | 663 |
| The effect of thyroid extract administration in the normal dog | 664 |
| Dog 814 ♂, bassethound × Saluki $F_2$ | 664 |
| Dog 868 ♂, bassethound × shepherd $F_2$ | 666 |
| Dog 881 ♀, bassethound × Saluki $F_2$ | 672 |
| Summary of the thyroid effects | 675 |
| The effect of thyroidectomy | 677 |
| Dog 866 ♂, bassethound × shepherd $F_2$ | 677 |
| Dog 869 ♀, bassethound × shepherd $F_2$ | 680 |
| Dog 864 ♂, bassethound × shepherd $F_2$ | 683 |
| Dog 1030 ♂, bassethound × Saluki $F_2$ | 687 |

|  | PAGE |
|---|---|
| The effect on behavior of the administration of parathyroid extract to the normal dog | 697 |
| Dog C-1 ♀, bassethound × shepherd $F_2$ | 697 |
| Dog 814 ♂, bassethound × Saluki $F_2$ | 698 |
| The effect of complete thyro-parathyroidectomy | 699 |
| Dog 869 ♀, bassethound × shepherd $F_2$ | 699 |
| Dog 856 ♂, bassethound × Saluki $F_2$ | 702 |
| The influence of the pituitary upon behavior | 709 |
| The effect of the administration of a general extract of the anterior lobe in the normal dog | 709 |
| Dog C-1 ♀, bassethound × shepherd $F_2$ | 709 |
| The effect of hypophysectomy | 710 |
| Dog 492 ♂, bassethound × shepherd — bx bassethound | 710 |
| Dog C-1 ♀, bassethound × shepherd $F_2$ | 716 |
| Dog C-2 ♀, bassethound × shepherd $F_2$ | 719 |
| The influence of the suprarenals upon the behavioral reactions | 723 |
| The effect of administration of adrenalin on behavior in the normal dog | 723 |
| Dog 868 ♂, bassethound × Saluki $F_2$ | 723 |
| Dog 742 ♂, bassethound × English bulldog $F_1$ | 724 |
| Dog C-1 ♀, bassethound × shepherd $F_2$ | 727 |
| The effect of bilateral adrenalectomy | 730 |
| Dog 1398 ♂, bassethound × Saluki $F_2$ | 730 |
| The influence of the gonads upon the behavior reactions | 736 |
| The effect of castration in the male | 736 |
| Dog C-6 ♂, bassethound × shepherd $F_2$ | 736 |
| Dog 1150 ♂, bassethound × shepherd $F_2$ | 737 |
| The effect of ovariectomy | 738 |
| Dog C-4 ♀, bassethound × shepherd $F_2$ | 738 |
| Discussion | 740 |
| Comparison and correlation of the results | 740 |
| The probable rôle of the glands in the production of behavioral types in the dog | 746 |

# SECTION I

CHARLES R. STOCKARD

INTRODUCTION

*Statement of the problem.* The most promising prospect for an understanding of the mechanisms of growth and postnatal development in man and the higher animals is the analysis and regulation of the internal secretions in conjunction with the genetic constitution of the individual. Advances in knowledge along these lines may open the way for proper control of physical and mental development, as well as of susceptibility to deficiencies and infectious disease. Such possible regulation and control will, of course, always depend to a considerable extent upon the genetic constitutions of the individuals concerned. Certainly all individuals cannot respond similarly to exactly the same experiences. This fact in itself demands analysis and explanation.

It is urgently important at the present stage of our knowledge of this subject to attempt an estimate, based upon controlled experiments, of the interrelations of the rôles played by genetic constitution and the endocrine secretions in both normal and modified types of physical development and functional expression. Only a few scattered contributions to this intricate problem have as yet appeared. Some of these show in a definite way that modified conditions in the glands of internal secretion are clearly hereditary and are correlated with structural and functional peculiarities in the animal body. A study of the inheritance of a bulldog type in cattle by Crew ('23), a preliminary statement by the writer ('23 a, '23 b), followed by more recent reports ('26, '27 a, '27 b, '28, '30, '31, '32 a, '32 b, '32 c, '34, '35, '36 a, '36 b, '36 c, '37, '38 a, '38 b) on the significance of dog breeds in this connection, the studies on the creeper-fowl by Landauer ('31, '32, '33) and Landauer and Dunn ('30), the investigation of an hereditary dwarf mutation in mice associated with defective pituitary glands by Smith and MacDowell ('30, '31) and the reports by Mohr ('26, '29) and Mohr and Wriedt ('30) on hereditary defects in cattle are among the few contributions most closely related to the physical and morphologic side of our present problem.

In the dwarf mice of Smith and MacDowell we have a simple hereditary deficiency of the pituitary giving an internal environment unfavorable for normal growth and development. These dwarf individuals, when supplied with pituitary secretion, respond and grow to normal size and adult function, and this reaction to pituitary treatment is exactly comparable to that of the dwarf cretin with deficient thyroid secretion to the administration of thyroid extracts. These cases are examples of the developmental failure of an essential organ through an hereditary defect, just as albinism is due to an hereditary absence of melanin pigment, hemophilia to the absence of fibrinogen in the blood plasma, and color blindness to a retinal deficiency; all other tissue constituents in such individuals may be normally developed.

An insufficient amount, or the complete absence of thyroid or pituitary secretions, results in a deficient chemical environment within the body of the developing mammal, either before or after birth, and the tissues are unable to grow and develop in the usual manner in this defective milieu. However, if the missing substances are added to the environment, the animal may recover its normal development.

The growth reaction of the dwarf mice in response to pituitary treatment has not been interpreted by all investigators in so general a way. Some writers have claimed this reaction to indicate that the pituitary secretion contains a growth stimulating substance; yet such a growth stimulating hormone has not been postulated for the thyroid even though it brings about an equally remarkable growth response when administered to the cretin. It could be claimed, however, that the growth of the cretin results from a stimulating effect upon the pituitary caused by the thyroid administration, but there are many facts to contradict such a claim. A more acceptable explanation for both cases is that the addition of glandular secretion relieves the deficiency and restores the entire internal chemical environment to normal, and by so doing facilitates the proper growth response. Growth is a universal property of protoplasm or life itself and occurs even where no specific pituitary hormone is known to exist. It scarcely seems logical to imagine the phenomenon of growth as depending specifically upon such a hormone, though of course it may be that in higher animals the kind and degree of growth is regulated, controlled and modified by it. In the developing body there most certainly must exist a very definite mechanism for insuring coordination of growth among the various organs and systems in order to bring about the harmonious size relations of all its parts and finally to limit increase in total size at a characteristic level. Very probably the function of the pituitary gland is highly significant in this adjustment of proportions and limit in body mass. Much material bearing directly upon these problems is presented in this study.

The bulldog calf of Crew and the creeper-fowl or "parrot chicken" of Landauer are quite different from the dwarf mouse of Smith and MacDowell and the well known thyroid cretin. In the former cases, the extremities and the skull undergo a marked modification of development during early embryonic stages and this distorted development is inherited in definite Mendelian manner and cannot be changed to the normal type by any form of glandular administration yet attempted.

For many years I have been investigating modifications of embryonic growth and development brought about by various chemical disturbances of the embryonic environment. These studies finally led to the problems involved in an analysis of those changes during postnatal growth which establish the individual type and constitution. In studying such problems, it becomes strongly evident that the differences in genetic composition among individuals have so great an influence in determining their response to any modifying cause that an understanding of postnatal development and final expression of type must involve both genetic and developmental studies upon one specific type of material. It has been shown (Stockard, '21), for instance, that the eggs from two closely related species may differ in so gross a performance as the production of twin embryos in response to the same modification in environment.

Among human beings it is well known that the most exaggerated deviations in type and constitution are associated with various modifications and diseases of the glands of internal secretion. There is strong probability in many cases that to a large extent the diseased gland is the causative agent, bringing about the marked changes in physical type, and in certain of these cases there is indication that hybridization or other genetic modifications are very probably concerned. Certain clinical investigators have tended to emphasize the possibility that human giants, dwarfs, midgets and other peculiarly modified individuals owe their unusual conditions directly to functional deviations in their endocrine systems. However, that the conditions may in general be largely hereditary has not been clearly recognized, and the character and details of such heredities have remained almost entirely unknown.

In considering such problems it becomes evident that an analysis of the inheritance and endocrine influences involved in the origin of these types would be difficult, and could not be undertaken with any hope of completion through a study of human beings. However, this fact does not seriously affect the problem. Among the species of several lower mammals we find distortions of the normal anatomical form closely similar to those found in man. I have recognized for many years ('23 a) that the numerous breeds of dogs probably furnish the best example of such distortions. Many of the present dog breeds have been carefully preserved for generations and now constitute the most ideal material for an extensive investigation and analysis of the interrelations of heredity and the influences of internal secretions in bringing about distortion of structural types and behavioristic modifications in the higher animals. The understanding of such processes in grossly modified types can undoubtedly aid our understanding of the slight expression of these tendencies which exists in almost all so-called normal or ordinary individuals.

Modern dog breeds have been developed entirely by sportsmen and "fanciers" who have carefully selected and bred the various strange mutations spontaneously occurring in the stocks. Many of the stocks were probably of hybrid origin. After the breeds have once been established, they are perpetuated and perfected by careful selection. Many breeds are now old and highly homogeneous in genetic quality, as our experiments will show. Fortunately for the experimenter, in many cases the dog breeds have been established and handed over to us with more than a century's start toward the analysis of our present problem. The lifetime of an investigator would scarcely be long enough for the preparation of the breed stocks, even had the mutations from which they arose appeared before his eyes.

Only a few scientific studies on the genetics of the dog breeds have been made, and of these few none has had as its aim the problems now under consideration. There have been several studies of color inheritance in dogs, among which are those by Warren ('27) on the greyhounds, Little and Jones ('19) on the great Danes, Darling ('32) on bull terriers, Darling and Gardner ('33) on Irish wolfhounds, and Dahl and Quelprud ('37) on the German boxer. Plate ('30) studied the inheritance of hairlessness, hair color and erect ears in crosses between the hairless Ceylon dog and the dachshund, but gave no consideration to the possible endocrine implications. A short report was published in 1910 by Lang on a cross between a St. Bernard dog and a dachshund. This single hybrid litter exhibited points which might have been of interest to our present problem, but the breeding was not continued and the condition of the internal secretions received no consideration at all, nor could it have been appreciated from our present standpoints at that time. The study by

Lang was in no sense an experiment aimed towards the investigation of the problems we are now discussing. So far as our knowledge goes, the present study is the initial attempt on anything like a sufficiently large scale to analyze the structural qualities of the dog breeds on the basis of their hereditary constitutions and their endocrine conditions. It should be clearly understood that our aim is to give an experimental analysis of constitution in a comprehensive manner and not simply to report on the genetics of isolated characters among dogs. A preliminary consideration of the general significance of these problems was given after a survey of the histological conditions of the glands in numerous breeds, and the earlier results of the hybridization experiments were considered in several chapters of my book on personality ('31).

The purpose of this report is to present the results of an extensive series of new experiments and to discuss the investigations as a connected whole, since the various problems concerned are so closely interrelated that they cannot be fairly considered or properly analyzed in any other way. The considerations must involve the inheritance and development of the finished type, both from the morphologic and functional standpoints. We fully recognize that much is lacking at present in our knowledge of the chemistry of the functional side. Most of the phases, as would be expected in so large a problem, are still in their early stages, and we appreciate quite fully that this investigation has extensive boundaries, the thorough survey of which is a future accomplishment. Nevertheless, we believe that the present attack outlines a logical and productive means of approach, and that the evidence presented in this contribution analyzes to some extent the significance of the genetic constitution in determining developmental and growth reactions of bodily tissues and parts in their responses to different internal chemical or endocrine environments. Numerous results of the functional modifications which accompany definite structural and glandular deviations from the normal type are also recorded, as well as studies of the modifications in instinctive behavior and psychologic reactions. The expression of instinctive and conditioned reactions as definite hereditary entities has also been investigated.

*Varieties of form among the dog breeds.* No other species of mammals presents such wide diversities in structural type and general behavior as are shown among the breeds of domestic dogs. More than 100 separate breeds now exist. The exhibits in kennel shows in America and the European countries bring together most remarkable examples of structural deviations from a wild or ancestral dog type. These deviations involve, in the first place, the size of the individual, as illustrated by the tiny midget Chihuahua of less than 1 kilogram adult weight, as well as the Pomeranians, sleeve Pekingese, midget pinchers and others almost equally tiny. Such toy breeds are contrasted with the gigantic great Danes, St. Bernards and Irish wolfhounds, the largest specimens of which weigh nearly 100 kilograms. In other words, adult dogs at opposite ends of the size scale differ in weight by 100 times. Equally striking contrasts are seen in head shapes, from the round head with flat muzzle of the Brussels griffon, the pug and the bulldog, to the long, slender muzzle and head of the ancient Saluki and greyhounds. Body shapes and proportions range from short, stocky and rounded to long and tapering and, further, to a peculiarly emaciated thinness. The legs are extremely long in the wolfhound, long and very slender in the greyhound, and long and strong in the great Dane and shepherd dogs, while they are short and strong in other hounds, still shorter but straight and stocky in the bulldogs and finally extremely short, bent and twisted in posture in the dachshund, bassethound, Pekingese and others. In the latter breeds, the long bodies may actually at times drag on the ground. Tails also differ greatly among dog breeds, from the long, slender and straight tails of the pointers, setters and foxhounds, to the heavy, short and curled tails of the huskies, chows and Pomeranians, still further to the even shorter and tightly curled tail of the pugs, and finally to the short, bent and deformed screw-tail of the bulldogs.

Hair coats differ among the dog breeds in thickness, texture and length, as shown by the almost polar bear-like coats of the huskies and chows, heavy coat of the shepherd, long, silky coats of sheep dogs and some terriers, thin, silky and fringe-like coat of the Saluki, short stiff coats of the so-called short haired dogs and finally to an almost complete absence of hair in the Mexican, South American and Ceylon hairless dogs. Most of the breeds lose their hair in quantity twice a year and grow new coats, thin in summer and heavy in winter, but some dogs, such as the Irish Kerry blue terriers, never shed the hair *en masse* and do not change their coats. The great differences in coat color and in patterns and markings among the dog breeds are well known.

Some of the dog breeds are so grossly deformed in structure as to be rendered almost helpless and unable to maintain an independent existence, being entirely dependent upon the attentions of their masters. Other breeds are modified in localized parts of their bodies, which renders them especially suitable for one activity and somewhat useless for others. The legs of the dachshund and bassethound are useful for burrowing and struggling through heavy undergrowth, but are poorly fashioned for fast running in the open field. The Saluki, greyhound and whippet are admirably adapted for high speed in open country and are poor at burrowing or running through dense brush. In some breeds the tail may serve as a useful rudder while running and other breeds are almost tailless. The jaws are powerful and wolf-like in most dog breeds, but in the bulldog types are deformed and poorly suited for biting. In most breeds the teeth are splendidly set and strongly developed, but in some, such as the bulldogs, toy griffons, Pekingese, and pugs, they are ill-set and poorly developed. There are wide differences in acute-ness of hearing, sight and smell, as well as great differences in intelligence and learning ability. Certain breeds are par-ticularly useful for hunting a definite kind of game; for example, there are badger-hounds, rabbit-hounds, foxhounds, and deerhounds, and bird-dogs for land birds and water fowl. On the other hand, some dogs are incapable of hunting anything and are prized only for their daintiness as lap dogs, or their extreme grotesqueness, or because they are difficult animals to breed or cultivate. In spite of all these differences among the many characters of the various breeds of dogs, there is one characteristic which all have in common—a peculiar devotion to man. Their association with human beings may differ in degree, but every breed of dog lends itself to human companionship.

The internal organs and functional reactions among different breeds show wide deviations from the known wild dog pattern. Certain breeds reproduce with high fecundity and show well-expressed reproductive instincts, while others contain many sterile individuals or produce litters of only one to four puppies, as contrasted with eight to fifteen in the breeds with highest fecundity. The maternal instincts are vitiated to various extents among the individuals of some breeds. The glands of internal secretion which are known to influence these behaviors often show remarkable peculiarities, both in gross proportions and microscopic structure.

In view of these facts, the question arises as to whether the characteristic structural and functional peculiarities found among the various breeds might not be due to genetic mutations which brought about primary changes in the glands of internal secretion. The affected glands would then secondarily induce the characteristic modifications. Such conjecture would interpose the glands of internal secretion as the *modus operandi* through which the mutant genes may finally give rise to the many modified types of both anatomical and physiological characters. For example, does the shortened head of the bulldog develop as a result of modified pituitary-thyroid reactions which have arisen from a definite genic mutation? The alternative query would be, does genic mutation impress each growing tissue in such a way as to cause it to develop modified structural arrangements apart from influence of the internal secretions, or in spite of the quality of such secretions? If the latter proposition were true, the bulldog head could be inherited as such with no relation to the nature of the endocrine secretions as long as these were sufficiently normal to permit development at all. Does the genic constitution of the tissues themselves determine their pattern of development in every environment sufficiently favorable to permit development? Or again, to contrast these propositions by concrete query, is giant growth only possible from those tissues genetically constituted as giant, or may the potencies for normal size be stimulated, or better, liberated for giant growth through the action of peculiar internal secretions? And finally, a combination of the alternative propositions presents itself: are modified endocrine glands and peculiar growth deviations correlated characters, both resulting from a common genetic change, or, returning to the initial question, is the one primarily and the other secondarily the consequence of a genetic change? Definitely localized modifications of growth in the separate regions of the body, as are present in some dog breeds, supply material of unique value for an analysis of these questions. In fact, many of the most pressing problems of constitution, development and growth are subject to analysis when the array of dog breeds is appreciated as peculiarly favorable material for the investigation of these problems.

*Resemblances of growth deviations in man to the modified forms in dog breeds.* A knowledge of the dog races from the biological and medical points of view impresses one with the fact that many of these breeds are characterized by peculiarities of type and structural modifications comparable in close detail to certain unusual and so-called pathologic conditions found among other mammals, particularly in human families. The human giant, for example, may be a well proportioned, overgrown individual, in type and form entirely comparable to the giant Irish wolfhound or the great Dane dog. In addition to these well proportioned giants are others showing an excessive heaviness of skin and facial features as well as a disproportionately heavy lower jaw and overlarge hands and feet. Such characteristics constitute well recognized symptoms of the distortion known as acromegaly. Pierre Marie (1889) first recognized that acromegaly in human beings is closely correlated with abnormality and degeneration of the pituitary gland. It is now generally thought to result directly from pituitary disease. Several breeds of dogs constantly exhibit acromegalic patterns, and are bred true for this peculiarity. Both the giant St. Bernard breed and the bloodhound show most exaggerated acromegalic characteristics, having heavy overgrowth of bone and skin along with the functional deficiencies. The large Newfoundland dog is acromegalic to a lesser degree. The members of these acromegalic breeds frequently show considerable modification in the histology of their pituitary glands and distortions of their reproductive processes—characteristics which will be fully considered in following chapters.

In human beings of ordinary size, acromegalic tendencies with overgrowths are clearly shown at times as an accompaniment of age degeneration in the pituitary. Occasionally similar conditions appear in the normal sized young person, taking the form of unusually large and chubby hands and feet and thickened and furrowed facial features. Among dogs, the bloodhound, although only slightly if at all larger than the wild ancestral types, has developed a most exaggerated acromegaly of the skin, accompanied by heavy bones and large feet. The skin overgrowth is often more pronounced in the bloodhound than in the acromegalic giant St. Bernard dog. These dogs present many of the physiological symptoms which characterize the human acromegalic, and their voice, postures and behavior are similar to those of their human prototype to an almost uncanny degree.

Among both dogs and men, dwarf and midget individuals are even more common than giants. These small persons are known to occur in all human races and are to be seen as the commonest freaks of the circus and stage. Dwarf and diminutive persons, like the giants, are of two general types. The midgets or ateliotic dwarfs exhibit normal proportions of head, body and extremities in greatly reduced dimensions, but are gracefully formed tiny persons weighing in extreme cases less than 10 kilograms. Among the dogs this type is well known and perfectly illustrated by the tiny Chihuahua, the toy Pomeranians and, still more perfectly for normal proportions, by the diminutive toy pinchers. These little dogs are gracefully formed, with head, body and legs in fairly standard relations; they are miniatures of the ordinary shepherd or hound dog. The prize specimens among toy dogs may weigh less than 1 kilogram.

The other sub-normal sized type among humans is the so-called stocky dwarf, or achondroplasic individual. Such persons may have a full sized head and trunk accompanied by abnormally short extremities and are consequently low of stature to varying degrees. Not only are the long bones of the arms and legs abbreviated, but the base of the cranium is disproportionately short so that the face is flattened and depressed at the nasion, and the forehead, as a consequence, prominently rounded. The epiphyseal cartilages in the extremities and the basicranial cartilage in the head are deficient, with more or less connective tissue hyperplasia, and fail to give the usual amount of growth for the production of normal bone length. In the achondroplasic dwarf dog, therefore, the face or muzzle is short and flattened due to arrest of the cartilage growth in the basicranium, and the fore and hind limbs are short and twisted in shape through the growth deformity of their long bones. The French bulldog shows this condition to a high degree, while the Asiatic Pekingese dog is a perfect example. Fully expressed cases of human achondroplasic dwarfism are seen as rare members of the population in almost all communities of the world. Aside from the fully typical condition, every degree of variation in achondroplasic growth is met among human beings, and slight expressions in this direction give very sturdy persons with a determined demeanor.

The Pekingese and the French bulldog, which are among the several breeds exhibiting achondroplasia, have wide, rounded heads with nose and muzzle that are short and set back, giving the flat-faced physiognomy. The legs of the Pekingese are short and show a peculiar twisting due to spiral rather than straight long bone growth. This twisting is very noticeable in the fore legs, the hind legs showing it to a slight degree only. The extreme shortness of legs causes the body of the animal to appear unusually long. In the French bulldog, the legs are not noticeably achondroplasic but the tail is decidedly short and twisted, a result of distorted growth with ankylosis of caudal vertebrae. In the Pekingese, the tail escapes the modification almost completely, being well developed and carried curled gracefully over the rump.

The human stocky dwarf is round headed or brachycephalic. The nose bridge is flat and the palatal region shortened, causing the mandible to protrude beyond the upper jaw and producing the so-called "undershot" condition. The face is characteristically wide and flat with sunken nasion, making the appearance commonly termed "dish-faced." Such a physiognomy is comparable in every detail to the face of the bulldog and the Pekingese.

The coccygeal vertebrae are fused and bent in direction in some human dwarfs and resemble the like condition in the bulldogs. We possess the skeleton of such a specimen in the collections at Cornell University.

The extremities of the human achondroplasic are short and considerably bowed and twisted. As a rule the proximal segment of both extremities, the humerus and femur, are more shortened than the forearm and leg; the hands and feet may be simply stocky and wide in appearance yet the long bones in both are comparatively short. The posture of the hands and feet tends to abduct or outspread the digits to varying degrees. The arms and hands of the achondroplasic person are moved in a characteristic manner. The hand cannot be brought to the mouth without abducting and raising the elbow almost shoulder high, a condition caused by the spiral twist in the long bones affecting the plane of flexion of the elbow joint. There is thus a generous, wide movement in bringing the hand to the mouth.

Many weird explanations of the causes of achondroplasia have been offered in a serious scientific manner. One of the most fantastic of these attributed the clear-cut modified histogenesis of achondroplasia in both cranium and extremities to the influence of amniotic pressure on the developing fetus. This thesis, with beautiful illustrations, was presented by Murk Jansen ('12), a Dutch orthopaedic surgeon, and the late Sir G. Elliot Smith, the British anatomist, wrote an introduction of strong approval. In the light of our investigations on the genetics and development of this condition in dogs, as well as the studies of Landauer on fowls and of Knötzke ('29) on the morphology and histology of this distorted bone growth, such explanations of the histologic processes involved are altogether untenable.

Achondroplasia, or chondrodystrophy, the deficient growth of bones derived from a cartilage matrix, may, in a certain sense, be interpreted as an opposite reaction to that of gigantism or acromegalic overgrowth of bone. As in acromegaly, much evidence for a strong correlation between the dwarf growth reactions and modifications of the pituitary gland is found. In these dwarf cases one would expect the pituitary deviations to differ from or even directly oppose those associated with the giant growths. If modifications of the pituitary are the causative elements in both the giant and the dwarf growth deviations, one would assume the glandular abnormality associated with overgrowth or acromegaly to be a contrasted and opposite condition to that associated with the deficient dwarf growths. Yet as a result of hybridizing certain dog breeds, we have been faced with a very remarkable situation in which achondroplasic dwarfing in certain parts and acromegalic overgrowth in other parts are produced in one and the same individual.

Not only do we obtain peculiar mixtures of growth reactions on crossing different breed types, but modified structural responses are sometimes localized or limited to certain narrow regions, while other parts of the animal conform to the usual or normal pattern. Extreme structural disharmonies as well as minor disharmonious relations among structures and functions are frequently found to occur in hybrids.

Many of the pure-line dog breeds are in themselves characterized by localized deformities. The dachshund and basset-hound, for example, are quite normal in body and head form, having perfectly normal axial skeletons with long tails, but their extremities show exaggerated achondroplasia and are twisted and much reduced in length. On the other hand, the King Charles spaniel, Boston terrier, Brussels griffon and several other breeds have quite normally developed long, straight legs, while the head, and in some cases both head and tail, exhibit extreme shortness and distortion due to achondroplasia of the basicranium and jaws and, in those in which the tail is also involved, of the caudal vertebrae. Localized growth distortions of closely similar nature also occur among human beings. Certain individuals with quite normally proportioned heads and bodies may have disproportionately short, twisted arms and lower extremities; these might be classed as human bassethound or dachshund types. Again, there are persons with long, straight extremities who show a much flattened face with depressed, sunken nasion, short maxillary region and protruding lower jaw—a bulldog-faced man. Sharply localized overgrowths, such as excessive thickening and wrinkling of the skin in the head and shoulder regions, also occur in human individuals.

All these localized peculiarities and mixtures of type make it difficult to credit a specific endocrine disturbance as the sole causative agent for any one of them, since the same endocrine secretions necessarily surround, and are in contact with all parts of the body. The nature of the localized or specific tissues themselves—their genetic constitutions—must be suspected and investigated. There is still another possibility: that a temporary glandular modification acting for only a short time during development may have impressed certain organs then at a critically susceptible stage. This possibility is subject to genetic proof and in the cases tested we have found it to be inapplicable.

Familiarity with these exaggerated modifications of growth equips the observer with the basic knowledge for detecting mild degrees of the same expressions which are commonly seen in normal individuals. A satisfactory and practical understanding of human types can probably be arrived at most easily through a thorough analysis of these strongly modified expressions. If a correlation exists between the inherited qualities of endocrine secretions and peculiarities of structural features, no doubt such associations can be more readily recognized and analyzed in fully manifested cases. The less marked conditions in the so-called "normal" individuals may then later lend themselves to more refined and expert analysis.

Among dogs, just as among people, mild degrees of bullhead, short legs and certain skin and bone overgrowths, exophthalmos with restlessness, tendencies toward thin and emaciated conditions, or the reverse, an excessive accumulation of fat and overweight, are constantly observed. Closely the same functional reactions and typical behaviors as found in individuals with extreme manifestations are associated with even these mild expressions in different species of animals. Deviations in the function of endocrine glands during different periods of the individual's existence are well known to bring about, or be associated with, structural and functional changes of diagnostic significance, yet how much responsibility for these changes can be attributed to the glands as *prima-facie* cause it is difficult to determine in the natural occurrences. Probably the initial cause lies behind the gland modification and this change can scarcely be thought to arise spontaneously within the gland itself, in spite of our ignorance of the initiating process. No one knows precisely the initiating cause for so common a phenomenon as the changes during mammalian puberty. One can only say in general that these changes result from a biologically harmonious state which develops with time. (A more completely indefinite statement would be difficult to compose!) The progressive development and change in the constitutional nature of the individual is the only determining or causative element in the response of which we are certain.

In many cases the removal and transplantation of endocrine glands bring about typical changes in structure and function, but these changes in themselves do not necessarily show the extent to which the particular gland under consideration is ordinarily responsible for such processes. The responses are usually brought about by a long series of functional adjustments which develops as a result of the initial operation. Castration, for example, changes the bull into the ox, which is taller, of different form and proportions, and more easily fattened. The accumulation of fat may be caused by changes in the thyroid, pituitary and other glands, as well as the central and sympathetic nervous systems, and is certainly not alone a result of the removal of the gonads. As a matter of fact, similar or probably the same changes may operate to produce fattening of the bull under certain conditions even in the presence of the gonads. Many other questions might be asked and examples enumerated which would strongly indicate that a study of the inheritance and development of peculiar body types in association with modified endocrine quality is a very necessary step towards the full and complete understanding of endocrine reactions in the animal constitution, as well as their rôle in health and disease.

*Modified types among other domestic animals.* Although man and the dog probably show the widest and most highly modified deviations from stem type in size and form, they are by no means the only examples of such phenomena among the domesticated animals.

Among domestic horses there are well known giant and dwarf breeds—the powerful, slow-moving, heavy truck horses and the diminutive Shetland ponies. There are also slender greyhound-like race horses. All these animals deviate from the normal size and form of the wild horse. There are, however, no well expressed acromegalic conditions among horses and no large variety of dwarfs and midgets, as occur among dogs and human beings. The domestic horses have in all probability been derived from a less widely hybridized ancestry than the dogs and this may possibly account in part for the fact that they show fewer divergent and mutant types. It must also be recognized that horses are used by man for working and riding; their selection and breeding have been limited to a fulfillment of these purposes and not to the gratification of a desire to preserve the odd, grotesque or useless. Again, the entire nature of the horse, its size, reproductive qualities and instincts, lacks the appeal for which man has selected the dogs. Should achondroplasia or acromegaly appear among horses, the individuals so affected would be discarded rather than selected for the establishment of new breeds, nor would the affected animals be reared to maturity for the sentimental or humane reasons that preserve the human freak individuals.

Domestic cattle probably have a more diverse wild ancestry than does the horse, and they likewise show tendencies toward the production of more divergent and freak types, although these again are not preserved or perpetuated. Exaggerated bulldog types, which are usually non-viable, have long been known to occur among cattle, and their inheritance and glandular conditions have recently been investigated by Crew and Mohr. However, the large size and slow reproductive processes of cattle, as well as their economic value, prevent extensive experimental study of such material. Several dwarf types of cattle are bred and some of these show mild degrees of achondroplasia. Giant individuals considerably above normal size occur sporadically and are occasionally exhibited, although they are not stabilized by breeding.

Many of the varieties of domestic swine differ widely in type and form from the wild hog and have been selected chiefly for tendencies towards high accumulation of fat. There is one variety, the Japan pig (*Sus pliciceps*, Gray), which is an almost bulldog-St. Bernard combination in type. This hog has an extraordinary appearance, with shortened muzzle and broad frontal region, a heavy fleshy condition of the ears, and skin that is thickened and deeply furrowed into folds about the neck and shoulders, suggesting in some respects the condition in the bloodhound and St. Bernard dogs. The Japan pig is an old and well established race, breeding true. The highly modified skull has led some taxonomists to rank it not only as a distinct species, but to place it in a separate section of the genus. Others have considered it to be only a domesticated variety of *Sus indicus*, a short-eared Chinese breed. Darwin knew of all these breeds and felt that if the latter interpretation were correct the Japan pig furnished a wonderful example of the amount of modification which could be effected under domestication. The modern interpretation is that the Japan pig has arisen as a distinct mutant race.

Not alone these mammalian forms, but the far removed domestic fowls present wide diversity in size and type among the various breeds throughout the world. Many of these breeds are hybrid in wild origin and thus complicated in their hereditary composition. In general it is believed that the breeds of domestic fowl were probably derived from the small wild *Gallus bankiva* of India in combination with the larger Cochin fowl of Asia. There are at present giant races, larger than either of these wild types, and dwarf and bantam varieties, as well as the short legged creeper fowl, all showing conditions closely comparable to the modified forms in mammals. Landauer ('33) has recently shown that a homozygous condition in the creeper fowl brings about an extreme state of chondrodystrophy, giving badly deformed head and extremities in non-viable individuals. Some evidence of modified endocrine glands in these fowls has also been presented.

Other domestic animals, such as sheep and goats, do not show such marked violations of their original type and size. These may be less widely hybridized in their origins, coming from a more closely related ancestry. However, there is among sheep a sporadic tendency to give rise to strange mutant types. The classical case of the ancon ram was, in the light of present knowledge, very clearly an achondroplasic mutant in sheep. Many years ago I reported ('07) the case of legless lambs sired on two different occasions by the same ram paired with related ewes. Amelia, or leglessness, is at times associated in its occurrence with achondroplasic stocks. We shall refer to a few such instances that have recently occurred among achondroplasic dogs in our experiments. Such freaks among sheep and goats are, however, extremely rare.

During recent years wild stocks of rabbits have been crossed in numerous ways under domestic conditions. Some of these stocks have lately been reported by Greene, Hu and Brown ('34) of the Rockefeller Institute to give rise to structural distortions and deficiencies comparable in many ways with those known for man and the dog, but as far as behavior is concerned these animals are again poorly suited for constitutional studies. One of the most important problems in the ultimate aim of our present investigation relates to the influences of constitutional differences upon behavioristic and psychological patterns. Few lower animals are suitable material for such research, and none is so favorable as the dog.

*Divergent forms among the vertebrate species.* Strange and divergent body forms are not alone confined to man and the domestic mammals and birds, but very closely comparable peculiarities in size and type are found among numerous species in other classes of vertebrate animals. Tiny, almost microscopic varieties occur among the bony fishes, and there may be reasons for considering these as truly midget types or mutants from a much larger ancestral stem form. On the other hand, there are gigantic species of fish with body and type strongly suggesting the giant mutants among mammals.

Most remarkable of all deviations from normal stem size have occurred among the fossil and modern reptiles. Giant reptiles attained an exaggeration in size during the Triassic period which surpasses the performance of modern mammals. The mutations giving rise to these enormous individuals might be imagined to have produced a pituitary reaction in the total glandular complex that was *par excellence* the acromegalic giant combination.

The living reptiles still present clear examples of exaggerated types. The giant crocodile and alligator, as well as some giant lizards, show an excessive overgrowth of loose wrinkled skin along with other acromegalic symptoms. It is also important that many of these animals do not attain a limited adult size but continue to grow throughout their lives. Their reproductive functions do not cease with age and they show none of the usual symptoms of senility. The nature of the pituitary function in these animals is entirely unknown.

There are, at the other end of the reptilian size scale, tiny active midget lizards with definite uniformity of body size, and also sluggish achondroplasic bulldog-like lizards of the "horned toad" type. Whether or not modified growths and varieties of form are primarily caused by changes in endocrine secretion, there is the peculiar fact that such reactions, in mammals at least, are almost constantly associated or correlated with definite glandular peculiarities.

The fact that the above forms are clearly recognized animal species does not preclude definite comparisons of their size and type with those of the newly established dog breeds or with the unusual growth modifications which occur among human beings. Much evidence is accumulating to indicate that nature brings about growth deviations from a stem pattern in closely similar ways among widely different species. We have considerable justification for considering the achondroplasic reactions shown by man, dogs and cattle to be of the same nature and origin as "parrot head" and shortened legs in the far removed creeper fowl. Changes in size and structural quality are the phenomena which occur in the evolution of animal species, judging only from the nature of those specimens living today. Modifications in structural quality of bone, skin, endocrine glands, *et cetera* are the processes which we are attempting to analyze in our study of the different dog breeds and their hybrids. The further these studies progress the more certain it becomes that along with structural qualities the functions and behaviors of individuals are the products of a definite genetic constitution interacting within a correlated chemical environment regulated to an important degree by the endocrine glands. This position has gradually been reached through the recently accumulated knowledge of genetics and the illuminating experimental studies by many workers on the influences of the endocrine secretions on the growth processes and the functional reactions of the organs and tissues within the body. Slight disturbances, as well as normally rhythmical variations in endocrine secretions, bring about prompt modifications and alterations in the functional reactions of the tissues, and particularly in the instinctive behaviors and the reactions of the nervous systems. One may logically suppose that any genetic change or mutation which affects the endocrine glands, either directly or indirectly, must very probably be of the highest importance in giving rise to new species as well as to new domestic breeds. This interplay within the single endocrine system may be the reason for the reappearance of the same or comparable patterns among very widely separated families and classes of animals as well as among closely related species.

*Genetic mutations in dogs and the evolution of structurally modified species.* At the present time peculiar genetic changes are taking place within some breeds of dogs which may parallel in ways and degrees the evolutionary processes which give rise to strangely modified animal species. Several such type modifications and glandular alterations have been referred to above. I recently ('36 a) reported an hereditary loss of motor neurones in the lower portions of the spinal cord in certain dog breeds and their hybrids which results in degeneration and functional alteration of the hind extremities, clearly suggesting the evolutionary loss and modification in the posterior extremities of aquatic mammals. It is well known that animals with rudimentary limbs, such as the flightless birds with their undeveloped wings, have a much reduced cervical enlargement of the spinal cord, while completely limbless animals, such as the snakes, show no enlargements of the cord in either the cervical or lumbosacral regions. All the motor neurones which usually supply the muscles of the extremities are absent from these spinal cords. It is very probable that the neurones failed to appear or were lost during development before the leg itself began to degenerate. At any rate, it is quite certain that if through a mutation the quota of motor neurones designed to supply the muscles of the arm should fail to arise, the arm would necessarily be motionless and eventually would wilt. Thus the course of evolution in the modification or the loss of limbs might have its origin in a mutation which is lethal for the motor neurones in the cord supplying the limb, followed by the resulting modifications and loss of muscles and other tissues. Marine mammals, such as walruses, seals, porpoises and whales, show different degrees of modifications, or more exactly, of the degeneration and almost complete loss of the posterior extremities. This is brought about by the loss of many motor neurones and a reduction of the lumbosacral enlargement of the spinal cord. It is difficult to imagine that the entire change necessary to give this loss of nerve cells in the spinal cord and these strangely altered posterior extremities could come about as a single mutation. It would seem far more probable that a series of mutations or a certain complexity of genic rearrangements was gradually evolved in bringing about this modification of a walking extremity into a flipper-like paddle. A careful study of the skeletons of such animals shows evidence of achondroplasic reaction, and other features suggest modified pituitary function. Here, as in the dogs, the genetic history is associated with deviations in endocrine constitution and considerable change may result from a single point mutation. Yet just as the modified achondroplasic head of the prize bulldog is a character depending upon the homozygous condition of several genetic factors for its complete expression, as we shall indicate in a subsequent chapter, so the flippers of the seal with their achondroplasic-like skeleton, modified muscular arrangements and fin-like metamorphosis of the foot probably originated from an initial mutation causing the loss of spinal neurones and a subsequent series of mutations associated with the specialization of the limb.

In two giant breeds of dogs there is the tendency to produce individuals with a lameness resulting from degeneration following paralysis of the thigh muscles. The condition varies in its expression depending upon the homozygosity of the more or less complete complex of probably three dominant mutant genes. The more nearly homozygous the individual becomes for all three of these genes, the more pronounced and extensive is the degeneration. Possibly the completely homozygous complex might give highly modified lower extremities, though such an individual has probably not yet been bred. All the thigh muscles are not paralyzed and quite definite ones persist and compensate in such ways as to give hyperextension and eversion of the leg, producing a gait suggesting closely the peculiar ambling of the seal. The inheritance of this paralysis may in some way be genetically associated with the inheritance of skin overgrowth and certain acromegalic features which are further associated with a modified pituitary reaction, since all the breeds involved show these characters. It is of further interest to note that most of the aquatic mammals have thickened and wrinkled overgrowth of skin, as well as heaviness of the anterior body regions and a tendency towards the accumulation of fat. The head, neck and shoulders of the paralyzed dogs are large, strongly muscled and covered with excessively loose rolls of skin, while the rump and thighs of such animals are wilted and disproportionately small. The pituitary and other glands are almost uniformly modified. The genetic complex which is associated with acromegalic growth and alteration of the pituitary also seems to be associated in some cases with a tendency towards loss of spinal neurones and a resulting disappearance of certain muscles of the extremities. Such tendencies may be readily imagined to progress as the race becomes more homozygous for the mutant condition leading to more extensive loss and modification of the posterior extremities and then spreading or becoming more generalized to involve the anterior extremities as well. These changes would qualify the animal for a floating or swimming existence rather than for locomotion by dragging the heavy body on land.

Certain modified breeds of dogs show another peculiarity suggesting the possibility of water living tendencies. The slightly acromegalic giant Newfoundland dog is frequently web-toed, and the toes of short legged achondroplasic dogs such as the dachshund are often webbed almost to the tips. Acromegaly and achondroplasia are not altogether mutually exclusive reactions, but, as mentioned above for dogs, each may occur in different parts of the same individual. And this is also true for the marine mammals. Webbing of the feet, a fin-like symptom in water birds as well as aquatic mammals, does seem in many cases to be associated or correlated in some way with growth distortions such as achondroplasia, and likewise with a peculiar pituitary disturbance in the breed.

These introductory speculations and comparisons, which are presented in an entirely theoretical manner, are intended to indicate that the study of a highly diversified stock, such as the domestic breeds of dogs, may furnish information leading towards an understanding of the origin and development of not only individual form and types but also of deviations and changes away from an ancestral pattern which well might give rise to new varieties and distinct species of animals. Very probably, as has been pointed out by Sir

Arthur Keith ('28), the present writer, and several other workers, hereditary modification in the qualities of endocrine secretions has played an important rôle in the evolution of the types and races among domestic mammals, including man.

### The Primitive or Wild Ancestral Dog Type

What was the ancestral or wild primitive type or types of dog from which the modern breeds have been derived? This question deserves serious attention in connection with our present considerations.

The literature regarding the wild origin of the domesticated dog presents a great diversity of opinion. This results from two facts. In the first place, it is commonly agreed by Studer ('01, '05), Breuil ('12), Elliot ('25), Osborn ('15), Allen ('20), and others that the dog was the earliest animal domesticated by man. This taming of the dog occurred in distant prehistoric times. The early savage man and the wild dog joined in a hunting combination that was of peculiar advantage to both, and in offensive and defensive battles the tool-using hand of man and the powerful jaws of the dog with its tearing teeth were more than a single species adversary could successfully overcome. In time the man and his dog became masters of the forest. Possibly this was the beginning of the impounding or domestication by man of a lower animal species, and in those early stages of the process the mutual benefits which accrued to each from this association would dignify it as a true example of commensalism. In this connection it is difficult to resist propounding the idea that the wild dog may have initiated the association with man rather than that man first domesticated the dog. In other words, may not the dog have primarily domesticated man, and from this association may not man have become aware of the possibility of furthering such associations and the usefulness of other animals? The dog is instinctively more inclined to cling to man than is man to the dog. No other domestic animal exhibits the dog's deep attachment for man, nor so strong a tendency for a close association with him.

The second reason for the uncertainty regarding the wild origin of the domestic dog breeds is that this did not involve simply a single species of wild canine, but was probably more complex, involving a number of species or kinds in various regions of the world. The ancestry of the dog probably reaches back to several stocks rather than to a single stem, and since domestication took place so early in prehistoric times, the lines of descent have long since become too hazy for accurate tracing.

Darwin, in his classical treatise on *The Variation of Animals and Plants under Domestication*, epitomized in 1875 the opinions of that time regarding the origin of the modern dogs as follows:

"Some authors believe that all have descended from the wolf or from the jackal or from an unknown and extinct species. Others again believe, and this of late has been the favourite tenet, that they have descended from several species, extinct and recent, more or less commingled together. We shall probably never be able to ascertain their origin with certainty. Palaeontology does not throw much light on the question, owing, on the one hand, to the close similarity of the skulls of extinct as well as living wolves and jackals, and owing, on the other hand, to the great dissimilarity of the skulls of the several breeds of the domestic dogs. It seems, however, that remains have been found in the later tertiary deposits more like those of a large dog than of a wolf, which favours the belief of DeBlainville that our dogs are the descendants of a single extinct species. On the other hand, some authors go so far as to assert that every chief domestic breed must have had its wild prototype. This latter view is extremely improbable; it allows nothing for variation; it passes over the almost monstrous character of some of the breeds; and it almost necessarily assumes that a large number of species have become extinct since man domesticated the dog . . ." (p. 15, v. 1.)

Isidore Geoffroy Saint-Hilaire (Hist. Nat. Gén. 1860, T. III, p. 107) stated his belief that most dogs descended from the jackal although some may have descended from the wolf.

These views expressed by the leading biologists of two generations ago are in many respects as correct as any that could be advanced today. However, at that time it was entirely impossible, without our modern knowledge of genetics and mutations, to understand the origin of the diversified breeds of dogs. We now know from numbers of examples among various animal species, including even man himself, that strange freak individuals are constantly appearing as mutations which definitely transmit their characteristics and which may be used for the creation of new true races or breeds.

Nevertheless, Darwin, through his broad knowledge of the animal kingdom, was surprisingly close to a correct understanding of what modern experiments have demonstrated to be true. He recognized the fact that the short legged dachshund pattern appeared from time to time among various species, and he apparently also appreciated the fact that such sports or mutants might give origin to certain breeds. Referring to carvings on Egyptian monuments from the fourth to the twelfth dynasties, i.e., from about 3400 B.C. to 2100 B.C., which represent several varieties of dogs, Darwin states:

"Most of them are allied to greyhounds; at the later of these periods a dog resembling a hound is figured, with drooping ears, but with a longer back and more pointed head than in our hounds. There is, also, a turnspit, with short and crooked legs, closely resembling the existing variety; but *this kind of monstrosity is so common with various animals*[1], as with the ancon sheep, and even, according to Rengger, with jaguars in Paraguay, that it would be rash to look at the monumental animal as the parent of all our turnspits: Colonel Sykes (Proc. Zoolog. Soc., July 12, 1831) also has described an Indian pariah dog as presenting the same monstrous character." (p. 17, v. 1.)

Darwin thus recognized that breeds might arise from monstrosities and that similar breeds from different parts of the world may have originated independently since the same

[1] Italics supplied.

monstrosity could occur in different stocks in various countries.

The dog represented on the most ancient Egyptian monuments is a greyhound-like animal and resembles very closely the present day Saluki of Northern Africa. The ancient monumental type had long, erect, pointed ears instead of the hanging ears of the Saluki, and is represented with a somewhat shorter, curled tail. Mr. E. V. Harcourt, an English sportsman of 50 years ago, stated that the Arab boar-hound of that time was "an eccentric hieroglyphic animal, such as Cheops once hunted with, somewhat resembling the rough Scotch deer-hound; their tails are curled tight round on their backs, and their ears stick out at right angles." (From Darwin, p. 18, v. 1.)

There is this graphic evidence that at periods four and five thousand years ago various breeds, such as pariah dogs, greyhounds, common hounds, mastiffs, house dogs, lap dogs, and turnspits existed, and that they more or less resembled some of our present breeds.

The bones of canine animals from much earlier times have been found in the Danish Middens of the Neolithic period and these ancient dogs were succeeded in Denmark during the Bronze period by a large kind which was in turn replaced during the Iron age by a still larger animal. Remains of dogs found in Switzerland indicate that closely similar animals lived there during the same periods. The succession of the different kinds of dogs in Switzerland and Denmark is thought to be due to the immigration of conquering tribes who brought their dogs with them; this view is in agreement with the belief that different wild canine animals had been domesticated in different regions.

There is no *a priori* difficulty in the belief that several canine species have been domesticated. Members of the dog family were aboriginal in almost all parts of the world; and several species agree rather closely in structure and habits with the several domesticated dogs. It would have been, as

Darwin expresses it, a strange fact if only one species had been domesticated throughout the world.

The natives of Guiana partially domesticated two aboriginal species of wolf and crossed their dogs with them. The two species belonged to a quite different type from the North American and European wolves. Rengger (Naturgeschichte der Säugetiere von Paraguay 1830 S. 151) gives reason for believing that a hairless dog was domesticated when America was first visited by Europeans. This naked dog is quite distinct from that found preserved in the ancient Peruvian burial places. It is not known whether these two kinds of dogs are the descendants of native species.

Several old European dogs closely resemble the wolf. The shepherd dogs of Hungary were almost indistinguishable from wolves several generations ago. The European wolf differs slightly from that of America and has been classed as a distinct species. The common wolf of India has been classed as a third species and here again we find a marked resemblance to the pariah dogs of certain districts.

Isidore Geoffroy Saint-Hilaire (Hist. Nat. Gén. 1860 T. III, p. 101) claimed that not one constant difference could be pointed out between the structure of the jackal and that of the small races of dogs. These also agree closely in habits. Jackals, when tamed, wag their tails, lick the master's hand, roll on their backs and in general exhibit many habits exactly similar to those of the dog. Several of the early students of mammals have expressed strong arguments with respect to the resemblance of the half-domestic dogs of Asia and Egypt to jackals. It has also been claimed that the domestic dogs of lower Egypt and certain mummified dogs have as their wild type a species of wolf, whereas the domestic dogs of Nubia and certain other mummified dogs are closely related to a wild species of the same country, *Canis sabbar*, which is but a form of the common jackal. The general statement has been made that in the East jackals and dogs sometimes cross naturally.

Darwin has made a further important statement concerning the multiple origin of dogs:

"From the resemblance of the half-domesticated dogs in several countries to the wild species still living there,—from the facility with which they can often be crossed together,—from even half-tamed animals being so much valued by savages,—and from the other circumstances . . . which favour their domestication, it is highly probable that the domestic dogs of the world are descended from the two well-defined species of wolf, (viz. *C. lupus* and *C. latrans*), and from two or three other doubtful species, (namely, the European, Indian, and North African wolves); from at least one or two South American canine species; from several races or species of jackal; and perhaps from one or more extinct species." (p. 26, v. 1.)

Following this statement, Darwin characteristically points out certain objections:

"The belief that our dogs are descended from wolves, jackals, South American Canidae, and other species, suggests . . . important difficulty. These animals in their undomesticated state, judging from a widely spread analogy, would have been in some degree sterile if intercrossed; . . . these animals keep distinct in the countries which they inhabit in common. On the other hand, all domestic dogs, which are here supposed to be descended from several distinct species, are, as far as is known, mutually fertile together." (p. 31, v. 1.)

"Notwithstanding the difficulties in regard to fertility, . . . when we reflect on the inherent improbability of man having domesticated throughout the world one single species alone of so widely distributed, so easily tamed, and so useful a group as the Canidae; when we reflect on the extreme antiquity of the different breeds; and especially when we reflect on the close similarity, both in external structure and habits, between the domestic dogs of various countries and the wild species still inhabiting these same countries, the balance of evidence is strongly in favour of the multiple origin of our dogs." (p. 34, v. 1.)

"The intercrossing of the several aboriginal wild stocks, and of the subsequently formed races, has probably increased the total number of breeds, and . . . has greatly modified some of them. But we cannot explain by crossing the origin of such extreme forms as thoroughbred greyhounds, bloodhounds, bulldogs, Blenheim spaniels, terriers, pugs, etc., unless we believe that forms equally or more strongly characterized in these different respects once existed in nature. But hardly anyone has been bold enough to suppose (this) . . . No instance is on record of such dogs as bloodhounds, spaniels, true greyhounds having been kept by savages . . . The number of breeds and sub-breeds of the dog is great; Yonatt, for instance, describes twelve kinds of greyhounds.'' (p. 35, v. 1.)

Darwin also points out that different breeds of dogs become adapted to different climates under which they have long existed, and states, with reference to importation of European breeds into India: "It is positively asserted that when bred there for a few generations they degenerate not only in their mental faculties, but in form." (p. 39, v. 1.) This appears to be the case with hounds, greyhounds and pointers, but spaniels apparently are not so affected. Darwin further calls attention to the fact that bulldogs bred for fighting and bull baiting not only fall off after two or three generations in pluck and ferocity, but lose the under-hung character of their lower jaws; their muzzles become longer and their bodies lighter.

In other countries there is a similar degeneration or modification of imported breeds, though this fact is not widely realized. Many of our American dogs are largely derived from imported European breed stocks and the characters and points on which these breeds are judged are determined by European fanciers and judges. For several years I have observed that American bred dogs, although carefully selected from the best imported champion stock, usually fail to win in point competition against the European bred animals imported for a kennel show. A breed developed in Europe is partially the product of that environment, and its type becomes somewhat modified when reared under different conditions in another part of the world. The breed characteristics would seem to be, to a slight degree at least, the product of the environment in which they were primarily developed. No doubt the development and interaction of the endocrine glands, particularly in highly modified types, are influenced by the environmental conditions of climate and food under which they exist.

With our present knowledge of the influences of slight dietary deficiencies and of light and other climatic conditions on growth and development, and the modifications which take place in habit and form as well as fecundity of wild species when transplanted from one part of the world to another, the degeneracy of breed types among imported dogs is not surprising. No doubt much is to be learned from careful study of such reactions.

In discussing the origin of dog breeds, Darwin stated more clearly than in any other connection his ideas of the possible origin of species, through mutations, use-inheritance and selection. He states:

"Some of the peculiarities characteristic of the several breeds of dog have probably arisen suddenly, and, though strictly inherited, may be called monstrosities; for instance, the shape of the legs and body in the turnspit of Europe and India; the shape of the head and the under-hanging jaw in the bull- and pug-dog, so alike in this one respect and so unlike in all others. A peculiarity suddenly arising, and therefore in one sense deserving to be called a monstrosity, may, however, be increased and fixed by man's selection. We can hardly doubt that long-continued training, as with the greyhound in coursing hares, as with water-dogs in swimming —and the want of exercise, in the case of lapdogs—must have produced some direct effect on their structure and instincts. But we shall immediately see that the most potent *cause* [2] of change has probably been the selection, both methodical and unconscious, of slight individual differences,—the latter kind of selection resulting from the occasional preservation, during hundreds of generations, of those individual dogs which were the most useful to man for certain purposes and under certain conditions of life." (p. 40, v. 1.)

In the absence of modern knowledge of mutations and the mechanism of inheritance this statement of 60 years ago is remarkable in parts and completely out-dated in others. The origin and inheritance of the legs of the turnspit and the

---

[2] Italics supplied.

head of the bulldog through mutation is keenly correct, while lack of exercise as the causative agent in the production of the lap dog is highly improbable. Lack of exercise in the Asiatic chow dog could scarcely be imagined as the basic factor in the origin of the Pekingese, one of the oldest of the lap dogs. The Pekingese is just as probably the product of mutation as is the turnspit or the bulldog, and this is equally true for the Pomeranian lap dog.

At an early date in England, when greyhounds were used for hunting large game, they were supposed to have been crossed with a mastiff or bulldog to improve their courage. Youatt ("The Dog" 1845) claims that after the sixth or seventh generation not a vestige was left of the form of the bulldog, but his courage and indomitable perseverance remained. Such a statement is, of course, open to very great doubt. At an early date the English setter was probably crossed with the pointer, while the pure Irish setter shows no signs of such a cross. The bulldog seems to have originated from the mastiff and it is highly probable that it existed as the bulldog before 1630 though then of much larger size than the modern breed. We shall find much evidence to indicate that careful selection of numerous mutations was necessary in the development of the present day bulldog, while the ancient turnspit and the more recent dachshund and bassethound were readily established by selection of only a single mutation in so far as their most characteristic feature, the short achondroplasic leg condition, is concerned. Pointers are descended from a Spanish breed but were known in England before 1688. The Newfoundland dog was certainly brought into England from that country, but has been so modified that it does not now resemble any existing native dog in Newfoundland. This dog probably originated from a cross between the huskie and a large French hound.

Wide crosses between dog breeds have been made from time to time with ideas of strengthening or modifying the stock and for study of color and hunting ability, but before the present study was begun none had been made from the standpoint of physiologic differences or of the symptoms indicating modified internal secretions.

*Hybridization for new combinations and recombinations of modified glands and type tendencies.* The strongly contrasted types and the sharply localized structural distortions which occur among the dog breeds are often correlated or associated with definite peculiarities of the endocrine glands. These conditions offer probably the most unique possibilities to be found among the mammals for making new combinations of normal and modified glands and of contrasted growth tendencies. Through crossing or hybridizing the various dog breeds, the experimenter is able to break down certain complexes of structural and functional modifications and to build up new complexes or recombinations of characters in the second hybrid generation. Thus he is able to devise crucial tests for determining the functions and degrees of influence of the endocrine secretions in regulating the development and growth of tissues and organs in different genetic constitutions. The results of such tests are to be recorded in detail in the following sections.

Since prehistoric time, hybrid breedings of many kinds have occurred at random among the different races of human beings. Such race crossings may have tended to stimulate mutations and genic instability, thus bringing about freak reactions and functional disharmonies just as are found to occur among dogs. The chief difference has been that in dogs a master hand has selected the freak individuals according to fancy and purified them into the various dog breeds. No such force regulates the mongrel mixing of human beings, and dwarf, giant, achondroplasic and acromegalic tendencies have not been selected out or established in pure form. On the contrary, individuals carrying different degrees of these tendencies are constantly being absorbed into the general human stock, possibly to render the hybridized races less stable and less harmonious in their structural and functional complexes than were the original races from which they were derived. Mongrelization among widely different human stocks has very probably caused the degradation and even the elimination of certain human groups; the extinction of several ancient stocks has apparently followed very closely the extensive absorption of alien slaves. If one considers the histories of some of the south European and Asia-Minor countries from a strictly biological and genetic point of view, a very definite correlation between the amalgamation of the whites and the negroid slaves and the loss of intellectual and social power in the population will be found. The so-called dark ages followed a brilliant antiquity just after the completion of such mongrel amalgamation. Contrary to much biological evidence on the effects of hybridization, racially prejudiced persons, among them several anthropologists, deny the probability of such results from race hybridization in man. There is no doubt that unstable individuals with structural and functional disharmonies arise from crosses between contrasted breeds of dogs, and probably the same conditions to lesser or greater degree result from hybridization among other mammals, including man himself. Certainly no answer to these debatable and very important questions can be scientifically arrived at by any method other than careful experimentation on higher mammals, and, in the light of such experiments, an impartial study of the unregulated human results.

*The pure breeds selected for hybridizing and their strongly contrasted characters.* Many biologists and workers in the medical sciences, as well as specialists in endocrinology and genetics, have only limited knowledge of the detailed characteristics of the various dog breeds. In spite of this fact, it is scarcely in line with our present purpose to devote space to a detailed survey of the characteristics of all the breeds we have employed. It seems much more desirable to describe the characters of the different pure breeds in connection with particular experiments aimed at an analysis of the nature and significance of these characters. Proceeding in this manner we are quite certain that the reader will be able to appreciate the experiments and their results without personal acquaintance with the breeds concerned. The characters to be considered are strongly pronounced and readily recognized as such regardless of the breed in which they occur. Only in the most incidental way is this investigation concerned with dog breeds from the points of interest to dog fanciers.

However, in considering any so-called altered or modified character, two basic and very important questions must of necessity arise: *From what* is the character altered or modified? And what is the *degree* of modification? To answer these questions a control standard or normal dog breed must be determined, for in no other way can we have a basis of comparison. This animal should approach the normal wild or ancestral type dog in bodily size, characteristics and proportions. It is also very essential that it possess, in so far as we are able to diagnose, typically normal endocrine glands.

It is not surprising to find, in surveying the great number of breeds, that very few satisfy the requirements for an ancestral type or normal control. The Labrador huskie and other northern more or less wild and isolated breeds are quite wolf-like and normally proportioned in most respects; but many carry their tails in an abnormally twisted and bent-over fashion lying flat on the rump. The Asiatic chow dog, a wild type, and the European pug, a lap dog type, and others as well, carry their tails in the same manner. This is certainly not an ancestral or common tail position for the dog and involves modifications in both skeleton and muscles. The ancient Saluki is also not a fair control, since it shows unusual narrowness of type and greyhound-like structure clearly associated with high metabolism and excessive activity. Even the common hounds, pointers, setters and other physically well balanced breeds practically all show on careful examination slight degrees of structural peculiarities which make them unfit as all-round controls for this particular study. The excessive growth of skin and long hanging ears in the hounds, and the loose flews or hanging lip-folds of these, the setters and other breeds, might be the mild indications of certain conditions we were seeking to analyze. There are the characteristic instincts, such as various hunting reactions and definite postures, which are found among some otherwise control type dogs, and these, of course, make them unfit for use as controls in connection with studies on the relationship of form and type to instinctive and reflex behavior. The control, if possible, must be a dog showing not even mild deviations from an harmoniously balanced pattern and with no disproportions of structure or parts.

The breed which seemed to us most nearly to approach a standard or ancestral dog type is the German shepherd dog, *Schaefferhund*, sometimes called police dog. This dog, in its general type, structure, functions and behavior, deviates very slightly if at all from a standard or control type. There is no excessive growth of skin, neither its ears nor lips are pendulous, and the shape of head, length and width of muzzle and body form are well on standard canine type. The legs are long and strong, not too slender nor too short and heavy. In size, the shepherd is quite wolf-like, not oversize, having no symptoms of gigantism, and not undersize. The posture, gait, position of the tail, and the instinctive behavior of this animal are all of the standard wild canine type; it is normally canine in all its reactions and is an unusually intelligent companion to man. No other dog fits so closely into the pattern which one would imagine for the early hunting and fighting associate of prehistoric man, and no other breed of dog differs so little from the present living species of wild Canidae. The glands of internal secretion of the German

PLATE 1

EXPLANATION OF FIGURES

Some of the types of pure breed dogs used in connection with this study.

| 1 St. Bernard. | 5 Bassethound. | 9 French bulldog. |
| 2 German shepherd. | 6 Foxhound. | 10 Boston terrier. |
| 3 Saluki. | 7 Dachshund. | 11 Brussels griffon. |
| 4 Great Dane. | 8 English bulldog. | 12 Pekingese. |

All photographs are of animals from the Cornell Anatomy Farm with the exception of figure 6 (AKC American Foxhound Champion, Mr. Ely's Sable—photograph courtesy of Mr. W. Newbold Ely, Jr.).

PLATE 1

shepherd show no consistent deviations in their gross morphology and microscopic structure from what would be considered normal. Various abnormalities in the endocrines may be found in individual cases but these are not consistent for the breed and are certainly to be expected when it is realized that many of these animals are reared and kept under the most abnormal conditions in so far as their diet and behavior are concerned. These dogs are not usually permitted to breed normally as wild animals would, have too little exercise and freedom, and eat an artificial diet, all of which might tend to modify their endocrine glands. We do not claim for them, or any animal, immunity to endocrine disturbances; but in general their endocrine glands are normal and may well serve as a standard for comparison with the glands of other breeds, particularly since all the animals are kept under the same uniformly regulated regime.

# SECTION II

CHARLES R. STOCKARD

## ACHONDROPLASIA OF THE EXTREMITIES; A DEFINITELY LOCALIZED AND HIGHLY ALTERED GROWTH REACTION

The careful study of the genetics and development of a strongly expressed but sharply localized alteration in growth would seem to be the simplest mode of approach to our general problem of the interrelation of the genetic constitution of the tissues and the endocrinic influences in determining structural quality and form. The extremely short and deformed legs of the dachshund and the bassethound breeds offer the most clear cut examples of the condition desired. The modified legs in these dogs are found to result from a typically achondroplasic growth reaction. The epiphyseal growth cartilages in the extremities fail to give the usual longitudinal proliferation of cartilage cells as forerunners for the normal growth in length of the long bones. Instead, the cartilage is abnormally scant and the cellular proliferation and growth take place in transversely spiral and other irregular directions, exactly as has been frequently reported for human achondroplasia and is clearly illustrated and discussed by Knötzke ('29). This chondrodystrophy and modification of subperiosteal bone formation are exactly the kinds of growth distortions thought to result from diseased or defective conditions of the endocrine system, and particularly of the pituitary. They are commonly treated clinically from this standpoint.

The fact of extreme importance in connection with the dachshund and bassethound breeds is the sharp limitation of chondrodystrophy to the skeleton of the extremities, while the axial skeleton—the skull and vertebral column—completely escapes. If abnormal endocrine secretion is the causative agent in producing this skeletal deformation, why should one part of the skeleton suffer and other parts completely escape, while all parts are necessarily exposed to the influences of the same body fluids? This question presents considerable difficulties, yet there are possible answers. It may be recalled, for example, that in embryonic development comparable growth stages of limb and axial skeleton are reached at different embryonic periods. An endocrine disturbance modifying limb growth may possibly occur temporarily during a critical period in the development of the limb and then disappear, leaving a normal environment during the critical stage of origin for the cartilages of the basicranium and the vertebral column. Temporary endocrinal and chemical disturbances are of so common occurrence during postnatal life that it is logical to suppose that during embryonic existence similar disturbances may occur for short periods and then disappear. If embryonic distortions of endocrine glands are responsible for the deformed legs of the bassethound and dachshund, such glandular disturbances are not detectable in later life, since, as we shall see in the histological section of this study, the endocrine glands of mature individuals of these two breeds show no decided deviations from the normal type. Therefore, if a disturbance in endocrine balance or quality occurs during a brief embryonic period to modify limb skeletons, it becomes ineffective during later embryonic periods and completely disappears, leaving no mark that can be found in the endocrine glands of the adult.

The simple examination of these dogs themselves cannot furnish a very satisfactory basis for determining whether the short legs are primarily genetic in origin or are a secondary reaction to a peculiar endocrine condition, which may be in itself primarily genetic. With the hope of arriving at a more satisfactory understanding, an extensive study has been made of the inheritance of short, achondroplasic legs as a contrasted condition to the normal long leg. Three breeds of dogs with typical short achondroplasic legs have been employed: the bassethound, dachshund and Pekingese. The bassethound, a normal sized foxhound typed dog with very short twisted legs, and the well-known dachshund, a dwarf hound typed dog, are both European breeds and may have arisen from a common mutant origin; thus the leg defect might show the same genetic reactions in both. The Pekingese, however, probably arose as an achondroplasic dwarf mutant from a chow-like ancestor and is almost certainly independent in its origin from the other two breeds. This suggests a question: does the short leg of this dog behave in inheritance in the same way as the legs of the other two breeds?

The most dependable stocks available were procured from reliable registered kennels, and the pedigrees without exception have proven to be correct for breed purity in leg form. Results of hybridization experiments offer conclusive proof of this purity.

THE GENETICS OF LIMB ACHONDROPLASIA IN THE BASSETHOUND

The short legged bassethound was crossed with the contrasted long legged normal or standard dog type, the German shepherd; with the slender, very long legged greyhound-like Saluki; with the English bulldog, which has short and stocky but straight non-achondroplasic legs; and finally with the short legged dachshund. The problem of central interest is the manner of inheritance for the achondroplasic growth of the legs and the determination of the part played by the endocrine secretions in the mode of expression for this character.

*Bassethound-shepherd hybrids.* The bassethound is short haired, with an irregular color pattern, the body spotted white and black and the head and ears a reddish brown. It has the large, long, pendulous ears of the hound, and the skin area is excessive, loosely fitting and sagging into folds in the neck and chest regions. The tail is carried in a raised curve and sometimes in an almost vertical position. The bassethound is prized for trailing and hunting rabbits, foxes and other small mammals through heavy undergrowth. It runs with head down, scenting the game with the nose close to the ground; when the trail is found the dog barks as it runs, carrying a so-called open or noisy trail.

The German shepherd dog differs from the bassethound in almost all characteristics. It has longer hair and a wolf-like coat pattern of brown agouti and gray. The coat colors vary from black to a light cream but there is never any spotting. The average weight of the shepherd is somewhat more than that of the bassethound. Its ears are much smaller, being of medium size, and are held erect, as in the wolf. The tail is long and moderately bushy and is carried in a drooping or semi-raised position. Plate 2 (figs. 1 and 2) illustrates the physical differences between the two animals. Shepherd dogs are often good natural hunters and may be trained to hunt in various ways as well as to trail human beings. They hunt and run with the head lifted instead of with the nose to the ground and do not bark while trailing and hunting the prey, though they may bark when they are close in and the prey is at bay. They also offer a sharp contrast to the bassethound in instinctive behavior and posture. The bassethound is much less active and less excitable than the shepherd, being more inhibited, and its thyroid gland is proportionally larger than that of the shepherd, with larger follicles and more colloid.

The genetic behavior for many contrasted characters in the various dog breeds has been followed in our experiments and will be discussed in its possible connection or association with the structural quality and function of the endocrine glands in the several sections of this report. At this place the consideration is entirely devoted to the genetics of the achondroplasic short legged character in the bassethound.

Two pedigreed and registered shepherd bitches were mated to three prize winning registered bassethound males from the pack owned by the late Mr. Erastus T. Tefft who at that time owned one of the only two packs of these hounds in the eastern part of the country. The pedigree records of these animals are as reliable as can be had from breeding kennels. Since such animals are very valuable, the males at times selling for as much as five hundred dollars, there is little chance of their owners permitting unrecorded cross-breed matings. One of the bassethound males, "Leader," had one foxhound grandparent which had been introduced and recorded in the line, carrying out an idea that this lessened the tendency to have knocked wrists which inhibit the running speed for the highly achondroplasic leg. The other two bassethound males used were homozygous for short legs.

One of the first matings made was between the shepherd bitch "Thea" 111 ♀, and "Pathfinder," a pure line bassethound. Four puppies were whelped, two males and two females, all of which lived to maturity. All four puppies were short legged, since the achondroplasic leg of the bassethound is dominant over the normal leg of the shepherd. Photographs of the skeletons of two of these $F_1$ bassethound-shepherd hybrids, 123 ♂ and 124 ♂, are shown in plate 3 (figs. 4, 5 and 6).

The same shepherd bitch, 111 ♀, was then mated to the dog "Leader," a typical bassethound in appearance but having one long-leg foxhound grandparent. This mating also produced four puppies that lived to maturity, two males and two females. Of this litter one male and one female were long legged and the other two were short legged. This clearly indicates that the father was heterozygous for the dominant short leg, carrying the genes for both long and short, and the expectation from his mating with a long legged bitch is equal numbers of long and short legged puppies, which, by chance, were produced.

These two litters from the German shepherd bitch 111 ♀ indicate in themselves that the achondroplasic short leg of the bassethound is a single factor dominant character.

A second shepherd bitch, "Else" 118 ♀, was then mated to a third bassethound male, "Drifter," from pure short-leg lines. This mating whelped seven puppies, three males and four females; two of these animals are shown in plate 2 (figs. 3 and 4). Again the short leg dominates the normal long and all members of this litter of seven are uniformly short. Thus an apparently complex achondroplasic short-leg character would seem to depend upon a simple single genic factor for its inheritance. The further proof of this fact will be shown below.

The reciprocal cross was now made, with two bassethound bitches mated to three different German shepherd males. The pure-line bassethound "Paula" 277 ♀ was mated to a champion shepherd male and whelped five puppies, two males and three females. All five hybrids showed short achondroplasic legs.

The second bitch, "Staridge Jill" 83 ♀, was a perfect bassethound in type, yet she again carried the long leg factor from the foxhound ancestor, as did the dog "Leader" cited above. "Jill" was mated to a pure shepherd dog and whelped a litter of eight puppies, four males and four females. Five of these were short legged and three were long. "Staridge Jill" was later mated to a different shepherd, 1132 ♂, and whelped seven puppies, four males and three females; only one of these was long legged, while six were short.

The achondroplasic short leg of the bassethound definitely dominates the normal long leg in these crosses with the shepherd dog. When pure stock is employed, all members of the first, $F_1$, hybrid generation have short legs. The legs of the heterozygous $F_1$ group are not so extremely achondroplasic nor so fully short as those of the pure homozygous bassethound. The $F_1$ hybrids all carry, of course, the factor for long from the shepherd parent, and the achondroplasic short condition is not so fully expressed when the allelomorph

PLATE 2

EXPLANATION OF FIGURES

Cross between the long legged German shepherd and the achondroplasic short legged bassethound showing inheritance of leg length as well as other physical characters in the first and second hybrid generations.

1 German shepherd 118 ♀.
2 Bassethound 220 ♂.
3–4 $F_1$ brother and sister 246 ♀ and 248 ♂.
5–11 One litter of seven $F_2$ hybrids.
  5  866 ♂.    9  868 ♀.
  6  865 ♂.  10  863 ♂.
  7  864 ♂.  11  862 ♂.
  8  869 ♀.

PLATE 2

$P_1$ 1 2

$F_1$ 3 4

$F_2$ 5 6 7 8 9 10 11

for long is paired with that for short as in the homozygous state with both allels for short. There is also another possible reason why the $F_1$ hybrid is not so short legged as the bassethound. In general, the leg bones of hounds are not so slender and long as those of the German shepherd dog and there is the possibility that the shepherd type of bone is more dominant in the $F_1$ and not so extremely shortened by achondroplasia. In other words, the constitutional type of the bone itself may modify the expression of the achondroplasic condition. Both the above possible explanations for the incomplete shortening of the $F_1$ leg have been analyzed by studying the later generations and backcrosses of this combination as well as by testing the chondrodystrophic response in the bone types of other breeds.

Before considering leg inheritance in the further generations of the shepherd-bassethound cross we may mention in general some of the other qualities and characters of these $F_1$ hybrids. Without exception they show the coat of the shepherd dog, the hair being thicker than in the bassethound and moderately long, with a color pattern closely similar to that of the shepherd. The ears are of medium size, much smaller than those of the hound, but are pendulous or hanging as in the bassethound and are never held erect. The tail is carried in a shepherd-like manner. The $F_1$ hybrids are more active than the bassethound, but when running free to hunt, or when being led on a leash, drop their heads down and scent with the nose to the ground just as does the bassethound parent. The voice and barking reactions are not completely hound-like yet are fuller and somewhat different from the shepherd. They are shepherd coated and colored but are short legged with hanging ears, and physically are hound-like rather than shepherd. These hybrids are large, heavy and very vigorous. Their glands of internal secretion, as we shall show in a subsequent chapter, are quite normal, the only peculiarity being that their thyroid glands are proportionally quite large. The reproductive reactions in these $F_1$ bassethound-shepherds are normal and they produce from five to nine pups in a litter. The female maternal reactions are very good, and all puppies are usually reared to adulthood.

These $F_1$ hybrids are surprisingly uniform in their characters and are mistaken for a standardized breed even by persons familiar with dogs. This uniformity in appearance of a first hybrid generation can only result from crosses between two very pure parent stocks. If the original stocks are not homozygous for their breed characteristics, variations in the qualities of the $F_1$ hybrids will appear as indications of the impurity in the parent stocks. Thus the uniformity in qualities of the $F_1$ generation is the crucial test for the purity of the parent breeds involved.

Returning to the special problems related to the inheritance of achondroplasia in the legs, we may now consider this character in the $F_2$ generation produced from *inter se* matings among the uniformly typed $F_1$ hybrids. Twenty-three fertile matings of $F_1$ hybrids have whelped 144 puppies during a period of 8 years. Approximately one-fourth of these $F_2$ hybrids have long, straight legs with no symptoms of achondroplasia and three-fourths have typical achondroplasic short legs. On further examination the short legged animals may be separated into two groups, the smaller number having extreme achondroplasia with very short legs and a larger group, about twice as many, having achondroplasic legs that are less shortened and show almost exactly the same condition as that found in the $F_1$ parents. The $F_2$ generation is thus divided into three leg-length groups: one-fourth have very short and badly twisted extremities, one-fourth have normal long legs, and half are intermediate in leg condition. In other words this is the typical 1:2:1 Mendelian ratio for the behavior of contrasted expressions of a given character which depends for its inheritance on a single point genetic factor or one gene. Achondroplasic growth of the leg bones is dominant over normal long bone growth and results from the presence of a single allel for this expression. In the heterozygous or mixed condition the influence of the allel for achondroplasia is less pronounced than when the two similar allels are present in homozygous state. A single litter of seven $F_2$ animals shown in plate 2 illustrates these facts. Two animals (figs. 5 and 6) are homozygous for short legs; two (figs. 10 and 11) are homozygous for long legs; and three (figs. 7, 8 and 9) are heterozygous for leg length, carrying the allels for both short and long, and are therefore intermediate in length. This single litter group presents the 1:2:1 ratio as nearly as is possible with seven members; one intermediate leg-length is lacking.

The skeletons from three generations of this cross are seen in plate 3, the contrasted parent skeletons at the top (figs. 1, 2 and 3), the middle line showing the $F_1$ hybrids (figs. 4, 5 and 6) and the bottom row (figs. 7–11) illustrating the three degrees of leg length in $F_2$ skeletons.

A number of other contrasted characters from the parent stocks are redistributed and often occur in new combinations among the $F_2$ hybrids. The recessive tricolor spotting of the bassethound reappears in some of both the short and long legged animals, and the shepherd color and pattern predominate in both leg types, as is illustrated in plate 4. There is no linkage between coat texture and color pattern and leg length. In fact, dogs, with their large number of chromosomes, have not yet definitely yielded a linkage among the single factor characters studied. There are apparent correlations and associations between some conditions and certain elements in multiple factor complexes, but few of these are clearly marked. The erect position of the ears of the shepherd is complex in inheritance and not one of the

PLATE 3

EXPLANATION OF FIGURES

Skeletons of the cross between the German shepherd and bassethound showing contrast in leg length and form in the pure breeds and the resulting condition in the first and second generation hybrids.

1 2 German shepherd 111 ♀.    4 5 $F_1$ 124 ♂.
3 Bassethound 214 ♀.    6 $F_1$ 123 ♂ (brother of 124 ♂).
7–11 Three members of a litter of eight $F_2$ hybrids.
7–8 404 ♂.    9 and 11 402 ♀.    10 403 ♂.

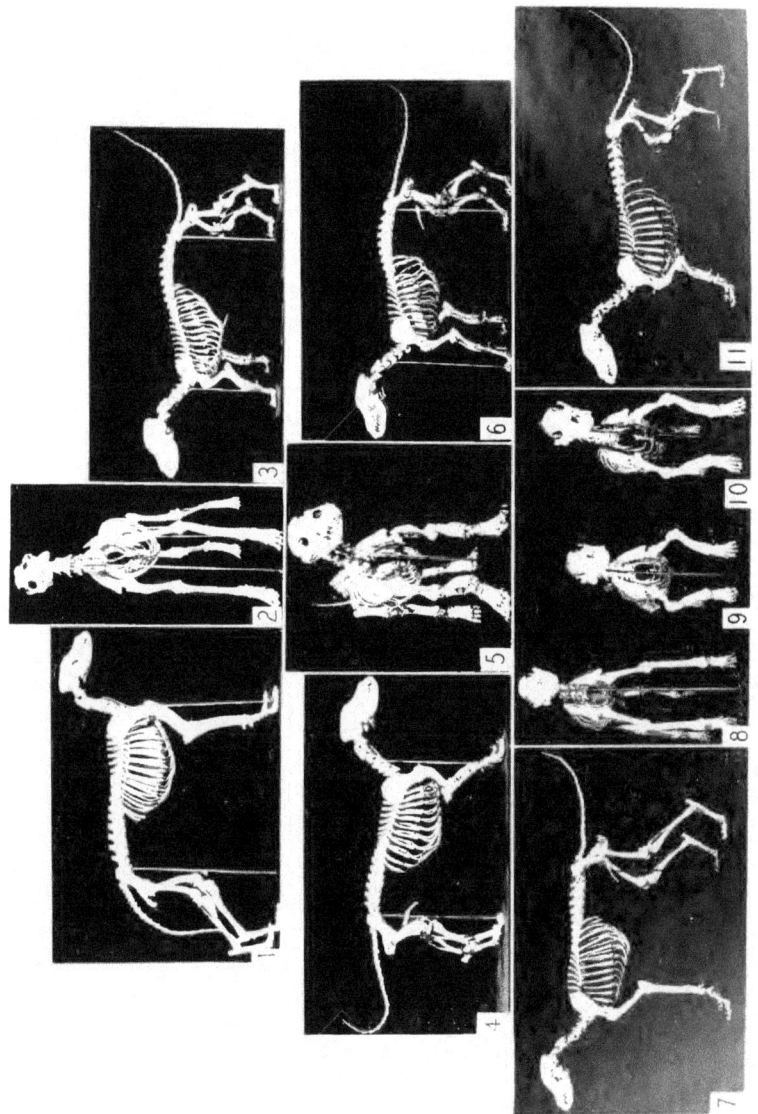

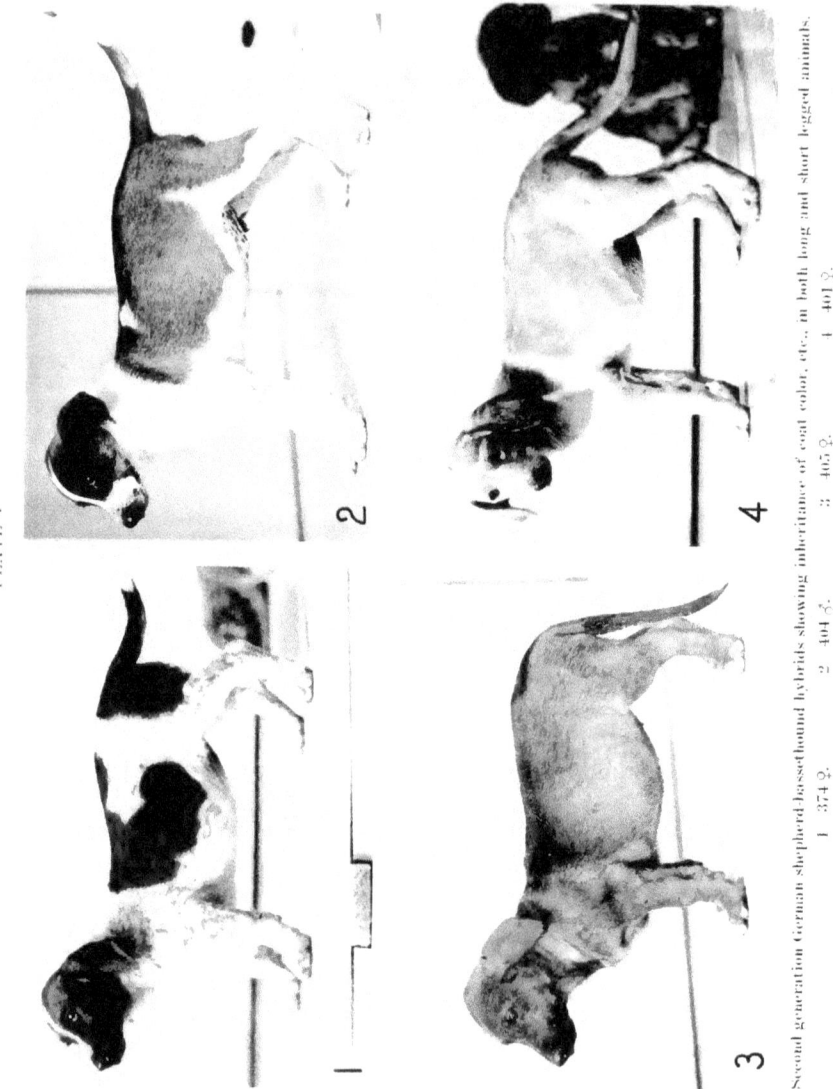

Second generation German shepherd-bassethound hybrids showing inheritance of coat color, etc., in both long and short legged animals.

1  374 ♀.    2  404 ♂.    3  405 ♀.    4  401 ♀.

almost 150 $F_2$ animals has erect ears, although many show a semi-raised ear posture. The size of the ear among these $F_2$ combinations rarely approaches the large ear of the hound. Some of the $F_2$ hybrids are excitable in behavior, resembling the shepherd grandparent; others are less active and less nervous, approaching the bassethound in disposition.

Among the tall $F_2$ animals, some show long, slender, shepherd-like legs while others have a less slender, rather foxhound typed leg. Some of the achondroplasic legs are slenderer and seem comparatively less shortened than others. We shall discuss further the importance of bone quality after other breed crosses have been considered.

*The $F_1$ bassethound-shepherd backcrossed with the shepherd parent stock.* Nine fertile matings were made between the $F_1$ shepherd-bassethound hybrid and the pure shepherd stock. The backcrosses were arranged in some cases between a female $F_1$ and the male shepherd and in others between the female shepherd and the male $F_1$. The results were the same for both kinds of matings. In all, sixty-two offspring were produced from nine matings between the pure long legged parent stock and the heterozygous short $F_1$. The average litter size was about seven, the smallest litter containing only two puppies, and the largest ten. The backcross hybrid puppies were divided for leg length into approximately equal groups of long legged and short legged individuals. If we represent the factor for long leg by the letter $l$ and the factor for short by $s$ and consider the germinal quality of the pure shepherd as $ll$ and the hybrid $F_1$ as $sl$, we obtain the expected 50:50 ratio of $ll$ and $sl$ combinations. The types of legs among these backcross hybrids are either fully long as in the shepherd or intermediately short as in the $F_1$ shepherd-bassethound; no pure $ss$ legs are possible.

In common language, these backcross hybrids would be termed three-quarter shepherd, but, as may be seen by reference to any one character, such a fractional expression is genetically entirely incorrect. For example, the long, non-achondroplasic leg is not three-quarters shepherd but entirely shepherd, *ll*, while the achondroplasic intermediate-short leg results from half bassethound and half shepherd effects, *ls*. These reactions accord with the principles of Mendelian segregation of characters in inheritance and are mentioned here since many workers in fields bearing on other phases of this investigation are unfamiliar with genetic conceptions.

In the smallest of the backcross litters there were only two individuals, and by chance one of these was long legged and one short legged. Plate 5 illustrates the contrast in leg length between these litter mates, 652 ♂ *ll* and 653 ♀ *sl*, when 4 months old (fig. 3) and as adults (fig. 5), with the parent types pictured above. The skeletons from these two dogs in front and side views are shown in plate 6. Comparing these two skeletons vividly illustrates the effect of the single allel for achondroplasia as derived from the bassethound. In figure 3 of plate 6 the very short and bent tibia from 653 ♀ is shown on the left and the long and almost straight line tibia from the brother on the right. The contrast between the growth patterns in these two bones is extreme and it is surprising to realize that in a mammal the presence of only one modified gene may give rise to so great a distortion in form and size. The difference between the achondroplasic short and twisted humerus and the normal humerus is shown by figure 4. This modification in growth is strictly confined to the skeleton of the extremities; the axial skeletons of these two animals are alike and normal, as is clearly shown by the lateral aspects in figures 5 and 6 of plate 6.

PLATE 5

EXPLANATION OF FIGURES

Backcross of the $F_1$ German shepherd-bassethound having intermediate legs with the pure long legged shepherd parent. The expectancy here is equal numbers of intermediate and long legged hybrids.

1 German shepherd 118 ♀.
2 $F_1$ 251 ♂.
3 Backcross hybrids 653 ♀ (intermediate legs) and 652 ♂ (long legs) at 4 months.
5 Same two dogs at 18 months of age.
4 Backcross 501 ♂. The head and body of this animal are very like the pure shepherd, but the legs are achondroplasic like the bassethound. Note the erect ears as in the shepherd parent.

PLATE 5

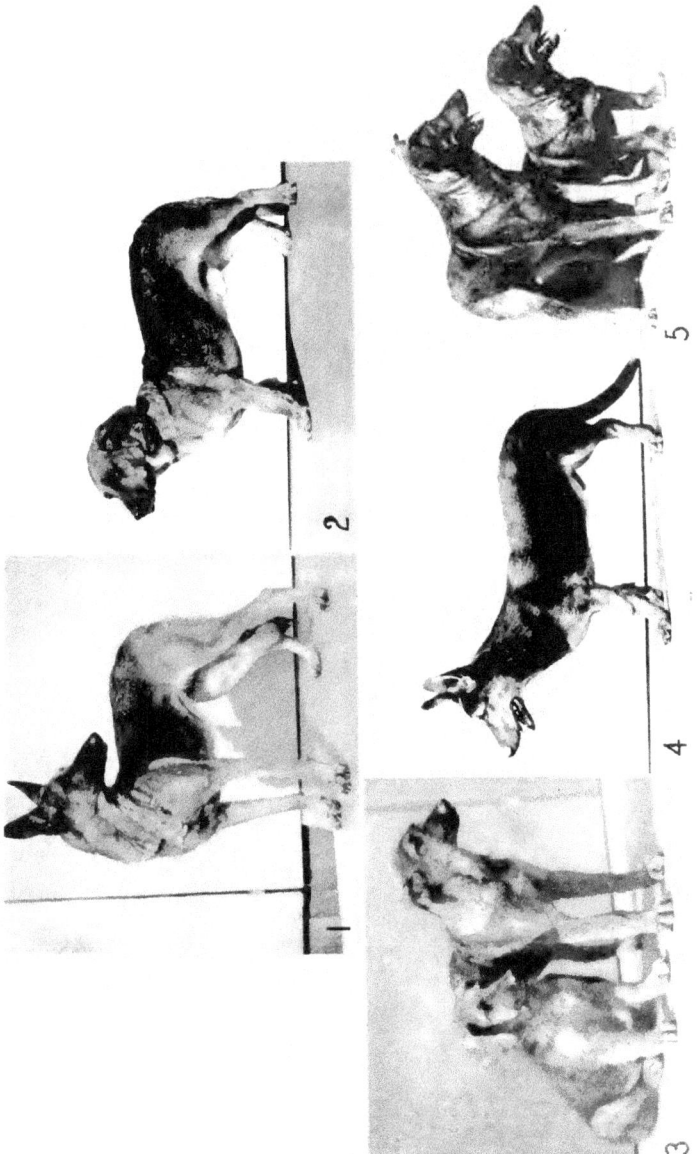

PLATE 6

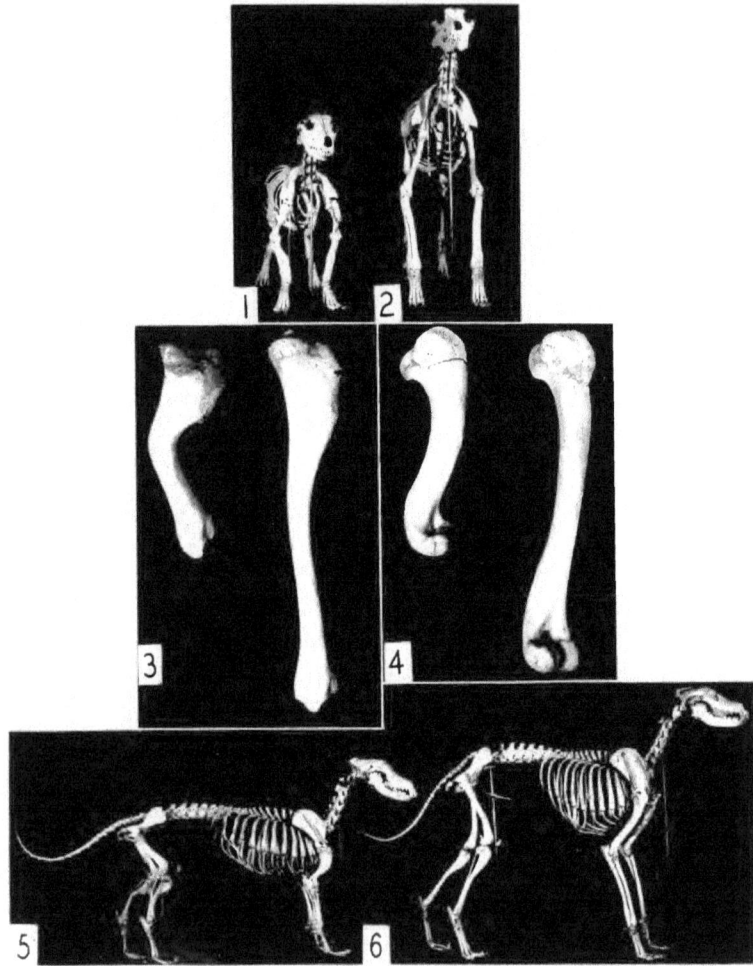

Skeletons and leg bones of two contrasted litter mate backcross shepherd-bassethound-shepherd hybrids (photographs from life in plate 5). No. 653 ♀ has inherited one gene for achondroplasia from the $F_1$ parent, and 652 ♂ is pure for long legs.

    1 and 5   653 ♀        3 tibia of 653 ♀ (left) and 652 ♂ (right).
    2 and 6   652 ♂        4 humerus of 653 ♀ (left) and 652 ♂ (right).

The backcross hybrids exhibit the hair texture and coat pattern of the shepherd, as seen in plate 5. Some of these are also quite shepherd-like in behavior. Only one among the fairly large number of animals, however, had perfectly erect, typically shepherd typed ears although two others showed ears which were almost erect. The backcross animal with erect ears is shown in plate 5 (fig. 4). The head and body of this dog would be mistaken for pure shepherd and the tail is also shepherd-like, but strangely enough the body is carried upon achondroplasic bassethound legs. When the reader places his hand over the photograph so as to cover the legs of this dog, its shepherd type then becomes more strongly pronounced; when the hand is removed the strange appearance due to the short legs is exaggerated.

The erect ear of the shepherd is a complex character depending in its inheritance upon multiple factors, of which most are recessive in expression, as is illustrated by its rare appearance in these backcross hybrids. As is well known, the breeders of pure shepherd dogs frequently have difficulty in maintaining strongly erect ears in their stocks. This is no doubt due to its complex and recessive nature.

Summarizing our present point of interest in the backcross of the $F_1$ shepherd-bassethound with the shepherd parent, it is clear that the normal leg of the shepherd is recessive to achondroplasia on a single factor basis.

*The $F_1$ bassethound-shepherd backcrossed with the bassethound.* The $F_1$ bassethound-shepherd was also crossed back on the bassethound parent stock. On the basis of the leg conditions in the $F_2$ generation as already discussed, and the results of the backcross on the shepherd given in the preceding section, we should expect the bassethound backcross to produce only achondroplasic short legs. Furthermore, we should expect these short legs to be of two different classes. Since the pure bassethound is homozygous for achondroplasia of the leg we may represent the genes chiefly concerned as *ss*, and since the $F_1$ shepherd-bassethound is heterozygous or hybrid for this condition of the leg its genic composition will be *sl*. On crossing two such animals the only possible recombinations will be *ss* and *sl*, since every germ cell from one parent carries an *s*, and from the other parent half will carry *s* and half *l*; thus, half the fertilizations will give *ss* and half *sl*.

Plate 7 illustrates in the case of one litter of six animals, the realized expectation of three extremely short *ss* puppies (fig. 3) and three intermediately short *sl* (fig. 4). In none of the offspring from this backcross can long legs ever appear since there is no possibility of the arrangement *ll*. In the preceding section with the shepherd backcross it was equally impossible to obtain the extreme achondroplasic shortness since the homozygous condition necessary for this, *ss*, could not occur.

In all, six matings were made between the $F_1$ shepherd-bassethound and the pure bassethound. Both $F_1$ males and females were used in this backcross, with similar results. Thirty-six puppies were whelped in litters of from four to eight individuals. On careful measurement and examination from puppyhood to adult size it was estimated that very short legs and intermediate shortness occurred in about equal numbers. There is the possibility that the hound leg bone and the shepherd leg bone are not equally susceptible to the achondroplasic reaction; the one might be more shortened by this effect than the other. Since the different qualities of bone from the two ancestral pure stocks are involved in an estimation of the degree of shortness, it is almost impossible

PLATE 7

EXPLANATION OF FIGURES

Backcross of the $F_1$ German shepherd-bassethound having intermediate legs with the pure short legged bassethound. The expectancy here is equal numbers of short legged and intermediate legged offspring.

1  Bassethound 83 ♀.
2  $F_1$ 248 ♂.
3–4  Litter of six backcross hybrids.
   3  (L to R) 412 ♂, 407 ♂, 410 ♂ (short legged).
   4  (L to R) 409 ♂, 408 ♂, 411 ♀ (intermediate legs).

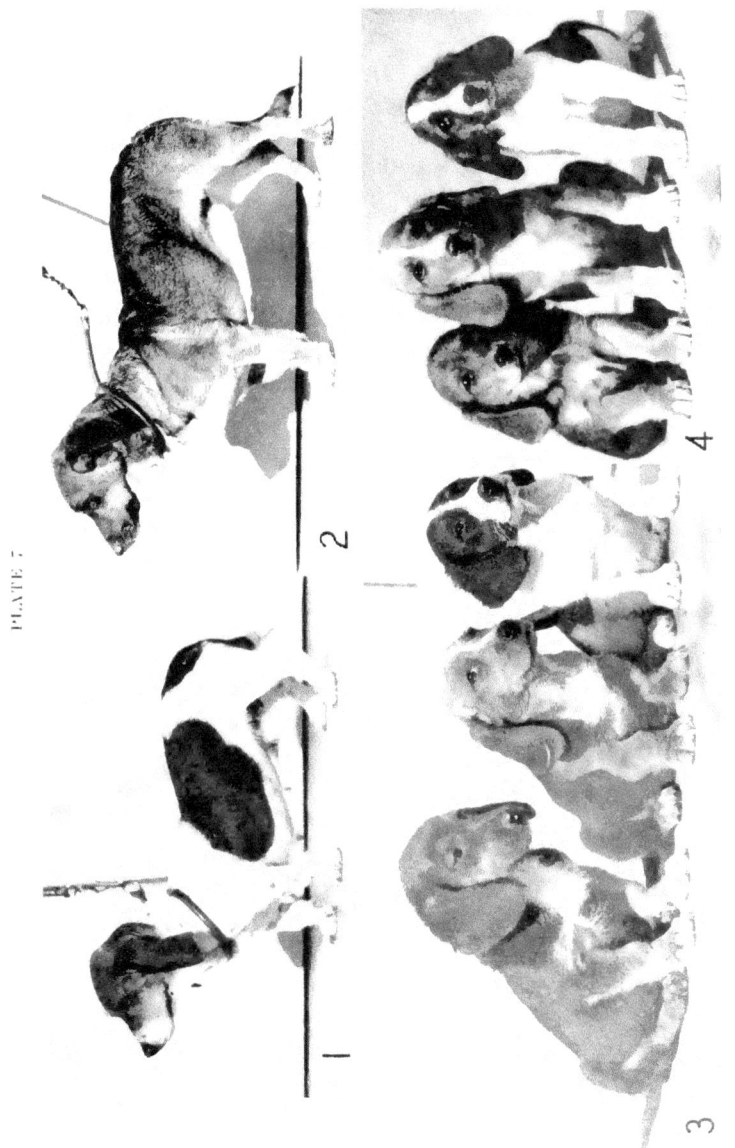

PLATE 7

in some cases to know simply from the morphology and without genetic tests whether an individual should be classed as homozygous and extremely short, or mixed and intermediate. In most cases, however, the diagnosis is quite clear and certain.

The crucial proof of the constitution in the questionable cases must, of course, depend upon the genetic test, and these we have made from time to time, as will be discussed below.

## THE ENHANCED EFFECTS FROM TWO ALLELOMORPHS FOR ACHONDROPLASIA AS COMPARED WITH THE EFFECTS FROM ONLY ONE SUCH GENE

Mammals are so much more highly complex than are the lower forms on which most genetic problems have been analyzed that it may be permissible to discuss in connection with these studies on dogs certain propositions that from an orthodox genetic standpoint seem quite well established. Such a proposition concerns the question of whether there may be contamination of the gene for normal leg growth after an association with the allel for achondroplasia. For example, an $F_1$ bassethound-foxhound hybrid having short legs will supposedly carry the allelomorphic genes $s$ for short and $l$ for long legs in close contact in a chromosomal pair. Will the gene for long, $l$, or likewise the gene $s$ for short, be

PLATE 8

EXPLANATION OF FIGURES

Cross between the pure German shepherd and a mixed shepherd-bassethound-foxhound female carrying two genes for long legs, one of which was associated with the allelomorph for short in the chromosomal pairs of her bassethound-foxhound father. Had the gene for long been contaminated by association with the gene for short, half the offspring would show a decrease in leg length. All hybrids from this mating were long legged.

1 German shepherd 112 ♀.

2 213 ♀, produced by mating a pure shepherd female to a bassethound-foxhound male.

3 Litter of nine hybrids (Nos. 356–364) produced by mating 213 ♀ to a pure shepherd male.

modified as far as later genetic influence is concerned on account of this close contact? We have made breedings which bear on this question.

In one case, a pure shepherd bitch was mated to a heterozygous bassethound-foxhound male and produced two long legged and two short legged offspring, as was expected on the chance basis. A long legged daughter (plate 8, fig. 2) is $ll$ for leg length, but one of the allels for long in this animal's cells was previously associated with the allel for short in the chromosomal pairs of her bassethound-foxhound father. Has the former contact with the $s$ gene affected half the genes for long contained within this daughter? To answer this question the bitch was mated to a pure shepherd male, and nine puppies were whelped, all of which lived to adulthood (see lower line of dogs in plate 8). Every one of these animals had long legs and there was no indication of decrease in leg length, as may have occurred in half of them had the gene for long been contaminated in the heterozygous short legged maternal grandfather. The experiments previously discussed show that the gene for achondroplasic short leg, $s$, is dominant in its influence over the gene $l$ for long legs, and neither the $l$ nor the $s$ gene is modified by allelic association with the other. Yet each of these genes probably exerts an influence when in the other's presence. As evidence of this last statement, it has been mentioned above that individuals which are homozygous for short legs, $ss$, develop more extremely shortened legs than do those animals which are mixed or heterozygous, $sl$. In other words, a single gene in the mammalian constitution may exert a profound modification in the development of long bones and decidedly modify the animal type. The presence of two similar allels for inducing the achondroplasic condition gives a more enhanced effect than does only one gene. The enhancement may be due to a summation of effects from the two genes in the homozygous case, but, on the other hand, the weaker achondroplasic effect in the heterozygous animal may be due to some competition with the gene $l$ for normal leg length. These reactions are so pronounced that the observer may diagnose the limb conditions resulting from the influence of two genes as contrasted with the conditions due to only one such gene. The two groups, short and intermediately short, are so clearly distinguishable, and the number of animals making up each group follows so exactly Mendelian expectations, that it is highly probable that the very short group is homozygous and the group with less deformed legs is heterozygous. The crucial proof for the correctness of these suppositions is the genetic test which has been applied in a number of cases.

Plate 9 illustrates the results of such a genetic test. Figures 1 and 2 show two $F_1$ shepherd-bassethound dogs with achondroplasic legs of intermediate length, the mixed heterozygous condition. At the left in figure 3 is an $F_2$ animal, 560 ♂, with very short legs, which was diagnosed as homozygous $ss$. At the right in figure 3 is a long legged, $ll$, $F_2$ litter mate sister, 562 ♀. To prove our diagnosis correct, a mating between this brother and sister should produce only offspring with intermediate-short legs. The mating was made and ten $F_3$ puppies were whelped, all having intermediate length short legs. Figures 4, 5 and 6 of plate 9 show eight members of this litter which lived to adulthood, and the heterozygous short state of the legs is clearly comparable with the condition shown by the $F_1$ hybrids (figs. 1 and 2). This mating thus furnished genetic evidence of practical certainty that the $F_2$ male 560 (left in fig. 3) is homozygous, $ss$, for short legs, as we had diagnosed from morphological examination. It is of considerable importance to know that so complex a deformity as chondrodystrophy of the extremities, involving as it does the length and shapes of bones and muscles as well as other less evident arrangements, arises from the presence of a single gene which is largely dominant in its influence over the normal allel for long legs. Further, we repeat, one is able to diagnose the animal as genetically mixed or pure for the achondroplasic condition simply from the degree of the morphologic reaction.

PLATE 9

Genetic proof of diagnoses of leg length from morphological examination. Shepherd-bassethound hybrids.

1  $F_1$ 246 ♀.
2  $F_1$ 251 ♂.
3  $F_2$ 560 ♂ (L) and 562 ♀ (R).
4–6  $F_3$s (Nos. 940–947).

The two $F_2$s in figure 3 were diagnosed as pure for short (ss) and pure for long (ll), respectively. Offspring produced by mating these two animals (figs. 4–6) all show the intermediate leg condition of the $F_1$s, thus proving the diagnoses correct.

The consideration of different crosses in which other breeds were employed will add to the above analysis and extend our understanding of these growth distortions, as well as others of somewhat different degrees and quality.

## Bassethound-Saluki Hybrids

The general type and chief characteristics of the bassethound have been described at the beginning of the chapter in the introduction to the consideration of the bassethound-shepherd cross. The reader unfamiliar with this breed may review the type by referring to page 47.

The Saluki, which has existed since ancient times in Asia Minor and northern Africa, is far more strongly contrasted in type with the bassethound than is the normal standard shepherd dog. The Saluki deviates from the shepherd dog type in an almost opposite direction from that of the bassethound, and the contrast between the Saluki and the bassethound is extreme. While the bassethound is built for heavy running through low growing woods and thick underbrush, the Saluki is the light-footed, swift-speeding greyhound type adapted for chase in the open country.

An almost exact representation of the modern Saluki type can be seen in carvings on the oldest monuments in both Asia Minor and Egypt. It is surprising, when one considers the history of wars and human migrations in these regions, that a breed of dogs could have maintained any degree of purity in type through thousands of years. Nevertheless, the Saluki of today definitely resembles in outline the drawings and carvings of a dog depicted from time to time through long ages. The disposition of the Saluki may in some way account for the persistence of its type. This dog is quite indifferent and almost unfriendly toward the members of many other breeds, and it is equally true that some individuals of other breeds fail to recognize the Saluki as belonging to their species and will occasionally attack it without provocation. Among the large number of breed crosses made in our experiments, none of the cross-matings has been more difficult to manage than that involving the Saluki, unless it be those with the Labrador huskies. Both males and females of these breeds which have come under my observation seem slow to recognize the member of another breed as one of their kind, and when a Saluki and a huskie are brought into the same compartment for mating, one usually attacks the other in a vicious fashion before realizing the object of the meeting. To prevent an attack the master must introduce the two animals slowly and with great care until such time as the male has scented the fact that the bitch is in heat and until the bitch has shown that she is properly inclined to accept the male. This hesitation to associate and mate with members of other breeds is not strongly pronounced in most dogs although there is often a slight tendency to mate more willingly with individuals of the same breed. This preference, however, is very rarely strong enough to inhibit the acceptance of males of other breeds by a proud bitch or to discourage most males from pursuing any bitch that may be in heat.

Possibly the tendency towards exclusiveness in the Saluki has aided in maintaining the purity of its type. A factor of equally great importance would seem to have been the preference of the Arabs and Egyptians for the Saluki as a hunting hound. These people were not disposed to keep or even tolerate deformed and worthless dogs. In addition, the frequent scarcity of food and the lack of proper care would probably be contributing factors. This dog is more independent and a more capable forager than any other of which I know, and such characteristics might save it under adverse conditions sufficient to eliminate many another breed. Whether or not we accept these explanations, the fact still remains that the Saluki has the qualities of the persistent type and has maintained a high degree of purity for long ages.

Salukis become attached to the master in a very casual way, not with the exaggerated devotion shown by many breeds. Their tendency is to wander long distances from home and to return at irregular intervals. On such trips they hunt and forage for food and when approached by strange persons, or even by their own masters, avoid being caught and frequently run away. They are typically negative in their instinctive response and are often unwilling to do the master's bidding. Such a reaction is sometimes interpreted by trainers as a lack of intelligence or inability to learn. However, this estimation is based entirely on misinterpretation; the Saluki is a truly intelligent dog and appreciates the situation quickly, but is an unwilling negative individual not at all times interested in the things the trainer may wish him to do. A docile agreeable dog may learn the task set by a trainer more readily than a less agreeable animal, yet this does not necessarily indicate differences in intelligence since the degree of attention to the task is of different magnitude in the two cases. The degree of attention measures interest in the given problem rather than intelligence of the individual.

In physical form, the Saluki is extremely lank, slender and greyhound-like (see fig. 1, plate 10). The head is long, with a slender but strong muzzle, and the body is thin and deep chested, the ribs having a tendency to show even when the animal is well fed. The Saluki, among all the dogs, is more nearly comparable to what one may think of among persons as an individual with a highly active thyroid—the normal high-thyroid type. It is alert though not nervous, and is *par excellence* the linear typed individual. The long bones of the limbs are slender and of dense hardness. The muscles are also long, drawn out, and slender, yet the animal has great strength. A 30 kilo Saluki can support the sudden weight of a 70 kilo man upon its back.

The legs of the Saluki are proportionately longer than those of the shepherd dog and are also much slenderer. The ratio of circumference to length in the leg bones of the Saluki is only about half that of the shepherd, and the contrast between the long, slender leg of the Saluki and the short, chondrodystrophic leg of the bassethound is extreme. Saluki bone growth deviates from the standard control in an opposite direction from chondrodystrophy. The questions arise: will the very slender Saluki bone be affected by the inheritance of chondrodystrophy, and if so, will it be affected to the same degree as is the shepherd bone? The fact that achondroplasia of the extremities in the bassethound-shepherd cross is inherited as a single factor dominant character over normal leg growth need not necessarily mean that this condition is dominant for all crosses nor that all types of bone will be susceptible to such growth reactions. The investigation of such growth distortions must be made on many different breeds and must be extended to other degrees and forms of distorted expression in order to fully analyze these problems.

The $F_1$ bassethound-Saluki hybrids. A tested pure bassethound bitch, "Paula" 277 ♀, was crossed with a perfectly typed Saluki male, 323 ♂. This male was the offspring of a pair of highly prized Salukis imported from Egypt by Mr. Erastus T. Tefft. Five $F_1$ hybrids, three males and two females, were whelped from the cross-mating and all lived to maturity.

Two $F_1$ bassethound-Salukis are shown in plate 10 (figs. 3 and 4) and in somewhat less reduced photographs in plate 11 (figs. 1 and 2). All the $F_1$ hybrids are almost exactly the same in form and behavior, and this uniformity is in itself indicative of the purity or genetic homozygosity of each of the parent stocks. These hybrids have a slenderer and seemingly longer head than the bassethound and show the peculiar almond shaped and obliquely slit Mongol-like eyelid openings of the Saluki. The Saluki (fig. 1) and $F_1$ (fig. 3) in plate 10 show this characteristic eye, and in figures 2 and 3 of plate 11

PLATE 10

EXPLANATION OF FIGURES

Cross between the long, slender legged Saluki and the achondroplasic bassethound to determine whether the hybrid reaction for leg type follows the same pattern in this cross as in the shepherd-bassethound cross.

1   Saluki 323 ♂.
2   Bassethound 220 ♂.
3   $F_1$ hybrid 505 ♂.
4   $F_1$ hybrid 504 ♂.
5–11  Seven members of one litter of $F_2$ hybrids.
   5  1441 ♂.   6  1440 ♂.   7  1442 ♂.   8  1439 ♂.   9  1443 ♂.
                10  1444 ♂.   11  1445 ♀.

PLATE 10

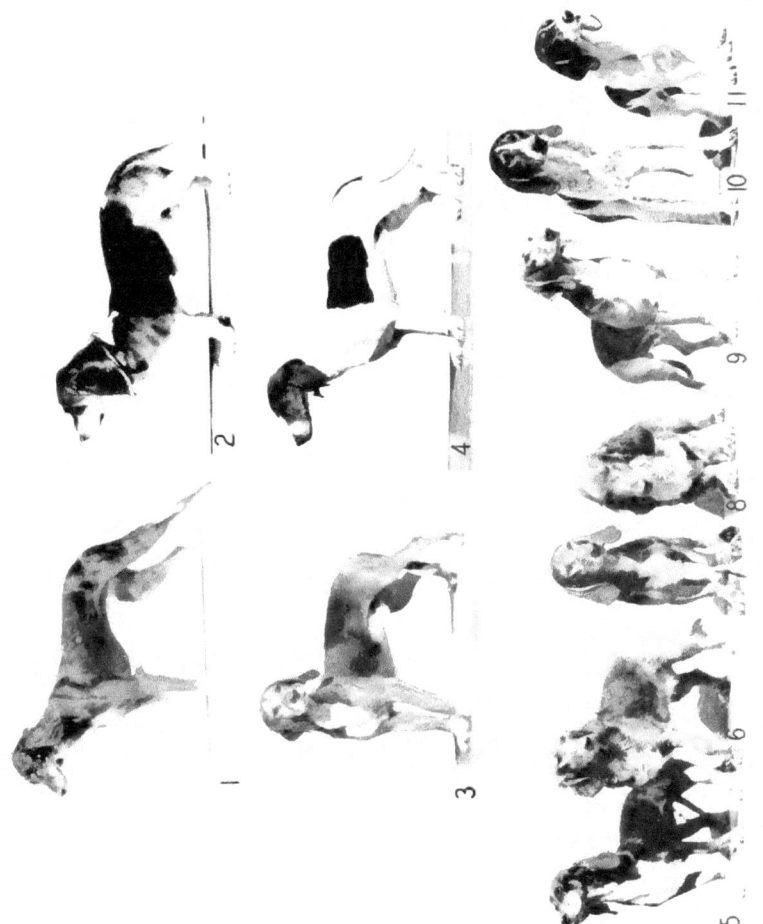

the same feature, less reduced in size, can be seen. The body of the $F_1$ is slender and its movements and postures are closely similar to those of the Saluki. This similarity is noticeable even in the photographs.

The $F_1$ bassethound-Saluki has the short hair of its bassethound parent. The Saluki body coat of silky hair of medium length with the long fringe on the legs and tail and the long wavy hair about the ears seems to be recessive to the bassethound short hair, whereas, it will be recalled, the full shepherd coat is dominant over the short hair of the bassethound. Two of the five $F_1$s, a male and a female, were spotted, and three were brown and tan with white markings on the chest. The male Saluki of the parent cross, though black and tan, carried a recessive for spotting and the mating to the spotted bassethound bitch therefore resulted in an almost equal number of spotted and uniformly colored offspring. The spotting in these breeds is recessive.

The legs of the $F_1$s are short with mild symptoms of the twist in shape and abduction at the wrist common in achondroplasia. These features are not nearly so strongly pronounced as in the $F_1$ bassethound-shepherd. There is also considerable tendency in these $F_1$ bassethound-Saluki hybrids toward Saluki slenderness of bone, which would indicate that this quality bone is largely dominant over hound quality.

*The $F_2$ bassethound-Saluki hybrids.* Eleven litters of $F_2$ bassethound-Saluki hybrids, totaling eighty-two individuals, have been whelped. The litters were uniformly large, containing from six to nine members, and the $F_2$ puppies were unusually vigorous; only a very small percentage of them failed to reach maturity.

The sex ratios in the litters produced by the two $F_1$ bassethound-Saluki mothers were quite strongly contrasted. From one mother the ratio was three to one for males, and from the other it was only one to three. The female $F_1$ 507 ♀ produced thirty-three males to twelve females, while the sister, 508 ♀, produced nine males to twenty-eight females. In the case of 507 ♀ there was a litter of eight, a litter of six and a litter of seven, each containing only one female puppy, while the sister, 508 ♀, gave a litter of eight and a litter of six with only one male pup each, and a litter of seven and a litter of nine with only two males each. Other litters produced by both mothers were more nearly divided for males and females.

The $F_2$ generation showed most instructive conditions in leg length and bone type. The bottom row of plate 10 illustrates a single litter of seven $F_2$ adult animals. Three of these, 1441 ♂ (fig. 5), 1439 ♂ (fig. 8), and 1445 ♀ (fig. 11) are double short or *ss* for achondroplasia; three, 1440 ♂ (fig. 6), 1442 ♂ (fig. 7), and 1443 ♂ (fig. 9) are intermediate or mixed, *sl*; and one animal, 1444 ♂ (fig. 10) shows very long, *ll*, Saluki legs. Thus in this litter appear the three expected kinds of legs: the dominant pure short *ss*, mixed short *sl*, and the recessive pure long *ll*. But an element which was not so noticeable among the bassethound-shepherd $F_2$ animals, although it was present, is clearly presented in these. The Saluki typed bone and the bassethound typed bone tend to segregate in a rather definite manner, while at the same time the achondroplasic growth occurs with both bone types. This fact introduces a second element in the determination of leg length and pattern and the degree of achondroplasic reaction, and because of this second element the three animals, figures 5, 8 and 11 in plate 10, although diagnosed as double short, *ss*, are not all equally short. No. 1445 ♀ (fig. 11) is the tallest and 1439 ♂ (fig. 8) the shortest of the three. These two animals are better shown and less reduced in size in plate 11 (fig. 3, right, and fig. 4). The shortest one, 1439 ♂ (fig. 4) is seen to have a most pronounced achondroplasic distortion of the stocky, bassethound-like front legs. The two factors, *ss*, for short affecting this stocky bassethound bone produced a very pronounced reaction. Conversely, the pure *ss* short condition acting upon the slender Saluki typed bone in 1445 ♀ (right in fig. 3), produced a less marked effect, and this dog shows legs almost as long as the mixed *sl* $F_1$ hybrids (figs. 1 and 2) and with even slenderer bone. This animal appears to have almost pure Saluki typed bone and the achondroplasic modi-

PLATE II

Further details of the inheritance of leg length and bone type, as well as other physical characters, in the cross between the Saluki and bassethound.
1. $F_1$ 504 ♂.    2. $F_1$ 505 ♂.    3. $F_2$ 1444 ♂ (L.) and 1445 ♀ (R.).    4. $F_2$ 1439 ♂.

## PLATE 12

Influence of bone constitution on the homozygous state for achondroplasia. Saluki-bassethound second generation hybrids.

1 Litter mate brothers 1214 ♂ (L) and 1211 ♂ (R). No. 1214 ♂ has inherited the homozygous condition for achondroplasia on Saluki typed bone, while 1211 ♂, although also homozygous for achondroplasia, has inherited almost pure bassethound quality bone.

2 Litter mate brothers 1441 ♂ and 1439 ♂, also both homozygous for achondroplasia. No. 1441 ♂ has inherited Saluki bone type. No. 1439 ♂ shows an exaggerated condition of achondroplasia on thick, stocky bone type and is more extreme for this condition than the bassethound.

fication shortens such bone to a lesser degree than either shepherd typed or bassethound typed bone. The constitution of the bone itself is of consequence in determining the degree of shortening from chondrodystrophy. This fact must be taken into account when diagnosing an individual as genetically mixed *sl* or pure *ss* for the achondroplasic condition.

The above facts are somewhat better illustrated by the photographs in plate 12. The two dogs in figure 1 are brothers. No. 1214 ♂ at the left carries the homozygous condition, *ss*, for achondroplasia and has, in addition, inherited the factors for the slender typed Saluki bone; while a brother, 1211 ♂, also homozygous, *ss*, for leg length, has inherited almost pure bassethound quality bone and consequently shows stockier legs, larger, more outspread feet with more pronounced abduction at the wrist, and finally a much lower swung body. Figure 2 in plate 12 shows two brothers from a different litter. These again are both homozygous, *ss*, for the achondroplasic short extremities. Judging from its development and bone type, the animal on the left, 1441 ♂, has inherited almost pure Saluki bone quality. The brother, 1439 ♂, at the right presents a most exaggerated chondrodystrophic short leg with stocky, thick bone, extreme abduction at the wrist and greatly enlarged, outspread feet, much more exaggerated than its bassethound grandparent. This animal would appear to possess a new quality of bone, different from that of either parent stock and derived from its own peculiar combination of ancestral factors, the result of which is this exaggerated expression of achondroplasia.

PLATE 13

EXPLANATION OF FIGURES

Second generation bassethound-Saluki hybrids showing various conditions of leg length and bone type, as well as other physical characters.

| 1 931 ♂. | 4 932 ♂. | 7 817 ♂. | 10 798 ♀. |
| 2 929 ♂. | 5 933 ♀. | 8 792 ♂. | 11 797 ♀. |
| 3 930 ♂. | 6 791 ♂. | 9 816 ♂. | 12 795 ♀. |

Figures 1 to 5 are litter mates, as are figures 7 and 9, and figures 6, 8, 10, 11 and 12.

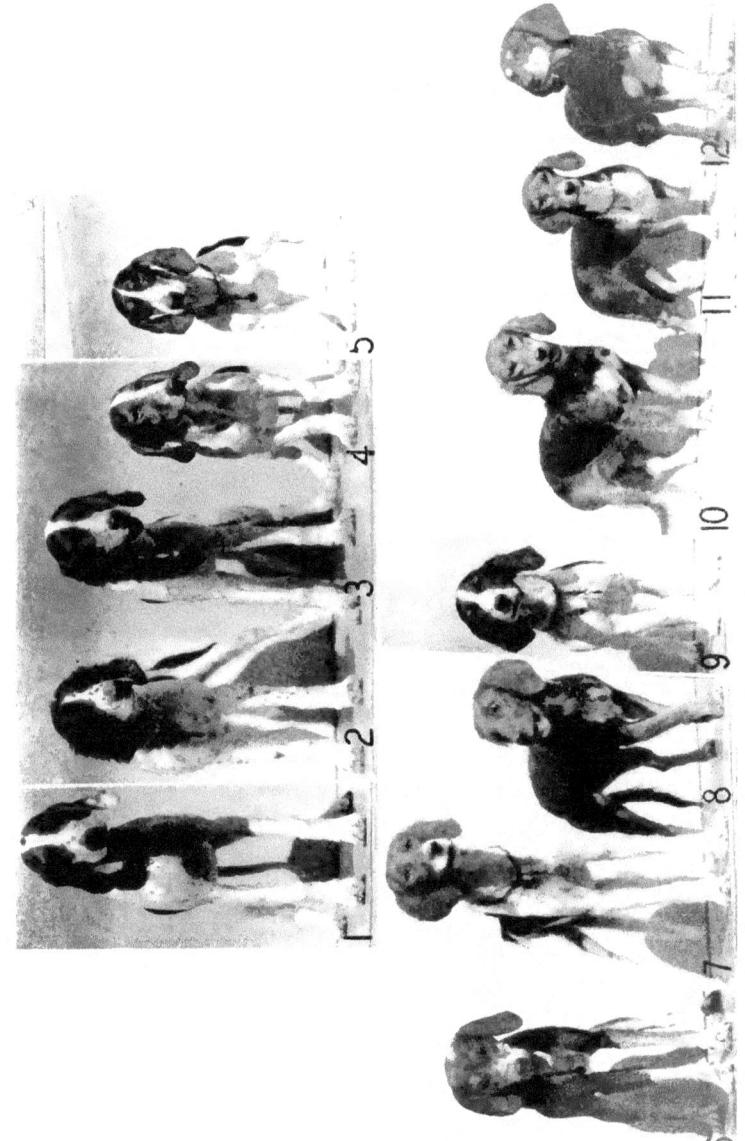

PLATE 13

The segregation of bone constitution and type is also shown among the recessive long legged $F_2$s. Some of these have the long slender greyhound-like legs of the Saluki while others have heavier and somewhat shorter legs resembling those of the foxhound and the setter. The latter animals have inherited, we assume, the bassethound bone type, free or segregated away from the factors for chondrodystrophy.

Plate 13 illustrates still other bassethound-Saluki $F_2$ hybrids. Figures 1 to 5 show five adults from a litter of six; three are long legged, one was judged to be pure for short, and the other intermediate, sl. Nos. 932 ♂ and 933 ♀ (figs. 4 and 5) are strongly Saluki in bone type. One of the tall dogs (fig. 2) tends toward hound bone type and the other two (figs. 1 and 3) have rather definite Saluki bone type. In the lower group in this plate, 817 ♂ and 816 ♂ (figs. 7 and 9) are members of a litter of eight. The two long legged dogs (figs. 6 and 7) are both of Saluki type, the two short (figs. 11 and 12) are pure for short but with Saluki typed bone, and the three intermediates (figs. 8, 9 and 10) are mixed, sl, for leg length but with Saluki bone.

The Saluki constitution, as indicated in the $F_1$ hybrids, is largely dominant, and the $F_2$ generation shows the characteristics of the Saluki segregating and reappearing in very definite form in a large majority of the individuals. It is aside from our present problem to consider in detail the inheritance of many of these features, since only a few of them have been suspected of an association with endocrine types of diseases. The strange, obliquely placed almond shaped eye openings of the Saluki would seem to be a single factor dominant character and is very prevalent among the $F_2$ dogs, as the illustrations show. Types of coat and color pattern and several characteristic attitudes and postures among these hybrids are available for investigation, but are to be reported in other places.

On hybridizing widely contrasted types, such as the bassethound and Saluki, we have occasionally obtained strange, almost grotesque individuals in the $F_2$ generation, some of which are non-viable. These conditions result from the accidental association of contrasted tendencies or from new combinations of genic interaction. A very unusual individual of this sort occurred in the $F_2$ bassethound-Saluki generation. This dog, 1439♂, has been referred to in connection with the exaggerated shortness and grossness of its legs, and is shown as figure 4 in plate 11. The animal was very large and heavy of body, being longer and heavier than either of the parent stocks; its head was much exaggerated in length and the long straight muzzle gave to the face an almost horse-like appearance. The kennel attendants named this animal "Duckbill," doubtless because of the long face and the low duck-like amble in walking. He was kept alive until 3 years of age at which time his appearance and behavior were those of a rather old animal, although he had been in perfect health throughout his lifetime. Morphologically he showed what may be classed as certain symptoms of acromegaly; there was excessive growth of much thickened skin over the neck, shoulders and front legs. His hair was of unusually heavy fur-like texture, completely different from that of either parent stock and much like the thickened fur of several shepherd-bassethound dogs in our kennels from which the pituitaries had been removed. Respiration was labored and the dog was rather inactive and slow-moving, usually panting with the tongue hanging out while other dogs were breathing normally. Several attempts to mate this animal were made, but all were unsuccessful. While his gonads seemed well developed, he was incapable as a stud. The texture of his bones was slightly coarse and his endocrine glands showed some modifications, as will be described in a following chapter.

*The $F_1$ bassethound-Saluki backcrossed with the Saluki.* In order to further test the genetic reaction for chondrodystrophy in the leg bones of the bassethound-Saluki combination as well as the apparent dominance of Saluki bone constitution over that of the bassethound, backcrosses were made between the $F_1$ hybrids and both parent stocks. We shall consider first the findings in breeding back to the Saluki.

An $F_1$ bassethound-Saluki, 506 ♂, was mated to a pure Saluki bitch, 833, and a litter of six puppies was whelped. This litter is shown in plate 14 (figs. 4–9). Figure 2 of the same plate shows the pure Saluki mother, and the $F_1$ represented (fig. 3) is a brother of the sire. The six backcross animals were adults when photographed. Two of these are tall, slender, Saluki-like males; figure 4 is short haired like the bassethound and figure 9 is Saluki-coated, and might easily be mistaken for a pure bred Saluki. The other four members of this litter have the intermediate leg condition of the $F_1$ father. If only one of the dogs with intermediate legs had had long legs instead, this litter would show the correct 50:50 expectation. The recessive Saluki coat with the fringe on legs and tail and long hair about the ears appears exactly according to expectation, as is shown by figures 7, 8 and 9. The six animals all possess slender, Saluki typed bone, as should be the case if this type of bone dominates the heavier foxhound-like bone of the bassethound, which it does. Two members of this litter were bred to further follow the expression of bone type and leg length. The long legged male, 1012, (fig. 4, pl. 14; fig. 1, pl. 15) was mated to his sister, 1016, with legs of intermediate length (fig. 5, pl. 14; fig. 2, pl. 15). This mating whelped four female puppies, which are seen in plate 15 (figs. 3 and 4). Two of these have long, slender legs and the other two have slender, intermediately long legs with

PLATE 14

EXPLANATION OF FIGURES

Backcross of the $F_1$ bassethound-Saluki with the pure Saluki to further test the genetic reaction of achondroplasia in the leg bones as well as the apparent dominance of Saluki bone constitution.

1   Bassethound 216 ♀.
2   Saluki 833 ♀.
3   $F_1$ 504 ♂.
4–9 One litter of six backcross Saluki hybrids.
    4   1012 ♂.   6   1013 ♂.   8   1015 ♀.
    5   1016 ♀.   7   1017 ♀.   9   1014 ♂.

PLATE 13

only mild indications of the single factor for chondrodystrophy present in their genotype. The result of this mating is in exact accord with expectation on the basis of a single dominant gene for the expression of achondroplasia. This result is also in line with the probability that the Saluki type of bone is inherited as a dominant condition over that of the bassethound. All four animals have long, slender heads and thin bodies on the exact pattern of their Saluki grandmother and great-grandfather.

*The $F_1$ bassethound-Saluki backcrossed with the bassethound.* The same male $F_1$, 506 ♂, used in the previous backcross mating was now mated to the pure bassethound bitch 216 ♀ (fig. 1, pl. 14). From this mating six puppies, three males and three females, were whelped, five of which lived to maturity. These five backcross bassethounds are shown in plate 16. The expectation for leg length from this backcross would be equal numbers of double short, $ss$, and intermediate, $sl$, and the plate shows three dogs with intermediate legs at the left and two with double short at the right, in accord with this expectation. Although these dogs have one pure bassethound parent and one half-bassethound hybrid parent, half of them still show certain dominant features of the Saluki, as would be expected. For example, on careful examination of plate 16, the reader will find that three of the dogs, the first, third and fifth, have the characteristic almond eye of the Saluki.

PLATE 15

EXPLANATION OF FIGURES

Results of a mating between two members of the litter of backcross Saluki-bassethound-Saluki hybrids shown in plate 14 to further follow the expression of bone type and leg length.

1 Backcross Saluki 1012 ♂.
2 Backcross Saluki 1016 ♀.
3–4 Hybrids produced from a mating between 1012 ♂ and 1016 ♀.
    3 (L to R) 1385 ♀ and 1384 ♀.
    4 (L to R) 1384 ♀, 1383 ♀, 1385 ♀, 1382 ♀.

PLATE 15

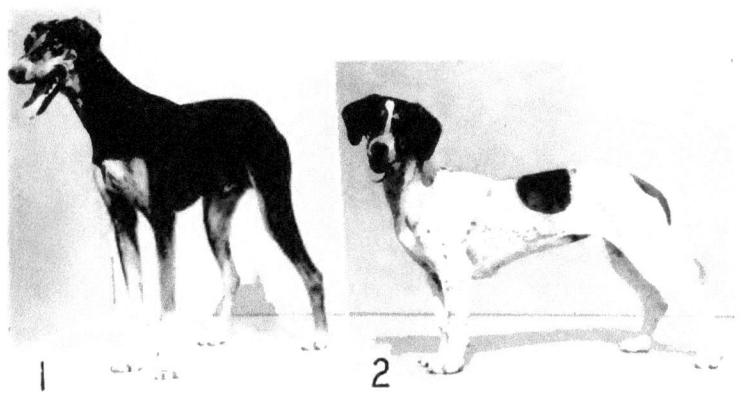

PLATE 16.

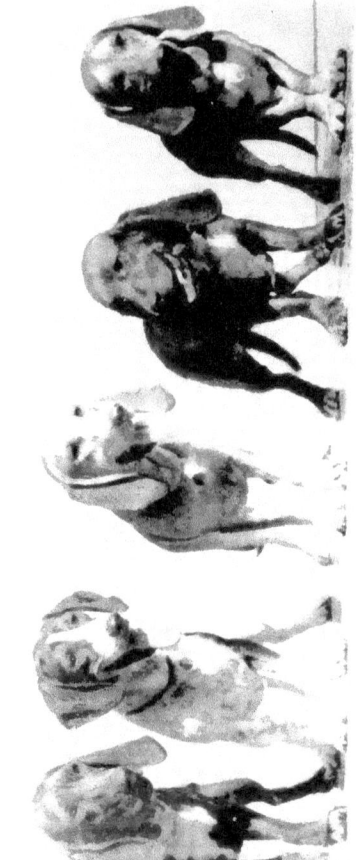

Backcross hybrids produced by mating an $F_1$ bassethound-Saluki to a pure bassethound. The expectancy for leg length here is half short (ss) and half intermediate (sl).
L to R: 857 ♂, 856 ♂, 860 ♀ (sl); 859 ♀, 858 ♂ (ss).

The shortness of legs in the three intermediates at the left is more pronounced than in the intermediates shown in plate 14, and abduction of the foot is more pronounced in the intermediate backcross bassethound than in the intermediate short legs of the backcross Saluki. Both these differences in growth expression are due to differences in relative completeness of the dominant Saluki typed Lone which seems to be a multiple factor character. Although there is some indication of certain dominant factors for Saluki type even in the backcross bassethounds, yet this type is not nearly so complete as in the backcross on the Saluki itself. These facts indicate that although the Saluki constitution for bone quality is quite dominant in this cross, complete dominance depends upon more than one influencing factor rather than upon only a single genic reaction, as is the case in the transmission of chondrodystrophic growth.

A second backcross with a different $F_1$ male, 505, and a different pure bassethound bitch, 277, whelped a litter of four puppies. These showed conditions closely similar to those discussed above.

A further test mating using these backcrosses was made in an effort to determine as clearly as possible whether the heterozygous condition, that is the presence of only one gene for chondrodystrophic short leg, gives a morphological expression of this distortion differing to a clearly distinguishable degree from the expression resulting from a pair of genes or the homozygous condition for such growth. In other words, in so complex a phenomenon as the dwarfing in skeletal development of the limb in higher mammals, can differences be consistently recognized which are simply due to the presence of either the single gene or the pair of genes determining this dominant condition? Since the possibilities for variations are not so great in the backcrosses, the leg conditions of intermediate $sl$ and double $ss$ should be morphologically distinguishable with somewhat more certainty than they are among the $F_2$ hybrids.

The double short, *ss*, backcross bassethound male 858, at the right in plate 16, was mated to an intermediate sister, 860, the center dog in the same group. These two animals are shown in a side view photograph in plate 17 (fig. 1), and in this position the two different degrees of leg condition are clearly contrasted. No. 860 ♀ has a short leg with a twist at the wrist, indicated by the bulge just above the white foot, while the legs of 858 ♂ are even shorter, and the top of his head is but slightly higher than the sister's shoulder. In the male, the knob at the wrists is also more pronounced. On the basis of the morphological appearance of the legs of these two animals, they were diagnosed for the achondroplasic reaction as of the genotypes *sl* and *ss*. If this deduction from the phenotypic differences is correct, then their mating should produce only *sl* and *ss* individuals in about equal numbers. No long legs, *ll*, should appear unless the diagnosis for *ss* is incorrect and *sl* the correct interpretation.

A litter of five puppies was whelped from this mating, three males and two females. Two puppies had very short legs like those of the father, and three had legs of a lesser degree of shortness like those of the mother. In figure 2 of plate 17, four of the five animals are shown. The two dogs in the center have legs of intermediate shortness, *sl*, and the left and right animals are very low and short legged, *ss*. This result proves the correctness of our diagnosis of the degree of chondrodystrophy in the legs of the parents.

The above mating, along with the comparable one between the backcross Saluki hybrids illustrated in plate 15, proves conclusively that it is possible to distinguish the difference between growth deformities of the legs resulting from the presence of the one or the two genes for the modification, and that the growth expression when the allelomorphs are heterozygous differs from that when homozygous.

A consideration of the skeletons of the extremities from the animals in these crosses further substantiates the above interpretations. This will be fully illustrated and discussed in a chapter following the presentation of the leg conditions in the bassethound and English bulldog cross.

## PLATE 17

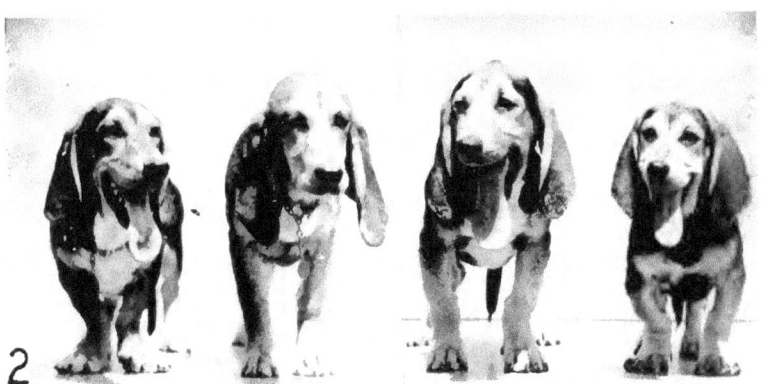

Test mating to determine whether the heterozygous (sḷ) condition for leg achondroplasia gives a morphological expression of this distortion differing to a clearly distinguishable degree from the expression resulting from the homozygous (ss) condition. Bassethound-Saluki hybrids.

1 Backcross bassethound-Saluki-bassethound hybrids S60 ♀ (diagnosed as sḷ) and S58 ♂ (diagnosed as ss).

2 Hybrids produced by mating S60 ♀ and S58 ♂ (from litter 1398–1402). Since no long (ll) offspring were produced, the diagnoses for achondroplasia in the parents are proved correct.

## The Bassethound and English Bulldog Hybrids in Connection with Dwarf Leg Growth

The reader may again refer to page 47 for the discussion of the general type and characteristics of the bassethound.

The English bulldog, commonly known among dog fanciers as simply the bulldog, offers probably the most perfectly suited material for an investigation of the interrelationships between genetic constitution and the endocrine glands in the development, growth and functions of the mammalian body. No other deviation from a standard of type in any known breed shows such consistent uniformity in the modified histological condition of its endocrine glands in association with characteristically extreme distortions in the growth patterns of the head, body and tail, and certain defective conditions in the skeleton of the appendages. The bulldog also deviates to a marked degree in behavior and psychology from what one would accept as the reactions of the standard or ancestral dog type.

The bulldog is a fairly old and well established breed although it is not perfectly homozygous in its genetics for the determining factors of all its characteristics. The breed has existed more or less in its present form for well over a century. The earliest bulldogs were not so grossly deformed as the present day animals but were more mastiff-like in character. Very probably the bulldog was originally derived from a series of mutations which gave rise to structural deviations, passing through a stocky mastiff type and from this to the more highly modified bulldog through the addition of later mutations. The animal used for bull-baiting and dog fighting a century ago in England was a far less deformed individual than our present day bulldog in which the mouth and teeth are so defective as to make its biting ability very poor. The structures and characters of the bulldog will be more fully considered in the chapters beyond in connection with the investigations on head types, endocrine histology and instincts and behavior. In the present consideration we are concerned only with the growth of the extremities and the quality of the leg bones in this breed as contrasted both structurally and genetically with the comparable characters in the bassethound.

The legs of the English bulldog are short and sturdy and the front legs are set far apart, making the chest appear extremely wide and giving rise to the term "bench-legged." Figure 1 in plate 18 is a good illustration of this condition in the legs of a highly prized champion specimen of the breed, "Lorne's Latest" A.K.C. 651313, our 903 ♂, which has been used in these experiments as a sire. The legs are perfectly straight boned and show no evidence of twist in growth and no overhang at the wrist or abduction of the foot. In other words, there is no evidence of achondroplasic growth in the long bones of the extremities in the bulldog. This fact is of great interest since the skull, tail and at times other regions of the axial skeleton show the most exaggerated conditions resulting from pronounced chondrodystrophy. These facts, as we shall emphasize in later sections, form an ideal contrast with the bassethound which, as we have seen, shows chondrodystrophy in the appendicular skeleton and perfectly normal development in the axial skeleton.

*Test for absence of achondroplasia in the legs of the bulldog.* In order to be genetically certain that the bulldog had no factors for chondrodystrophy in the long bones of the extremities, a test cross breeding with the control type German shepherd dog was made. From evidence in the experiments already discussed it could be presumed that if the bulldog had any basis for achondroplasia of the legs this would show itself in the hybrids from the shepherd cross. Another possibility suggested itself: even though the bulldog might have no basis for achondroplasia of the legs, the highly expressed achondroplasia localized in the axial skeleton might possibly become generalized and spread to other skeletal parts on hybridizing. A test of this possibility was highly desirable.

A pure German shepherd bitch, 118 ♀, of perfect long leg type, a niece of the bitch shown in plate 18 (fig. 2), was mated with the champion bulldog pictured in figure 1. Three pups, a male and two females, were whelped from this mating. The three hybrids lived to be adults and were all closely similar in their physical characters as well as their behaviors. They were sturdy, stocky, handsome animals resembling in general the mastiff-like dog known as the German boxer. One of these hybrid females is shown as figure 4. The physical characters of both the shepherd and the bulldog are almost completely lost in this hybrid, and persons familiar with dog breeds fail to guess the origin of the bulldog-shepherd $F_1$ more frequently than that of any other cross or breed in our kennels. The legs of this bulldog-shepherd bitch are perfectly straight and well set, resembling more those of the shepherd than the bulldog. Certainly there is no dominant symptom of achondroplasia to be found in the legs of these hybrids, and in the light of the foregoing discussion of the genetics of this condition, we must presume that the bulldog does not carry factors for this type of leg modification. Further, in this cross at least, there is no spreading or generalizing of the achondroplasia in the axial skeleton of the bulldog. On the basis of this test our diagnosis of the English bulldog's appearance as due to localized achondroplasic growth in the skull and axial skeleton without modified growth in long bones of the extremities, is very much strengthened.

We must make one qualification in the statement that chondrodystrophy in the bulldog is strictly confined to the axial skeleton. For this reason we have emphasized its absence from the long bones of the leg rather than from the entire appendicular skeleton. The cartilage growth in both the pectoral and pelvic girdles is affected. The labial cartilages of the glenoid fossa on the scapula and of the acetabular fossa of the pelvic bones are somewhat deficient and thin, causing the fossae to be abnormally shallow. In such cases the heads of the humerus and the femur may be dislocated from the shallow sockets. This occurrence is not rare in the bulldog but as a rule the sockets are sufficiently deep to prevent easy luxation. In cases of dislocation of either one or both shoulder joints, one or both hip joints, or all four joints, the condition

PLATE 18

Cross between the English bulldog and German shepherd for genetic proof of the absence of achondroplasia in the long bones of the extremities of the bulldog, as contrasted with cross between the bulldog and the achondroplasic bassethound.

1 English bulldog 903 ♂.
2 German shepherd 111 ♀.
3 Bassethound 220 ♂.
4 $F_1$ English bulldog-shepherd 658 ♀.
5 $F_1$ bulldog-bassethound 694 ♂.
6 $F_1$ bulldog-bassethound 602 ♀.

As indicated in figure 4, the $F_1$ bulldog-shepherd shows no symptoms of achondroplasia, while the $F_1$ bulldog-bassethound hybrids in figures 5 and 6 show clearly marked expressions of this distortion due to the gene for achondroplasia inherited from the bassethound parent.

93

becomes evident when the young puppy first attempts to raise the body in order to stand or walk. The dislocated limb or limbs are abducted by muscle pull and body weight so that they project out laterally from the body. The puppies are unable to maintain the limb or limbs in a vertical position and sprawl in outspread fashion. When this deficiency involves only one or two joints the animal gradually learns to compensate for it by modifying the use of the other legs and by redirecting the body weight. Such an animal may later walk with the affected limb in normal position, its muscles having strengthened and compensated so that almost normal posture is developed. The skeletons of adult bulldogs sometime show an old dislocation of the shoulder or hip joint that was not apparent in the living animals.

The $F_1$ hybrids of the bulldog-shepherd cross have shown no symptoms of these articular deficiencies, but the number of these hybrids studied is very small.

*Leg growth in the bassethound-bulldog $F_1$ hybrids.* Crossing the straight long legged bulldog with the short legged bassethound produces, of course, a very different leg condition from that found in the bulldog-shepherd hybrids discussed above. But the bulldog-shepherd experiment offers confirmation of the belief that the modified leg in the bassethound-bulldog hybrids is inherited from the bassethound parent only, with no contribution from the bulldog. Figures 4, 5 and 6 of plate 18 contrast the results of these two crosses. Figures 5 and 6 show the bassethound-bulldog-hybrid in front and lateral views. The legs are extremely achondroplasic, short and much bent. In fact the condition in this hybrid seems as fully pronounced as in the bassethound itself even though the hybrid is heterozygous, carrying only the single gene for leg chondrodystrophy. This exaggerated expression is what forced us to test the bulldog against the shepherd in order to determine whether the bulldog contained in its genotype some factor or combination not evident in its phenotype but which would nevertheless give rise to achondroplasia of the long bones. After the negative results of this test we must now account for the exaggerated condition in the $F_1$ bassethound-bulldog leg in some other way.

The bulldog and bassethound parent stocks are illustrated in figures 1 and 2 of plate 19, and three $F_1$ hybrids from this cross are shown in figures 3, 4 and 5 of the same plate. The legs in all the hybrids are fully as short or shorter than those of the pure bassethound parent (fig. 2).

Four matings were made between two tested pure bassethound bitches and two prize stock highly typed bulldogs. These matings whelped litters of eight, two, seven and six puppies, a total of twenty-three $F_1$ hybrids. All were quite uniform in body size and form and in the characteristic condition of the leg deformity, and were fairly vigorous animals in spite of their distorted appearance. A large majority of them lived to adult life, were mated, and produced 150 offspring. Many important modifications in the head and body will be considered in other connections.

*Leg growth in the bassethound-bulldog $F_2$ hybrids.* Twenty-three fertile matings were made between $F_1$ hybrids, using seven bitches as matrons and four males for stud. Among these are both brother-sister matings and cross-line matings. The twenty-three whelpings gave litters varying in size from only a single pup up to ten in the litter. In all 150 individuals were produced in the $F_2$ generation. This gives a large statistical sample for analysis of the genetics of the leg conditions.

The $F_2$ generation hybrids from this cross again showed, as has been seen for the bassethound-shepherd and bassethound-Saluki crosses, the typical Mendelian segregation expected for a single factor dominant character. Among the 150 individuals, approximately three out of every four had short, bent legs and one out of four had long, straight legs. The diagnoses for leg condition were made in some cases on puppies which died when quite young, and although these are probably correct, they cannot be as accurate as the measurements and estimates made from the large number of adult animals later available for study. The legs of the newborn and 1 week old puppy in all breeds are rather short but in almost every case can be distinguished from the short leg of achondroplasia by the slender form and narrow, smaller foot, as well as by the differences in length among the short legs of litter mates. With this bassethound-bulldog cross the error in leg classification is very small, if any, and would not warrant the amount of work necessary for an histologic examination in order to verify the classification.

The achondroplasic $F_2$ animals in this cross again fall into two groups: those very pronounced and probably homozygous for the condition, and those with a less severe expression. Yet in these hybrids the separation of the short legs into the two groups cannot be done with such clearness as is possible with both the bassethound-shepherd and the bassethound-Saluki crosses. On the other hand, the long legged $F_2$ animals in this cross are more clearly separated into two classes of leg length than was possible in either of the former crosses. Some of the long legged $F_2$ animals have straight legs of about the same length as those in the foxhound, while others have a much stockier and shorter leg, similar to that of the bulldog.

These differences in length of long legs and in thickness of bones are due to differences in bone type. The leg bones of the bulldog are thicker and shorter than the bones of the foxhound, of which the bassethound is considered the achondroplasic leg mutant. On crossing the bulldog and the bassethound, the bone type or bone constitution of the bulldog is

PLATE 19

EXPLANATION OF FIGURES

Cross between the bassethound and English bulldog showing inheritance of leg length and other physical characters.

1  English bulldog 903 ♂.
2  Bassethound 216 ♀.
3–5  $F_1$ litter mates.
  3  694 ♂, 695 ♂.  4  694 ♂.  5  740 ♂, 694 ♂.
6–9  $F_2$ litter mates.
  6  917 ♂.  7  916 ♂.  8  918 ♀.  9  919 ♀.

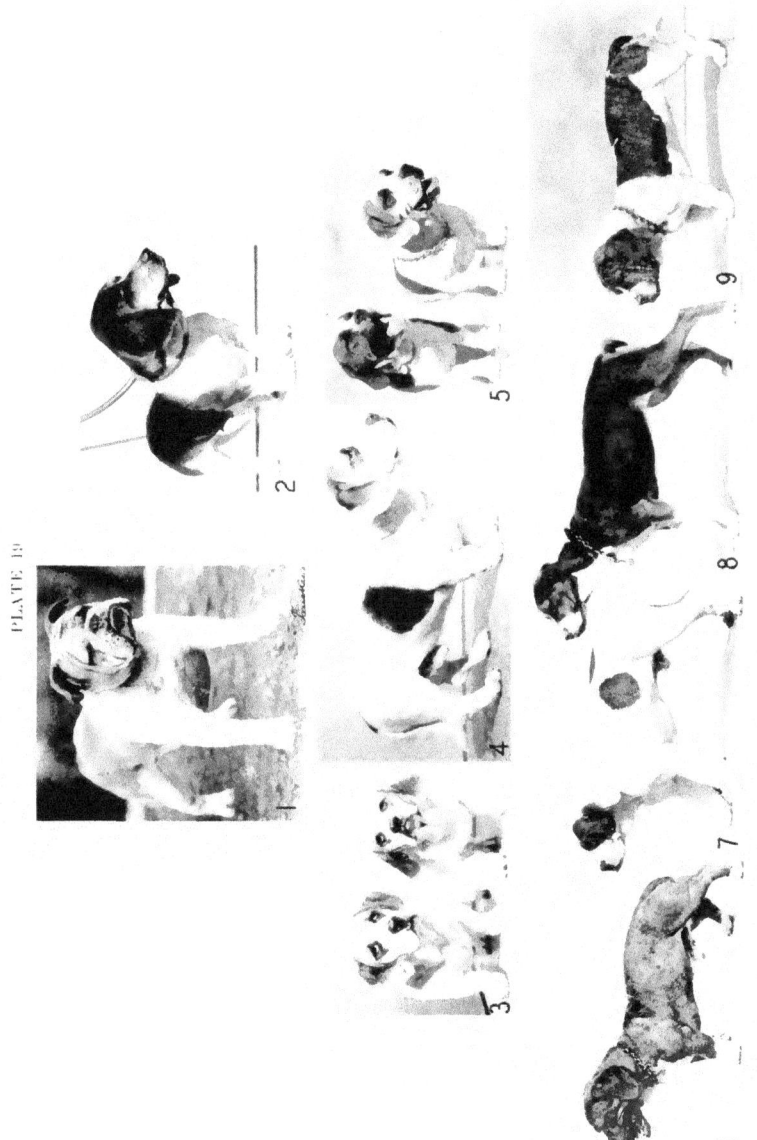

PLATE 19

largely dominant over hound typed bone. We have seen that the $F_1$ bassethound-bulldogs have legs as short as the pure bassethound. The reason for this is that a single factor for achondroplasia, acting in association with the constitution for bulldog bone, induces a greater or more complete achondroplasic effect than is the case for other types of bone. Bulldog bone is in type short and stocky, as contrasted, for example, with the long and slender type of Saluki bone. We have much evidence for the statement that short and stocky bone is more completely affected in the presence of the achondroplasic leg gene than is the long, slender type of bone. After further consideration of the $F_2$ bassethound-bulldog legs we shall discuss the bone types in more detail.

Figures 6–9 of plate 19 show four litter mate $F_2$ bassethound-bulldogs, two of which have achondroplasic legs and two normal legs. Figure 7 has typical bulldog legs as in the grandfather (fig. 1). The skeleton of this animal, 916 ♂, is shown in plates 20 and 21 (figs. 8), and from both aspects the leg is seen to be closely similar to that of the bulldog, shown as figure 1 in these two plates. Figure 8 in plate 19 shows a sister, 918 ♀, which also has long legs, but of an entirely different type. These legs are those of a foxhound, almost as long and slender as the legs of the German shepherd. The bone types of the bulldog and hound parent stocks are thus again segregated out among these $F_2$s.

Figures 6 and 9 of plate 19 show animals with achondroplasic legs, and we have diagnosed animal 917 ♂ (fig. 6) from both life and a study of the skeleton as short ss for achondroplasia on hound typed bone. The skeleton of this dog is shown in plates 20 and 21 (figs. 5). The short legged animal in figure 9 of plate 19 gives all evidence for bulldog typed bone and is diagnosed from life and a study of its skeleton as heterozygous for short achondroplasic legs on bulldog bone. The skeleton of this animal, 919 ♀, is shown as figure 7 in plates 20 and 21 and should be compared with the two $F_1$ skeletons in the middle row of both plates, since we have interpreted the leg conditions in the three as being the same.

PLATE 20

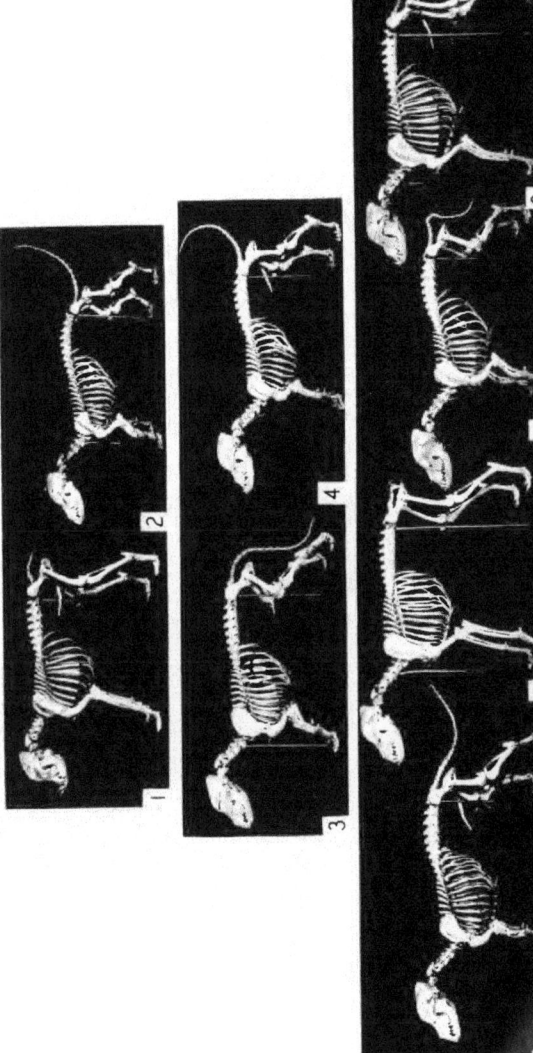

Skeletons of the cross between the English bulldog and bassethound showing contrast in leg length and bone constitution in the pure breeds and the resulting conditions in the first and second generation hybrids.

1. English bulldog 303 ♂.
2. Bassethound 214 ♀.
3. $F_1$ 759 ♂.
4. $F_1$ 605 ♂.
5. $F_2$ 917 ♂.
6. $F_2$ 918 ♀.
7. $F_2$ 919 ♀.
8. $F_2$ 916 ♂.

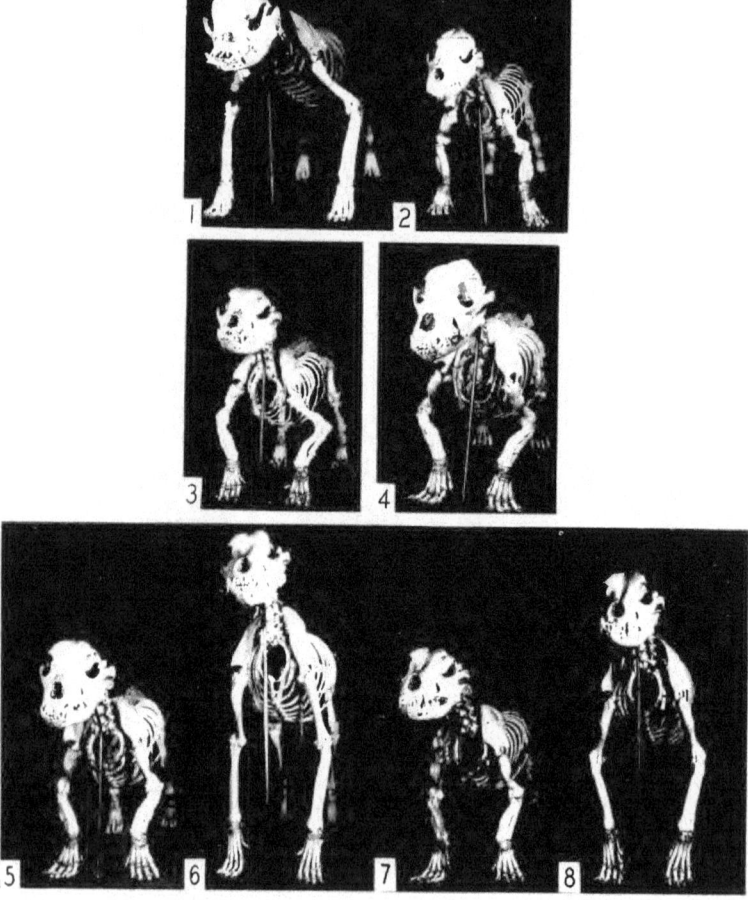

Further details of skeletons shown in plate 20. English bulldog-bassethound cross. 1 English bulldog 903 ♂. 2 Bassethound 214 ♀. 3 4 $F_1$ hybrids. 3 695 ♂. 4 739 ♂. 5-8 $F_2$ hybrids. 5 917 ♂. 6 918 ♀. 7 919 ♀. 8 916 ♂.

The skeleton of 917 ♂ (fig. 5), with double short ss on hound typed bone, is no shorter than the two single short F₁s on bulldog typed bone.

This litter shows both tall and short animals, with hound typed and bulldog typed bone in both classes. Bone constitution or type is an important element in influencing the length of legs in hybrids and, further, is significant in effecting the degree of expression in achondroplasic growth.

Three male F₂ animals are illustrated in plate 22. No. 1311 ♂ (figs. 1 and 4) has long bulldog bone legs, and 1312 ♂ (figs. 2 and 5) has long legs with incomplete hound typed bone. Animal 1313 ♂ (figs. 3 and 6) is double short for achondroplasia on hound typed bone. Deformed legs on this type of bone are no thicker than the long legs of the brother with bulldog typed bone (figs. 1 and 4).

*The F₁ bassethound-bulldog backcrossed with each of the parent stocks.* Three fertile matings were made between F₁ hybrids and the bassethound parent stock. These matings produced litters of seven, six and nine puppies, a total of twenty-two. The results from this backcross, as concerns leg growth, were exactly as would be expected in view of the foregoing crosses. The individuals in this generation have short, achondroplasic legs; about half of them show the condition to a limited degree and half have fully deformed short legs.

Four backcross matings were made in the opposite direction, that is, on the bulldog parent stock. These matings gave litters of three, five, seven and six puppies, a total of twenty-one. About half these animals had long, straight legs of bulldog type and half had very short, achondroplasic legs. Although these short legged animals are heterozygous for leg length, the deformity is highly marked in its expression because of the dominant bulldog quality of their bone. The significance of bone quality in these growth reactions has been referred to in several connections, but the relation of differences in types of bone constitution to differences in growth reaction is more fully discussed in the chapter following.

PLATE 22

## The Effects of Different Breed Constitutions on the Fundamental Growth Pattern of the Limb Skeleton as Responses to a Single Gene or to a Homozygous Allelic Pair

In our efforts to determine whether gross deviations from normal type are of direct genetic origin or arise indirectly due to developmental modifications in the internal environment, it was deemed desirable to perform the same experiments on more than one breed. The employment of several breeds has facilitated the analysis of this complex condition to a great extent and has thrown some light on the significance of the general constitution in modifying reactions to specific responses. The genetically rather simple phenomenon of achondroplasic growth in the skeletons of the extremities has proven very valuable in demonstrating the differences in degrees of expression of a growth phenomenon as related to different constitutional types. The full meaning of the problem is best brought out as we follow it through.

In connection with the inheritance of dwarf growth in the leg, we have discussed hybrids resulting from crosses involving four different breeds. The dwarf leg of the bassethound was tested against the German shepherd, our standard control, and, toward one extreme, against the long, slender greyhound typed leg of the Saluki, and in opposite direction against the shorter, stocky typed leg of the bulldog. In figure 1 of plate 23 the skeletons of the right front legs from these

PLATE 22

EXPLANATION OF FIGURES

Second generation English bulldog bassethound litter mates illustrating differences in leg length and bone type.

1 and 4   1311 ♂ long legs (ll) on bulldog bone.
2 and 5   1312 ♂ long legs (ll) on incomplete hound bone.
3 and 6   1313 ♂ short legs (ss) on hound bone.

The pure long legged animal with bulldog bone (figs. 1 and 4) has legs fully as thick as the animal in figures 3 and 6 which is homozygous for achondroplasia but has hound typed bone.

four breeds have been photographed on a single plate to facilitate comparison. For our present purposes, the front leg skeletons have certain advantages over those of the hind legs, for although the hind limb skeletons would show the same conditions, it would not be so clearly presented for comparative purposes.

The long, slender and graceful leg skeleton of the Saluki is at the left in figure 1. The scapula is somewhat rectangular in shape and much longer dorso-ventrally than in anterior-posterior width, and the index of width to length is low. The humerus in this dog is longer and straighter than in the other three legs and has but a very slight curve. The lengths of the radius and ulna in the Saluki leg are even more exaggerated than the length of humerus, and these bones are very slender in comparison with the same two bones in the other three breeds. The lower half of the Saluki ulna is not only slender but almost attenuated, as is clearly shown in the figure and emphasized by comparison with the other skeletons. It must be carefully noted that the distal epiphysis or process of the ulna in this leg extends far below the distal end of the radius and thus insures the straight front position of the foot, rendering an abducted posture impossible. The metacarpal bones in the Saluki fore-foot are also long and slender in comparison with the other skeletons.

The second leg skeleton in figure 1 is that of the German shepherd dog. This is not so long nor so straight in total posture as the Saluki skeleton. The bones are thicker and heavier with the processes for muscle attachments more strongly pronounced. The width to length of the scapula gives a higher index than in the Saluki. The straightness in posture of the foot is also less decided. The skeleton of the shepherd dog is a normal standard and shows no tendency to incline towards any specific modification. This skeleton would seem to be the intermediate norm from which the deviations have departed.

The third leg skeleton in this figure is that of the bulldog, and it differs from the shepherd skeleton in quite opposite ways than does the Saluki. Compared with the shepherd, the scapula is somewhat wider for its length and all the bones are shorter and with higher indices for width to length. The humerus is much shorter than in the shepherd but almost equally as thick. The radius and ulna are short and stocky but very straight. The distal condyle or epiphysis of the ulna does not extend very far below the radius, as is the case in the first two legs, but it is sufficiently long to prevent the carpal bones from rotating beneath it to any abnormal extent. Nevertheless, the front foot of the bulldog has a tendency to abduct, as may be observed in many specimens of the breed. The metacarpals and bones of the toes are seen to be much shorter in this foot than in the first two.

The "bench-legs" of the bulldog bring about a slightly outward or lateral rotation of the leg skeleton which is noticeable in the photograph. The four leg skeletons of this group had been placed in as nearly identical positions as possible, yet in such position the bones of the fore-leg and foot of the bulldog are seen to be so rotated that an undue amount of front surface is shown in this lateral view.

The fourth skeleton in figure 1 illustrates the much distorted bassethound leg. This leg presents deviations from a standard type very different from the comparative differences shown among the first three. The scapula in the bassethound extremity has a very high index and is almost as wide as it is long. This increase in scapular index is always found in the achondroplasic leg. The humerus of the bassethound leg is only about half as long as that of the shepherd and in addition is much bent, chiefly towards the distal end; this bend exaggerates the usual spiral twist of the humerus. The head of the humerus sets somewhat insecurely in the fossa of the scapula and the elbow joint juts out laterally from the body. The radius and ulna are greatly reduced in length and much bent, as well as twisted on their long axes. The epiphysis or distal condyle of the ulna is almost undeveloped and does not extend below the end of the radius. On this account the ulna gives no opposition or fixation against outward rotation of the carpal bones in the wrist joint, and under this condition the pressure of the body weight directing the leg bones medially rotates the unobstructed carpals and abducts the front foot in a manner characteristic of achondroplasia, with the wrists knocked in close together (see the front views of animals in plates 11, 12, 16, 17, 18, and 19). This modification of the extremity, as we have shown in the foregoing genetic experiments, arises through the influence of a single dominant gene which in the homozygous state accentuates the expression.

Figure 2 in plate 23 shows the right foreleg skeletons from $F_1$ hybrids between the bassethound and the three other pure breeds from which the leg skeletons in figure 1 were taken. The $F_1$ skeletons are arranged in an order comparable to the pure group, that is, the bassethound-Saluki at the left, the bassethound-shepherd next, and the bassethound-bulldog last. Just as in the pure breeds the Saluki bone is longest and slenderest, so in the $F_1$ hybrids the bassethound-Saluki leg skeleton is longest, least modified, and slenderest.

The scapula in each of the $F_1$ skeletons is much broader than that of the long legged parent and approaches the high index of the bassethound parent. The humerus in the three $F_1$ legs is longest, and least bent and twisted in the bassethound-Saluki (left); shorter and more bent and twisted in the bassethound-shepherd (center); and shortest, most decidedly bent and twisted in the bassethound-bulldog (right), as the photographs very clearly illustrate. The radius and ulna are progressively more modified in length and form as we compare the skeletons from the bassethound-Saluki through the bassethound-shepherd to the bassethound-bulldog. The radius and ulna of the $F_1$ bassethound-Saluki are not badly bent nor twisted when compared with the normal long leg, but they are much shorter and thicker than in the leg of the pure Saluki. The distal condyle of the ulna in the $F_1$ bassethound-Saluki extends about as far below the distal articular surface of the radius as in the case of the foreleg of the pure bulldog shown in the parent group. Lateral out-

PLATE 22

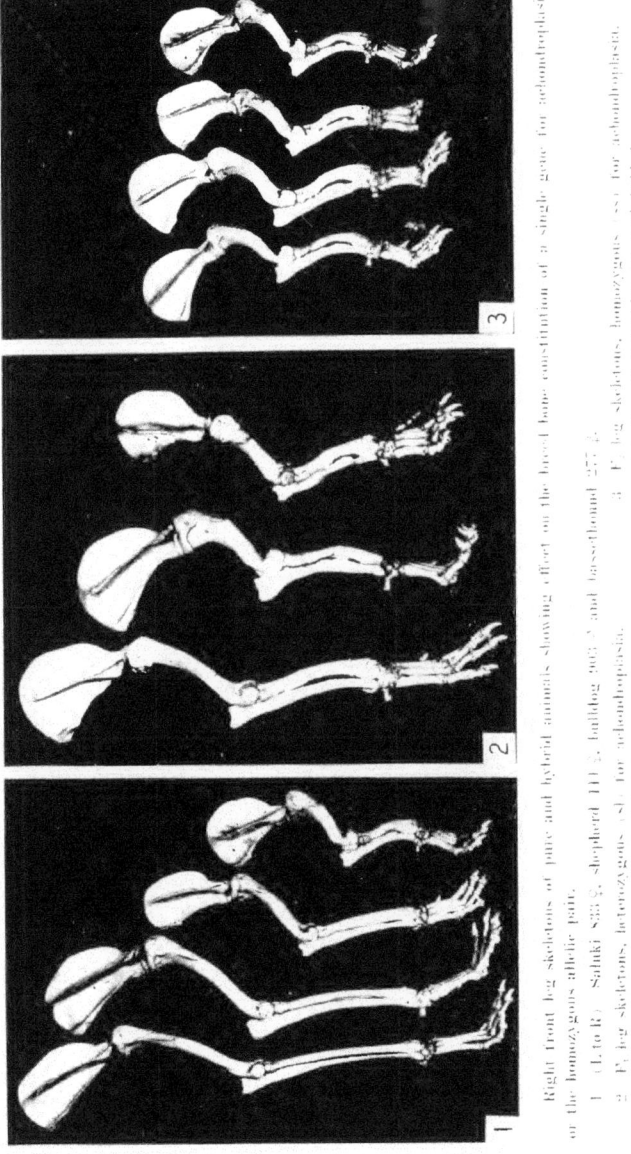

Right front leg skeletons of pure and hybrid animals showing effect on the breed bone constitution of a single gene for achondroplasia or the homozygous allelic pair.

1 (L to R) Saluki 828 ♀, shepherd 717 ♂, bulldog 905 ♂ and bassethound 277 ♀.
2 F₁ leg skeletons, heterozygous (+a) for achondroplasia. 3 F₂ leg skeletons, homozygous (aa) for achondroplasia.
 (L to R) F₁ Saluki bassethound 504 ♂. (L to R) F₂ Saluki bassethound 1211 ♀.
  F₁ shepherd bassethound 216 ♂. F₂ shepherd bassethound 1401 ♀.
  F₁ bulldog bassethound 602 ♀. F₂ bulldog bassethound 1144 ♀.
  Bassethound 277 ♀ for comparison with F₂.

107

ward rotation of the carpal component of the wrist is partly blocked by the moderately long distal process of the ulna, and consequently the $F_1$ bassethound-Saluki shows only a slight lateral bend at the wrist and mild abduction of the front foot, as may be seen from life in plate 11 (fig. 1). The foot skeleton in the $F_1$ is intermediate when compared with those of the Saluki and bassethound.

The leg skeleton from the $F_1$ bassethound-shepherd hybrid (second in fig. 2) is of a pronounced achondroplasic type. The scapula is wide and the humerus short, thickened and decidedly twisted on its long axis. The radius and ulna are much deformed. Unfortunately the photograph does not clearly indicate that the distal end of the ulna extends only a little below the end of the radius and does not therefore entirely prevent lateral rotation and some abduction of the front foot. The $F_1$ bassethound-shepherd leg may permit a wider degree of abduction of the foot than does the bassethound-Saluki leg.

Finally, the $F_1$ bassethound-bulldog leg skeleton (third in fig. 2) could pass for the fully expressed achondroplasic type. The scapula is very nearly the same as in the bassethound. The humerus is also much the same, but the radius and ulna are not quite so severely bent. The distal process of the ulna falls entirely short of the end of the radius so that the foot of the $F_1$ bassethound-bulldog is twisted and abducted about as fully as would be found for the pure bassethound. This is illustrated clearly from living specimens in plate 19 (p. 97).

The three $F_1$ leg skeletons in figure 2 of plate 23 show that the single factor for achondroplasic leg growth produces different degrees of this deformity in different breed combinations. These three specimens are heterozygous for the achondroplasic factor which we have designated as $s$. They carry as the allelomorph of this gene the factor $l$ for normal growth in length. However, the three $F_1$ leg skeletons indicate that the $l$ factor is not in all cases equally strong in counteracting the effect of the $s$, or a more likely possibility is that the entire complex for the bone constitution typical of a given breed determines the degree of response to the dominant gene underlying the achondroplasic reaction. In other words, the genetic complex which causes the pure bred Saluki bone to express the greyhound-like type in contrast with the shepherd type also causes the Saluki bone to respond to the achondroplasic factor to a lesser degree than does the shepherd bone. One might say that the Saluki bone is further away from the achondroplasic defect than is the shepherd bone, and that it is therefore more difficult to turn its growth reaction toward such a pattern.

The homozygous $ss$ achondroplasic legs which appear among the $F_2$ hybrids from these crosses furnish very important material in the elucidation of the above questions. In the first place, we have proven genetically in the foregoing experiments that the very short achondroplasic legs in the $F_2$ groups are possessed by animals homozygous, $ss$, for the short condition. In these animals the allelomorph $l$ for long legs is completely absent and therefore cannot enter into modification in the degree of the action of the gene for achondroplasic legs. Should all the $F_2$ dogs homozygous, $ss$, for achondroplasia not show exactly the same condition in their leg bones, the variations must be due to differences in interaction between the genes for achondroplasia and the breed constitutions of the bones concerned.

The first three leg skeletons of figure 3 in plate 23 are from $F_2$ hybrids homozygous for leg achondroplasia, and the fourth leg skeleton is that of a pure bassethound, placed here for comparison. The skeletons are placed in the same order as in the first two groups and are, from left to right, bassethound-Saluki, bassethound-shepherd, bassethound-bulldog and pure bassethound. The $F_2$ bassethound-Saluki skeleton was selected as showing full achondroplasia $ss$ upon Saluki typed bone. In spite of the homozygous condition for short, the bones of this leg are slenderer and more graceful than those in the other three skeletons. The scapula is not quite so squared and the humerus is thinner for its length and not so twisted. The radius and ulna of the bassethound-Saluki leg are not as thickened nor so gnarled with exostoses as in the other three. This is the only one of the four leg skeletons in which the distal process of the ulna projects slightly beyond the end of the radius, and the foot in this $F_2$ bassethound-Saluki is less abducted than in the other $F_2$ skeletons.

The $F_2$ bassethound-shepherd, the second skeleton in figure 3, shows the pure achondroplasic reaction on shepherd typed bone. The bones in this leg are thicker in proportion to length than in the first leg of this group, and the scapula is very wide for its length. The ulna does not extend below the radius and the wrist is free to rotate and abduct the forefoot. The first two leg skeletons in this figure are both longer than the pure bassethound leg seen at the right end.

The third skeleton of figure 3 is from an $F_2$ bassethound-bulldog. It is as completely achondroplasic in shortness and form as that of the pure bassethound at its right. These two leg skeletons are bone for bone almost exactly alike. The ulna falls short of the radius in its lower extent, thus rendering the wrist joint very unstable, and the foot is badly abducted. The excessive shortness of bones in the legs of the $F_2$ group homozygous for achondroplasia is appreciated more clearly by comparing them with the leg skeletons from the heterozygous $F_1s$ (fig. 2, pl. 23). Comparisons made among the several leg skeletons in each of these groups make it clearly evident that the influence of the dominant gene for achondroplasia of the extremities differs, depending upon the breed constitution of the animal involved. The functioning of the same gene gives different results when acting upon different constitutions. Among these breeds of dogs the Saluki constitution is the most resistant to the effects of the gene for short achondroplasic legs and the bulldog bone is the most responsive. The hound typed bone of the bassethound itself is probably not so responsive as that of the bulldog, and on this account a heterozygous $F_2$ bassethound-bulldog with bull typed bone may be equally as low and short legged as a homozygous $F_2$ bassethound-bulldog with hound typed bone. Mistaken diagnoses between homozygous and heterozygous conditions among the $F_2$ generation are sometimes due to the complication resulting from differences in degree of expression on different bone constitutions. The bone constitution is inherited quite independent of the achondroplasic leg factor in the crosses we have made.

Further facts relative to constitutional differences in bone response are found by examination of the leg skeletons from the several groups of $F_2$ hybrids.

*Leg skeletons of the $F_2$ bassethound-shepherd.* In addition to the segregation of factors for normal and achondroplasic growth of the extremities in the $F_2$ generation of the bassethound-shepherd cross, there is some evidence for segregation of hound and shepherd bone type. Plate 24 shows photographs of six right front leg skeletons. The first is from a pure long legged German shepherd dog and the other five are from $F_2$ bassethound-shepherd hybrids.

The first $F_2$ leg skeleton is an extracted recessive long with bone of almost exactly the same type as that of the pure shepherd to the left. If these two long legs had been photographed on a straight base line they would show identical lengths and proportions. Other long legged $F_2$ animals of this cross show a somewhat shorter, stockier leg approaching the foxhound type.

The third and fourth leg skeletons are classed as heterozygous for short, genotype *sl*, and are much like the skeletons from the $F_1$. The bone types in these legs are somewhat mixed, yet the third skeleton inclines towards the shepherd bone type and has a longer, lower epiphyseal process on the ulna, less rotation of the wrist with less abduction and a slightly narrower scapula than does the fourth skeleton of the group at its right, which is more hound bone in type. The metacarpal and phalangeal bones of the foot in achondroplasia are shortened on the same comparative proportions as are the other bones. Type differences among the feet of the $F_2$ hybrids can also be seen.

PLATE 24

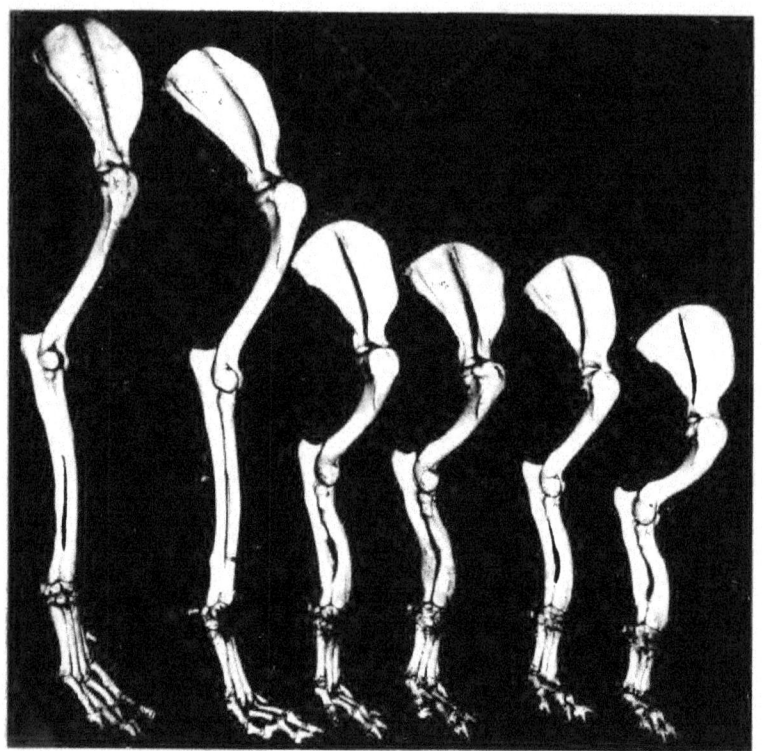

Segregation of bassethound and shepherd bone constitution in normal long (ll), short (ss), and intermediate (sl) leg conditions among second generation hybrids. Right front leg skeletons.

L to R. German shepherd 1132 ♂ (for comparison).
    F₂ 1150 ♂ ll, shepherd bone.
    F₂ 1492 ♂ sl, mixed bone tending toward shepherd.
    F₂ 1490 ♂ sl, mixed bone tending toward hound.
    F₂ 1493 ♀ ss, almost pure shepherd bone.
    F₂ 1491 ♂ ss, hound bone.

The last two skeletons, the fifth and sixth in the group, are considered to be homozygous or pure for achondroplasic shortness, $ss$. In spite of the same genotype for this defect, there is considerable difference between the degrees of deformity shown in the two leg skeletons. The scapula of the fifth specimen is much narrower than the scapula of the heterozygous hound bone to the left. The humerus is longer, slenderer and less deformed in the fifth skeleton than in the sixth. The foreleg bones of the two differ in a similar way and in the fifth leg the end of the ulna extends as low as the radius, but does not do so in the sixth. The foot is rotated in both, but can be more widely abducted in the sixth specimen than in the fifth. The fifth skeleton shows its deformity on what is interpreted as almost pure typed shepherd bone, while the last specimen shows an accentuation of the same deformities on pure hound typed bone. These two bone constitutions cannot be considered as extremely different in type, but they nevertheless do give rather clearly differentiated responses to the genic influences for the achondroplasic growth defect of the leg.

*Leg skeletons of the $F_2$ bassethound-Saluki.* Among the second generation hybrids from the cross between the bassethound and Saluki, differences in slenderness of leg without regard to differences or similarities in leg length are constantly observed. These differences in slenderness depend upon whether the animal has developed bone more nearly that of the Saluki or that of the hound. The bone constitution in this case, as in the cross considered above, influences the degree of expression in the achondroplasic deformity.

The skeletons of the right front legs from six litter mate $F_2$ bassethound-Saluki hybrids are shown in plate 25. Beginning at the left they are as follows: one recessive long slender leg, two heterozygous $sl$ short legs, and three homozygous $ss$ more fully shortened legs. The animals from which these leg skeletons were taken are shown in plate 10 (p. 73). Figure 5 (pl. 10) is $F_2$ 1441 ♂ whose leg skeleton is fourth in plate 25 and who is again shown in plate 12 (p. 77) as homozygous ss for achondroplasic legs on Saluki typed bone in comparison with a brother, 1439♂, also homozygous but with modified hound typed bone and much more shortened and deformed legs. Figure 6 (pl. 10) shows animal 1440♂, from which the third leg skeleton in plate 25 was taken; this animal is intermediate-short on impure Saluki typed bone. No. 1442♂ (fig. 7, pl. 10) is the donor of the fifth leg skeleton in plate 25; he is diagnosed as homozygous for short on Saluki bone. Figure 8 (pl. 10), 1439♂, has been described previously as a grossly modified and divergent type. The leg skeleton of this member of the litter is the only one not pictured in plate 25, since he was being retained for further study in life when his six litter mates were autopsied. Figure 9, plate 10, 1443♂, is clearly seen to be intermediate for short legs on Saluki typed bone; its front leg skeleton is second in plate 25. This animal is almost indistinguishable from members of the $F_1$ generation. The only long legged dog of the litter is 1444♂ (fig. 10, pl. 10); his long leg skeleton is first in plate 25. This dog is almost pure Saluki in bone type, as the leg skeleton quite definitely indicates and as one could readily recognize from observation during life. The only female in the litter, 1445♀, is shown as figure 11 in plate 10 and in larger view in plate 11 (right in fig. 3) by the side of her long legged brother. This bitch is a perfect example of the homozygous expression for achondroplasia of the extremities in an almost purely developed Saluki type. The front leg skeleton of this animal is at the right in plate 25.

The examinations and measurements made on the living animals of this litter, as well as the large total number of $F_2$ bassethound-Saluki hybrids, show the Saluki type, as a physical complex, to be largely dominant in its inheritance over the bassethound type. The photographs of the $F_1$ and $F_2$ hybrids in plates 10, 11 and 12 clearly illustrate this fact to anyone having some knowledge of dog breeds. In the above statement we are, of course, excluding the achondroplasic leg inheritance from the composite breed constitution or type.

PLATE 25

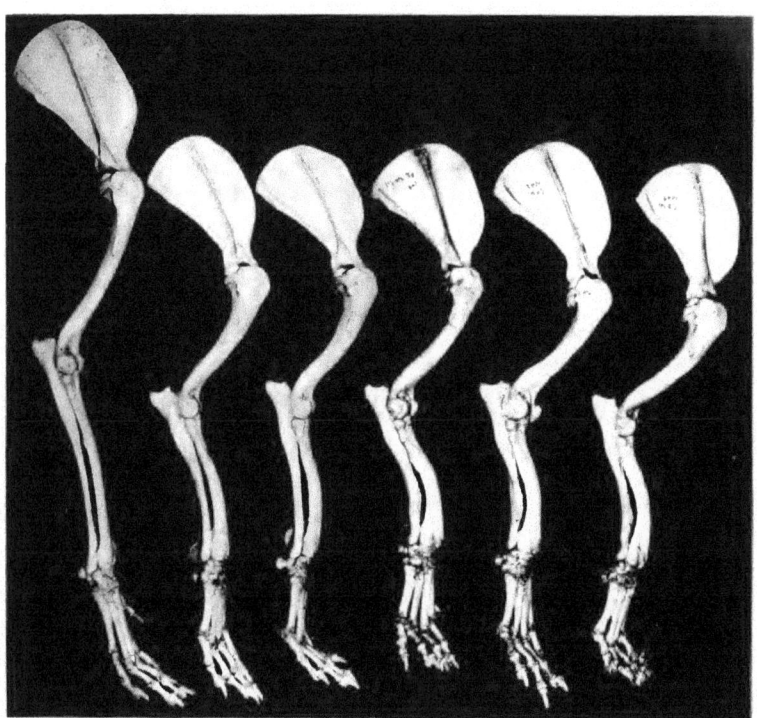

Response of the dominant Saluki type bone to factors for achondroplasia in second generation Saluki bas-ethound hybrids. Right front leg skeletons.

L to R  1444 ♂, ll, Saluki bone.
        1443 ♂, sl, Saluki bone.
        1440 ♂, sl, impure Saluki bone.
        1441 ♂, ss, Saluki bone.
        1442 ♂, ss, Saluki bone.
        1445 ♀, ss, Saluki bone.

On this constitutional basis, a comparison of the leg skeletons of $F_2$ bassethound-shepherd hybrids in plate 24 and the $F_2$ bassethound-Salukis shown in plate 25, clearly demonstrates well marked differences in the degree of response to the achondroplasic factors in the two combinations of breed types. There is no doubt that Saluki bone is much less responsive to the factor for achondroplasia in the leg than are the shepherd and the hound bone types.

Plate 26 illustrates the comparative effects of one gene or two genes for achondroplasia of the legs. The first skeleton is from $F_2$ 1440 ♂, which was shown as the third leg skeleton in plate 25. This leg was diagnosed as heterozygous, $sl$, having but a single gene for achondroplasia, on Saluki typed bone. The second skeleton is from $F_1$ 504 ♂ and must of necessity be heterozygous, $sl$, for the short factor. The two photographs show these skeletons to be almost exactly alike, the only slight difference being that the $F_2$ leg may be somewhat more nearly complete for Saluki bone than the $F_1$, as indicated by its slenderer form. In both skeletons the distal end of the ulna projects below the articular surface of the radius and obstructs carpal rotation and excessive abduction of the foot. The state of this arrangement is a reliable index of the degree of achondroplasic deformity.

The third leg skeleton in plate 26 differs greatly from the other two. The $F_2$ animal, 1211 ♂, from which this leg skeleton was taken, had been clearly recognized in life as having the most extreme degree of leg shortness to be found among bassethound-Saluki hybrids. This dog, which had slightly long hair, is photographed from life in plate 12 (right in fig. 1) and is standing beside a short haired brother whose more purely developed Saluki typed bone was evident even in life. No. 1211 ♂ was classed as homozygous or $ss$ for achondroplasia and the leg skeleton illustrates how much this defect is accentuated when pure $ss$, instead of the mixed or single $sl$ genic condition for short leg, reacts on this type bone. The distal end of the ulna in this skeleton falls short of the end of the radius and offers no obstruction to outward

PLATE 26

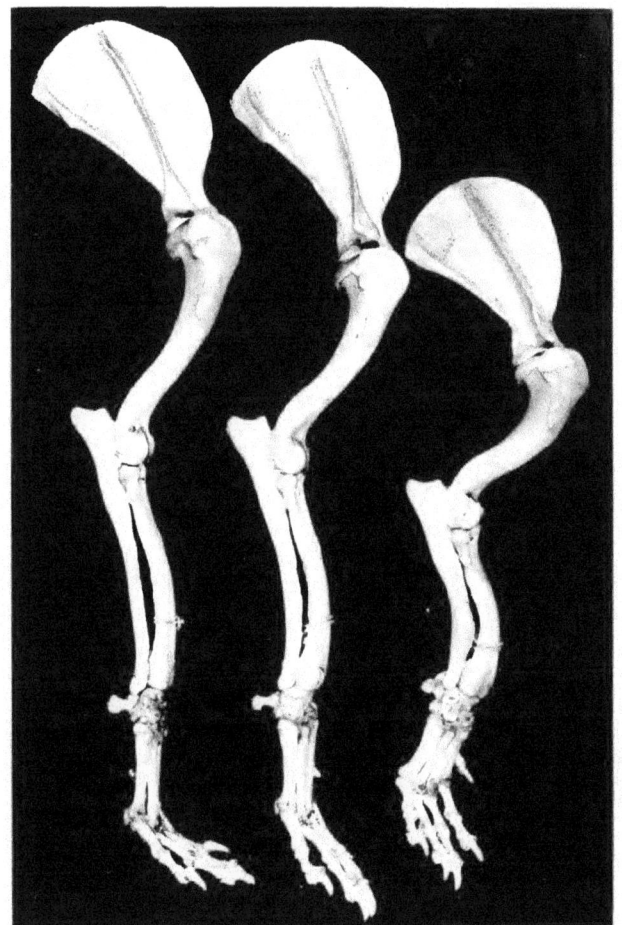

Comparative effects of one or two genes for achondroplasia.
L to R   $F_2$ Saluki-bassethound 1440 ♂, sl.
         $F_2$ Saluki-bassethound 504 ♂, sl.
         $F_2$ Saluki-bassethound 1211 ♂, ss.
Note difference occasioned by homozygous condition in 1211 ♂ and heterozygous condition in 1440 ♂ and 504 ♂.

rotation of the wrist joint. The dorsal surface of the foot loses its forward position and is rotated outward laterally. The entire foot abducts widely, with the wrist, as a consequence, knocked in medially and almost contacting the similarly bent wrist of the other front leg.

*Leg skeletons of the $F_2$ bassethound-bulldog.* Many complicating factors are involved in the structural patterns of the bassethound-bulldog hybrids and these will be discussed in various connections in the further chapters of this study. As we have seen, the achondroplasic short legged condition is limited to an entirely separate or independent growth reaction and follows the same genetic basis in these hybrids as was found for the two foregoing breed crosses. In the $F_2$ generation of bassethound-bulldog hybrids, we find individual sports toward dwarf size and others in an opposite direction toward gigantism. These conditions will be discussed later, but some attention to leg size is necessary at this time. Many of these complicating growth reactions more or less obscure the breed type of bone inheritance which stands out so clearly in the previous crosses. Even so, there are definite indications of inheritance of bull typed and hound typed bone.

Plate 27 shows the right front leg skeletons from six $F_2$ bassethound-bulldog hybrids and, for comparative purposes, the leg of an $F_1$ (at the right end). The first three skeletons are extracted recessive long legs with no achondroplasic symptoms, yet it is quite evident that they differ greatly in size and type. The first skeleton is from a large male $F_2$ animal which was definitely oversized when compared with either of the parent stocks and weighed almost 50% more than his litter mates; he was rather like a St. Bernard dog in living appearance as well as in skeletal type. Comparing the leg skeleton from this animal, 1312 ♂, with the third and fourth skeletons which came from two litter brothers, it is seen to be much larger, with heavier bone, than either of the other two. This rather St. Bernard typed bone arises in the $F_2$ generation as a neomorph, probably due to a strange and new genetic complex largely different in type from that of either the bassethound or bulldog stock. This then, on a size basis for the breeds concerned, is a giant leg from a large St. Bernard-like animal. It might be mentioned in passing that this dog had a large, meaty thymus gland.

The second skeleton, from 1488 ♀, is of a long, straight leg very similar in size and type to that of a foxhound. This is the recessive long, normal leg with the ancestral hound bone type.

The third specimen, from 1311 ♂, is the long legged skeleton of a bulldog typed animal weighing about 20 kilograms. His head was bulldog-like and, in contrast to his giant brother 1312 ♂, he had very scant thymus tissue. The leg skeleton is closely similar to that of the bulldog shown as the third skeleton in figure 1, plate 23. The scapula, humerus and forearm bones are quite the same as those of the bulldog, and the end of the ulna does not extend far below the distal articular surface of the radius, this causing the foot to be somewhat rotated laterally into the typical bulldog posture. We find, therefore, among the long legged dogs in the $F_2$ generation of this cross, the long hound leg and the bulldog leg derived from the parent stocks, as well as mixtures of these two; in addition giant types with long legs arise, and, in an opposite direction, dwarf and almost midget-like animals, none of which has so far failed to show achondroplasia of the legs. There may be, in this cross, some linkage between achondroplasic legs and dwarf body size.

The fourth leg skeleton is from 1313 ♂, a short legged brother of the first and third specimens. This animal had a bassethound-like body and a slight amount of thymus tissue, merely mentioned here in connection with the large thymus of the giant brother. The leg of this animal is interpreted as mixed, $sl$, for achondroplasia. It compares very closely to the $F_1$ leg skeleton shown at the right of the plate. The bone type of this mixed $sl$ $F_2$ is more bulldog-like than that of the $F_1$ although, as we have pointed out before, bulldog type is largely dominant over hound bone and the $F_1$ does show bull bone type. This was shown by comparisons with the $F_1$ bassethound-shepherd.

The next two leg skeletons, the fifth and sixth, are from litter sisters, 1581 ♀ and 1583 ♀. Both these show fully developed achondroplasia and are also judged to be $ss$ in genotype. In bone type these legs are much like the $F_2$ hound bone bassethound-shepherd hybrids. The fifth specimen, 1581 ♀, shows some bulldog quality of bone, but 1583 ♀ is quite typically double short on hound typed bone and, as the photograph shows, this skeleton is unusually small and dwarf for the breeds concerned. The scapula is very wide in both, and the humerus is short, typically bent and twisted on its axis as in fully developed achondroplasia. The forearm bones are characteristic of the defect; the deficiency of the ulna is complete and the foot is everted and widely abducted laterally from the leg axis. These two pure or double short $ss$ legs with largely hound typed bone are only slightly if any more deformed than the mixed short $sl$ leg of the $F_1$ on the dominant bull bone type.

The high accentuation of the reaction in the bulldog typed bone to the gene for achondroplasia is illustrated most strikingly in the contrast between the two leg skeletons in plate 28. The leg skeleton on the left is from the pure double short $ss$ $F_2$ bassethound-Saluki 1211 ♂, which is photographed from life in plate 12 (right in fig. 1) (p. 77). This dog was one of

PLATE 27

EXPLANATION OF FIGURES

Right front leg skeletons showing inheritance of leg length and bone type in English bulldog-bassethound hybrids.

L to R  $F_2$ 1312 ♂, ll. (This animal was definitely oversized and rather St. Bernard-like in living appearance as well as skeletal type.)
 $F_2$ 1488 ♀, ll, hound bone.
 $F_2$ 1311 ♂, ll, bulldog bone.
 $F_2$ 1313 ♂, sl, bulldog bone.
 $F_2$ 1581 ♀, ss, hound bone with some bulldog bone quality.
 $F_2$ 1583 ♀, ss, hound bone (skeleton unusually dwarfed for the two breeds concerned).
 $F_1$ 602 ♀, sl (for comparison).

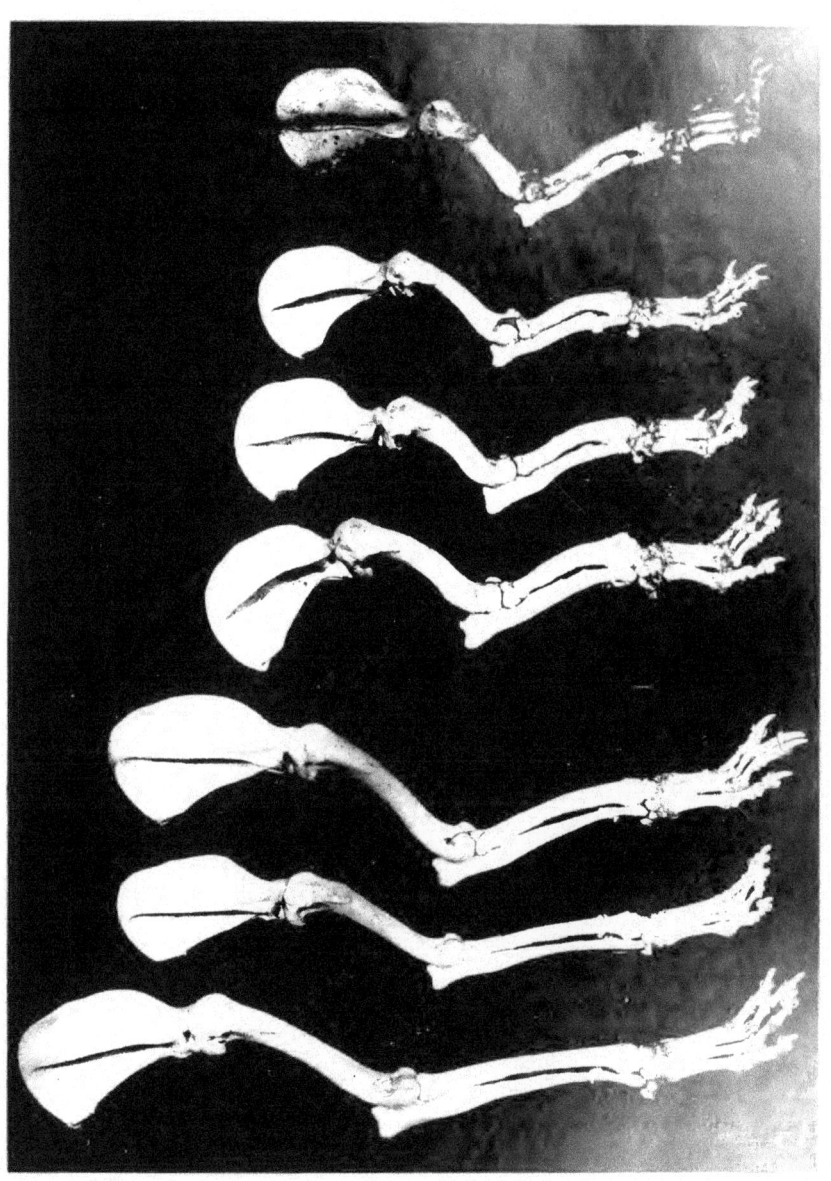

the shortest of the eighty-two animals in his generation. There is little doubt that he presents the most pronounced reduction in leg length that can be produced in the bassethound-Saluki cross. Plate 26 also shows this leg skeleton in company with the $F_1$ skeleton and a mixed $F_2$ to illustrate the increased degree of the achondroplasic reaction in the presence of the genic composition $ss$ as compared with $sl$.

The leg skeleton to the right in plate 28 shows the chondrodystrophic reaction of the bulldog constitution to the presence of only a single gene for leg achondroplasia paired with the allelomorph for long. The heterozygous state of this single factor dominant for short achondroplasic legs exerts a considerably greater effect when acting on the bulldog constitution than does even the homozygous double gene for this dominant expression when acting on the bassethound-Saluki constitution. This fact is vividly shown in plate 28. There is no question that the bassethound-bulldog 1479 ♂ from which the leg skeleton at the right was taken is genetically $sl$. This animal was derived from a backcross between an $F_1$ bassethound-bulldog bitch and a pure bulldog sire and so could only acquire a single $s$. The leg skeleton from this animal, along with that of its tail, is again shown in plate 80 (p. 395) and the animal itself, pictured from life with three other members of his litter, in plate 79 (p. 393). This is indeed a most impressive phenomenon: to observe in the complex mammalian body clearly marked differences in morphologic development due to the presence of only a single or double gene in the genetic constitution. The influence for better or worse of one strange gene in the constitution of higher mammals and of man himself gives a thoughtful person adequate reason for concern regarding racial hybridization. In spite of superficial generalities on the part of so-called authorities who claim that all human races are highly mongrelized anyway, available knowledge at present forces us not to accept this statement as correct for many racial characteristics.

PLATE 28

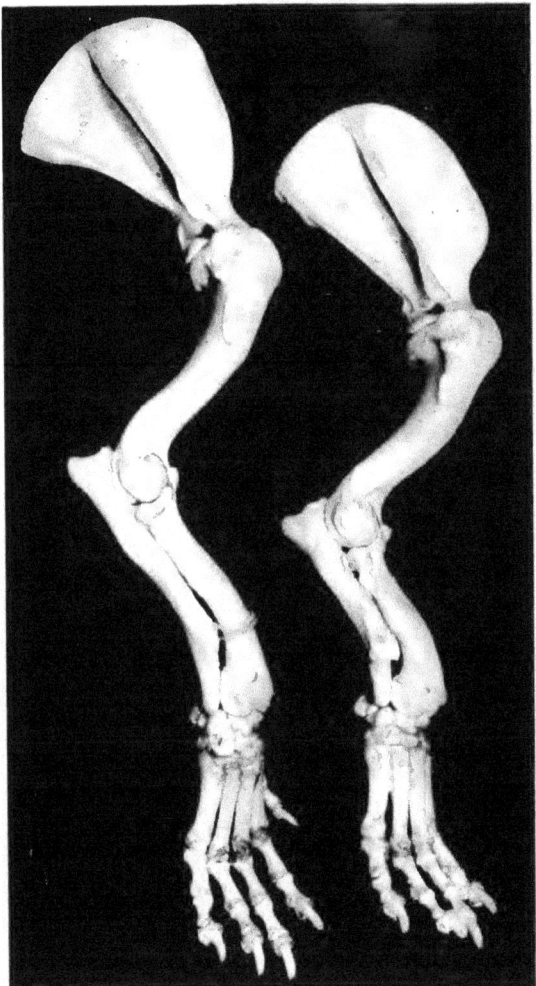

Contrasting the degree of reaction to achondroplasia of bulldog and Saluki-bassethound bone constitutions.

L. $F_1$ Bassethound-Saluki 1211 ♂, ss.
R. Backcross bulldog-bassethound-bulldog 1479 ♂, sl.

The heterozygous condition for achondroplasia of 1479 ♂ exerts a considerably greater influence on its bull bone constitution than does the homozygous condition of 1211 ♂ on the Saluki-bassethound bone constitution.

## LOCALIZED ACHONDROPLASIA IN THE EXTREMITIES OF THE DACHSHUND AND THE PEKINGESE

The reader no doubt appreciates by this time that we have fully tested the inheritance of short achondroplasic growth in the extremities as transmitted by the bassethound when hybridized with widely different stocks. However, a question still remains—whether the short leg condition found in other breeds, such as the dachshund and the Pekingese, is transmitted in the same genetic fashion. We have mentioned in an earlier section that the short leg deformity appeared very early in the history of the dog and that a low turnspit-like animal probably arose independently in several widely separated parts of the world. Did this modification of the legs always arise from a single point mutation which affected the same gene in all breeds or races? It is a matter of considerable genetic importance to learn whether in the complex constitution of higher mammals, such as the dog, there is a tendency for the same mutation to appear in different stocks and, after arising, to react in inheritance in only one way when paired with non-mutant allelomorphs.

If each gene in a series is a different complex protein molecule, then a given gene which exerts its most noticeable influence on a particular character may be very closely or exactly the same kind of compound in all the species in which this character occurs. In other words, exactly the same gene probably exists in many different animals and functions in a similar way in all of them. If the gene is somewhat unstable in composition and tends to mutate by shifting or dropping a secondary or side chain compound, one may imagine that the same modification would repeatedly tend to occur at the least stable point rather than at a different point each time. Chemical compounds usually build up or break down by definite steps instead of changing first in one way and then in another. The same mutation has been found to occur in many different stocks of the fruit fly, *Drosophila*. Against the above supposition, however, is the fact that a few cases of several allelomorphs for the same gene are known, and this probably means that an original gene had mutated in more than one way or by more than a single type of change.

The short legged condition not only occurs in several dog breeds but, as will be recalled from our earlier discussions, a closely similar growth reaction is found among many widely different animals, such as cattle, sheep, birds, and the human race. No one can deny that the mutations giving rise to the distorted short extremities in these very different forms may have occurred independently. Among the dogs, however, there is a possibility that man introduced the short legged condition into the different breeds from one original mutant source. The history of several recent short legged breeds would indicate that they doubtless were produced in this manner. In spite of this possibility there is strong probability that several of the short legged dog breeds have entirely independent origins. There is no satisfactory evidence to indicate that the bassethound and the dachshund derived their short legs from a common ancestral origin, yet the chance for this must be acknowledged since both breeds have been developed in nearby European countries. However, the Pekingese, with its short achondroplasic legs, arose in a far distant region of Asia, and from old illustrations we are led to believe that the breed has existed as such for more than a thousand years. There is little possibility that the origin of the achondroplasic legs of the Pekingese dog is in any way connected with the origin of short legs in the European dogs, or vice versa.

With these questions and problems in mind it seemed highly desirable to widen our study of the short leg character by further breed crosses using the dachshund and Pekingese.

THE EXTREMITIES IN THE DACHSHUND-BOSTON TERRIER CROSS

Except for its dwarf size, the dachshund is very similar in general type to the bassethound. The same extreme degree of localized achondroplasic growth is found in the extremities, while the axial skeleton—the skull and vertebral column—shows no indication of achondroplasic defects. The head is well formed with a long slender muzzle and the tail is long and normally motile. As in most hound breeds, the ears are long and pendulous and the skin moderately loose. The dachshund weighs less than half as much as a normal sized hound. This dog is thus an ideal animal for the investigation of the origin and development of chondrodystrophic extremities.

The Boston terrier breed is highly contrasted in type with the dachshund except that it also is a dwarf. The legs of this animal are long and perfectly straight. The head and tail are bulldog-like in pattern, which is due to a decided chondrodystrophic reaction at both ends of the axial skeleton (a characteristic to be considered in a later section of this study). The defective growth of cartilage and bone is sharply localized in the skull and caudal end of the vertebral column; the bones of the extremities grow in a perfectly normal manner. At this time we shall limit our consideration entirely to the contrasted extremities of the Boston terrier and the dachshund.

In our cross matings between dachshunds and Boston terriers, members of both breeds have been used as sires and dams. The $F_1$ offspring from the dachshund mother and the Boston terrier father are indistinguishable from those with a Boston terrier dam and a dachshund sire. All members of the first hybrid generation have short achondroplasic legs, never the long straight legs of the Boston terrier parent. The short legs of the dachshund are dominant when crossed on long legged stock just as are those of the bassethound, and again the legs of the $F_1$ animal are not so short nor completely achondroplasic as those of the short legged parent. The heterozygous $sl$ condition gives an intermediate length to the $F_1$ leg. Plate 29 shows photographs of the dachshund (fig. 1) and Boston terrier (fig. 2), with their extreme contrast in leg length. The two $F_1$ animals in figures 3 and 4 are dachshund-Boston terriers and the three in figure 5 are

PLATE 29

Results of a cross between the two dwarf breeds, the dachshund and Boston terrier, as a further study on the inheritance of achondroplasia of the extremities.
1  Dachshund  255 ♀.
2  Boston terrier  435 ♀.
3–4  F₁s 127 ♀ and 129 ♂.
5  F₁s (L to R) 553 ♂, 554 ♀, 555 ♀.

Boston terrier-dachshunds (the breed name of the mother is placed before the hyphen).

These $F_1$ hybrids, when bred *inter se*, give rise to an $F_2$ generation showing the same differences in leg conditions as have been described previously for the bassethound crosses. The long straight legs of the Boston terrier grandparent reappear in about one-fourth of the $F_2$ animals, as would be expected in Mendelian segregation for a single factor recessive character. About three-fourths of the $F_2$ generation have achondroplasic short legs, but again, not all are equally short. The majority of the short legs are intermediate like those of the $F_1$ parent while about one-third are very short and probably *ss* in genotype, like the dachshund grandparent. In other words, the short legs of the dachshund are transmitted as a single factor dominant character and the $F_2$ generation is approximately divided into the expected ratio of one short leg *ss* to two intermediate short *sl* to one normal long *ll*.

Plate 30 shows photographs of sixteen $F_2$ hybrids. Of the two animals in figures 6 and 7, figure 6 illustrates the homozygous pure short leg condition and figure 7 the intermediate heterozygous leg condition. Great differences in size are found among litter mates, as illustrated by the animals in figures 1 to 5. Further points of interest shown by these animals will be discussed in other connections.

Plate 31 gives a family tree of the skeletons in this cross. The low skeleton of the dachshund is shown in figures 1 and 2. The characteristic shortness and typical posture of the leg bones are evident. The skeleton of the Boston terrier is shown in figure 3. The deformed skull and short, bent tail offer marked contrast to the long skull and fine tail of the dachshund skeleton, while on the other hand the legs of the Boston terrier show to great advantage over those of the dachshund. An $F_1$ skeleton is seen from two aspects in figures 4 and 5. Figures 6 to 11 show four skeletons from $F_2$ animals: a puppy skeleton is shown in two aspects (figs. 6 and 7), a midget with intermediate legs (fig. 8), a short leg

PLATE 30

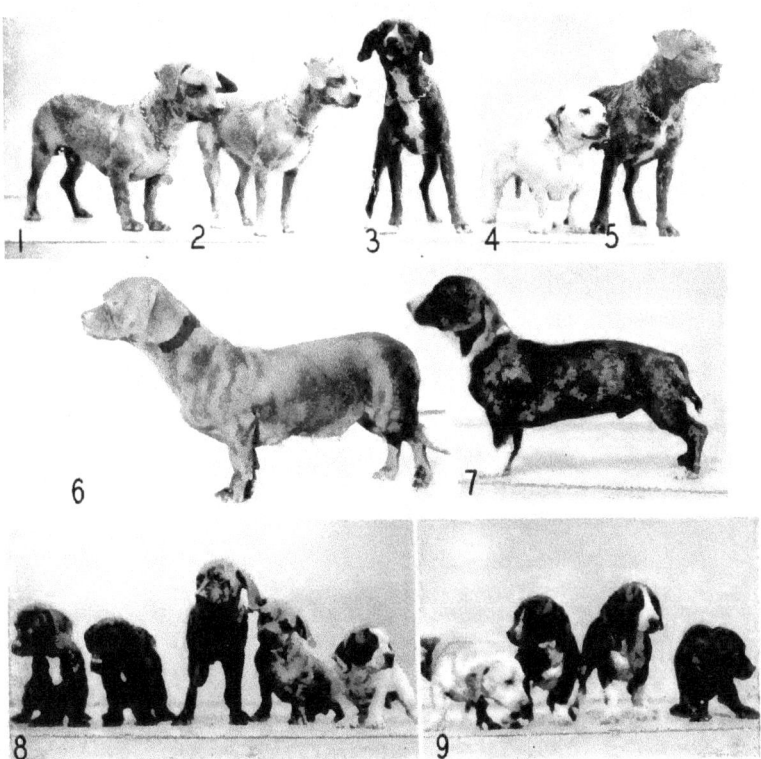

Second generation dachshund-Boston terrier hybrids showing the same differences in leg length and variations in size and other physical characters as found for the bassethound crosses.

1–5. One litter of five hybrids.
  1  782 ♂.      4  779 ♂.      6  296 ♀.      8  Litter 1517–1521.
  2  781 ♀.      5  780 ♂.      7  1522 ♂.     9  Litter 1522–1526.
  3  778 ♂.

130                CHARLES R. STOCKARD

skeleton (fig. 9), and two aspects of a recessive long leg skeleton (figs. 10 and 11). The leg conditions as shown by these skeletons compare very closely with those for the bassethound-shepherd cross, illustrated in plate 3 (p. 55), and the bassethound-bulldog cross shown in plates 20 and 21 (pp. 99 and 100).

The $F_1$ dachshund-Boston terrier hybrid has been backcrossed with both parent stocks with a resulting distribution of leg lengths exactly as would be expected on the basis of our knowledge of the bassethound-shepherd cross. Plate 44 (p. 247) shows the backcross of the $F_1$ on the Boston terrier parent with the two possibilities for leg length, pure long $ll$ and intermediate short $sl$. The backcross in the opposite direction, with the dachshund stock, is illustrated in plate 45 (p. 248). Here the recessive long leg is completely absent since all specimens must carry the gene for short. We find the two types of short leg, the very short $ss$ and the incomplete short $sl$, in about equal numbers.

*Leg skeletons of the dachshund-Boston terrier hybrids.* Skeletons of the right forelimbs from three different $F_2$ dachshund-Boston terrier litter groups are illustrated in detail in plate 32. Figure 1 shows two recessive long legs and an intermediate short $sl$. The first long bone skeleton shows much heavier and more nearly hound typed bone than does

PLATE 31

EXPLANATION OF FIGURES

Skeletons of the dachshund-Boston terrier cross showing contrast in leg length, skull formation, tail, etc., in the pure breeds and the resulting conditions in the first and second generation hybrids.

1–2  Dachshund 84 ♀.         6–11 $F_2$ hybrids.
3    Boston terrier 106 ♀.        6–7  1697 ♂ (puppy).
4–5  $F_1$ 130 ♀.                   8    779 ♂ (midget).
                                    9    782 ♂.
                                    10–11 352 ♂.

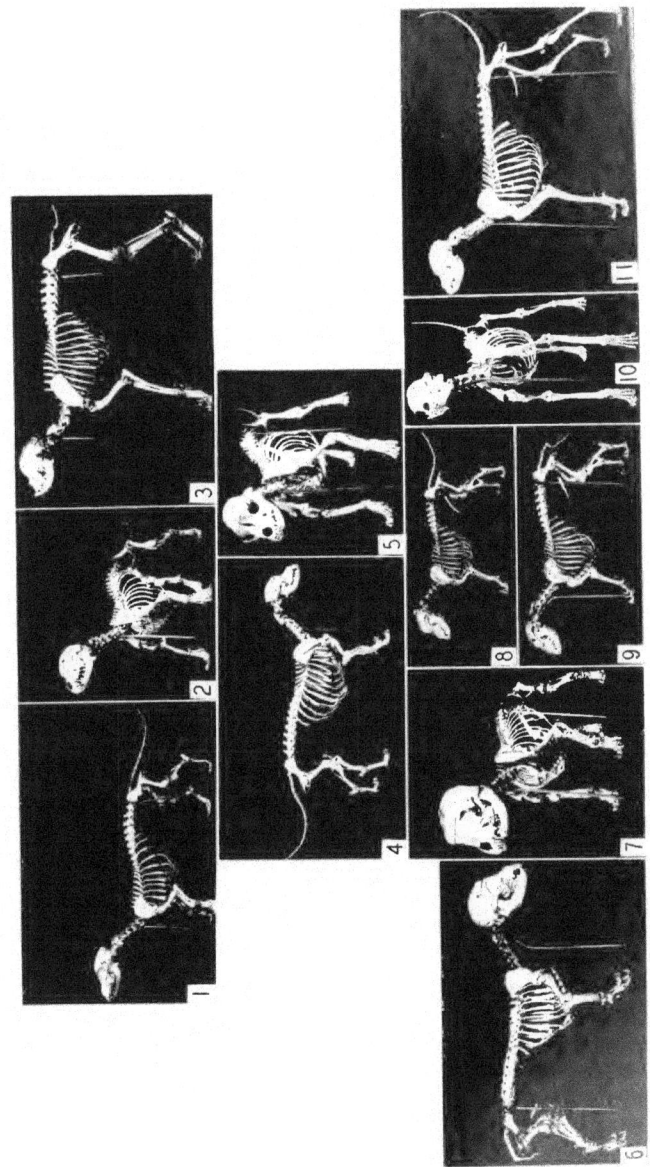

the second with its slenderer Boston terrier-like quality of bone. The scapula in each of these limbs is long and narrow and the humerus, as well as the radius and ulna, is long and normally shaped. The distal epiphysis of the ulna extends well below the end of the radius and prevents lateral rotation and abnormal abduction of the foot.

The foot in the first skeleton, from 1696 ♂, shows a very rare abnormality. The fourth metacarpal bone is abnormally short, only about half normal length, and the proximal phalanx of the fifth toe is raised into the position that should be occupied by the distal half of the metacarpal. The middle phalanx of the toe is reduced to a knob and fused with the ungual segment. This is clearly an abnormality occurring in a normal long leg and having no connection with our present subject. Had it arisen in a short achondroplasic leg it might have been suspected of association with the other skeletal deficiencies.

The third skeleton from this litter illustrates the incomplete short $sl$ condition. The scapula, which is short and broad in shape, has a higher index of width to length than in the two long skeletons. The anterior border changes direction with a sharper angle as the articular end of the scapula is approached, giving a rectangular rather than an ovoid outline to the shoulder blade. This tendency is frequently seen in the achondroplasic limbs of the other crosses. The humerus is shortened and characteristically twisted in shape. The radius and ulna are short, allowing excessive lateral rotation and abduction at the wrist joint.

The four right front leg skeletons in figure 2 of plate 32 are from another litter of $F_2$ dachshund-Boston terrier hybrids. The first skeleton in this group is long and of rather Boston terrier bone type and the other three are classed as intermediate, $sl$, for short. The same differences between shapes of scapula and length and form of humerus, radius and ulna noted in the first group are again found here. The foot in the long leg has the normal straight-to-the-front position while the other three feet are rotated laterally and

PLATE 32

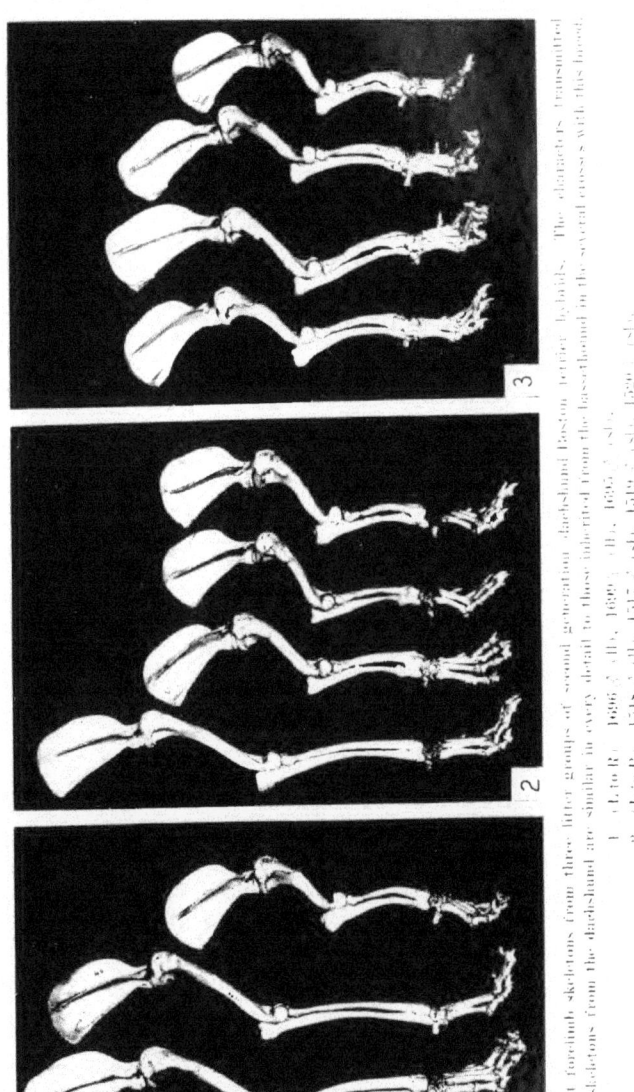

Right forelimb skeletons from three litter groups of second generation dachshund-Boston terrier hybrids. The characters transmitted to these skeletons from the dachshund are similar in every detail to those inherited from the base-hound in the several crosses with this breed.

1 (L. to R.) 1686 ♂ db, 1699 ♀ db, 1695 ♂ db.
2 (L. to R.) 1578 ♂ db, 1515 ♂ db, 1519 ♂ db, 1580 ♂ db.
3 (L. to R.) 1352 ♀ db, 1522 ♂ db, 1523 ♂ db, 1526 ♂ db.

abducted away from the normal straight line. The characteristics transmitted to these front leg skeletons from the dachshund are the same in every detail as those inherited from the bassethound in the several crosses with this breed.

The last group of litter mate skeletons (fig. 3) shows three intermediate and one pure short leg skeleton from the $F_2$ dachshund-Boston terrier hybrids. The extreme modification in the homozygous short leg at the right is clearly appreciated by comparison with the three intermediates. The scapula is wider and shorter with a sharper anterior angle than in the other three, and the humerus is more shortened and more fully twisted, and the radius and ulna much shorter and more strongly bent. The distal end of the ulna in this completely achondroplasic specimen falls completely short of the end of the radius, allowing free rotation and wide abduction of the foot at the wrist joint.

A comparison of the dachshund-Boston terrier leg skeletons in plate 32 with the bassethound-shepherd, bassethound-Saluki and bassethound-bulldog hybrid skeletons shown in plates 24, 25 and 27, respectively, will convince the observer that the achondroplasic growth reaction developed in the bassethound and dachshund is transmitted and expressed in their hybrid descendants in the same manner, even to minute details.

DACHSHUND-FRENCH BULLDOG CROSS FOR EXTREMITY TYPES

The French bulldog is a dwarf of terrier type resembling in many ways the Boston terrier, although it is somewhat larger and heavier in stature. In the formation of its head and tail the French bulldog is a more pronounced bull type than is the Boston terrier and its legs, as in all bulldog breeds, are straight and of normal length with no symptoms of achondroplasia.

Crosses between the dachshund and the French bulldog gave exactly the same results for growth distortion of the extremities as has been described for the dachshund-Boston terrier hybrids. These hybrids were produced more for a study of their skull and other features than for the simple inheritance of the achondroplasic extremities. However, they add material to further substantiate the results recorded in previous pages. Examination of plate 46 (p. 261) will show the manner of short leg inheritance following the cross of these two pure stocks. The dachshund (fig. 1) and French bulldog (fig. 2) are beautifully contrasted types and the $F_1$ hybrids (figs. 3 and 4) are almost indistinguishable from the $F_1$ dachshund-Boston terriers. Four litter mate $F_2$ animals are seen in figures 5 to 8, and the same four specimens, carefully mounted, are shown in plate 47 (p. 263), each facing its own skeleton which was arranged to stand in as closely comparable a position as possible. The short, wide scapula and short legs deviate from the normal long legged skeletons in the same ways as those with which we are familiar from previous descriptions of extremity skeletons.

DACHSHUND-BRUSSELS GRIFFON CROSS FOR EXTREMITY TYPES

This cross was also made primarily for its importance in an analysis of skull types and their modifications. Incidentally, however, it supplied further data on inheritance of contrasted conditions in the extremities.

The Brussels griffon is a tiny midget dog with a flat monkey-like face. Many specimens have practically no muzzle and lack entirely the normal protruding jaws of the dog. The legs of this midget are long, slender and straight. When crossed on the dachshund the short achondroplasic extremities are inherited by the hybrids as a single factor dominant character just as has been found in all other crosses. Figures 1 and 2 in plate 33 illustrate the extremely contrasted features of the two pure breeds. Figure 3 shows the $F_1$ hybrid, and figures 4 to 7 animals derived from a backcross of the $F_1$ on the dachshund parent. The extremities seen in these illustrations are exactly what would be expected from previous experience.

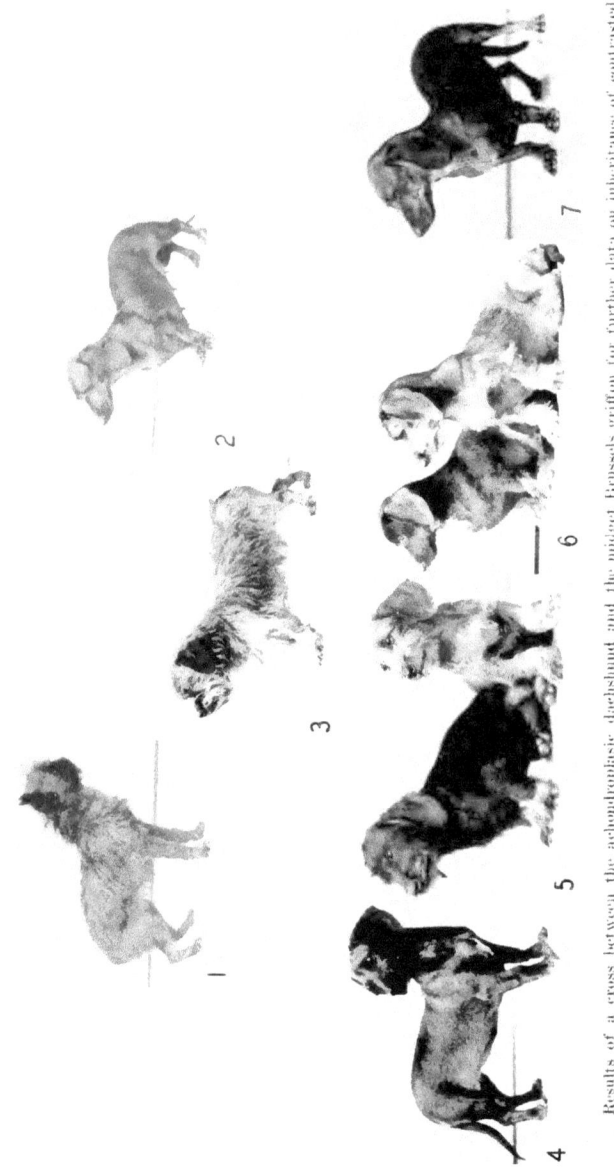

PLATE 33

Results of a cross between the achondroplasic dachshund and the midget Brussels griffon (for further data on inheritance of contrasted leg conditions).

1 Brussels griffon 278 ♀.  4–7 Backcross of $F_1$ with dachshund.
2 Dachshund 255 ♀.  4 337 ♀.  6 334 ♂ (L) and 338 ♀ (R).
3 $F_1$ 134 ♂.  5 335 ♂ (L) and 338 ♀ (R).  7 336 ♀.

136

## The Extremities in the Hybrids Between the Pekingese and Saluki

We have shown that the short achondroplasic extremities of the bassethound and the dachshund are inherited in identical fashion when crossed with a number of normal long legged European dog breeds, and it would seem that the genetic basis for this distorted growth is the same in both cases. It was further desired, however, to secure an achondroplasic breed of unquestionably different origin from either of the above two in order to learn whether the short leg character would always react in its inheritance in the same way. We felt such evidence might help to determine whether an independent identical mutation giving rise to the same deformity of the extremities had occurred independently in several breeds. There is also the further point of interest in that this short leg distortion frequently occurs in widely different species, and its genetic behavior in these may some day demand study. The final question for future approach is whether the same chemical change in the genic complex of the germ cells in these widely different animals produces the same growth modifications in the development of their extremities.

The Pekingese dog, which is a very ancient Chinese breed, has short, bent achondroplasic extremities, as well as achondroplasia of the skull. This latter condition need not interest us here. This dog is probably the most completely perfect achondroplasic dwarf to be found among the many breeds and we shall consider its nature from several standpoints and in connection with other problems. The Saluki dog of Egypt and Asia Minor is one of the most ancient of present day breeds. It is very tall and slender and greyhound-like in type, as we have already called to attention in connection with its cross on the bassethound. No two dogs could be much more widely different in type than are the Pekingese and the Saluki.

We have had the good fortune to successfully mate a Saluki bitch to a Pekingese male. The bitch whelped two $F_1$

puppies, a male and female, both of which lived to produce several litters of $F_2$ hybrids.

Plate 34 illustrates the two parent types (figs. 1–4), and an $F_1$ tan male (fig. 5) and his black and tan sister (fig. 6). The extremities in both $F_1$s have fallen far short of the Saluki and are typically heterozygous achondroplasic legs. A single litter of five $F_2$ animals is shown in figures 7 to 11. It is quite obvious from even these small photographs that here again we have a Mendelian segregation of the single factor dominant short leg character. The $F_2$ animal in figure 7 has straight long legs though certainly not of slender Saluki bone pattern. The second animal (fig. 8) has intermediate length legs like the $F_1$ parents. The next two (figs. 9–10) show legs of questionable shortness; they seem shorter than the $F_1$s, but this may be due to the action of the heterozygous condition on Pekingese bone type, just as the long legged bitch in figure 7 is not a tall dog and certainly does not possess Saluki typed bone. The fifth member of this litter (fig. 11) has unquestionably pure completely short extremities. It is very short with knocked-in wrists closely resembling the Pekingese grandparent. Two other litters of $F_2$ animals bear out the supposition that the achondroplasic short extremities of the Asiatic Pekingese are due to a genetic background which, on crossing with normal long legged animals, reacts in exactly the same way as does the achondroplasic extremities in European breed crosses.

PLATE 34

EXPLANATION OF FIGURES

Cross between the Pekingese and Saluki to determine whether the short leg character in the Pekingese (an Asiatic breed) reacts in its inheritance in the same manner as in the bassethound and dachshund (European breeds).

1 Pekingese 1119 ♀, Saluki 835 ♀.
2 Pekingese 1118 ♂.
3 Saluki 833 ♀.
4 Saluki 835 ♀, Pekingese 1118 ♂.
5 $F_1$ 1295 ♂.
6 $F_1$ 1296 ♀.

7–11 One litter of five $F_2$s.
7 1941 ♀.
8 1942 ♀.
9 1940 ♂.
10 1939 ♂.
11 1938 ♂.

PLATE 34

### TESTING THE LOCATION OF THE GENE WHICH INDUCES ACHONDROPLASIA OF THE EXTREMITIES BY CROSSING THE DACHSHUND WITH THE BASSETHOUND AND WITH THE PEKINGESE

The germ cells of the dog contain such a large number of chromosomes—more than forty—that it is extremely difficult to associate a given gene influencing a certain character with any individual chromosome. As previously mentioned, no two characters among the many which we have studied in the dog are clearly linked together in inheritance, although certain of the head features in the bulldog have given some indication of linkage. The difficulty in finding associated characters is due, of course, to the high number of different gene groups or chromosomes.

We have, however, attempted to ascertain whether the single gene necessary for achondroplasia of the extremities is located in the same chromosomal pair in the different breeds transmitting this character, particularly the bassethound, dachshund and Pekingese dog. If this single factor dominant character is due to the presence of a specific gene located in a given chromosomal pair in the bassethound, and in the same or comparable chromosome of the dachshund, then all individuals in the hybrid generations resulting from a cross between these two breeds would constantly show fully short achondroplasic extremities; there could be no intermediate condition and no normal long legs. As far as this character is concerned, the cross would be the same as the pure line breeding.

On the other hand, if the gene for this character is located in different chromosomal pairs in the two breeds, the expectation for the second generation, $F_2$, hybrids would be three different classes of extremity lengths—as indicated in the diagram (text-fig. 1), in which we may assume that the gene for achondroplasia in the mother is carried by the round chromosomes, while in the father it is located in the long chromosomes. Normal legs should appear among the $F_2$ individuals, since one in sixteen would fail to receive a

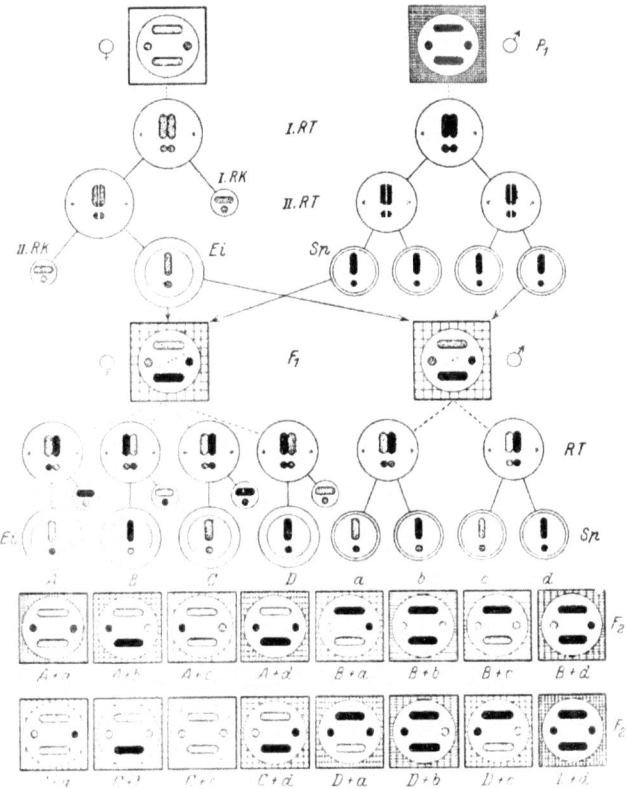

Text-figure 1. Diagram showing expectancy for achondroplasic reaction in the $F_2$ generation if the gene for this factor is located in different chromosomal pairs in the two parent breeds. If it is assumed that the achondroplasic gene is carried in the round gray chromosome of the female, and the long black chromosome of the male, there will be sixteen possible combinations in the $F_2$ generation, as shown at the bottom of the diagram. From K. Belar.

chromosome carrying the gene for achondroplasia (A + a); four in sixteen would receive only one chromosome carrying the gene (A + c, A + d, C + a, D + a) and would therefore show the intermediate condition; while all others of this generation would show fully achondroplasic extremities due to the presence of at least two genes for the condition. There is also the possibility that some of these animals, in fact, a fourth of them, would carry three such genes (B + c, B + d, C + b, D + b) and one in sixteen, being homozygous through two pairs of chromosomes (one pair from each parent stock) could have four genes for achondroplasia (B + b). These animals with an excessive number of genes for achondroplasia might give rise to exaggerations of the deformity and be almost or completely legless. Therefore, the expectations for the transmission of this deformity to the hybrids, provided the modifying genes were located in different chromosomes in the two breeds, would be exactly the same as in any case of a character dependent for its transmission upon genes in two different chromosomes. The long legs would appear as a double factor recessive in the one $F_2$ out of sixteen (A + a) which failed to receive a chromosome carrying the gene for short from either of the two responsible chromosomal pairs.

The results of crossing the bassethound and the dachshund do not show such different varieties in extremity forms. All the hybrids in both the first and second generations were uniformly short with achondroplasic extremities.

Two slightly related bassethound bitches were bred to two distantly related dachshund males, and litters of eight and five $F_1$ puppies were whelped. Animals from these two $F_1$ litters were mated in various combinations and produced fifty-four $F_2$ offspring which showed various conditions of size, color patterns, etc. Some of these will be referred to later. But the achondroplasic short leg character was uniformly consistent in its expression in the fifty-four $F_2$ animals. All were diagnosed as fully short and were apparently homozygous individuals, indicating that the genes for achondroplasia in the bassethound and the dachshund were quite certainly carried by comparable pairs of chromosomes.

Because both above breeds are European in origin, the mutation giving rise to achondroplasic extremities may have appeared in the germ cells of ancestors common to both of them and on this account it was deemed desirable to conduct an experiment with breeds derived from two widely distant parts of the world as had been done in the previous contrasted crosses. We again used the European dachshund, this time crossing it with the Asiatic Pekingese dog. There is no indication of any relationship whatsoever between these two breeds as such. Therefore the achondroplasic leg character found in both breeds very probably arose through independent mutations. The question is again presented: does this character always depend upon a mutation which affects the same gene? And if it does, is this gene always located in the same chromosome in all the breeds involved? It has been clearly shown by Dobzhansky ('37) for the fruit fly that a given gene is not always carried in the same chromosome in all varieties of these flies. Whether or not this is true for the germ cells in the higher animals, and particularly in mammals, no one has determined. At present the only way to detect such a discrepancy in the location of a given gene in different varieties or breeds of a mammal is through crossing widely separated breeds that chance to show the same single point mutation.

The dachshund and the Pekingese both have achondroplasia of the extremities which we have demonstrated above to be transmitted independently as a single factor dominant character. These breeds were crossed a number of times in both directions and the details of these crosses will be discussed in other connections. At this time we shall merely summarize briefly the results as they concern the growth of the hybrid extremities.

Fifteen $F_1$ dachshund-Pekingese hybrids were produced and all showed fully short achondroplasic extremities; five members of this generation may be seen in plate 67 (p. 345).

No intermediate legs typical of the $F_1$ hybrids between short and tall dogs occur in this cross. A number of matings were made among the $F_1$ hybrids and these resulted in twenty-three $F_2$ puppies, all of which showed uniformly short extremities; there were no intermediate and no exaggerated forms, and all were of exactly the same type as in the two pure parent stocks (see pl. 67, p. 345).

This result indicates quite conclusively that the modified extremities in these breeds are due to a mutation which affected the same gene in both breeds, and further, that at the present time this gene is located in the same pair of chromosomes in each breed. This is significant since the two breeds arose long ago in widely separated parts of the world.

On the basis of the facts obtained from the many breed crosses considered for leg length, it would seem possible that all animals in which the achondroplasic defect of the extremities occurs, including man himself, must possess this same specific gene. There is a possibility that a given gene consists of one or more specific protein molecules and that the same gene or same protein molecule might occur in a great number of animal species. Further, it is possible that in the various species of animals in which achondroplasia occurs, a mutation of one specific gene common to all gave rise to modified extremities in the mutant individual. Only by investigating some such suppositions as these can we attempt to understand why the same type of modification can be inherited in almost all higher classes of vertebrates. The fact that in these problems our chemical knowledge is very far behind should not discourage investigation of the genetics and development of these characters. Such studies may in the end lead the way to a knowledge of the chemistry involved. Certainly the chemist cannot hand the biologist the composition of chromosomes and genes until he is directed by the biologist to the sources of material. Biological assays and reactions were necessary before the chemist could start an approach to thyroxin or oestrin (theelin). The performance of the chemists in the solution of biological problems must necessarily lag behind the discovery of the problems. Not only is this difference in time of performance evident in the interdependence of two different sciences, such as biology and chemistry, but the same may be true for two related fields of the same science. Those familiar with the progress of genetics will know that our knowledge of the cytology of germ cells continually lagged behind genetic discoveries until, it may be said, genetics finally pulled cytology into its own.

After the foregoing survey of the genetic behavior of the achondroplasic distortion of the extremities, we may finally epitomize the facts regarding this condition as follows:

Achondroplasic extremities occur among a number of mammalian species, including man, as an isolated or localized structural deformity in otherwise normal individuals.

This condition exists in several of the domestic breeds of dogs from widely distant countries, and in all cases where animals showing the condition are crossed with those having normal extremities, the distorted growth is inherited as a single factor dominant character.

The influence of the factor for leg achondroplasia differs in degree of severity depending upon the bone constitution of the breed concerned. The Saluki or greyhound typed bone has the greatest resistance to this growth distortion, the shepherd dog bone is affected to a somewhat greater degree, the hound bone to a still greater degree, and the bulldog bone gives the most pronounced response.

The presence of only a single gene in the heterozygous genotype for limb achondroplasia gives rise to an incomplete or intermediate degree of expression in the phenotype, and the homozygous condition, with both allelomorphic genes for achondroplasia, brings about a complete or full expression of the defect. On the basis of morphologic expression alone, the observer is able to diagnose the difference between the mixed or heterozygous animal carrying only one gene for the condition and the pure homozygous animal with two genes. These diagnoses have been substantiated in several cases by crucial genetic tests. It is surprising to realize that the influence of either one or two genes acting on so complex a phenomenon as the growth and development of the mammalian extremity will give rise to two different degrees of distortion so readily differentiated. It is equally surprising that so complicated a disturbance as achondroplasic development of the extremities results from only a single mutant or modified gene within the entire hereditary complex (unless it be from several modified genes within the same chromosome).

Evidence has been presented which indicates that the same modified gene is the basis of achondroplasia of the extremities in all dog breeds carrying this short leg deformity, and that this gene is carried within a comparable pair of chromosomes in the different breeds in which it occurs, even though many of these may have arisen independently centuries ago in widely separated regions of the world.

Since this defect of the extremities occurs in man and many other mammals as well as in other classes of vertebrates, it is suggested hypothetically that a gene of identical chemical nature may exist in widely different members of the animal kingdom and that this gene plays a consistent rôle in the development of individuals.

The possible influence of unusual endocrine secretions in this modified growth reaction, as well as the possibility of primary inheritance of endocrine conditions bringing about the distortions of the extremities as a secondary effect, are reserved for consideration in a later section of this study.

# SECTION III

CHARLES R. STOCKARD
and
A. L. JOHNSON

# THE CONTRASTED PATTERNS AND MODIFICATIONS OF HEAD TYPES AND FORMS IN THE PURE BREEDS OF DOGS AND THEIR HYBRIDS AS THE RESULTS OF GENETIC AND ENDOCRINIC REACTIONS

## THE PROBLEMS INVOLVED IN THE STUDY OF HEAD TYPES AMONG DOGS

In the preceding chapters we have considered the widely contrasted differences in structural growths and arrangements found in the extremities of the pure dog breeds. Most pronounced deviations from the ancestral or wild type occur as strictly localized deformities in leg length and shape, while all other parts of the animal are perfectly normal in their expression. The present chapter will deal with the heads and underlying skull structures among the different dog breeds which we shall find are as strongly modified and contrasted as are the extremity types. However, the head involves a greater number of features and is much more complex than the extremities, and necessitates the calculation of indices for comparisons. In some breeds we again find that the head distortions are a strictly localized modification in an animal with otherwise normal structural arrangements. The King Charles spaniel and the Brussels griffon, though midget dwarfs in size, are well formed and normally proportioned in all regions of the body with the exception of their skulls, which deviate enormously from the wild dog pattern. The English bulldog, French bulldog and Boston terrier show highly modified conditions of the skull as a growth complex quite independent of the less pronounced modifications occurring in other regions of the body.

The skull modifications in certain breeds are accompanied by characteristic arrangements of teeth which differ from those of the standard shepherd. Moreover, there are constitutional defects in dentition in some breeds and deficiencies in tooth structure, such as hyperplasia of the enamel and pitting of the tooth surfaces. These dental defects are exactly similar in some cases to those which have been reported as resulting from vitamin deficiencies in the dog and other animals, yet in the present cases these malformations of the teeth are constitutional reactions arising in certain typed animals whose litter mates develop perfectly normal teeth under identical vitamin supply and other living conditions.

The modified leg condition was found to be a simple single factor dominant expression, but the genetics of the short achondroplasic head modification, such as found in the bulldog and other breeds, is much more complex. Certain factors in the complex influence only definite distinct parts of the head in either a dominant or a recessive fashion, while others affect entirely different features. These modifications of different elements among the structures of the head are inherited more or less independently, and as a consequence frequent disharmonies occur among the parts, often disturbing functional efficiency. The so-called processes of developmental regulation are ineffective in bringing about structural adjustments in the hybrids resulting from crosses between breeds with widely contrasted head forms.

The maladjusted conditions found in the skulls of deformed dog breeds, and particularly of their hybrids, are frequently comparable with well known modifications and distortions which occur in human beings. Structural disharmonies in the growth of the jaws, giving various degrees of dental malocclusion, may be cited as a widely prevalent condition common to both dogs and man. The association of a number of different maldevelopments with modifications of the endocrine glands and the difficulty in differentiating between correlation and causal relation in the interpretation of many of the conditions are considered in the following pages. The strongly contrasted proportions of bodily structures and wide differences in quality of the endocrine glands in different dog breeds give us almost ideal material on which to investigate the significance of these relations.

The differences in skull shapes, cranial capacities and facial arrangements exhibited among the dog breeds are of special interest as correlated with the behavior of the individuals, since milder degrees of the same expressions in human beings are frequently associated with modifications in behavior and mental reactions. It is well known that dogs of different breeds behave in widely different ways, and many of the instinctive reactions found in one breed may be entirely different or actually lacking in another. Whether these deviations in behavior are consistently associated with definite differences in head forms, and whether a given head form is the developmental result of a characteristic endocrine quality or balance, are questions that can be studied to greater advantage in contrasted dog types than in either human beings or other mammalian species.

With such considerations in mind, it seemed very desirable to analyze the differences among dog skulls in some detail and with as much accuracy of measurement as could be attained. After the many skull differences had been established, their hereditary significance among the hybrids of contrasted breeds was carefully followed. We further made an extensive study of both gross and microscopic conditions of the endocrine glands from all these animals. In the following sections of this report the findings for the various glands and their possible relation to the structural and functional modifications found among the pure breeds and their hybrids will be discussed. Finally, some of the instinctive and conditioned behaviors accompanying the various head types will be recorded in an effort to determine in what ways structural changes may be correlated with modified types of functional behavior. Experimental modification of the endocrine balance and its influence on behavior in the different morphologic types will be considered from these standpoints.

It is intended at this point to present the contrasts in morphologic characters as shown among the dog skulls, and to consider the mode of hereditary transmission of these characters and the developmental reactions involved in their expression. It is safe to say that the skulls of no other single mammalian species can approach in variety the series derived from the domestic breeds of dogs. Starting with those having long narrow crania, a high sagittal bony crest and a long, projecting, strongly developed facial skeleton largely formed by ferocious jaws, we may pass to the opposite extremes showing almost spherical crania with smoothly rounded or flattened tops and no trace of the sagittal crest, and with a rounded forehead overhanging a facial skeleton with defective jaws reduced to such an extent as not to project beyond the bulge of the forehead, and with practically no dental occlusion. The face in such a skull is as flat as that shown by the apes or even man (see figs. 7 and 8, pl. 50, p. 275). Between these extremes almost every variation and deviation can be demonstrated in our collection of about 1000 pedigreed specimens.

### The Normal or Standard Dog Skull

It is not difficult to agree on the type of skull which one could accept as ancestral or normal for the dog. Several dog breeds still possess skulls resembling much more closely those of the wolf or wild Canidae than of numerous other dog breeds. In other words, in spite of the large variety of skull patterns and the extreme deviations they present, many breeds still retain the normal or standard typed skulls from which these modifications must have arisen. This is of great advantage to the investigator since it enables him to determine the exact kind and degree of the alterations occurring in a number of different regions and structures of the skull. The ancestral form is often lost or obliterated in many animal groups which have deviated widely from the original stem, and the presence in the dog company of the perfectly formed wolf-like skull of our standard control German shepherd dog is very fortunate indeed.

Three different aspects of the shepherd skull photographed with comparable views of the English bulldog skull are shown in plate 50 (p. 275). If these two skulls were found as fossils, a paleontologist would hesitate to class them as belonging to any one family of Carnivora. The shepherd skull is in all aspects closely reminiscent of the skull of the wolf.

A check of the literature on the dog breeds did not bring to light any exact information on the growth of the skull in the dog, and no comparative measurements showing the contrasts among the various dimensions found in the skulls of different breeds are available. The fixed points from which growths take place in order to give the characteristic skull forms for the dog have not been determined. We were forced, therefore, to plot the numerous dimensions of these skulls in order to determine which were significantly important in the comparison of types. Linear measurements of a complex object such as this are not alone sufficient, and indices have been determined to facilitate more complete comparisons. The measurements in themselves are not difficult to make, yet it is often hard to locate the measurement between two points or the index of a region which would be consistently and significantly indicative of an inclination toward one or another type. It was thus decided to map a number of points on the skull and record a complete series of measurements between certain of these, the expectation being that such measurements derived from a sample group of skulls from different breeds might be compared graphically so as to determine the lines of type differences and agreements.

Plate 35 illustrates the points and lines which were decided upon for making these measurements. Figure 1 shows the two sagittal measurements made from the dorsal aspect of the skull: *cranial length*, the straight distance between the supraoccipital spine and the nasion, line H–I in the figure;

PLATE 35

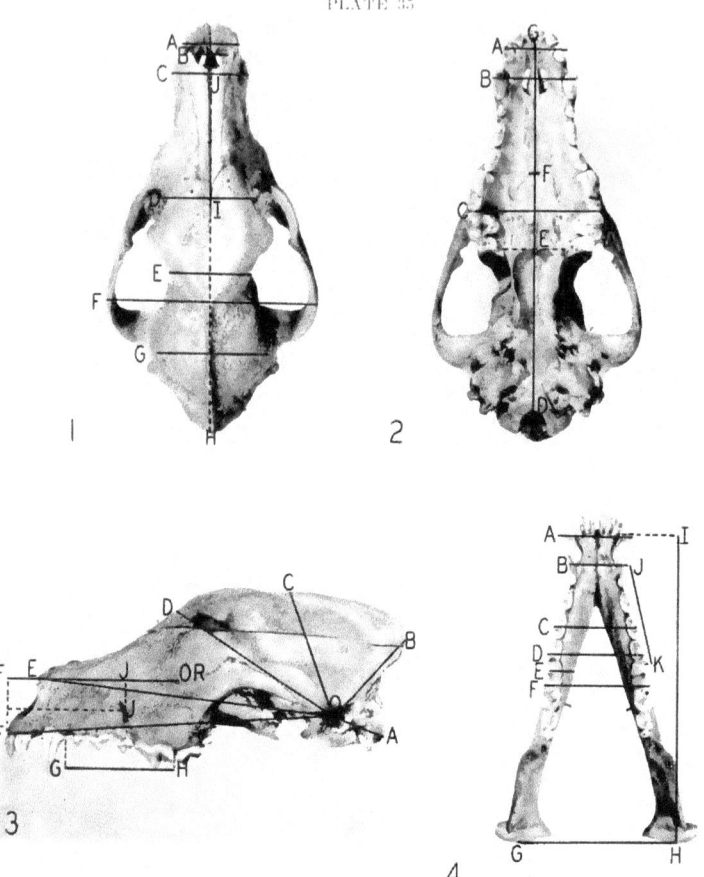

Four aspects of the dog's skull illustrating linear measurements and points forming bases for computation of indices in the comparison of skulls of different types.

1   A   Incisal alveolus width
    B   Nasal width
    C   Canine alveolus width
    D   Interorbital width
    E   Least frontal width
    F   Zygomatic width
    G   Cranial width
    H–I Cranial length
    I–J Nasal length
2   A   Third incisor tips
    B   Canine tips
    C   Palatal width
    D–G Total skull base
    E–G Palatal length
    E–F Palatal processes of palate
3   O   Auditory meatus
    A   Occipital condyles
    B   Supraoccipital spine
    C   Bregma
    D   Nasion
    E   Anterior nasal
    F   Superior dental alveolus
    G–H Premolar region
    OR  Orbit
    J   Infraorbital foramen
4   G   Intercondylar
    H–I Condyle symphysis
    A   Inter canine tips
    B   Inter canine alveoli
    C   3rd premolar tip
    D   4th premolar tip
    E   Mandibular thickness
    F   Inter 1st molar high cusp
    J–K Mandibular premolar region

and *nasal length*, from the nasion to the anterior end of the sagittal suture of the nasal bones, line I-J. A series of transverse measurements was also taken. Beginning anteriorly, they are: line A, *incisal alveolus width*, the straight distance between the alveoli of the right and left third incisors; B, *internasal width*, the distance between the anterolateral spines of the two nasal bones; C, *canine alveolus width*, the distance between the posterior alveolar borders of the canines; D, *interorbital width*; E, *least frontal width*, the narrowest line of the frontal region; F, the *zygomatic width*; and G, the *cranial width*.

The measurements taken on other aspects of the skull may be readily seen and understood by an examination of the figures and accompanying explanations. We need only comment on some of the measurements shown in the lateral view (fig. 3). The orifice (O) of the external meatus proved to be the most satisfactorily fixed point from which to measure distances to other points on the skull. The head-spanner was used to determine straight distances between this point and the posterior border of the occipital condyle, the supraoccipital spine, the bregma, the nasion, the anterior end of the internasal suture and the most anterior limit of the superior dental alveolus. We shall find that certain measurements are almost consistently of the same length in all skull types, while others show great differences and are of primary importance in the differentiation of types.

The control shepherd dog skull presents the measurements shown in the second column of table 1 (p. 208) of pure breed skull dimensions; the averages, probable errors and standard deviations are indicated. The length of skull base averages 19.27 cm with a standard deviation of 10.5 mm. The zygomatic width is 10.8 cm, giving a total skull index of 56, which means, of course, that the skull is very long and narrow. The cranial index is 51. A further study of the table will bring out the dimensions of this skull in reference to the points and lines illustrated in the diagrams of measurements (pl. 35). This control skull as such is more fully appreciated as we proceed with the considerations of the various head types.

COMPARISONS OF LINEAR MEASUREMENTS MADE ON A GROUP OF SEVENTY ADULT DOG SKULLS INCLUDING VARIOUS BREEDS FROM THE LARGE ST. BERNARDS AND GREAT DANES TO THE SMALL PEKINGESE AND TOY DOGS

These measurements were a necessary initial step in our attempt to determine for the seventy individuals representing the various breeds those skull dimensions showing similarity or uniformity as contrasted with those showing significant differences. In the accompanying charts a series of comparisons between given measurements and a number of other dimensions is made. On the basis of a given computation, the skulls were arranged in sequence from greatest to smallest, and the same sequence then followed in charting other dimensions for the same skulls. This method will be readily appreciated by proceeding at once with our first series.

All measurements in these studies were made with the best calipers obtainable, accurately calibrated for anthropological use.

*Zygomatic widths compared with other skull widths.* The distance between the widest lateral points of the zygomatic arch (pl. 35, fig. 1, F) was used in arranging a selected group of skulls from seventy dogs of different breeds, the sequence being from greatest to least zygomatic width. The group of skulls included those from various breeds and types, from great Dane and St. Bernard giants to Pekingese and dwarfs, as well as from dogs with bulldog-like distortions. Text-figures 2 to 10 indicate the skull measurements. Each line in the several charts represents a dimension on one skull and the sequence of the skulls is the same in all charts.

The zygomatic widths (text-fig. 2) form a quite regularly graded series and range from a high of 140 mm to a low of only 72 mm, the broadest skull being twice the width of the narrowest. Is this due only to the fact that some of the skulls in the group are large and some are small? Or does the zygomatic arch form a wider lateral curve in some skull types than in others of the same general size? If the latter is true, can differences in the degree of curvature be correlated with other characteristics of the skull? In order to answer such questions, these same skulls were charted for eight other dimensions.

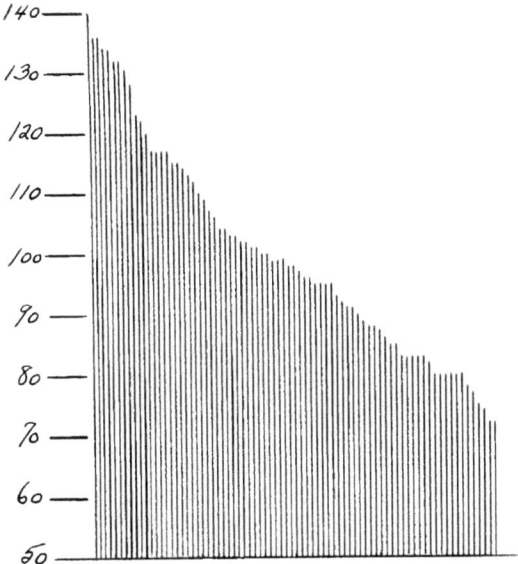

Text figure 2. Sequence A. Zygomatic width. Group of seventy skulls arranged in sequence from greatest to least distance between the widest lateral points of the zygomatic arch.

Text-figure 3 represents the cranial widths of the skulls (pl. 35, fig. 1, G) arranged in the same sequence as for zygomatic arch measurements, and these range from 65 to 45 mm. In spite of the size differences among the skulls, the widest cranial measurement is only 50% greater than the narrowest. A comparison of this chart with that for zygomatic widths shows no accord between the two. The thirty-second skull in the cranial width series, for example, is among the widest for this measurement but is more than half way down the slope in the zygomatic series. There is no correlation between the width of the head at the zygomatic arch and the broadness of the cranium, and this lack of correlation is quite independent of differences in skull size.

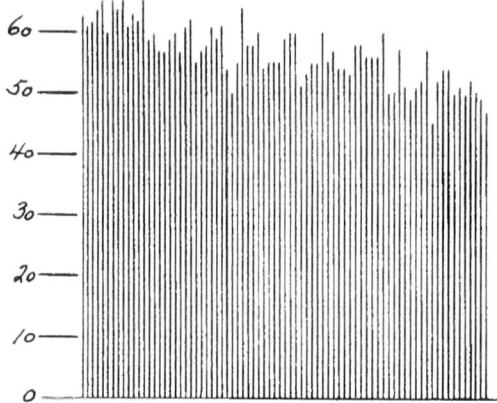

Text-figure 3. Sequence A. Cranial width. Same skull sequence as text-figure 2.

One other transverse cranial measurement, the least frontal width (pl. 35, fig. 1, E) has been taken. The values for this measurement are represented in text-figure 4. The least frontal width ranges from 49 to 27 mm, a proportion of about 7:4. Again there is not the slightest correlation between this width and that of the zygomatic arch.

The series of interorbital widths (pl. 35, fig. 1, D) is indicated in text-figure 5. These range from 57 to 22 mm or about as 5:2. As might be anticipated, there is here a fair degree of accord with the zygomatic widths although many individual irregularities occur. The mode of divergence of the zygomatic process of the maxillary bone has an effect on both the zygomatic width and the interorbital width and this no doubt underlies to some extent the accord between these two measurements.

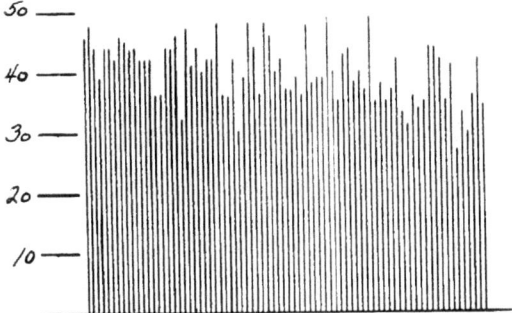

Text-figure 4. Sequence A. Least frontal width. Same skull sequence as text-figure 2.

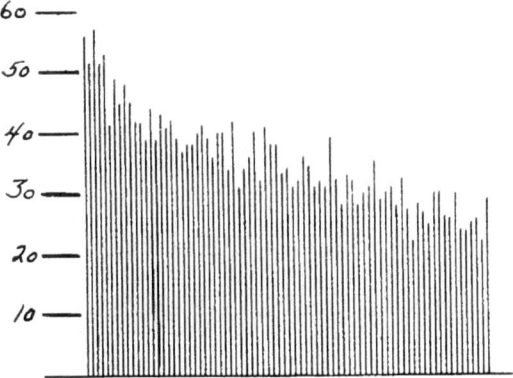

Text-figure 5. Sequence A. Interorbital width. Same skull sequence as text-figure 2.

Nasal width, the distance between the anterior lateral spines of the nasal bones (pl. 35, fig. 1, B) ranges in this series of skulls from 37 to 13 mm, the greatest distance being almost three times the smallest. Text-figure 6 indicates only a slight and irregular accord between these nasal widths and the sequence of zygomatic widths.

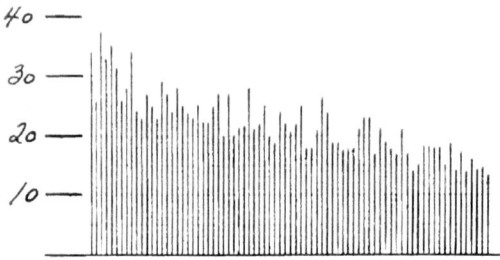

Text figure 6. Sequence A. Nasal width. Same skull sequence as text-figure 2.

The palatal widths in this series of skulls (pl. 35, fig. 2, C) range from 79 to 40 mm or as 2:1. There is fair but irregular accord between this measurement and that of the zygomatic width, as a comparison of text-figures 7 and 2 will show. The range is about the same for the two dimensions and the sequence follows without violent irregularities.

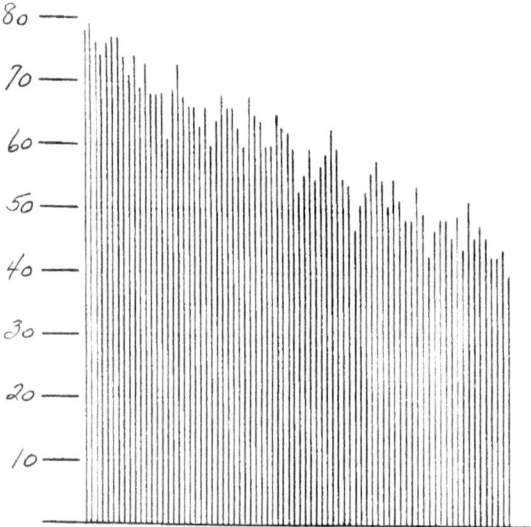

Text figure 7. Sequence A. Palatal width. Same skull sequence as text-figure 2.

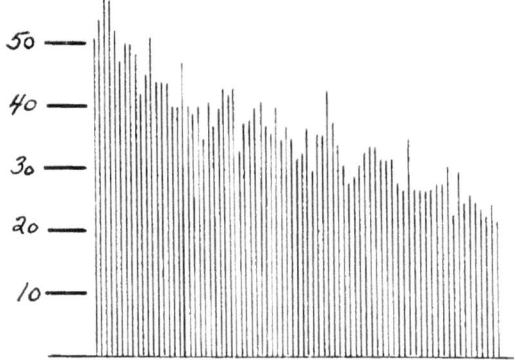

Text-figure 8. Sequence A. Distance between maxillary canine tips. Same skull sequence as text-figure 2.

The distance between the tips of the maxillary canine teeth (pl. 35, fig. 2, B) ranges from 58 to 22 mm or as 2.65:1. Here again, as indicated in text-figure 8, there is good but irregular accord with the sequence of zygomatic widths. The mandibular canine widths (pl. 35, fig. 4, A) are closely comparable to the maxillary, although the tips of the mandibular canines do not spread to so great an extent. The range for this measurement is from 37 to 14 mm or as 2.66:1. Text-figure 9 indicates that the accord of this measurement with the zygomatic width sequence is also good, but with strong individual

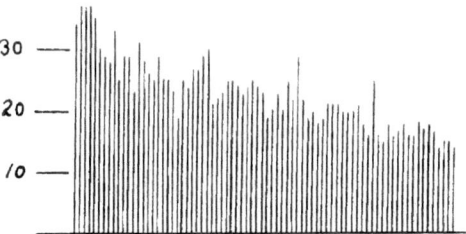

Text-figure 9. Sequence A. Distance between mandibular canine tips. Same skull sequence as text-figure 2.

irregularities. The individual discords in both canine charts are due to the lateral flaring of the canines in bulldog-typed heads.

The maxillary incisal alveolar widths (pl. 35, fig. 1, A) are arranged in text-figure 10. This measurement ranges from 40 to 13 mm or as 3:1, and there is a general but irregular accord with the sequence of zygomatic widths. This accord is much the same as that for the palatal widths. All three charts show a somewhat rhythmical discord in spite of the general similarity in slope.

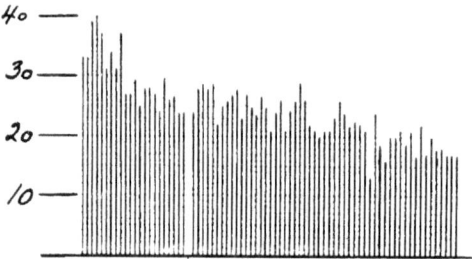

Text-figure 10. Sequence A. Maxillary incisor alveolus width. Same skull sequence as text-figure 2.

The comparison of zygomatic widths with the eight different groups of measurements in this series of skulls brings out several interesting facts. In the first place, zygomatic and cranial widths are quite independent of each other, and a wide or narrow cheek may occur in heads with the same cranial width measurement. In addition, there is much less range in cranial widths than in zygomatic widths.

Secondly, the interorbital width, although to some extent involving cranial bone, follows with fairly close accord the zygomatic width. This agreement is associated with the fact that the maxilla joins the frontal bone in forming part of the orbit as well as giving the zygomatic process to form the anterior portion of the zygomatic arch. The degree of lateral divergence of this process of the maxilla affects both the zygomatic width and the interorbital width and brings about an accord between these two measurements. Wide interpupillary distance and wide cheek bones are also thus correlated in the heads of human racial types.

In the third place, the last five groups of measurements, made entirely on the facial skeleton, all agree in general with the zygomatic width series, yet even these show strong individual discords which are due more largely to type than to size differences among the skulls. The zygomatic width is definitely a facial measurement quite unrelated to cranial width. Disproportionately wide zygomatic arches are associated with short, wide facial skeletons, and thus the total skull sizes do not show strict accord in series with zygomatic widths.

*A comparison of widths at different cranial regions.* A second series of measurements was made in order to determine whether the widths across three different regions of the cranium showed a close correlation. In other words, if a cranium is broad in the posterior region, is it also wide in the anterior region? To determine this, the seventy skulls were arranged in a graded sequence from widest to narrowest according to the individual cranial width (pl. 35, fig. 1, G). This arrangement is represented in text-figure 11, and a gentle and quite regular slope from a width of 65 mm down to 45 mm is shown. The difference between the narrowest and widest crania is only as 1.44:1.

When the measurements for the least frontal widths (pl. 35, fig. 1, E) are plotted in the same sequence, the chart shown as text-figure 12 results. These widths range from 49 mm down to 27 mm, the greatest and least differing from one another about as 1.75:1. A curve drawn along the tops of the lines in this figure shows that no relation whatever exists between this curve and the one for cranial widths, in which the same skulls are in identical sequence. It is surprising to find that in the crania of the different dog breeds there is no correlation between cranial widths and least

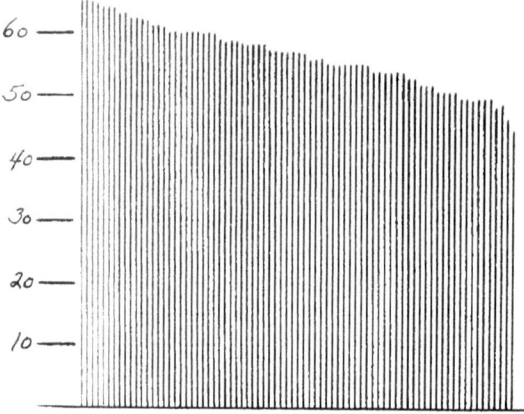

Text-figure 11. Sequence B. Cranial width. Group of seventy skulls arranged in sequence from greatest to least cranial width.

frontal widths or between the broadness of the posterior and anterior portions of the cranial case. The outlines of cranial shape as seen from the dorsum may be wide anteriorly and narrow posteriorly, or vice versa.

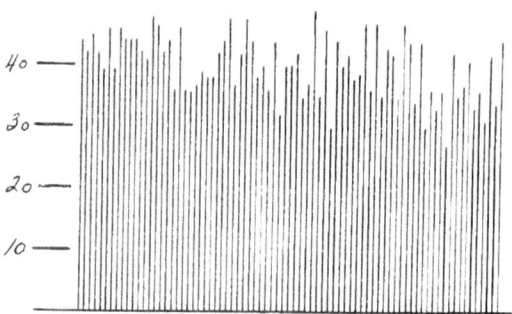

Text-figure 12. Sequence B. Least frontal width. Same skull sequence as text figure 11.

The interorbital distance (pl. 35, fig. 1, D), which is to some extent involved in the anterior cranial region through the influence of the frontal bone on this measurement, was plotted for the skulls in the same cranial width sequence. A comparison of text-figures 13 and 11 shows no smooth accord between cranial width and interorbital width and there is a much greater range in dimensions in these interorbital widths than in the other two cranial width measurements. Interorbital widths range from 57 mm down to only 22 mm, the extremes differing as 2.6:1.

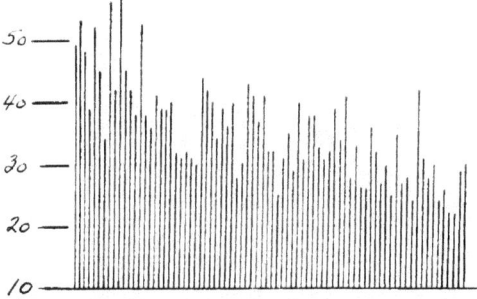

Text figure 13. Sequence B. Interorbital width. Same skull sequence as text figure 11.

It is somewhat surprising to find that there is such wide variation in the interrelations of these three measurements among the seventy skulls of the different dog breeds. This fact indicates that cranial shapes of different dog breeds are considerably contrasted on the basis of the widths at different regions. The differences in cranial lengths have not thus far entered into the picture, though we shall later see that such differences are even more important than differences in width.

It is difficult to determine from text-figures 12 and 13 whether there is any definite accord between least frontal widths and interorbital widths. For this reason the measurements were rearranged for interorbital width in a sequence from widest to narrowest, and the least frontal widths were then placed in the same sequence. With this arrangement (text-fig. 14), a gentle and regular slope for interorbital widths results, but the measurements for least frontal width in the same sequence (text-fig. 15) give an entirely different

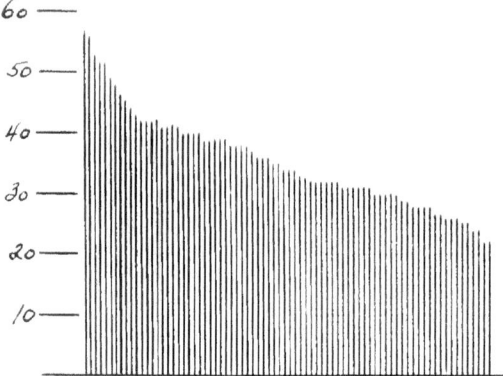

Text-figure 14. Sequence C. Interorbital width. Group of seventy skulls arranged in sequence from greatest to least interorbital distance.

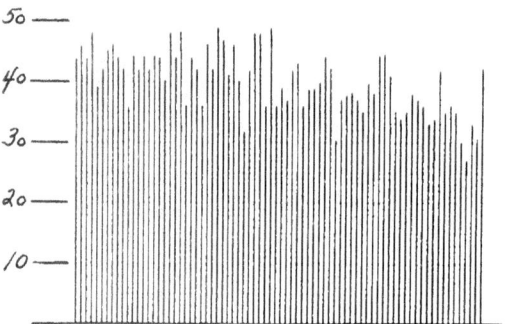

Text-figure 15. Sequence C. Least frontal width. Same skull sequence as text-figure 14.

picture. There is absolutely no correlation between these two measurements in this series of skulls. We conclude, therefore, that in the skulls of the different dog breeds no two of these three cranial width measurements follow any close accord.

*A comparison of cranial height and width measurements among different breeds.* The relation of height to width in the mammalian cranium is of considerable significance. A high, wide cranium usually means a large brain, but in the final analysis the size of the brain depends, of course, upon cranial length as well. The cranial index, as discussed in a later section of this paper, is of interest in connection with these height to width comparisons.

The height of the cranium is indicated in these measurements by the straight distance between the orifice of the auditory meatus and the bregma, that point on the sagittal line where the parietal and frontal bones meet (pl. 35, fig. 3, O-C). In addition to height, an element of width is partially involved in this measurement, but height is the larger factor.

In text-figure 16, measurements on this group of seventy skulls were arranged in sequence from the longest to shortest straight distance from auditory meatus to bregma. These distances range from 73 mm down to 41 mm, the extremes being to one another as 7:4. This difference is not great in view of the fact that both giant and midget dog skulls are included. A curve drawn along the tops of the lines in this chart forms a regular and quite gentle slope, the only sharp fall being between the sixth and seventh dimensions.

It is quite evident from a comparison of this chart with text-figure 17, which shows least frontal widths in the same sequence, that there is no correlation between cranial heights and least frontal widths. The six very high crania indicated at the left in text-figure 16 are equalled or surpassed for their frontal widths by ten skulls scattered almost throughout the series in text-figure 17. The range of measurements for least frontal widths is almost identical with that for cranial

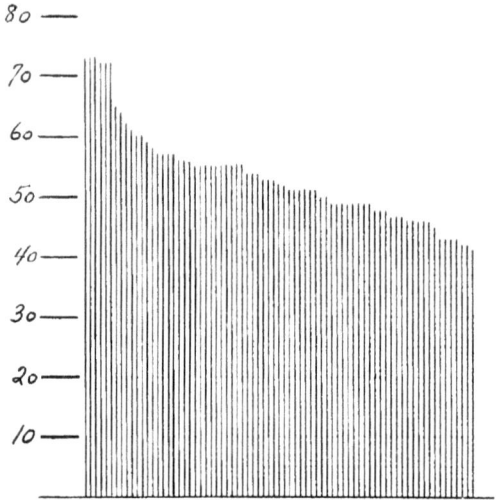

Text-figure 16. Sequence D. Cranial height. Group of seventy skulls arranged in sequence from longest to shortest straight distance from auditory meatus to bregma.

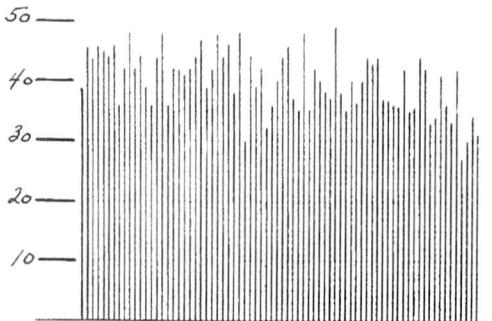

Text-figure 17. Sequence D. Least frontal width. Same skull sequence as text-figure 16.

heights, the distance from auditory meatus to bregma, but the top of the graph for frontal widths forms a broken and irregular curve quite out of accord with that for cranial height. Thus the least frontal width of a high cranium may be either wide or narrow.

*The least frontal width of the cranium as related to length of total skull base.* As shown in text-figure 18, the least frontal measurements were arranged in sequence from widest to narrowest, the range of measurements being from 49 mm to 27 mm or as 7:4.

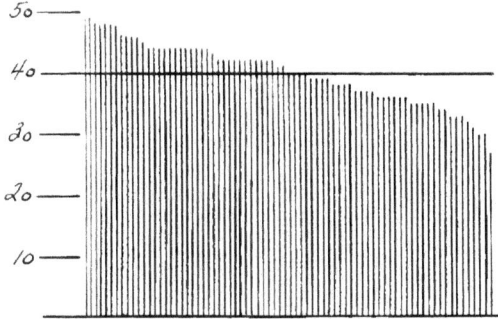

Text-figure 18. Sequence E. Least frontal width. Group of seventy skulls arranged in sequence from widest to narrowest least frontal measurement.

The lengths of the total skull base, from the posterior edge of the occipital to the anterior lingual alveolus along a median line (pl. 35, fig. 2, D–G) were arranged in text-figure 19 in comparable sequence to the above. These measurements range from 210 mm down to 67 mm, the length of the longest skull being more than three times that of the shortest. A comparison of the two charts clearly indicates that in the different dog breeds there is no correlation whatever between cranial width in the frontal region and skull length.

Thus far we have found that not all measurements of widths in various skull regions are correlated, and also that some widths are not directly increased with an increase in

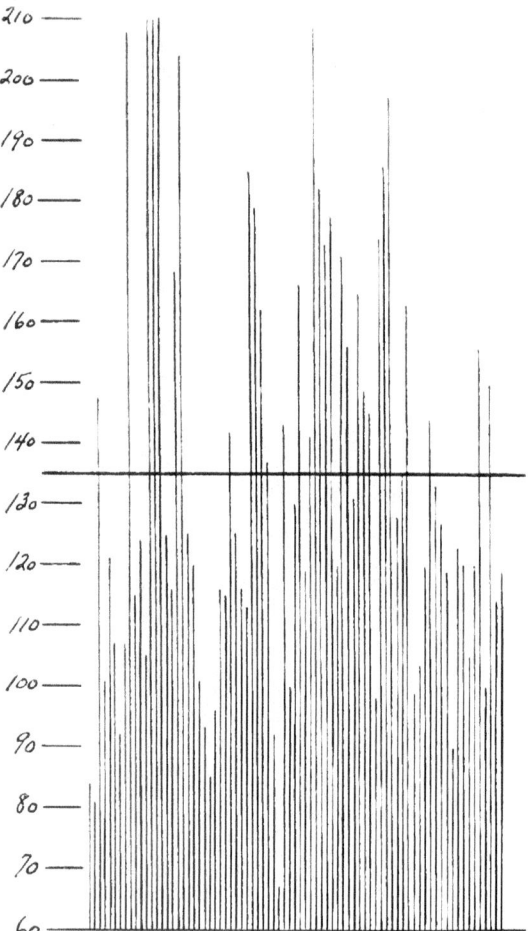

Text figure 19. Sequence E. Total skull base. Same skull sequence as text-figure 18.

length. We shall now compare anteroposterior lengths of the several parts of the facial skeleton in an effort to determine whether these measurements are related.

*Comparisons of the lengths of various facial parts and regions of the skull.* The charts plotted for this series of skull measurements show the lengths of different parts of the facial skeleton all placed in a sequence based on the

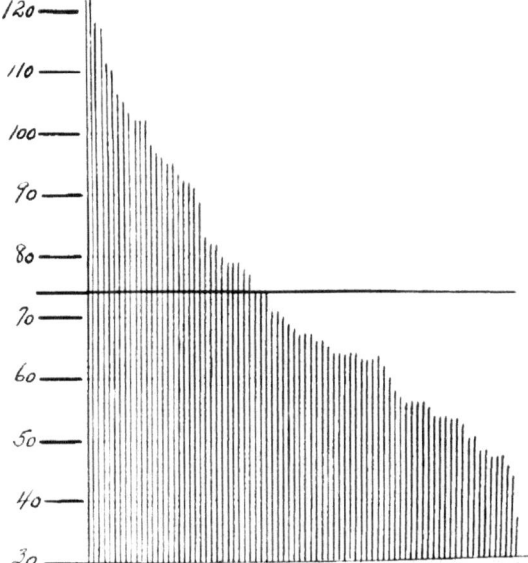

Text-figure 20. Sequence F. Palatal length. Group of seventy skulls arranged in sequence from longest to shortest bony palate.

value of palatal lengths, from the specimen with longest bony palate down to the one with the shortest. These palatal length measurements, shown in text-figure 20, range from 122 mm to 36 mm, the longest being to the shortest as 3.4:1. A curve drawn along the top of the lines in this chart is fairly smooth and steep. Five other measurements of length on various skull parts in these specimens were plotted for comparison with the palate lengths.

Text-figure 21 represents the shortest anteroposterior distance from the infraorbital foramen to a vertical line passing the anterior incisal alveolus (pl. 35, fig. 3, J–F). A curve along the top of this chart is closely similar to that for palatal lengths; only a few mild irregularities occur. The range of measurements from the infraorbital foramen to the

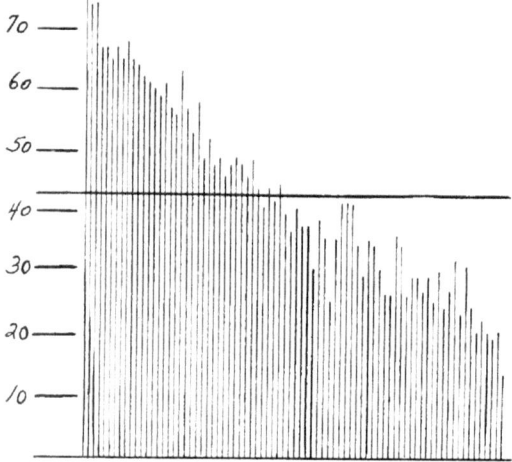

Text-figure 21. Sequence F. Infraorbital foramen to incisal alveolus. Same skull sequence as text-figure 20.

line of the incisal alveolus is from 75 mm down to only 14 mm. The longest is 5.4 times greater than the shortest. Both the above groups of measurements involve features in the skulls that differ widely in length but are nevertheless closely related.

The distances from the sagittal point of union between the frontal and nasal bones to the anterior end of the internasal suture (pl. 35, fig. 1, I–J) gave a third series of measurements for these skulls. These measurements (text-fig. 22) range from 98 mm down to only 10 mm, the longest being to the shortest as 9.8:1. Some breeds of dogs have long noses, while in other breeds the nose is extremely short. The series of measurements for nasal lengths accords very closely with the series for the two other facial features represented in text-figures 20 and 21.

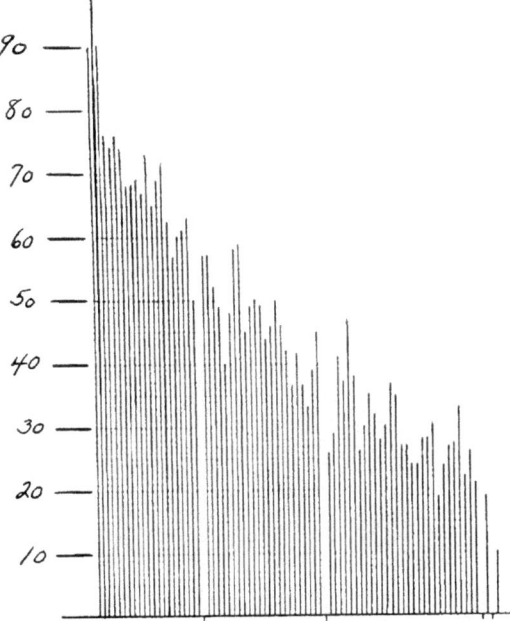

Text figure 22. Sequence F. Nasal length. Same skull sequence as text-figure 20.

The lengths of mandibles in the same sequence of skulls are represented in text-figure 23. The method used in measuring mandibular length is shown in plate 35 (fig. 4, H–I); that is, the mandible was placed in a vertical position with the condyles resting on a flat surface, and the distance from this

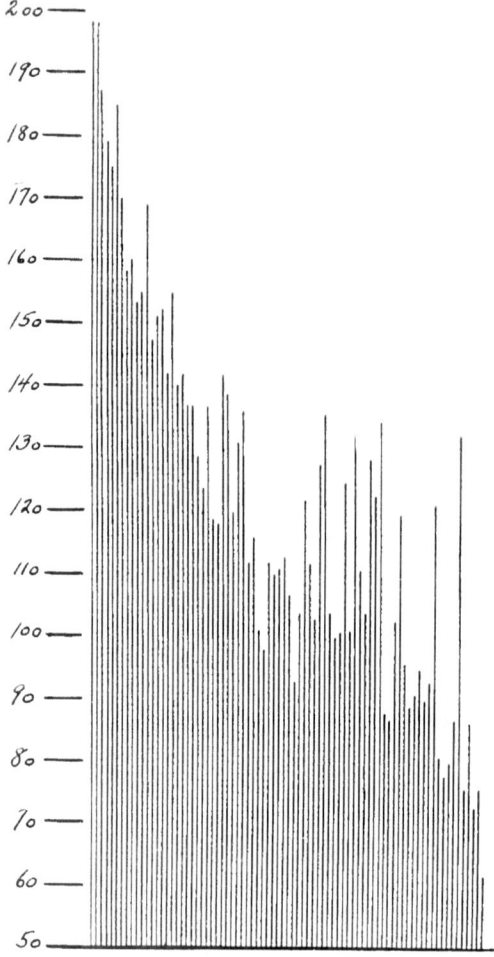

Text figure 23. Sequence F. Mandibular length. Same skull sequence as text figure 20.

surface to the anterior end of the mandibular symphysis was measured. The range of these mandibular lengths is from 198 mm to 62 mm or as 3.2:1. These lengths, although agreeing in general with the above three dimensions, show violent individual deviations which are due to the presence of the bulldog skulls with their extremely shortened maxillary and nasal regions.

The fifth series of measurements in this sequence represents the maxillary premolar regions, the distance from the

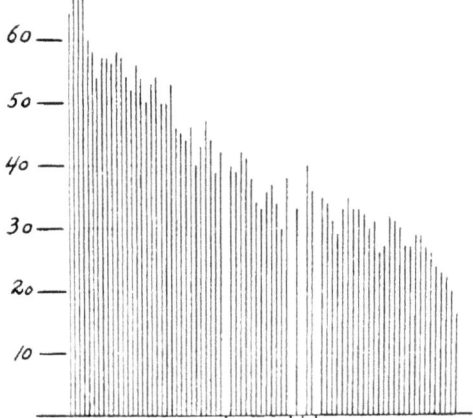

Text-figure 24. Sequence F. Maxillary premolar region. Same skull sequence as text-figure 20.

posterior tip of the canine alveolus to the posterior border of the fourth premolar tooth (pl. 35, fig. 3, G–H). These distances range from 67 mm to 16 mm (text-fig. 24), the extremes differing as 4.2:1. The slope formed by the measurements in this chart follows very closely those for palatal length, length of muzzle from infraorbital foramen and length of internasal suture, but here again are individual disagreements with mandibular lengths.

Finally, the skulls in this sequence were measured for the sum of the greatest anteroposterior dimensions of the four maxillary premolar teeth (text-fig. 25). Certain specimens in which teeth were missing were necessarily omitted; this particularly involved the short muzzled bulldog-like skulls which have poorly imbedded teeth. The sums of the anteroposterior widths of the premolars ranged from 56 mm to 23 mm, the greatest being to the least as 2.4:1. The sums of the premolars show a general trend of accord with palatal lengths and the other facial measurements, although in detail this resemblance is not very striking.

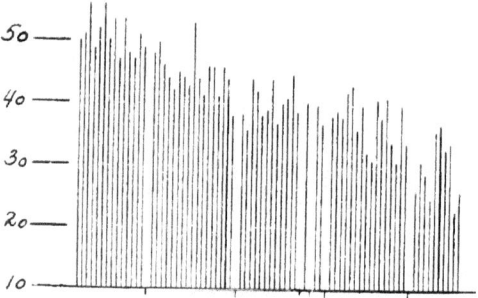

Text-figure 25. Sequence F. Sum of the anteroposterior dimensions of the maxillary premolar teeth. Same skull sequence as text-figure 20.

Detailed comparisons among the six charts in this sequence, all of which involve measurements of anteroposterior lengths in the facial skeleton, indicate very clearly that the different parts of the face tend to vary in length in a closely comparable manner. It is almost necessarily true that a short muzzled skull will have a short maxilla, a short palate, short premolar region and short nasal bones, though the shortness may not be proportionately the same in the several parts. The only marked deviation from this general harmony in facial skeleton dimensions is found in the lengths of the mandible. Mandibles may be either disproportionately short or long for the associated upper facial skeleton. A prognathism of the upper jaw in some cases or the lower jaw in others may thus result.

## Does the Length of Jaw Directly Determine Tooth Size?

Disharmony between the lengths of the upper and lower jaws in certain types of dog skulls, a condition pointed out in the previous section, made it seem desirable to compare the sizes of teeth in the upper and lower jaws in order to learn whether jaw size has a direct effect on tooth size. The sum of the anteroposterior widths of the four premolar teeth was selected as the most significant measurement, since the extent of the premolar region of the maxilla differed more than any other dental region in the various typed skulls of comparable size. And, as we have seen, the premolar region

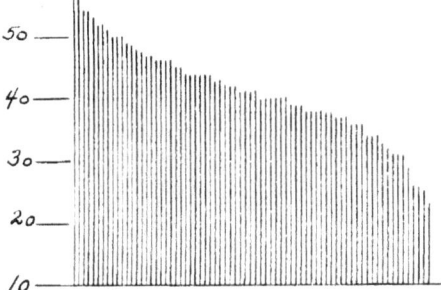

Text-figure 26. Sequence G. Sum of the anteroposterior dimensions of the maxillary premolar teeth. Group of seventy skulls arranged in sequence from greatest to least total dimension.

of the lower jaw in certain breed types does not closely follow such variations in extent of the maxillary premolar region. Thus, a given skull may possess much abbreviated maxillary premolar space while the mandibular premolar space may be long and spacious.

The sequence of skulls for this comparison was arranged on the basis of the sum of the anteroposterior dimensions of the maxillary premolars (text-fig. 26). The measurements range from an extreme of 56 mm for total widths down to only 23 mm or as 2.4:1. The top of this chart forms an almost uniformly regular slope.

Similar measurements for the mandibular premolar teeth (text-fig. 27) range from 42 mm down to only 16 mm, or as 2.6:1. The range in size is about the same for both series, but the mandibular premolars are definitely smaller in all typed jaws. The largest total mandibular premolar dimensions are only three-fourths as much as the greatest total maxillary premolar dimensions, and the sum of the smallest maxillary premolars is one and one-half times greater than the smallest mandibular total.

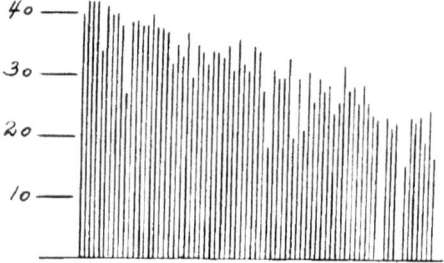

Text-figure 27. Sequence G. Sum of the anteroposterior dimensions of the mandibular premolar teeth. Same skull sequence as text figure 26.

A comparison of text-figures 26 and 27 shows that there is a fair general accord in total widths of premolar teeth in the upper and lower jaws. However, great individual deviations are indicated. For example, the fifth skull in the series totals 53 mm for the maxillary premolar teeth against only 34 mm for the mandibular; and in the tenth skull this relation is 50 mm against 27 mm, the sum of the anteroposterior dimensions of maxillary teeth being nearly twice that of the mandibular teeth. These facts, along with other knowledge of the teeth which we shall present, indicate that in these highly modified dog skulls the size of the teeth is quite independent of the size of the jaw.

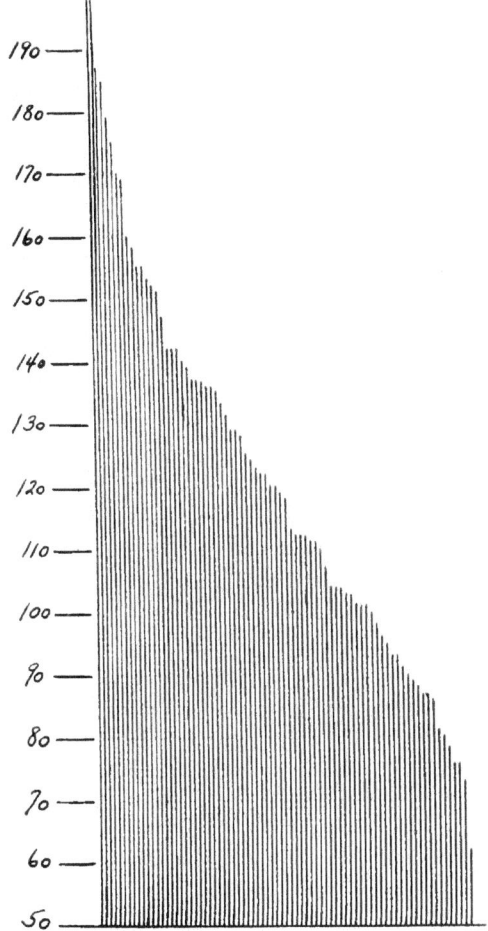

Text-figure 28. Sequence H. Mandibular length. Group of seventy skulls arranged in sequence from greatest to least distance from condyles to a line parallel to the anterior tip of the mandibular symphysis.

## Comparisons of Mandibular Length With Other Mandibular Dimensions

The mandibular lengths of the seventy skulls from different dog breeds show a wide range and a steep slope when represented by lines placed in a sequence for magnitude of this measurement (text-fig. 28). Mandibular length is estimated as a vertical line from the condyle to the level of the anterior end of the symphysis (pl. 35, fig. 4, H–I). These lengths range from 198 mm down to 62 mm, the extremes being as 3.2:1. Measurements of other mandibular features show no such wide range. Although the differences in mandibular length in various dog breeds are strongly emphasized, the angles of divergence between the mandibular rami, and the distances between the condyles, may in some cases be more significant for the differentiation of the types.

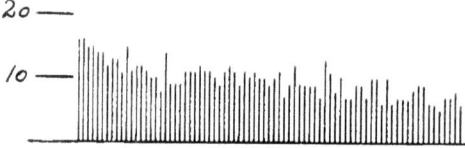

Text-figure 29. Sequence H. Mandibular thickness. Same skull sequence as text-figure 28.

Mandibular thicknesses, measured in the region of the first molar tooth (pl. 35, fig. 4, E) range from 16 mm down to 5 mm or as 3.2:1 (text-fig. 29). This chart shows a loose general agreement with that for mandibular length but there are wide individual disagreements throughout.

The measurements of the mandibular premolar regions (text-fig. 30) show somewhat closer agreement with total mandibular lengths, but here again there are strong individual irregularities. The sum totals of the anteroposterior widths of the mandibular premolar teeth (text-fig. 31) are slightly more out of accord with the chart for mandibular lengths than is the curve for premolar regions. Some short jaws have teeth of large anteroposterior dimensions owing to the fact that although the jaw itself is short it may be possessed by a large dog.

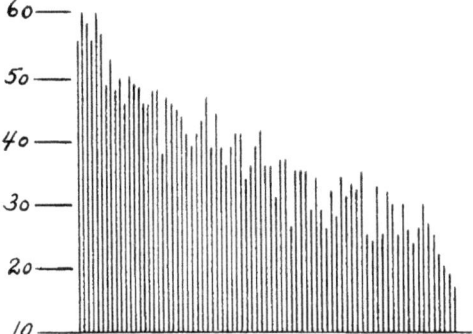

Text-figure 30. Sequence II. Mandibular premolar region. Same skull sequence as text-figure 28.

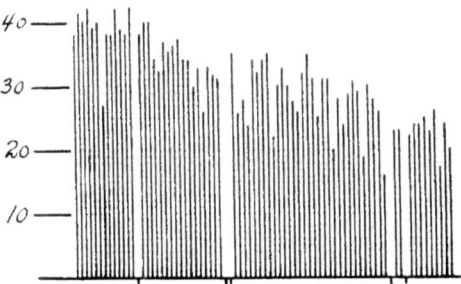

Text-figure 31. Sequence II. Sum of the anteroposterior dimensions of the mandibular premolar teeth. Same skull sequence as text-figure 28.

There is a general trend of agreement among the different dimensions of the dog's mandible, but sharp individual exceptions occur in the jaws of the bulldog-like breeds.

### THE RELATION OF THE BONY PALATE TO THE SKULL BASE AND TO THE SIZE OF THE PALATAL PROCESS OF THE PALATE BONE

The proportional percentage of hard palate (pl. 35, fig. 2, E–G) to total skull base (pl. 35, fig. 2, D–G) ranges from 60 down to 48 per cent (text-fig. 32). These percentages, arranged in sequence from largest to smallest palatal proportion, give a very gentle and regular slope.

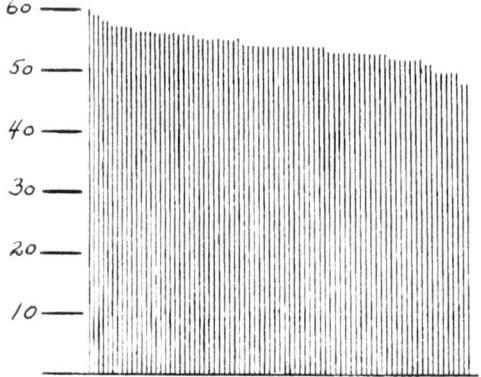

Text-figure 32. Sequence I. Proportional percentage of hard palate to total skull base. Group of seventy skulls arranged in sequence from largest to smallest percentage.

As is well known, the anterior region of the bony palate is composed of the palatal processes of the maxillae, and the posterior region is composed of the palatal processes of the palatal bones. These two components do not always constitute the same relative amount of the total palate of the dog skull. The proportional percentage of length of palatal processes to total length of palate is shown in text-figure 33, and the curve offered by this chart is very irregular and of an almost opposite inclination to that in text-figure 32. The dissimilarity between the two charts indicates that in many specimens in which the total palate forms a large fraction of the entire skull base, the palatal process of the palate bone may form a smaller fraction of the total palate than it does in skulls where the proportion of total palate to total skull base is lower. In other words, skulls with long muzzles and long palates receive a proportionally greater contribution of palatal plate from the maxilla than do those with short muzzles and short palates, or, to state it still another way, variations in palatal length are principally due to variations in maxillary contribution, since the contribution to the total palate from the palate bone itself is comparatively uniform in all types of dog skulls of a common size.

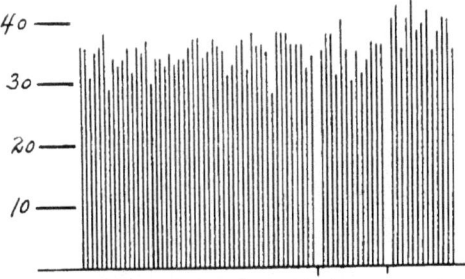

Text-figure 33. Sequence 1. Proportional percentage of length of the palatal processes to the total length of palate bone. Same skull sequence as text-figure 32.

The percentage of palatal processes of the palatal bone to the total palate length ranges from 44 per cent down to 28 per cent, that is, from a little less than half to a little more than one quarter of the entire palate. The proportions of palatal process length to entire palate length are highest in the skulls represented to the right in text-figure 33; these proportions are for the same skulls having the smallest proportion of palate to total skull base, as indicated in text-figure 32.

The above relations are somewhat more clearly illustrated by text-figure 34 (fig. 1). The numbers along the vertical line give the percentage of palatal process contributed by the palate bone to the total hard palate and those along the horizontal line indicate the percentage of palate length to the total length of the skull base. The direction of the curve indicates that as the palatal process of the palate bone forms a smaller and smaller portion of the total palate, the palate as a whole forms a larger and larger fraction of the total skull base.

This curve, however, gives no indication of the types or lengths of skulls in which the palate forms a higher or a lower proportion of the total skull base. Are the higher proportions of palate length found among the longer or the shorter skulls? The curves in figure 2 of text-figure 34 were plotted to answer this question. The solid line in this graph represents the snout index, the dashed line the palatal index and the dash-dot line the skull index. The manner of calculating indices is discussed beyond and need concern us only briefly at present. In each of these cases the width of the region involved is multiplied by 100, and this product divided by the length of the region. The resulting quotient or index will obviously be high if the region is wide and short, and low if the region is narrow and long. The figures on the vertical line represent the values of the indices and those along the base line indicate proportional percentages of the palatal length to total length of the skull base.

When the snout index is high, the palatal index is likewise high, as is also the skull index. Starting at the left and comparing the three indices, we find that a short wide skull has a palate which is proportionately wide for its length, and the muzzle or snout of such a skull is comparatively more abbreviated than is the skull as a whole. The first snout index is 162, while the total skull index of this specimen is 103. A study of the three curves throughout their extent shows that in short skulls the indices for the two regions plotted deviate widely from the index for the skull as a whole, while in the longer skulls, with lower indices, the two regions tend to show indices closely the same in magnitude as that for the total skull.

# GENETIC TYPE AND THE ENDOCRINES

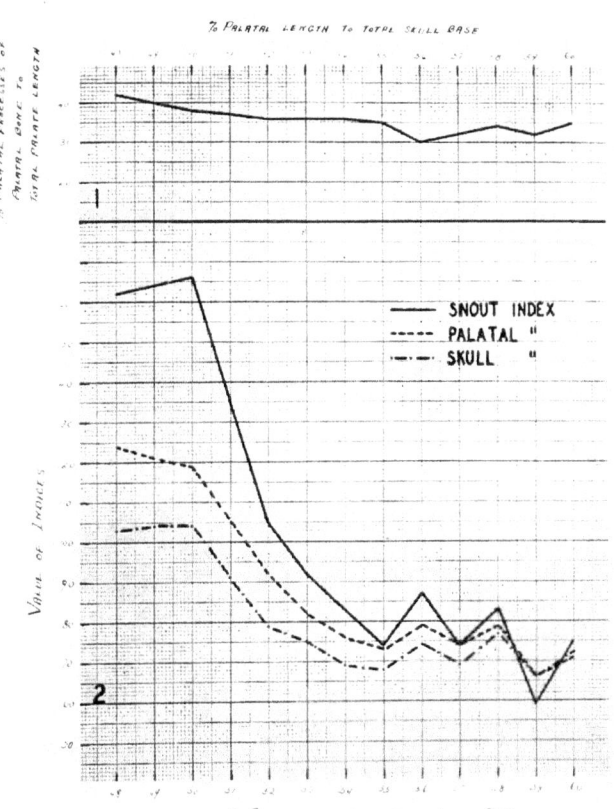

Text figure 34. (1) The percentage of the total palate formed by the palatal processes as related to the percentage of the total skull base formed by the palate. (2) The relationship of three skull indices to the percentage of total skull base formed by the bony palate.

The percentages of palatal length to total skull base clearly show that in short skulls with short muzzles the proportional percentage of palate to total skull base is very small, but that this percentage increases in those skulls that are longer and have longer muzzles. Thus we find that the percentage of palatal length to total skull base is a very significant relation, for when this proportion is known one may accurately estimate the type of skull concerned. Comparing the curves with the figures along the base line, one can be quite certain that when the palate forms less than 53 per cent of the total skull base, the skull as a whole is short and wide, and further, that as the percentage of palate length to total skull base increases beyond 53 and on to the maximum of 60 per cent, the skulls are long and narrow.

## Comparison of Measurements from the Orifice of the Auditory Meatus to Several Definite Points

The measurements to be considered at this time were taken by placing the ear rests of the head-spanner in the orifice of the auditory meatus and the tip of the scale at a definite selected point. The measurement was then read from the scale. The distances thus represent the shortest lines between the two points irrespective of the intervening angles and curvatures of the skull.

For this series of comparisons, the seventy skulls were arranged in a sequence based on the distance from auditory meatus to bregma (pl. 35, fig. 3, O–C). These measurements (text-fig. 35) show a range of from 73 mm down to 41 mm, the extremes being as 1.78:1. Between the two extremes the lines representing the various skulls form a rather regular and gradual slope. The differences among these measurements are surprisingly small when one considers that the series contains not only the normal and highly modified skulls, but giant and midget skulls as well.

Four other groups of measurements were made for comparison with the auditory meatus to bregma series, and were plotted with the skulls in the same sequence.

Text-figure 36 represents the distance from the orifice of the auditory meatus to the nasion (pl. 35, fig. 3, O–D). The range for this measurement is much greater than for the bregma measurements, being from 103 mm down to 44 mm or as 2.34:1, against the proportion of as 1.78:1 found for the bregma series. When arranged in the same sequence as for the meatus-bregma measurements, the measurements from the auditory meatus to the nasion also show much greater irregularity. Some skulls with a short distance between meatus and bregma show a much greater distance from

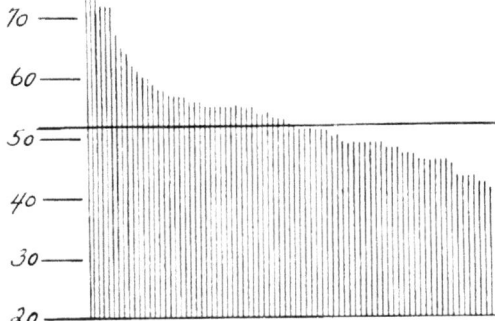

Text-figure 35. Sequence J. Auditory meatus to bregma. Group of seventy skulls arranged in sequence from greatest to least straight distance between these two points.

meatus to the nasion. This is shown in a striking manner by comparison of the measurements in the right half of the two figures. One of the longest recorded measurements from meatus to nasion occurs in a skull with a shorter than average meatus-bregma distance. The two charts are in general but irregular accord and there are wide individual discords.

The distance from the auditory meatus to the anterior end of the internasal suture (pl. 35, fig. 3, O–E) supplied the measurements for text-figure 37. These measurements show an almost total lack of relative agreement with the values for distance from meatus to bregma. Some of the skulls in which the meatus to bregma measurement is very short may show an extremely long distance between meatus and the anterior end of the internasal suture.

The slight general agreement in the slopes of text-figures 35, 36 and 37 is more largely due to range in total size of the various skulls than to type differences. However, the

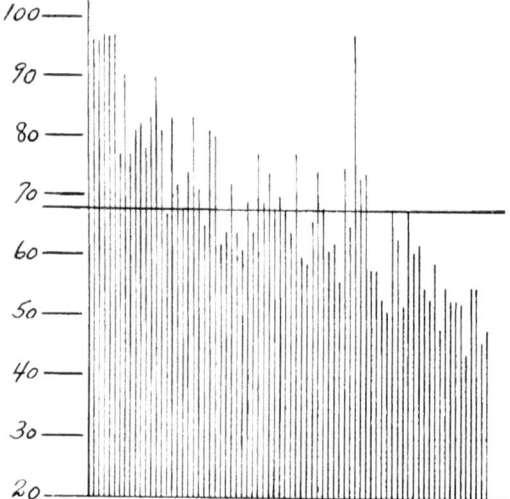

Text-figure 36. Sequence J. Auditory meatus to nasion. Same skull sequence as text-figure 35.

wide variations in height of adjacent lines in text-figure 37 are due to the presence of some strongly pronounced types. In the auditory meatus to bregma measurements there is no evidence of these pronounced types, and this particular measurement is insignificant for contrasting types. The distance from meatus to the anterior end of the internasal suture, however, is highly significant as an indication of the skull

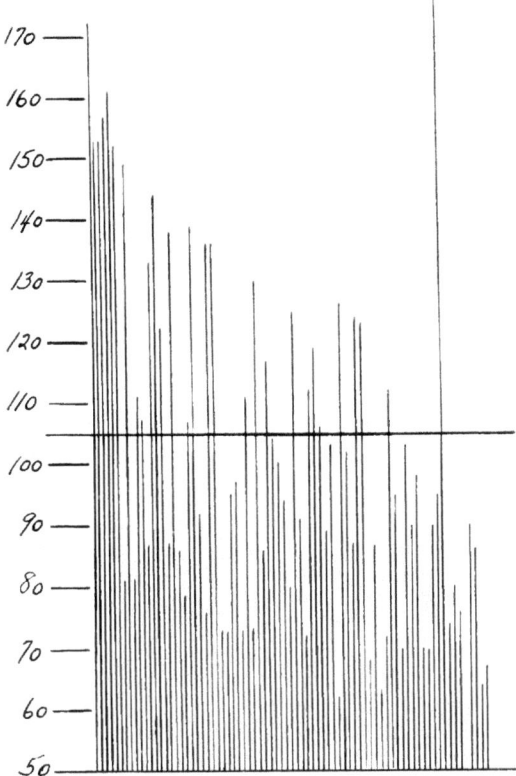

Text-figure 37. Sequence J. Auditory meatus to anterior end of internasal suture. Same skull sequence as text-figure 35.

type in the dog. Arranging the skulls in a sequence on the basis of a comparatively unimportant measurement such as distance from meatus to bregma permits other measurements to show strong contrasts. In such sequence adjacent skulls and groups may show the widest differences for a type significant.

Wide differences again stand out when the distances from the orifice of the auditory meatus to the anterior tip of the superior dental alveolus (pl. 35, fig. 3, O–F) are arranged in sequence based on the regular decrease in distances from the meatus to the bregma. A comparison of text-figures 38 and 35 illustrates quite vividly the contrast between type significant and insignificant measurements. The measurements from the meatus to the tip of the superior dental alveolus range from 200 mm down to only 57 mm, or as 3.5:1. Text-figure 38, for this measurement, is the most widely irregular in the series and shows no correlation whatever with the meatus-bregma measurements. It indicates more clearly than the other charts, however, the enormous deviations in type characteristics which exist in these dog skulls from many different breeds.

The length of muzzle in the dog is the determining feature in numerous types of skulls, and the nature and origin of reductions in muzzle length is a problem of primary importance in connection with the influences of modified internal secretions on the growth and development of structural patterns. We shall discuss these features more completely in other parts of this report.

Finally we may make a comparison between the measurements of distance from the auditory meatus to bregma and from the meatus to a more posterior point on the skull. This may serve to indicate whether the posterior skull region is as variable in length as we have found the anterior portions to be. Measurements were made from the orifice of the auditory meatus to the supraoccipital spine (pl. 35, fig. 3, O–B). It should be recalled at this point that the skulls of certain breeds show a pronounced occipital crest which has at its posterior end the supraoccipital spine, while other dog skulls are quite flat with a poorly expressed spine. The flat topped cranium is as a rule wider than the crested type, yet to some extent a prominent crest and spine no doubt exaggerate and vitiate the relative distances from the meatus

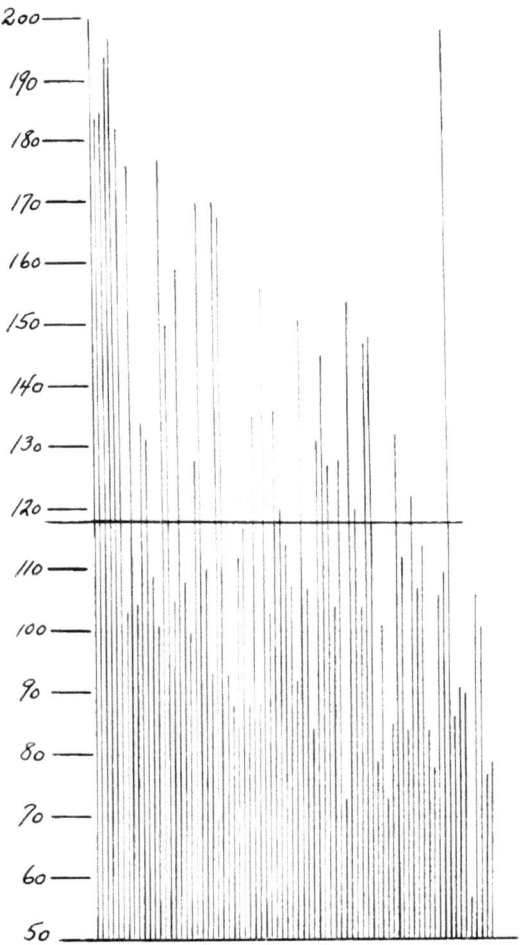

Text figure 38. Sequence J. Auditory meatus to anterior tip of the superior dental alveolus. Same skull sequence as text-figure 35.

to the supraoccipital spine. The range of measurements (text-fig. 39) is from 72 mm down to 26 mm or as 2.7:1. There is a loose and irregular conformity between the curve of this chart and that for the meatus to bregma measurements, with, however, some fairly marked differences between adjacent skulls which make it quite evident that there is only a slight correlation between the two. The region of the skull posterior

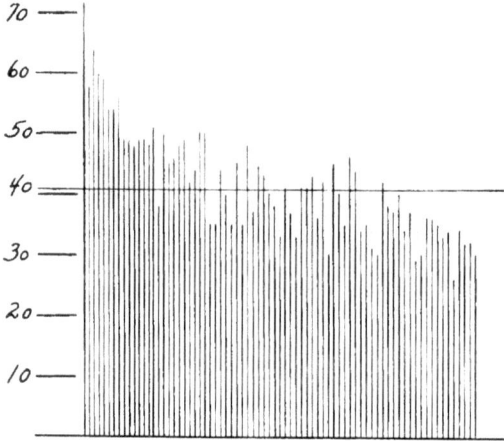

Text-figure 39. Sequence J. Auditory meatus to supraoccipital spine. Same skull sequence as text-figure 35.

to the bregma is shown to be almost as variable among the dog breeds as are the measurements from the meatus to the nasion in the anterior region (compare text-figs. 36 and 39). These measurements are definitely confined to the cranium, and the variations among them do not approach in significance the wider differences found among the anterior or facial dimensions of the skull. The most violent variations and disharmonies to be found in the dog's skull occur anterior to the nasion.

### Comparison of the Same Skull Dimensions Arranged in Another Sequence

When the sequence of skulls is arranged on the basis of a somewhat more significant measurement than that of meatus to bregma, which was used in the preceding series, there is a tendency toward closer agreement in the curves representing the various measurements. The sequence we are now to follow is based on measurements from the orifice of the auditory meatus to the nasion, an anterior cranial dimension.

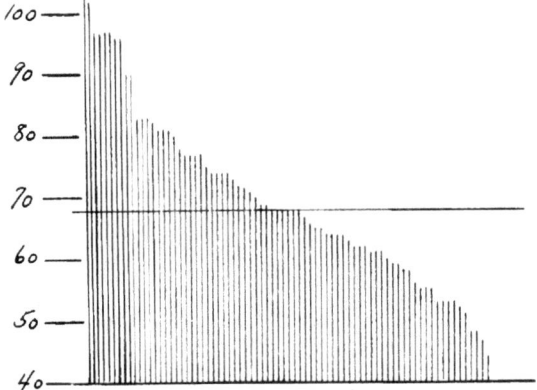

Text-figure 40. Sequence K. Auditory meatus to nasion. Group of seventy skulls arranged in sequence from greatest to least distance between these two points.

These measurements range from 103 mm down to 44 mm, the extremes being to each other as 2.34:1; the curve formed by the lines representing these measurements (text-fig. 40) shows a very regular and fairly steep decline.

Text-figures 41 and 42 represent the measurements from the auditory meatus to the anterior end of the internasal suture, and from the meatus to the anterior superior dental alveolus, respectively. The curves formed by the lines representing the two series of measurements show a smooth general downward trend. These two figures are in marked contrast to text-figures 37 and 38 for the same measurements arranged in the less significant sequence of distance from meatus to bregma. There is a general accord among the

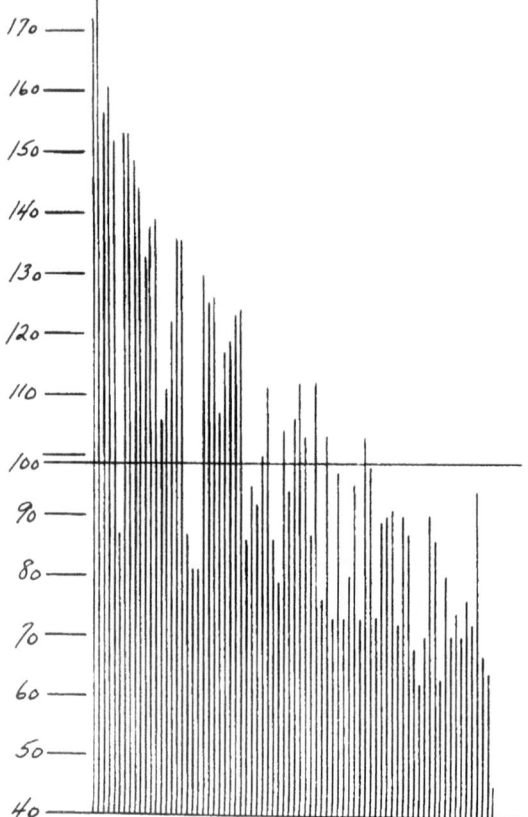

Text-figure 41. Sequence K. Auditory meatus to anterior end of internasal suture. Same skull sequence as text figure 40.

GENETIC TYPE AND THE ENDOCRINES 195

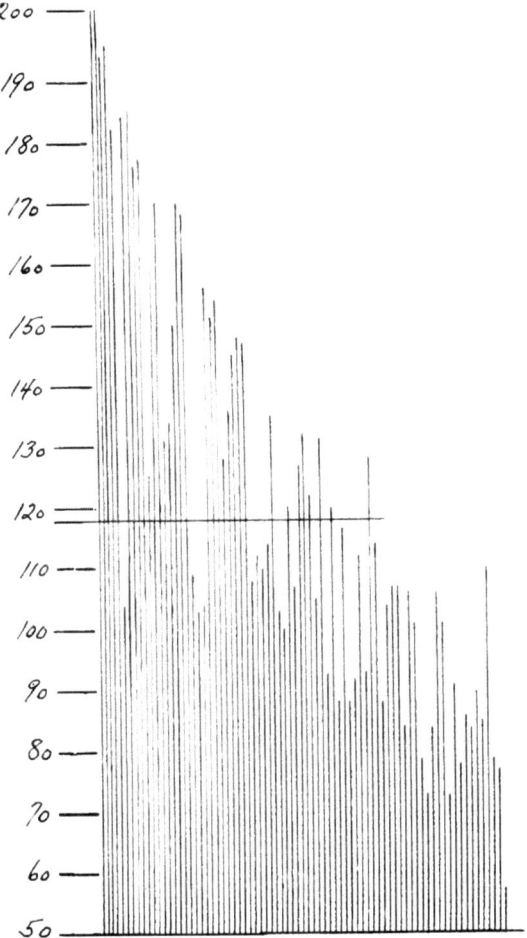

Text-figure 42. Sequence K. Auditory meatus to anterior tip of the superior dental alveolus. Same skull sequence as text-figure 40.

three charts (text-figs. 40, 41 and 42), and indication of a slight correlation between the anterior cranial measurement, meatus to nasion, and the other two of this sequence which involve muzzle length.

A comparison of these figures warrants the statement that in general a long anterior cranial region is associated with a long facial skeleton or a long muzzle. There are, however, wide exceptions to this generalization. In certain types of skulls a long anterior cranium is contrasted with a much abbreviated facial skeleton. The specimen which gave the measurements represented by the sixth line from the left in each of the three charts is a striking example of the association of one of the longest crania in the series with two of the shortest facial features. Numerous skulls of this type may be detected in the group by comparing the corresponding lines of the three charts.

Obviously the distances from auditory meatus to the anterior nasal point and from the meatus to anterior dental alveolus are closely correlated. This correlation in individual detail may be accurately demonstrated by arranging the sequence of skulls on the basis of one of these measurements. Text-figure 43 represents the sequence of measurements from greatest to smallest distance from the auditory meatus to the anterior end of the internasal suture. The range for these measurements is from 176 mm down to only 45 mm, the longest being almost four times the length of the shortest. A very regular and steep decline is formed by the tops of the lines in this figure.

The measurements from the auditory meatus to the superior dental alveolus are recorded in an identical sequence in text-figure 44. The range of measurements in this chart is from 200 mm down to 57 mm or as the ratio 3.5:1. This range of measurements is not quite so wide as that represented in text-figure 43, but on the whole the general outline of the two charts is very similar. Yet even here we find small individual deviations. Such differences among the elements

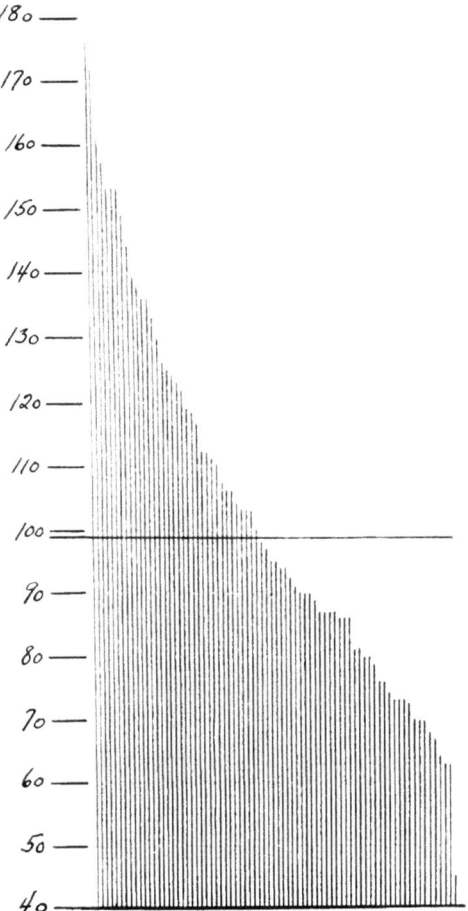

Text-figure 43. Sequence L. Auditory meatus to anterior end of internasal suture. Group of seventy skulls arranged in sequence from greatest to least distance between these two points.

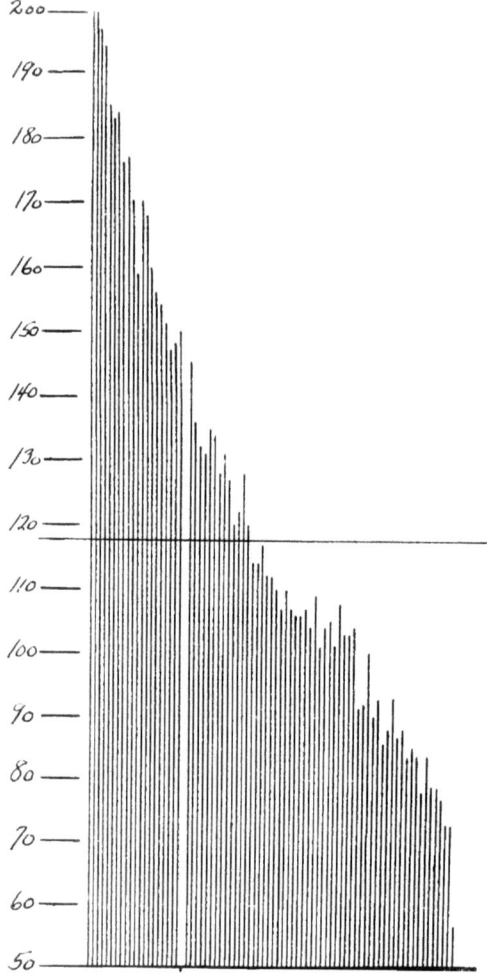

Text figure 44. Sequence L. Auditory meatus to anterior tip of superior dental alveolus. Same skull sequence as text figure 43.

composing similar skull regions are difficult to detect except by the arrangement of the measurements under consideration in a proper sequence. The sequence used for text-figures 40-42, although comparatively fair, could give no ready indication of the several important deviations easily detected by comparing text-figures 43 and 44.

The length of the floor of the anterior nares is the element producing the chief discrepancies between the curves in text-figures 43 and 44, and, as indicated by a few of the lines scattered throughout the latter, the floor of the anterior nares is disproportionately long in some skulls and abnormally short in others. Text-figure 47 gives the measurements for a region almost corresponding to those above, that is, from the anterior end of the internasal suture to the anterior superior dental alveolus. These measurements range from 52 mm down to 14 mm, the extremes differing as 3.7:1. A comparison of text-figures 43 and 44, in conjunction with 47, indicates that the length of floor of the anterior nares does not directly follow the total muzzle length, but may show independent variations. Thus text-figure 47 aids in an understanding of the small and irregular differences found between the measurements of length from the auditory meatus to the anterior end of the internasal suture and from the meatus to the anterior superior dental alveolus.

## Comparisons of Measurements Between Given Points Along the Mid-Dorsal Line of the Skull

The sequence of skulls in these sagittal measurements was arranged according to the distance from the bregma to the nasion (pl. 35, fig. 3, C-D). These measurements range from a longest of 82 mm down to a shortest of 31 mm, the extremes differing as 2.66:1. Text-figure 45 shows the first two measurements at the left to be much greater than the third, but from there on a regular and gentle decline in the magnitudes of this dimension is shown.

The second measurement was taken along the mid-dorsal line from the nasion to the anterior end of the internasal suture (pl. 35, fig. 3, D-E). This measurement is a direct forward continuation of the one above. A comparison of text-figures 45 and 46 shows practically no correlation. Strong disagreements stand out all along the series in the two figures. Two adjacent skulls which are closely the same for

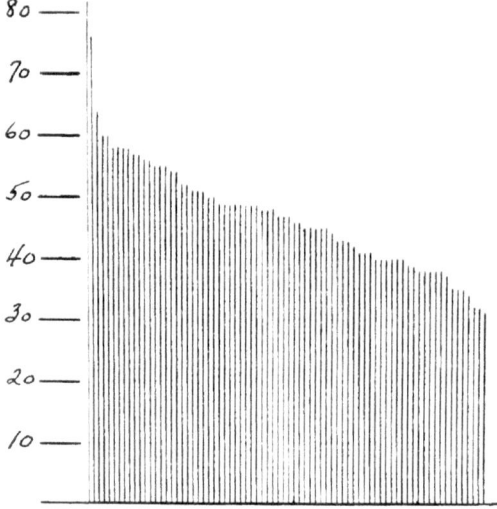

Text-figure 45. Sequence M. Bregma to nasion. Group of seventy skulls arranged in sequence from greatest to least distance between these two points.

bregma to nasion distances may be extremely far apart for lengths of internasal sutures. The last two lines to the right in each figure strongly emphasize this point; the bregma-nasion distances for the two skulls differ by only 1 mm, while the internasal suture length is 3.3 times longer in one of these skulls than in the other. A number of other almost equally wide divergencies between closely adjacent lines representing internasal suture lengths can be seen.

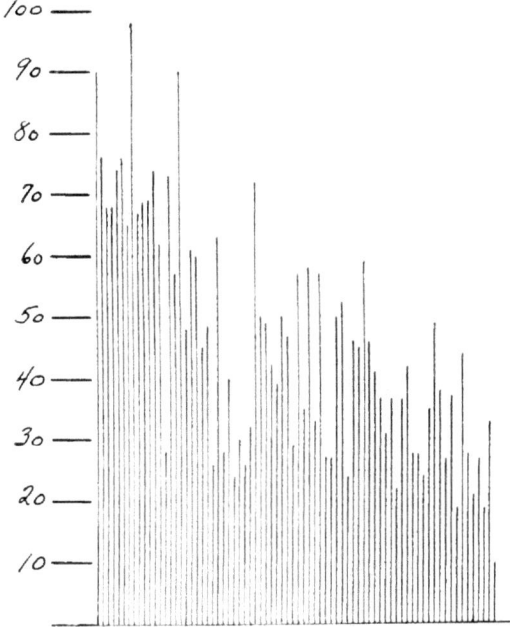

Text-figure 46. Sequence M. Nasion to anterior end of internasal suture. Same skull sequence as text-figure 45.

Text-figure 47 represents measurements from the anterior end of the internasal suture to the anterior superior dental alveolus (pl. 35, fig. 3, E–F). We have already referred to the differences in the lengths of this measurement as being chiefly responsible for the disagreements between individual skulls in text-figures 43 and 44. Arranged in the present sequence, these measurements, which involve practically the total length of the floor of the anterior nares, show a general correlation with the lengths of the anterior cranium, bregma to nasion (text-fig. 45). But again it is seen that many wide individual disagreements exist between these two measurements. While adjacent skulls may differ only slightly in bregma to nasion lengths, the lengths of the floor of the anterior nares may show wide variations. The existence of such pronounced disagreements makes it evident that the appearance of a general accord between the two figures is more largely due to a gradation in size of the skulls than to differences in skull type.

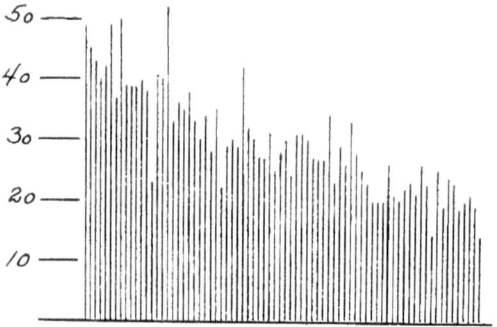

Text-figure 47. Sequence M. Anterior end of intermasal suture to anterior tip of the superior dental alveolus. Same skull sequence as text-figure 45.

Finally, text-figure 48 represents measurements of posterior cranial length, from bregma to supraoccipital spine (pl. 35, fig. 3, B–C), for comparison with the anterior cranial measurements from bregma to nasion. The range of measurements from bregma to the supraoccipital crest is from 80 mm down to 36 mm, or as 2.2:1. This range is not quite so great as the one for anterior cranial length, and there is practically no accord between the slope formed by the tops of lines representing bregma to nasion lengths (text-fig. 45) and the very irregular series for the measurement from bregma to supraoccipital spine (text-fig. 48).

These charts of mid-dorsal measurements indicate that in the different typed dog skulls there is little correlation in length between the portion of the cranium anterior to the bregma and that posterior to it. There is also no correlation between either of these cranial measurements and the length of the bony nose or the length of the snout.

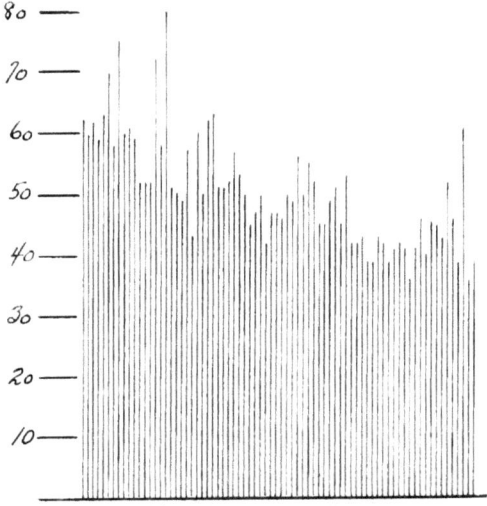

Text figure 48. Sequence M. Bregma to supraoccipital spine. Same skull sequence as text-figure 45.

## Length of Skull Base in Relation to Anteroposterior Length of Premolar Tooth Crowns

The lengths of skull base in this group of skulls range from 210 mm down to 67 mm, the extremes differing as 3.13:1. It seemed a matter of possible importance to determine whether the size of teeth, as indicated by anteroposterior dimensions of the tooth crowns, could be directly correlated with the total skull length. The number of teeth or dental formula is quite uniform in all dog breeds and, since this is the case, an animal with a long jaw would need larger teeth to fill the allotted space than would one with a much shorter jaw. Text-figure 49 gives a series of lines representing length of skull base in dogs of different breeds; these are arranged in sequence from longest to shortest.

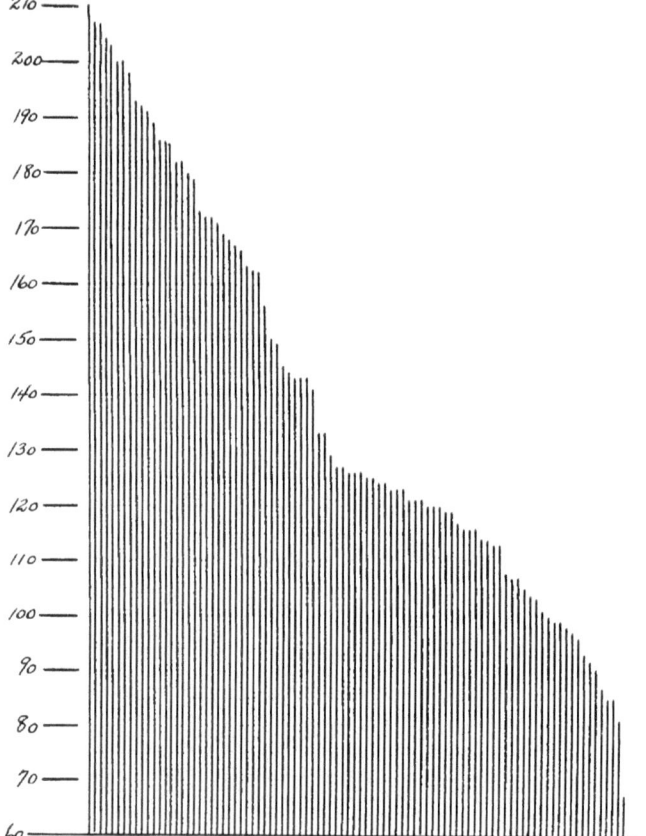

Text-figure 49. Sequence X. Total skull base. Group of seventy skulls arranged in sequence from longest to shortest length of skull base.

The four maxillary premolar teeth were measured for greatest anteroposterior width of crown, and the sum of the widths is represented for each skull by the lines in text-figure 50. The sequence in this figure is the same as that for the skull base.

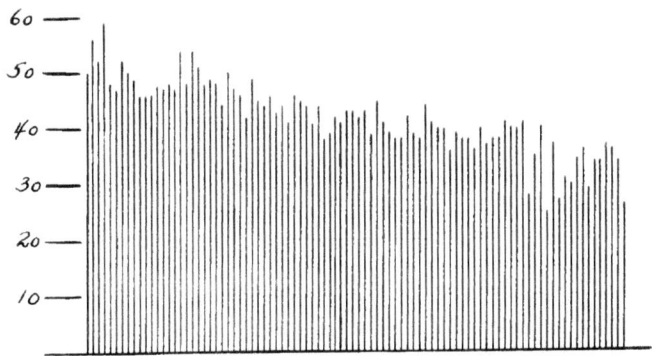

Text-figure 50. Sequence X. Sum of the anteroposterior dimensions of the maxillary premolar teeth. Same skull sequence as text-figure 49.

The range of total premolar measurements is from 59 mm down to 25 mm, the extremes differing as 2.4:1. A comparison of text-figures 49 and 50 shows no detailed exactness in correspondence of length of skull and size of teeth, but there is indication of a general though irregular agreement which is probably due to a large extent to size differences among the skulls.

### Résumé of Deductions from Linear Measurements Made on Different Skull Types

From the foregoing rather comprehensive survey of linear measurements on a group of dog skulls which included a wide range of differences in size and type, we may make the following deductions.

In the first place, there would appear to be little if any correlation between the linear dimensions of the cranium and the wide variations found in the skeleton of the face. In general, a long cranium is associated with a long face, but striking disharmonies in which a long cranium is associated with a short muzzle are found. In dog skulls, therefore, no estimation of facial length can be safely deduced from cranial length.

Different linear dimensions of the cranium itself are found to be quite unrelated in their variations. On the other hand, most of the longitudinal dimensions of the facial skeleton vary in an evidently correlated manner, as for instance the transverse dimensions of the facial skeleton, which, though not correlated with cranial widths, are interrelated in their variations among the different typed skulls.

The relation of length of the bony palate to total skull base forms a very significant proportion in the differentiation of skull types. The proportional lengths of the contributions from the maxilla and palate bones to the total bony palate are also consistently related to this differentiation. The longer the palatal process from the maxilla, the longer the total skull base and the lower the proportion of palatal process contributed by the palate bone. A smaller fraction of the total skull base is formed by the hard palate in short bulldog-like skulls than in long shepherd-like skulls.

Although these linear measurements may furnish a number of dependable correlations in an estimation of the several skull types, they fail to indicate in a satisfactory manner the existence of many of the important type characteristics. This linear survey has been quite essential in the obtaining of a detailed familiarity with the numerous deviations from the wild typed skull, but as is common practice in a study such as this, a more complete differentiation both within a given type as well as among the different types depends upon a comparison of indices for the various regions.

## DETERMINATION AND COMPARISON OF SKULL INDICES AMONG VARIOUS DOG BREEDS

The indices of various skull regions permit somewhat more instructive comparisons than do the previously discussed linear measurements, in that indices involve more than one dimension. They express, as a rule, two dimensional relations, these usually involving a width and a length, or transverse to longitudinal relationship. For example, the conventional cranial index is obtained by multiplying the greatest cranial width by 100 and then dividing the product by the cranial length. Multiplying by 100 enables one to express the index as a whole number rather than a fraction, thus facilitating comparisons in a series of indices. A high cranial index indicates that the cranium is comparatively wide for its length, while a low figure means a long, narrow cranium. With the exception of the upper facial index (see p. 217), all indices used in the present discussion are to be understood as based on similar calculations.

A number of indices and measurements for the skulls of pure breed dogs are arranged for comparison in table 1. Measurements have been made on both male and female skulls in most of the breeds represented. Rather consistent differences between the two sexes frequently occur among the pronounced breed types, these suggesting probable endocrine influence for the differential structural expression. In this table, as well as tables 2, 3, and 4, each group of three values for specific measurements and indices shows first, the average for the females; second, the average for the males; and third (bold-faced type), the average for the breed. The number of animals of each sex which were measured are indicated. It is very difficult with such material as this to have large numbers of measurements for each breed, but probable errors as well as the coefficients of deviation are indicated in the table.

TABLE 1

| | SALUKI 1♀ 1♂ | | | GERMAN SHEPHERD 4♀ 3♂ | | | POINTER | GREAT DANE 3♀ 1♂ | | | ST. BERNARD 6♀ 1♂ | | | BASSETHOUND 2♀ 1♂ | | |
|---|---|---|---|---|---|---|---|---|---|---|---|---|---|---|---|---|
| | Av. | P.E | S.D. | Av. | P.E. | S.D. | ♂ | Av | P.E. | S.D. | Av. | P.E | S.D | Av. | P.E | S.D. |
| Cranial Index. | 59. 70. 64.5 | 2.624 | 5.5 | 51. 52.* 51.333 | .860 1.431 .757 | 2.550 3. 2.749 | 59. 59. | 52.50** 50. 51.667 | .716 .66 | 1.50 1.70 | 53.00 45. 51.36 | .81 .879 | 2.94 3.45 | 65. 63. 64.433 | 1.908 1.324 | 4.0 3.399 |
| Skull Index. | 55. 58. 56.5 | .716 | 1.5 | 55.5 56.667 56. | .439 .183 .385 | 1.303 .471 1.512 | 63. 63. | 60.33 61 60.50 | .49 .38 | 1.25 1.12 | 60.20†† 60. 60.17 | .723 .604 | 2.40 2.192 | 62. 61. 61.667 | 1.431 .971 | 3.0 2.494 |
| Palatal Index. | 57. 58. 57.5 | .239 | .5 | 61.25 60. 60.714 | .602 .486 .512 | 1.785 1.247 2.01 | 69. 69. | 69.33 66. 68.5 | 1.47 1.20 | 3.77 3.57 | 62.5 62. 62.43 | .377 .300 | 1.369 1.178 | 64. 65. 64.333 | 1.431 .971 | 3.0 2.491 |
| Snout Index. | 55. 51. 53. | .954 | 2. | 60.5 61.333 60.857 | .439 1.116 .598 | 1.303 2.867 2.357 | 72. 72. | 68.33 69. 68.50 | 1.08 | 3.68 3.20 | 75.0 77. 75.286 | .616 .704 | 2.236 2.762 | 62.5 63. 62.667 | 2.147 1.434 | 4.5 3.682 |
| Upper Facial Index. | 121. 113. 117. | 1.939 | 4. | 105.25 109.5* 106.667 | 2.663 1.670 1.939 | 7.896 3.5 7.040 | 98. 98. | 99. 107 101. | .50 1.26 | 1.291 3.74 | 111. 118. 112. | 1.002 .884 | 3.641 3.47 | 105. 105. 105. | 1.431 .954 | 3.0 2.449 |
| Breadth-hgt. Index. | 91. 88. 89.5 | .716 | 1.5 | 97. 108. 101.714 | 1.093 1.908 1.727 | 3.241 4.899 6.776 | 93. 93. | 98.67 105 100.25 | 2.57 2.14 | 6.60 6.34 | 109. 118. 110.28 | 1.440 1.471 | 5.228 5.77 | 83.5 82. 83. | .239 .318 | .5 .816 |
| Palate total Skull Base. | 55. 54. 54.5 | .239 | .5 | 55. 56. 55.426 | .238 .551 .300 | .707 1.414 1.178 | 55. 55. | 52.33 53. 52.50 | .37 .29 | .94 .87 | 54.†† 54. 54. | .443 .389 | 1.549 1.414 | 56.5 56. 56.333 | .239 .183 | .5 .470 |
| Palatal total Palate. | 31. 34. 32.5 | .716 | 1.5 | 34.666† 33.333 34. | .734 .734 .551 | 1.885 1.886 2.0 | 37. 37. | 34.67 38. 35.5 | 1.01 .91 | 2.62 2.69 | 36.2†† 36. 36.167 | .638 .560 | 2.231 2.034 | 32.5 33. 32.667 | .239 .183 | .5 .470 |
| Orb.OrbFr/ Orb.Inc.Alv. | 26. 27. 26.5 | .239 | .5 | 26.5 27. 26.714 | .608 .551 .425 | 1.803 1.414 1.666 | 24. 24. | 26. 26. 26. | 1.10 .83 | 2.83 2.45 | 25. 26. 25.143 | .693 .601 | 2.517 2.356 | 24.5 24. 24.3 | .239 .183 | .5 .470 |
| Max.PreM. PreM. Region. | 75. 82. 78.5 | 1.607 | 3.5 | 83.5 82. 82.857 | .695 1.146 .659 | 2.062 2.944 2.587 | 87. 87. | 80. 85. 81.25 | .84 .96 | 2.16 2.86 | 79.833 78. 79.571 | 1.370 .952 | 4.975 3.736 | 90. 84. 88. | 1.431 1.457 | 3.0 3.742 |
| Mandibular Index. | 45. 45. 45. | | | 43. 43.333 43.143 | .477 .486 .345 | 1.414 1.247 1.355 | 52. 52. | 43.667 48. 41.25 | .84 .68 | 2.16 1.92 | 46. 40 45.143 | .421 .646 | 1.528 2.532 | 50. 47. 49. | .954 .841 | 2.0 2.160 |
| Mand.PreM. PreM. Region. | 65. 71. 68. | 1.431 | 3.0 | 74.5 70.5 73.333 | .136 2.147 1.279 | 4.023 4.5 4.643 | 77. 77. | 67.** 75. 69.67 | 2.385 .216 | 5.00 5.55 | 67.8†† 68. 67.833 | .431 .370 | 1.509 1.344 | 80.5 80. 80.333 | 1.193 .800 | 2.5 2.055 |
| Ant.Post.Dim. of Max.PreMs. | 43. 44. 43.5 | .239 | .5 | 47.5 52 49.429 | .377 .954 .769 | 1.118 2.449 3.017 | | 48.33 51. 49. | .486 .533 | 1.247 1.581 | 50.667 50. 50.571 | .757 .651 | 2.749 2.555 | 44.5 42 43.667 | .716 .662 | 1.5 1.70 |
| Ant.Post.Dim. of Mand.PreMs. | 33. 34. 33.5 | .239 | .5 | 37.5 40.5 38.5 | .377 1.670 .724 | 1.118 3.5 2.630 | | 35.33 40. 36.5 | .971 .994 | 2.494 2.958 | 39.4†† 38. 39.166 | .409 .370 | 1.897 1.344 | 35.*** | | .5 |
| Zygomatic Width. | 96. 98. 97. | .477 | 1.0 | 103.5 114.333 108.143 | 1.694 2.048 1.905 | 5.024 5.26 7.473 | 108. 108. | 123. 131. 125. | .55 1.24 | 1.41 3.67 | 131.2†† 136. 132. | 1.903 1.840 | 6.660 6.683 | 97.5 100. 98.333 | .239 .486 | .5 1.247 |
| Lt. Frontal Width. | 35. 37. 36. | .477 | 1.0 | 36.5 40.333 38.143 | .292 .486 .552 | .866 1.247 2.167 | 35. 35. | 42.33 45. 43.00 | 1.10 .86 | 2.59 2.45 | 41.833 44. 42.143 | 5.84 5.35 | 2.115 2.100 | 37.5 36. 37. | .239 .318 | .5 .816 |
| Orbital Width. | 33. 34. 33.5 | .239 | .5 | 39.75 48.333 43.429 | 1.201 2.408 1.645 | 3.562 6.183 6.455 | 36. 36. | 48.** 49 48.33 | 2.39 1.60 | 5.00 4.11 | 52. 57. 52.714 | .595 .677 | 2.160 2.657 | 33. 32. 32.667 | .954 .662 | 2.0 1.700 |
| Nasal Width. | 22. 21. 21.5 | .239 | .5 | 26.5 29.333 27.714 | .169 .486 .425 | .5 1.247 1.666 | 25. 25. | 30.** 35. 31.67 | .95 1.12 | 2.00 2.87 | 34. 37. 34.429 | .425 .381 | 1.544 1.495 | 22.5 25. 23.333 | .239 .486 | .5 1.247 |
| Skull Base. | 174. 169. 171.5 | 1.193 | 2.5 | 185.75 202. 192.714 | 1.314 3.611 2.676 | 3.897 9.274 10.496 | 171. 171. | 204.667 215. 207.25 | 1.88 2.03 | 4.84 6.02 | 218.2†† 228 219.83 | 2.894 2.367 | 10.127 8.591 | 157.5 163 159.333 | 4.055 2.885 | 8.5 7.409 |
| Mandibular Thick. | 9. 8. 8.5 | .239 | .5 | 11.75 12.667 12.143 | .280 .486 .287 | .829 1.247 1.125 | 12 12. | 12.67 13. 12.75 | .183 .146 | .471 .433 | 14.833 16. 15. | .189 .193 | .687 .756 | 10. 9. 9.667 | .477 .367 | 1.0 .943 |
| Mand.1st M.Width. | 39. 39. 39. | | | 44.25 50. 46.714 | .146 .954 .837 | .433 2.449 3.283 | 49. 49. | 58.33 61. 59. | .671 .533 | 1.723 1.581 | 56.833 56. 56.714 | .553 .523 | 2.007 2.050 | 44. 45. 44.333 | .954 .662 | 2.0 1.700 |
| Mand.4th.PreM.Width. | 35. 35. 35. | | | 41.667† 48.333 45. | .159 .143 .370 | .471 .368 1.342 | 45. 45. | 52. 59. 53.75 | .636 1.128 | 1.633 3.345 | 54.6 60 55.5 | .897 .910 | 3.137 3.304 | 39.5 41. 40. | 2.147 1.457 | 4.5 3.742 |
| Mand.3rd.PreM.Width. | 28. 31. 29.5 | .716 | 1.5 | 36. 40 37.714 | .860 .841 .791 | 2.550 2.160 3.104 | 36. 36. | 42. 48. 43.50 | .636 .994 | 1.633 2.958 | 45 50 45.714 | .746 .779 | 2.708 3.057 | 33. 35. 33.667 | 1.431 1.022 | 3.000 2.625 |

Av.—Average  P.E.—Probable error  S.D.—Standard deviation
Averages based on: 2♂ only—*; 3♀ only—†; 2♀ only—**; 5♀ only—††; 1♀ only—***.

TABLE 1

| | DACHSHUND 4♀ | | | COCKER SPANIEL 2♀ - 1♂ | | | ENGLISH BULLDOG 3♀ - 6♂ | | | FRENCH BULLDOG 3♀ - 1♂ | | | BOSTON TERRIER 5♀ | | | PEKINGESE ♀ | MALTESE POODLE | BRUSSELS GRIFFON | CHOW | LABRADOR HUSKIE ♀ |
|---|---|---|---|---|---|---|---|---|---|---|---|---|---|---|---|---|---|---|---|---|
| | Av. | P.E. | S.D. | Av. | P.E. | S.D. | Av. | P.E. | S.D. | Av. | P.E. | S.D. | Av. | P.E. | S.D. | | | | | |
| | 69.75 | ±.730 | 2.165 | 72.5 | ±1.670 | 3.55 | 69.667 68.833 69.111 | ±.918 2.118 1.447 | 2.357 7.692 6.437 | 73. 75. 73.5 | ±.945 .773 | 2.449 2.292 | 77.2 77.2 | ±.749 .749 | 2.482 2.482 | 84. 84. | 69. 69. | 84. 84. | 60. 60. | 59. 59. |
| | 69.75 | .730 | 2.165 | 71.667 | 1.204 | 3.091 | | | | | | | | | | | | | | |
| | 66.5 | .167 | .5 | 68.5 66. 67.667 | .716 .662 | 1.5 1.700 | 102.667 110.333 107.778 | 1.943 2.548 2.571 | 4.989 9.253 9.211 | 103.676 99. 102.5 | 2.778 2.059 | 7.134 6.104 | 105.2 105.2 | 1.227 1.227 | 4.069 4.069 | 107. | 72. | 103. | 72. | 64. |
| | 66.5 | .167 | .5 | | | | | | | | | | | | | | | | | |
| | 66.25 | .499 | 1.479 | 76. 73. 75. | .954 .841 | 2.0 2.160 | 120.667 124. 122.889 | 1.434 2.749 1.589 | 3.682 9.983 7.069 | 117. 111. 115.5 | .954 1.131 | 2.449 3.354 | 119.6 119.6 | 2.104 2.104 | 6.974 6.974 | 122. | 80. | 125. | 80. | 69. |
| | 66.25 | .499 | 1.479 | | | | | | | | | | | | | | | | | |
| | 61. | .983 | 2.916 | 72.5 70. 71.667 | .716 .662 | 1.5 1.700 | 167. 173.667 171.444 | 5.940 6.220 5.445 | 15.253 22.586 24.217 | 164.667 142. 159. | 4.826 4.904 | 12.392 14.543 | 155.6 155.6 | 3.861 3.861 | 12.8 12.8 | 179. | 74. | 183. | 76. | 67. |
| | 61. | .983 | 2.916 | | | | | | | | | | | | | | | | | |
| | 96.5 | .499 | 1.479 | 77.5 93. 82.667 | .239 2.850 | .5 7.318 | 39.333 42.5 41.444 | .971 1.604 1.167 | 2.494 5.824 5.189 | 40. 45. 41.25 | 1.101 1.102 | 2.828 3.269 | 38. 38. | .763 .763 | 2.53 2.53 | 23. | 65. | 25. | 83. | 111. |
| | 96.5 | .499 | 1.479 | | | | | | | | | | | | | | | | | |
| | 84.75 | .839 | 2.488 | 90.5 89. 90. | .716 .551 | 1.6 1.414 | 91.332 94.833 93.667 | .971 1.060 .912 | 2.494 3.848 4.055 | 97.5 95. 96.667 | 1.193 .918 | 2.5 2.357 | 90.2 90.2 | .749 .749 | 2.482 2.482 | 87. | 91. | 90. | 98. | 98. |
| | 84.75 | .839 | 2.488 | | | | | | | | | | | | | | | | | |
| | 59. | .238 | .707 | 56.5 56. 56.333 | .239 .183 | .5 .470 | 49.333 50.667 50.222 | .367 .687 .495 | .943 2.494 2.200 | 53.333 53. 53.25 | .733 .553 | 1.886 1.639 | 52.6 52.6 | .560 .560 | 1.855 1.855 | 54. | 52. | 52. | 52. | 55. |
| | 59. | .238 | .707 | | | | | | | | | | | | | | | | | |
| | 33.5 | .843 | 2.0 | 34.*** 35. 34.5 | .239 | .5 | 41.333 37.833 39. | 2.704 .701 1.081 | 6.944 2.544 4.807 | 32. 32. | | | 34.2 34.2 | .883 .883 | 2.926 2.926 | 33. | | 31. | 34. | 32. |
| | 33.5 | .843 | 2.0 | | | | | | | | | | | | | | | | | |
| | 23. | 1.60 | 4.744 | 17.5 22. 19. | .239 .841 | .5 2.160 | 13.333 17.5 16.111 | 2.386 1.270 1.242 | 6.128 4.610 5.516 | 15. 13. 14.5 | 3.033 2.294 | 7.789 6.801 | 10. 10. | .739 .739 | 2.449 2.449 | 12. | 14. | 8. | 24. | 24. |
| | 23. | 1.60 | 4.744 | | | | | | | | | | | | | | | | | |
| | 97.5 | 1.407 | 4.172 | 105.5 105.5 | 2.625 2.625 | 5.5 5.5 | 119. 123. 121.667 | 1.272 2.759 1.924 | 3.266 10.017 8.602 | 138. 129. 135. | 2.385 2.293 | 5.0 5.888 | 148.333 148.333 | 2.069 2.069 | 5.31 5.31 | 162. | | 98. | | |
| | 97.5 | 1.407 | 4.172 | | | | | | | | | | | | | | | | | |
| | 51. | .631 | 1.871 | 51. 51. 51. | .477 .318 | 1.0 .816 | 64. 63.667 62.778 | 1.272 .468 .528 | 3.266 1.700 2.347 | 67.667 66. 67.25 | 1.503 1.153 | 3.859 3.419 | 71.4 71.4 | .984 .984 | 3.262 3.262 | 73. | 55. | 70. | 54. | 53. |
| | 51. | .631 | 1.871 | | | | | | | | | | | | | | | | | |
| | 84.5 | .773 | 2.292 | 100.*** 89. 94.5 | 2.624 | 5.5 | 73.333 71.8 72.375 | 5.455 1.420 2.227 | 14.008 4.707 9.338 | 81.5 125 96. | 4.089 7.495 | 10.5 22.226 | 115.667 115.667 | 3.517 3.517 | 9.031 9.031 | 118. | | | | |
| | 84.5 | .773 | 2.292 | | | | | | | | | | | | | | | | | |
| | 37. | .318 | .816 | 39. 39. | | | 38. 40.333 39.556 | .318 .821 .610 | .816 2.981 2.713 | 36.5 40. 37.667 | 1.670 1.285 | 3.5 3.300 | 34. 34. | | | 26. | | 46. | | |
| | 37. | .318 | .816 | | | | | | | | | | | | | | | | | |
| | 28.75 | .280 | .829 | 33. 33. | | | 29.667 29.400 29.5 | 1.022 .777 .620 | 2.625 2.577 2.598 | 21. 21. | .477 .477 | 1.0 1.0 | 25.5 25.5 | .506 .506 | 1.5 1.5 | 20. | | | | 29. |
| | 28.75 | .280 | .829 | | | | | | | | | | | | | | | | | |
| | 79. | .924 | 2.739 | 81.5 87 83.33 | .716 1.116 | 1.5 2.867 | 120.333 127.333 125. | 1.116 1.098 1.561 | 2.867 3.986 5.142 | 99. 100. 99.25 | 1.682 1.298 | 4.320 3.849 | 89.6 89.6 | .845 .845 | 2.80 2.80 | 72. | 74. | 63. | 107. | 112. |
| | 79. | .924 | 2.739 | | | | | | | | | | | | | | | | | |
| | 30.5 | .422 | 1.25 | 37.5 39. 38. | .239 .318 | .5 .816 | 43.667 46.667 45.333 | .918 1.256 .930 | 2.337 4.561 4.137 | 48.333 44. 47.25 | .183 .648 | .471 1.920 | 46.4 46.4 | .702 .702 | 2.332 2.332 | 42. | 35. | 43. | 38. | 35. |
| | 30.5 | .422 | 1.25 | | | | | | | | | | | | | | | | | |
| | 25.25 | .368 | 1.090 | 27. 29 27.667 | .367 | .943 | 42. 46. 44.667 | .954 .746 .892 | 2.449 2.708 3.968 | 37.667 40. 38.25 | .674 .499 | 1.732 1.479 | 33.8 33.8 | .296 .296 | .980 .980 | 22. | 26. | 26. | 37. | 37. |
| | 25.25 | .368 | 1.090 | | | | | | | | | | | | | | | | | |
| | 17. | .238 | .707 | 19. 21. 19.667 | .367 | .943 | 25.333 25.5 25.444 | .367 .443 .321 | .943 1.607 1.423 | 20. 20. 20. | .318 .238 | .816 .707 | 19.2 19.2 | .418 .418 | 1.386 1.386 | 14. | 16. | 13. | 23. | 26. |
| | 17. | .238 | .707 | | | | | | | | | | | | | | | | | |
| | 119.25 | 1.128 | 3.345 | 118.5 131. 122.667 | 2.147 2.704 | 4.5 6.944 | 117.333 116. 116.444 | 2.117 1.834 1.418 | 5.437 6.658 6.309 | 96. 101. 97.25 | 3.667 2.845 | 9.416 8.437 | 85.2 85.2 | .942 .942 | 3.124 3.124 | 67. | 103. | 61. | 150. | 174. |
| | 119.25 | 1.128 | 3.345 | | | | | | | | | | | | | | | | | |
| | 6.75 | .146 | .433 | 8. 9. 8.333 | .183 | .470 | 11. 11. 11. | .318 .159 .500 | .816 .577 .667 | 9.667 10. 9.75 | .183 .146 | .471 .433 | 8. 8. | | | 6. | 6. | 4. | 11. | 12. |
| | 6.75 | .146 | .433 | | | | | | | | | | | | | | | | | |
| | 35.5 | .735 | 2.183 | 38. 38. 38. | .954 .636 | 2.0 1.623 | 54.333 57.667 56.556 | .734 .851 .712 | 1.886 3.091 3.166 | 42. 46. 43. | 2.085 1.669 | 5.354 4.950 | 39.8 39.8 | .773 .773 | 2.561 2.561 | 31. | 31. | 30. | 48. | 48. |
| | 35.5 | .735 | 2.183 | | | | | | | | | | | | | | | | | |
| | 32. | 1.101 | 2.828 | 34.5 36. 35. | .239 .318 | .5 .816 | 52.333 54.833 54. | 1.434 .877 .800 | 3.682 3.184 3.559 | 40.** 46 42. | 1.908 1.682 | 4.0 4.430 | 38.4 38.4 | .452 .452 | 1.497 1.497 | 27. | | 27. | | 44. |
| | 32. | 1.101 | 2.828 | | | | | | | | | | | | | | | | | |
| | 25.75 | .768 | 2.278 | 27. 29. 27.667 | .477 .486 | 1.0 1.247 | 40. 40.8 40.5 | 1.682 1.543 1.156 | 4.320 5.115 4.848 | 36.** 35 35.667 | .477 .367 | 1.0 .943 | 31.4 31.4 | .409 .409 | 1.356 1.356 | 21. | 23. | | | 36. |
| | 25.75 | .768 | 2.278 | | | | | | | | | | | | | | | | | |

An appreciation of the extent of the character differences among the many dog types may be clearly brought out by comparing the first four indices at the top of table 1 for the Saluki and German shepherd dog, with the same indices for the English bulldog, the Pekingese and the Brussels griffon. The cranial index for the Saluki is 64, and for the German shepherd only 51; while in the English bulldog this index is 69, and in the Pekingese and Brussels griffon 84. The two dogs last mentioned have wide, almost spherically shaped cranial cases which are in strong contrast to the long, narrow cranium of the shepherd dog. In spite of the general linear type of the Saluki it would seem to have a somewhat more rounded cranium than the shepherd dog, but this is an apparent rather than a real condition and is due entirely to the fact that the shepherd skull has a high dorsal crest and prominent supraoccipital spine, which adds to its length; the Saluki skull is flat dorsally and has almost no crest or spine.

The second index in the table represents the skull as a whole and is calculated on the basis of the relation of zygomatic width to length of skull base (pl. 35, fig. 1, F; fig. 2, D-G). The skull index for the Saluki and German shepherd dog is only 56, while for the bulldog and Pekingese it is 107, and for the Brussels griffon 103. The three latter skulls have indices almost double that of the shepherd. The bulldog-like skulls are wider than long and the shepherd skull is often twice as long as wide. These must be recognized as enormous differences in the head shapes occurring within a single species.

The palatal index, determined on the basis of palatal width to length, is 60 for the German shepherd as against 122 for the bulldog and Pekingese and 125 for the Brussels griffon. The palatal indices of the short skulls are more than double that of the shepherd.

The fourth line of figures in table 1 represents the snout indices. These indices are based on the relation of the width at the alveolar border of the maxillary canine teeth (pl. 35, fig. 1, C) and the length of the snout (pl. 35, fig. 3, J-F).

This snout index is 60 for the long German shepherd skull and only 53 for the narrow muzzled Saluki skull, as contrasted with 171 for the bulldog, 179 for the Pekingese, and 183 for the Brussels griffon. No other index calculated, with the possible exception of the upper facial index, shows such enormous deviations from the control or standard shepherd type.

The differences shown in three of the above four indices between the wild or ancestral typed dog skull and the divergent or mutant types are of such magnitude that confusion of the types would be impossible.

It is unnecessary in this text to further pursue the details of table 1; the significance of the figures is sufficiently clear and they can be followed by the reader to his own satisfaction. However, it is very difficult to make comparative estimates of values among the large numbers of detailed measurements contained in the table, and we have attempted to express these in graphic fashion by the charts discussed below.

GRAPHIC COMPARISONS OF MEASUREMENTS AND INDICES AMONG SIMILAR AND CONTRASTED SKULL TYPES

In this section, groups of similar typed skulls will be compared in order to discover how closely alike they are in their indices and dimensions, and also which characteristics are most variable or likely to differ among even those breeds of the same general type. For this purpose we separated and classified the skulls according to outstanding characteristics of size, structure, etc. The first group contains the long typed skulls, those from the German shepherd, the foxhound and the Saluki. These three breeds have standard wolf-like skulls which may be thought to represent the original wild type from which the modified skulls have been derived.

The St. Bernard, great Dane and dachshund make up the second somewhat divergent group of skulls. Although the St. Bernard is of giant size with definite acromegalic symptoms, the basic type of the skull is closely similar to that of the simple giant great Dane and, strange to find, both these large skulls are closely comparable to the skull type of the partially dwarfed dachshund. Feature for feature, the skulls in this second group are not very widely different from those in the first group, but in total pattern they form a quite distinct type.

The English bulldog, French bulldog and Boston terrier make up the third group of skulls, and it will be found that this group is widely different in type from the other two groups. Although the skulls from these three breeds are highly distorted and more variable than the others, they yet adhere to a pattern which is just as consistent for its type as that of the wild or standard type of dog skull.

An examination of text-figure 51 gives a very clear conception of the features for the standard dog skull. The indices of the German shepherd are represented by the solid black columns, those of the foxhound by cross-hatched columns and those of the Saluki by the diagonal columns. The relative dimensions of the three skulls are represented in outline at the top of the figure. The close similarity of the outline patterns of these skulls is readily evident.

Nine indices and eleven different dimensions and proportions are represented in this figure. The unshaded space at the top of each column indicates the total variation both above and below the average for a given index or dimension. The measurements represented in the chart were made on seven shepherd skulls, three foxhound skulls and two Saluki skulls. Skulls of these breeds are so uniform in size and type that measurements from a large number of animals are unnecessary for the present purpose.

These three breeds of skulls show no large differences in any of the indices or any of the linear dimensions represented. The breadth-height index, the zygomatic width and the orbital width seem to be the only very variable features. All other indices and dimensions not only fall surprisingly close together in the three breeds, but, as indicated in the unshaded areas at the tops of the columns, these features show but slight variations in individuals of the same breed. This type skull is evidently quite definitely and uniformly established.

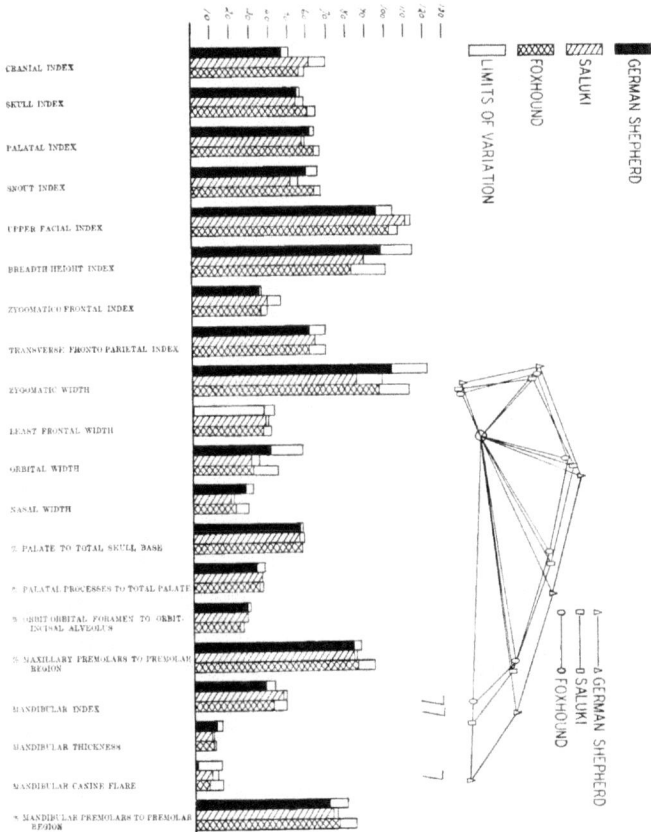

Text-figure 51. Comparison of skull measurements and indices of the German shepherd, foxhound and Saluki. The values indicated are based on averages of actual measurements of seven German shepherd, three foxhound and three Saluki skulls.

Text-figure 52 shows the same general arrangement for comparing the indices and dimensions of the St. Bernard, great Dane and dachshund skulls. The solid black columns represent values for the St. Bernard, the cross-hatched for the great Dane and the diagonal for the dachshund. The outlines of the three skulls in relative dimensions are shown

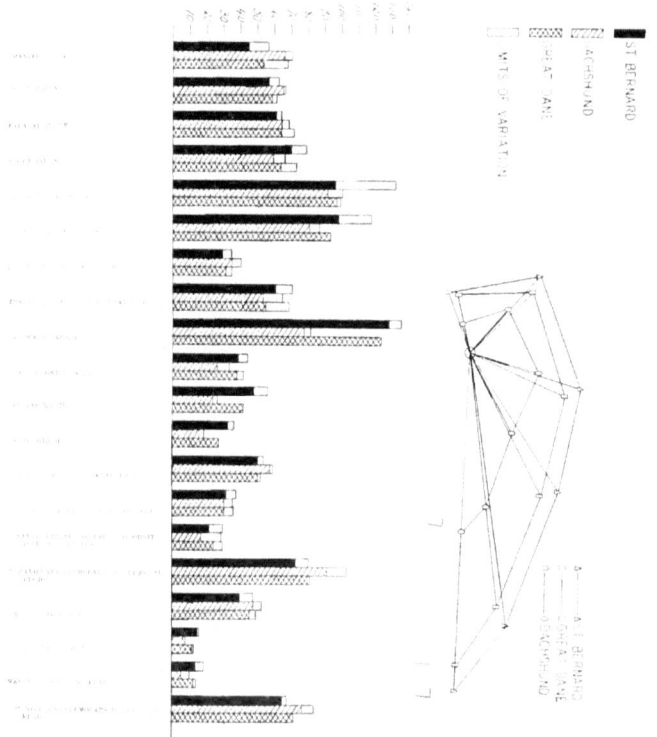

Text-figure 52. Comparison of skull measurements and indices of the St. Bernard, great Dane and dachshund. The values indicated are based on averages of actual measurements of seven St. Bernard, four great Dane and four dachshund skulls.

at the top of the chart. The St. Bernard skull is very large, the great Dane is slightly smaller, and the dachshund skull only about half the size of either of the first two. In spite of this discrepancy in size, the outlines of the three skulls are on an almost identical pattern.

The columns in this figure represent the averages for seven St. Bernard, four Dane and four dachshund skulls. The St. Bernard skulls, as indicated by the blank spaces at the top of the black columns, are more variable for indices and dimensions than the other two. The upper facial index and the breadth-height index in the skull of this dog are very variable although the averages for these indices are quite similar in the three breeds. The skull variations in the St. Bernard are very probably associated with differing degrees of the acromegalic reaction in the skulls of this breed.

The dachshund falls well below the other two skulls for zygomatic width and orbital width, but these differences are due solely to the smaller size of the skull and are in no sense indicative of deviations in type. In general the twenty sets of columns shown in this chart indicate that there is a surprisingly close uniformity in type among the skulls from these three very different dog breeds.

The skulls represented in text-figure 53 are almost entirely different in pattern from those represented in the two previous figures. At the top of the chart, outlines of relative dimensions are given for the three skulls. These three outlines are just as closely uniform in their patterns as are those of the standard typed skulls in text-figure 51. As indicated in table 1, the characters were measured from the skulls of nine English bulldogs, four French bulldogs and five Boston terriers. The bulldog typed skulls are shown by this figure to be more variable for indices and dimensions than are those of the two previous groups, and in most of the characters indicated the English bulldog skull is more variable than those of the Boston terrier or the French bulldog. In spite of this variability, the average indices for the three skulls are remarkably close together for all features indicated. In zygomatic width the English bulldog is far above the other two, but this is due almost entirely to the general differences in skull size, and the type value of this character is about equal in all three skulls.

The relation of the total anteroposterior dimensions of the maxillary premolar teeth to the maxillary premolar region is highest in the Boston terrier, next in the French bulldog and lowest in the English bulldog. The same relation holds for the total mandibular premolar anteroposterior dimensions to mandibular premolar region. This means, of course, that

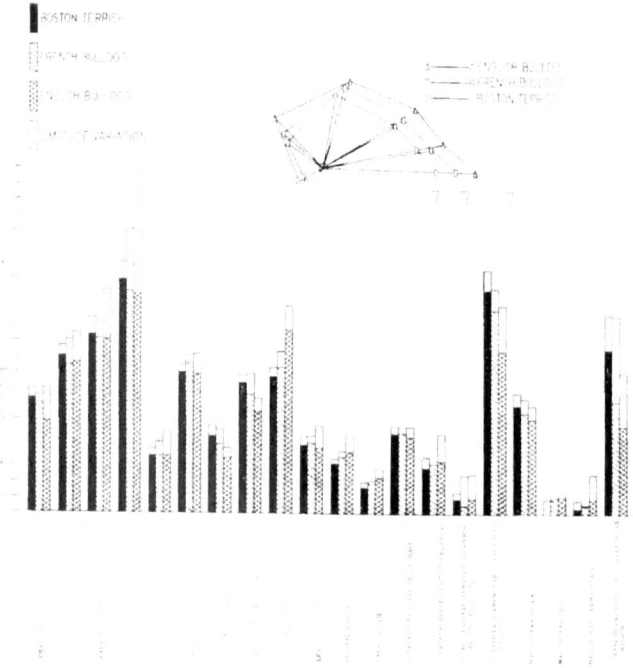

Text figure 53. Comparison of skull measurements and indices of the Boston terrier, French bulldog and English bulldog. The values indicated are based on averages of actual measurements of nine English bulldog, four French bulldog and five Boston terrier skulls.

the teeth are more closely set and crowded together in the jaws of the Boston terrier than in either the French or English bulldogs. The relations in size of premolar teeth to extent of premolar regions differ more among these three breeds than does any other characteristic charted.

It will be noticed in this chart that while all other indices are high, indicating short wide skulls, the upper facial index is low. This is due to the fact that the upper facial index was calculated in a manner the opposite to that used for the other indices, that is, the upper facial index was based on nasal length divided by palatal width while in general the indices were determined by dividing widths by lengths. The manner of calculating these indices was reversed simply as an aid for contrasting the types, as we shall see beyond. This index is also reversed in the two previous charts.

An inspection of text-figure 53 as a whole shows that the bulldog skulls are uniformly close together and exhibit an harmonious type agreement quite equal to that for the shepherd, foxhound and Saluki skulls (text-fig. 51). Although the bulldog skulls are highly aberrant in form and very abnormal, with pronounced structural disharmonies, they nevertheless constitute a definite type with clear cut characteristics.

Finally, the position of the anterior inferior dental alveolus is indicated below the sagittal outlines at the top of text-figure 53. The lower jaw of the English bulldog projects far in front of the upper jaw; the prognathism of the mandible in the French bulldog is not quite so pronounced; and, as a breed characteristic in the Boston terrier, the incisor teeth are in opposition, since the upper and lower jaws are almost equal in length.

A final chart of this series was made to contrast in a graphic way the indices and dimensions of representative skulls from the two different types found in text-figures 51 and 53. In text-figure 54, the skull indices and dimensions of the standard German shepherd skull are arranged beside the values for the same characteristics in the English bulldog skull. At the top of this figure, the sagittal outlines of these two skulls are given. The outline of the shepherd skull forms a long pattern which is strongly contrasted with that of the shortened and proportionately much higher outline of the English bulldog skull. The contrast is further emphasized when these two outlines are compared with those shown at the top of the three previous charts.

The indices and measurements represented by the columns in text-figure 54 were furnished by the skulls of seven pedigreed pure-line German shepherd dogs and nine pedigreed English bulldogs. The chart as a whole shows great differences in height between the diagonal columns representing the shepherd characteristics and the cross-hatched columns representing those of the bulldog. The skull index, palatal index, snout index, upper facial index and mandibular index all show wide differences for these two skull types. The cranial indices of the two breeds differ in the same direction though not so strongly. The upper facial index, as mentioned before, was calculated in a manner the reverse of that for the other indices, and thus appears high for the shepherd and low for the bulldog. This index is widely different in the two skull types.

The breadth-height index (distance from auditory meatus to bregma divided by cranial width) gives no contrast between the breeds and is an insignificant feature. The relations of zygomatic width to the width of frontal bone and of frontal width to parietal width are about the same for the two types and are also insignificant. The right half of the chart illustrates the almost complete inadequacy of linear measurements for differentiating types among strongly contrasted skulls. The zygomatic widths are the only linear measurements which give a true picture of the variations between these two highly different types of skulls.

The degree of variability above and below the average for the measurements shown in the chart is again represented by the blank space at the top of each column. The bulldog skull is much more variable in all the characteristics represented in the chart than is the skull of the shepherd, with possibly one or two insignificant exceptions. This instability

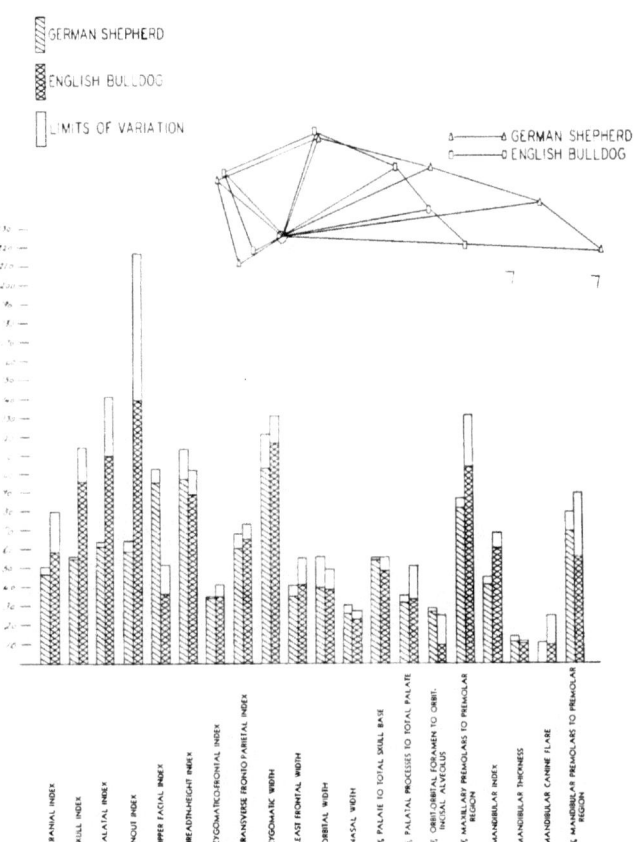

Text-figure 54. Comparison of skull measurements and indices of the contrasted German shepherd and English bulldog. The values indicated are based on averages of actual measurements of seven German shepherd and nine English bulldog skulls.

might indicate that the development of these characteristics in the bulldog skull is quite susceptible to variations in internal environmental conditions, such as functional modification in the endocrine glands. Or variations in such characters might with equal probability be due to lack of homozygosity in the multiple factor complex underlying the completed patterns of the bulldog skull. Whether one or both these possibilities are responsible for this variability in pattern we shall attempt to determine by a study of hybrid conditions.

The differences between the long type of skull and the shortened bulldog type are brought out with even greater clarity in the curves shown in text-figure 55. Six different pure breeds having long typed skulls—the German shepherd, Saluki, bassethound, St. Bernard, great Dane and dachshund—are represented by the six continuous or solid lines in the chart. Round typed skulls from five pure breeds — the English bulldog, French bulldog, Boston terrier, Pekingese and Brussels griffon — are indicated by the broken lines. The figures in the vertical column give the values of the indices and the proportional percentages for the twelve features listed at the bottom of the chart. These curves indicate in a remarkably clear fashion the characters in which the two types of skulls differ strongly, those which are not so widely contrasted, and finally the features which are quite similar for all skull types.

Examining this figure in detail we find that there is only a slight difference in the cranial indices of these two groups; skull indices differ more, palatal indices still more and snout indices differ to the greatest degree. The snout indices for the long skull group range from 53 to 75, but in the short skull group they range from a low of 155 up to a high of 183. The differences in snout index between the long skulls and the short skulls are seen to be almost three times as great as the range of this index within either group.

The upper facial index, again calculated on the reverse basis of nasal length to palatal width, is very different in the two types. With this manner of calculation, the short skulls

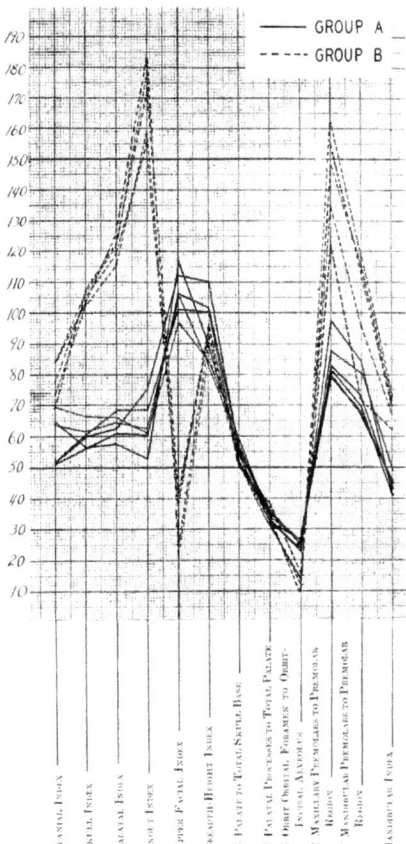

Text-figure 55. Curves showing contrasts and similarities in skull measurements and indices in the two main types of dog skulls—long and short. Group A (long type): Saluki, great Dane, St. Bernard, German shepherd, bassethound and dachshund; group B (short type): English bulldog, French bulldog, Boston terrier, Pekingese and Brussels griffon.

have a very low index, ranging from 23 to 43, while the long skulls range from 97 to 117. The range within each type is only 20, while the difference between the highest index of one type and the lowest of the other is 54, or 2.7 times greater than the range within the types.

The breadth-height indices (distance from auditory meatus to bregma divided by the greatest cranial width) show an overlapping in the curves for the two types and are clearly of no significant value in type differentiation.

The proportion of palate to total skull base, as well as the proportion of palatal process from the palate bone to the total palate, is seen to differ only slightly among the breeds. It will be recalled, however, that the series of seventy skulls of various breeds gave clear indication of the significance of these palatal proportions, and we are quite certain that these proportions are valuable for type differentiation in spite of the only slight differences shown in this graph.

The distances from the rim of the orbit to the infraorbital foramen and from the rim of the orbit to the anterior superior incisal alveolus differ only slightly in the two types of skulls. Any variations in these two measurements are definitely linked; either both are short or both are long and the relation of one to the other does not change.

The relation of total anteroposterior dimensions of the maxillary premolars to length of the maxillary premolar region differs in the two types. In the long skulls the premolar region is definitely longer than the sum of the widths of the premolar teeth, while in the short skulls the teeth have a greater total extent than does the premolar region. The latter condition causes the teeth to be crowded out of position. The curves for this characteristic indicate that these differences in premolar arrangement are of significant value for separation of the skull types.

Similar relations between size of the mandibular premolar teeth and premolar regions are not so significant for differentiation of types. At this point there is an overlapping of the curves for the two types, but there is also a general tendency to be in accord with the maxillary premolar condition.

The mandibular index is distinctly lower in the long typed skulls than in the short bulldog typed, but the difference for this feature is not very great. The divergence of the rami of the mandible is greater in the bulldog typed skull than in the shepherd dog type.

We may conclude from the several charts based on skull measurements (text-figs. 51–54) and the curves in text-figure 55 that the skulls of the long muzzled dog breeds differ in various respects within their group, yet all exhibit characteristics clearly contrasted with those of the short faced breeds. We may term these two groups, for simplicity, the long-skull and short-skull types.

The skull characteristics which are most important for distinguishing the long and short types are indicated by the indices rather than the linear measurements, and the curves in text-figure 55 show that for this purpose certain indices are far more significant than others. In some breeds of both groups the cranial indices almost overlap, while the mandibular index shows no overlapping between the two types, and the skull index, palatal index and upper facial index are increasingly far apart for the long and the short skulls. The values for snout index show the maximum difference between the two types.

The only linear comparisons which bring out the differences between the types are those concerning the relations of total anteroposterior width of the premolar teeth to the premolar regions of the upper and lower jaws, and the proportion of palate length to length of skull base.

Whether the several differences between these skull types are inherited primarily and independently as separate characters or whether the divergent patterns of the dog skulls result from definitely modified endocrine functions may be analyzed by a study of the hybrids resulting from crosses between the extreme types. We have attempted to analyze the modifications found in the bulldog skull by selecting pure breeds with strongly pronounced head characters and crossing these with standard wolf-like long-skull breeds showing no symptoms of the short bulldog head. In the study of so complex a condition as the development of the skull, it has been necessary to resort to several different breed crosses, just as was done for the study of the achondroplasic leg conditions discussed in previous chapters.

### Crosses Between Dog Breeds With Highly Contrasted Types of Skulls

The foregoing survey of skull measurements and indices for the different pure breeds of dogs emphatically demonstrates that the skull is a complex of structures, many of which are quite independent in their mode of expression. It is found, for example, that two parts intimately related in function, such as the upper and lower jaws, may develop along very different lines, causing extreme structural disharmony and consequent impairment of efficiency. Also such closely related parts as the maxilla and the teeth which it supports may be strangely out of accord. Maldevelopment of the nose and upper face rendering respiration difficult and noisy is a constant characteristic in certain dog breeds.

These and a number of other less marked distortions result as peculiar growth reactions distinctly deviating from the original canine pattern. Our general problem is to determine whether such growth distortions are the results of modifications in the endocrine systems of the different breeds or whether they are due to genetic mutations which give rise to such developments even in a normal endocrine environment, or again, whether there may be a genetic linkage or association between these structural distortions and modifications of one or several of the endocrine glands.

Early surgical removal of endocrine glands and the feeding of gland products or the injection of glandular extracts cannot supply conclusive answers to the above problems. Such experimental procedures have yielded most valuable results tending toward an understanding of the influences of the internal environment on developmental expression, but they have supplied almost nothing to aid in the understanding of the significance of the genetic constitution in determining the responses. Do the constitutions of certain tissues force them to give definite structural reactions in spite of various internal modifications? For instance, must there always be a genetic basis for the typical acromegalic modification as seen in nature, or may this be experimentally induced in any individual? These and many other similar questions of serious importance have not been answered with any degree of satisfaction by experimenting with glandular ablations or hormonal applications.

Human families, as has been frequently mentioned, may possess modified structural features of the cranium and face closely the same as are found among the dog breeds. It is evident that a complete understanding of the nature and origin of such peculiarities involves a careful analysis of the genetic background along with a consideration of the endocrine complications which may accompany these distorted expressions. The most valuable material available for this genetic and endocrinal analysis is found to be the long established and carefully selected dog breeds of distorted types. This fact has been previously emphasized in other connections.

In attempting the analysis of head types and distortions, we have employed several different crosses between highly contrasted breeds. Thus we are able to determine whether a given peculiarity arises in the same way in all cases or breeds, and whether it behaves in similar genetic fashion for all cross combinations. Whether or not the peculiarity is irregular and highly variable in its genetic reactions or in its expression is of much importance.

For this study the Boston terrier, French bulldog and English bulldog were selected as representing three different and quite uniformly established degrees of bulldog modification of the skull.

The short headed "pug-nosed" Boston terrier was crossed with the long skulled, long and slender nosed dachshund, and the French bulldog, having a more pronounced bull typed skull, was also crossed with the dachshund. All three breeds are partially dwarfed. The English bulldog, which is of normal size and possesses an extremely shortened skull with prognathous lower jaw, abbreviated muzzle and upturned nose, was crossed with both the German shepherd and the bassethound. The latter two breeds are also of normal size and possess the primitive wolf-typed skull with long, perfect biting jaws.

The Pekingese has a spherical cranium and almost completely abbreviated facial skeleton, and, although not of typical bulldog pattern, has an extremely achondroplasic skull. We have crossed this dog with the long faced, partially dwarfed dachshund as well as with the normal full sized Saluki, which possesses one of the longest and slenderest of dog skulls. Finally we employed the flat "monkey faced", almost round skulled midget Brussels griffon in crosses with the dachshund. These hybrid matings furnish a wide variety of combinations for head types in association with both the normal sized and dwarfed proportions.

Without further introduction we may now proceed to survey the head types and conditions which arise in these several hybrid groups.

### THE GENETICS AND EXPRESSION OF SKULL CHARACTERISTICS IN HYBRIDS BETWEEN THE BOSTON TERRIER AND THE DACHSHUND

This cross has been made in both directions with individuals of each breed serving as sire and as dam in the production of the first hybrid generation. The several matings and the numbers of individuals concerned in the different generations have been previously referred to in connection with the discussion of achondroplasia in the dachshund. Therefore we shall refer only briefly to these facts in the present discussion.

The measurements and indices of the skull of the Boston terrier and the dachshund are given in table 1, and again

TABLE 2

| | DACHSHUND $4\frac{1}{2}$ | | | | BOSTON TERRIER $3\frac{1}{2}$ | | | | $F_1$ $3\frac{1}{2} \times 4\frac{1}{2}$ | | | | $F_2$ $9\frac{1}{2} \times 5$ | | | | Bx BOSTON TERRIER $1\frac{1}{2} \times 4\frac{1}{2}$ | | | | Bx DACHSHUND $2\frac{1}{2}$ | | | |
|---|---|---|---|---|---|---|---|---|---|---|---|---|---|---|---|---|---|---|---|---|---|---|---|---|
| | Av. | P.E. | S.D. | | Av. | P.E. | S.D. | Av. | P.E. | S.D. | Av. | P.E. | S.D. | Av. | P.E. | S.D. | Av. | P.E. | S.D. | Av. | P.E. | S.D. | | |
| Cranial Index | 69.75 | ±.730 | 2.165 | | 77.2 | ±.749 | 2.482 | 73.667 | ±.749 | 2.482 | 70.75 | ±.631 | | 70.75 | ±1.116 | 2.867 | 71.75 | ±2.000 | 5.932 | 69.5 | ±.716 | 1.5 | | |
| | 69.75 | .730 | 2.165 | | 77.2 | .749 | 2.482 | 71. | .749 | 2.482 | 70.6 | .881 | | 76.6 | .924 | 2.739 | 75. | .924 | 2.739 | 69.5 | .716 | 1.5 | | |
| Skull Index | 66.5 | .167 | .5 | | 105.2 | 1.227 | 4.069 | 73. | .763 | 2.53 | 72.642 | .584 | | 72.642 | .636 | 1.633 | 74.875 | 1.102 | 4.622 | 70.5 | .239 | .5 | | |
| | 66.25 | .199 | 1.479 | | 119.6 | 2.104 | 6.974 | 77.5 | .749 | 2.482 | 79.857 | .948 | | 79.857 | .559 | 1.659 | 90.75 | 1.534 | 4.548 | 70.5 | .239 | .5 | | |
| Palatal Index | 66.25 | .499 | 1.479 | | 119.6 | 2.104 | 6.974 | 82.25 | .749 | 2.482 | 84.0 | .888 | | 84.0 | .730 | 2.165 | 92.125 | .994 | 4.166 | 71.5 | .239 | .5 | | |
| Snout Index | 61.0 | .983 | 2.916 | | 155.6 | 3.861 | 12.8 | 80. | .863 | 2.926 | 84.571 | 1.503 | | 84.571 | 2.231 | 6.615 | 97.125 | .625 | 2.619 | 70.5 | 1.670 | 3.5 | | |
| Upper Facial Index | 96.5 | .499 | 1.479 | | 38. | .763 | 2.53 | 68.75 | .739 | 2.449 | 69.357 | 1.594 | | 69.357 | 1.458 | 4.323 | 116.25 | 2.327 | 9.756 | 86.5 | 1.670 | 3.5 | | |
| Breadth hgt. Index. | 84.75 | .839 | 2.488 | | 90.2 | .749 | 2.482 | 88.25 | 1.855 | 2.482 | 90.643 | .690 | | 90.643 | .499 | 1.479 | 93.875 | 1.543 | 6.470 | 88. | .477 | 1.0 | | |
| % Palato total Skull Base. | 59. | .238 | .707 | | 52.6 | .560 | 1.855 | 56.25 | .883 | 2.926 | 55.357 | .211 | | 55.357 | .499 | 1.479 | 55.75 | .503 | 2.107 | 57.5 | .239 | .5 | | |
| % Palatal total Palate. | 33.5 | .843 | 2.0 | | 31.2 | .883 | 2.926 | 33.25 | | | 33.5 | .287 | | 33.5 | .804 | 2.385 | 36.375 | .237 | .992 | 35. | .477 | 1.0 | | |
| % Orb.Orb.Fr/ Orb.Inc.Mx. | 23. | 1.60 | 4.744 | | 10. | .739 | 2.449 | 16.5 | | | 16.143 | .720 | | 16.143 | 1.228 | 3.640 | 10.75 | .672 | 2.817 | 21.5 | .239 | .5 | | |
| % Max.PreM./PreM. Region. | 97.5 | 1.407 | 4.172 | 148.333 | | | | 106.5 | 2.069 | 5.31 | 104.786 | 1.884 | | 104.786 | .876 | 2.598 | 131.143 | 3.757 | 14.740 | 104. | 1.908 | 4.0 | | |
| Mandibular Index. | 51. | .631 | 1.871 | 71.4 | .984 | | 3.262 | 57. | | | 59.286 | 1.188 | | 59.286 | .716 | 2.122 | 64.25 | 1.085 | 4.548 | 52.5 | .716 | 1.5 | | |
| % Mand.PreM./PreM. Region. | 84.5 | .773 | 2.292 | 115.667 | 3.517 | | 9.031 | 95.25 | | | 89.545 | 1.525 | | 89.545 | 1.177 | 3.491 | 101. | 5.381 | 17.837 | 94. | 2.862 | 6.0 | | |
| Ant.Post.Dim. of Max.PreMs. | 37. | .318 | .816 | 34. | | | | | | | 34.273 | .814 | | 34.273 | .841 | 2.160 | 33.875 | .795 | 3.333 | 40.5 | .716 | 1.5 | | |
| Ant.Post.Dim. of Mand.PreMs. | 28.75 | 2.80 | .829 | 25.5 | .506 | 1.5 | | 30.667 | .506 | 1.5 | 25.3 | .895 | | 25.3 | .486 | 1.247 | 24.25 | .661 | 2.773 | 31.5 | .716 | 1.5 | | |

Av.—Average  P.E.—Probable error  S.D.—Standard deviation

separately in connection with their hybrid progeny in table 2. Figure 1 in text-figure 56 (p. 239) serves particularly well in familiarizing the reader with the highly contrasted patterns of these pure breed skulls. The solid line in this figure represents the sagittal outline of the dachshund skull from exact measurements. This outline is very long, drawn-out and low. The broken sagittal outline is of the Boston terrier skull and is superimposed on the dachshund as closely as possible. This skull is short and proportionately much higher than that of the dachshund. The two angles drawn below the sagittal outlines, one in solid line and the other in broken line, represent the positions of the anterior alveolar ends of the mandibles in reference to the anterior tips of the upper jaws. The dachshund mandible lies in a normal position, that is a little posterior to the end of the upper jaw, while the mandible of the Boston terrier lies immediately below the anterior tip of the upper jaw, which indicates malocclusion of the teeth; that is, instead of normal occlusion of the lower incisors, these incisors are in end to end opposition to those of the upper jaw.

The differences between these two skulls are shown in a more comprehensive way in plates 36 and 37. Figure 1 in plate 36 illustrates the long, normally proportioned dachshund skull. The upper face, jaws and teeth are typical of the standard typed dog skull. The dental occlusion is perfect, with the lower incisors fitting in closely behind the upper incisors and the lower canine tooth locking into the interval between the third upper incisor and the upper canine. This arrangement is responsible for the efficient, sharp and tearing

PLATE 36

EXPLANATION OF FIGURES

Skulls of the cross between the dachshund and Boston terrier showing contrasting characteristics of the pure breeds and the resulting conditions in the first and second generation hybrids.

1  Dachshund 84 ♀.      4  $F_2$ 294 ♀.
2  Boston terrier 76 ♀.  5  $F_2$ 296 ♀.
3  $F_1$ 130 ♀.           6  $F_2$ 295 ♀.

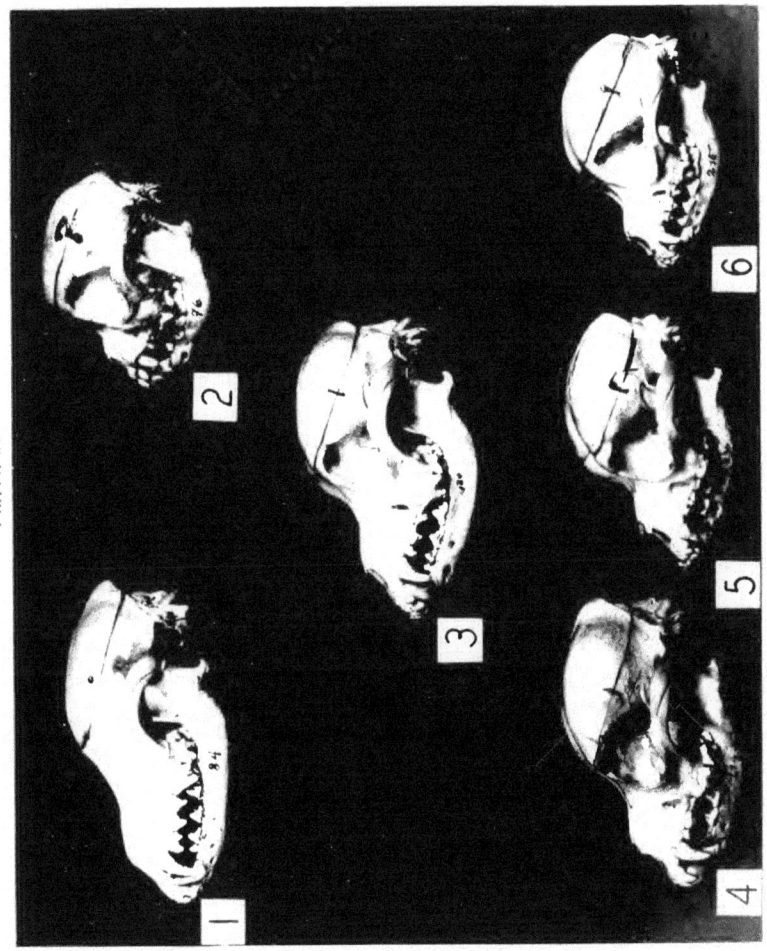

bite of the dog. The four upper and lower premolar teeth are set with abundant space and without occlusal contact, which is a normal arrangement and provides for the holding and carrying of objects in an almost non-biting region of the mouth. As is well known, a dog may handle delicate and breakable articles and carry them without damage for long distances. When changing the nest, the bitch frequently carries the tender young puppies in her mouth without injury to or complaint from the puppies. Further, this premolar interval with no occlusal contact enables the dog to hold and carry an object with a minimum of muscular effort. The molar teeth of the dachshund skull show a well adapted occlusion. These form the jaws' strongest pulling and crushing arrangement. In taking hold to tear and chew the food from a carcass, the dog opens his jaws wide and twists his head far to one side in order to secure a strong grip on the tough tissues with the molar teeth. As the photograph clearly shows, the dachshund's jaws are properly formed to function in these several ways.

Figure 2 in plate 36 illustrates the Boston terrier skull. This skull as a whole is high and short when compared with that of the dachshund. The cranium approaches a spherical shape and is smooth dorsally, with no sagittal crest and only a feebly expressed occipital spine. The frontal region is strongly arched, giving prominence to the forehead and exaggerating the depression at the nasion. The zygomatic arch is short and strongly curved, making the skull wider than it is long; this is clearly seen in figure 4 of plate 38. The jaws in this dog are much shortened and are poorly

PLATE 37

EXPLANATION OF FIGURES

Mandibles of the cross between the dachshund and Boston terrier showing contrasting characteristics of the pure breeds and the resulting conditions in the first and second generation hybrids.

1  Dachshund 255 ♀.  4  $F_2$ 294 ♀.
2  Boston terrier 76 ♀.  5  $F_2$ 296 ♀.
3  $F_1$ 130 ♀.  6  $F_2$ 295 ♀.

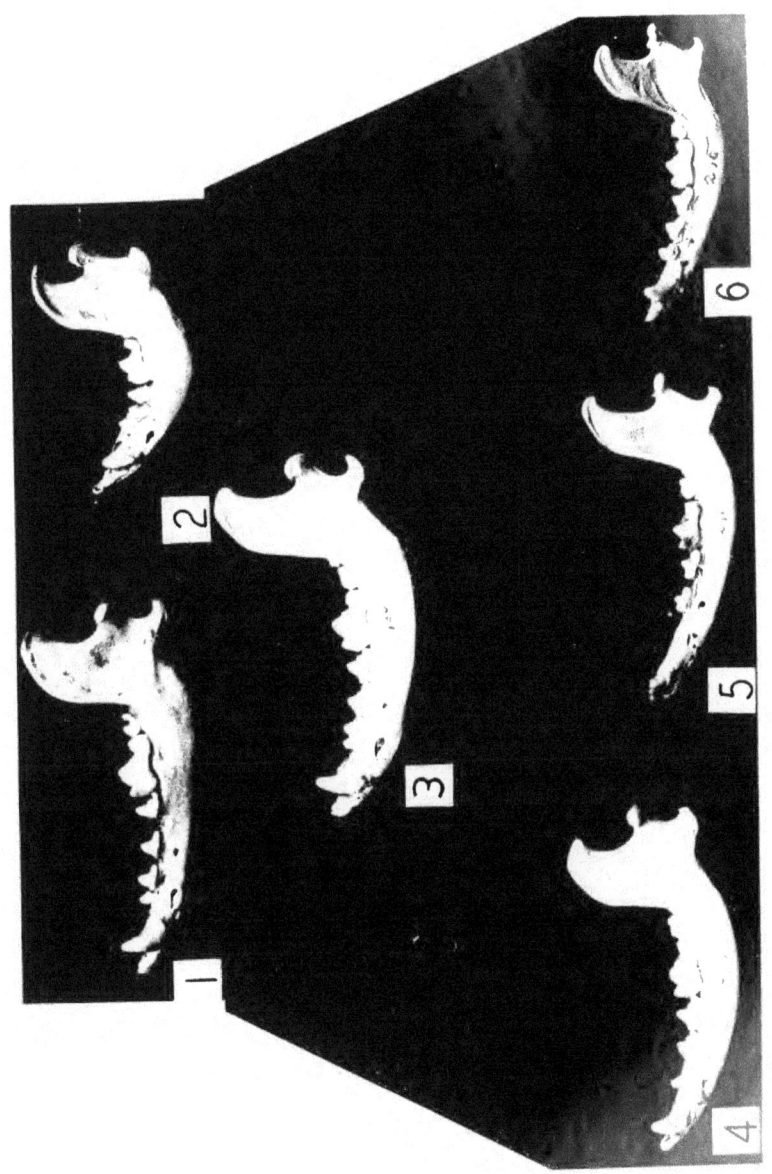

designed for the functions of the normal dog which were so perfectly seen in the dachshund. The edges of the upper and lower incisor teeth are seen in the photographs to be in end to end relation. This disturbs a proper occlusion of the canines which interfere with and grind against one another in various ways. The premolar carrying interval is very short in some Boston terrier skulls and entirely lost in others. As shown in plate 38 (fig. 4), the upper fourth premolar may be set transversely across the jaw, that is, at right angles to the normal position for this tooth. The upper molar teeth, instead of being arranged in an almost straight line as in the dachshund, follow an angular course, the apex of which projects out laterally. Malocclusion of the molars is present to various degrees.

The poor dental accommodation of these short, deformed jaws is associated with numerous defects of the teeth themselves. Improper occlusion tends to loosen the teeth and wear them down in abnormal ways. As clearly shown in plate 38, resorption of alveolar bone may occur as a result of improper pressure. The teeth may be defective in structure with hypoplasia of the enamel; this may also be seen in the photographs of the Boston terrier skulls. Figure 2 in plate 37 shows that the lower jaw of the Boston terrier is not only short, but curved as well, with the anterior end directed upward. This is in direct contrast to the long, straight lower jaw of the dachshund (fig. 1).

The differences between the skulls from these two pure dog breeds are so readily distinguishable and are so numerous that before attempting to compare their detailed indices and measurements with those of their hybrids it would be best to proceed with a general consideration of the gross appearance of these hybrids during life.

Photographs from life of the Boston terrier and the dachshund and five of their $F_1$ hybrids are shown in plate 29 (p. 127). The hybrid skull and lower jaw are illustrated in plates 36 and 37 (figs. 3). The sagittal outline of the $F_1$ skull is drawn in solid line in figures 2 and 3 of text-figure 56; in

PLATE 38

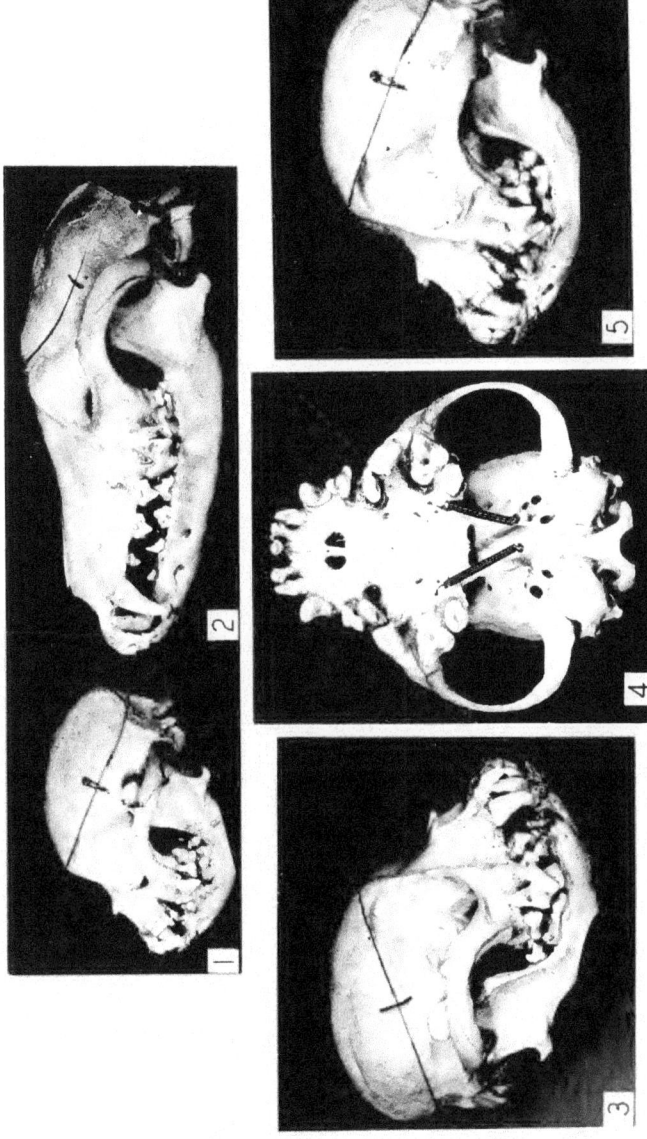

Several views of the deformed Boston terrier skull showing condition and arrangement of teeth, resorption of the alveolar bone and other typical characteristics. The long, slender Saluki skull is shown for comparison.
1, 3, 4, 5, Boston terrier 136 L.   2, Saluki 328 L.

figure 2 the $F_1$ outline is superimposed over the sagittal outline of the dachshund skull, and in figure 3 over the outline of the Boston terrier skull. The fit with the dachshund skull is closer than that with the Boston terrier skull. The $F_1$ hybrids, as shown in plate 29, resemble in general the dachshund more closely than they do the Boston terrier. As in the dachshund, the legs are short, the tails are long and the ears droop or hang. Although the $F_1$ head is larger and less slender than that of the dachshund, it shows even greater deviation from the typical Boston terrier head. The face is shortened and the region of the nasion is decidedly depressed; the zygomatic arch is more strongly curved than is usual in the long skull, and the lower incisors project beyond the upper, giving a slight degree of undershot jaw. The features of this skull are in many ways a combination of the two parent types.

These hybrids were vigorously active and normal in behavior, having advantages in both size and stamina over both the pure stocks.

Of the eight $F_1$ individuals produced, four were breeding bitches, and sixty-five offspring were whelped as a second, $F_2$, hybrid generation. The living $F_2$ animals exhibited wide differences in size, body form and head type and can be seen in plates 30 (p. 129), 39 and 40. Figures 1 and 2 in plate 39 show litter mate sisters, one with an almost Boston terrier head and the other with an almost dachshund-like head. Photographs of the skulls of these sisters are seen as figures 4 and 5 in plate 36; figure 4 approaches the dachshund skull somewhat more closely than does the skull of the $F_1$ (fig. 3). The dental occlusion in these $F_2$s is normal, and the teeth are perfectly developed and strong. The zygomatic arch is not so strongly bowed as in the $F_1$ skull, and the nasion is not very deeply depressed.

Figure 5 in plate 36 is a high, short skull, and some of its features are quite different from either parent stock. The maxilla is short and there is almost complete dental malocclusion. The teeth in this skull show an extreme state of enamel hypoplasia. This condition is identical with the hypoplasia of enamel usually attributed to dietary deficiencies, but such deficiencies cannot be considered the contributing cause in this case, since, as stated above, this animal was a litter mate of the one supplying the skull in figure 4 which contains perfect teeth, and both these animals were reared under identical dietary conditions. They developed in the same uterus, suckled the same mother and fed from the same dish. The environment and diet were fully adequate for perfect dentition in one animal, while under the same conditions the second individual produced defective, malformed teeth with deficient enamel. The constitution of the animal itself was no doubt at fault rather than that there were deficiencies of environment. A further consideration of dental defects occurring in abnormal constitutions is given in a chapter beyond.

Figure 3 in plate 39 shows a puppy with spherical and enlarged cranium and pronounced internal hydrocephalus. The facial features of this puppy were Boston terrier-like, and there was pronounced exophthalmos. Figures 4–7 in this plate illustrate other, very different head and facial features occurring in the second hybrid generation. A large percentage of the $F_2$ hybrids have a protruding lower jaw, the undershot condition, while a few of them show an opposite arrangement with a prognathous upper jaw extending beyond the anterior end of the mandible and giving a "rat-nose" or overshot condition. It is strange to find such reversed arrangements in the skulls of animals derived from the same cross breeding.

The lengths of upper and lower jaws are inherited independently, and when a member of a breed with long jaws is crossed with a short jawed dog, the $F_2$ hybrids show various disharmonious combinations and may have either a long upper jaw associated with a very short mandible or the reverse, a short muzzle associated with a long prognathous mandible. Figure 5 in plate 39 and the photographs in plate 40 illustrate the prognathous maxilla or the "rat-nose" de-

PLATE 39

Second generation dachshund-Boston terrier hybrids showing wide differences in head type and the structural disharmony between upper and lower jaws.
1 296 ♀.  2 294 ♀.  3 353 ♀.  4 780 ♂.  5 620 ♂.  6 782 ♂.  7 781 ♀.

feet. Figure 1 of plate 40, as well as others of this type, would seem to have inherited the upper face and maxilla of the dachshund in association with the abbreviated and curved lower jaw of the Boston terrier. If when such a dog is alive the hand of the observer is placed in the mouth of the animal so as to hide the lower jaw, the head takes on the typical appearance of a dachshund, but if the hand is placed so as to cover the upper face, allowing a view of the lower jaw and chest only, the resemblance is that of a Boston terrier, even to the white hair on the chin and chest. Were the internal chemical environment alone responsible for the patterns of growth, it would be difficult to imagine the lower jaw developing on one pattern while the upper jaw of the same head followed an entirely different mode. Rather does this disharmony between the two jaws appear to be a mosaic condition, with dachshund tissues in the maxilla and Boston terrier constitution in the mandible.

Be this as it may, the structural disharmony between the upper and lower jaws in these hybrids is extremely pronounced, and the resulting functional inefficiency is such that the animal is unable to eat food from a flat surface or shallow plate. Such dogs must be fed from a deep pan so that the abbreviated lower jaw may aid in grasping the food. The growth in length of the face occurs largely after the early weeks of puppy life, and the act of suckling the mother is thus not seriously impaired by these subsequently developed malformations of the mouth. As puppies, these dogs are the same as those of other breeds, all of which have, at birth, a short muzzle and rather flat face with upper and lower jaws of almost equal length.

The genetic basis for the disproportionately short mandible is definitely transmitted. The male $F_2$ in plate 40 (fig. 1) was mated with a non-related $F_1$ Boston terrier-dachshund, and some of the puppies produced exhibited the same prognathous condition of the upper jaw. A male offspring of this mating is shown from two aspects in figures 3 and 4. Several other such matings between the $F_2$s and $F_1$s have

Dachshund-Boston terrier hybrids showing the "rat nose" defect resulting from the inheritance of the long upper jaw of the dachshund associated with the short mandible of the Boston terrier.
1 F₁ 620 ♂ (see also fig. 5, pl. 39). 2-3 F₂ × F₁ 1246 ♂.

given similar results, and this phenomenon also occurs in hybrids from crosses of other long and short jawed breeds.

Attention may be called to the fact that the Boston terrier is bred for the white on its chest and chin, as shown in plates 29 (fig. 2) and 43 (fig. 1) (pp. 127 and 245). The dachshunds, as seen in the same plates, never show such markings. In the hybrids from this cross, the short Boston terrier-like lower jaw has the white markings underneath, and the chests are also white, as plate 40 indicates. The appearance of these animals suggests that the anterior ventral region is Boston terrier in constitutional type while the rest of the head and the body clearly resembles the dachshund.

A fair impression of the general range in type of the hybrid skulls may be obtained by again referring to plates 36 and 37 and text-figure 56. Plate 36 shows the entire skulls, and

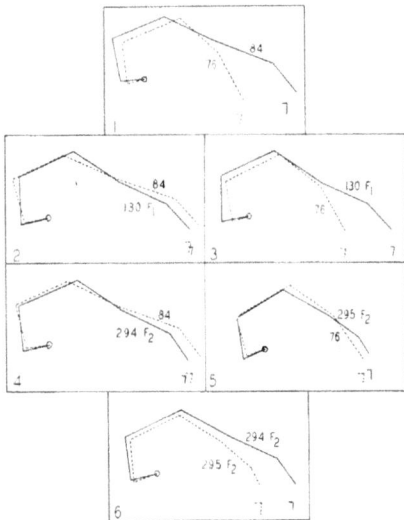

Text-figure 56. Sagittal outlines based upon exact measurements of the skulls of the Boston terrier and dachshund, and of the first and second generation hybrids from this cross. (1) 84 ♀ dachshund and 76 ♀ Boston terrier; (2) 84 ♀ dachshund and 130 ♀ $F_1$; (3) 76 ♀ Boston terrier and 130 ♀ $F_1$; (4) 84 ♀ dachshund and 294 ♀ $F_2$; (5) 76 ♀ Boston terrier and 295 ♀ $F_2$; (6) 295 ♀ $F_2$ and 294 ♀ $F_2$.

plate 37 shows the mandibles arranged in the same manner as the skulls. We have called attention before to the characteristics of the two parent types. In the $F_1$ hybrids the skulls are very closely alike, as should be the case when two parent stocks are homozygous or pure for their skull types. The $F_1$ skull and lower jaw are seen to be a combination of the two parental types, the total complex for neither type being completely dominant. Certain elements of the skull of the Boston terrier, such as the strongly curved arch of the zygoma and the depression at the nasion, may be found in combination with the long facial skeleton and strong dentition of the dachshund. Evidently all these different features are transmitted in a somewhat independent fashion; they are certainly, at least, expressed in such a manner.

Figures 4, 5 and 6 in these two plates illustrate the skulls and mandibles of three litter mates in the second hybrid generation. These skulls show various recombinations of the features derived from the two parent types. Figure 4 approaches somewhat nearer the dachshund type than does the $F_1$ skull, yet the approach is by no means complete. Figure 5 has more the features of the Boston terrier and has also extremely defective dentition and malformed teeth with hypoplasia of the enamel. Figure 6 could almost be that of a Boston terrier with imperfect facial type. In rather rare cases the pure bred Boston terriers may diverge from type to as great an extent as does this last skull.

In text-figure 56 (figs. 4 and 5) the sagittal outlines of two of these highly different $F_2$ skulls are superimposed

PLATE 41

EXPLANATION OF FIGURES

Ventral view of the mandibles of the dachshund, Boston terrier and their first and second generation hybrids showing concave articular surface of the condyles in the dachshund as opposed to the convex surface in the Boston terrier, and the expression of this character in the hybrids. The difference in the degree of divergence of the mandibular rami in these two breeds and its expression in the hybrids is also clearly shown.

1 Dachshund 255 ♀.   2 Boston terrier 536 ♀.   3 $F_1$ 130 ♀.
4 $F_2$ 722 ♂.   5 $F_2$ 1522 ♂.   6 $F_2$ 781 ♀.   7 $F_2$ 810 ♂.

GENETIC TYPE AND THE ENDOCRINES 241

PLATE 6

over outlines of the dachshund and the Boston terrier skulls. In the one case (fig. 4), the fit with the dachshund is very close while in the other (fig. 5), the $F_2$ skull closely approaches the outline of the Boston terrier. The sagittal outlines of these two $F_2$ skulls are shown for contrast in figure 6.

The appearance of such divergent patterns in the skulls of $F_2$ litter mates makes it quite certain that external environment and dietary elements have little if any responsibility in the differential expression of these types. The various structural responses are due to the differences in the basic constitutional complexes possessed by the several individuals. The chance that two animals in the second hybrid generation will ever receive exactly the same total genetic composition from their $F_1$ parents is extremely small, and as a consequence members of this generation differ greatly in size, form and proportions, as the photographs in plate 30 very well illustrate. The instincts and behaviors of these $F_2$ animals are also widely variable.

A minor peculiarity of the mandibular condyle in the dachshund skull was found to be inherited in this cross as a single factor recessive character. Figure 1 in plates 41 and 42 shows that the articular surface of the condyle in the dachshund mandible is concave rather than convex as in other dog skulls, illustrated for the Boston terrier in figure 2 of these plates. Figure 3 illustrates an $F_1$ mandibular condyle approaching the Boston terrier in type although the expression is not complete. The four $F_2$ mandibles (figs. 4–7) were selected to illustrate the distribution and expression of the character in this generation. About one fourth of the condyles are typically convex as in the Boston terrier, half are slightly flattened as in the $F_1$, and one fourth show

PLATE 42
EXPLANATION OF FIGURES

Enlarged photographs of the condyles of the same mandibles as shown in plate 41 showing in more detail the differences in the articular surfaces in the pure breeds and the resulting expression in the hybrids.

1 Dachshund 255 ♀.  2 Boston terrier 536 ♀.  3 $F_1$ 130 ♀.
4 $F_2$ 722 ♂.  5 $F_2$ 1522 ♂.  6 $F_2$ 781 ♀.  7 $F_2$ 810 ♂.

PLATE 12

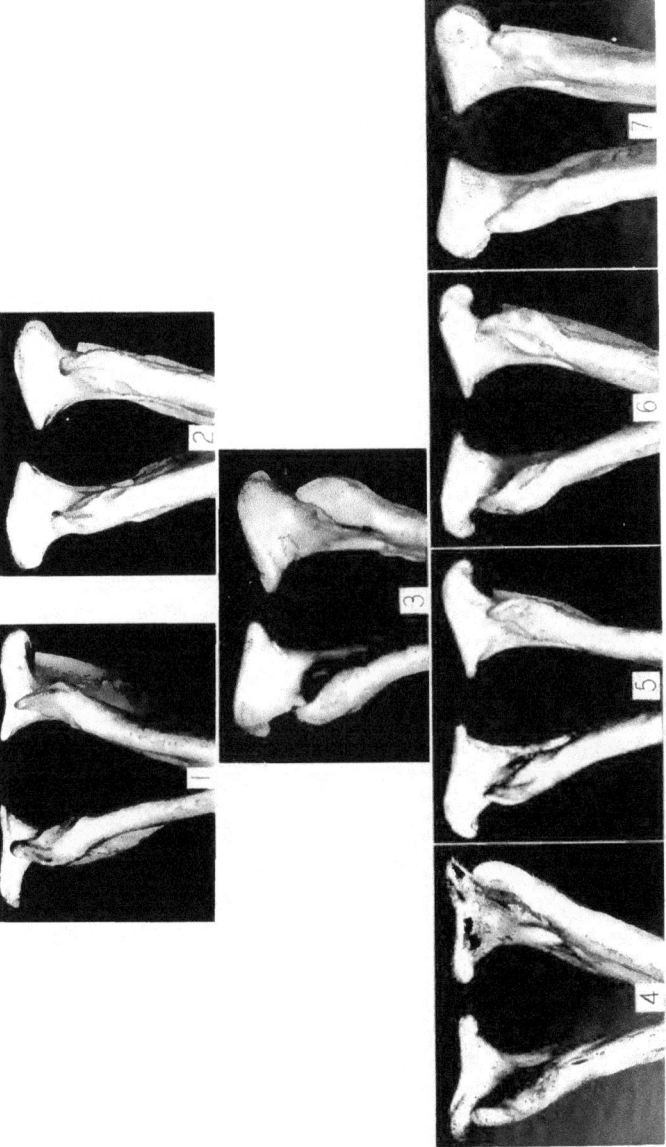

the fully concave dachshund condition. The character behaves as a typical single factor recessive, although in the heterozygous condition it is not completely suppressed and the convex pattern of the condyle is somewhat flattened.

In plate 41 the differences in the degree of divergence of the mandibular rami in the dachshund and Boston terrier are readily noticeable. This divergence is again uniformly intermediate in the $F_1$ hybrid while the $F_2$ hybrids present various degrees of divergence. The $F_2$ mandible in figure 4 shows a wide degree of divergence, as found in the Boston terrier, and associated with this condition is the concave condyle typical of the dachshund. This association indicates that the concave condyle of the dachshund is not genetically related or linked with the general form of the dachshund mandible.

*The backcrosses of the $F_1$ hybrid Boston terrier-dachshund on the two pure stocks.* Backcrossing the $F_1$ hybrid on the Boston terrier parent stock tends to give some quite well expressed Boston terrier heads in combination with various characters from the two stocks. Plate 43 illustrates the two parent stocks (figs. 1 and 2) and an $F_1$ male (fig. 3). Breeding such a male back to the Boston terrier female produced the hybrid photographed as a mounted specimen in figures 4 and 5. This backcross hybrid exhibits several peculiar combinations of characters from the two stocks. In the first place, the head is fairly typical of the Boston terrier. The ears are held in the erect Boston terrier position in spite of the fact that they are very large and long, a characteristic

PLATE 43

EXPLANATION OF FIGURES

Backcross of the $F_1$ dachshund-Boston terrier with the pure Boston terrier showing recombinations of characters of the two pure stocks.

1 Boston terrier 435 ♀.
2 Dachshund 255 ♀.
3 $F_1$ 128 ♂.
4–5 Backcross 634 ♂. Note the long dachshund-like ears carried in the erect Boston terrier position, and the short achondroplasic legs of the dachshund in combination with the short, bent tail and coat markings of the Boston terrier breed (see also fig. 4, pl. 44).

PLATE 43

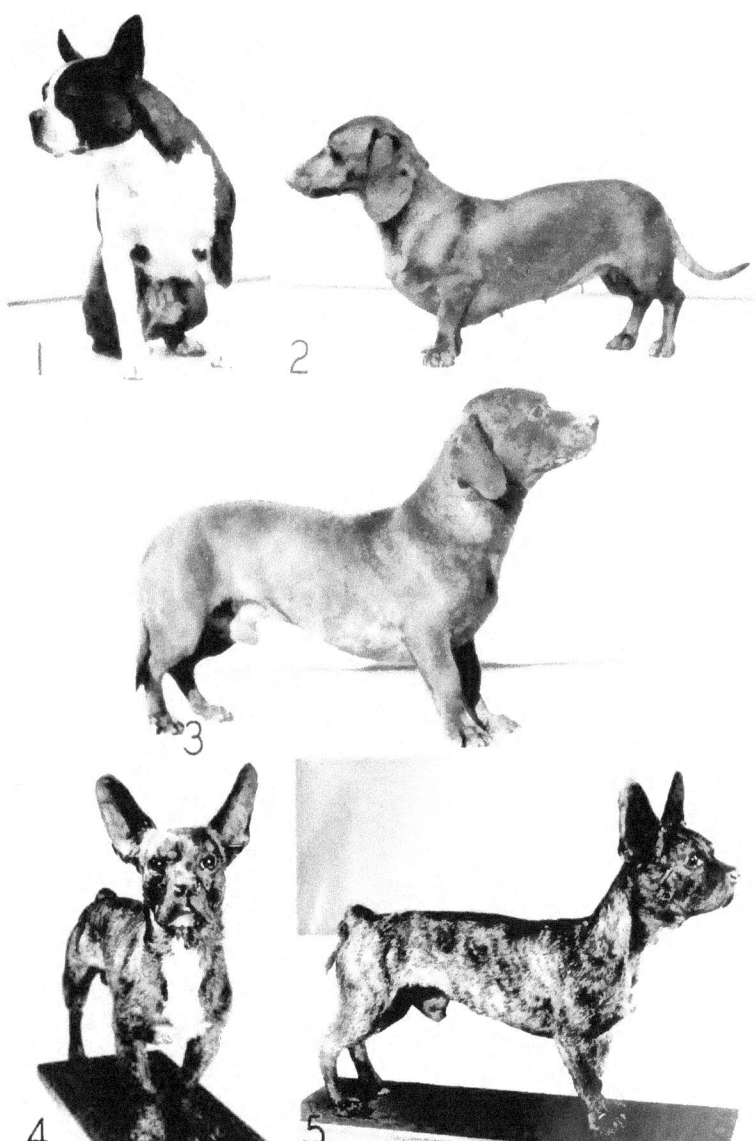

of the dachshund. A very strange and unusual appearance is produced by carrying the large ears of the dachshund in this erect Boston terrier manner. The body of the animal is long and the legs are short and achondroplasic as in the dachshund, yet the tail is short and much bent and the coat color is brindle with a white chest and chin as in the Boston terrier. This animal was a medley of strange combinations, yet a very pugnacious individual, easily dominating all other members of his litter.

The same animal, standing between a litter brother and sister, is shown photographed from life in plate 44 (fig. 2). Immediately below (fig. 4) is a photograph of the mounted specimen, and it is readily seen that the excellent mount in no way distorts the features of the living animal. Nine different backcross individuals showing a wide range of character differences are illustrated in plate 44. A great variation in size and type is found among them.

The backcross of the $F_1$ on the dachshund parent stock does not give nearly so wide a variety in form as when the cross is made on the Boston terrier. Plate 45 contains photographs of five backcross hybrids from two litters whelped by dachshund mothers. The bodies, legs and tails all closely resemble those of the dachshund, while white hair spots on some of the chests are reminiscent of the Boston terrier color pattern. All the heads approach the dachshund in general form. The ears are large and drooped, although in some animals they may be partially raised and on the whole can be more easily lifted and moved than is possible in the pure dachshund. The face in the backcross hybrid is long, the depression at the nasion mild and the forehead lowered, all in dachshund manner.

This survey of the general appearance of the living animals in the several filial generations and backcrosses and the examination of the general skull characteristics in the hybrids have prepared the way for a more exact and detailed consideration of the inheritance and development of the individual characters in the hybrid skulls. It is on the basis of

PLATE 44

Hybrids derived from backcrossing the $F_1$ dachshund-Boston terrier with the pure Boston terrier stock showing the great variation in size, skull type and other physical characters.

1  525 ♀ (L) and 524 ♂ (R).   4  634 ♂.
2  (L to R) 636 ♀, 634 ♂, 635 ♂.   5  Litter 828-831.
3  525 ♀.

PLATE 45

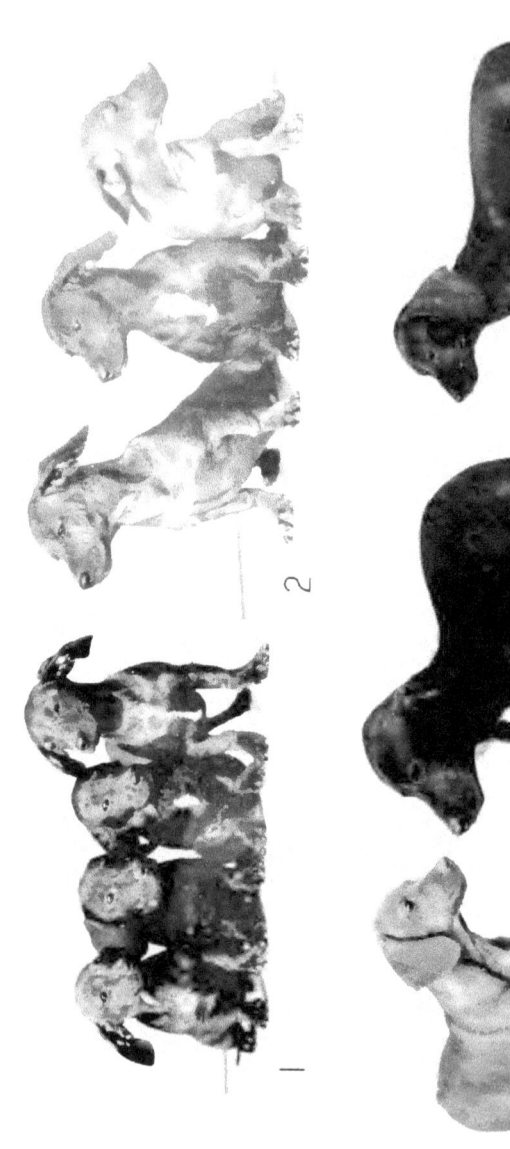

Hybrids derived from backcrossing the $F_1$ dachshund-Boston terrier with the pure dachshund stock. Hybrids from this backcross do not show nearly so great a variation in size and form as was shown for the backcross with the Boston terrier stock. In general they resemble the dachshund.

1 (L. to R.) 349 ♂, 350 ♂, 348 ♀, 348 ♀.   2 (L. to R.) 311 ♀, 312 ♀, 310 ♂.   3 340 ♀.   4 342 ♀.   5 350 ♂.

these characters that we hope in later chapters to evaluate the relations between the genetic constitution and the influences of various endocrinal modifications in the differentiation of structural and functional types.

*The expression of individual features in the skulls of Boston terrier-dachshund hybrids.* The indices and various proportional relationships which have been found significant for the differentiation of types among the skulls of the different pure dog breeds have been calculated for each of the several hybrid generations resulting from the Boston terrier-dachshund cross. The figures for these indices and proportions and the probable errors and standard deviations for the two parent stocks and their hybrids are recorded in table 2 (p. 227). The pure stocks are strongly contrasted in almost every skull feature, and in a large majority of these features the $F_1$ hybrids more nearly approach the dachshund than they do the Boston terrier.

The figures derived from the $F_2$ animals are interesting in that the averages for the various dimensions approach in value those recorded for the $F_1$ generation. Such average figures, however, completely conceal or level out the wide differences which exist among the $F_2$ skulls. The standard deviations also fail to convey a proper appreciation of the variation in skull measurements. In the cases of the most significant indices and proportions, however, the deviations in the $F_2$ column are larger than those in the $F_1$ column, in some instances even being several times as large.

The backcross of the $F_1$ on the Boston terrier also gives wide variations in skull form, and again high standard deviations are seen. In contrast to these, the backcross on the dachshund produces skulls with features nearly the same as those of the dachshund and without great variation in pattern. Although the number of skulls is not sufficient to fully demonstrate the latter point, numerous observations from other specimens confirm this statement.

The indices and proportions in table 2 are not derived from a large number of skulls and might readily be objected to as not having a sufficient statistical basis. This, however, is not the primary importance of the table. It is arranged simply to present the average values for the several skull features and show the tendency in the different hybrid generations to incline toward one or the other parent type. A discussion of the detailed figures in table 2 is unnecessary for present purposes, since the expression of the skull features in the hybrids may be more easily appreciated from a consideration of the following charts.

Text-figure 57 has been arranged to show the measurements of three skull features in the Boston terrier-dachshund cross. Each heavy vertical line represents the exact value of the dimension concerned in one particular skull.

The upper series in the figure represents the total skull index which is calculated by multiplying the zygomatic width by 100 and dividing this by the length of skull base. The value of the indices is indicated by the figures at the left. The four dachshund skulls have uniformly low indices, 66 to 67, while the four Boston terrier skulls are uniformly high, 100 to 107, these being as wide as or wider than they are long.

Three $F_1$ skulls fall between the two parent stocks for this index, their values being from 77 to 79; the deviation from the round head of the Boston terrier is about twice as great as from the long dachshund typed skull.

The skulls of eleven $F_2$ hybrids show a wide range of from 71 to 90 for this skull index. The lowest $F_2$ index is 4 units above the dachshund and the highest is 17 below the Boston terrier. Five of the eleven $F_2$ skulls are shorter than the $F_1$, five are about equal in index, and one is decidedly longer. In other words, the $F_2$ skulls tend to spread in two directions for this index, approaching the values of both parent stocks; but in the cases represented by the chart, they fall a little short of complete arrival in either direction. This important fact is altogether concealed by averaging the $F_2$ skull indices; an average would fall close to that of the $F_1$, as recorded in table 2. The standard deviation in this table is, however, three times as large for the $F_2$ index as for the $F_1$.

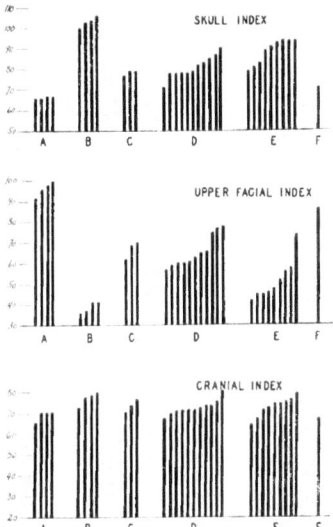

Text figure 57. Dachshund-Boston terrier cross. Each vertical line represents an index based on exact measurements of the skull, and the same series of skulls was used for the three charts. A, dachshund; B, Boston terrier; C, $F_1$; D, $F_2$; E, backcross of $F_1$ with the Boston terrier; F, backcross of $F_1$ with the dachshund.

When the $F_1$ hybrid is crossed back with the Boston terrier, the skull index of the hybrid offspring is raised. The indices for nine of these backcross hybrids range from 79 to 94. They approach more nearly the Boston terrier skull index than does the $F_2$ group, and eight are above the indices for the $F_1$s.

Only one skull represents the total skull index for the backcross of the $F_1$ on the dachshund. This skull is longer than the $F_1$ parent but is 4 units higher than the index for the dachshund skull.

These charts would suggest that the high and low skull indices are truly hereditary features, although they are definitely not simple or single factor dominant or recessive characters. The value of this index depends upon the influence of several genetic elements, and those tending to bring about the low or long skull index are somewhat more dominant in their influences than are the elements concerned in producing the short Boston terrier skull. For this reason the skull index in the $F_1$ hybrid approaches more nearly that of the dachshund.

The middle chart in text-figure 57 represents the values of the upper facial indices, nasal length to palatal width, for the same skulls, arranged in the same sequence as for the indices examined above. It will be recalled that the upper facial index has been calculated in a manner the opposite of that for the other indices, and thus the long skulls have high rather than low values.

The upper facial index in the four pure dachshund skulls ranges from 92 to 100, in contrast with only 36 to 41 for the four Boston terrier skulls. The $F_1$s range from 62 to 70 and again fall between the two parent types, being more nearly midway between them for this index than for the total skull index.

The eleven $F_2$ skulls have a wide range for upper facial index, from 57 to 78; five of these are below the $F_1$ range, having a broader facial skeleton, and three have a higher index than the $F_1$s. The $F_2$ with the lowest index fails to reach the Boston terrier index by 16 units and the $F_2$ with the highest index falls short of that of the dachshund by 14 units. Thus the $F_2$ range fails to reach the parent indices to about the same degree in both directions.

The upper facial index in the backcross of the $F_1$ on the Boston terrier ranges from 42 to 74. One of these skulls approaches to within only one unit of the Boston terrier index and thus is, for this feature, practically Boston terrier in type. In spite of the fact that five out of the nine backcross skulls closely approach the Boston terrier for this index, one of those among the other four is further from the Boston terrier than are the three $F_1$ skulls.

The single backcross dachshund skull with an upper facial index of 87 closely approaches this index in the pure dachshund.

From this chart it would appear that the upper facial index, like the skull index, is definitely hereditary and also depends upon the influences of more than one specific genetic element for the complete expression of its type. The expression of an index might very well be of this nature, since the factor or factors chiefly concerned in determining, for instance, nasal length, may not be the same as those influencing palatal width. Both these features are employed in calculating the values for the upper facial index.

The lower chart in text-figure 57 is arranged so that the cranial indices of the several generations of skulls may be compared. The differences in this index for the two pure stocks are quite definite although not so large as the two previous indices. The range for cranial index in the hybrid generations is also more limited than those shown in the above charts. In spite of these smaller differences, the cranial indices still follow very clearly the trends which have been pointed out for the two indices above. The $F_1$ cranial index lies between those of the parents. The indices among the eleven $F_2$s range completely down to those for the dachshund skull and, in the other direction, fully up to those for the Boston terrier skull. The backcross on the Boston terrier gives skulls with very variable cranial indices; although some return to the Boston value, others fall as low as those of the dachshund. All in all, this chart would seem to indicate in definite fashion that cranial indices are of different values in the dachshund and the Boston terrier skulls, even though the values for the two breeds differ to only a slight degree.

Text-figure 58 charts the very significant snout indices and palatal indices for the same series of skulls represented in text-figure 57. The snout index, as we may recall, is the character which presents the widest differences between the normal long skulls and the short bulldog typed skulls. The difference in palatal indices for the two types is also very great.

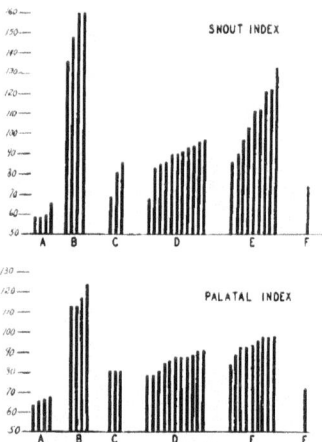

Text-figure 58. Dachshund-Boston terrier cross. Each vertical line represents an index based on exact measurements of the skull. The series of skulls for these two charts is the same as used for text-figure 57. A, dachshund; B, Boston terrier; C, $F_1$; D, $F_2$; E, backcross of $F_1$ with the Boston terrier; F, backcross of $F_1$ with the dachshund.

The long, narrow snout of the dachshund gives a very low index, which ranges from 59 to 66 for the four skulls represented. In wide contrast to this, the four Boston terrier skulls range from 136 to 160, the indices being between two and three times higher than for the dachshund skulls. The snout indices in the three $F_1$ skulls are very variable as compared with the three other indices discussed above. The features controlling this index are very delicate in their response, and their expression is dependent upon the degree of homozygosity of head factors in the genotype of the Boston terrier parent. We therefore made a particular effort to employ only carefully bred Boston terriers with fully pronounced skull types. The snout indices of the $F_1$ skulls approach more nearly those of the dachshund than the Boston terrier. The determination of the short muzzle for the Boston terrier is largely recessive in its expression.

The eleven $F_2$ skulls range for snout index from 68 up to 97, thus also tending to lie nearer the dachshund than the Boston terrier values and again emphasizing the complex and rather recessive nature of the determining influences which bring about the short muzzle in the Boston terrier. The highest snout index among the eleven $F_2$ skulls is 39 units below the lowest index for the four Boston terrier skulls and only 31 units above the highest dachshund index. In contrast to this wide divergence, the lowest $F_2$ index approaches to within 2 units of the range of the dachshund index, while it is 68 units below the lowest Boston terrier index.

The backcross offspring from the $F_1$ hybrid bred with the Boston terrier stock show a considerable range in snout index, from 86 to 133. The highest snout index in these nine skulls approaches close to the pure Boston terrier index, while the lowest is far higher than those of the dachshund. This backcross on the Boston terrier gives expression to much of the recessive quality for the short muzzle. Only one backcross on the dachshund skull is represented in the chart, and, as would be expected, its index is low and approaches the long muzzled type.

The chart for the palatal indices in these skulls closely follows, though in less pronounced manner, the spread of the snout indices. The three $F_1$ skulls have a closely uniform palatal index value, and the indices for the eleven $F_2$ hybrids fall almost midway between those for the two parents. The nine skulls from the hybrids produced by a backcross on the Boston terrier show indices only slightly higher than the $F_2$ levels although they are more uniform in their approach to the indices for the pure Boston terrier. The single skull from the $F_1$ backcrossed on the dachshund parent is close to the pure dachshund level.

The five charts for the several skull indices in text-figures 57 and 58 clearly indicate that these characters, all widely contrasted in the pure dachshund and Boston terrier breeds, are expressed in the hybrid generations in such ways as to suggest that they are strictly genetic in nature and not the results of dietary and environmental responses. Such records, however, are not sufficient for determining whether endocrine modifications or typical internal environmental changes are the primarily inherited qualities underlying the different growth and structural reactions indicated through these indices. Only the gross and microscopic examination of the endocrine glands and the observations on their functional reactions, which are to be presented in following chapters, can supply the additional necessary evidence from which to draw satisfactory deductions regarding these matters.

The curves in text-figures 59 and 60 give a clear picture of the records for the five indices just considered, and illustrate as well seven other skull features from the different generations of this cross breeding. In text-figure 59 the solid line represents the dachshund parent and the dash-dot line the Boston terrier parent; the average of skull features for the $F_1$ hybrid generation is shown by the line of dashes, and the dotted line illustrates the average for the second, $F_2$, generation. The figures at the left vertical border of the graph indicate the values for the several points along the curves. The different indices and proportions considered are listed immediately below the points on the curves which represent their values. The cranial indices of the two parent stocks are not widely different and the average indices for both hybrid generations fall about half way between them. Other readings on the graph are readily understood. The main points of interest are that the average indices for every feature in the first and second generation hybrids are near together and that the curves for these indices follow more closely the curve of the dachshund parent than the Boston terrier.

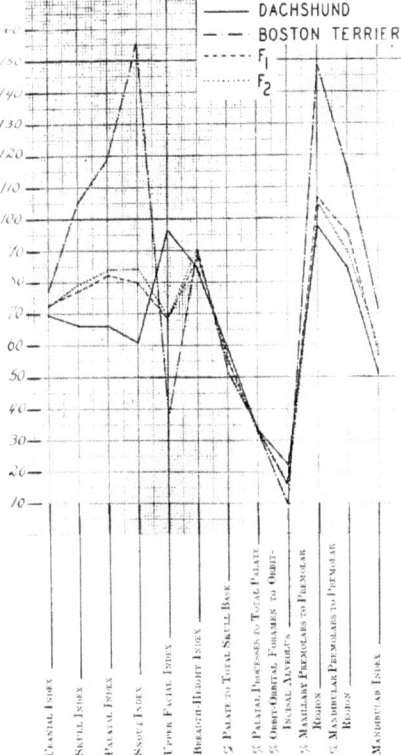

Text-figure 59. Dachshund-Boston terrier cross. Comparison of skull measurements and indices of the pure breeds and their first and second generation hybrids.

In text-figure 60 the dotted line represents the average record for the backcross of the $F_1$ with the Boston terrier, and the dashed line the backcross of the $F_1$ with the dachshund. All other arrangements are the same as in text-figure 59. The curve for the Boston terrier backcross follows the curve of the pure Boston terrier, and in most features approaches it very closely. The backcross dachshund curve lies even closer to that of the pure dachshund.

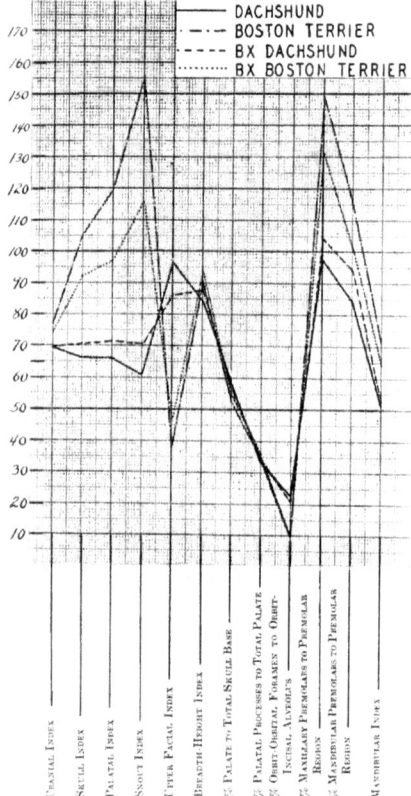

Text figure 60. Dachshund Boston terrier cross. Comparison of skull measurements and indices of the pure breeds and their backcross hybrids.

Both sets of curves indicate that in general the individual features of the long normal dachshund typed skull tend to dominate comparable features in the short wide skull of the Boston terrier.

### THE BEHAVIOR OF SKULL CHARACTERISTICS IN THE FRENCH BULLDOG-DACHSHUND HYBRIDS

A second cross was made between the dachshund and another dog of bull type, the French bulldog, in order to discover whether the hybrid reactions would be similar to those in the cross between the Boston terrier and dachshund. The French bulldog is somewhat different from the Boston terrier and is a more pronounced bull type. $F_1$ hybrids were again produced by crosses in both directions, and their general type and appearance were the same whether the dam used was a dachshund or a French bulldog.

Plate 46 illustrates the general appearance of the two pure parent stocks as well as that of their $F_1$ and $F_2$ hybrids. Through the descriptions in connection with the foregoing cross we are familiar with the dachshund characteristics (fig. 1). The French bulldog (fig. 2) is a European breed frequently spotted dark brindle and white, but in this country it is usually bred for a uniform brindle pattern. The head is much heavier and of more pronounced bull type than is the head of the Boston terrier. The mandible is prognathous or undershot, projecting beyond the maxilla in the same way as is strongly presented by the English bulldog. The forehead is high and rounded, and the eyes are somewhat exophthalmic, though not to so great a degree as in the Boston terrier. The rounded bat-like ears are carried erect. In action and behavior the French bulldog is not generally so nervous nor so excitable as the Boston terrier.

The two $F_1$ French bulldog-dachshund hybrids (figs. 3 and 4, pl. 46) are, in the photographs, almost indistinguishable from the $F_1$ Boston terrier-dachshund hybrids seen in plate 29 (p. 127). So close is the resemblance that it is very difficult to avoid confusing the living $F_1$ hybrids of these two crosses. They not only resemble one another physically, but behave very much alike. The French bulldog-dachshund $F_1$ is the somewhat stockier and slightly heavier of the two. Its head is far from the French bulldog type, and is shorter and with a more pronounced "stop" than that of the dachshund. The ten $F_1$s used in our experiments were all closely alike; five were used for adult comparisons and five were examined closely as young puppies. The matings among these $F_1$ hybrids produced four litters of $F_2$ animals, numbering six, seven, five and three puppies. These litter sizes are a little above the expectation for French bulldog whelpings but are easily within the fecundity expectations for the dachshund.

The $F_2$ generation of hybrids from this cross contains individuals of extremely varied form and type, just as was the case among the Boston terrier-dachshund $F_2$ progeny. Among the twenty-one $F_2$ specimens, a large majority were, as would be expected, short legged. A number of them showed prognathism of the lower jaw because of the abnormal shortness of the maxilla. In other cases there was opposition of the incisors, yet normal occlusion of these teeth was also presented. Sixteen of them had long straight tails as in the dachshund grandparent, one showed a long tail bent at several places, two had tails slightly shortened and bent and two possessed the typical short, twisted "screw-tail" of the French bulldog stock. Plate 46 (figs. 5-8) shows four litter mate $F_2$ French bulldog-dachshunds. It would be difficult to find four dogs of about the same body size differing more widely in type than do this male dog and his three litter sisters. The bitch in figure 5 has a typical dachshund head, body

PLATE 46

EXPLANATION OF FIGURES

Cross between the contrasted dachshund and French bulldog showing inheritance of skull characteristics and other physical features in the first and second generation hybrids.

1  Dachshund.
2  French bulldog.
3-4  $F_1$ hybrids.

5-8  $F_2$ hybrids.
5  668 ♀.     7  666 ♂.
6  667 ♀.     8  669 ♀.

GENETIC TYPE AND THE ENDOCRINES 261

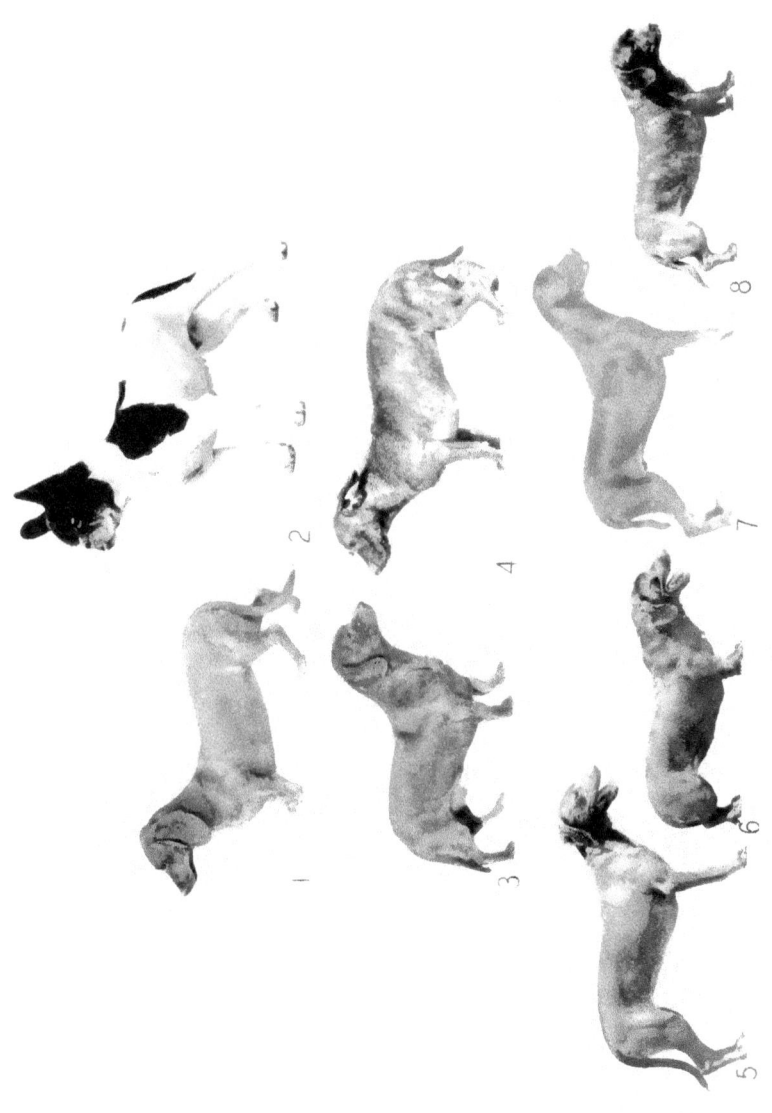

PLATE 46

and long tail, and associated with these, the long slender
hound typed legs; this animal on short legs would be an
almost perfect dachshund. Figure 7 shows the male dog with
stocky long legs nearer bull-bone type than hound. His head
is shortened and heavy but far different from the complete
bull type, and his tail is bent and partially shortened although
not to the extent of that of the typical French bulldog. The
other two members of this litter have short, dachshund legs.
The animal in figure 6 has a long dachshund-like head. The
sister in figure 8 shows a prognathous mandible below the
short upper jaw, and her head, though quite definitely modified, is of poor bulldog type.

The four litter mates just described were carefully prepared and mounted in life-like postures for a permanent
record of their wide differences in form. Photographs of
these mounted specimens, each facing its own skeleton, are
shown in plate 47. The contrasts in head form are clearly
seen, both from the mounted specimens and the skeletons.
The heads and skulls in the two upper photographs (figs. 1
and 2) approach the dachshund pattern, and figures 3 and
4 show bulldog features. Further comparisons of the living
and mounted specimens, as well as other $F_2$ individuals, may
be had by referring to the photographs in plate 48. An almost
completely bulldog-headed young animal is shown in figure
4 of this plate.

The general skull characteristics of this cross are seen
somewhat more clearly in plate 49. Figure 1 is from a pure
French bulldog and should be contrasted with the dachshund
skull (fig. 2). The typical $F_1$ hybrid skull is shown as figure
3. Figure 4, an $F_2 \times F_1$, shows a slight undershot condition
with opposition of the incisors; in figure 5, an $F_2$, the mandible
is undershot to a greater degree; and in figure 6, another $F_2$,
the occlusion of the teeth is quite normal. Since both jaws
are equally shortened, the premolar carrying interval in this
skull (fig. 6) is almost obliterated. A mild degree of enamel
hypoplasia on some of the teeth, mostly on the canines, is
seen in all three skulls.

## PLATE 47

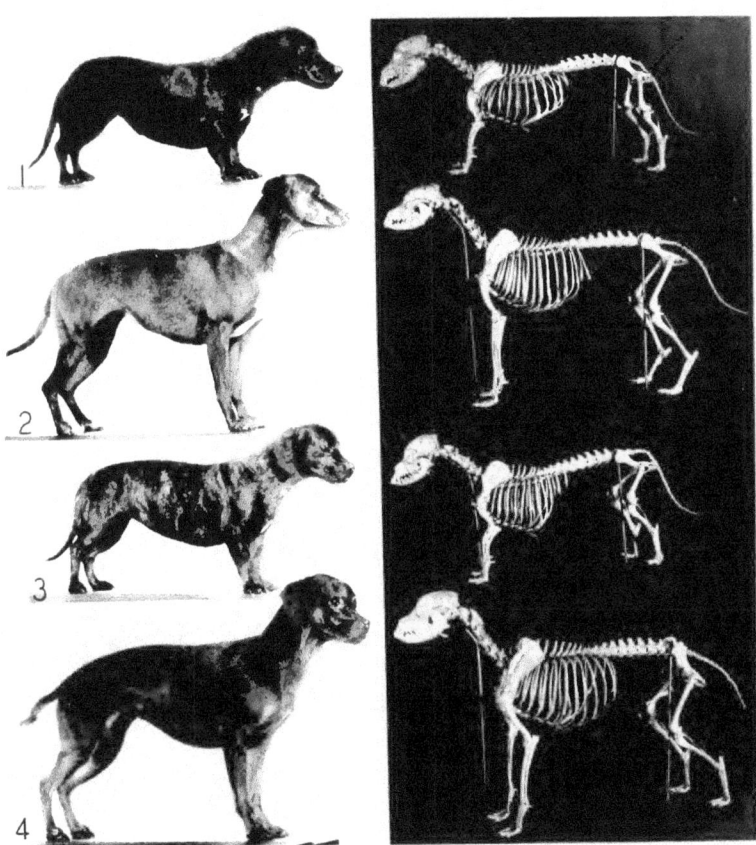

Dachshund-French bulldog second generation hybrids. The four animals shown from life in figures 5 to 8, plate 46, were carefully mounted for permanent record, and the mounted specimens are shown here, together with their skeletons, to emphasize the wide differences in form to be found among litter mates of this generation.

1  667♀.    2  668♀.    3  669♀.    4  666♂.

PLATE 48

Second generation dachshund-French bulldog hybrids showing the great variation in size, head characteristics and other physical features.
1 (L to R) 667 ♀, 669 ♀, 668 ♀, 666 ♂.    3 (L to R) 669 ♀, 668 ♀.
2 (L to R) 667 ♀, 666 ♂.                  4-6 Kennel numbers not noted.

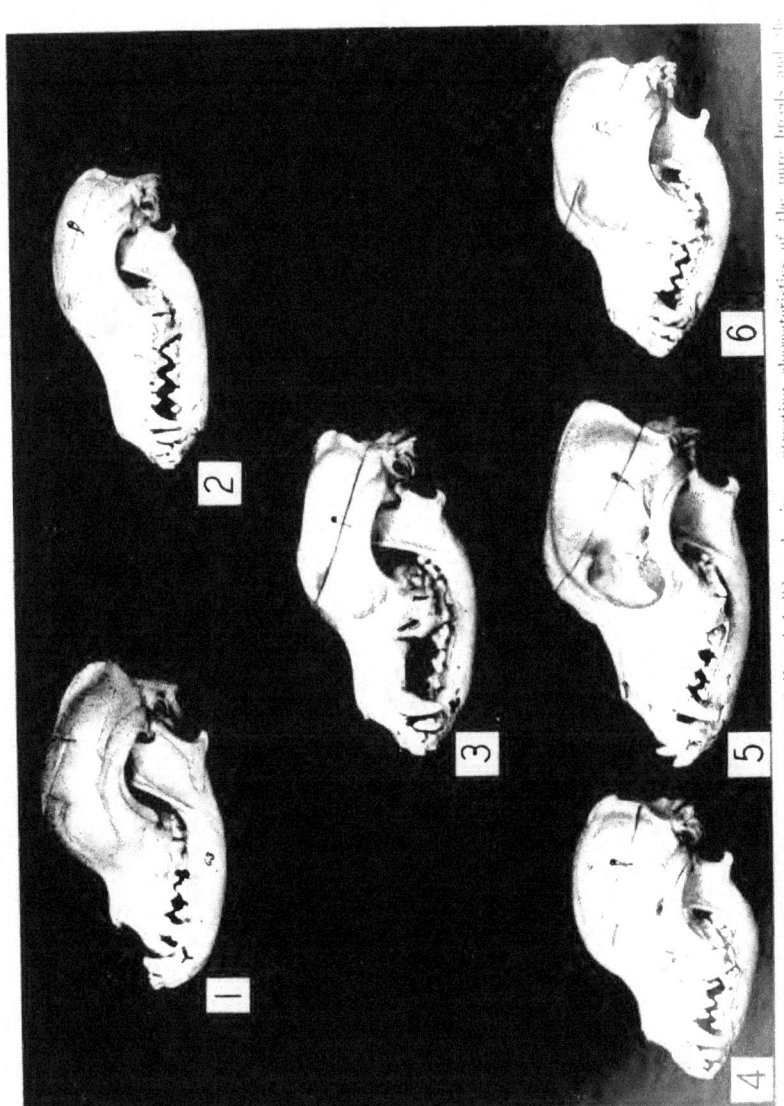

Skulls of the cross between the dachshund and French bulldog showing contrasting characteristics of the pure breeds and the varying conditions in the hybrids.

1. French bulldog ♂.  2. Dachshund 455 ♀.  3. $F_1$ 230 ♂.  4. $F_1$ $F_2$ 653 ♀.  5. $F_1$ 110 ♂.  6. $F_1$ 111.

The skull indices and proportions for the pure parent breeds and the averages for the same features in the $F_1$ and $F_2$ generations are given in table 3. The average indices for the three $F_1$ hybrid specimens are very similar to the averages for the eleven $F_2$ skulls, although the standard deviations for the $F_2$ group are, of course, much greater than for the $F_1$s. The deviations for some of the $F_2$ features are several times larger than they are for the same characters in the $F_1$. Again the average indices for the hybrid generations fall between the indices of the two pure stocks. The range in expression of the skull characters in the $F_2$ hybrids towards one or the other parent type is not evident from this table. In order to show this range, charts representing the indices for the individual skulls have been arranged.

Text-figure 61 presents charts representing the cranial index, total skull index and palatal index for the individual skulls of the two pure stocks and the hybrid generations.

The cranial index in the two pure breeds is not very different, although it is, on the whole, slightly lower in the dachshund. Considering the very elongated total skull of the dachshund, its cranial index is really quite high and approaches the bulldog index more closely than is usual for long skulls, such as those of the bassethound and foxhound.

The cranial indices in the $F_1$ skulls are well below those for the French bulldog and are actually lower than the index in three of the four pure dachshund skulls.

Eleven $F_2$ skulls show the full expectation for range in the cranial index. Four of these indices are lower than that of the lowest dachshund and two are as high as the highest cranial indices for the French bulldog. The $F_2$ indices also range well above and below two of the three $F_1$s. The average of the $F_2$ indices, as shown in table 3, completely conceals this wide range, but does indicate the tendency of the hybrid skulls to fall between the two parent types in this characteristic.

TABLE 3

PRENCH BULLDOG

| | DESHOUND | | | PRENCH BULLDOG | | | $F_1$ | | | $F_2$ | | |
|---|---|---|---|---|---|---|---|---|---|---|---|---|
| | Av. | P.E. | S.D. | Av. | P.E. | S.D. | Av. | P.E. | S.D. | Av. | P.E. | S.D. |
| Cranial Index | 68.75 | .730 | 2.165 | 73. | .945 | 2.449 | 67. | 1.670 | 3.5 | 70.714 | .880 | 3.452 |
| | | | | 75. | | | 61.5 | 1.204 | 3.091 | 67. | 1.370 | 4.062 |
| Skull Index | 69.75 | .730 | 2.165 | 73.5 | .773 | 2.292 | 65.333 | | | 69.363 | .833 | 4.096 |
| | 66.5 | .167 | .5 | 103.667 | .778 | 7.134 | 73.5 | 1.193 | 2.5 | 71.286 | 1.305 | 5.119 |
| Palatal Index | 66.5 | .167 | .5 | 99. | | | 72.5 | .800 | 2.055 | 75.75 | .935 | 2.773 |
| | 66.25 | .167 | .5 | 102.5 | 2.059 | 6.104 | 72.667 | | | 74.818 | .909 | 4.470 |
| Snout Index | 66.25 | .499 | 1.479 | 115. | .954 | 2.449 | 71. | .239 | | 76.571 | 1.187 | 4.656 |
| | 61.0 | .983 | 2.916 | 111. | 1.131 | 3.354 | 76.5 | .486 | 1.247 | 82.25 | 1.177 | 3.491 |
| Upper Facial | | | | 115.5 | 4.826 | 12.382 | 75.667 | | | 79. | 1.086 | 5.343 |
| Index | 61.0 | .983 | 2.916 | 164.667 | 4.904 | 14.543 | 71. | .716 | 1.5 | 76.429 | 1.988 | 7.789 |
| | 96.5 | .499 | 1.479 | 142. | 1.101 | 2.828 | 74.5 | .800 | 2.055 | 87.5 | 3.325 | 9.862 |
| Breadth hgt. | 96.5 | .499 | 1.479 | 159. | | | 73.333 | | | 80.455 | 2.057 | 10.120 |
| Index | 84.75 | .839 | 2.488 | 40. | 1.102 | 3.269 | 82. | 3.338 | 7.0 | 76.286 | 2.192 | 8.589 |
| | 59. | | .707 | 45. | 1.193 | 2.5 | 72. | 3.005 | 7.717 | 70.25 | 2.097 | 6.220 |
| % Palate total | | | | 41.25 | | | 75.667 | | | 74.091 | 1.695 | 8.339 |
| Skull Base | 59. | .238 | .707 | 97.5 | .918 | 2.357 | 91. | 1.908 | 4.0 | 92. | .452 | 1.772 |
| % Palatal total | 33.5 | .843 | 2.0 | 95. | .733 | 1.886 | 94. | 1.272 | 3.266 | 96. | 1.768 | 5.244 |
| Palate | | | | 96.667 | .553 | 1.639 | 94. | | | 93.455 | .806 | 3.963 |
| % Orb.Orb.Pr/ | 33.5 | .843 | 2.0 | 53. | | | 56. | .239 | .5 | 57.571 | .186 | .728 |
| Orb.Inc.Alv. | 58. | .843 | 2.0 | 53.25 | | | 56.5 | .183 | .470 | 54.75 | .368 | 1.090 |
| % Max.PreM. PreM. | | | | 82. | | | 56.333 | | | 56.545 | .329 | 1.616 |
| Region | 58. | .843 | 2.0 | 32. | 3.033 | 7.789 | 36. | .716 | 1.5 | 55.167 | .189 | .687 |
| Mandibular Index | 23. | 1.60 | 4.744 | 15. | | | 36.5 | .486 | 1.247 | 57.5 | .343 | 2.5 |
| % Mand.PreM. PreM. | 23. | 1.60 | 4.744 | 13. | | | 36.333 | | | 36.1 | .431 | 2.022 |
| Region | 97.5 | 1.407 | 4.172 | 14.5 | 2.294 | 6.801 | 21. | 1.431 | 3.0 | 15. | 1.029 | 4.036 |
| Ant.Post.Dim. of | 97.5 | 1.407 | 4.172 | 138. | 2.385 | 5.0 | 15. | 1.457 | 3.742 | 17.75 | .602 | 1.785 |
| Max.PreMs. | 51. | 1.407 | 4.172 | 129. | 2.293 | 5.888 | 17. | | | 16. | .741 | 3.643 |
| Ant.Post.Dim. of | 51. | .631 | 1.871 | 135. | 1.503 | 3.859 | 108. | .716 | 1.5 | 112.286 | 3.148 | 12.349 |
| Mand.PreMs. | 84.5 | .773 | 2.292 | 65.667 | 1.153 | 3.419 | 111. | | | 115. | 3.530 | 10.469 |
| Av. Average | 84.5 | .773 | 2.292 | 66. | 1.089 | 10.5 | 109.5 | .716 | 1.5 | 113.273 | 2.393 | 11.771 |
| | 87. | .318 | .816 | 67.25 | 7.495 | 22.226 | 52. | .486 | 1.247 | 54.857 | .645 | 2.631 |
| | 37. | .318 | .816 | 81.5 | 1.670 | 3.5 | 51.5 | | | 51. | 1.601 | 4.744 |
| | 28.75 | .280 | .829 | 125. | 1.285 | 3.300 | 51.667 | 2.145 | 4.5 | 54.545 | .717 | 3.526 |
| | 28.75 | .280 | .829 | 96. | .477 | 1.0 | 100.5 | 1.457 | 3.742 | 94.429 | 2.594 | 10.168 |
| | | | | 40. | .477 | 1.0 | 101.5 | | | 98.75 | 2.149 | 15.270 |
| | | | | 56.5 | | | 101. | | | 96. | 2.529 | 12.429 |
| | | | | 37.667 | | | 11. | .239 | .5 | 38.857 | .652 | 2.167 |
| | | | | 21. | | | 12. | .954 | 2.0 | 44. | .233 | .707 |
| | | | | 21. | | | 41.5 | .662 | 1.700 | 41.364 | .511 | 2.513 |
| | | | | | | | 52. | | | 20.286 | .204 | 1.979 |
| | | | | | | | 33. | | | 31. | .413 | 1.225 |
| | | | | | | | 32.667 | | | 31.636 | .507 | 2.496 |

P.E. Probable error     S.D. Standard deviation     1 male only.

Seven cranial indices are given for the skulls of hybrids derived from crosses between the $F_1$ and $F_2$ generations. These indices have a wide range and are quite comparable to those of the $F_2$ group. The $F_2$ female employed in producing these hybrids was almost indistinguishable in type from an $F_1$ animal. Therefore her progeny, sired by an $F_1$

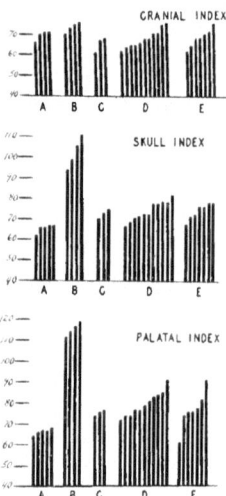

Text-figure 61. Dachshund-French bulldog cross. Each vertical line represents an index based on exact measurements of the skull, and the same series of skulls was used for the three charts. A, dachshund; B, French bulldog; C, $F_1$; D, $F_2$; E, $F_1 \times F_2$.

male, might be expected to follow rather closely the true $F_2$ group.

The total skull indices represented by the middle chart in text-figure 61 furnish a much wider contrast between the two pure types than do the cranial indices discussed above. Five dachshund skulls range for total skull index from 62 to 67. Four French bulldog skulls range in total skull index from 94 to 111, two of these being almost as wide as long and the other two showing greater width than length. Thus the skull types of these breeds are extremely divergent for the total skull index.

Three $F_1$ hybrid skulls show total skull indices from 70 to 75, the lowest being only 3 units above the dachshund group while the highest falls 19 units below the index for the longest French bulldog skull. For this feature, therefore, the $F_1$ skull is very close to that of the dachshund.

Among the eleven $F_2$ skulls, the total skull indices range from 67 to 82. The lowest of these indices reach those of the dachshund, while the highest is 12 units below the lowest skull index for the French bulldog and 29 points below the highest. When crossed with the dachshund typed skull, this character is equally as recessive in composition in the skull of the French bulldog as it is in the Boston terrier skull.

The palatal index, also a highly different character in these two types of skulls, is shown in the bottom chart in this figure, and its record is closely the same as that for the total skull index. Again the hybrid generations tend to approach more nearly the largely dominant dachshund pattern.

Text-figure 62 records the snout index and the upper facial index for the same skulls as are represented in the previous figure. The top chart shows the snout index to be the most highly contrasted feature in the skulls of the dachshund and the French bulldog, just as was found for the skulls of the Boston terrier and dachshund. The upper facial index is again represented as derived from a method of calculation the reverse to that for the other indices, and thus the long face is indicated by the large rather than the small index value.

The snout indices for the $F_1$ skulls are very far from those for the French bulldog but comparatively close to those for the dachshund. The $F_2$ indices vary; the lowest is down to those for the dachshund, but the highest is only about half as much as the French bulldog values.

270   CHARLES R. STOCKARD AND A. L. JOHNSON

The lower chart, which represents the upper facial index, indicates a close parallel between this index and the snout index.

The indices of the various skull features and the relative proportions between certain linear dimensions in the skulls of the French bulldog and the dachshund, along with the

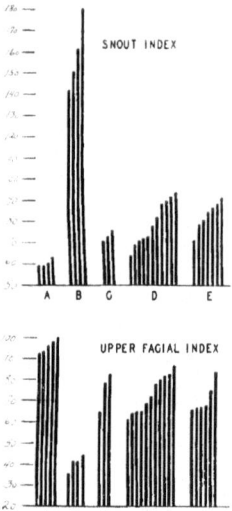

Text-figure 62. Dachshund-French bulldog cross. Each vertical line represents an index based on exact measurements of the skull. The series of skulls for these two charts is the same as used for text-figure 61. A, dachshund; B, French bulldog; C, $F_1$; D, $F_2$; E, $F_1 \times F_2$.

averages for these characters in the $F_1$ and $F_2$ hybrids, are indicated clearly by the curves in text-figure 63. The curve of values for the dachshund is drawn in continuous line, for the French bulldog in a dash-dot line, for the $F_1$ in a dashed line and for the $F_2$ in a dotted line. The magnitudes of the indices and the relative linear proportions are indicated by the figures along the left border of the graph. The features recorded are listed immediately below the points on the curves which indicate their values.

At the points indicating cranial index values, the curves for the two pure parent stocks are close together, and from there on show increasing divergence for skull index, palatal

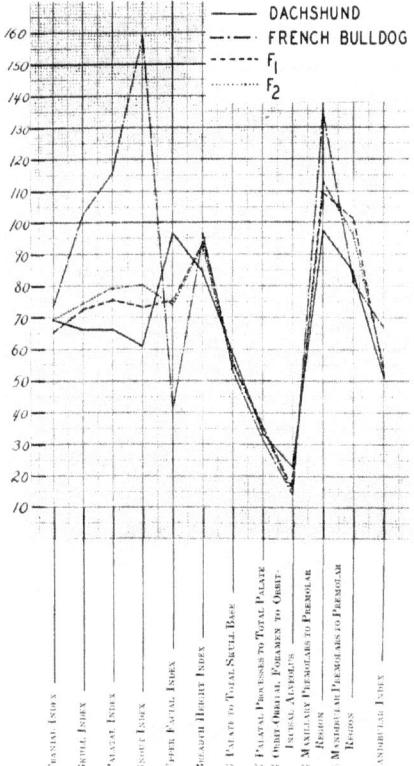

Text-figure 63. Dachshund-French bulldog cross. Comparison of skull measurements of the pure breeds and their first and second generation hybrids.

index and snout index. They again converge to within 50 units of one another for the upper facial index and are quite close together for all other features indicated, with the exception of the relation of total size of premolar teeth to the extent of the maxillary and mandibular premolar regions. The reader may follow without difficulty these points along the curves.

Curves based on the averages for the indices and linear proportions in the $F_1$ and $F_2$ skulls lie between the curves for the parent breeds. In the six indices and the relative linear proportions plotted, the hybrid curves almost without exception follow more closely that for the dachshund than for the French bulldog. These results are in close accord with those found for the Boston terrier-dachshund cross, and confirm the conclusion that the various features differentiating these skull types are responses which definitely depend upon a genetic complex of factors having a dominant inclination towards the normal long typed dog skull as opposed to the divergent short and wide bulldog-like skull. The nature of these expressions in relation to the influence of the endocrine systems and other developmental factors must be left for later consideration.

### The Bulldog Achondroplasic Skull; Its Modified Growth and Development

The discussion of the head and skull features in the two foregoing crosses between animals with bulldog and normal head types makes it necessary, before proceeding further, to inquire into the morphologic nature and development of the aberrant bulldog skull. This is not simply a short, wide skull as compared with the usual type, but one showing consistent modifications in many important structural arrangements, some of which result in gross disharmonies and evident impairment of function. As mentioned in a previous discussion, the bulldog typed skull is not confined to the dog species alone; a closely comparable type of skull modification appears in many different species of animals, including man himself.

The general appearance and behavior of persons with this bulldog-like depression of the face and consequent protrusion of the lower jaw have led physicians to suspect an association between these modified features and either a defective or disturbed endocrine system. The bulldog type of face and head, as found in the human race, is usually confined to short, stocky, dwarfed persons with abnormally shortened extremities. The behavior of such persons may be loosely diagnosed as stolid and deliberate, and the more intelligent among them are recognized as strongly determined in their actions. In popular parlance, they are said to have "bulldog tenacity." There have been very few reports on either the morphology or physiology of the endocrine glands from such human individuals. A number of years ago Symmers and Wallace ('13) recorded the abnormal condition of the glands and other tissues from an adult achondroplasic dwarf with bulldog typed face and head. The thyroid in this individual showed well marked modifications.

The general morphology and the behavior of bulldog typed individuals are so consistently uniform that they deserve serious investigation. This type probably offers the most valuable material available for an analysis of the relationships between morphologic form and nervous functions. For such reasons it is important to know whether the bulldog head has a similar origin and whether it develops on a common plan in all the many different animal species in which it is found.

We may again refer to plate 38 (p. 233), and to plate 50, for clear illustrations of the wide differences between the normal long skull and the modified bulldog typed skull. In plate 50 the skulls of the German shepherd dog and the English bulldog have been photographed from three aspects. In lateral view, the abbreviated face, increased skull height and enormously protruding mandible of the bulldog skull stand out conspicuously (fig. 1). From the dorsal aspect (fig. 3) the bulldog skull presents a widened cranium with smooth flattened top, an exaggerated lateral curve of the wide zygomatic arch and an extreme reduction in forward extent of the facial skeleton. All these characteristics are in striking contrast with the comparable features of the German shepherd skull. The ventral surface of the bulldog skull (fig. 5) shows with equal emphasis the wide spread of the anterior dental region, the tightly contracted premolar region and the marked angle at the junction between the premolar and molar teeth. Also shown is the flat and convex rather than concave oral surface of the bulldog bony palate; the very short basicranium; and a persistent ventral foramen, not always present, which permits a membranous connection between the epithelium of the pharynx and the anterior lobe of the hypophysis.

Figures 7 and 8 in plate 50 show two views of the extremely modified skull of a midget dog, the Brussels griffon. The griffon is one of the smallest of the dog breeds and has a head and face far more reminiscent of a small, flat-faced monkey than of a dog. The cranium is almost spherical and the facial skeleton makes up but a small fraction of the total skull, a reverse condition to that usually found in the dog. The chondrodystrophy of the basicranium in the Brussels griffon contrasts in a striking manner with the long muzzled midget Pomeranian poodle. The griffon skull has a rounded, protruding forehead; little depth of orbit; and an extreme reduction in the jaws, affecting not only the maxilla, as in the typical bulldog, but the mandible as well. This pattern, although tending toward bull type, is in many features far more divergent from the standard than is that

PLATE 50

EXPLANATION OF FIGURES

Comparison of the normal, long skull of the German shepherd with the deformed English bulldog skull and the still more divergent skull of the Brussels griffon.

1, 3 and 5   English bulldog 1233 ♂.
2, 4 and 6   German shepherd 714 ♀.
7 and 8   Brussels griffon.

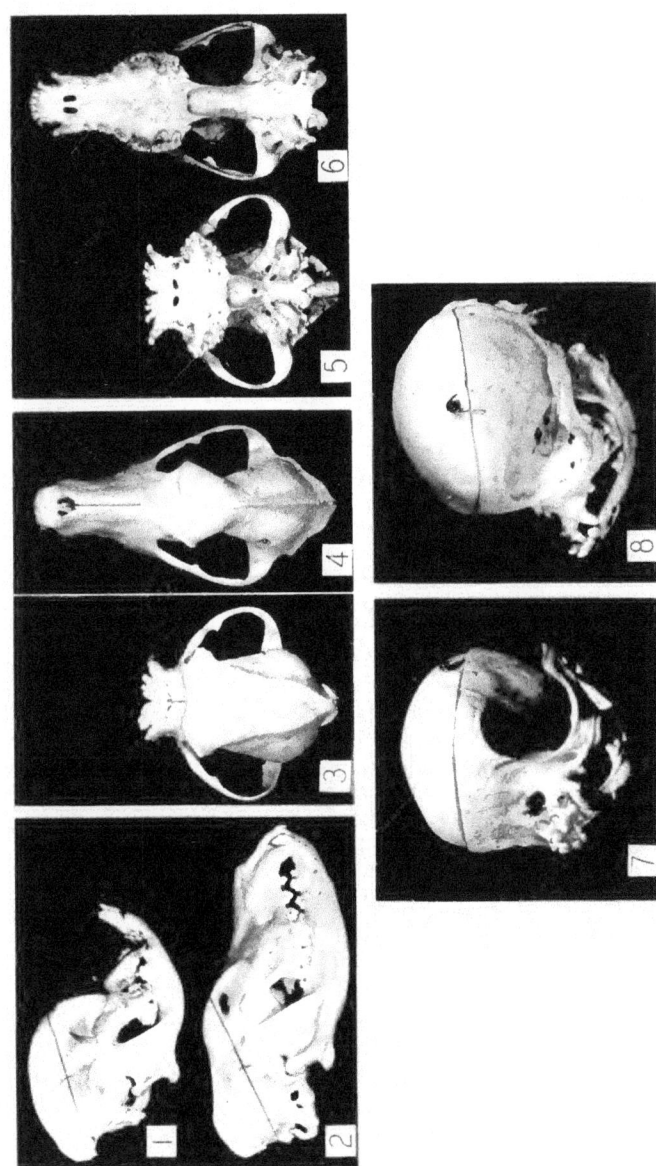

of the bulldog. The extreme facial reduction surpasses that of the bulldog, and the mandible is so shortened as to almost correspond with the maxilla. The Brussels griffon is highly nervous and excitable in its behavior, differing completely from the stubborn and persistent nature of the bulldog.

Plate 38 illustrates the long skull of the greyhound-like Saluki in contrast with several aspects of the dwarfed and partially expressed bull typed Boston terrier skull. The characteristics of the Boston terrier skull as compared with those of the English bulldog are readily evident.

These two plates of skull types may be supplemented by referring again to text-figure 54 (p. 219). At the top of this figure a dimensionally proportioned outline of the bulldog skull is shown superimposed over the outline of the German shepherd skull, illustrating the differences in length and height from point to point in these two skull patterns.

With the foregoing features in mind, we may now examine, for comparative purposes, the so-called bulldog typed skull from another animal species. The bulldog deformity in a human skull is illustrated in plate 51, which shows crown and basal views of three human skulls. Figure 2 illustrates a long dolichocephalic skull with a cranial index of 72.58. Figure 3 is a short, wide brachycephalic specimen with an index of 100; this skull is exactly as wide as long. For comparison with these two, the top and bottom aspects of an achondroplasic human bulldog typed skull with a cranial index of 80.79 are shown in figure 1.

The basal views of the three skulls have been photographed with the oral surface of the bony palates on as nearly as possible an exact horizontal plane. With the skulls in this position, the observer looks directly down on the complete more or less circular outline of the foramen magnum of the two normal though different typed skulls. The long skull differs from the extremely brachycephalic skull simply in details of shape; the structural arrangements are quite similar. The basicranium of the brachycephalic skull is some-

PLATE 51

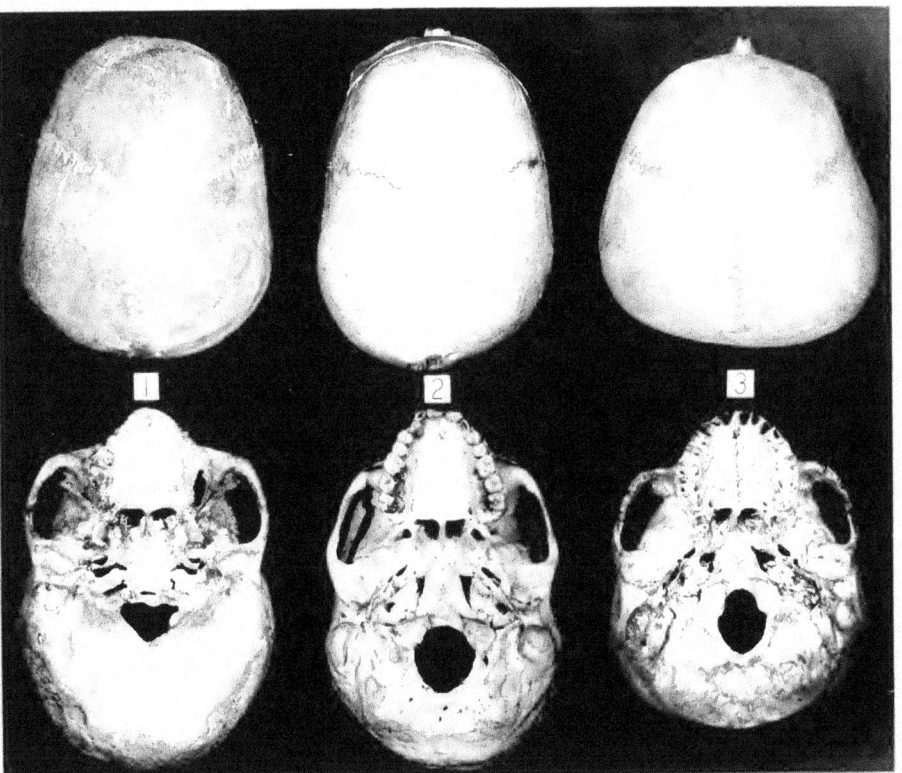

Comparison of a human achondroplasic skull with two normal though different typed skulls.
1  Achondroplasic skull, cranial index of 80.79.
2  Dolichocephalic skull, cranial index 72.58.
3  Brachycephalic skull, cranial index 100.

what short, but its position and general inclination are the same as in the long skull. The palate in the round type is short and broad, almost semicircular, and in the long skull is much longer and narrower; but in both it is concave transversely and anteroposteriorly.

The ventral region of the bulldog typed skull in figure 1 is different in structure from this region in the other two skulls. Unfortunately, the teeth and portions of the dental alveolar processes are missing from this human achondroplasic skull which was received at the Anatomical Laboratories of Cornell University many years ago. The method used in preparing skulls at that time caused more corrosion than present methods, and in this skull the spongy bone of the alveolar region was almost destroyed; in other respects, the specimen is perfectly good. The dental malocclusion which very probably existed during the life of this person may have been partly responsible for the toothless condition and partial resorption of alveolar bone.

In making the photographs, the palate of this achondroplasic skull was placed on as nearly as possible a horizontal plane, comparable to the position of the other two skulls. With the dwarf skull, this position fails to give an observer, looking directly downward, the flat view of the border of the foramen magnum possible in each of the other skulls. In the achondroplasic skull the outline of the foramen magnum is inclined obliquely upward and forward so that were a plane surface placed over the opening it would incline forward and slightly downward instead of directly down.

Through the basicranium of this skull, a short distance in front of the anterior border of the foramen magnum, there is a natural transverse opening which is seen in the photograph as a dark transverse line. This opening is the result of defective union in the ankylosis of the basioccipital and the basisphenoid bones to form the base of the cranium. The basioccipital, which normally makes the larger contribution to the formation of the basicranium, is in this skull but a narrow strip of bone between the border of the foramen magnum and this open defect. All the basicranium in front of this opening is entirely basisphenoid bone. The oral surface of the palate in this skull is convex both transversely and anteroposteriorly, a direct contrast to the normal skull which is concave in both these directions. The entire palate is abnormally short. This skull also differs from the other two shown in that the zygomatic arch is short and sharply curved in a lateral direction.

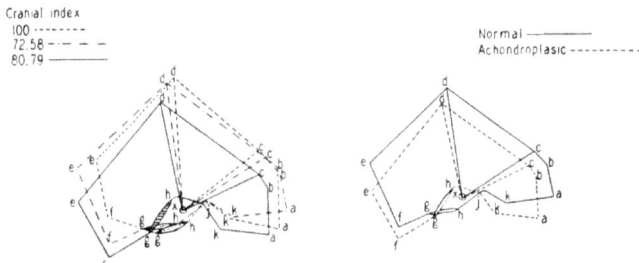

Text figure 64. Sagittal outlines of the three human skulls shown in plate 51. These outlines are based on measurements of the straight distances from the auditory meatus to the points designated. a, superior dental alveolus; b, anterior nasal; c, nasion; d, bregma; e, occipito-parietal suture; f, occipital protuberance; g, posterior margin foramen magnum; h, anterior margin foramen magnum; j, base of vomer; k, posterior palate; x, auditory meatus.

In text-figure 64, comparable outlines of these three human skulls are shown. These outlines were determined by measurements of the straight distances from the auditory meatus to designated points along the sagittal border of the skull, and the outlines of the skulls have been superimposed as nearly as possible. In the outlines comparing the three skulls, the long skull is indicated by a dot-dash line, the round skull by a dashed line and the bulldog typed skull by the solid line. The positions of the foramina magna in the sagittal plane are indicated by the three spindleform outlines at the bottom of the figures. The outlines for the long and the round skulls correspond from point to point in fairly symmetrical fashion, and the positions in inclinations of the foramina magna are close together. The solid outline of the achondroplasic skull not only diverges from the general pattern of the other two, but the outline for the skull base departs completely from that for the normal types. The spindleform outline of the foramen magnum inclines upward and forward instead of being in almost horizontal position. In the bulldog typed skull, the mid-line of the skull base from the anterior border of the foramen magnum curves strongly *downward* as it passes forward to the base of the vomer, whereas in the normal skulls this line passes from the anterior border of the foramen magnum *upward* and forward to the base of the vomer. In the bulldog skull there would seem to be a pull toward the occipito-sphenoidal junction in the basicranium, bringing the lower frontal and occipital regions toward each other ventrally, and causing the region around the border of the foramen magnum and the basicranium to bend upward and give the strongly arched mid-line shown in the outlines.

At the right in text-figure 64, the achondroplasic specimen, represented in dotted line, is matched against the solid outline of the dolichocephalic skull. The contrasting directions of the lines indicating the basicranium, the posterior border of the vomer and the bony palate are more clearly shown in this figure with only the two skull outlines involved.

After examining the arrangements at the base of the skulls, we are now prepared to interpret the cranial index of the achondroplasic skull as compared with those for the normal. The top views of the three crania (pl. 51) are quite different in outline. The dolichocephalic skull is long anteroposteriorly and narrow transversely, and when viewed from the top its outline forms an elongated oval. This form gives the low cephalic index. As the name indicates, the brachycephalic cranium (fig. 3) is short anteroposteriorly and broad transversely and is seen as a shortened ovate when viewed from the top. We have already seen that the basicranial pattern is closely the same for both these skulls.

The cranium in the achondroplasic skull (fig. 1) is shorter and somewhat wider than in the long skull, thus making its cranial index apparently high. When we recall, however, that the base of this skull is strongly arched upward, as illustrated in the outlines in text-figure 64, and that the lower parts of the occipital and frontal regions must, as a result of this, be brought closer together with consequent anteroposterior shortening of the cranium (clearly shown in this figure) it becomes evident that this skull may be primarily of dolichocephalic tendency. If we imagine the skull to be plastic so that the lower occipital and frontal regions could be lifted and pulled farther apart in the sagittal plane, the exaggerated arch of the basicranium would be flattened and the cranial length increased by this force, thus giving an approach toward the dolichocephalic pattern. The achondroplasic specimen may have had dolichocephalic ancestry, and had it been able to develop normally its cranial index would have been quite low.

The peculiar modifications in the adult bulldog typed skull are largely the consequence of definite alterations in the development of the cartilaginous structures forming the basicranium. In the normal immature human skull, there is a thick epiphyseal growth cartilage separating the anterior surface of the basioccipital bone and the posterior surface of the basisphenoid bone. This cartilaginous plate is the most important element in producing the increase in length or forward growth of the basicranium, and this growth in turn accentuates the growth of the vomer and nasion, stimulating the development of a high nasal bridge and a strong forward growth of the face leaving behind a vertical or receding, but not bulging, forehead. The prominent growth of the nose is also closely correlated with the forward extension of the maxilla.

Plate 52 (fig. 1) shows the central portion of the basal aspect of a skull from a four year old child. The basioccipital bone is shield-shaped in outline and separated from the lateral occipital portions by thin plates of cartilage, shown as dark transverse lines, near the anterior ends of the condyles. The anterior surface of the basioccipital is separated from the basisphenoid by a wide space which was, in life, occupied by the thick growth cartilage. In the human skull this cartilage persists until between the twentieth and twenty-second year and functions to produce the bone growth which brings about an almost continuous lengthening of the basicranium with the forward development and strengthening of the upper facial skeleton. At about the age of twenty years this basicranial cartilage becomes ossified, and complete ankylosis is established between the basioccipital and basisphenoid bones. The ossification of the cartilage ends the growth in length of the basicranium.

The formation of the achondroplasic skull, bulldog type head, centers very closely around a defective growth reaction of the basicranial epiphyseal cartilage. This defective growth, however, is anticipated by an earlier deficiency in the cartilaginous matrix which is the precursor of the basioccipital and basisphenoid bones themselves. A section through the sagittal plane of the head of a normal newborn human (fig. 2) shows, in dark color, the well formed and strongly developed hard basioccipital and basisphenoid bones, with, in lighter color, the thick epiphyseal growth cartilage between them. A similar section from the head of a newborn human achondroplasic (fig. 4) shows a very different condition. The basioccipital bone is short and defective in outline, and the bony basisphenoid is irregular in shape and much below normal in size. These two bones are, at the time of birth, already fused together in places, and the growth cartilage is very dystrophic. These facts were well described by F. Knötzke in 1929 in a report on the pathological anatomy of chondrodystrophy in a newborn baby, and figures 2 and 4

PLATE 52

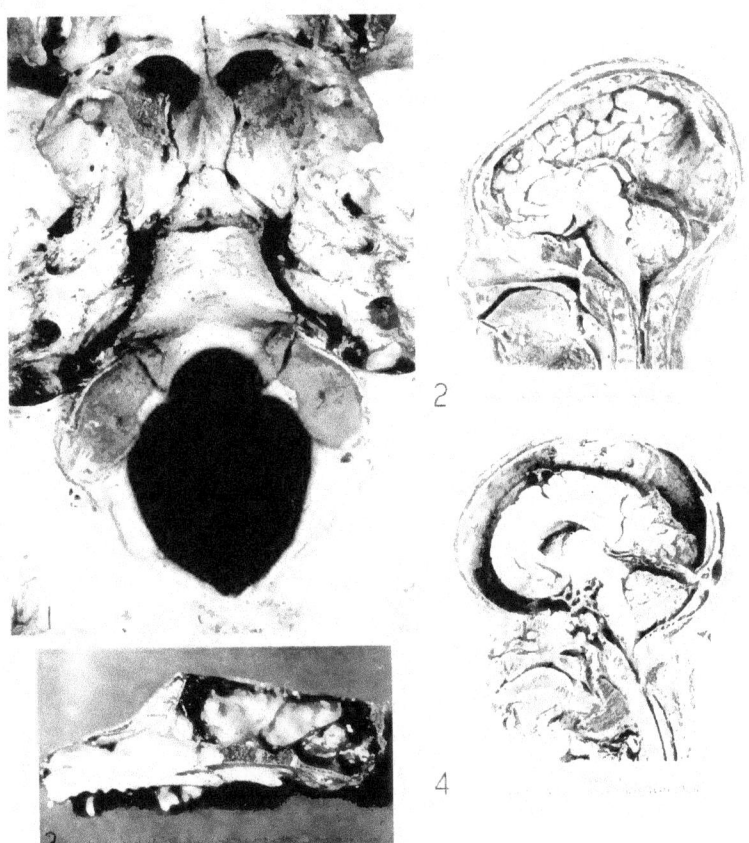

Structure of the basal portions of the immature human and puppy skulls.
1  Central portion of basal aspect of the skull of a 4 year old child.
2  Sagittal section through the head of a normal newborn infant. From Knötzke.
3  Sagittal section through the skull of a young puppy.
4  Sagittal section through the head of an achondroplasic newborn infant. From Knötzke.

in plate 52 are from his report. The deficiency in basicranial length fails to give enough support in a forward direction to the unions between the wings of the sphenoid and the frontal bones. This apparently insufficient support causes the ethmoid bone and the orbital plates of the frontal bone to sag inward and back, depressing the nasion and causing the bulging rounded shape to the forehead. The mature face of the human achondroplasic is wide, with a depression at the nasion; the nose bridge is low and the nose short and inclined to be upturned at the nostrils; and the maxilla is short and somewhat set-back, causing prognathism of the mandible which projects beyond the maxilla with the lower incisors biting in front of the upper. All these facial conditions are quite directly related to the shortened and defective basicranial bones.

A photograph of the skull of a young puppy cut through the sagittal plane is shown in figure 3. In the puppy, the basicranium is composed of three parts, instead of two as in the child, and this arrangement may have some connection with the production of a long muzzle and extension of the entire facial skeleton. The posterior basicranial epiphyseal cartilage in the puppy skull lies between the basioccipital and basisphenoid bones, and thus corresponds to the single cartilage in the same location in the human skull. The more anterior basicranial cartilage in the puppy is inserted immediately in front of the part of the sphenoid forming the sella turcica, and it therefore intervenes between two parts of the immature sphenoid bone. The base of the dog's skull grows in length by means of these two cartilages. The effects on skull pattern due to this growth are quite similar in both the human and the dog. The newborn puppy of all breeds is round headed and rather flat faced, and the long jaws and muzzle of the adult dog are almost entirely postnatal developments.

The skulls of two newborn puppies are photographed together from the ventral aspect in plate 53 (figs. 1 and 2).

GENETIC TYPE AND THE ENDOCRINES

PLATE 53

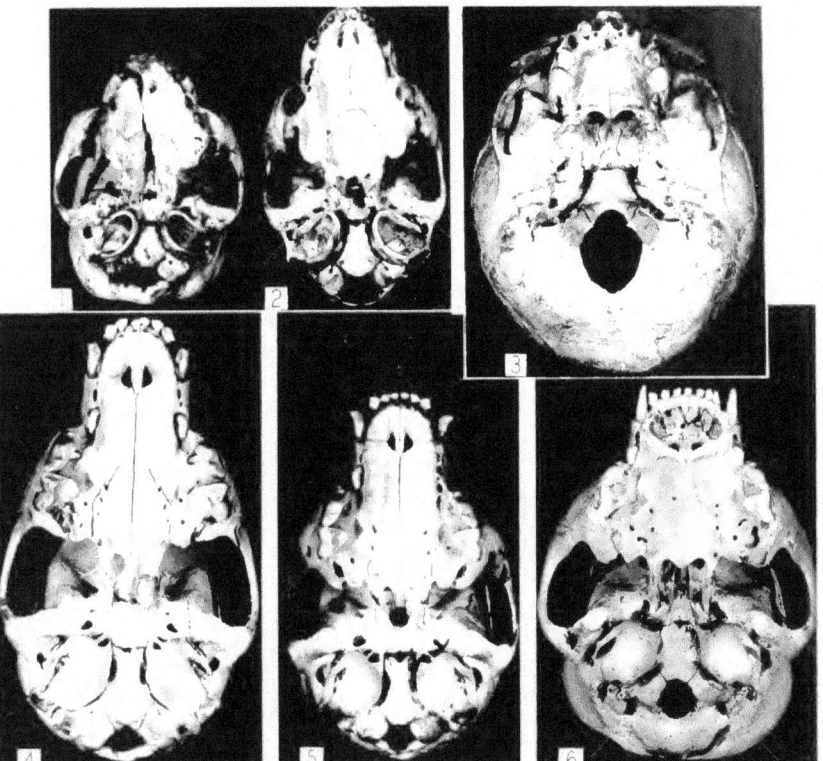

Structure of the basal portions of the skull in puppies of different cross breeds. An immature human skull is shown for comparison.
1  $F_2$ Bassethound-English bulldog 1358 ♂ (newborn).
2  $F_2$ St. Bernard-great Dane 1412 ♂ (newborn).
3  Four year old child.
4  $F_2$ Bassethound-Saluki 1913 ♀ (39 days).
5  $F_2$ Bassethound-English bulldog 1970 ♂ (56 days).
6  Backcross English bulldog-bassethound-English bulldog 1365 ♀ (2½ months).

Figure 2 is from a hybrid Dane by St. Bernard, both of which breeds are long skulled. The foramen magnum in the puppy is in the same relative position as in the adult. The basioccipital bone is very long. The posterior segment of the basisphenoid, which contains the sella turcica on its dorsal surface, shows a large opening which represents an arrest in the closure of the foramen, Rathke's pouch, through which the hypophysis grows from the stomodaeum up into the cranium. The black transverse line a short distance in front of this foramen shows the position of the anterior epiphyseal growth cartilage of the basicranium. This skull is quite normal in general respects and has the facial skeletal proportions typical of the rather flat faced newborn puppy.

The highly modified skull of a newborn bulldog typed puppy is illustrated in figure 1. In addition to the usual bulldog characteristics, this skull shows a cleft palate, which is a rather common anomaly among such typed skulls. This defect in the present case serves our purpose to advantage by permitting a full view of the basicranium throughout its extent. Through a rounding of the plate of the occipital bone in this specimen, the foramen magnum is placed somewhat more forward than it is in the long skull. The basioccipital is short, but not disproportionately so. Through the cleft in the palate it is seen that the two segments of the basisphenoid are widely separated and that both are abnormally short. At this age, the basicranial cartilages are present, but are known to be dystrophic and deficient in their growth reactions.

Three other skulls from older puppies are illustrated in figures 4, 5, and 6. One of these (fig. 4) is a fairly typical long skull, one is partially bulldog in type (fig. 5), and the third (fig. 6) is a fully expressed bulldog type.

The two long skulls have the foramen magnum in the usual posterior position with the plane of the opening facing ventro-posteriorly. In the bulldog typed skull (fig. 6), the foramen magnum is more anterior in position and the plane of the opening faces directly ventral, a strikingly different placement from the other two. It may be recalled that this foramen is quite similarly altered in its position in the human achondroplasic skull, as shown in plate 51. The location of the two basicranial cartilages is clearly seen in all three skulls. The segments of the basicranium are shorter and wider in the complete bulldog typed skull than in the other two.

At 2 months of age, the hybrid bulldog skull again shows the presence of an enormous hypophyseal foramen in the posterior segment of the basisphenoid (fig. 5). The pharyngeal epithelium still retains its embryonic connection with the arrested glandular pituitary through this huge foramen. Such foramina, along with other evidence on the histology of the pituitary which is to be presented, make it apparent that considerable arrest in hypophyseal development is associated with both acromegalic giant and achondroplasic bulldog types. The embryonic arrests in these breeds are significantly involved in adult abnormalities of the pituitary.

The two posterior segments of the basicranium of the complete bulldog skull (fig. 6) are drawn more closely together than in the other two although all three dogs from which the skulls were taken were of about the same age. The lateral parts of the epiphyseal space in the bulldog skull are almost obliterated through an early ankylosis of the bones due to chondrodystrophy of the growth cartilage.

The anterior part of the palate in the bulldog skull has been dissected away to expose the bone underlying the small erupted milk teeth. There are four deciduous incisors on the right side instead of the usual three, and this dissection was made to find whether an accessory permanent tooth was also present. The immature permanent incisor may be seen crowded into a posterior position between the median and the middle right incisor tooth germs. Numerous anomalies of this kind, which are probably associated with an unstable mutational type, are frequently present in these highly modified skulls.

These general considerations of the structural characteristics and developmental modifications in the bulldog type prepare us for an understanding of the genetic and environmental influences which are involved in the origin of such expressions. A genetic analysis of the conditions has been attempted by employing in the experimental studies the grotesquely featured English bulldog with its extremely achondroplasic skull, and crossing members of this breed with breeds having a normal wild typed hound skull.

## The Contrasted Skulls of the English Bulldog and the German Shepherd

Only a limited test of the genetic reactions of the factors involved in the production of the full typed bulldog skull when contrasted with the normal standard shepherd skull was made, this being due to the fact that both breeds are not dependable as breeders nor sufficiently prolific to be well suited to such experiments. The bulldog-bassethound cross proved far more favorable, since the bassethound is a steady and reliable breeder and genetic tests could be readily made through its offspring in all necessary directions. Nevertheless, certain points of value were derived from the bulldog-shepherd cross and these will be given briefly.

A registered German shepherd, "Else" 118♀, who was of carefully pedigreed lines with a perfect typed head, was bred to "Lorne's Latest," A.K.C. 651313, a bulldog of champion stock with a well expressed bulldog head. Fortunately, this bulldog was a remarkably good sire and was used in these experiments a number of times. He lived to be only slightly more than 5 years of age and died suddenly while out walking with his master. Within a few hours after death this animal was sent to our laboratory for autopsy and the fresh endocrine glands were obtained for study. His skeleton was also prepared and mounted to serve as a permanent record.

The mating between these two dogs whelped three hybrid puppies, two females and a male, all of which lived to adulthood. A photograph of one of the $F_1$ bitches is shown in plate 54 (fig. 3). She was a handsome animal of strong, mastiff-like appearance and a quite vicious attitude toward other dogs. She is taller and larger in body than the bulldog and stockier than the shepherd. Her head, as the photograph shows, is much like that of an English mastiff and not very different from the German boxer dog; it is heavier and shorter than that of the shepherd, but has only a mild expression of the typical bulldog pattern. This is one of the few $F_1$ hybrids in the experimental kennels which even a person familiar with dog breeds is invariably unable to diagnose for hybrid origin. There are almost no features which clearly suggest the shepherd dog, and the stocky features resemble more closely those of breeds other than the bulldog. The three $F_1$ shepherd-bulldogs were remarkably alike in general appearance.

The male $F_1$ died at maturity and so no second generation hybrid offspring were produced. However, a sister, 659♀, was successfully used for the backcross with both parent stocks, and the resulting hybrids have supplied some definite indications of the genetic relations between the extreme bulldog skull and the normal long German shepherd type.

The behavior records of these two $F_1$ shepherd-bulldog sisters are particularly interesting. One, 658♀, remained in the kennels for 3 years without whelping a puppy although she was mated several times with productive studs of record. This bitch also missed several oestrous periods. Her sister, 659♀, now more than 6 years old, had at 4 years of age produced five whelps of eight, eleven, ten, twelve and nine puppies, a total of fifty offspring. Of this number she succeeded in rearing twenty-seven to over 3 months of age, which is in general a good record.

The whelping behavior of 659♀, however, was far from calm. She was shy and wild in her reactions. More care and

PLATE 54

Cross between the English bulldog and German shepherd to determine the genetic relations between the bulldog skull and the normal long shepherd skull.

1 English bulldog 885 ♀.   3 F₁ 658 ♀.   5 Backcross shepherd 1231 ♀.
2 German shepherd 112 ♀.   4 Backcross shepherd 1228 ♂.   6 Backcross shepherd 1227 ♂.

arrangements were necessary in order to prevent this bitch from harming her puppies than was necessary with almost any other bitch in the kennels. Her first litter of eight puppies was born in a whelping compartment splendidly arranged for the purpose; it had proved to be an altogether agreeable whelping environment for about 200 bitches of many breeds. Yet this bitch was very nervously shy in the compartment and was much disturbed by the occasional presence of the attendant to supply food and water. The disturbed state was expressed by the instinctive reaction to move the nest and hide her puppies. She would take one after another of the puppies in her mouth and carry it about as though seeking escape. She finally recovered from this disturbed state and was quite calm and well behaved until the pups began, at 10 days or 2 weeks of age, to crawl on the whelping board and cry from time to time for food. The crying seemed to excite and anger the bitch so that she snapped and bit the puppies on the head and body as though to force them to be quiet. This treatment, of course, provoked louder cries, and as a result of the maternal reactions only one puppy was alive after a few days. This lone survivor lived to maturity.

Following this experience, arrangements were made outside the whelping kennel so that the bitch could hide away and whelp in seclusion and at the same time be free to leave the nest for food. Such an arrangement was quite successful with this animal, although it has not been necessary nor beneficial in the other cases where it was tried.

A backcross mating between this $F_1$ shepherd-bulldog hybrid and a good typed German shepherd dog was made. This being the second mating for the $F_1$ female, she whelped a litter of eleven puppies, six males and five females. Five of the puppies died within 2 days after birth because of an initially poor maternal reaction. Fortunately, however, the bitch's reactions were adjusted very promptly, and four males and two females were reared to adult age.

Three of these backcross bulldog-shepherd hybrids are shown in plate 54 (figs. 4–6). Figure 5 is an adult female and the other two are adult brothers. Their size, shape, posture, coat and color pattern are closely similar to the same features in the shepherd. The heads are all very shepherd-like. The bitch (fig. 5) has a head almost identical with that of the pure shepherd in figure 2. When these hybrids were pointed out to persons of wide experience with dog breeds, no trace of the grandparent bulldog features has ever been recognized. Their appearance, behavior and voice are those of an ordinary German shepherd dog with partly drooped ears. These six backcross hybrids were surprisingly uniform in type, and the photographs in plate 54 could serve for any one of them. The mild indications of bulldog features in the head of the $F_1$ hybrid, which seemed to partly dominate the long shepherd character, failed to be re-expressed in any one of the six backcross shepherds. If the shortened features of the $F_1$ were due to certain single factor dominant elements from the bulldog, these should again appear in half the backcross shepherd offspring.

The same $F_1$ shepherd-bulldog bitch was on three occasions crossed back with different males of the bulldog stock, and a total of thirty backcross bulldog hybrids was whelped. Thirteen of these hybrids lived to be adults. They showed just as little resemblance to a German shepherd dog as the shepherd backcross had to the bulldog.

Plate 55 contains photographs of eight adult backcross bulldog-shepherd-bulldogs. Four of these are males (figs. 1–4), and four are females (figs. 5–8). All were whelped in the same litter and were vigorous, strong specimens, as the photographs indicate clearly. Only one of the eight (fig. 4) shows

PLATE 55

EXPLANATION OF FIGURES

Backcross of the $F_1$ English bulldog-shepherd with the pure bulldog. These hybrids present varying degrees of bulldog head features, indicating that a complex of factors is essential for a complete expression of the bulldog type.

| 1 1449 ♂. | 3 1448 ♂. | 5 1452 ♀. | 7 1455 ♀. |
| 2 1447 ♂. | 4 1451 ♂. | 6 1453 ♀. | 8 1454 ♀. |

PLATE 35

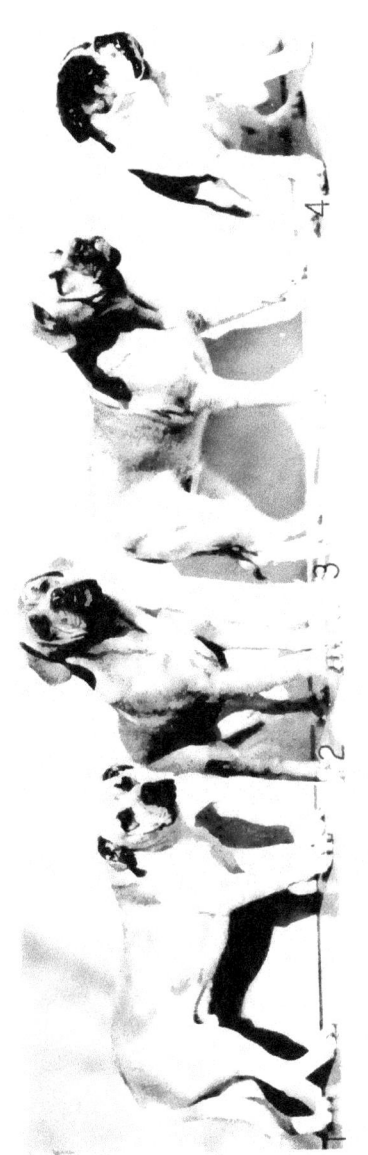
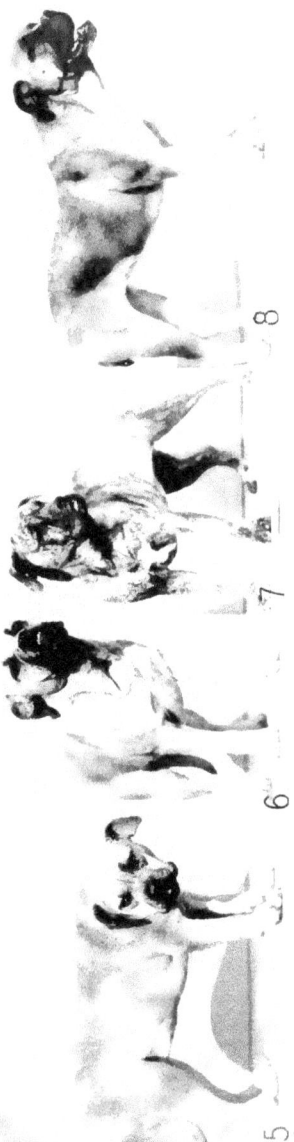

a fully expressed bulldog head and face. This dog could readily pass as a pure bred English bulldog. He has the short stocky body, wide chest and straight, wide apart "benched" front legs. The cranium is wide and round and the forehead high with a deep depression at the nasion giving the "stop." The nose is short and set back on the short upper jaw. The underswung lower jaw projects forward beyond the upper, and the lower incisors are visible when the jaws are closed.

The behavior of this bulldog-like hybrid was carefully tested and found to be similar to that of a slow and stupid bulldog. Examination after the animal's death showed that the ventricles of the brain were enlarged to a marked degree through internal hydrocephalus. This is a common condition in the bulldog brain, as it is in several of the achondroplasic and acromegalic skull types; the condition is very prevalent in the Dane-St. Bernard hybrids and in all the bulldog combinations we have studied.

The two males in figures 2 and 3 have very short heavy heads with an excessive formation of skin producing loosely hanging folds or wrinkles. As found for the shepherd-bulldog hybrids discussed previously, these strong stocky animals resemble very closely the heavy typed German boxer dog as well as certain breeds of the mastiff. The male in figure 1 is of least pronounced bull type.

The four females are of much the same type as their brothers. Two (figs. 6 and 7) show fairly pronounced bulldog heads with, however, an excess of muzzle, or too much nose for the bulldog, but with the characteristic protruding upswung lower jaw and exposed lower incisor teeth. The bitch in figure 5 has a near boxer typed head; and an almost perfect picture of the German boxer is seen in figure 8. This last bitch has the recessive short bulldog tail, as does the brindle sister (fig. 7) and the male in figure 4; the other five all have long straight tails.

This cross between the English bulldog and the normal shepherd dog would indicate that the bulldog head is genetically complex in origin, being influenced in its expression by some factors which tend to be dominant for the normal head type and others which tend to be recessive. If all the bulldog head features were recessive to the normal, the $F_1$ hybrid would not show a shorter and heavier head than that of the shepherd. In breeding the $F_1$ hybrid back to the shepherd, these modifications of the long head type are almost completely lost. The great variety in degree of expression for bulldog head or the difference among phenotypes shown by the hybrids from the backcross of the $F_1$ with the bulldog, clearly indicates the presence in the underlying genotype of a complex of factors which are essential for the fully expressed bulldog head.

The analysis of the bulldog head and of the general characteristics associated with it, necessitates the study of an abundance of hybrid material which could only be derived from a more productive breeding stock than the shepherd-bulldog cross has proved to be. On this account we resorted to the far more prolific cross between the bulldog and the bassethound. So far as our experience goes, this cross has enormous advantages in such a study, and on this basis the general analysis of the bulldog characteristics is considered in the following chapter.

## GENETIC CONSTITUTION AND ENDOCRINIC ABNORMALITY AS FACTORS IN THE GROWTH AND STRUCTURAL MODIFICATIONS OF THE ENGLISH BULLDOG-BASSETHOUND HYBRIDS

In a previous section, we considered the inheritance and development of the extremities in the cross between the English bulldog and the bassethound. It will be recalled that the bassethound is of normal dog size, possessing a normal head of the hound type, a well proportioned body, and a long, straight tail, while the extremities are very short with extreme achondroplasic deformities. The legs of this animal furnish one of the most striking cases of sharply localized chondrodystrophy in an otherwise normal skeleton. The behavior and hunting instincts of the bassethound are closely the same as those of an ordinary hound.

The English bulldog, with its various growth distortions, forms an almost perfect contrast to the bassethound. The extremities in the bulldog are stocky and straight, and the long bones of the leg give no evidence of chondrodystrophy, either from genetic or morphologic examinations. In this dog, the head and the tail, the two opposite ends of the axial skeleton, show distortions due to chondrodystrophy in the basicranium of the skull and the epiphyseal cartilages in the vertebrae of the tail. The intermediate parts of the axial skeleton are usually perfectly normal, but in unusual cases chondrodystrophy in the cervical and other regions of the vertebral column has been found. To our knowledge, however, the long bones of the extremities in the bulldog are never achondroplasic. The instincts and behavior of the bulldog are not entirely those of a normal dog; it has almost lost the hunting instinct, and its breeding reactions are frequently defective.

The question arises whether these modifications in nervous function are the results of the structural distortions and abnormal endocrine conditions in the bulldog. We hope to give at least a partial answer to this question in the pages beyond.

In view of these localized growth modifications in the bodies of animals otherwise normal in gross structure, it seemed theoretically possible that other and even more sharply localized modifications and combinations might be obtained by cross breeding such dogs with contrasted characters. For example, in hybrids from such cross breedings, the head of the bulldog might be associated with the short legs of the bassethound; or the bulldog head might occur in an animal with long, straight, normal tail; or, still more important, the short, bent "screw-tail" might be produced as the only deviation from normal. Is it possible for chondrodystrophic growth to occur only at the head end or only at the tail end of the axial skeleton and nowhere else in the body? If so, such distortion of growth can scarcely be due to strange endocrine environment. If such localized distortions could be produced in a consistent manner among these hybrids, it might be possible to determine whether the genetic constitution of the individual induces the growth pattern of its parts independent of differences in the quality of the endocrine secretions. In other words, might the modifications in the structural pattern usually attributed to endocrine disturbance occur in a limited body region which is necessarily in the same endochemical environment as are all other organs and parts which are progressing on a perfectly normal plan?

The occurrence of achondroplasia in the domestic fowl as a result of manganese deficiency, recently suggested by the work of Lyons and Insko ('37), is beset by the same difficulty in offering an explanation as is the endocrine explanation in answering this problem of localized chondrodystrophic reactions.

One of the most important questions in mammalian development is: just how far are genetic modifications of the endocrine glands the contributing factors in bringing about typically hereditary growth deviations? A definite proposition may further clarify the problem: does a disturbance of the pituitary gland constitute the initial cause of acromegalic gigantism, or is a mutation in the genetic complex of the individual responsible for both the modification of body form and size and the defective pituitary? Are diseased pituitary and acromegalic growth reactions two genetically correlated characteristics of the giant constitutional complex, and both therefore merely symptomatic of the common cause? Gland operations and injections of glandular extracts have failed to furnish answers to such inquiries.

We have made extensive studies on bulldog-bassethound hybrids in an effort to solve some of these problems. Two pure line bassethound bitches were each mated to two highly typed well bred bulldog sires. Four litters of eight, two, seven and six $F_1$ hybrids were obtained, a total of twenty-three individuals. Seven of these $F_1$ females were paired with various $F_1$ males to give twenty-three litters of $F_2$ pups. These $F_2$ litters ranged in size from only a single puppy to a litter of ten, and the twenty-three whelpings gave a total of 150 $F_2$ hybrids. Three backcross matings between the $F_1$ and the bassethound were made, producing litters of seven, six and nine, a total of twenty-two backcross bassethounds. The reverse backcross by the $F_1$ with the bulldog gave four litters, containing three, five, seven and six puppies, a total of twenty-one backcross bulldog hybrids. In all, 216 hybrid animals from various combinations between the bassethound and bulldog were produced in our kennels. These hybrids were studied during life for growth and behavior; and after death their endocrine glands and various other tissues were studied both in the gross state and microscopically. From these various studies we hoped to approach an understanding of the interrelations among the endocrine modifications and the genetic constituents in determining the morphologic types of animals.

### The Head and Skull Features in English Bulldog-Bassethound Hybrids; New Types from New Constitutional Complexes

From the previous chapters of this study we are familiar with the highly altered achondroplasic skull and head of the English bulldog. We have also seen the normally well developed quality of the bassethound skull and head as shown by the indices and measurements in table 1 (p. 208). It is to be recalled that both these pure breeds are of ordinary size with neither dwarf nor giant growth tendencies. Photographs of highly typed specimens of the bulldog and bassethound breeds, along with their $F_1$ hybrids and a litter of four $F_2$ animals, may be seen by again referring to plate 19 (p. 97). Skeletons of the same groups are photographed in plates 20 and 21 (pp. 99 and 100).

The indices for various skull proportions and the relative dimensions of several skull parts in the bassethound-bulldog cross are tabulated in table 4. The average numerical values of features based on three pure bassethound skulls and nine English bulldog skulls are given in the first two columns of the table.

The bulldog cranial index is only slightly higher than the bassethound, while the total skull index, palatal index and snout index are enormously high. The width-length relations on which the latter three indices are calculated have in each case a dimension in width that is somewhat greater than the length of the part involved, and for the palatal and snout indices the width is much greater. The same indices in the bassethound skull are low, being only about half the value of those for the bulldog. The three indices in the bassethound are also much more nearly of uniform value.

The upper facial index for these skulls is calculated in a reverse manner of length-width relation; therefore, it is very high in the bassethound, since the nasal length in this skull is much greater than the palatal width. The value of this index is less than half as great for the bulldog skull as for the bassethound skull, the bulldog nasal length being considerably shorter than the palatal width. This reverse facial index, along with the three previous indices, is very useful for detecting the slight degrees of bulldog tendency in contrast with the normal. The breadth to height index of the total skull is higher for the bulldog than for the bassethound, and the mandibular index is still higher; these also add their evidence for differentiating such skulls.

The sum of the anteroposterior dimensions of the four maxillary premolar teeth in the bassethound equals about 88 per cent of the length of the maxillary premolar region, while the total of the same tooth dimensions in the bulldog is almost 122 per cent of its maxillary premolar region. This means, of course, that in the jaws of the bulldog these teeth are crowded and twisted into crosswise position, as is clearly

shown in plate 56 where the three posterior premolar teeth are set at right angles to the normal position seen in the accompanying long skull.

The mandibular premolar teeth occupy 80 per cent of the length of the mandibular premolar region in the bassethound, which is about the same proportion as for the upper jaw. It is a surprising fact to find that the premolar teeth in the mandible of the bulldog occupy an even lower percentage of this region, about 72 per cent, than they do in the bassethound. The teeth of the bulldog are not so large and strong as those of the hound.

The peculiar phenomenon of the crowding together of the premolar teeth in the upper jaw of the bulldog and the free spacing in the lower jaw is due to the fact that the mandible in this deformed skull is much less reduced in length than is the upper face and maxilla. Judging from the conditions found in other short faced breeds, to be discussed later, the mutations which shortened the upper face and maxilla of the bulldog have not progressed to a point where the mandible is correspondingly shortened.

The third column in table 4 represents the average values for the skull characters of three $F_1$ bassethound-bulldog hybrids. In general the indices and proportions for the $F_1$ skulls are between the values of comparable features in the two parent stocks, but in all cases where the indices of the bulldog and the bassethound differ considerably, the $F_1$ falls much closer to the bassethound. For example, in the skull index, palatal index and snout index, the $F_1$ values are each about ten above the bassethound and, respectively, 36, 47 and 97 below the same indices for the bulldog. Taking average indices for comparisons between $F_1$ hybrids and the parent stocks is a fair procedure, since the $F_1$ animals are almost as uniform in type as are the pure breeds, this uniformity of the $F_1$ hybrids being proof of the purity of the parent stocks. If the parent stocks are not largely homozygous for

PLATE 56

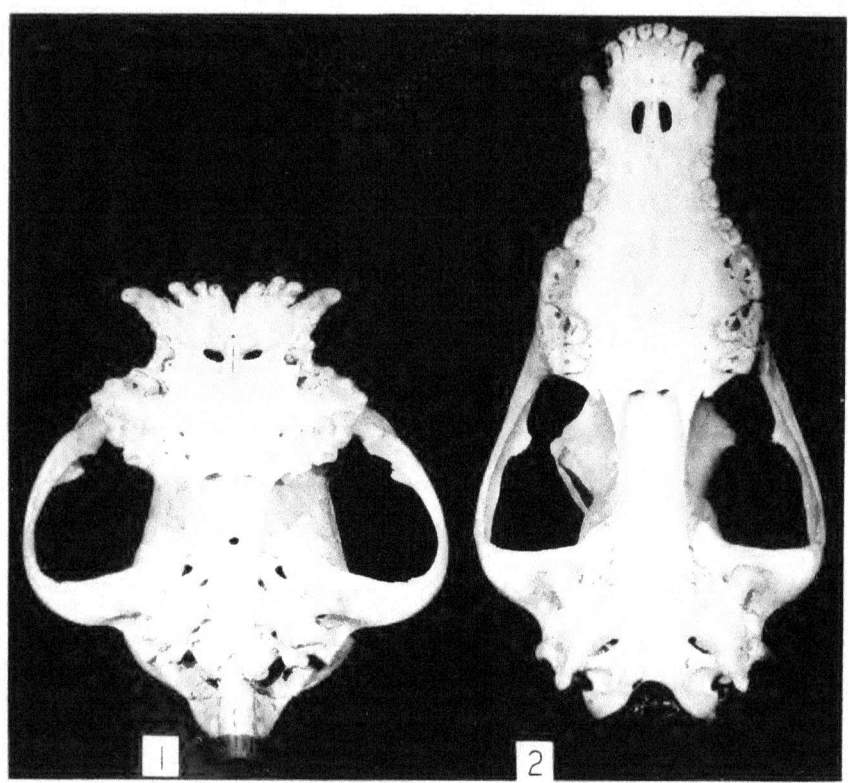

Crosswise arrangement of the maxillary premolar teeth in the skull of the English bulldog in contrast to the normal position in the German shepherd skull.

1 English bulldog 1233 ♂.
2 German shepherd 714 ♀.

type and features, the several $F_1$ hybrids would individually inherit very different complexes of the factors involved.

The skull as a whole in the $F_1$ hybrids is shorter than in the bassethound but the hybrid mandible is not equally shortened. Among the twenty-three individuals of this generation, seventeen show prognathism of the mandible, or the so-called undershot condition characteristic of the bulldog skull.

The average indices and proportions for the skulls of thirty $F_2$ bassethound-bulldog hybrids are recorded in the fourth column of table 4. These average indices are found to be almost the same as those for the $F_1$ hybrids. The standard deviations in the $F_2$ group are, however, much higher, being in the highest case thirteen times greater than the standard deviation for the $F_1$ group. Nevertheless, even these differences in deviations do not convey an adequate picture of the great variety of type modifications exhibited among the $F_2$ hybrids as compared with the $F_1$ hybrids in this cross. These facts we shall demonstrate in other ways. The average indices in the fourth column of table 4 are still important as showing that thirty $F_2$ skulls selected at random may lend their features for an average amalgamation into the indefinite $F_1$ type in spite of the highly pronounced and divergent characteristics which exist among them. From the biological standpoint, there can be, of course, no average for these $F_2$ skulls, since the most significant thing about them is the fact that they are so generally and widely different, having been obtained from hybrids having new and unique genetic complexes derived from the recombination of factors from the widely contrasted parent stocks. The profitable study of these hybrids in our present problems does not depend so heavily upon large numbers and statistical methods, but more directly upon a thorough analysis of the individual differences in structural and functional features exhibited among the members of each hybrid generation.

Plate 57 (p. 321) presents a series of fourteen $F_2$ skulls, and a mere casual examination of these will indicate how very different each of the fourteen is from the others.

The last column in table 4 gives the records of skull measurements for backcross hybrids from the $F_1$ on the English bulldog. The indices for these backcross bulldog skulls, as would be expected, approach more nearly the pure bulldog values than do the other hybrid measurements. Yet in those features for which the bulldog skull is extreme, the backcross from the $F_1$ on the bulldog deviates considerably from the pure parent type.

In order to make further comparisons among the indices and features of individual skulls in contrast with comparisons of average conditions, we have plotted charts for several of the bulldog-bassethound indices, and these will be discussed in the following section.

### INDICES AND PROPORTIONS IN INDIVIDUAL SKULLS FROM THE BASSETHOUND-BULLDOG CROSS

Several different indices for the individual skulls of the bassethound-bulldog cross are indicated in text-figures 65 to 68. The upper chart in text-figure 65 gives the cranial index values. The three bassethound skulls have values of 61, 67 and 68, a range of 7 units, while the eight bulldog skulls range from an index of 58, which is lower than any for the bassethound, up to a high index of 80. The cranial index in the bulldog has a range of 22 units, roughly three times greater than the range for the bassethound skulls. However, three of the eight bulldog skulls show less range for this index than do the three bassethound skulls, and one might be justified in concluding that if more skulls were represented, the cranial index of the bassethound might be as widely variable as it is in the bulldog; but on the basis of measurements from many living animals we know this to be untrue. The bulldog cranium varies in its shape much more widely than does the cranium of the bassethound.

The cranial index is of about the same value in each of the three $F_1$ skulls and is very close to the average index for the bassethound. The twenty-one $F_2$ skulls range in their cranial indices from a low of 56 to a high of 73, which is about the same as the range in the pure bulldog.

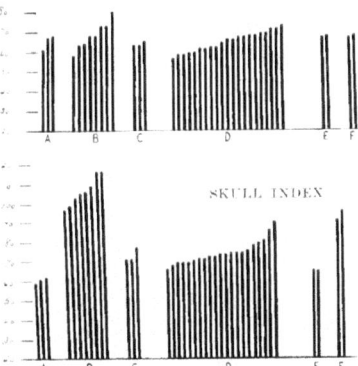

Text-figure 65. Bassethound-English bulldog cross. Each vertical line represents an index based on exact measurements of the skull, and the same series of skulls was used for both charts. A, bassethound; B, English bulldog; C, $F_1$; D, $F_2$; E, backcross of $F_1$ with bassethound; F, backcross of $F_1$ with bulldog.

This chart shows, as much previous data have already indicated, that the cranial index is not always a highly significant feature for the differentiation of types among dog breeds. Cranial indices are more variable within certain breeds than they are within others, but there is nearly always considerable overlapping in values among widely different skulls. Part of this variability and overlapping is due to the presence or absence of the sagittal crest; it is difficult to control the effect of this on index values. In spite of the somewhat uncertain importance of the cranial index in the dog skull, we have presented it because of its extensive employment in the study of human skulls.

Referring again to table 1 of measurements for pure breed dog skulls, we find that certain of these, such as the German shepherd, great Dane and St. Bernard, do have low cranial indices clearly distinguishing them from the small round cranial types, the Boston terrier, French bulldog and the still more brachycephalic Pekingese dog and Brussels griffon. The bassethound, English bulldog and dachshund fall between these extremes, and their cranial indices are therefore not so strongly contrasted with one another.

The total skull index is a much more highly significant character for contrasting the bassethound and the bulldog skulls than is the cranial index. The lower chart in text-figure 65 represents the skull indices for the same series of bulldog-bassethound skulls as were shown above for the cranial index. The three long bassethound skulls have about equally low skull indices, 59 to 62, while the short wide bulldog skulls have high indices, varying from 96 to 115. Six of the eight bulldog skulls are over 100 in skull index, which means that the zygomatic widths are greater than the lengths of the total skull base from foramen magnum to anterior incisor alveolus. There can be no question of the differential value of this index in the bulldog and bassethound.

The three $F_1$ hybrid skulls range from 71 to 77 for total skull index, which places them for this width to length relation nearer the value for the skull of the bassethound than for that of the bulldog. The twenty-one skulls from $F_2$ hybrids range from 66, slightly above the bassethound index, to 89, which is 7 units below the lowest bulldog index. The majority of these skulls have an index close to the $F_1$ range. This would indicate that the genetics of the skull index involves much more than a single or simple factor and depends upon a number of factors influencing the growth of various parts. Among the twenty $F_2$ individuals not one received in its inheritance the entire complex necessary to give a completely short and wide bulldog skull.

The two backcross bassethound skulls have skull indices of 65, which is close to that of the pure bassethound, while the two backcross bulldog skulls likewise approach the pure bulldog with indices of 90 and 95. The higher of the latter two backcross skull indices is still 20 units below the two highest indices of the eight bulldog skulls, although it is only 1 unit under the lowest. Such relations would indicate that most of the factors influencing those characters which determine this index are dominant for the bassethound long skull, while a few factors for the short and wide growth of the bulldog head tend to dominate sufficiently to modify the long normal condition. The short achondroplasic skull of the bulldog by no means bears the same simple genetic relation to the normal long skull as was found for the short achondroplasic legs of the bassethound when contrasted genetically with the normal long legs of the shepherd dog. Achondroplasic shortness of the extremities is inherited as a single gene dominant, while the achondroplasic short head results from a complex of genic influences of which most, but not all, are recessive to the genes for normal.

The chart for snout index (maxillary canine width in proportion to snout length) is given in text-figure 66. These indices show greater differences between the bulldog and bassethound skulls than any other proportional dimensions recorded. The six bassethound skulls have snout indices of 58, 58, 65, 66, 69 and 71. The same indices for the ten bulldog skulls range from 139 up to 200, or from about two to almost three times higher than the bassethound indices. This contrast is due to the fact that the bassethound skull has the common long protruding upper jaw or muzzle of the ordinary dog while the upper jaw of the bulldog is short and wide; in poor typed bulldog skulls it is only about two-thirds as long as wide, and in high typed skulls about half as long as wide. The range for this index among the six bassethound skulls is only 13 units, as against 61, almost five times more, among the ten bulldog skulls.

The snout index for the nine $F_1$ hybrid skulls is low, overlapping and extending only a little above the bassethound range. The thirty-seven $F_2$ skulls range in snout index from the bassethound low level of 58 up to almost 120, or, in other words, from long, narrow skulls to those in which the width of the jaw is greater than its length. However, this maximum for the $F_2$ falls far short of the pure bulldog proportion with a length of only two-thirds to one-half as

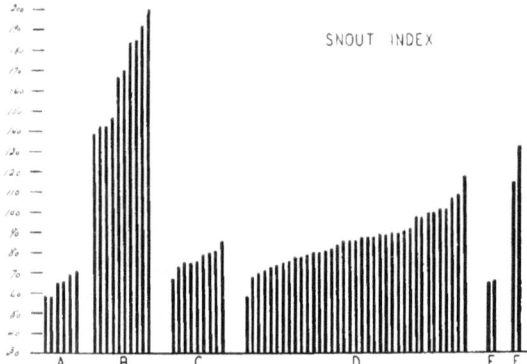

Text figure 66. Bassethound-English bulldog cross. Each vertical line represents an index based on exact measurements of the skull, and the series includes those used in text figure 65 as well as a number of additional skulls. A, bassethound; B, English bulldog; C, $F_1$; D, $F_2$; E, backcross of $F_1$ with bassethound; F, backcross of $F_1$ with English bulldog.

great as the width for the upper jaw. Almost half the $F_2$ skulls again fall for this index within the $F_1$ range. The trend of $F_2$ indices is considerably closer to that of the bassethound than to that of the bulldog.

The two skulls measured for this index from backcross bassethound hybrids have the exact values of those for the pure bassethound. In contrast, the two backcross bulldog hybrids have short snouts with high indices of 115 and 133. The higher of these is only 6 units below the lowest index among the ten pure bulldogs, but is more than 50 units below the three highest.

The snout index again represents a complex of several characters which are influenced in their expression by a number of different genetic factors. The normal length of snout growth tends to dominate in a general way the short bulldog muzzle.

The relation of width to length of the palate has been expressed as the palatal index and is shown in text-figure 67. In the same figure, the mandibular index is represented by the lower chart. A close comparison of these two indices is particularly important since the first one may be taken as the most representative for the upper jaw while the mandibular index expresses, of course, the width to length proportion for the lower jaw. The mandible in the bulldog skull is less shortened than is the palatal or upper jaw region, and the charts show the differences for palatal index between the bulldog and the bassethound to be much greater than for mandibular index.

The bulldog skulls are fairly uniform in their palatal indices but even more so in their mandibular indices. In both these indices the $F_1$ hybrids are much nearer to the bassethound skull pattern than to that of the bulldog. Three $F_1$ palatal indices are shown to be close to the bassethound, and the nine $F_1$ mandibular indices are also more bassethound-like.

The twenty-one $F_2$ bassethound-bulldog skulls measured for palatal index range from 74, which is about the same as the highest bassethound index, to 96, which is 14 units below the lowest bulldog index of 110. The bony palate is wider than it is long in all eight bulldog skulls, but in not one of the twenty-one $F_2$ skulls is this the case. The majority of the $F_2$ skulls are within the $F_1$ range and in general approach the bassethound skull more nearly than they do that of the bulldog.

The range in mandibular index is shown in the lower chart of text-figure 67. Not only do the bassethound and bulldog skulls differ less in mandibular index than in palatal or upper jaw index, but the $F_2$ hybrids range all the way from 1 unit above the lowest bassethound index up to the level of the lowest bulldog index. The skulls of the $F_2$ hybrids fail to reach only the highest values for the bulldogs. In contrast with this, the upper chart shows that the highest

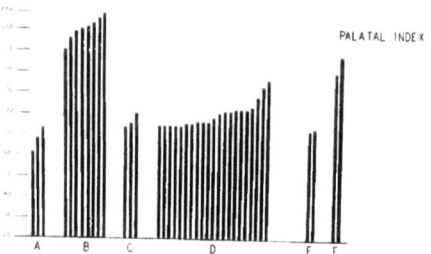

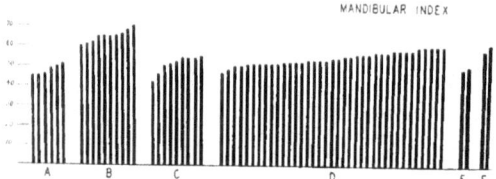

Text-figure 67. Bassethound-English bulldog cross. Each vertical line represents an index based on exact measurements of the skull. The series of skulls for palatal indices is the same as used in text-figure 65, and for mandibular indices the same as used in text-figure 66. A, bassethound; B, English bulldog; C, $F_1$; D, $F_2$; E, backcross of $F_1$ with bassethound; F, backcross of $F_1$ with English bulldog.

palatal index among twenty-one of the same $F_2$ skulls falls 14 units below the lowest bulldog palatal index. In other words, the skull of the $F_2$ hybrid may attain the typical bulldog mandibular index far more readily than it can the bulldog upper jaw or palatal index. Although the bulldog lower jaw is longer than the upper, it is not an entirely normal mandible; there is not only some shortening but a definite modification in its form. This modification is partly genetic, as indicated by other breeds—the Boston terrier, Pekingese, etc.—and partly a mechanical adaptation to the achondroplasic short skull.

The backcross bassethound hybrid shows bassethound values for both the palatal index and the mandibular index. The backcross bulldog hybrid has a palatal index approaching much nearer the value of the pure bulldog index than do the

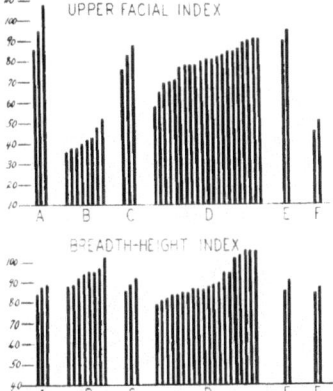

Text-figure 68. Bassethound-English bulldog cross. Each vertical line represents an index based on exact measurements of the skull, and the series of skulls is the same as used for text-figure 65. A, bassethound; B, English bulldog; C, $F_1$; D, $F_2$; E, backcross of $F_1$ with bassethound; F, backcross of $F_1$ with English bulldog.

highest $F_2$ indices, while the mandibular index in this backcross hybrid is as completely high as that of the pure bulldog. All these relations are due to the fact that the upper face of the bulldog is more extremely modified than its lower jaw.

The top chart in text-figure 68 represents the values for upper facial index in this series of skulls. It will be recalled that the upper facial index (the proportion of nasal length to palatal width) is calculated in a manner the reverse of that for the foregoing indices, and for this reason the bassethound long skull type is represented by high indices and the short bulldog skull by low. The contrast between the two types is, of course, shown with equal clearness by calculating the proportion of length to width or by doing the reverse.

The $F_1$ skulls again approach close to the bassethound values for this proportion of nasal length to palatal width. The value of the $F_2$ skulls ranges almost down to that of the bulldog skulls and completely as high as the lowest bassethound value. The majority of $F_2$ indices lie within the range of the $F_1$ values.

The two skulls from the backcross on the bassethound show upper facial index values on a level with the highest pure bassethound indices. This index for the backcross between the $F_1$ and the bulldog sinks completely down to the lowest levels of value for the poorest or least modified pure bulldog skulls.

The upper facial index is of definite significance for differentiating between the normal long bassethound skull and degrees in tendency toward the deformed short bulldog skull. In crosses between the bassethound and the bulldog, the elements concerned in the calculation of the upper facial index are dependent upon a genetic complex of factors; some of these factors are dominant in the direction of normal expression while others are recessive for normal growth when in contact with those factors which influence the modifications toward the bulldog skull. Such an interpretation is indicated by the range shown for this index in the twenty-one $F_2$ hybrid skulls. The inclination of the pattern of the backcross hybrid skulls in the direction of the parent stock on which the backcross is made also indicates the complexity of the characters from which this index is calculated.

The lower chart in text-figure 68 represents the values of the breadth-height index. This index, based on the relation between the distance from the auditory meatus to bregma

and the cranial width, tends to be low for the long bassethound skull and higher for the bulldog skull, a relation
similar to those in text-figures 65, 66 and 67 where widths
of skull regions are divided by lengths. The straight distance
as measured from auditory meatus to bregma involves to
some extent cranial width as well as height. The width enters
into both the measurements involved in the estimation of this
breadth-height index. The breadth-height index concerns
strictly cranial measurements, as does the cranial index itself.
In neither of these indices are the pure skulls of this cross
clearly differentiated by their values. Cranial indices for
the three bassethound and eight bulldog skulls overlap, as
do also the breadth-height indices, although the overlapping
in the latter is not nearly so great in extent. The breadth-
height index seems to differentiate between the skulls of
the two types more effectively than does the cranial index.

The three bassethound skulls range in value for breadth-
height index of the cranium from 84 to 89, while the eight
bulldog skulls show values ranging from 88 to 102. Only two
of the eight bulldog crania are down within the bassethound
range; the others are well above, and one of these far beyond
the bassethound indices. This, along with what was found
for the cranial indices, would show that while cranial shape
and proportions in the bassethound and bulldog skulls are
not greatly different, there is nevertheless a definite short-
wide inclination in the bulldog cranium. This shape may be
a secondary effect of the shortened basicranium on the upper
cranial curvatures and, therefore, not always clearly pronounced. Such a suggestion is emphasized by referring back
to plate 51 (p. 277) in which the photographs of a human
achondroplasic dwarf skull, and skulls of low and high cranial
indices are shown. The top of the cranium of the achondroplasic skull is definitely inclined in outline toward the long
dolichocephalic type. The reduction in length of the cranial
dome is due to the chondrodystrophic shortness and upward
arching of the basicranium, as is illustrated in the sagittal

outlines of the skulls (text-fig. 64, p. 279). The bulldog-like head may occur in a family of dolichocephalic type just as certainly as in a brachycephalic family, and this deformity involves the basicranial and facial skeletal growths more than it does the growth and shape of the upper cranial domes. The bulldog skull modification is in no sense connected with a transformation from the long into the normal short cranial type. Further, this modification may be superimposed on both the dolichocephalic and brachycephalic cranial types. This fact may be a possible reason why certain specimens in the series of pure bulldog skulls overlap the bassethound in their strictly cranial measurements, and at the same time other specimens of the bulldog series depart far away from the bassethound indices. The bulldog mutation has probably arisen among several European dog breeds, but in each case the mutant is typically bulldog in spite of the type of its ancestral origin. These mutants from various origins have been selected and amalgamated during the past century to form the present day English bulldog breed. Breeders selecting for prize bulldog type ignored almost entirely the features concerned in cranial indices, since these enter only slightly into the grotesque head pattern and expression of the champion bulldog.

The breadth-height index chart shows the $F_1$ bassethound-bulldog hybrids to be more or less intermediate with regard to the parental stocks, although possibly they approach a little nearer the bassethound index. The $F_2$ skulls range in values for this index from 79 to 105. The lowest indices are thus well below the bassethound values while the highest are above the bulldog range. Only a few intermediate specimens show values within the $F_1$ range. This spread in the $F_2$ indices could be interpreted to mean that there has been a genetic resorting which separates these crania into the two ancestral types and, in addition, gives new combinations further tending to accentuate the extremes in both parental directions.

Strangely enough, the two backcross bassethound skulls and the two backcross bulldog skulls show no definite inclination for the breadth-height index. These same backcross skulls also showed no differences for cranial indices in the upper chart of text-figure 65. The breadth-height index and the cranial index charts both show that there are no consistent genetic differences between the cranial proportions of the bassethound and the bulldog, and this means that the measurements concerned do not involve the base of the cranium in a consistent manner.

Curves have been plotted in text-figure 69 to indicate the average of the index values for the individual skulls given in the foregoing charts. The average for the bassethound indices is represented by the solid line, for the bulldog by the dash-dot line, for the $F_1$ by a dashed line, and for the $F_2$ by a dotted line. The several indices and the proportions represented by the curves are listed at the bottom of the chart immediately below the points on the curves which indicate their values.

The average indices for the bulldog and bassethound skulls show the cranial index in the two breeds to be only 5 points apart and the breadth-height index slightly more. These are the only two upper cranial proportions shown.

The averages for total skull index, palatal index and snout index place the two skull types increasingly far apart. The curves for snout index averages are separated by 110 units, the widest divergence shown. The reversed upper facial index shows a difference of 64 units between the two skull types.

The several regional proportions as designated below the curves show only slight differences, except in the case of the relation between the total anteroposterior width of the maxillary premolar teeth and the anteroposterior extent of the premolar region. The bassethound and bulldog skulls differ from one another for this proportion by 33 units of percentage.

The curves for averages of indices and proportions in the $F_1$ skulls almost invariably lie closer to the bassethound averages than to those of the bulldog, and this is particularly true in all cases where the two parent skulls are widely separated.

The average indices for the $F_2$ hybrid skulls shown by the dotted curve follow the $F_1$ curve very closely. This illustrates again the importance of individual records rather

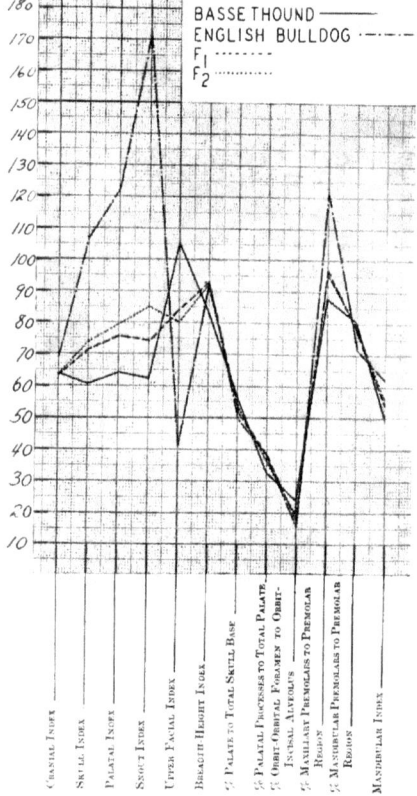

Text figure 69. Bassethound-English bulldog cross. Comparison of average skull measurements and indices for the pure breeds and their first and second generation hybrids.

than statistical averages in the study of characters exhibited by $F_2$ hybrids—thus the important value of the above review of these charts for individual indices. It might be mentioned in this connection that most human individuals are of at least the second generation in regard to almost all their separate features and characters, and that they therefore do not lend themselves to a reduction to community averages in any effort which might be made to properly understand the given characters and tendencies among them. With this in mind we shall return to a further brief consideration of the individual animals in the $F_2$ and backcross hybrid generations between the bulldog and the bassethound.

A second arrangement of curves may serve to bring out the individual differences in the same series of indices and proportions. In text-figures 70 and 71, the range of the characters in three bassethound skulls is represented by the area in solid horizontal lines. The range of values for the same characters in twelve bulldog skulls is shown by the dotted area enclosed in dash-dot outline. In text-figure 71, the range for three $F_1$ skulls is plotted in solid black, and in both figures the range in values for thirty $F_2$ skulls is represented by the area in dashed horizontal lines. The characters concerned are again listed at the bottom of the figures, each being immediately below the place on the curve which represents its value. Although the individual deviations from the average are represented in this pattern of curves, yet the skull characters concerned are so complex in their composition that the range of the $F_2$ hybrids fails to either reach or overlap the parent ranges for those characters which are highly contrasted in the two parent skull types. The snout index of the bulldog, for example, would seem to involve so extensive a complex of hereditary factors that extremely large numbers of $F_2$ animals would be needed to furnish the chance recovery of the exact genetic combination which is necessary to induce its fully expressed condition. In spite of some discouragement to which these curves may give rise in an isolated study of skulls as such, we have found that careful investigations of all parts and functions in the living animal, along with a histological study of the endocrine glands in connection with these skull measurements and head types,

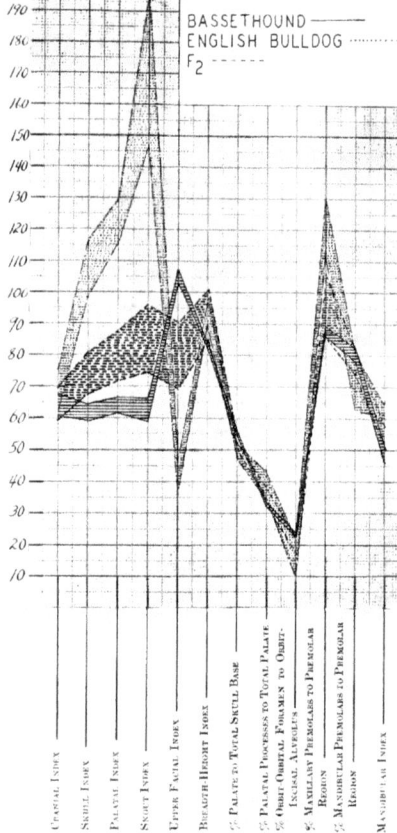

Text figure 70. Bassethound-English bulldog cross. Comparison of the range in skull measurements and indices for the pure breeds and their second generation hybrids.

GENETIC TYPE AND THE ENDOCRINES 319

have supplied a mass of knowledge which is of much aid in the interpretation of individual constitution as related to the genetic background and the functional reactions of the endocrines.

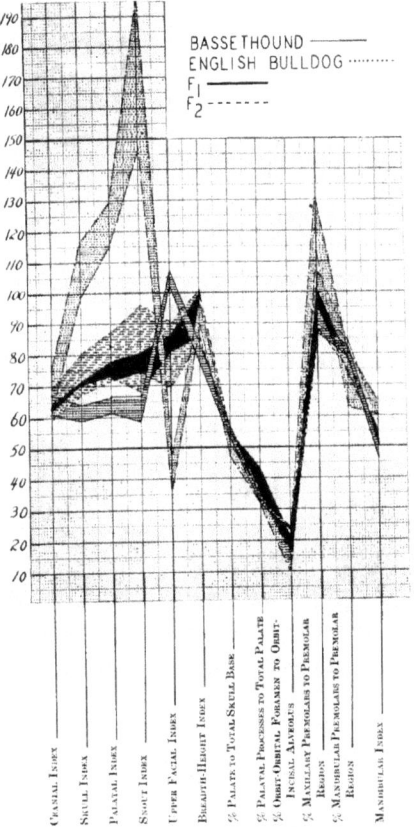

Text-figure 71. Bassethound-English bulldog cross. Comparison of the range in skull measurements and indices for the pure breeds and their first and second generation hybrids.

An examination of the dorsal views of individual skulls as shown in plate 57 will serve to emphasize the complexity of the reactions we are attempting to analyze. The skull of a highly typed bulldog is shown in figure 5, a typical bassethound skull is shown in figure 3, and the $F_1$ bassethound-bulldog hybrid skull is shown in figure 4. This hybrid skull is intermediate in its resemblance to the two parent types. It shows a prognathous condition of the lower jaw as in the bulldog, but the type of the mandible and the position of the projecting incisor and canine teeth resemble more closely these characters in the bassethound. What has actually happened is that the upper facial skeleton has been somewhat shortened while the mandible has not.

The backcross of this $F_1$ hybrid on the bulldog gave rise to the two skulls in figures 6 and 7. These may be diagnosed, using the bulldog parent for comparison, as bulldog skulls which are too long for perfect type. Each of these skulls is also quite different from the other.

The backcross of the $F_1$ on the bassethound stock produced the two skulls in figures 1 and 2. In general these are closely similar to the pure bassethound skull although, as comparison shows, they are too short for pedigreed type. These two backcross skulls are very closely alike.

PLATE 57

EXPLANATION OF FIGURES

Skulls of the bassethound-English bulldog cross showing contrast in size and features in the pure breeds and the resulting condition in the hybrids, particularly the remarkable size differences to be found among members of the second generation.

1 Backcross bassethound 1010 ♀.
2 Backcross bassethound 1011 ♀.
3 Bassethound 277 ♀.
4 $F_1$ 695 ♂.
5 English bulldog 104 ♀.
6 Backcross bulldog 875 ♂.
7 Backcross bulldog 876 ♂.

8–21 $F_2$ hybrids.

8  1053 ♂.
9  1359 ♂.
10 1145 ♂.
11 1052 ♂.
12 1171 ♂.
13 1175 ♀.
14 991 ♂.

15 1055 ♀.
16 977 ♂.
17 995 ♀.
18 978 ♂.
19 1147 ♂.
20 902 ♀.
21 1056 ♀.

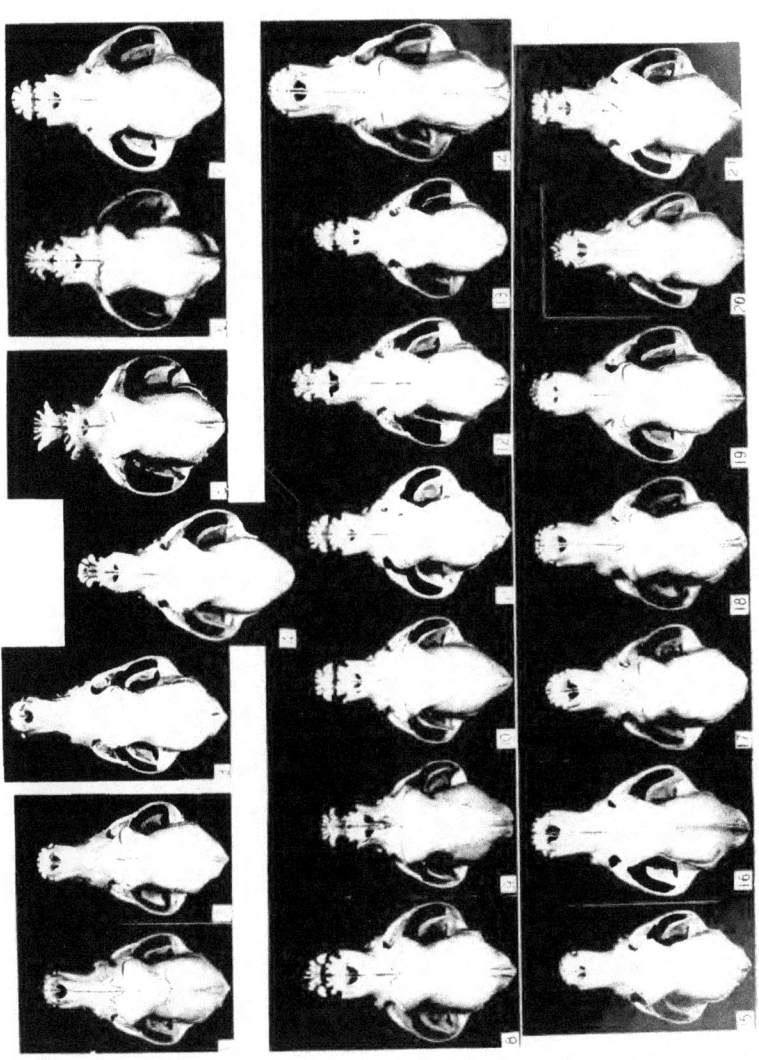

## BOTH GIANT AND DWARF REACTIONS FOR BODY SIZE AMONG $F_2$ BASSETHOUND-BULLDOG HYBRIDS

The two lower rows of skulls in plate 57 (figs. 8–21) are from fourteen bassethound-bulldog $F_2$ hybrids. All photographs in the plate were reduced to the same degree, and the skulls are therefore accurately comparable for size and shape.

No two of the fourteen $F_2$ hybrid skulls are closely alike in all respects. In the first place, the group offers remarkable differences in size; this is particularly outstanding in view of the fact that the two ancestral stocks are of about the same normal size, as are also the $F_1$ hybrid parents. Figure 8 is somewhat oversized and quite bulldog-like. Figure 9 is smaller and shows congenital absence of the entire nasal bones, the only such case on record for the dog. Figures 10, 11 and 12 show varied conditions inclining toward the bulldog type. Figure 13, as well as figure 20, is decidedly small and dwarf in type; figure 13 is rather bulldog-like and figure 20 is nearer the bassethound type. $F_2$ dwarfs similar to those furnishing these two skulls are photographed from life in plate 58 (fig. 7) and plate 59 (figs. 3 and 5). These plates were arranged to show dwarfs standing close to their large litter mates, and all animals were photographed at the same age. All photographs were reduced to the same degree and the animals are therefore directly comparable for size.

In plate 57, the skulls in figures 14, 16 and 18 are giant in size when compared with the parent stocks. These skulls, as well as the animals from which they were obtained, exhibit certain symptoms of acromegaly. In many of their features the skulls resemble more closely the skull of the giant St. Bernard dog than they do those of either parent stock. Plate

PLATE 58

EXPLANATION OF FIGURES

Second generation bassethound English bulldog hybrids showing both giant and dwarf body sizes among members of the same litter, as well as other growth distortions, such as an excessive amount of skin area.

1  991 ♂.   2  995 ♀.   3  996 ♀.   4  992 ♂.   5  977 ♂.   6  980 ♂.   7  979 ♂.

(Figs. 1 to 4, litter mates; 5 to 7, litter mates.)

PLATE 5.

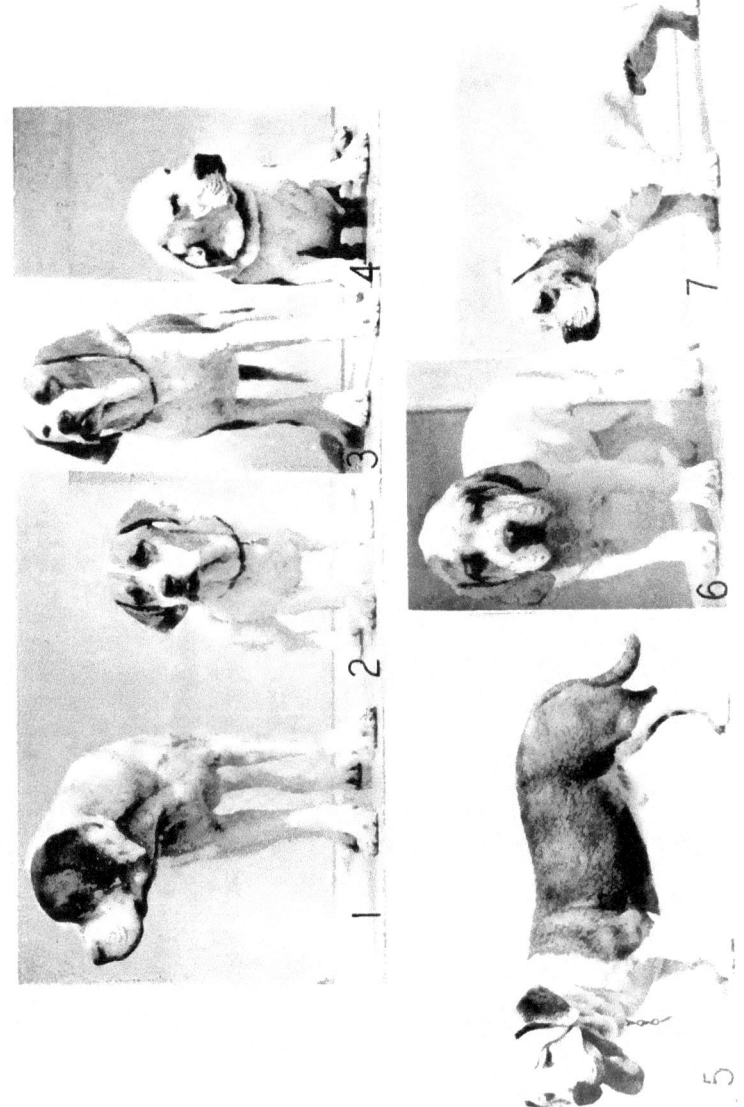

PLATE 59

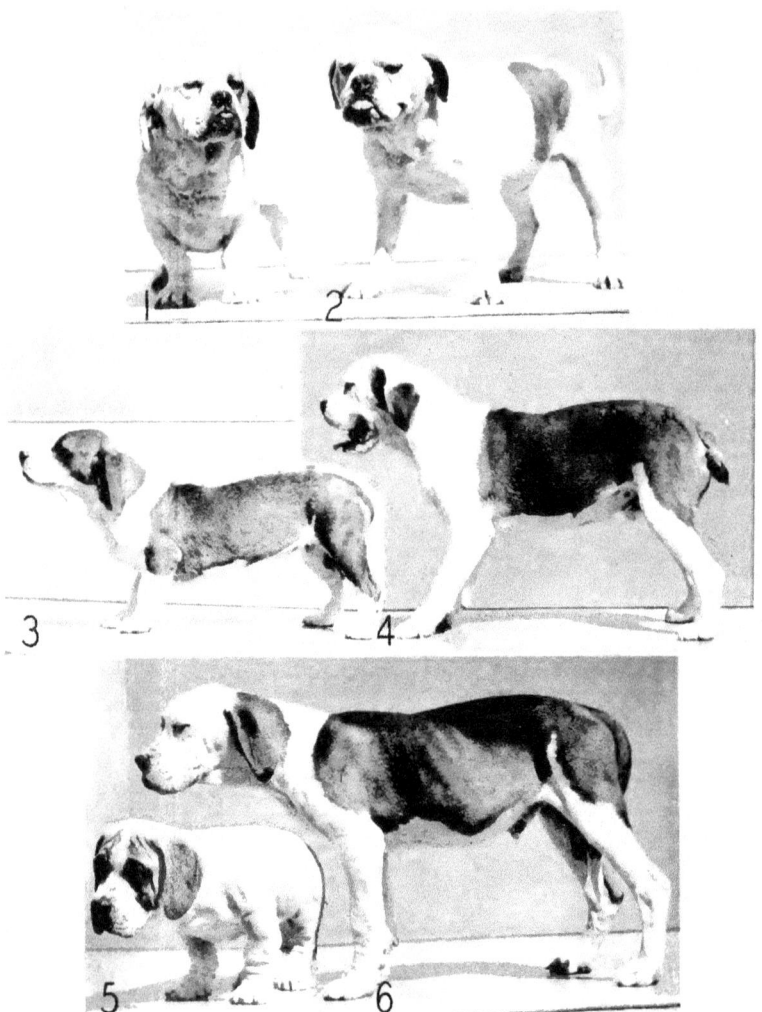

Second generation bassethound-English bulldog hybrids. A further comparison of size differences and skin area among litter mates.
1 1053 ♂.  2 1052 ♂.  3 1055 ♀.  4 1054 ♂.  5 1135 ♂.  6 1134 ♂.
(Figs. 1 and 2, litter mates; 3 and 4, litter mates; 5 and 6, litter mates.)

60 shows two giant $F_2$ bassethound-bulldog skulls (figs. 1 and 4) and two pure St. Bernard skulls (figs. 2 and 3). All four skulls were reduced to the same degree. The heavy wide muzzle of the St. Bernard skull is seen to be closely imitated by the bassethound-bulldogs, and the set and occlusion of the teeth in both are similar. The giant skull in figure 14 (pl. 57), from 991 ♂, is equally as pronounced for St. Bernard type as are the skulls in plate 60.

Figure 1 in plate 58 (991 ♂) is the $F_2$ bassethound-bulldog which furnished the skull in figure 14 of plate 57. He is seen to be of giant frame, and persons familiar with dog breeds recognized in him the splendid type of the short-haired St. Bernard dog, and found nothing reminiscent of either the bulldog or the bassethound.

It is of peculiar interest to find giant size of the entire body as well as overgrowth of certain parts, and also dwarfism and deficiencies of growth, all appearing among hybrids derived from two normal sized parent stocks. Both these opposite typed growth reactions are thought to be associated with derangements of the pituitary gland, and some writers have been bold enough to claim that gigantism and overgrowths are brought about by the hypersecretion of a certain pituitary product, the hyposecretion or absence of which results in cessation of growth and dwarfism. Such reasoning presumes that quite opposite pituitary conditions are related to each of these directly contrasted growth responses. Certainly the pituitary disturbance that might be associated with the inability to attain normal size could scarcely be the same as that associated with an excess of growth to double normal size, always provided, of course, that one accepts the pituitary as the controlling element and the tissue constitution as of secondary or of no importance. Whether either or both giant and dwarf growth patterns are initiated through pituitary anomalies, both certainly develop in the strange constitutional complexes which arise from the new combinations of factors occurring in the $F_2$ bassethound-bulldog hybrids. And still

PLATE 60

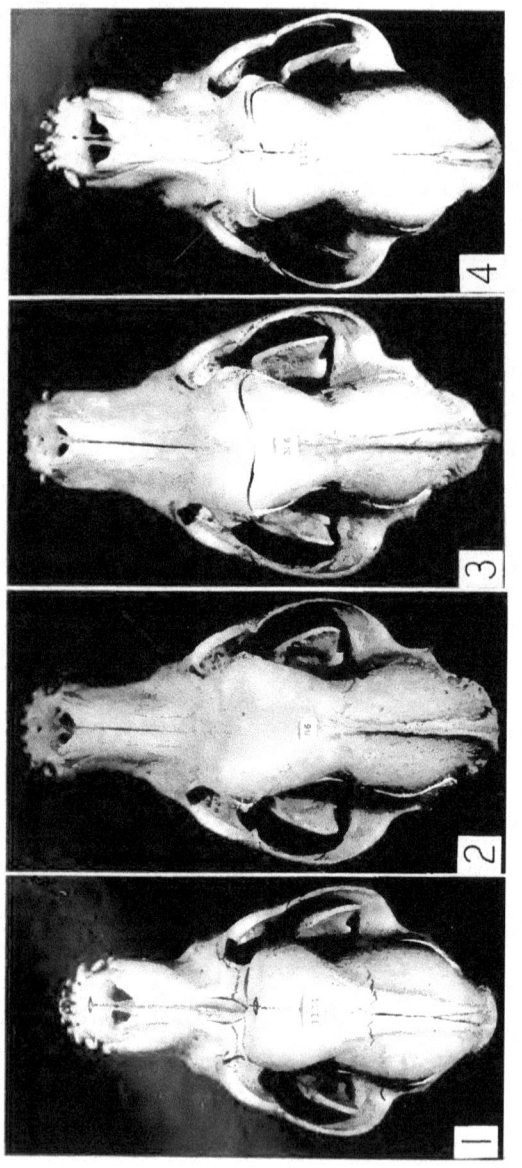

A comparison of two giant F₁ bassethound-English bulldog skulls with the pure St. Bernard. In many skull features, these F₁s resemble the St. Bernard much more than they do either the bassethound or bulldog parent stocks.
1. F₁ Bassethound-bulldog 1134 ♂.   2. St. Bernard 86 ♀.   3. St. Bernard 226 ♀.   4. F₁ Bassethound-bulldog 1172 ♂.

more difficult of endocrine explanation is the fact that a single hybrid individual may show symptoms of both types of growth distortion, being dwarf in body size with an overgrowth of skin or other parts.

The regulatory mechanisms for adjusting growths to normal size and form must be quite stably balanced among pure breeds, or there could not be so large a majority of individuals with fairly uniform measurements. It is difficult to believe that the constitutional complex which tips this adjustment towards gigantism and acromegaly is the same as that which in an identical environment lowers it towards dwarfism and chondrodystrophy. However, the occurrence of these contrasted patterns among the bulldog-bassethound second hybrid generation might indicate that the distortions of size in both directions are the consequence of strange genetic associations which arise in hybrid combinations. As pure breeds, neither the bassethound nor the bulldog shows tendencies toward giant or dwarf body size, and yet both breeds have localized chondrodystrophy in their skeletons, along with an excessive production of loose-fitting skin. Chondrodystrophy is commonly found among dwarf types, and overgrowth of skin is common among giant breeds. When dog breeds carrying these two qualities are crossed, the hybrids show new variations in total body size, and individuals both larger and smaller than the parent types are produced.

This is an entirely different phenomenon from inheritance of breed size when large and small breeds are crossed. Breed size in some cases is inherited in a very simple manner, while in others it is more complex and the members of the $F_1$ generation may be larger in size than either parent stock. One of the simplest examples of size inheritance is the cross between the full sized bassethound and the small dachshund. Total body size in this cross follows a rather definite Mendelian behavior. The $F_1$ hybrids are uniformly intermediate in size when compared with the parent stocks, although they are probably somewhat nearer the dachshund. The large majority of $F_2$ hybrids are of about the same size as the $F_1$; a few are as small as the dachshund and a few are of bassethound size. These size differences are definite, and there is no overlapping.

The individuals in the several generations of the bassethound-dachshund cross have already been recorded in a previous section under a discussion of the inheritance of short legs. The inheritance of skull size is well illustrated in plate 61. Two dachshund skulls (figs. 1 and 2) are seen to be much smaller than the bassethound skull (fig. 3). The $F_1$ skull (fig. 4) is of intermediate size. Of the four skulls from one litter of $F_2$ hybrids, two (figs. 5 and 6) are intermediate in size and very close to the $F_1$, one (fig. 7) is as small as the dachshund and is also without the sagittal cranial crest, and one (fig. 8) is as large as the bassethound skull and shows the same high sagittal crest along the top of the cranium. This $F_2$ litter chances to show the expected ratio of size differences, having one small, two intermediate, and one large member. The large size and bassethound cranial crest are recessive to small size and dachshund flat-top cranial pattern.

In this cross between two breeds of different body size, no hybrids of more diminutive or of greater size than the parent stocks have appeared. This is also true for a number of other crosses between large and small breeds. The giant and dwarf specimens arising from the cross between the equal sized bulldog and bassethound stocks are distinctly new types due to strange genetic combinations.

## Excessive Skin Area and Other Disharmonies of Growth in Hybrids from Breeds with Bulldog Deformities

Not only do giant and dwarf body sizes appear among the bulldog-bassethound hybrids, but limited and localized growth distortions occur as well. One of the most pronounced of the limited distortions is confined to the exaggerated overgrowth of skin. In specimens with this peculiarity, the skeletal frame and total body proportions are of normal size, but

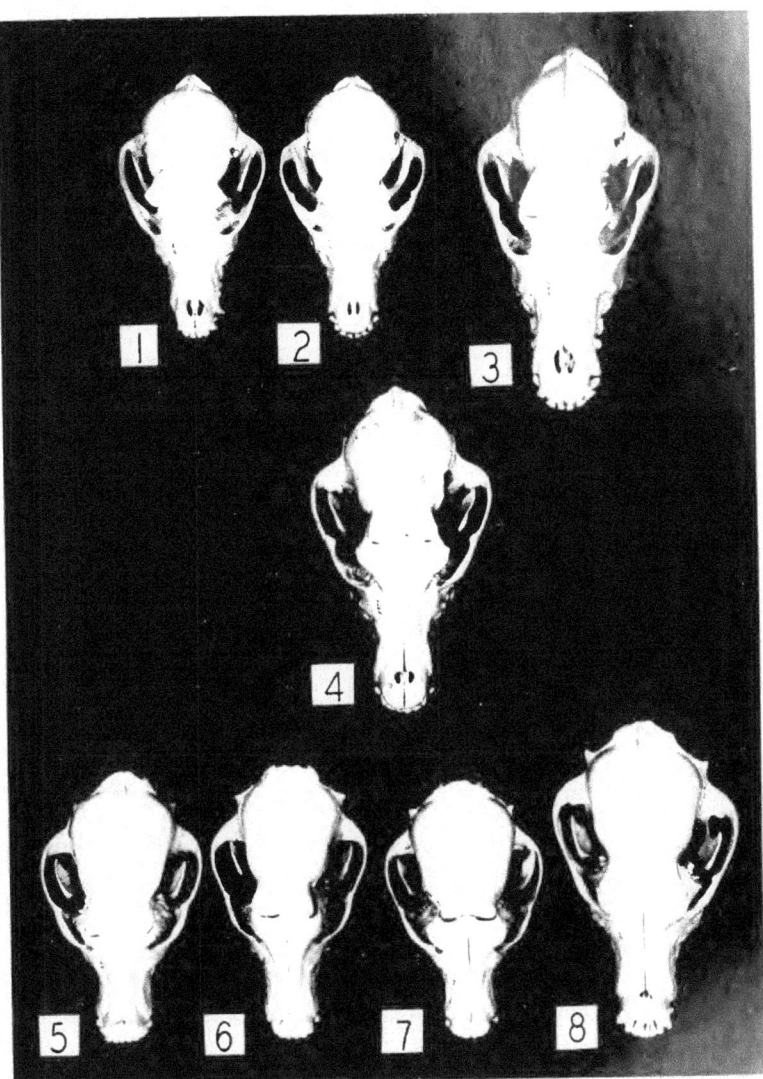

Skulls of the bassethound-dachshund cross illustrating, as a contrast to the bassethound-English bulldog cross, one of the simplest examples of size inheritance.

1. Dachshund 84 ♀.　　3. Bassethound 277 ♂.　　5, 8. $F_1$s.
2. Dachshund 255 ♀.　　4. $F_1$ 1263 ♂.　　　　　6, 7, 1035 ♀.

the area of the skin surface is excessively increased to more than double the necessary amount. The excess skin hangs in loose wrinkles and folds about the head, neck, shoulders and legs. The $F_1$ bulldog-bassethound has a considerable amount of excess skin, and among the members of the $F_2$ generation some individuals show an extreme overgrowth of skin surface while others show quite normal, close-fitting skin. The seven $F_2$ animals in plate 58 all have loose skin hanging in excessive folds about the head and neck. In plate 59, figures 3 and 4 are almost normal in this respect while figures 1, 2, 5 and 6 show skin that is wrinkled and folded.

The four brothers illustrated in plate 62 are from one $F_2$ litter and have been especially chosen to demonstrate the exaggerated production of skin in these hybrids. These four dogs, photographed from life in figures 1–4, all have loose wrinkles and heavy folds of skin about the head, neck, shoulders, back and legs.

In order to demonstrate the extent of skin overgrowth, the two brothers in figures 3 and 4 were killed and treated as follows. No. 1146 ♂ (fig. 4) was mounted as true to life as possible by an expert in mammalian taxidermy. The skin was placed on an accurately measured model and the folds were carefully patterned after those in the living animal. This mounted specimen is shown in figures 6 and 8, and the skeleton of this animal, photographed at exactly comparable scale, in figure 7. There are no symptoms of overgrowth in this skeleton, and body weights and sizes for all four brothers were closely the same. The skin area of this animal was, however, sufficient to cover twice his body size, and the excess formed the wrinkles on the forehead, the deep folds over the cheeks sagging into the low hanging flews or pendulous lips of the upper jaw, the folds along the sides of the neck with the loose double dewlap swinging from the chin to the sternum, and the circular folds covering the short bent legs. The skin is loose along the back and sides of the trunk, but better fitting over the rump and thighs.

PLATE 62

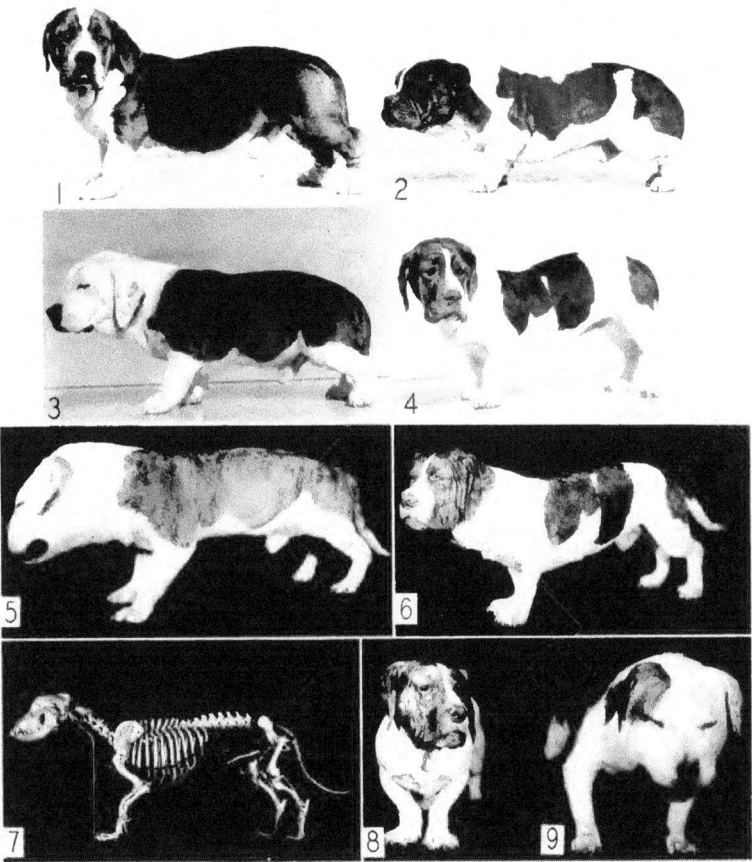

Further details of the enormous amount of skin area to be found among the second generation bassethound-English bulldog hybrids.

1   1143 ♂.
2   1145 ♂.
3   1144 ♂.
4   1146 ♂.
5   1144 ♂ (mounted specimen; animal prepared to show full extent of skin area).
6   1146 ♂ (mounted specimen; skin folds carefully patterned after those in the living animal).
7   1146 ♂.
8   1146 ♂ (mounted specimen).
9   1144 ♂ (mounted specimen).

A brother of this animal, 1144 ♂ (fig. 3), was mounted in an entirely different manner by the same taxidermist. The skin, carefully prepared so as to avoid any possible stretching, was completely stuffed so that there were no folds or wrinkles and the full extent of its area could be demonstrated. Figures 5 and 9 show this dog as it would have looked had its body frame been such as to take up the excess skin.

The excessive overgrowth of skin in either pure line dog breeds or these hybrids is associated with developmental arrests resulting in both histological and cytological abnormalities of the pituitary gland. The defective condition of these pituitary glands is illustrated and discussed in a further section of this study.

An exaggerated overproduction of skin comparable with the most extreme conditions found among the $F_2$ bulldog-bassethound hybrids is obtained by backcrossing the $F_1$ hybrid with the pure bulldog stock. Figure 1 in plate 63 shows the bulldog to have a degree of looseness of skin about the neck and shoulders. In this case, however, the wrinkles about the head and face are due to suppression of the underlying parts of the face and upper jaw without equal reduction in the rather normal amount of overlying skin. If the reader will imagine the skeletal structures of the muzzle of the dog in figure 2 to be flattened back as in the bulldog, he may readily appreciate that the skin covering would also be pressed back in accordion fashion, forming the cheek folds of the bulldog. Figure 2 is of an $F_1$ bassethound-bulldog hybrid having somewhat looser skin than the bulldog.

Figures 3 to 6 in plate 63 show the skin conditions in the hybrids derived from backcrossing the $F_1$ on the bulldog. Figure 3 shows sagging skin about the approximately half-typed bulldog head, and figures 4, 5 and 6 illustrate the high degree of skin overgrowth in these hybrid animals.

The excess in skin area over body size is a definite case of structural disharmony. The size of the skeletal frame and the muscular form are far too small and out of accord with

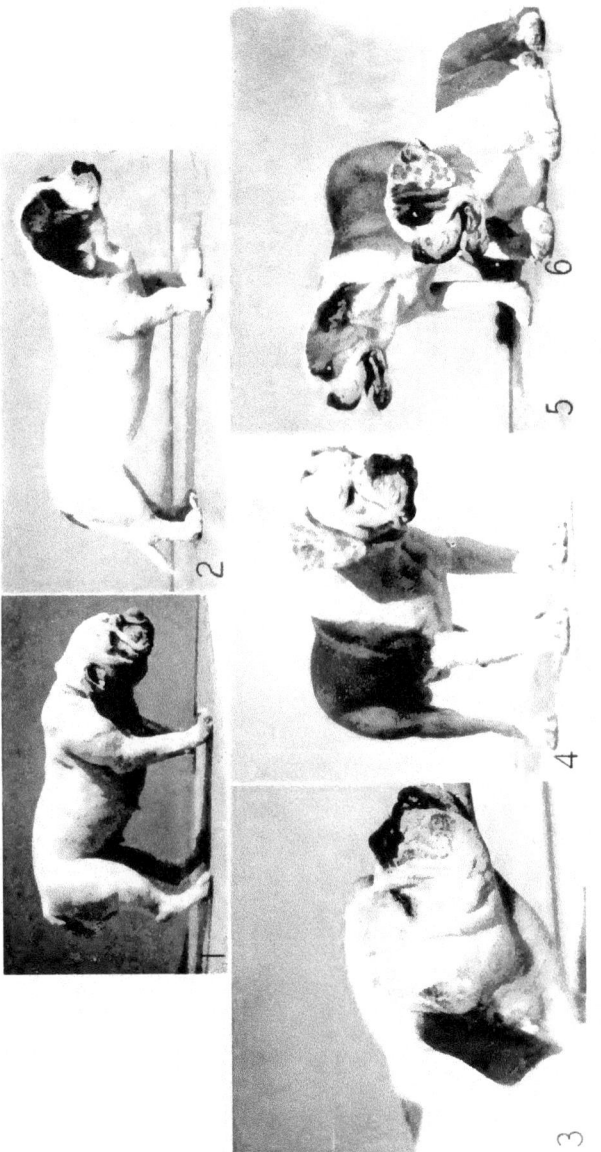

PLATE 63

Excess growth of skin in head and neck regions in hybrids produced by backcrossing the $F_1$ bassethound English bulldog with the pure bulldog stock.

1. English bulldog 885 ♂.  2. $F_1$ bassethound bulldog 692 ♀.  3 and 5. Backcross bulldog 875 ♂.  4 and 6. Backcross bulldog 876 ♂.

the dermal coat. An animal is handicapped by this condition. The drag of the skin often misplaces the opening of the eyelids and in some cases obscures the vision. The flews or upper lips are so excessive and pendulous as to inconvenience the dog when feeding, and the unusually thick, hanging skin makes locomotion heavy and cumbersome. The skin is excessive in thickness, as well as too large in area, and may be fully one centimeter thick over the dorsum of the neck.

This disharmony between skin area and body size, although differing in many ways from the misfit between upper and lower jaws which we have previously discussed, is in some respects a comparable structural mixup resulting from hybrid confusion of genetic qualities.

We may recall another disharmony of similar type, that of leg length in the $F_2$ hybrids between the short legged dachshund and the slender legged Brussels griffon. Some of these $F_2$ animals have disproportionately long hind extremities which raise the level of the hips high above the level of the shoulders. Referring to plate 65 (p. 340) we see that the animal in figure 1 has a partially expressed rabbit-like disproportion between the front and hind legs, while the sister (fig. 2) shows the proper balance in extremity length.

In other sections of this study we have discussed a number of different structurally disharmonious conditions, such as the skin overgrowth in several giant breeds, inadequate dental accommodation in the short jawed breeds, inadequacy of the optic fossa to accommodate the eyeball in the flat faced Brussels griffon and Pekingese and so on. The one character common to all these breeds and hybrids in which structural misfits occur is an abnormality of the pituitary gland. Such an array of growth disharmonies in association with pituitary abnormality makes it seem highly probable that the pituitary secretions are largely concerned with the normal regulation and adjustment of growth among the organ systems and bodily parts. It should be remembered that many of these disharmonious arrangements are strictly inherited in very definite fashion. This fact may mean that the related peculiarity of the pituitary is the primarily inherited character, while the structural derangements are secondary results due to the failure in harmonious growth regulation by the genetically modified pituitary gland.

Slight structural disharmonies in pure stocks may often be enormously increased by hybridization. For example, both the bulldog and bassethound have a mild degree of looseness and wrinkling of the skin, but hybrids between these two stocks show an exaggerated degree of skin overgrowth far beyond that attained by either pure breed. A careful observer may frequently notice similar accentuations of characters in the hybrids between human racial stocks.

## THE BULLDOG MODIFICATION IN COMPARISON WITH OTHER SHORT MUZZLED AND ROUND HEADED DISTORTIONS IN NON-RELATED BREEDS

The bulldog-like breeds thus far considered have all originated either directly or indirectly within a limited region of western Europe. These breeds not only show similarities in their head features, but are more or less similar in many of their general characteristics. For example, all are short and stocky in body form, and have short, stiff hair, brindle coloring, a tendency for lifting or erecting the ears, etc. It is highly probable that the typical modifications in the features of the head and skull in the English and French bulldogs and in the Boston terrier have been derived from one original complex or series of mutations which occurred somewhere in their common ancestry.

It was impossible to learn from a study limited to the skulls of these three breeds whether the bulldog-like deformities occurring in entirely unrelated dog breeds and other animal species were of similar genetic complexity and developed on the same modified pattern. It seemed very desirable to extend the investigation to include other breeds which had independently developed comparable bulldog distortions of the old ancestral dog head pattern.

For this purpose, two other bulldog-like breeds were chosen, the Brussels griffon and the Pekingese. The first of these is of probable European origin supposedly non-related for the deformity to the above three breeds, and the second is an Asiatic flat faced animal of entirely distinct origin. The midget Brussels griffon has previously been referred to in connection with the extremely aberrant skull shown in plate 50 (p. 274). This skull differs from that of the typical bulldog in its more infantile form and the disproportionately huge spherical cranium, with which is associated an extremely abbreviated facial skeleton with a mandible that is as severely reduced as the upper jaw. It will be recalled that in the typical bulldog deformity there is a marked prognathism of the mandible due to the fact that the lower jaw is only partially involved in the facial abbreviation.

The Brussels griffon was crossed with the long muzzled dachshund in order that the genetic behavior of the head conditions could be compared with that in the bulldog-dachshund hybrids previously considered.

The second cross involved the Pekingese poodle. This dog is thought to have arisen in China several thousand years ago, and early bronze effigies and figures leave no doubt that this breed has existed in its present form since ancient times. One may be reasonably certain that the peculiar form and structure of the Pekingese head had an independent origin from that of the head type of the European bulldogs as well as of the Brussels griffon. This dwarfed Pekingese dog was crossed for head type with, again, the small dachshund. We have further made the cross between the Pekingese and the tall, slender and greyhound-like Egyptian Saluki. This latter cross involves the widest extremes of breed and type brought together during our hybridization experiments.

A brief discussion of these crosses in reference to the inheritance and development of head form will be given in order to add to the more extensive results derived from the crosses between bulldogs and the long headed types.

### The Head Features in Brussels Griffon-Dachshund Hybrids

Two midget Brussels griffon males of the best breed lines were crossed with two pedigreed dachshund females. The extreme contrast between the flat monkey-like face of the griffon and the long slender muzzle of the dachshund is clearly shown in figures 1 and 2 of plates 33 (p. 136) and 64. The long straight legs of the griffon are also sharply contrasted with the short achondroplasic legs of the dachshund. The genetics of leg length in this cross has been presented in an earlier section.

Achondroplasia of the extremities is transmitted as a single factor dominant character completely independent of the factors determining the flat face or the long muzzle. Among the second generation hybrids the shortened muzzle may appear in association with either the long or short legs, just as was the case among the bulldog-bassethound hybrids.

Figures 3–6 in plate 64 illustrate the first generation, $F_1$, dachshund-Brussels griffon hybrids. They all show the dominant short leg of the dachshund and the long, rough hair of the griffon. The muzzle is considerably shorter than that of the dachshund and the depression at the nasion, the "stop," is much more pronounced. Yet in comparison with the head of the Brussels griffon, the $F_1$ muzzle is very long and the jaws very strong.

The mandible in the $F_1$ is not always so much shortened as is the maxilla. Among ten specimens of this generation, six showed prognathism of the mandible, "undershot" malocclusion, and one female had opposition of the incisors rather than the proper occlusion with lower incisors fitting behind the upper. This again emphasizes the fact that the abbreviation of the face in the short headed deformity is due to a complex of genetic influences, some dominant and some recessive, and all quite independent of one another, so that different parts are not always affected in a corresponding manner in a given individual. Structural disharmonies with

PLATE 64

Cross between the long muzzled dachshund and flat faced Brussels griffon to determine whether the expression of head type in the hybrid generations is of the same genetic complexity and develops on the same modified pattern as was found for the bulldog deformity in the bassethound English bulldog cross. The expression of other physical characters is also indicated.

1  Dachshund 255 ♀.
2  Brussels griffon 278 ♀.

3–6  $F_1$ hybrids.
3  134 ♂.
4  1675 ♀.
5  1676 ♀.
6  135 ♂.

7–10  $F_2$ hybrids.
7  kennel number not noted.
8  1946 ♂.
9  1947 ♀.
10  1948 ♀.

misfits, such as dental malocclusion, are common among these hybrids in both the first and second generations, and more serious maldevelopment of the face has proved fatal at the time of birth to some individuals of the second generation. Here again, as in the bulldog, the head condition in the carefully bred and selected Brussels griffon is so complex in its genetics that the best specimens are rarely completely homozygous for the entire complex; hence, the variability in head structures among the members of the $F_1$ generation.

In general behavior, the $F_1$ hybrids show a variety of reaction combinations derived from both parent breeds. They are very nervous and restless and almost constantly on the run, thus resembling somewhat the jumpy behavior of the griffon; but at the same time they are extremely shy and snappy towards people, and in this characteristic resemble more closely the dachshund.

Three $F_1$ bitches have whelped five litters of second generation, $F_2$ hybrids. The litters contained six, three, eight, four, and eight puppies, a total of twenty-nine. About half of these lived to maturity. Four of the litters contained one or more maldeveloped and grossly deformed puppies which were dead at birth. The small litter of three was the only one without a maldeveloped specimen, but since it was so small it is very probable that defective fetuses had died *in utero* before term. The deformities chiefly involved head structures, early arrests of the extremities tending toward amelia, with delayed development and lack of hair at birth.

Four $F_2$ hybrids are shown in plate 64 (figs. 7–10), and seven others are shown in plates 65 and 66. As will be recalled from the discussion in a previous section, these $F_2$ individuals have long, intermediate and short legs, and the majority have long, rough hair. They are peculiarly susceptible to mange infection and to rickety bones in spite of careful diet and vitamin feeding. The latter reactions indicate a defective and disturbed assimilation of calcium which cannot always

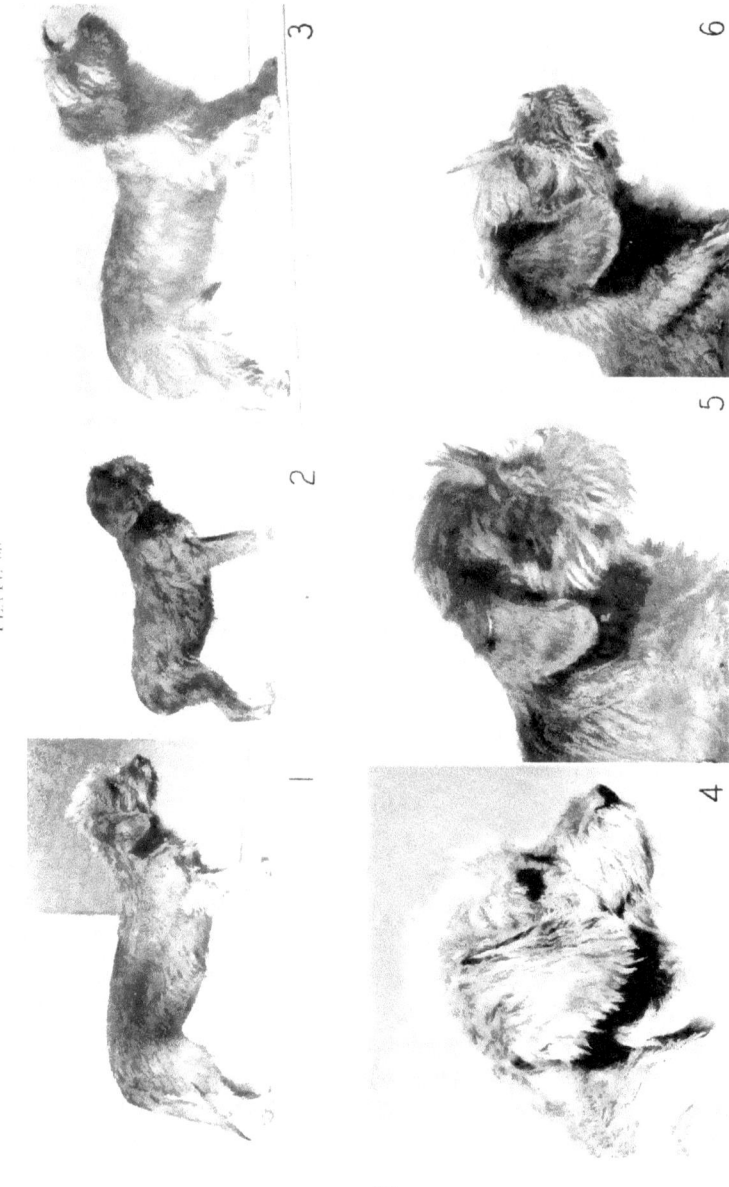

Second generation dachshund-Brussels griffon hybrids showing head form and other physical characters. 1 and 4, Kennel number not noted. 2 and 3, 1947 ♀. 5, 1946 ♂. 6, 1948 ♀.

PLATE 66

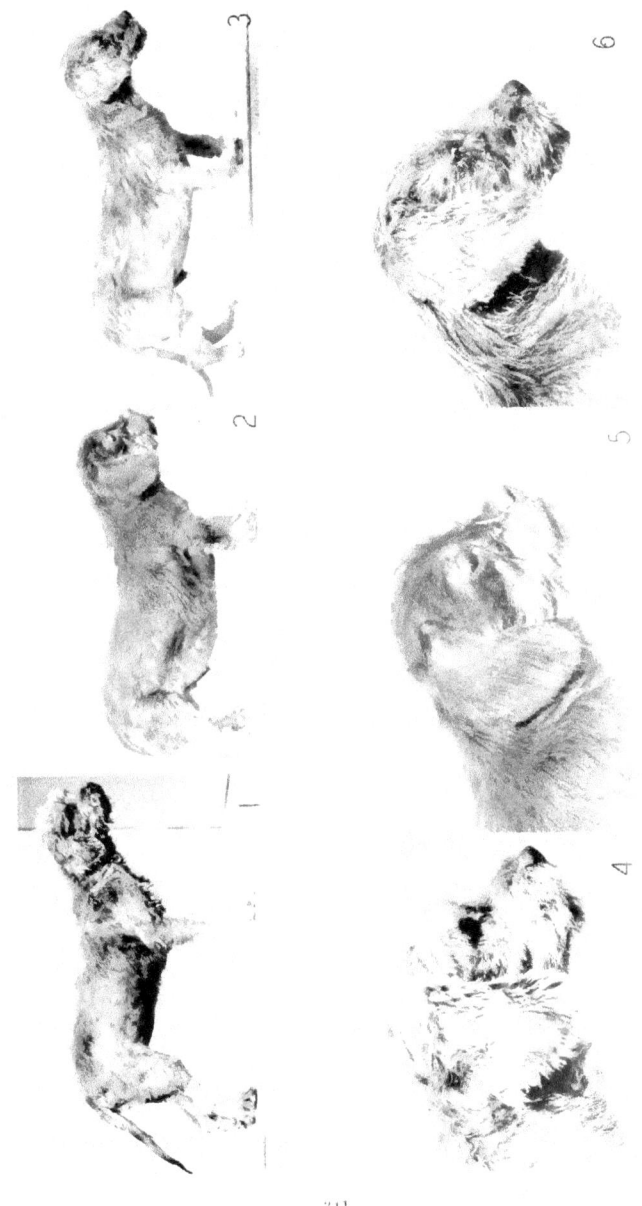

Second generation dachshund-Brussels griffon hybrids showing head form and other physical characters.
1 and 4—2656 2. 2 and 5—2656 3. 3 and 6—2656 4.

be overcome by well administered bone meal and vitamin D. These hybrid animals are constitutionally defective in their bone and skin reactions, and there is evidence of a defective pituitary-parathyroid complex not yet fully analyzed.

The head shapes of the $F_2$ hybrids vary widely, from the long and slender almost dachshund-like head seen in figures 3 and 6 in plate 66, to the short muzzled monkey-like face approaching the griffon (pl. 65, figs. 2 and 5). Between these two extremes are various modifications in shapes of the cranium and face. Figures 1 and 4 in plate 65 show a high spherical Brussels griffon-like cranium with a strong depression at the nasion, while the muzzle is slender and somewhat short and the jaws are well developed with normal dental occlusion. As mentioned above, the head of the animal in figures 2 and 5 (pl. 65) is shortened, and the prognathism of the mandible is hidden by the long hair. Figure 6 shows another short face and rounded cranium. The "undershot" prognathism of the lower jaw in this dog is clearly seen in the photograph.

Plate 66 illustrates three other $F_2$ Brussels griffon-dachshund hybrids. The heads have been photographed in profile at somewhat larger scale and are shown below the picture of the entire animal. The three specimens show evidence of the hypersensitive condition of the skin and there is an infection of mange about the eyelids and other places; the animal in figures 3 and 6 was, in addition, afflicted with rickets. Other puppies living under identical conditions of food and care were not so afflicted, and this is true even of litter mates with different constitutional compositions.

The short faced condition as expressed in these hybrids differs in several ways from the typical bulldog pattern, particularly in the mandible which is much more shortened. There is also no excessive wrinkling of the skin, as in the bulldog breeds. The mutations giving rise to the flat face in the Brussels griffon have involved factors which influence the growth in length of the mandible much more directly than did the mutations in the bulldog. This may represent an additional step in the mutational series bringing about the flat face. Prognathism of the mandible is only mildly expressed in the $F_2$ Brussels griffon-dachshunds and is in contrast to the long, protruding and up-curved mandible in the bulldog and the bulldog-bassethound hybrids. In this cross the head forms are again found to be expressed as a complex of characters influenced in their development by a number of genetic factors. Some of the mutant or modified factors are dominant and others recessive to the determiners for normal form.

The $F_1$ Brussels griffon-dachshund was backcrossed with the dachshund parent, and eight hybrids were whelped. These, as would be expected, were quite dachshund-like in quality. All had long muzzles, some of which were almost typically dachshund, and others showed a considerable depression at the nasion as a last character from the Brussels griffon. All were short legged, and about half the individuals had long hair, in some cases rough and in others silky. Plate 33 (p. 136) illustrates five of these backcross dachshund hybrids.

## The Head Features in Dachshund-Pekingese Hybrids

In the Asiatic Pekingese dog the reduced muzzle projects very little if at all beyond the overhang of the bulging forehead. This pattern of growth is quite definitely the result of achondroplasia in the basicranium and the facial skeleton, similar in kind to the growth disturbances giving form to the bulldog head. The high bred Pekingese, with its wide, flat face, large, protruding grape-like eyes, snoring pug nose and tight, snappy mouth can scarcely be claimed to have arisen from the same ancestral stock giving origin to the bulldog breeds in Europe. It seems logical to imagine that an Asiatic dog resembling the chow was the ancestral forerunner from which a mutation or series of mutations brought about the development of the achondroplasic dwarf Pekingese dog. The bodily characteristics of this achondroplasic sport from the Asiatic dog are closely similar to the characteristics produced by a comparable mutation or series of mutations among the European dogs in giving rise to the present day bulldog breeds. The series of factors involved in the two complexes may not, of course, be identically the same. In addition, the mutant changes might be thought of as progressive and as not having gone equally far in all cases. In the European bulldog, the point mutations effecting the reduction in length of the mandible have not progressed so far as in the Pekingese; the mandibular reduction has, however, been as fully accomplished in the European Brussels griffon as in the Pekingese.

It is quite evident after a long study of different breeds with various distortions of the head and other body regions that a series of very similar mutations tends to arise in the germ plasm of many breeds, not only within limited localities but in different regions of the world as well. These similar mutations have appeared in apparently independent fashion in the different dog stocks.

In order to determine whether the characters of the Pekingese head are inherited in a manner similar to that for the bulldog and the Brussels griffon, we have expended considerable time and effort in securing hybrid generations between the Pekingese and the dachshund. This cross is not in itself difficult to make, but it is very difficult to rear a satisfactory number of the hybrids even under careful kennel conditions. However, we have succeeded in accomplishing this.

*The $F_1$ dachshund-Pekingese hybrids.* Two litters of six and one litter of five $F_1$ dachshund-Pekingese hybrids have

PLATE 67

EXPLANATION OF FIGURES

Cross between the long muzzled dachshund and the short muzzled Pekingese for inheritance of head type as a further comparison with the expression of the bulldog deformity in the basset-hound-English bulldog cross.

1 Dachshund 255 ♀.
2 Pekingese AKC 795872 (not a kennel dog).
3-7 $F_1$ hybrids.
    3 1888 ♂.   4 2046 ♂.   5 1886 ♂.   6 2047 ♀.   7 1891 ♀.

PLATE 67

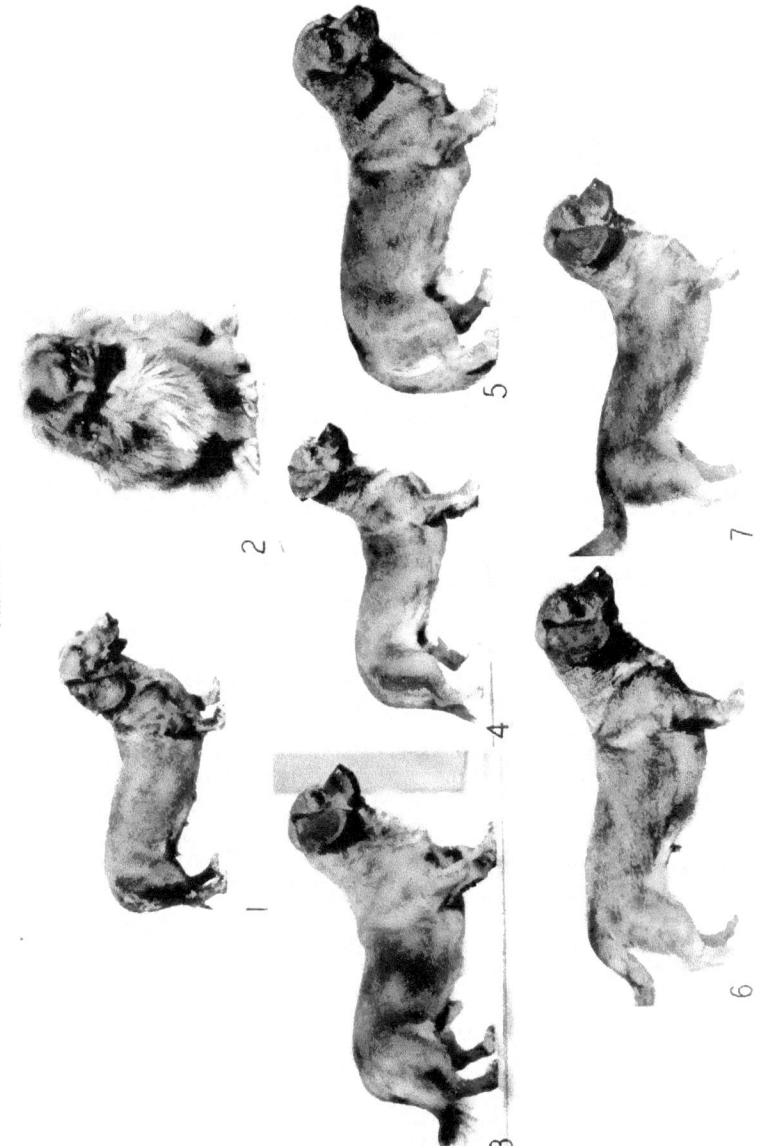

been obtained by crossing two pedigreed, high typed dachshund dams with a pronounced type Pekingese sire of champion stock. In addition, one litter of five $F_1$ reciprocal hybrids was obtained from a strong typed Pekingese dam by a good male dachshund. There have been twenty-two $F_1$ hybrids in all, and these are very uniform in size and type irrespective of whether they were whelped from Pekingese or dachshund dams. The hybrids are larger and more vigorous than either parent stock and are capable of living through severe winters in out-door kennels.

In plate 67, a typical dachshund bitch is shown (fig. 1) together with a less reduced photograph of a high typed Pekingese dog (fig. 2). Actually the dachshund is larger and heavier in weight than the Pekingese. The extremely contrasted head forms of the two breeds may be clearly seen in these pictures and are even more strikingly shown by plate 68 (figs. 1 and 2). The dachshund head has a long, slender muzzle and the jaws are perfectly formed, efficient in action and with proper dental occlusion. On the other hand, the facial skeleton of the Pekingese is extremely shortened, so much so that the muzzle, which is so characteristic of the dog family, is almost eliminated. The jaws are poorly formed and the teeth are irregularly set with extensive malocclusion. In the prize typed Pekingese, the mandible should not protrude beyond the maxilla; it should be equally shortened, so that the lower incisors fit in opposition with the upper. However, there is considerable tendency towards slight prognathism of the lower jaw, and even very carefully bred specimens frequently show mild degrees of this defect. In spite

PLATE 68

EXPLANATION OF FIGURES

Dachshund Pekingese cross. Further study of the contrasted head features in the pure breeds and the resulting expression in the first generation hybrids.

1 Dachshund 1177 ♀.
2 Pekingese 1118 ♂.
3–7 $F_1$ hybrids (same animals as shown in pl. 67, figs. 3–7).
  3 1888 ♂.  4 2046 ♂.  5 1886 ♂.  6 2047 ♀.  7 1894 ♀.

PLATE 68

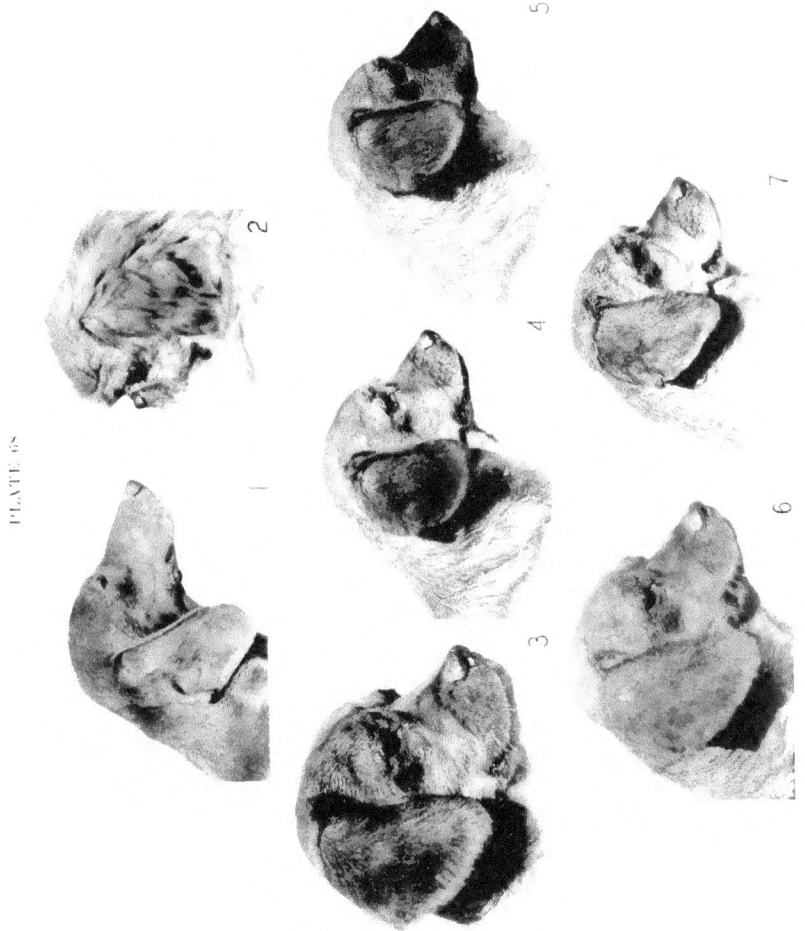

of this, the lower jaw in the Pekingese has clearly undergone mutation for pronounced reduction in length, as contrasted with the normal dog mandible as well as with the condition in the bulldog head.

Three $F_1$ males are shown in figures 3 to 5 of plate 67, and two $F_1$ bitches in figures 6 and 7. Larger photographs of the heads of these five animals are arranged in the same relative positions in plate 68.

These $F_1$ dachshund-Pekingese hybrids are very attractive in both appearance and behavior and were favorites with all the kennel attendants. As plate 67 indicates, the dachshund ancestry is clearly recognizable in their general form. The short legs are derived from both parent stocks, but the length of body and position of the tail suggest the dachshund. The posture of the head and neck is reminiscent of the haughty bearing typical of the Pekingese. These $F_1$ hybrids also behave with more assurance and boldness than the dachshund. Their coats are somewhat intermediate; not so completely short and much heavier than in the short haired dachshund, but much shorter and not so feathery as in the Pekingese. The $F_1$ animals are quite uniform in size and appearance and individuals can be distinguished from one another only by carefully recording the minor differences in color and markings. The size differences shown in the photographs of plate 67 are due to different degrees of reduction; no such noticeable variations exist among the animals.

The heads of these animals, as seen in plate 68, are strong and well proportioned. The cranium is slightly more spherical than in the dachshund, the depression at the nasion, the so-called "stop," more pronounced, and the muzzle shorter and apparently heavier. In other words, there is a general reduction of the long headed condition through combination with the flattened face and rounded head of the Pekingese. The upper and lower jaws of the $F_1$ hybrids are fairly equal in length, and in the majority the occlusion of the incisors is normal; the mandible is very slightly undershot in a few cases. The almost complete absence of prognathism of the mandible in this $F_1$ hybrid is in contrast to the strong prevalence of this condition in the $F_1$ bulldog-bassethounds, and emphasizes the fact that in the bulldog the largely dominant mutation for shortening the mandible has only begun to arise, although it seems to have been almost entirely accomplished in the Pekingese. In this connection we should also recall that the $F_1$ hybrids between the flat muzzled Brussels griffon and the dachshund are in most cases decidedly undershot. Although it has probably not been derived from the same stock as the typical bulldog, and even though the lower jaw shows greater reduction than this breed, yet the Brussels griffon has not attained the same degree of genetic purity for the mutant factors determining the short mandible as has the far more ancient Pekingese breed. This interpretation for these variations is far more plausible than would be the simple assumption that the lower jaw of the Pekingese is more dominant in character than that of the bulldog. It is not more dominant; it is more fully modified by mutations for shortness. We shall return to this matter in connection with the disharmony between the jaws in members of the second hybrid generation, in which both the genetic and developmental independence of maxilla and mandible are clearly demonstrated.

*The variety of head characters in the second generation dachshund-Pekingese hybrids.* Four $F_1$ bitches were mated with four $F_1$ males, and eight litters of $F_2$ dachshund-Pekingese hybrids were whelped. These litters contained eight, eight, five, eight, four, one, eight and five individuals, a total of forty-seven, more than half of which lived to adult age. Photographs of seven of these $F_2$ hybrids are shown in plate 69.

The $F_2$ hybrids vary considerably in size, ranging from small, even midget-like, individuals to dogs equal in size to the dachshund. Not one member of this generation possesses a complete expression of the typical Pekingese coat; the hair is either short, intermediate, or moderately long and varies

PLATE 69

Second generation dachshund-Pekingese hybrids showing variation in size, coat color and length, and head form.
1 2213 ♀. 2 2095 ♂. 3 2214 ♂. 4 2094 ♀. 5 2212 ♂. 6 2108 ♀. 7 Kennel number not noted.

in texture from soft and silky to rather coarse and hard. This would indicate a rather complex basis for the feathery hair and plume-like coat of the Pekingese. In color, the coats are various combinations of the parental stocks—black and various shades of red with white spotting. By chance an albino factor was carried in one of the parent breed lines and the brother-sister matings among the $F_1$ hybrids brought out this recessive factor. The albino dog is shown in figure 2 of plate 69. In not one of these hybrids is the tail held curled over the rump, Pekingese fashion. Such a tail position, characteristic of the Pekingese and Pomeranian poodle as well as the chow and other Asiatic dogs, would seem from this cross to be a character of complex genetics. All the $F_2$ animals have short achondroplasic legs, typical for both the dachshund and the Pekingese parent stocks, and the large ears of the dachshund are found to be quite dominant. The various head shapes in these hybrids are shown in plate 69 and again in profile in plate 70.

Beginning with figures 1 and 2 (pl. 70), 2213 ♀ and 2093 ♂, the cranial region is seen to be rounded or almost spherical, and as we continue toward the right it becomes progressively longer until in figure 7 we find an almost typical dachshund outline. In this head there is almost no "stop," or depression of the nasion, which is so pronounced in figures 1–4. These heads range from long and slender with long normal muzzles and shallow nasion depressions to those with short deep muzzles and high rounded foreheads. In none of the $F_2$ hybrids, however, is the muzzle so completely short as to give the flat Pekingese face, even though in a few it is greatly reduced and similar to what may be found in a poorly typed pure Pekingese.

The dental occlusion in these hybrids varies in a most significant manner. A few of them show the upper and lower jaws to be of about equal length with normal occlusion of the incisors; about the same number are slightly undershot having the lower incisors rising in front of the upper, the

PLATE 70

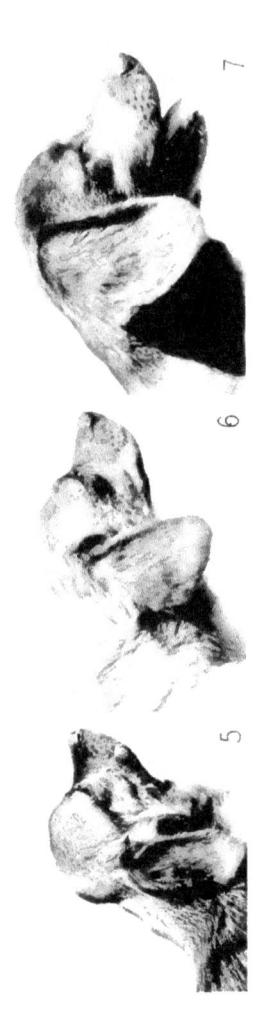

Further details of head form in second generation dachshund-Pekingese hybrids (same animals as shown in pl. 69).

1 2213 ♀.   2 2095 ♂.   3 2212 ♀.   4 2094 ♀.   5 2112 ♂.   6 2108 ♀.   7 kennel number not noted.

condition so common in the bulldog; while the most frequent expression in the $F_2$ hybrids is varying degrees of prognathism in the upper jaw, this causing the upper incisors to project far in front of the lower. The prognathism of the maxilla is often so extreme that even when the mouth is closed the tongue protrudes and hangs down in front of the chin. The long upper jaw in such specimens is apparently inherited in independent fashion from the dachshund line while the lower jaw is short and broad through a dominance of the Pekingese. In such an animal the misfit and disharmony of the jaws make feeding from shallow pans difficult, since the nose strikes the pan far in advance of the biting end of the short lower jaw.

In these crosses the genetic factors influencing growth in length of the mandible are transmitted quite independent of those influencing length of the maxilla and the basicranium. The two latter characters, however, are genetically linked, at least to a large extent. The independence in growth of the upper face to that of the lower jaw seems to be the rule for several widely separated dog breeds.

When long and short muzzled breeds are crossed, the members of the first hybrid generation show only mild degrees of disharmony between the upper and lower jaws, probably due to the complex genetic basis and only partial dominance of the factors for determination of either long or short jaws. Members of the second generation, through a recombination of factors separately influencing the length of each jaw, may show four possible combinations. In the first place, both jaws may be long. Secondly, both may be short and structurally harmonious with normal dental occlusion. A third condition is a short maxilla in association with a long undershot mandible, a disharmony of structures causing complete dental malocclusion. Finally, a fourth condition presents the reverse arrangement—long maxilla in association with short reduced mandible, the overshot disharmony with again complete dental malocclusion.

Plate 71 illustrates three of these jaw arrangements in $F_2$ dachshund-Pekingese hybrids. To facilitate comparisons, profiles of the long muzzled dachshund with normal dental occlusion and the flat faced, short muzzled Pekingese with fair occlusion are again shown. The $F_2$s in figures 4 and 6 show an extreme overshot condition, having a short Pekingese lower jaw in association with a fairly long dachshund upper jaw. Figure 3 has fortunately inherited an equally shortened condition of both the upper and lower jaws, and in length these are fairly intermediate between the dachshund and Pekingese. The dental occlusion in this animal is also good. Figure 5 shows prognathism of the mandible, the undershot lower jaw in association with a shortened upper jaw; the nose is slightly pugged, a character from the Pekingese. The disharmony between upper and lower jaws in this animal again causes complete dental malocclusion.

Disharmonies between the growth reactions of two jaws in the same head make it seem evident that the quality of the endocrine environment cannot be altogether responsible for the inhibition of growth in one jaw and stimulation of growth in the other. It would seem logical to expect that a modified internal chemistry would affect the simultaneous growth of two related structures in much the same manner. The old idea of a "developmental regulation" insuring harmonious structural adjustments is also seriously questioned by these evident contradictions. The commonly accepted point of view of the embryologist that the upper and lower jaws are derived from closely related branchial structures

PLATE 71

EXPLANATION OF FIGURES

Further details of the jaw arrangements and dental occlusion to be found among members of the second generation dachshund-Pekingese hybrids.

1  Dachshund 1177 ♀.
2  Pekingese 1118 ♂.
3–6  $F_2$ hybrids.
3  2213 ♀ (normal dental occlusion).
4  2212 ♂ (overshot).
5  2094 ♀ (undershot).
6  2214 ♀ (overshot).

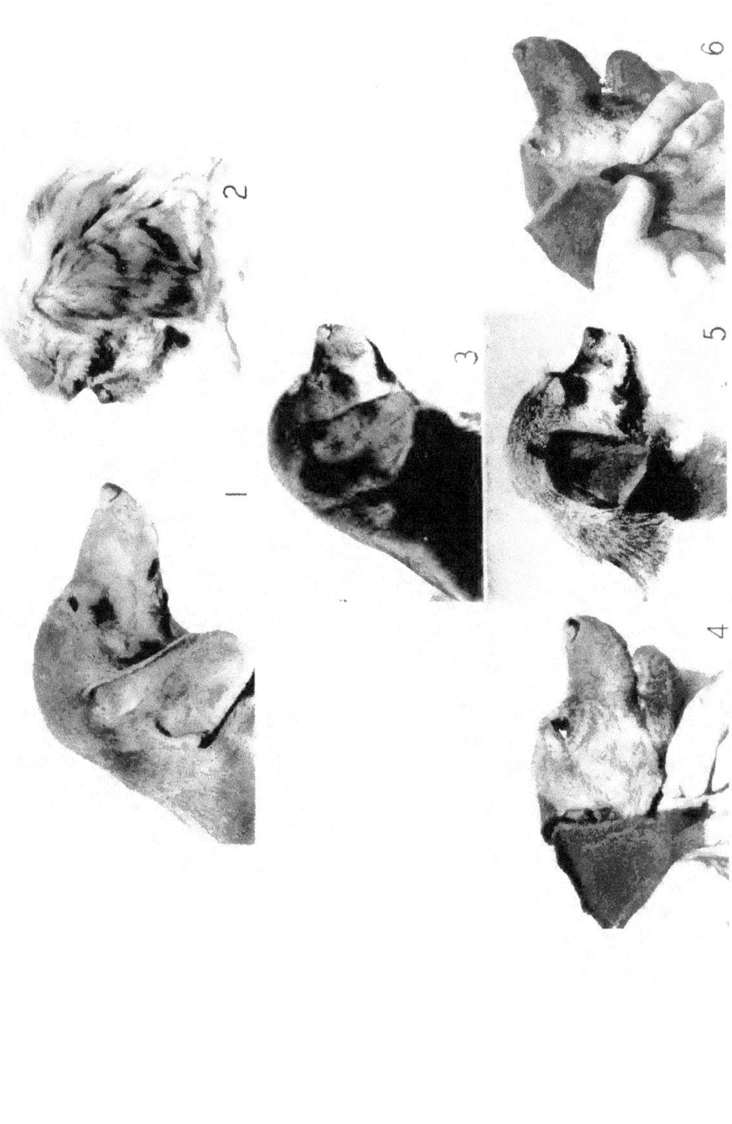

PLATE 72

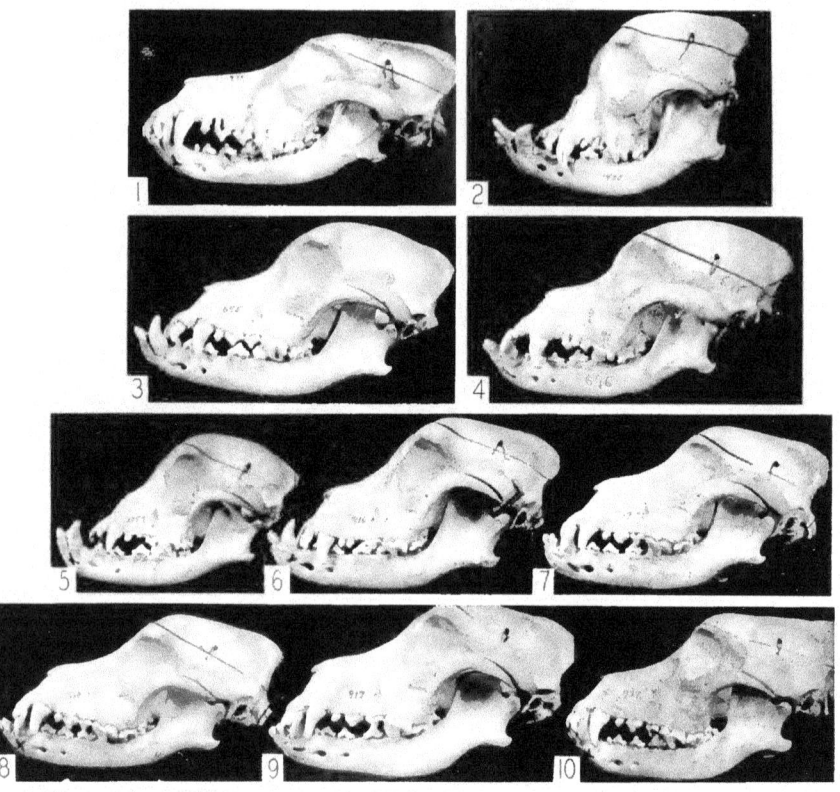

Skulls of the cross between the bassethound and English bulldog showing jaw arrangement and dental occlusion in the pure breeds and the resulting expression in the first and second generation hybrids.

1. Bassethound 277 ♀.
2. English bulldog 903 ♂.
3. F₁ 695 ♂.
4. F₁ 696 ♀.

5-10 F₂ hybrids.
5. 1359 ♂.
6. 916 ♂.
7. 919 ♀.
8. 918 ♀.
9. 917 ♂.
10. 977 ♂.

which differentiate in parallel directions and become functionally coordinated would lead one to expect a close correspondence in their reactions to stimuli tending to modify their growth and development. Yet the evidence from the dachshund-Pekingese cross, as well as from other crosses already discussed, shows quite clearly that the genetic basis for the pattern of the maxilla is entirely distinct and independent of the genetic background for the mandibular size and form. And further, the genetic constitution of the individual influences the patterns of the two jaws separately in spite of the quality of the internal environment as influenced by the endocrine glands. The genetic constitution of the tissues themselves determines their mode of growth and development as long as the environment is sufficiently favorable to permit the expression of the structure concerned.

Mutations have arisen in the ancestry of several different dog breeds which tend to suppress the growth in length of the face. The mutant factors which shorten the upper face and maxilla are not closely linked with other factors influencing the length and pattern of the mandible. Thus, in the English bulldog and the French bulldog, mutations have brought about a severe reduction of the usual canine muzzle, but the mutations for a corresponding reduction in length of the lower jaw have not reached completion. In the Boston terrier, the mandibular mutation is more nearly accomplished and there is only a slight or no undershot condition; and in the Brussels griffon and Pekingese the mandible is fully shortened in association with the completely flattened face. These three latter breeds with the shortened, wide lower jaw all occasionally show the overshot as well as the undershot condition. The reduction in length of each jaw is influenced by a complex of factors, some of which are dominant and some recessive to the normal jaw length, and not all members of the several short faced breeds are pure or completely homozygous for the entire mutant complex governing the reduction in length of each jaw. The $F_2$ hybrids arising from crosses between the flat faced and the long muzzled breeds furnish evidence of importance in the analysis of the nature of these facial patterns.

Structural disharmonies closely similar to those under discussion are very common in the faces of human beings. There are faces of narrow, wedged, sharp type and wide flat type with very distinct differences in patterns for the two jaws, and a careful observer may commonly see the hybrid combinations of these jaw patterns. Orthodontists are constantly attempting to correct the dental malocclusion of children with the overshot condition or maxillary prognathism, and people are continually losing their teeth because of malocclusion due to the undershot prognathous mandible. The overshot prognathous upper jaw is very common and very disfiguring, and the undershot jaw associated with a somewhat flat upper face is met with in every community. There is little doubt that these disharmonies can be registered among those ills resulting from type and racial hybridization.

We shall next consider the final and most striking breed cross that has been made in our efforts to understand the transmission and development of these strange and highly modified facial structures.

### The Cross Between the Pekingese and the Saluki

The inheritance and development of the achondroplasic flat faced head of the Pekingese was finally tested by crossing this dog with the extremely slender and long faced Saluki greyhound. The cross between these two widely different breeds is most difficult to accomplish, and we have not yet secured a large number of the hybrids. The characters under study, however, are so highly contrasted that this cross offers important results even in its present uncompleted state.

In a previous section we discussed the simple dominance of the short achondroplasic leg of the Pekingese over the long, slender Saluki leg. The genetics of leg length will be clearly seen by referring again to plate 34 (p. 138). It is well at this time to recall the inheritance of achondroplasia in the extremities since it differs so largely in its simple genetic basis from the more complex genetics for the closely similar growth phenomena of basicranial achondroplasia and the reduction of growth in the jaws. In plate 34 (figs. 1-4), the Pekingese is seen to have very short and typically bent front legs in contrast with the long, straight and slender legs of the Saluki. The two $F_1$ hybrids (figs. 5 and 6) have both developed short, bent legs resembling those of the Pekingese, although not fully as short. This strongly indicates that short legs result from the presence of a simple dominant factor, and is convincingly demonstrated by the $F_2$ hybrids (figs. 7-11). Figures 9-11 are homozygous for short, bent Pekingese legs; figure 8 is heterozygous for the short factor and shows legs of intermediate shortness as in the heterozygous $F_1$; while figure 7 has the recessive long, straight legs and contains no factor for short legs, even though not constitutionally the slender Saluki type.

The Pekingese round head and flattened face with extremely reduced jaws and muzzle is a complex arrangement involving a number of modified characters, each of which may have its own independent genetic basis. And the inheritance of each of the different elements in this complex of characters may be compared to the inheritance of the achondroplasic leg. The head of the Pekingese is not to be thought of as a mass character inherited through multiple factors, but rather as a multiplex of characters whose separate elements are independently influenced by different genetic factors, some dominant and others recessive to the allelomorphs for normal expression. And yet as one studies the structural modifications in these breeds and their hybrids it becomes more and more evident that simple chondrodystrophy is the common growth modification or deficiency underlying the development of most of these seemingly different structural distortions. The surprising fact then arises that this common disturbance, dystrophy in cartilage formation, may be minutely localized through the influence of genetic factors which do not disturb other cartilage growths even in near-by regions. It would seem as though there are separate genetic influences for the direction of development in each limited place throughout the general cartilage matrix of the entire skeleton. These are the discreet influences which make possible abnormal and distorted growth of sharply localized regions, such as the upper jaw or the lower jaw, while all other parts of the individual are developing in perfectly normal fashion. Both the normal growth and the modified growth reactions are taking place while in contact with the same body fluids, that is, within the same internal chemical environment. The elements responsible for the local discrepancies in growth are contained within the constitution of the individual tissues themselves.

The appreciation of these definitely inherited and sharply localized modifications of structural form and quality in otherwise normal bodies is highly important in comparing the results of these genetic experiments with the ordinary growth disturbances which follow the operative removal of endocrine glands or the administration of glandular extracts. The modifications in skull form toward the bulldog type as obtained by Dye and Maughan ('29) following the removal of the thyroid gland in puppies, and the more recent study by Todd and Wharton ('34) of similar modifications in the skulls of sheep after removal of the thyroid gland from the lamb, are definitely concerned with the general inhibition of skeletal growths resulting from induced alterations of the internal environment. These experimental operations with consequent deficiencies in the internal bodily environment furnish little evidence for analyzing the nature of developmental disharmonies and sharply localized distortions of form as met with under normally vigorous conditions in the bodies of man, the dogs and many other mammals. The prognathous mandible or undershot jaw of the thyroidless dog and sheep is not of the same nature as the undershot jaw of the bulldog.

although there is similarity in appearance. In the operated animal the upper and lower jaws are about equally shortened, and in addition the upper jaw is set farther back because of a similar arrest in the basicranium, resulting in a shortening of the upper face; consequently, the lower jaw, though short, projects in front of the upper. In contrast to this, the natural bulldog types may show many different degrees of disharmony between the two jaws because of the independent inheritance of length in each. The lower jaw may be much shorter than the upper, giving the overshot condition, or much longer, as in the undershot condition. In the artificial arrests due to gland removal, both jaws are about equally handicapped.

The above remarks are not to be misconstrued as a depreciation of the importance of surgical experiments. These have been very instructive. Our purpose is merely to show the difference between such artificial arrests in growth and those distortions in structure which arise from genetic disturbances.

With such points in mind we may examine the behavior of the head features in the Saluki-Pekingese hybrids. Plate 73 shows profile photographs of the two parent breeds and their hybrids at adult age. The Saluki, with typical long slender muzzle, is shown in figure 1, and the Pekingese, with its flat and muzzleless face in figure 4. Measurements and indices of the skulls for these breeds are given in table 1 (p. 208). The immature heads of $F_2$ animals at 5 months of age are shown in plate 74.

Figures 2 and 3 in plate 73 are heads of $F_1$ hybrids, a cream-colored male (fig. 2) and a black and white female (fig. 3). Both have well developed strong muzzles which show very little resemblance to the shortened muzzle in the Pekingese. The male is very slightly undershot; the female just a little more so. Both profiles show a combination of parental features rather than a similarity to either parent stock. The faces are much shorter and heavier than in the

Saluki and there is a more pronounced depression at the nasion. The teeth are strong and well developed as in the Saluki, but the mandible is slightly prognathous with the lower incisors fitting in front of the upper, giving somewhat disturbed dental occlusion.

The Saluki is of normal size while the Pekingese is a dwarf, as is clearly shown by figures 1 to 4 in plate 34. The height of the Saluki at the withers is about two and a half times that of the Pekingese. The $F_1$ hybrid, with its short legs, is only half as tall as the Saluki, but it is large and strong in body and weighs about as much as the Saluki and three times as much as the Pekingese. The two $F_1$ hybrids shown in plate 34 are closely alike in all their measurements and features with the exception of coat color, and this was mixed in the Saluki ancestry. The length and texture of coat is intermediate, being heavier and more uniform than in the Saluki and not so feathery as in the Pekingese. In disposition the $F_1$ is very active and playful. It also lacks both the elegance of posture of the Saluki and the haughty arrogance of the Pekingese.

The pair of $F_1$ hybrids just described produced four litters of six, four, five and two puppies. Eight of these seventeen $F_2$ offspring survived to adult age; nine were studied only as young and immature animals. Plate 75 shows the eight adult $F_2$ hybrids and plate 73 (figs. 5–12) shows profile views of the same animals arranged in a similar order.

None of these dogs carries the tail curled over the rump, as does the Pekingese, but several carry it as a high open circle over the back in Saluki fashion. No. 2111 ♂ (fig. 12,

PLATE 73

EXPLANATION OF FIGURES

Genetic behavior of the head features in the Saluki-Pekingese cross. Second generation hybrids at about 1 year of age.

1  Saluki 323 ♂.
2  $F_1$ 1295 ♂.
3  $F_1$ 1956 ♀.
4  Pekingese 77 ♀.

5–12  $F_2$ hybrids.
5  1942 ♀.
6  1941 ♀.
7  1940 ♂.
8  1939 ♂.

9   1938 ♂.
10  2112 ♀.
11  2113 ♀.
12  2111 ♂.

Further comparison of head features in the Saluki-Pekingese cross. Second generation hybrids at 5 months of age.
1 Saluki 323 ♂.  3, 6 F₂ hybrids.
2 Pekingese 77 ♀.  3 1942 ♀.  5 1940 ♂.
4 1939 ♂.  6 1941 ♀.

PLATE 25

Second generation Saluki-Pekingese hybrids at 1 year of age showing bodily size and form, coat length and color, and head features (same animals as shown in pl. 23, figs. 5-12).

1 1942 ♂, 2 1941 ♀, 3 1940 ♂, 4 1939 ♂, 5 1938 ♂, 6 2152 ♀, 7 2118 ♂, 8 2111 ♂.

pl. 73; fig. 8, pl. 75) shows the closest approach to the Pekingese coat pattern. The other animals all had moderately long hair. No. 1942 ♀ (fig. 5, pl. 73; fig. 1, pl. 75) gives the nearest approach to the Saluki coat style. Only one of the eight hybrids is long legged; the others are either intermediate or fully short.

A comparison of the profile views in plate 73 shows that the head features of the $F_2$ hybrids deviate from the $F_1$ in the direction of both parent stocks without completely arriving at the patterns of either. Figure 5 has a somewhat rounded cranial dome inherited from the Pekingese, but the muzzle is quite long and slender as in the Saluki. The maxilla is reduced more than the mandible which is almost fully Saluki length and actually projects forward beyond the tip of the nose. If the upper jaw in this animal had been long enough to be in perfect agreement with the mandible, there would have been a complete return to the Saluki muzzle. This case illustrates the independence of the factors concerned in the inheritance of form for each of the two jaws, and also shows the inability of coordinating influences in growth and development to adjust or smooth out the inherent disharmonies between the jaws. Figures 6 to 8 show a more fully expressed rounding of the cranial dome which gives prominence to the forehead and emphasizes the depression at the nasion, both of which are very definite Pekingese characters. The muzzles in these three dogs are short and are almost as wide as long; the upper and lower jaws are both reduced to about the same extent, and there is fairly normal dental occlusion. Figure 9 gives evidence of considerable mixing of the two sets of parental characters. The cranial dome and forehead are Pekingese, and had the face been suppressed, the type would have been almost complete. The upper jaw is very short and the nose slightly upturned, indicating the presence of much of the factor complex for the Pekingese face. However, the genetic factors for short Pekingese mandible are not complete and the lower jaw is disproportionately long and prognathous. Figures 10 and 11 are rather well proportioned and intermediate in character though both are slightly undershot. In life, the head of the dog in figure 12 resembled the Pekingese even more than the photograph indicates. This is the only $F_2$ hybrid that is overshot; the lower jaw is Pekingese-like and, as compared with the upper, is disproportionately reduced.

## STRUCTURAL DISHARMONY AND FUNCTIONAL MALADJUSTMENT BETWEEN THE UPPER AND LOWER JAWS IN BREED HYBRIDS

The Pekingese-Saluki cross, along with others previously surveyed, fully demonstrates the fact that the discrepancies in pattern between the upper and lower jaws in the mammalian head are inherited and developed as separate and independent characters. No doubt the strange lack of interrelation between both the genetics and development of the two jaws underlies the widespread disharmony in facial arrangements commonly seen among race and breed hybrids, one of the most frequent of which is faulty dental occlusion. Further, an abnormal reduction in length of one or both jaws is often associated with chondrodystrophy in the basicranium and other regions and leads one to suggest that cartilaginous growth plays a more important part in the early development and form of the maxilla and mandible than embryologists have generally recognized. Finally, the fact that the upper jaw may develop along one pattern, and the associated lower jaw on quite another plan, leads one to question the validity of the theory that their embryonic origin is from different portions of the same branchial arch.

A case bearing very directly on such embryological problems may be cited. In the cross between the bassethound and Saluki, two breeds having different skull proportions but without abnormal head distortions, some of the $F_2$ hybrids show very significant jaw arrangements. The Saluki, as already mentioned, has a long slender skull with almost no depression at the nasion. This skull is shown in lateral view as figure 4 in plate 76. The jaws are long and slender and decidedly narrowed in their anterior thirds, which can be clearly seen in the ventral view (fig. 1). Two views of the bassethound skull are shown in figures 3 and 6. This skull is shorter than that of the Saluki and has a curved depression in the region of the nasion; the jaws are also shorter and somewhat heavier. The skull of a second generation hybrid at 3 months of age is shown in figures 2 and 5. Careful inspection of these two figures shows the upper jaw of the $F_2$ hybrid, 1908♂, to be very Saluki-like in both lateral and ventral aspects; the maxilla is long and slender and projects some distance in front of the mandible. The lateral and ventral views of the mandible show it to be quite distinctly of the bassethound type, allowing, of course, for the puppy proportions and deciduous dentition. The angle of divergence between the rami and the general shape of the mandible approach the bassethound. But of most importance is the fact that this mandible is of proper length to function with the bassethound upper jaw, and falls far short of fitting the maxilla with which it is associated. Very clearly this puppy, 1908♂, inherited an upper face and maxilla from the Saluki in association with a mandible from the bassethound. The lower canine teeth fit behind the upper canines instead of in front as is normal for both the parent skulls.

Such a case shows conclusively that the genetic bases for breed quality in the two jaws of the dog's head are not one and the same. It further shows that the complex of genes for breed quality of the upper jaw is without linkage to the factors influencing the breed type of lower jaw. In other words, the hybrid individual descending from two stocks with different lengths or types of jaws may inherit the upper jaw from one stock in association with the different typed lower jaw from the other stock. In all probability this is equally as true for the race hybrids of man and other mammals as for dogs.

PLATE 76

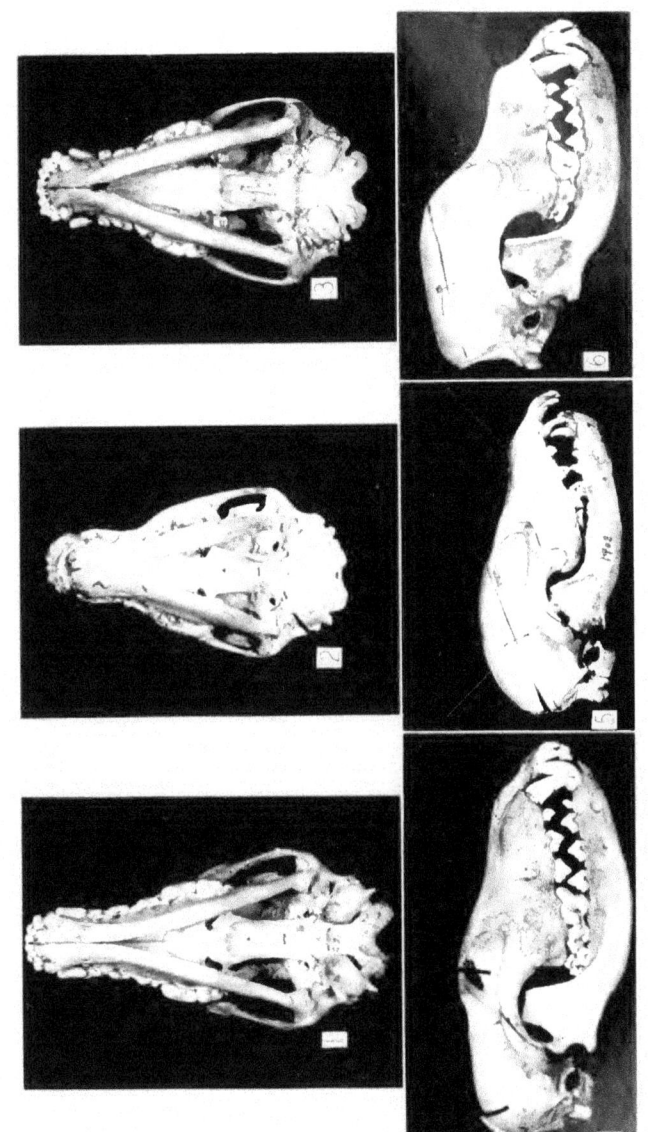

Structural disharmony between upper and lower jaws in a second generation Saluki-bassethound hybrid. 1 and 4, Saluki 276 ♂; 2 and 5, F₂ Saluki-bassethound 1908 ♂; 3 and 6, Bassethound 215 ♂.

In plate 77 (fig. 1) the same lateral view of the $F_2$ basset-hound-Saluki skull is again shown; the skull of a shepherd-bulldog hybrid with the opposite, undershot, condition is shown in figure 4. In the undershot skull, the face is short and the upper jaw is wide, with the flaring teeth of the bulldog in association with a long, strong mandible inherited from the shepherd dog. The upper canine tooth is in front of the lower canine in the overshot skull, while the prognathous mandible of the undershot skull throws its tusk-like canine tooth far in front of the upper canine. The common result of both these ill arrangements is complete dental malocclusion.

Exactly comparable conditions in the human are illustrated by figures 2 and 5 of plate 77. Figure 2 is a plaster cast of the dental arrangement in a case of maxillary prognathism in a child. The upper incisors project far in front of the lower, and all the mandibular teeth fall behind their proper positions, causing complete dental malocclusion. This is the overshot defect in the human and is similar in every detail to the derangement in association of the jaws in the puppy skull (fig. 1). These conditions in the child have been attributed to various causes, such as thumb sucking during babyhood, adenoid interference with nasal breathing, etc. Certainly no such causes underlie the condition in the puppy and probably rarely do in the child. The inheritance of a small lower jaw or defective mandibular development in association with other types and proportions for the upper jaw is to be suspected as a frequent cause of this disharmonious arrangement.

PLATE 77

EXPLANATION OF FIGURES

Comparison of abnormal dental occlusion in two hybrid puppies with the same conditions in the human.

1. $F_2$ Saluki-bassethound 1908 ♂ (overshot).
2. Plaster cast of overshot condition in a child.
3. Plaster cast of normal dental occlusion in the human.
4. Backcross of $F_1$ bulldog-shepherd with bulldog 1454 ♀ (undershot).
5. Plaster cast of undershot condition in a child.

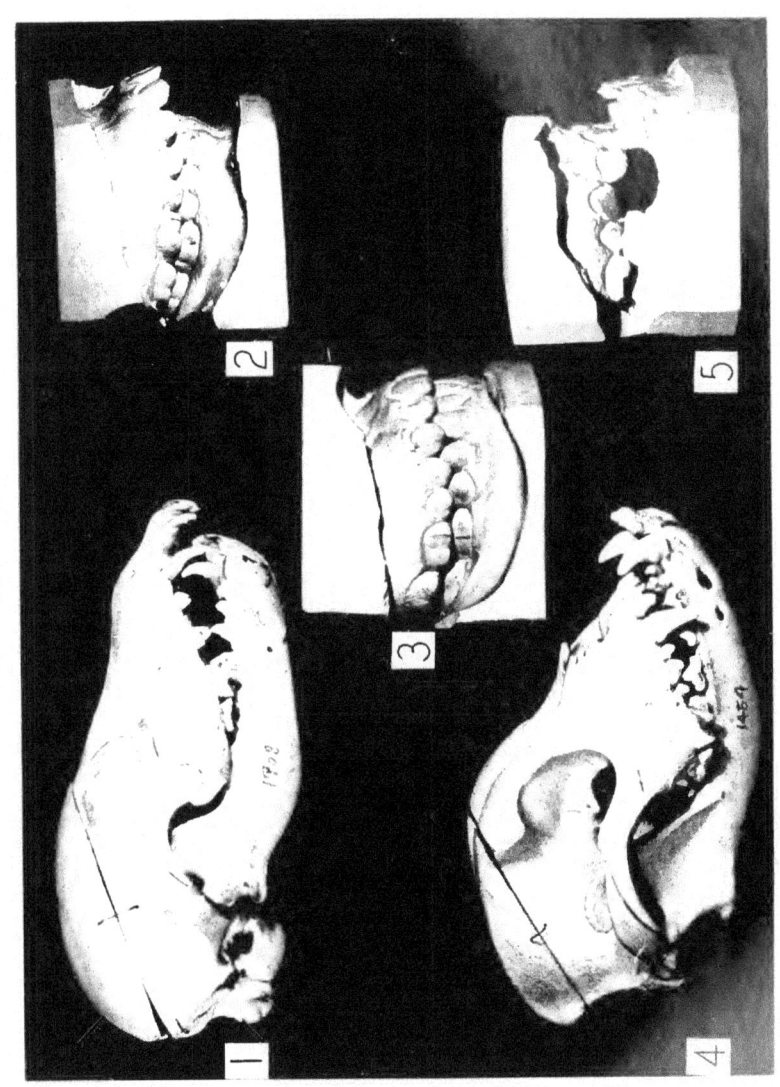

Figure 5 illustrates the cast from an extreme case of mandibular prognathism in a child. The exact similarity to the bulldog jaws (fig. 4) is obvious. For comparison, a cast illustrating the normal dental occlusion of the human mouth is shown in figure 3.

The human achondroplasic dwarf very commonly presents mandibular prognathism caused by the same conditions as are responsible for prognathism in the bulldog. The undershot condition may be due, however, to entirely different causes. The upper facial arrangement may be flat and short, as is the type in certain human families, and yet be associated with a large, long lower jaw which necessarily projects beyond the upper. The orthodontist, in attempting to correct malocclusion, continually finds that two patients with apparently similar kinds and degrees of malocclusion respond very differently to the same mechanical treatments. Some patients are much less responsive to one method than others, and some truly achondroplasic cases may not respond at all, or at least not in the ordinarily expected way.

## The Question of Permanence and Age of Establishment for Dental Occlusion

With such facts as those presented in the foregoing section in mind, we have attempted to determine whether there may be a definite relationship between some of the skull indices and the degree of perfection in dental occlusion. It seemed important also to determine the periods of growth at which the dental occlusion in the long jaws of the dog is established. In both man and the dog the permanent dentition with adult sized teeth becomes stabilized sometime before the jaws have completed their growth. The jaws of the prepubescent child, and of the puppy until it is 5 months old, are too small to accommodate freely the adult sized permanent teeth, with the result that they appear in crowded and misplaced arrangement until the growth of the jaw to adult size supplies the needed accommodation. The general shape and size of the jaws and teeth differ among the dog breeds, as well as among human races, and the hybrid individuals in both species may include misfits having large teeth in association with small jaws and vice versa. The breed hybrids among the dogs constantly emphasize the structural disharmony and functional maladjustments which necessarily arise from type and race mixtures.

In the cross between the giant St. Bernard dog and the large great Dane there is considerable variability and irregularity in the occlusion and relative positions of the upper and lower incisors. For these reasons a litter of seven $F_2$ hybrids from this cross was selected as material for a study of the growth of the jaws and the final establishment of dental occlusion (pl. 78).

All puppies at birth have fetal-like flat faces with only slight prominence of the muzzle. The upper and lower jaws are of about equal length, and there is little evidence of the pronounced prognathisms which are later to develop in many of the animals; the growth of the jaws to give the typical muzzle as well as the modified conditions which we have seen is largely or entirely a postnatal process. The discoordinated growths in the two jaws of the modified breeds begin to be noticeable during the first few weeks of age, and at about 8 weeks, when the deciduous teeth have appeared, the undershot and overshot prognathism can be very reliably diagnosed. The type of occlusion present at this time may remain permanently, or may gradually change due to inequality in the further growth of the two jaws.

The late growth reactions are well illustrated by the various conditions of incisal occlusion in the litter of seven great Dane-St. Bernard hybrids. Photographs were made of the incisor teeth of these puppies at 6 months of age, just after the permanent dentition was completely established. The animals were killed 1 year later, when 18 months old and fully grown, and second photographs of the incisal occlusions were made for comparative purposes. In plate 78 the two photographs of each dog's teeth are placed side by side.

Figure 1 shows the dental occlusion in 1422 ♀. When the animal was 6 months old, the teeth were full sized and the lower canines were in normal occlusion, fitting between the upper canines and lateral third incisors. The relative positions of the teeth one year later are almost identical. Nos. 1417 ♂, 1419 ♀ and 1414 ♂ (figs. 5, 6 and 7) show very similar conditions of occlusion, and in each case there is little evidence of any change having occurred to affect the relative positions of the teeth during the 12 months which intervened between the making of the first and second pictures.

No. 1420 ♀ (fig. 2) shows a slight prognathism of the mandible, as indicated by the projection of the lower incisors in front of the upper. This condition in the young animal is very mild and scarcely passes beyond an almost direct opposition of the upper and lower incisors. The photograph of the jaws at 18 months of age shows that as a result of this slight malocclusion a definite spreading of the teeth had taken place during the 12 month interval. Figure 4, 1418 ♀, illustrates a closely comparable record.

No. 1416 ♂ (fig. 3) shows a more advanced condition of mandibular prognathism in the immature skull. Yet even here the lower canines do not lie in front of the upper incisors but rest against the third incisors at such an angle as to prevent a complete biting closure of the teeth. At the older age this condition has advanced and become somewhat more pronounced, with the teeth more widely separated than at the earlier stage.

PLATE 78

EXPLANATION OF FIGURES

Growth of the jaws and final establishment of dental occlusion. Comparison of second generation great Dane St. Bernard hybrids at 6 months and 18 months of age (one litter).

1  1422 ♀.   4  1418 ♀.   6  1419 ♀.
2  1420 ♀.   5  1417 ♂.   7  1414 ♂.
3  1416 ♂.

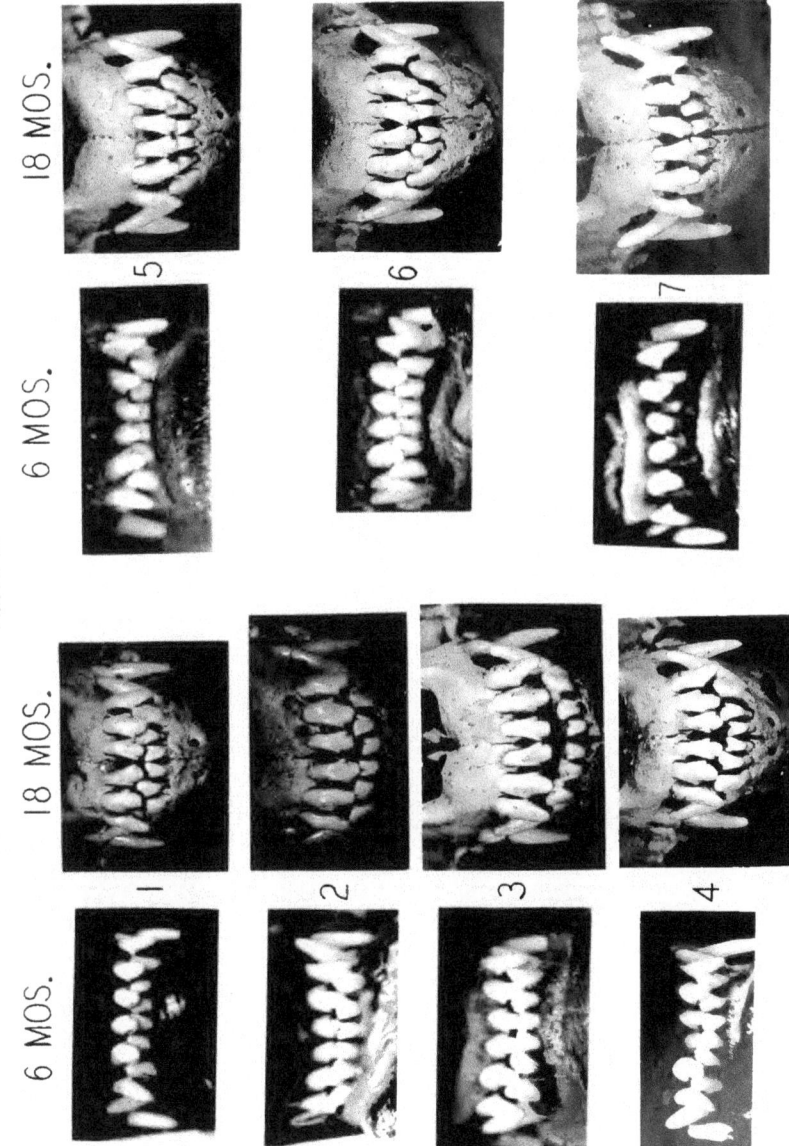

This series of photographs would indicate that the type of dental occlusion is about completed at the time permanent dentition is fully established, which is, in the dog, at about 6 months of age; at this time the animal is also approaching sexual maturity. But slight changes in the position of the teeth and their relative arrangements may occur after this time. The most extreme cases of mandibular prognathism may, in some bulldogs, continue to increase gradually up to about 15 months of age.

RELATION OF DENTAL OCCLUSION TO SKULL INDICES

On the basis of degree of dental occlusion, a collection of 184 adult skulls from different pure breeds and hybrids has been separated into the following seven groups:—Group A, forty-nine skulls with normal occlusion; group B, seventeen skulls with malocclusion of a few individual teeth; group C, seventeen skulls with incisors meeting in end to end opposition; group D, sixty skulls with mandibular incisors in front of the upper (undershot); group E, twenty-nine skulls with the entire mandibular series of teeth anterior to the proper position (undershot); group F, five skulls with the mandibular incisors or molars, or both, posterior to the normal position relative to the upper series (overshot); and, finally, group G, seven skulls with poor, irregular occlusion. The values of the five different skull indices were plotted for these seven occlusal groups in order to find whether definite relationships could be established between a given skull index or shape and the state of dental occlusion.

Text-figure 72 indicates the values for the total skull index of the individual skulls in each group. The total skull index expresses the relation of width across the zygomatic arch to entire length of skull base from foramen magnum to end of premaxilla, and is, therefore, low for long skulls and high for short. The skulls with normal dental occlusion range in total index from 72 down to 52 and may all be considered, on the basis of such indices, long, narrow skulls. The three groups, B with individual malplaced teeth, C with incisors meeting end to end, and D with the mandibular incisors anterior to the upper, all range much higher in total skull index than the group with normal occlusion. Practically every skull in these three groups is shorter than the average for the A group, but in the lower indices a number overlap or fall within the range of the highest indices in the normal group. The twenty-nine skulls in the completely undershot E group are all higher in index than any of those with normal occlusion. This would indicate that fully expressed

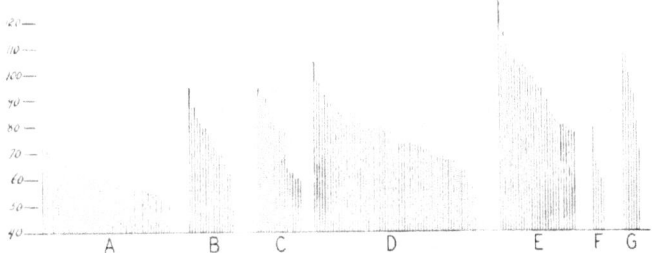

Text-figure 72. Relation of dental occlusion to total skull index in 184 skulls divided into groups as follows: A, forty-nine skulls with normal occlusion; B, seventeen skulls with malocclusion of a few individual teeth; C, seventeen skulls with incisors meeting end to end; D, sixty skulls with mandibular incisors in front of maxillary incisors (undershot); E, twenty-nine skulls with entire mandibular series anterior to maxillary series (undershot); F, five skulls with mandibular incisors or molars (or both) posterior to corresponding maxillary teeth (overshot); G, seven skulls with poor, irregular occlusion.

prognathism of the mandible is confined to short skulls of high index; in addition, group D shows that about 66 per cent of the skulls with but slight mandibular prognathism are also shorter than any in the normal group. In group G the seven skulls with deformed and irregular occlusion are all of higher index, that is, shorter than the normal group.

On the basis of total skull index, therefore, it is strongly indicated that normal dental occlusion in the dog is confined to the long typed primitive skull, while the modified short skulls tend to have various types and degrees of malocclusion, increasing in severity in almost direct proportion to the shortness of the skull.

This definite relation between the total shape of the head and the perfection of dental occlusion made it seem desirable to chart several regional indices for these skulls in order to determine what portions of the skull are most largely concerned with the disturbances of dental occlusion. Logically, of course, one would suspect the muzzle or facial region of being mainly concerned, but whether all parts of the muzzle are equally involved, and whether any other skull proportions play a rôle in these maladjustments, were points to be determined.

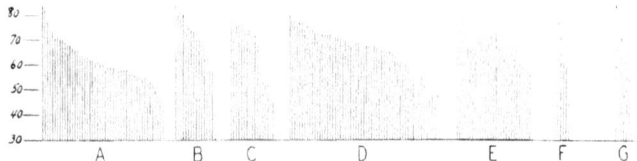

Text figure 73. Relation of dental occlusion to cranial index in 184 skulls divided into groups as indicated in text figure 72.

The cranial index (relation of cranial width to length) for the skulls in each of these seven occlusal groups is charted in text-figure 73. The forty-nine skulls with normal occlusion range in value for this index from 84 down to 47, and the six groups with various degrees of malocclusion all fall almost exactly within this range. This figure clearly indicates that there is no significant relationship between width-length proportions of the cranium and proper dental occlusion in these skulls. It therefore follows that the definite relation between the value of total skull index and type of occlusion must be due almost entirely to differences in facial proportions.

The muzzle index, width across maxillary canines relative to distance from nasion to tip of premaxilla, represents an almost total facial index. Text-figure 74 shows the range for this index among the several occlusal groups. This figure is strongly contrasted with text-figure 73 for cranial indices. The highest muzzle index with normal occlusion is 96, but this is exceptional; the forty-eight other skulls of this normal group range from 81 down to 51. In other words, only one member of the normal group has a muzzle almost as wide as it is long; in the others the muzzles are anywhere from slightly longer than wide to twice as long as wide. In contrast

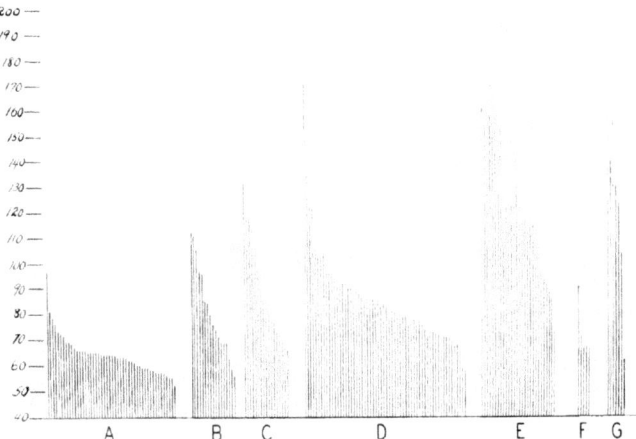

Text-figure 74. Relation of dental occlusion to muzzle index in 184 skulls divided into groups as indicated in text-figure 72.

to this, the malocclusal groups show very high muzzle indices reaching almost 200 in value, that is, the muzzles are nearly twice as wide as they are long. Group E, composed of skulls with decided mandibular prognathism, ranges for muzzle index from 193 down to as low as 73, but only six of the twenty-nine specimens have indices under 100. Therefore, all twenty-nine skulls have shorter muzzles than those of the normal group. The groups in text-figure 74 indicate that dental malocclusion in the dog's skull is directly associated with the increase in value for muzzle index.

In text-figure 75, the palatal index for these skulls is shown to be the most important fraction contained within the muzzle index. The group with normal occlusion ranges in palatal index from 80 to slightly below 60. The groups B, C and D, with slight degrees of malocclusion, average much higher for palatal index than do the skulls with normal occlusion, while group E, with general malocclusion, shows a range which lies entirely above the normal group. It is quite clear that short, wide palates are strongly and directly associated with dental malocclusion in the skull of the dog.

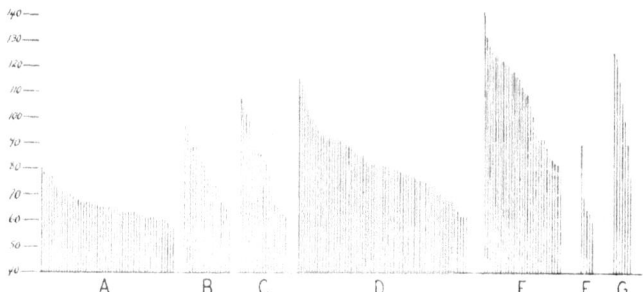

Text figure 75. Relation of dental occlusion to palatal index in 184 skulls divided into groups as indicated in text-figure 72.

The indices discussed thus far have involved upper facial dimensions with no consideration to the mandible or lower jaw. An important factor in our study of dental occlusion is to determine whether malocclusion is more largely due to disproportions in the upper jaw or the lower jaw, and to what degree each is responsible for such mechanical disharmony. To determine these important facts, the mandibular index, the relation of intercondylar width to length of mandible, has been charted in text-figure 76 for the seven groups of skulls. With the exception of three of the forty-nine normal specimens the range in value for this index lies between 54 and 41. This indicates that the general shape and proportions of the mandible are very uniform in the normal group. The range in values is steeper and wider in the B, C and D groups, and the tendency is toward higher mandibular indices. The indices for almost all the forty-nine mandibles in the normal group are about 50 or lower, while the majority in each of the three groups with minor malocclusions are higher than 50 and in a few specimens reach to above 70. In spite of these differences for the indices in the B, C and D groups, more than half the specimens lie within the range of the normal indices. These facts suggest very clearly that the mandibular index is not so directly concerned in

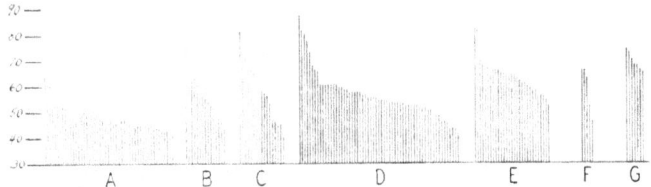

Text figure 76. Relation of dental occlusion to mandibular index in 184 skulls divided into groups as indicated in text figure 72.

dental malocclusion as is the palatal index represented in text figure 75.

The mandibular indices in group E, those specimens with complete malocclusion, range from above 80 down to 52. Thus these extreme cases are also within the upper limits of the normal range although they do not show indices with values so low as those in the first four groups. These prognathous mandibles have an average index well above the normal, yet they do show, as do the palatal index relations for the same skulls, an overlapping with the values for the normal group. Therefore, we can conclude that modifications in the palate and the maxilla are more largely responsible for dental malocclusion in the dog than are changes in width length relations of the mandible. In bulldog malocclusions, the upper jaw is the decidedly modified part; the lower jaw is much less modified in its proportions, and therefore projects forward beyond the shortened upper facial region.

These facts may be finally emphasized by a consideration of the upper facial index as charted in text-figure 77. It will be recalled from previous references that this index is calculated in a reverse manner, length to width proportion rather than width to length, and that therefore the long skulls have high indices and the short skulls low. This again is a particularly good index for indicating clear differences between skulls with normal occlusion and those with disturbed occlusal conditions.

The indicies for the normal group range in value from 74 to 124, while the indices for the three groups with partial malocclusion range from 36 to 132, or higher than the upper end of the normal range, although the large majority in each of these three groups have facial index values entirely below that for the normal group. Here again, the indices in group E with complete malocclusion lie almost entirely below and outside the range of those skulls with normal occlusion.

From these several charts of skull indices it is clear that the structural formation in localized regions of the skull determines the type of dental occlusion, and that it is the facial part of the skull which is of most importance in this connection. The palatal index, as a direct expression of the form of the upper jaw, is more intimately correlated with the nature of dental occlusion than is the index for any other skull feature. Modifications of the mandible in the dog skull are much less pronounced than those of the maxilla, and the responsibility of mandibular deformity for dental malocclusion is largely secondary. There is considerable probability that similar relations will be found to hold for man, since the disturbances of facial growth in the human infant and child are so readily comparable to the conditions in the skull of the puppy.

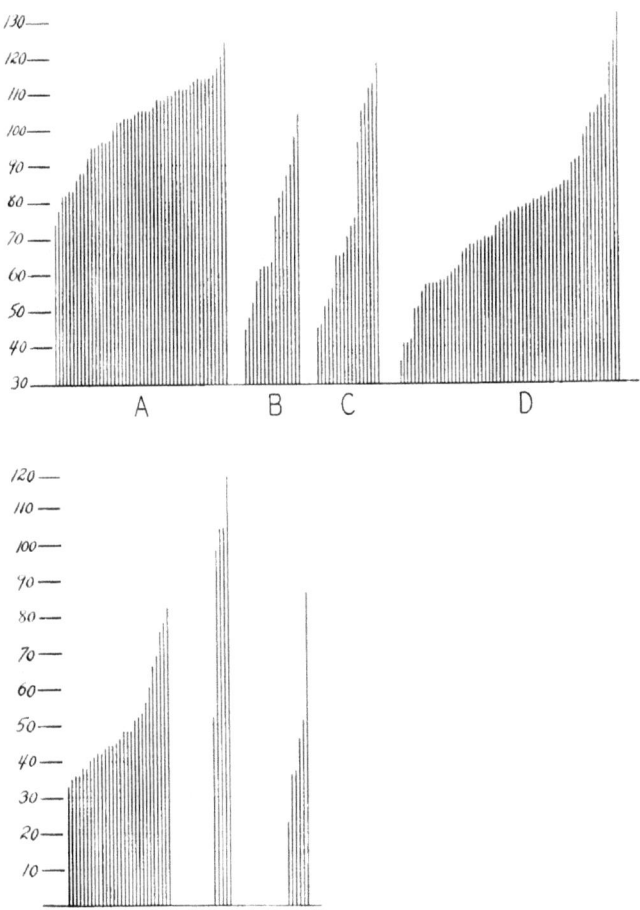

Text-figure 77. Relation of dental occlusion to upper facial index in 184 skulls divided into groups as indicated in text-figure 72.

# SECTION IV

CHARLES R. STOCKARD

## A CRUCIAL TEST OF GENETIC CONSTITUTION AS AGAINST ENDOCRINE DISTORTION IN DETERMINING THE TYPE OF STRUCTURAL FORMATION: THE "SCREW-TAIL" IN BULLDOG HYBRIDS

Many conditions have already been discussed which indicate that the genetic composition of the individual may bring about localized growth distortions in otherwise normal bodies. One of the most completely investigated cases of localized distortion is recorded in the earlier section on achondroplasia in the skeleton of the extremities. This condition is clearly inherited in a very simple fashion, but when considered alone there is, nevertheless, the possibility that an early and temporary endocrine modification may have been the primarily inherited character acting to initiate the chondrodystrophy in the extremity skeleton without similarly affecting the axial skeleton which at that particular period was not in a susceptible stage. The critically susceptible stages in the development of the appendicular and axial portions of the skeleton probably occur at different developmental moments.

The reverse condition of localized achondroplasic modification of the head and tail ends of the axial skeleton in a body with normal growth of the extremities, therefore, lends itself to a similar possible explanation. Also the further fact, brought out in a previous section, that the homozygous state for extremity achondroplasia brings about a more severe expression of this condition than does the heterozygous is still open to explanation on the basis of possible differences in degrees of endocrine modification resulting from mixed and pure allelic pairs. Even the different growth reactions shown by the upper and lower jaws in the same head may be due to momentary endocrine disturbances to which the growth of one jaw is more susceptible than the other. Such temporary endocrine disturbances are known to modify growth when acting during particularly susceptible periods.

It is very difficult in dogs, as it would be in man, to demonstrate that the genetic composition of the tissue determines its pattern of growth without regard to the general state of endocrine control. We felt that this problem would need to be studied on a limited part capable of development along several different patterns, and that further advantage might be gained were this part composed of a number of similar segments.

The deformities of the tail found in the bulldog breeds are particularly valuable for this investigation. These breeds show localized chondrodystrophic deformities at both the head and tail ends of the axial skeleton. In rare cases the deformity may extend to intermediate parts of the vertebral column, particularly the cervical and thoracic regions. This is also true for the similar disturbance in man. The epiphyseal cartilages in the tail vertebrae of the bulldog fetus are so dystrophic that the entire tail is deformed into a corkscrew-like twist, and shortened to a few centimeters in length.

When the screw-tailed bulldog is crossed with the basset-hound, which has a long, straight tail, all $F_1$ hybrids develop perfectly formed long tails, as shown in plates 19 and 20 (pp. 97 and 99). The deformed tail is, therefore, recessive to the normal. In the second hybrid generation, the tail deformity reappears in several different patterns. The majority of the $F_2$ animals have long, straight, freely jointed tails; others have long tails that are permanently bent at one or more places; a few have short, straight tails; still others have short tails with a simple bend; and finally a few, about one in sixteen, have the typical bulldog screw-tail. This break-up in tail condition follows the typical genetic behavior for a compound character consisting of two recessive elements. Plate 19 (figs. 6-9) shows one litter of four $F_2$ hybrids, and plate 20 (figs. 5-8) shows the skeletons of these animals. Three have long tails, and two of these long tails are permanently bent (figs. 7 and 9, pl. 19; figs. 7 and 8, pl. 20). Figure 8 in plate 19 presents the typical short twisted screw-tail (skeleton fig. 6, pl. 20). It should be observed that this screw-tailed $F_2$ bitch, 918♀, has long, straight legs and a strong, well developed, hound-like head. The screw-tail evidently developed in an endocrine environment which was sufficiently normal to permit a proper pattern of growth in all other body parts, the deformity of tail being directly due to the presence in this dog's genetic composition of the two recessive genes for short tail and the two recessive allels for bent tail characters. One could scarcely imagine this screw-tail to have resulted from a localized endocrine attack affecting only certain vertebrae of the tail.

The impossibility of such an explanation becomes more evident on examining the tail conditions in the backcross hybrids between the $F_1$ bulldog-bassethound and the pure bulldog stock. Here, of course, there is larger chance for the occurrence of the screw-tail condition than there is among the $F_2$ hybrids.

An examination of a large number of $F_2$ and backcross hybrids shows the following kinds of tails: long-straight, short-straight, long-bent, short-bent, and screw-tail. We may represent the genes concerned with these tail characters by the letters $L$ for long, $St$ for straight, $s$ for short and $b$ for bent. The screw-tailed bulldog would have the homozygous composition $ss$-$bb$, being pure for short and pure for bent, and only this particular genic arrangement can give rise to the extreme condition. The $F_1$ hybrid is heterozygous for both factors, $Ls$-$Stb$, and develops the dominant long-straight tail.

The sixteen possible genic combinations for the $F_2$ generation are shown in text-figure 78. As indicated in the squares, these combinations give rise to a definite distribution of tail patterns. Nine long-straight tails resulting from the combined presence of the dominant genes $L$ and $St$, and three long-bent tails due to the combination of the dominant $L$ for long tail with the double recessive $bb$ for bent, appear. Theoretically, there should be three short-straight tails resulting from combinations of the pure recessive *ss* for short and the dominant *St* for straight, but the short tail is straight only when homozygous for straight, *StSt*; when pure for short and heterozygous for straight, *Stb*, the short tail shows a simple bend. Therefore, in the F₂ generation only one tail in sixteen, instead of three in sixteen, is short and straight.

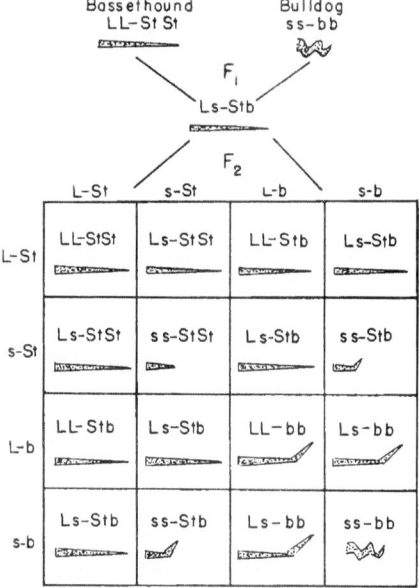

Text-figure 78. Diagram showing the sixteen possible genic combinations for tail length and structure in second generation bulldog-bassethound hybrids. L, long; St, straight; s, short; b, bent.

In combination with the homozygous allels for short, *ss*, straight is not fully dominant over bent, but it is completely dominant over bent in the long tail, as is shown by the scarcity of long-bent tails among more than 150 F₂ hybrids, and by the complete absence of bent tails among the F₁ generation, which is, of course, heterozygous for straight, $Stb$, in all individuals. Finally, the twisted screw-tail occurs as expected, that is, once in about sixteen individuals.

On backcrossing the $F_1$ with the bulldog, we obtain the following possible combinations of the four tail factors: $Ls$-$Stb$ = long-straight, $Ls$-$bb$ = long-bent, $ss$-$Stb$ = short with simple bend and $ss$-$bb$ = short screw-tail. As pointed out, long and straight are the dominant, and short and bent the recessive characters, but long dominates short more completely than straight dominates bent.

A single litter of four backcross bulldog hybrids is illustrated in plate 79. Figures 1 to 4 show the animals standing on the hind feet, their bodies vertical, and illustrate from life the relative lengths and conditions of the tails. Figures 4 to 8 are photographs of the tails, which were placed upon pieces of cardboard to better show their exact outlines. The bulldog-like heads of these four dogs are clearly illustrated in the small photograph (fig. 9).

Figure 1 in plate 79 has a long-straight tail, $Ls$-$Stb$, showing both dominant characters. Figure 2 has a short tail with a slight bend, $ss$-$Stb$, thus showing the recessive short condition in combination with the partially dominant straight character. Figure 3 shows a short, simply bent tail of the probable genic composition $ss$-$Stb$, the same constitution as the second dog. When animals with these short-bent tails are crossed with those having the complete screw-tail, only half the offspring have screw-tails; the other half show tails that are short with a simple bend. This is a common finding among pure stock bulldogs, many of which are not homozygous for bent and therefore fail to have the perfect screw-tail. Figure 4 shows the perfectly expressed screw-tail, $ss$-$bb$. Thus this single litter of four backcross bulldog-bassethound hybrids shows all the possible tail conditions for the double factor recessive deformity except the short-straight, $ss$-$StSt$, which cannot arise in the backcross, and the long-bent, $Ls$-$bb$ which is possible but did not appear in this litter. The long-bent

*Ls-bb* condition is well illustrated, however, by two of the $F_2$ hybrids in plates 19 and 20.

The skeletons of the tails and the right front legs from this litter of four backcross bulldog-bassethound hybrids are illustrated in plate 80. The long-straight tail (fig. 1) shows the perfect condition of the caudal vertebrae, all of which are freely articulated in a straight line arrangement. Figure 2 shows the short tail with a dorso-ventral bend and ankylosis and suppression of vertebrae near its base. There are also two short, deformed vertebrae near the tip, though in the photographs from life this tail seems almost straight. Figure 3 shows another tail skeleton, much shorter than the normal, with an ankylosed bend and short deformed vertebrae near its tip. This bend turns the tail toward the left and is thus more conspicuous from the ventral aspect than would be the dorso-ventral bend in the previous case. Figure 4 is the typical screw-tail, which not only has four bends, one of which is vertically over another and difficult to see in the photograph, but also a twisting of some of the vertebrae which causes rotation of their ventral surfaces into dorsal position. The angles formed by bending are permanently ankylosed.

These growth reactions bring out very emphatically the fact that the deformity of the tail depends directly and step-by-step upon the genetic composition of the individual and is in no recognizable way related to modifications in endocrine secretions. The very extreme type of bulldog-head may be present in an animal with a long straight tail, and vice versa, a fairly normal and long muzzled head may be

PLATE 79

EXPLANATION OF FIGURES

Tail length and structure in one litter of hybrids obtained by backcrossing the $F_1$ bassethound English bulldog with the pure bulldog.

1 and 5  1481 ♀ (Ls Stb),    3 and 7  1478 ♂ (ss Stb),
2 and 6  1479 ♂ (ss Stb),    4 and 8  1482 ♀ (ss bb).
9  (L to R) 1481 ♀, 1479 ♂, 1482 ♀, 1478 ♂.

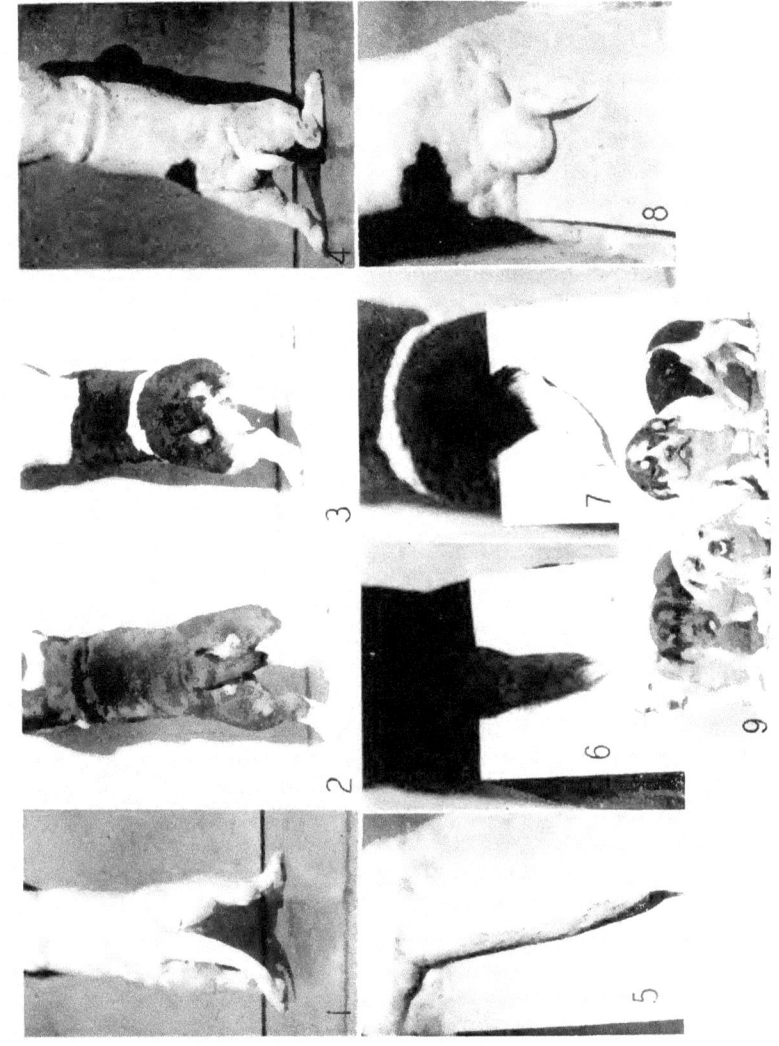

accompanied by a fully expressed short screw-tail (see 918 ♀ in plates 19 and 20).

The skeletons of the right front limbs in plate 80 are also of some interest in the present connection. All these show achondroplasia of the long bones, but are heterozygous for the condition, since they arose from the backcross of the $F_1$ hybrid on the long legged bulldog parent. We have previously pointed out that the dominant factor for achondroplasia in the extremities gives a more severe shortening in association with bulldog quality bone than with hound bone. It is fair to suppose that breed quality of bone may be dependent upon a large number of factors in the genetic constitution of the animal. It is further probable that individuals homozygous for the double factor recessive screw-tail condition derived from the bulldog parent will approach more nearly the genetic constitution necessary for the bulldog bone quality than do heterozygous individuals with long, straight tails, since the former carry certain bulldog chromosomes which the latter necessarily lack. In view of these facts, it is of interest to find that the leg skeleton accompanying the long-straight tail (fig. 1) is less shortened than the three others. This leg skeleton is probably nearer the basset-hound bone in quality than are those accompanying the short-bent and screw-tails. The more complete the bulldog constitution, the shorter will be the leg.

The fusion and shortening or abbreviation of caudal vertebrae bringing about a reduction in tail length is separated genetically from the vertebrae deformity which produces bending and twisting of the tail. Although these phenomena are two only slightly different distortions in cartilage growth, they are genetically separate and independently expressed.

PLATE 80
EXPLANATION OF FIGURES

Further details of tail length and structure in the backcross bulldog-basset-hound bulldog hybrids shown in plate 79, and a comparison of the tail and leg skeletons of these hybrids.

1  1481 ♀.     2  1479 ♂.     3  1478 ♂.     4  1482 ♀.

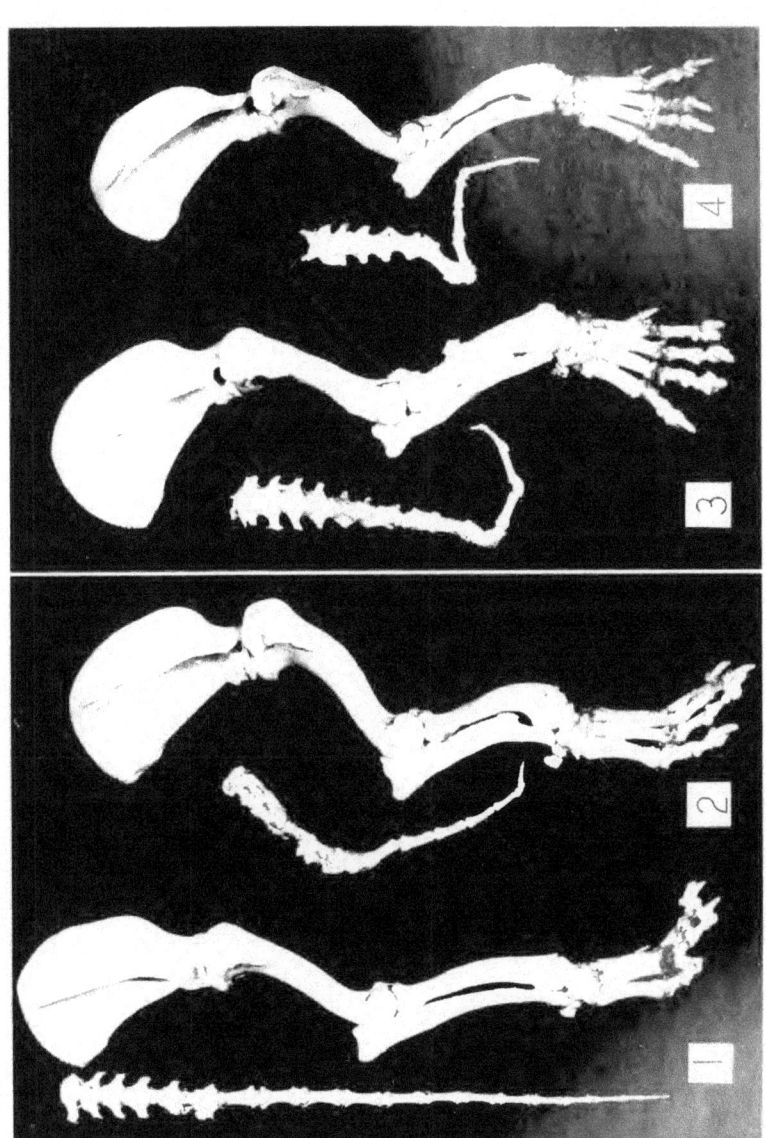

In these tails the genetic constitution of the tissues is the determining factor for their pattern of growth in spite of the composition of the endocrine environment. A similar statement is no doubt true in regard to a number of other modified growths which at first sight might seem to be responses to strange endocrine complexes. On the other hand, a number of structural modifications do result primarily from definitely inherited alterations in endocrine composition; overgrowth of skin and various disharmonious arrangements of parts are examples of this. The genetic constitution must determine the endocrine qualities, and the patterns of growth for certain tissues may be influenced by these, yet the pattern of growth for other tissues or parts may take place over and above such influences. These two courses of development in abnormal expression must constantly be differentiated, not only among these dogs but also for man and other mammals.

# SECTION V

CHARLES R. STOCKARD AND E. M. VICARI

## VARIATIONS IN PROPORTIONAL SIZE AND MODIFICATIONS IN HISTOLOGIC QUALITY OF ENDOCRINE GLANDS IN RELATION TO BODY TYPES AS FOUND AMONG THE DOG BREEDS

For several years before beginning the experimental part of this study, the endocrine glands from dogs of pronounced types were collected at the New York city pound. Since the exact ancestry and breed purity of such animals were uncertain, only those specimens showing well pronounced physical characteristics of the various breeds were selected. From a study of this material it became evident that the highly modified and deformed breeds, such as the achondroplasic bulldog types, showed marked abnormalities in the histologic structure of the thyroid and other glands. This evidence strengthened the initial idea that many dog breeds exhibit physical characteristics closely resembling the growth distortions found in human beings suffering from diseases of the endocrine glands, and we felt that the important problem was to ascertain whether modified endocrine glands might be the cause of hereditary growth distortions in the several dog breeds. Many secondary problems arising from this general investigation have been presented in previous sections of this paper. In this section the differences in gross proportional sizes and in microscopic structure presented by the endocrine glands of the various types of dogs will be discussed. Evidence will then be given of the inheritance of glandular size and quality as correlated with physical types in the various breeds and their hybrids.

Associated with the endocrine modifications found in the various pure breeds and their cross bred hybrids are many very striking functional peculiarities. For example, certain of the giant breeds, all of which have abnormalities of the pituitary, show most irregular records for fecundity. Many individuals in these breeds are poor producers, frequently failing to whelp at all or giving litters of only one to three puppies. In contrast, closely related individuals may produce from ten to seventeen puppies at a whelp. One such bitch in our colony produced fifty puppies within two years, while five of her highly typed relatives were perfectly useless breeders throughout their lives. The achondroplasic bulldog types produce only small litters, rarely more than four or five puppies, and often only one or two, while the normal typed dog produces from six to eight puppies at a time. First generation hybrids derived from crosses between types with distorted fecundity and the normal type are all fairly productive, while individuals of the second hybrid generation often show great irregularity in fecundity and some may be entirely sterile, as is not uncommon among the $F_2$ bulldog-bassethound hybrids. The entire question of the number of offspring to be produced at one litter is probably analyzable on the basis of the wide differences in litter size found among the different dog types.

Various deviations from the usual pattern of the normal canine are also presented by such breeds with abnormal endocrine glands. There are considerable differences in susceptibility to gross parasites as well as differences in resistance to infectious diseases. Such facts have emphasized the importance of a careful survey of the glandular characteristics among the different breeds in order to follow the inheritance of these characters in their hybrids. The correlations between the glandular deviations and the physical characters of the individuals in hybrid generations are of primary importance to the problem of constitutional and functional modifications.

Our attention has been centered mainly upon the more important of the endocrine glands—the pituitary, thyroid, parathyroids, suprarenals and gonads, with observations on the size and condition of the thymus. Glands from the pure breeds and hybrids have been systematically observed and studied in the fresh condition at autopsy and subsequently as fixed preparations.

## The Relative Sizes of Thyroid Glands in Contrasted Types of Pure Dog Breeds

There are usually two distinctly separate thyroid lobes in the dog. These are situated under cover of the ventral neck muscles, bilaterally on the right and left sides of the trachea a short distance caudal to the larynx. In some cases the two lobes are connected by an isthmus of thyroid tissue passing ventrally across the trachea. The isthmus varies in extent from a narrow, almost transparent strand of tissue to a strong wide band of thyroid material resembling to a mild degree the isthmus of the human thyroid. In our experience, the isthmus is found more often in the flat muzzled bulldog-like breeds than in the long jawed types. Several English bulldogs have shown the wide, strongly developed thyroid isthmus, and the flat faced Pekingese and its hybrids frequently possess a thin isthmus. However, this is not a consistent finding, and the bulldog may lack an isthmus entirely, while a long muzzled breed, such as the German shepherd, may possess one, though such cases are rare.

Also occurring in the dog is an additional mass of thyroid tissue in a more posterior position. Kampmeier ('37) has recently recorded the development of thyroid material in the region of the aortic and pulmonary arches in several mammals. Nonidez (unpublished results) has found thyroid tissue within the pericardium of a few of the puppies used in these experiments. And James, working at our kennels, has observed that after complete removal of both thyroid bodies from the neck region of the dog, the usual subsequent physiologic changes failed to develop in certain individuals, while others showed the expected ill effects. The animals showing no symptoms of thyroid deficiency after what was considered complete thyroidectomy were found to contain thyroid tissue in the mediastinum.

The volume of thyroid tissue from a large number of pure bred dogs and their hybrids was measured in both the fresh state and after fixation and, for comparative purposes, the amount of thyroid tissue in milligrams in proportion to kilograms of total body weight was calculated. Comparisons based on such calculations are, of course, not absolutely exact, and no account is taken of the occasional additional posterior thyroid material which, in the presence of the two usual thyroid lobes, is very insignificant. As is well known for several mammals, with particular reference to the studies by Brown ('29) on rabbits, there is great variation in relative thyroid size among perfectly normal individuals of the same breed. This individual variation is constantly found among the members of the several dog breeds which we have studied. Unless the proportion of thyroid material to body size were to differ very much more in two different breeds than among the members of a single breed, this quantitative variable could, of course, have no significant effect on the determination of physical type or functional pattern.

In order to analyze the thyroid proportions, we may first consider the individual differences in relative size found among the members of each of several pure breeds. Text-figure 79 indicates the amount of thyroid in milligrams per kilogram of body weight for the dachshund and Boston terrier, two partially dwarf breeds of strongly contrasted type. Text-figure 80 shows the same for the bassethound and English bulldog, both of normal canine size; and text-figure 81 gives relative weights for the great Dane and the St. Bernard, dogs of gigantic proportions.

The proportional sizes in milligrams of thyroid material to kilogram of body weight in the six adult Boston terrier females represented in text-figure 79 give the series 90–100–120–130–150–210, and the largest proportion of thyroid is $2\frac{1}{3}$ times greater than the smallest. The adjacent series of bars represents the proportional amounts of thyroid in seven adult dachshund bitches. The lowest of these is 100 milligrams per kilogram and the highest 320; the latter dog is therefore 3.2 times richer in thyroid material than the former. The other five individuals grade quite regularly between these two extremes. These figures indicate that the propor-

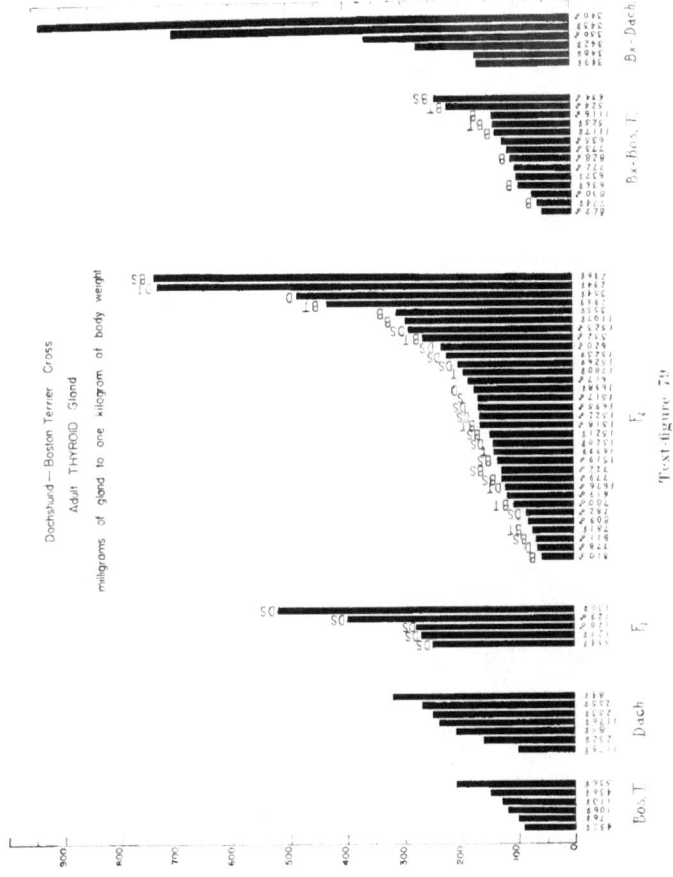

Text-figure 79

tional size of thyroid gland tissue varies very greatly among apparently normal adult dachshunds, and that the relative size of the gland very probably has little to do with determining the type, since the seven animals are closely alike in form. In other words, so far as influence on body form is concerned, the amount of thyroid material is not an important factor.

The series of bars at the left in text-figure 80 indicates relative thyroid sizes for thirteen adult English bulldogs, six bitches and seven males. The thyroid sizes of these animals show an enormous range, from 55 milligrams per kilogram of body weight to 305 milligrams per kilogram. The largest relative amount of thyroid is almost six times greater than the smallest and this difference is quite independent of sex. It is also important to note that bulldog 120 ♂, with the smallest relative amount of thyroid tissue, was as true and as strong an expression of his breed type as was 903 ♂ or 885 ♀, two of the dogs having the largest relative amounts of thyroid tissue. All these animals had been selected for their exaggerated expression of bulldog type. No. 885 ♀, having the largest amount of thyroid, is shown in plate 54 (p. 290), and 903 ♂, a champion type, is seen in plate 18 (p. 93). The dog 120 ♂, with the smallest amount of thyroid, could have been mistaken for either of these two. It is quite evident that an enormous variation of as much as 600% in proportional amounts of thyroid tissue does not modify the direction of type expression in these extremely distorted animals. Again we see, therefore, that the gross proportional amount of thyroid is not an important factor in determining either the degree or quality of thyroid function in the dog breeds.

The second group of bars in text-figure 80 represents the proportional sizes of thyroid glands in nine bassethounds, three of which were immature animals only 5 or 6 months old. Thyroid glands are proportionally larger in puppies than in adult dogs and the three highest bars represent the three immature bassethounds. The six other bars represent adult thyroids ranging from 160 to 370 milligrams per kilo-

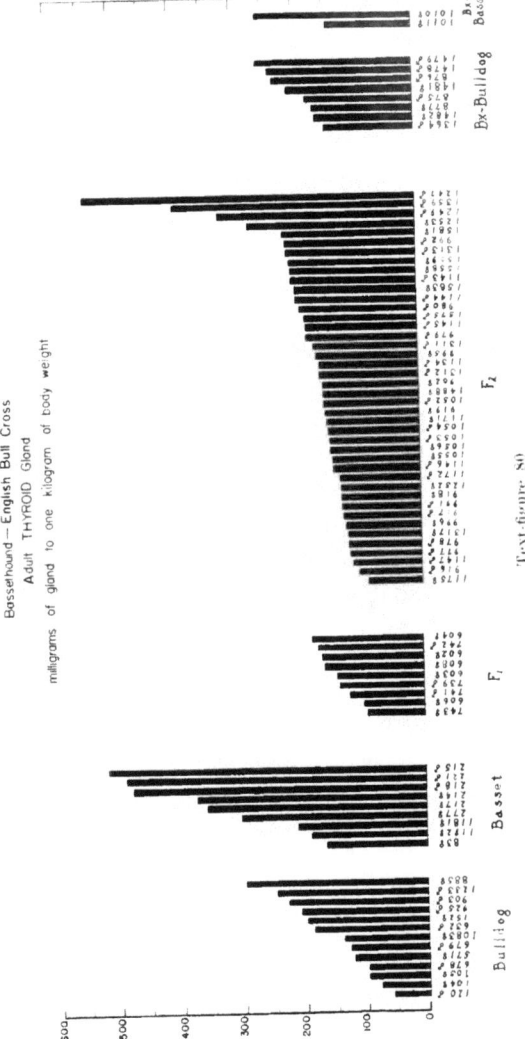

gram of body weight, the largest proportion being more than twice the smallest. The relative sizes of the thyroid in the bassethound show less than half the range in variability shown for the bulldog.

Text-figure 81 gives the relative sizes of the thyroid for the great Dane and St. Bernard, two giant breeds of dogs. The series of bars at the left represents two male and four female great Danes. The relative amounts of thyroid in these large animals, each weighing about 50 kilograms, are uniformly small, ranging from 80 to 130 milligrams per kilogram of body weight. The largest is only 1½ times greater than the smallest, a much lower variation in size than is shown for the two dwarf and the two normal sized breeds discussed above.

The next series of bars in text-figure 81 represents the relative thyroid sizes for ten adult St. Bernard dogs, two males and eight females. Several of these dogs weighed close to 100 kilograms and showed marked symptoms of acromegaly. The relative amounts of thyroid tissue are comparatively very low, being smaller than for any of the above five breeds. The range is from 45 milligrams per kilogram up to 125 milligrams, the upper extreme being almost three times the lower, with an average for the ten animals of only 85 milligrams.

These fairly representative groups of six pedigreed dog breeds of highly different types clearly indicate wide ranges of variability in the relative amounts of thyroid tissue possessed by closely similar specimens within each group. The greatest range of variability in relative thyroid size is among the English bulldogs. These may be said to differ more widely from the ancestral canine pattern than do any of the other five breeds discussed. Yet in spite of their extremely modified type, there is no evidence that the wide differences in proportional amounts of thyroid material are at all concerned with the degrees of development in their structural distortions.

The smallest range of variability in thyroid size is shown by the Great Danes. These dogs are of giant size, but of

# GENETIC TYPE AND THE ENDOCRINES 407

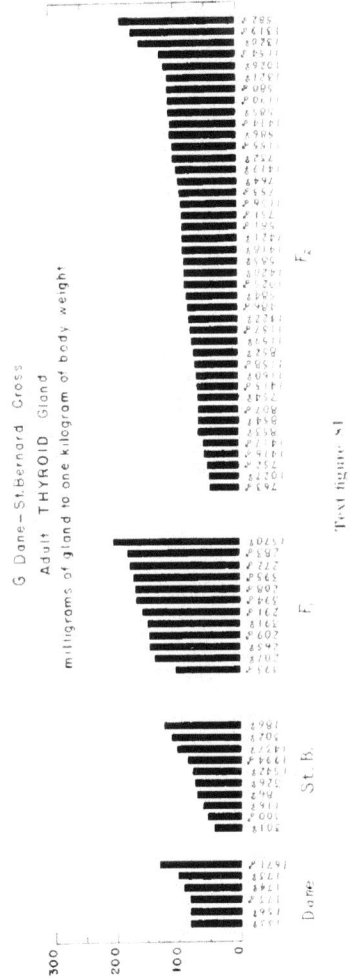

Text figure 11

uniformly normal canine proportions with a low degree of variability in the relative sizes of all their parts. The range in thyroid size for the great Dane is only as 1:1.5, while in the bulldog it is four times greater, or as 1:6.

The question now arises whether relative amounts of thyroid tissue might not differ widely enough between two breeds to indicate some bearing on breed differentiation. In attempting to answer this question, one must assume that relative thyroid proportions are probably of no breed significance unless the difference between two breeds is very much greater than the differences among similar members of a single breed. The six breeds already considered for individual thyroid variations are widely different types and serve admirably for these interbreed comparisons. The average relative sizes of thyroid to kilogram of body weight for each breed may be determined from the individual records in the charts, and these range as follows: six adult bassethounds, 267 milligrams; seven dachshunds, 224 milligrams; thirteen English bulldogs, 163 milligrams; six Boston terriers, 140 milligrams; six great Danes, 93 milligrams; and ten St. Bernards, 85 milligrams. In this series of averages—267–224–163–140–93–85—the highest value is three times greater than the smallest, that is, the average bassethound has about three times more thyroid material per kilogram of body weight than does the average St. Bernard. The individual charts also show that the lowest bassethound record of 160 milligrams is larger than the highest individual St. Bernard record of 125 milligrams. There is no overlapping between these two breeds. The lowest bassethound also has relatively more thyroid tissue than the highest recorded great Dane. There is also no overlapping in relative thyroid size between the dachshund and great Dane or St. Bernard. But the individual records of the bassethound, dachshund, bulldog, and Boston terrier do show considerable overlapping. This overlapping among breeds so highly contrasted in size and type is another strong indication that the relative quantity of thyroid tissue is of no significance in the determination of structural type or pattern.

On the other hand, the distinctly lower average for relative thyroid proportions shown by the giant breeds, as well as the fact that there is no interbreed overlapping of individual thyroid proportions between these and the several smaller sized breeds, might possibly indicate that a low thyroid ratio is conducive to large body size. Many facts concerning the rôle of thyroid influence on growth and differentiation in lower vertebrates, and in mammals as well, support such a possibility. Nevertheless, we should not lose sight of the fact that the breed with the largest average thyroid has only three times more thyroid than the one with the smallest. This difference in thyroid proportion may be unimportant when it is recalled that one dachshund may have relatively more than three times as much thyroid as another, and that one bulldog may possess six times more thyroid than another member of his breed.

Although quantity of thyroid tissue, within necessary functional limits, would seem to play no rôle in type determination, the relative size of the thyroid may yet be a definitely hereditary characteristic within itself. The three charts already referred to in connection with relative thyroid sizes for the pure breeds also contain data of interest in connection with the inheritance of thyroid size and its probable lack of correlation with physical type in the hybrids of widely different breeds.

*The relative sizes of thyroids in hybrids between pure breeds of contrasted types.* The relative thyroid sizes in the hybrid generations of the cross between the Boston terrier and the dachshund are represented in text-figure 79, to which we have already referred for pure breed records. Relative thyroid sizes for these two pure breeds are not very different, and the individual records overlap considerably. The thyroids in five adult $F_1$ Boston terrier-dachshund hybrids are shown in the chart to average somewhat greater in relative size than do the thyroids of the pure bred parent stocks. In general body type, the $F_1$ hybrids, as seen from life in plate 29 (p. 127), are nearer the dachshund than the Boston terrier, although they are somewhat larger in body size than either parent.

The next series of bars in text-figure 79 represents the relative sizes of thyroids for thirty-three $F_2$ hybrids. These sizes range from a mere 60 milligrams per kilogram of body weight up to the enormous proportion of almost 750 milligrams per kilogram. The highest amount of thyroid is thus more than twelve times greater than the smallest. These $F_2$ Boston terrier-dachshund hybrids also exhibit remarkable contrasts in type and in the recombinations of characters derived from the two parent stocks. This has been discussed in previous chapters and is well illustrated in plate 30 (p. 129). The contrasts in characteristics among members of the $F_2$ generation supply most valuable test material for determining the possible correlation between relative amounts of thyroid tissue and modified physical peculiarities. Taking into consideration the two most striking character differences among these $F_2$ hybrids—leg form, long-straight or short-bent; and head type, long muzzled dachshund form or short-wide Boston terrier shape—we find no relation whatever between the distribution of these different characters and the regularity of the slope formed by the bars representing relative thyroid sizes. Short-bent legs and long-straight legs occur in animals represented for relative thyroid sizes by adjacent bars throughout the series. Head shapes of Boston terrier pattern and dachshund pattern are also irregularly distributed among the individuals from one end to the other of the series for thyroid sizes. The animal with the smallest amount of thyroid has a Boston terrier typed head, while the next highest thyroid record is derived from an individual with a dachshund-like head. The two extremely large thyroid sizes in the $F_2$ series are recorded from litter mate sisters. One of these showed the mixed combination of short-bent dachshund legs and a Boston terrier typed head, while the other had long, straight Boston terrier legs and a dachshund-like head. These proportionally huge thyroids seemed to fit equally well into both structural complexes.

The initial letters B and D above the bars in text-figure 79 indicate, respectively, Boston terrier and dachshund characters in the head; and T and S indicate tall and short for legs. The reader may readily see the irregular distribution of these four characters throughout the slope of relative thyroid sizes as represented for the thirty-three $F_2$ Boston terrier-dachshund hybrids. Although no relation exists between proportional amounts of thyroid tissue and body form, there is an indication from these $F_2$ records that members of the same litter tend to have more or less the same relative amounts of thyroid tissue. This tendency might be interpreted to mean that richness in thyroid material is an hereditary or familial character.

The chart for $F_2$ thyroid sizes may be further interpreted as indicating that new genetic constitutions have arisen among these hybrid individuals which bring about relative thyroid proportions considerably smaller than either parental stock in some and very much larger in others. The proportionally huge thyroids are more than twice the relative size of the highest recorded for the parent stocks. These distorted proportions, deviating in both directions from the standard of the original breeds, are clear indications of the strange combinations in genetic constitutions which give rise to some of the $F_2$ hybrid individuals. The normal adjustment in proportional sizes of the various bodily organs is no doubt delicately controlled through both genetic and developmental influences, and in certain of these $F_2$ animals, organs other than endocrine glands are frequently distorted in proportion, and many of the puppies are non-viable. Several $F_2$ specimens have possessed such disproportionately large heads with internal hydrocephalus that they were unable to survive even though nursed with great care.

The backcross offspring of the $F_1$ hybrid and the Boston terrier parent show uniformly small relative proportions of thyroid material, as is indicated in the chart by the series of bars representing fourteen such backcross animals.

The records of six animals from the backcross by the $F_1$ hybrid on the dachshund parent show most widely variable relative amounts of thyroid tissue. The lowest of these proportions is less than 200 milligrams per kilogram of body weight, while the two highest specimens are 700 and 940 milligrams. Here again one doubtless finds entirely new constitutional complexes producing relative amounts of thyroid material entirely out of proportion with those shown for any of the pure dog breeds.

Text-figure 79, as a whole, clearly indicates that the relative amount of thyroid tissue in the dog is a widely variable proportion, and our examinations of the Boston terrier-dachshund cross again show that these differences in proportion are without significance in the determination of body form and type.

The relative sizes of thyroids in hybrids between the bassethound and English bulldog are represented in text-figure 80. Thyroid sizes in these two pure breeds overlap, though there is some indication that the bulldog has a smaller average amount of thyroid per kilogram of body weight than does the bassethound. Both breeds are widely variable in relative thyroid size.

The third series of bars in text-figure 80 represents gross thyroid proportions in nine $F_1$ bassethound-bulldog hybrids. The $F_1$ thyroids are fairly uniform in relative sizes and lie within the range of the parent breeds.

Members of the second hybrid generation from the cross between these two widely contrasted stocks are remarkably uniform in the relative amounts of thyroid tissue present. The records for forty-two individuals of this generation are indicated by the fourth series of bars in this figure. Thyroid sizes in thirty-eight of these forty-two individuals are represented by a gradually lengthening series of bars having values of from about 100 milligrams per kilogram of body weight to about 225 milligrams, all being within the bulldog range. In view of the wide variability in relative thyroid size occurring in both parent stocks, these $F_2$ records show remarkable uniformity. The four bars at the right end of the series break the uniformity, yet even these fall within the upper limits of the range for the bassethound grandparent. This record is very different from the Boston terrier-dachshund $F_2$ series which extended below and above the ranges of the two parent stocks. Since the Boston terrier-dachshund pure stocks are less variable for thyroid size than are the bassethound-bulldog breeds, it is difficult to account for the direction of differences between these $F_2$ records except on the grounds that the number of animals is small and the variability in relative thyroid sizes very great.

The backcross records in this cross are not important.

Relative thyroid sizes for the Dane-St. Bernard cross are represented in text-figure 81, and it is seen that both these giant breeds have small thyroid glands. The twelve $F_1$ hybrids recorded by the third series of bars would seem to give somewhat larger thyroid proportions than either parent stock, although in view of the small numbers the difference is not convincing.

The series of bars at the right in this figure represents the relative thyroid sizes for forty-two $F_2$ great Dane-St. Bernard hybrids. These sizes range from a low of about 50 milligrams of thyroid per kilogram of body weight to only 175 milligrams, showing the consistent tendency for low amounts of thyroid material in these large dogs. A comparison of this $F_2$ chart with the $F_2$ series in text-figures 79 and 80 shows that hybrids from the Boston terrier-dachshund dwarf breeds have an extremely wide range in relative amounts of thyroid; while animals of normal body size, the bassethound-bulldog hybrids, are less variable in relative thyroid amounts; and the giant dogs are least variable, having uniformly low amounts of thyroid tissue. In further support of previous conclusions, no correlation between structural type and relative thyroid size can be found in any of these crosses. If the thyroid gland exerts any specific control over the development of bodily proportions and structural form, it is not through the gross relative quantity of thyroid tissue, and we must examine into the histologic quality upon which its function depends for the possible relationship between thyroid activity and bodily type. However, a study of the differences in relative quantity of gland was necessary in order to know what, if any, effects size might exert before attempting to interpret the meaning of differences in histologic quality, and we now know that a small amount of gland seems fully capable of supplying the necessary amount of hormones, and only the quality of the gland would seem to be of prime importance.

GROSS RELATIVE SIZES OF THE PITUITARY GLANDS IN CONTRASTED BREED TYPES AND THEIR HYBRIDS

The relative amount of pituitary gland in milligrams per kilogram of body weight was estimated for the same six pure breeds for which the gross thyroid relations were discussed. An accurate measurement of volume and weight is more difficult to obtain for the pituitary than for the thyroid. In removing the pituitary from the base of the brain it is usually preferable to include with it a small amount of brain tissue in order to make sure of including the entire pars tuberalis and the infundibular stalk. The histologic and cytologic nature of this gland is known to play so important a rôle in the growth and structural development of the individual that there could be no sacrifice of histologic material in favor of more accurate gross proportions. For such reasons, variable small amounts of brain tissue are frequently included when calculating pituitary size; but definite effort has been made to control this extraneous tissue, and we are quite certain that the possible error is irregularly distributed throughout the records without advantage to any one group. The adhering membranes, often difficult to remove from the human pituitary, are not involved in the dog.

Text-figures 82, 83 and 84 indicate the relative sizes of pituitary gland for the same groups of dogs which furnished the thyroid records already examined in text-figures 79, 80 and 81. The individual mass of pituitary, as compared with

# GENETIC TYPE AND THE ENDOCRINES 415

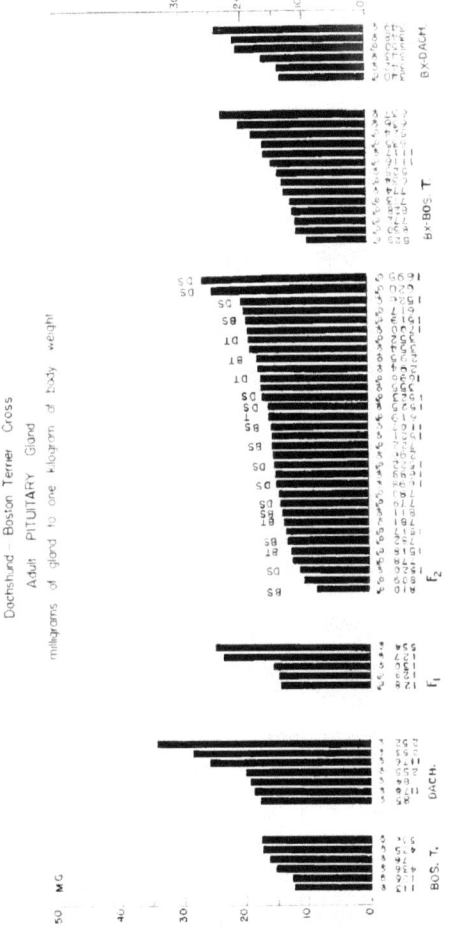

Text figure 8

the thyroid, is, of course, very small, and differences in relative pituitary sizes are not nearly so conspicuous as thyroid differences. This may be seen by comparing the wide range in thyroid size of the dachshund-Boston terrier groups in text-figure 79 with the uniformity of pituitary records for the same groups in text-figure 82. A detailed comparison of the relative positions of the individual animals of the $F_2$ series, as indicated below the bars in these two figures, brings out the fact that there is no relation, either direct or inverse, between the proportional sizes of thyroid and the proportional amounts of pituitary material. In other words, a relatively large amount of thyroid tissue is not regularly associated with either a high amount or a low amount of pituitary. Within wide limits, the gross quantity of these endocrinic materials seems to be of little functional significance.

A large number of investigators have recorded the weights of human pituitaries from both normal and diseased cases. The more important of these were conveniently tabulated in a recent study by Rasmussen ('38) and show, in the first place, that the human pituitary varies widely in size, ranging in adults from an approximate low weight of 200 milligrams up to a high of about 1300 milligrams. Rasmussen calls attention to the fact that some of the weight differences are undoubtedly due to the manner in which the pituitaries were cut from the brain or the infundibular stalk, as well as to the varying degrees of thoroughness with which the capsules were dissected off before weighing. In Rasmussen's own extensive series of human pituitaries, from 111 adult men and ninety-three women, in which both the capsule and infundibular stalk were completely removed, the male pituitaries ranged in weight from 358 to 788 milligrams and the female from 448 to 971 milligrams. The human female pituitary is distinctly larger than the male. Rasmussen's mean for the sexes being 618 milligrams for women and 526 milligrams for men. This difference is in accord with all other such investigations, and is of considerable significance. It is due entirely to the larger pars distalis in the female; the

# GENETIC TYPE AND THE ENDOCRINES 417

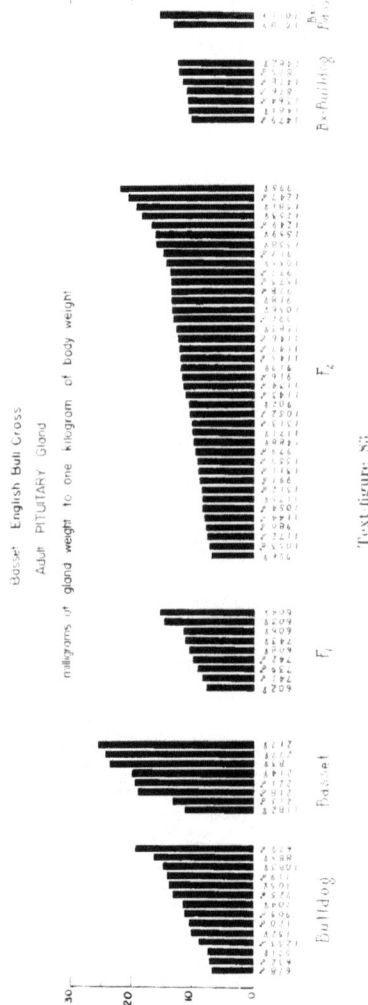

Text figure 83

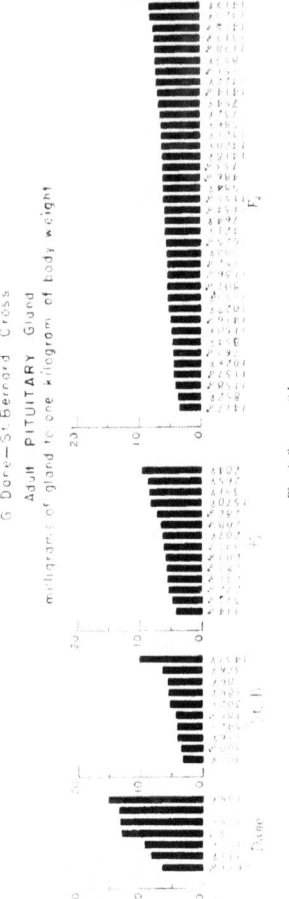

Text figure 84

pars infundibularis and pars intermedia are larger in the male. Since the body weight of women is less than that of men, the proportional size of the female pituitary exceeds the male even further than does its actual size.

Rasmussen is of the opinion that there is a distinct positive correlation between body length or height and the weight of the pituitary, and that this correlation is closer than the correlation between body weight and pituitary weight. In both human sexes, a person of large stature will be found to have a large pituitary. This is also true for the dog.

The large dog breeds have large pituitaries, and the small toy dogs have small pituitaries. However, the weight of pituitary in milligrams per kilogram of body weight is higher in the small dogs than in the larger breeds. This is clearly seen by comparing text-figures 82, 83 and 84. As shown in text-figure 82, hybrids from the dachshund and Boston terrier cross, each weighing about 10 kilograms, have pituitaries ranging in actual weight from less than 100 milligrams up to about 300. The bassethound-English bulldog hybrids represented in text-figure 83, each of which weighed more than 20 kilograms, have pituitaries ranging in weight from about 180 milligrams to well over 400 milligrams. The giant specimens represented in text-figure 84 range in body weight from about 40 to 100 kilograms, and the actual weights of their pituitaries vary from over 250 to over 600 milligrams. Therefore, in general it is true for dogs that the larger the stature the greater the weight of the pituitary, but also that the smaller the stature the greater the relative weight of pituitary per kilogram of body substance.

The pituitary in the dog is not nearly so variable in size as is the thyroid, nor do the size variations of these two organs seem to be directly related. The variability of pituitary weight in the dog is about comparable to the general ratio of variability for the heart, kidney and liver, which accords in general with the findings of Brown ('29) for normal rabbits.

The charts representing pituitary amounts per kilogram of body weight for the dachshund-Boston terrier cross, the bassethound-English bulldog cross, and the great Dane-St. Bernard cross, all fail to show recognizable correlation between gross pituitary proportion and pronounced structural distortions. This fact again leaves us free to interpret any relation between histologic quality and type characteristics without reference to variations in pituitary amounts.

The preliminary survey of the variations in gross proportions of the thyroid and pituitary glands leads to the consideration of the differences in histologic qualities of these and other endocrine glands from dog breeds of contrasted types in order to determine the possible significance of such differences in relation to the enormous deviations from the standard structural and functional type.

## Differences in the Histologic Qualities of Thyroid Glands from Dogs of Pure Breed

*Introductory view.* It is well known that each of the endocrine glands exerts some rather specific influence over the structural and functional reactions within the mammalian body. It is also generally recognized that the action of any one endocrine gland is not entirely independent of the influences of several or perhaps all other glands. The interactions of the thyroid and pituitary in influencing the gonadal functions is a well known example. There is, of course, a general interaction and dependence in functional relation among all the different organs and tissues of the animal body, but the interrelation among the members of the endocrine system is much more definite and specific. It has also been clearly established that most of the important alterations in endocrine gland function result from or are accompanied by definite modifications in the normal histologic patterns of the gland. Finally, it is now becoming widely recognized that severe and chronic illness and disturbed alimentary functions bring about various modifications in endocrine glands, many of which are evidenced by changes in the histologic structure of the gland. Much of the human material collected after death from protracted illness has been misinterpreted histologically because of the assumption that the patient had not suffered from endocrine disease. The possibility exists that a patient may die from the secondary disturbance of the endocrine glands. For example, it is known that suprarenal deficiency is very pronounced following certain systemic infections, and this deficiency brings about cardiac and circulatory symptoms of fatal significance. We have found that the endocrine glands from dogs dying of distemper and other diseases are modified, and therefore are not reliable material for a study of type or constitutional glandular differences. These elementary facts concerning the actions and interrelations of endocrine glands are of fundamental nature, particularly in establishing any existing relation between the endocrines and the differences in physical type.

At the time this study was begun, it was not realized, at least not in so far as our knowledge of the literature goes, that the widely different breeds of dogs might possess variously modified endocrine glands, and that there might be some correlation between the specific characters of the breed and the nature of its glands. The initial observations on glands from different breed types collected from the New York city pound showed wide differences in histologic structure, particularly among the thyroids. But, as stated above, this material was unreliable from the standpoint of both breed purity and individual physical history. The present discussion of the histology of endocrines in the different dog breeds and types is based entirely on material from pedigreed animals that were always, during life, under careful observation.

Other than several preliminary reports on these experiments (Stockard, '26, '27, '28, '31, '34, '35, '36), the only record of the histology of endocrine glands from pure line dog breeds that has appeared since our study began is an article from the Veterinary Institute of Bonn by Martin Frey in 1934. The material on which this study was based was collected from dogs killed at the station for animal disposal in Cologne; their history and age were hear-say, and the material is open to criticism on the grounds that the histologic conditions of many of the glands were modified by disease, and all the tissues were fixed simply with 5% formalin. The report gives histologic details of glands from only two breeds, the hound and dachshund; other breeds are tabulated. The dachshund is represented as possessing a thyroid showing desquamation and destruction of follicular epithelium with little colloid present, and a pituitary in which the pars distalis could be said to show acidophilic adenoma but for the fact, as he states, that forty-nine specimens gave identical pictures, showing this to be normal for the dachshund. On the basis of our experience with healthy tissues, these findings are entirely unreliable and incorrect, as the records beyond will show. According to Frey's second table, the thyroids of the dachshund and bulldog have the same histologic pattern; this is entirely incorrect. His brief discussion of types is based on a comparison of dwarf with full sized animals and shows no appreciation whatever of extreme differences in head shapes. His findings are generally out of accord with this report, and I regret that they fail to supply material for comparisons and need only be referred to in this brief way.

*Histologic techniques employed.* All glands and sample pieces of other organs used in this histologic study were fixed immediately after the animals were killed or at the time of autopsy. Several fixing fluids were used, and the same procedure was followed for all individuals in order to have the effects of technique comparable. The right thyroid gland was fixed in Bouin's fluid, and pieces of the left were fixed in Helly's, Zenker's or Susa's fluids, with usually one piece fixed in chloral hydrate for silver nitrate impregnation, a specific method to show the parafollicular cells. The right suprarenal was placed in 15% formalin for frozen sectioning and fat staining. The left suprarenal was divided, half being fixed in Bouin's fluid, the other half in Zenker's, Helly's or Susa's.

The fixative giving the most consistently reliable results for the pituitary was a modified Helly's fluid. Staining was most satisfactory with a modified form of Mallory's triple stain.

The thyroids and suprarenals were usually sectioned at seven microns thickness. Thyroids (including the internal parathyroids) were sectioned as thin as five or six microns. Some abnormal parathyroids were cut as thin as four or five microns in order to study nuclear details. Serial sections were made of the parathyroids, and special regions of the thyroid glands. The pituitaries were cut in serial sections through comparable regions at a thickness of four or five microns.

The stains most often used were Mann's hematoxylin-eosin (or erythrosin) and Mallory's triple stain. Heidenhain's iron-hematoxylin and eosin were frequently used for detecting nuclear types in the parathyroids. As supplement to the Mallory triple stain, the special stains of Altman and Masson were also used for the pituitary.

*Survey of histologic modifications in the thyroid.* The thyroid gland shows the most easily recognized histologic modifications to be found among the endocrines in the different breeds of dogs. For this reason its histology will be considered first, in order to give the general plan of analysis for determining what relationship if any is to be found between endocrinic modifications and the peculiar structural and functional characteristics of the dog breeds.

Plates 81, 82 and 83 show photomicrographs from typical sections of thyroids. Plates 81 and 82 have been arranged so as to show sections from the short muzzled bulldog-like breeds at the top and long muzzled, more nearly normal canine types at the bottom. This arrangement facilitates comparisons between the more highly modified breeds and the more nearly normal types and emphasizes the wide differences in thyroid structural quality and arrangements.

Those familiar with the histology of the thyroid gland will appreciate how practically impossible it is to select for a photomicrograph a single small spot which will fairly represent all the peculiar characteristics that might occur throughout the gland. The follicles are very rarely of equal size and of uniform distribution; neither are the supporting, vascular and other interfollicular tissues uniformly arranged in the different areas. The superficial and central portions of the gland usually differ considerably for follicular size and relative proportions of parenchyma to other tissues. In spite of regional variations which are common to all thyroid glands, it is possible, with the material under consideration, to select areas for photomicrographs which show particular patterns of thyroid structure that are more or less typically characteristic in a given breed of dogs.

In the discussion of the glands, definite effort will be made to bring out further points of importance that cannot be recognized from the photographs in the plates. Space prohibits, however, an unlimited treatment of all the details, many of which are without known significance. We shall discuss the structures with as much discrimination as is feasible.

The German shepherd and foxhound are normal or standard typed dogs, and the histologic structure of their thyroid glands furnishes a very satisfactory control pattern. Figure

PLATE 81

EXPLANATION OF FIGURES

Photomicrographs of typical sections of the thyroid glands from two short muzzled breeds (the English and French bulldogs) and two long muzzled breeds (the bassethound and foxhound). The contrast in histologic patterns between the two types is strongly marked.

1 English bulldog 149 ♂.
2 French bulldog 109 ♀.
3 Bassethound 277 ♀.
4 Foxhound 90 ♀.

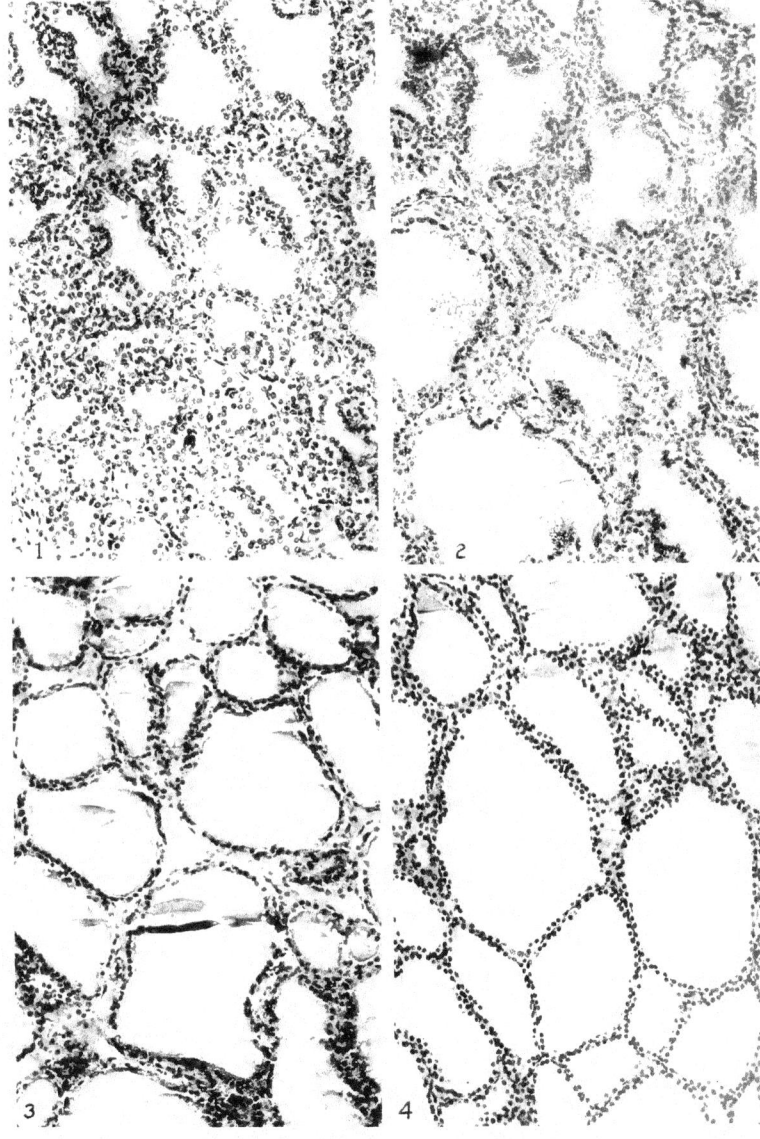

4 in plate 81 illustrates the normal histology of the foxhound thyroid. The follicles are large and fairly regular in outline and the epithelium is of a moderately active type. The fixed colloid tends to be hard and slightly brittle. Nests of parafollicular epithelial cells are seen lying in the sparse extrafollicular tissue. These cells have recently been discussed by Nonidez ('32 a, '32 b, '33), in our laboratory, and by other investigators. Their relative amounts are quite characteristic in certain breeds. The foxhound thyroid is similar in its histology to the normal human and other mammalian thyroids.

Figure 3 (pl. 82) illustrates the German shepherd thyroid. Again the follicles are large and regular in outline, but the epithelium is higher and more active than in the foxhound, as is indicated by the secretion droplets. Thyroid sections from two other German shepherd dogs are shown, for comparative purposes, in plate 83. The colloid of the somewhat more active shepherd gland is not so hard as in the foxhound and is less brittle. In general there are fewer parafollicular cells in the shepherd than in the foxhound thyroid. There are only small amounts of extrafollicular tissue in both these thyroids.

Most decided deviations from this normal pattern of thyroid histology are shown by the entire group of dog breeds possessing short skulls of the bulldog type. The general nature of the thyroid distortion in all the bulldog-like breeds is somewhat the same, yet wide specific differences are to be found among them.

Figure 1 in plate 81 is a highly characteristic and typical section of the English bulldog thyroid. We have studied thyroids from thirteen bulldogs, seven males and six females, and the type of histologic distortion in all these glands is remarkably consistent. One familiar with the histologic picture of its thyroid would undoubtedly feel that the English bulldog can be recognized almost as certainly from it as from the characteristic pattern of the head. Both characters vary about equally. Yet we must not be misunderstood as presuming at this time a direct causal relation between the two.

The follicles in the bulldog thyroid are very much smaller than normal, and are extremely variable and irregular in outline. The general picture is that of demoralization in follicular development, giving a somewhat adenomatoid character to the gland. Yet it will be recalled that these glands of the bulldog are of proportionally small size with no tumor-like reaction involved. The general irregularity and defective follicular formation result from early maldevelopment. In spite of the irregular form and often confluent nature of the follicles, the epithelium in many regions is high and very active, as indicated by abundance of secretory droplets around the periphery of the small colloidal masses within the irregular follicles. Such follicular conditions might at first sight give the impression of hyperactivity, but further study shows this gland to be very different from the histologic picture of the gland in common hyperthyroidism. The physiology of the bulldog also refutes the idea of thyroid hyperactivity. The basal metabolism is not high; the animal is slow and inactive and inclined to become fat, although a comparatively small eater. The photomicrograph of the bulldog thyroid shows an excessive amount of extrafollicular material. Some of this consists of epithelial cells not properly incorporated into follicles, and in some cases these cells seem to give rise to colloid which lies outside and between the follicles. However, there is no evidence of desquamation from the follicular epithelium which Frey claims to be a constant feature. The extrafollicular epithelial cells are not to be confused with the so-called parafollicular cells. The latter do not give rise to colloid and, in the dog, respond specifically, as Nonidez has found, to silver nitrate impregnation. Also the typical parafollicular cells, so common in the thyroids of most dog breeds, are practically absent from the English bulldog thyroid and are, when present at all, very scarce, as is shown by tests with the silver stain.

There is frequent evidence of developmental arrests in both the thyroid and parathyroids of the bulldog. We shall see beyond that there is also evidence of macroscopic arrests in the morphology of the pituitary gland, with large, plump suprarenals and frequent accompanying deficiencies in gonadal development, such as failure in descent of the testes, and defective oestrus with sterility and abnormally small litters in the female.

The microscopic structure of the thyroid gland in the French bulldog (fig. 2, pl. 81) is very much on the same general pattern as that for the English bulldog. The follicles in the French bulldog thyroid are extremely irregular in outline, although somewhat larger than in the English breed. Extrafollicular colloid is also found in this gland, and the microscopic picture of hyperthyroidism is somewhat more genuine, with high columnar epithelium and secretion droplets shown in most follicles. This dog is very nervous and hyperactive, with varying degrees of exophthalmos, all common symptoms of thyroid oversecretion. The thyroid, as in all the bulldogs, has an excessive amount of extrafollicular tissue, and lying within this are rather small groups of parafollicular cells. Although we have examined thyroids from only a few French bulldogs, their histology has been quite consistently of the same general pattern as shown in this photomicrograph.

Together with the bulldog sections in plate 81 are photomicrographs of the thyroids from the bassethound and the foxhound. The contrast in histologic patterns between the bulldog thyroids and those of the hounds is strongly marked. The bassethound, although having extreme chondrodystrophy of the legs, has a thyroid gland (fig. 3) almost indistinguishable in its normal histology from that of the long legged foxhound (fig. 4). If chondrodystrophy of the basicranium in the bulldog were related, either directly or indirectly, to the histopathology of its thyroid gland, certainly then the chondrodystrophy in the bassethound legs might be expected to accompany a somewhat similar thyroid condition. Since, however, this is not the case, the thyroid gland can scarcely be directly charged with the growth conditions in the head of the bulldog. The bassethound thyroid illustrated in the photomicrograph was functioning somewhat more actively at the time of death than that of the foxhound. This was due entirely to chance, and these two glands are, as a rule, about equally active, or, if there is a difference, the foxhound has the more active thyroid. After fixation the colloid in the bassethound thyroid is hard, and usually as brittle as in the foxhound.

The thyroids from two other breeds with short bulldog-like heads are illustrated by figures 1 and 2 in plate 82. Figure 1 shows the Pekingese thyroid to be quite bulldog-like, with small irregularly shaped follicles separated by abundant extra-follicular tissue. The follicular epithelium is in places high, columnar and quite active, forming a peripheral circle of secretion droplets about the colloid. The colloid, after fixation, is rather soft, indicating its freshness. There are extra-follicular epithelial cells and small nests of parafollicular cells lying between the follicles. This gland, as a whole, gives a fairly typical picture of so-called hyperactivity of the thyroid. There are no important indications of developmental arrest and the adenomatoid symptoms seen in the English bulldog are absent. The appearance and behavior of the Pekingese is also quite typical of the hyperthyroid individual. The animal is nervous, restless and excitable, with marked exophthalmos.

Figure 2 (pl. 82) illustrates the histology of the Boston terrier thyroid. This gland has small, irregularly shaped, hyperactive follicles. The hyperactive condition is shown in five of the Boston terrier thyroids examined, and in the case of the sixth individual, which was killed after a few day's illness, thyroid activity had ceased and the follicles are lined with low cuboidal epithelium. The latter specimen is shown in plate 85 (p. 443) and is from 76 ♀. This case is a good illustration of how promptly a general illness tends to arrest the hypersecretion of the thyroid. The colloid in the Boston terrier thyroid is harder after fixation than in the other bulldog types. This is difficult to explain.

Again we find in the Boston terrier abundant extrafollicular tissue, and at times extrafollicular colloid. The parafollicular cells are more abundant and occur in larger masses in this thyroid than in any other breed we have examined. These cells are most clearly shown in the thyroid of 76 ♀ (pl. 85). The parafollicular cells are epithelial in type, with large, lightly staining bodies, and not only occur between follicles but are occasionally present within the follicular epithelium, as may be seen by a careful examination of several of the follicles in the right half of the photomicrograph of the section from 76 ♀.

Figures 3 and 4 in plate 82 are sections of the German shepherd and St. Bernard thyroids. The histologic pictures of these two sections are closely the same. Both have large, well distended follicles filled with colloid of only medium hardness, the periphery of which is encircled by secretion droplets, although the follicular epithelium is not high and the glands are only moderately active. The extrafollicular tissue is very sparse and contains extremely few epithelial cells. All these features tend towards an extremely different condition from that illustrated by the thyroid sections from the Pekingese and the Boston terrier.

The histologic patterns of the thyroids from all German shepherd dogs are not exactly the same as that in plate 82, taken from 118 ♀. For comparison, sections of thyroids from two other German shepherd dogs, 111 ♀ and 1404 ♂, are illustrated in plate 83 (figs. 2 and 4). These were chosen

PLATE 82

EXPLANATION OF FIGURES

Comparison of thyroid sections from two short-muzzled breeds (the Pekingese and Boston terrier) and two long muzzled breeds (the German shepherd and St. Bernard).

1 Pekingese 77 ♀.
2 Boston terrier 536 ♀.
3 German shepherd 118 ♀.
4 St. Bernard 326 ♀.

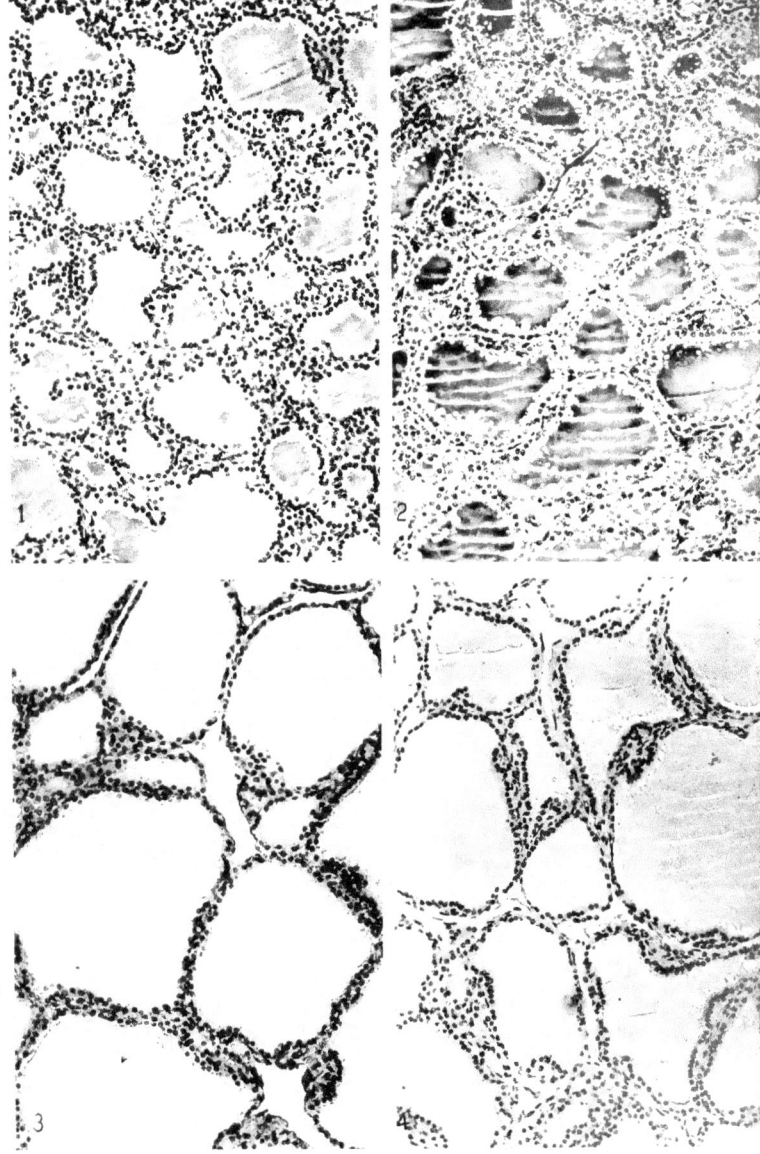

431

to show as wide a variation in histologic structure as could be found. The differences among the three sections photographed at the same magnification are very slight. The follicles in all are large, and the extrafollicular tissue is very scarce. The third section (fig. 4, pl. 83), with low cuboidal follicular lining and no droplets, shows much the lowest activity and was taken from a timid male dog that had never been a vigorous animal. It is used to illustrate the most aberrant condition found for shepherd thyroid histology. None of the differences among the shepherd thyroids tends to approach in the slightest degree the patterns shown by the bulldog typed glands, irrespective of whether they were active or inactive at the time of death.

Figures 1 and 3 in plate 83 illustrate for the St. Bernard thyroid the widest deviations from the typical section of 326 ♀ (fig. 4, pl. 82). Figure 1 is from the thyroid of 86 ♀. This section illustrates the nearest approach to hyperthyroid reaction found among glands from about one dozen adult St. Bernard specimens. All the sections are photographed at the same magnification, as can be seen by a comparison of nuclear size. Thus may we appreciate the excessively large sizes of the secretion droplets surrounding the colloid, as well as the extremely high columnar epithelium in this section. The animal from which this gland was taken was killed while suffering from an acute attack of gas formation throughout the gastro-intestinal tract. This distended the abdomen enormously causing severe pain. Until only a few hours before death the animal had always been in vigorous

PLATE 83

EXPLANATION OF FIGURES

Photomicrographs of thyroid sections from the St. Bernard and German shepherd. These sections were chosen to show the widest differences to be found in thyroid histological structure in the two breeds concerned and should be studied in conjunction with figures 3 and 4, plate 82.

1 St. Bernard 86 ♀.
2 German shepherd 111 ♀.
3 St. Bernard 186 ♀.
4 German shepherd 1404 ♂.

PLATE 83

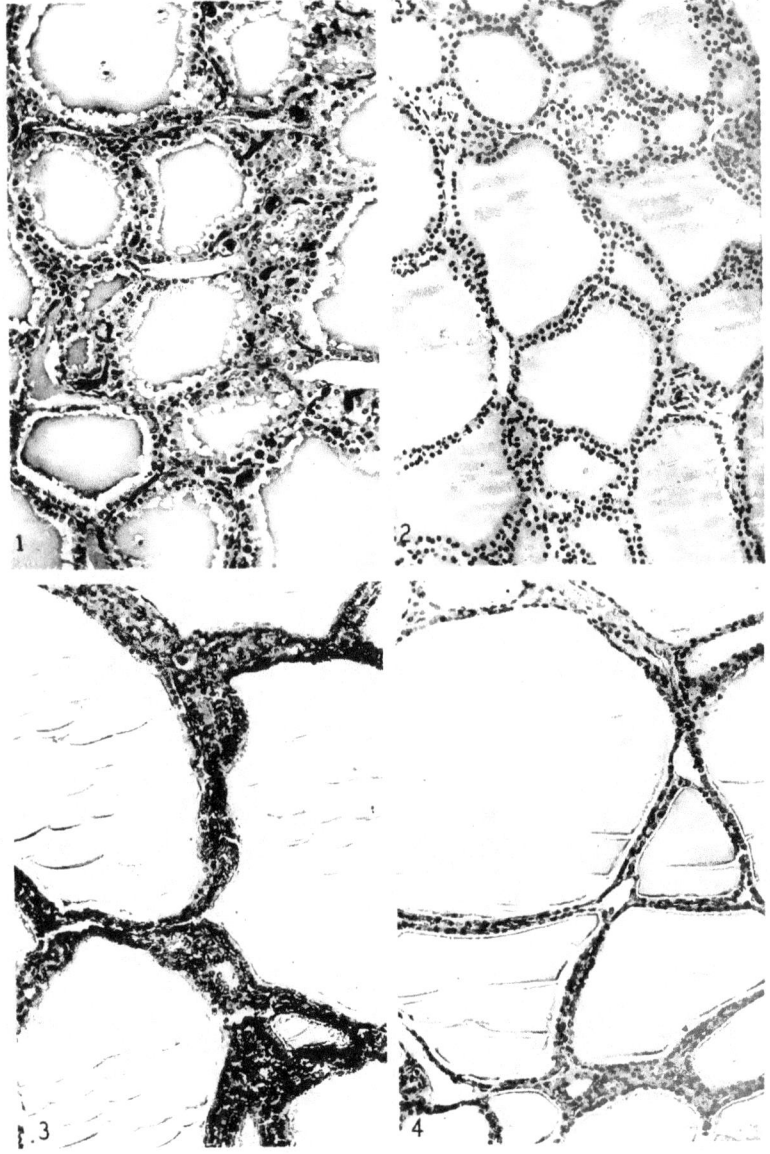

health. She was a most valuable matron bitch and had produced a record of fifty puppies within a period of two years. Very probably this high fecundity, with the production and nursing of litters of as many as fifteen puppies, may have indirectly brought about the hyperthyroid picture, although the appearance and behavior of the dog when in good health gave no evidence of such a condition.

The high columnar follicular epithelium seen in the photomicrograph of this hyperactive thyroid gives the superficial impression of abundant extrafollicular tissue. Closer examination of the section shows only a sparse amount of such tissue, and the general pattern of this thyroid is closely the same as that shown from 326 ♀ (pl. 82) which has large follicles and little extrafollicular material.

Figure 3 in plate 83 illustrates a thyroid section from another female St. Bernard, 186 ♀. This section differs from the two already described in having larger follicles with harder and more brittle colloid, giving the characteristic appearance of a lower functional level. The general histologic pattern in these three St. Bernard thyroids is closely the same, and the widely different appearances in the photomicrographs are due largely to the different states of activity existing in these thyroids at the time of death. No such explanation is applicable to the structural contrasts between the follicular patterns in the thyroids of the shepherd and St. Bernard and the Pekingese and Boston terrier (pl. 82). The excessive amounts of extrafollicular tissue in the Pekingese and Boston terrier thyroids consist of both parafollicular cells in groups of different sizes, and misplaced, irregularly distributed epithelial cells resembling those in the follicular wall and giving rise in many places to extrafollicular colloid. The general follicular formation is not normally and perfectly expressed in the glands from the breeds with short bulldog-like head shapes.

Finally we may examine the microscopic structure of the thyroid from two breeds of toy or midget dogs with almost spherical crania and much reduced facial skeletons. One of these is the Brussels griffon, in which the face is practically flat with no protruding muzzle, the most extreme reduction in jaw structure found among the dogs. The head and face of the Brussels griffon resemble much more closely these parts in a small monkey than in another dog. The second midget breed to which we refer is the ancient Maltese poodle. Here the cranium is spherical and the face is attenuated by protruding forward as a narrow and almost cylindrical muzzle. Such heads cannot be truly interpreted as of bulldog pattern, though they have in common the reduction of jaw structure and mal-accommodation of the teeth.

These two midget breeds show very similar conditions in the histologic pattern of their thyroids, which differ very much from that discussed for the bulldog, yet superficially resemble it in certain respects. Figure 1 in plate 84 illustrates the peculiar histology of the Brussels griffon thyroid. This section is from a perfectly typed bitch of more than 7 years of age, but it resembles almost exactly the familiar picture of the newborn gland from either the human or the puppy. There are a great number of follicles, all of which are very small and some extremely minute. These are true size differences among the follicles, as has been determined in serial sections, and are not simple apparent differences due to cuts through zones of various sizes. Some of the smallest bits of colloid are seen to be surrounded by uniformly cuboidal epithelium with no indication of tangential cuts through the follicular wall as are shown in other places of the section. There is an excessive amount of extrafollicular epithelioid tissue without definite arrangement, as well as very tiny follicles containing a mere drop of colloid. These conditions give to the section a compact and much more densely cellular appearance than is associated with the normal adult thyroid and its larger follicles.

It will be recalled that the Brussels griffon is inclined to rest and sleep much of the time, but when in action to be jerky and quick-moving, dancing about as it runs. Many specimens of this breed also show pronounced exophthalmos, but one would scarcely be justified in assuming that these actions or symptoms result from their peculiar thyroid histology.

The histologic picture of the Maltese poodle thyroid is shown by figure 2. The arrested fetal-like nature of this gland is even more marked than that of the griffon thyroid. The follicles are small and irregular in shape but the follicular epithelium is high columnar, as if there was more activity than in the griffon gland. Much of the epithelium in the poodle thyroid has failed to enter into follicular formation and is seen as ramifying plates and cords of epithelium in all parts of the gland. This thyroid shows extensive arrest in formation of the normal follicular pattern, and the small follicles that are present lie unusually far apart. The extent of histologic distortion in this thyroid is best appreciated by comparison with the normal glands (figs. 3 and 4 in this plate) of the dachshund and great Dane, which show wide contrast in structural pattern to figures 1 and 2 and again emphasize the defective follicular conditions in the griffon and poodle.

The dachshund section (fig. 3) contains large and medium sized follicles with low cuboidal epithelial walls. The colloid is of medium hardness and the gland is in a state of low activity. There are large groups of lightly stained parafollicular cells as well as some extrafollicular epithelioid tissue. The follicular arrangement and types of extrafollicular cells in the dachshund thyroid resemble in very close detail those

PLATE 84

EXPLANATION OF FIGURES

Photomicrographs of thyroid sections from two midget dog breeds with spherical crania and reduced facial skeleton (the Brussels griffon and Maltese poodle) and two long muzzled breeds (the dachshund and great Dane).

1 Brussels griffon 278 ♀.
2 Maltese poodle 79 ♂.
3 Dachshund 84 ♀.
4 Great Dane 175 ♀.

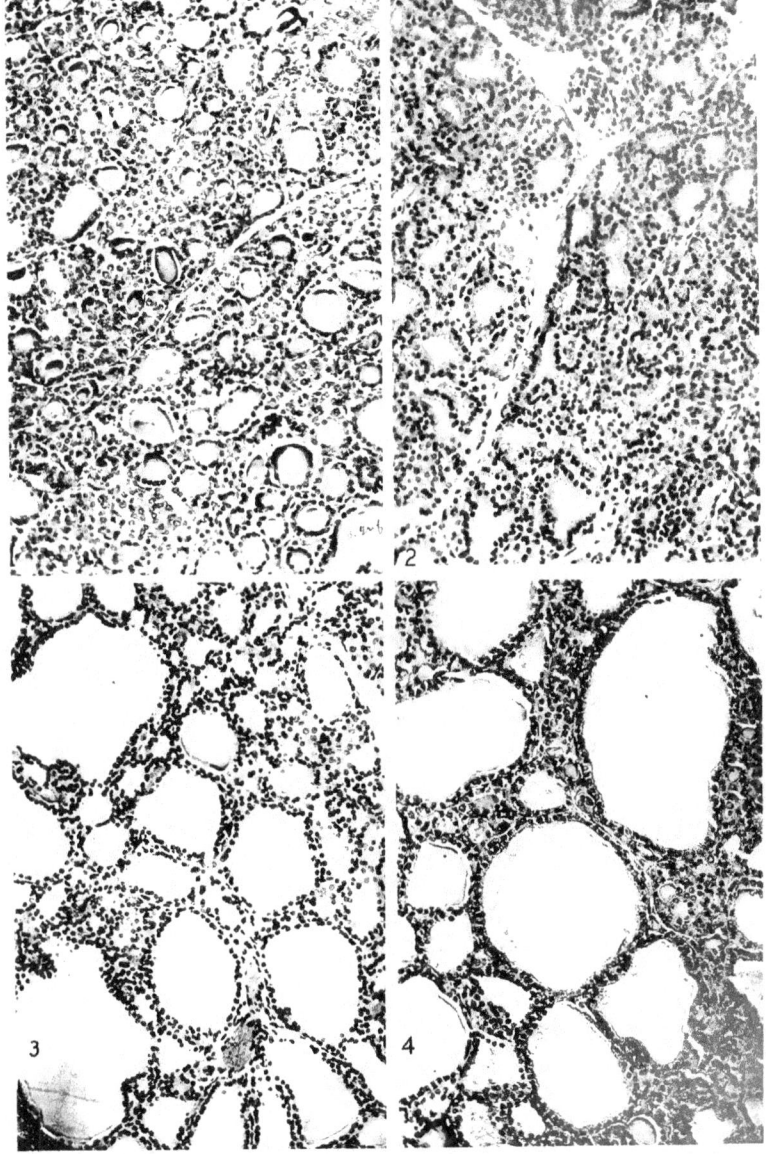

of the cocker spaniel, although the gland of the spaniel may be all in all somewhat more active. The point of interest is that the skull of the cocker, with its mild degree of basicranial chondrodystrophy, might be classed as the least pronounced of the bulldog series, and the round cranium associated with the long muzzle of the dachshund makes it an aberrant member of the long headed breeds. The dachshund falls near the end of the long-head series and the cocker spaniel stands at the beginning of the bulldog head group. The histologic patterns of their thyroids are similar, though as far as our knowledge goes this is mere coincidence.

Figure 4 (pl. 84) illustrates the histologic structure of the great Dane thyroid. This specimen was obtained from a bitch more than 7 years old. The follicles are large and the abundance of secretion droplets indicates a vigorously active epithelium without symptoms of hyperthyroidism. It will be particularly noticeable in this section that the epithelial cells on the left side of the follicles from which the droplets would seem to be exuding are higher and have more cytoplasmic material than the cells in other places where no drops are being formed. The extensive study of thyroids from several hundred dogs closely observed during life convinces one that the secretion droplets are a most reliable indicator for thyroid activity, although it is realized that some investigators using limited and less favorable material would question this. Lying among the large follicles of the Dane thyroid are very small follicles readily seen surrounding the oval bits of colloid, particularly in the right half of the photomicrograph. The presence of these tiny follicles is most unusual in a gland with well developed, large and typical follicles. Parafollicular cells are not abundant and the total epithelium is involved in the follicular formation.

The thyroid of the giant great Dane is not very different from that of the St. Bernard (pls. 82 and 83). Both have large follicles and are usually fairly active; but the very tiny follicles have been found only in the great Dane.

A summary examination of plates 81, 82, 83 and 84 makes it quite evident that the large, strongly developed follicles are present in the thyroids of all the long muzzled dog breeds, while the thyroids of dogs with bulldog typed heads and the dwarf breeds with defective muzzles, such as the Brussels griffon and Maltese poodle, all fail to develop large follicles of regular outline and usually show small, abnormally arranged follicles, often with defective walls. The extrafollicular tissue in the thyroids of the long muzzled dogs consists of the connective tissue supporting net with blood vessels and accompanying nerves, as Nonidez has so clearly described, and a sparse amount of light staining parafollicular cells. In almost all bulldog typed and flat muzzled dogs there is apparent arrest and disturbance of follicular development resulting in irregularly arranged extrafollicular epithelial cells, and in some cases these cells secrete extrafollicular colloid or form abortive follicles or, as in the poodle, show plates and cords of epithelial cells reminiscent of the fetal thyroid gland.

Our complete survey of pure breed glands is far more extensive than has been discussed or illustrated here, but the additional details are in full accord with what has been presented, and their further discussion is not necessary.

Whether the peculiarities of the thyroid are constantly or necessarily associated with the characteristic structural deformities of the several breeds cannot be stated with certainty from such a survey of pure breed thyroids even though some correlation may seem probable. For this reason we have attempted to analyze experimentally the relationships between the histologic nature of the thyroid and the physical type of the animal by crossing pure breeds which are contrasted in both the histologic patterns of their thyroids and gross bodily types. There should be material in the hybrid generations for determining whether the thyroid pattern of one parent breed might be associated with the structural type of the other breed. For example, in the $F_2$ hybrids from the Boston terrier-dachshund cross, may an individual with the Boston terrier head possess the typical dachshund thyroid histology? This is aside from the question of whether the thyroid gland within itself has the power to regulate the conformation of the bulldog head. The simple fact at this place is that pure line dogs with the bulldog head seem to have an accompanying distortion in histologic structure of the thyroid. Both these structural symptoms may be parts of a complex largely under pituitary or some other regulation. The nature of their cause or causes can only be approached after attempting to ascertain whether the two symptoms are necessarily inseparable. These statements are given in order to avoid misleading the reader into thinking that because we discuss head type in connection with thyroid structure a causal relation is inferred. A modified pituitary influence might induce the characteristic thyroid modification and possibly also the distortion of head growth. Thus the two alterations would necessarily accompany one another as results from a common cause.

## THE SIGNIFICANCE OF ENDOCRINE QUALITY IN RELATION TO PHYSICAL TYPE IN BOSTON TERRIER-DACHSHUND HYBRIDS

### The Inheritance of Contrasted Histologic Patterns of the Thyroid and Their Correlation with Physical Types in Boston Terrier-Dachshund Hybrids

It has been shown that in Boston terrier-dachshund hybrids no relation between the proportional amounts of thyroid tissue and the characteristic breed types can be established. We shall now attempt to determine whether histologic qualities of the thyroid are closely or directly related to the structural peculiarities of the individual.

A photomicrograph of a section of dachshund thyroid is shown in plate 85 (fig. 1), and a similar section from the Boston terrier is shown in figure 2. We see again, between these two thyroids, the differences which were pointed out on previous pages. In the dachshund, the follicles vary more widely in size, some of them being very large. The epithelium is low cuboidal and less active in appearance, and there is much less extrafollicular tissue in the dachshund than in the Boston terrier where we find an excessive abundance of parafollicular cells and no very large follicles. In other parts of this Boston terrier thyroid there are large confluent colloidal masses as if two or more follicles had joined. The Boston terrier thyroid approaches the infantile type but is quite active, and the dog itself is nervous and very excitable and shows varying degrees of exophthalmos. The dachshund is entirely different from the Boston terrier in disposition and behavior.

The $F_1$ hybrids from this cross, as we have seen in plate 29 (p. 127) are of uniform type, and somewhat intermediate when compared with the two parent breeds although they incline toward the dachshund in body form and the Boston terrier in cranial shape. A photomicrograph of a typical section of $F_1$ thyroid is seen in figure 3 (pl. 85). The variation from large to very small sized follicles, and the type of extrafollicular tissue, resemble more closely the histology of the dachshund thyroid than that of the Boston terrier. It may be recalled that the relative size of the $F_1$ thyroid is also in the direction of the dachshund. The thyroid glands from the five $F_1$ individuals studied are fairly uniform.

Thyroids from more than thirty $F_2$ hybrids have been examined and studied histologically. These form an almost complete series, with the fully typical dachshund thyroid at one end and an exaggerated or over-expressed Boston terrier gland at the other. Figures 4 and 5 (pl. 85) are striking illustrations of this fact, figure 4 being histologically extreme for the dachshund and figure 5 an over-expression of the Boston terrier thyroid.

The thyroid in figure 4 is from 620 ♂, which is shown from life in plate 39 (fig. 5) and plate 40 (fig. 1) (pp. 236 and 238).

This animal was in general a dachshund-like dog. The head, as the photographs show, was almost fully dachshund; the only typically Boston terrier feature is the marked reduction in mandibular growth giving an abnormally short lower jaw. Corresponding with the head and body type, the histologic structure of the thyroid is of the long muzzled dachshund pattern as found in the survey of pure breed thyroids. This gland is in a somewhat inactive condition, with rather brittle colloid.

Highly contrasted with the foregoing thyroid is the $F_2$ section in figure 5. This thyroid is from a 2 year old dwarf male, 779, which exhibited a considerable degree of short-wide head resembling the Boston terrier stock. The dog from life is shown as figure 4 in plate 30 (p. 129). The histologic picture of the thyroid of this animal shows only small irregular follicles with extremely high columnar epithelium and numerous droplets, an almost typical illustration of pathologic hyperthyroidism. Just above the center of the photomicrograph are several large nests of lightly stained parafollicular cells, and single cells of this type are richly scattered throughout the section, a feature very characteristic of the Boston terrier thyroid. This $F_2$ thyroid resembles much more exactly that of the Boston terrier in plate 82 (fig. 2) than it does the less active thyroid in plate 85 (fig. 2).

Photomicrographs from sections of four other thyroid glands from $F_2$ Boston terrier-dachshund hybrids are shown in plate 86 (figs. 1 and 2) and plate 89 (figs. 3 and 4) for comparison with those in plate 85. Figure 3 in plate 89 is histologically about the same as the thyroid of the dachshund;

PLATE 85

EXPLANATION OF FIGURES

Boston terrier-dachshund cross. Photomicrographs showing the inheritance of thyroid histological patterns in first and second generation hybrids.

1 Dachshund 84 ♀.
2 Boston terrier 76 ♀.
3 $F_1$ 128 ♂.
4 $F_2$ 620 ♂.
5 $F_2$ 779 ♂.

PLATE 85

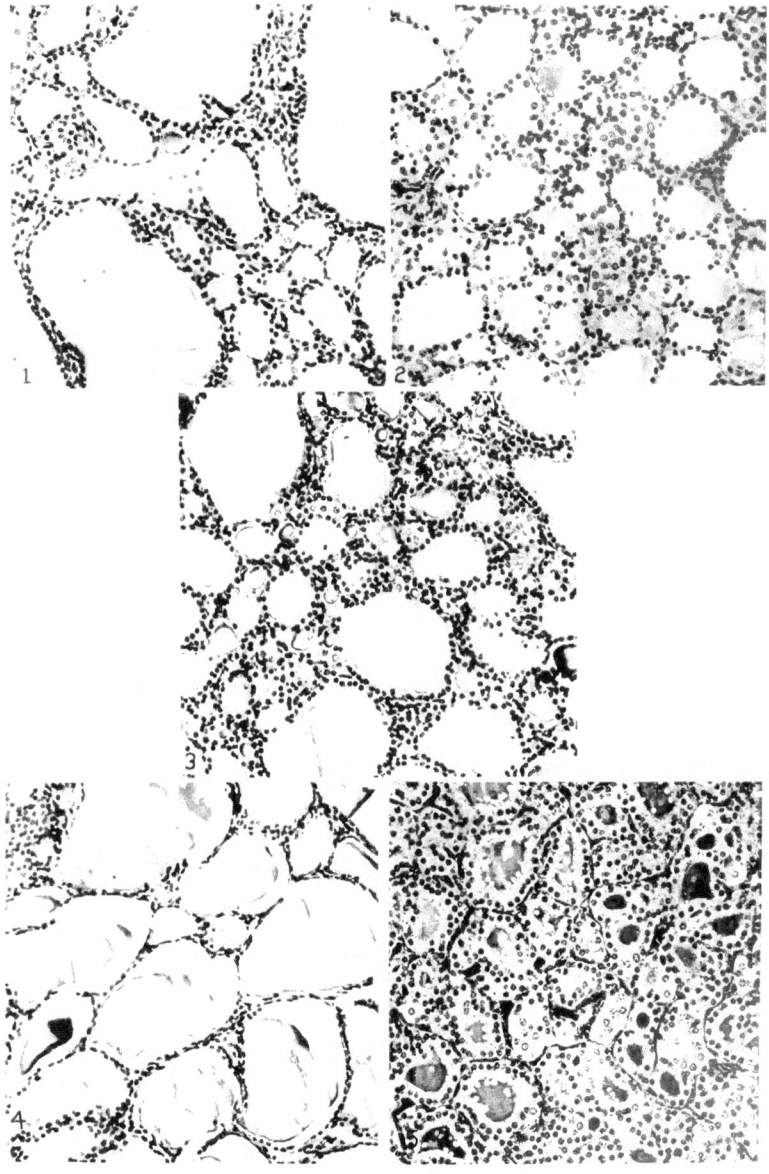

443

this is also true of figure 4 in plate 85. Figure 3 (pl. 89) is from $F_2$ 1523 ♂, which was closely dachshund in body type. A photograph of this dog while alive is at the right in figure 9, plate 30. The animal had a long muzzled dachshund head and short achondroplasic legs. As we shall find beyond, the pituitary of this animal is typically normal (plate 89, fig. 1).

Figure 1 in plate 86 shows a histologic pattern that might be interpreted as somewhat between those of the two parent stocks. The follicles are intermediate in size and of irregular outline with active cuboidal epithelium. There are smaller follicles and more abundant parafollicular cells than would be characteristic of the dachshund thyroid. The animal from which this gland was taken, 296 ♀, is shown as figure 1 in plate 39 (p. 236). This figure offers a fortunate profile view of the intermediate Boston terrier-dachshund head and face and should be compared with the more closely dachshund profile of a sister, 294 ♀ (fig. 2).

The photomicrograph in figure 2 (pl. 86) shows a rather mixed histologic pattern differing from both parent types. There are many tiny follicles containing only a drop of colloid, and other larger ones of irregular outline with active epithelium. This section of thyroid is from $F_2$ 352 ♂, a dog not shown from life in any of the illustrations. He was a long legged animal with a wide, strong head of boxer type, not closely resembling either parent stock.

Figure 4 in plate 89 is from $F_2$ 355 ♀ and approaches fairly closely the histologic pattern of the Boston terrier. This bitch possessed the head of a poor typed Boston terrier with a protruding undershot mandible. The photomicrograph of the thyroid section shows small follicles and an abundance

PLATE 86
EXPLANATION OF FIGURES

Boston terrier-dachshund cross. Thyroid histological patterns in second generation and backcross Boston terrier hybrids.

1  $F_2$ 296 ♀.
2  $F_2$ 352 ♂.
3  Backcross Boston terrier 524 ♂.
4  Backcross Boston terrier 525 ♀.

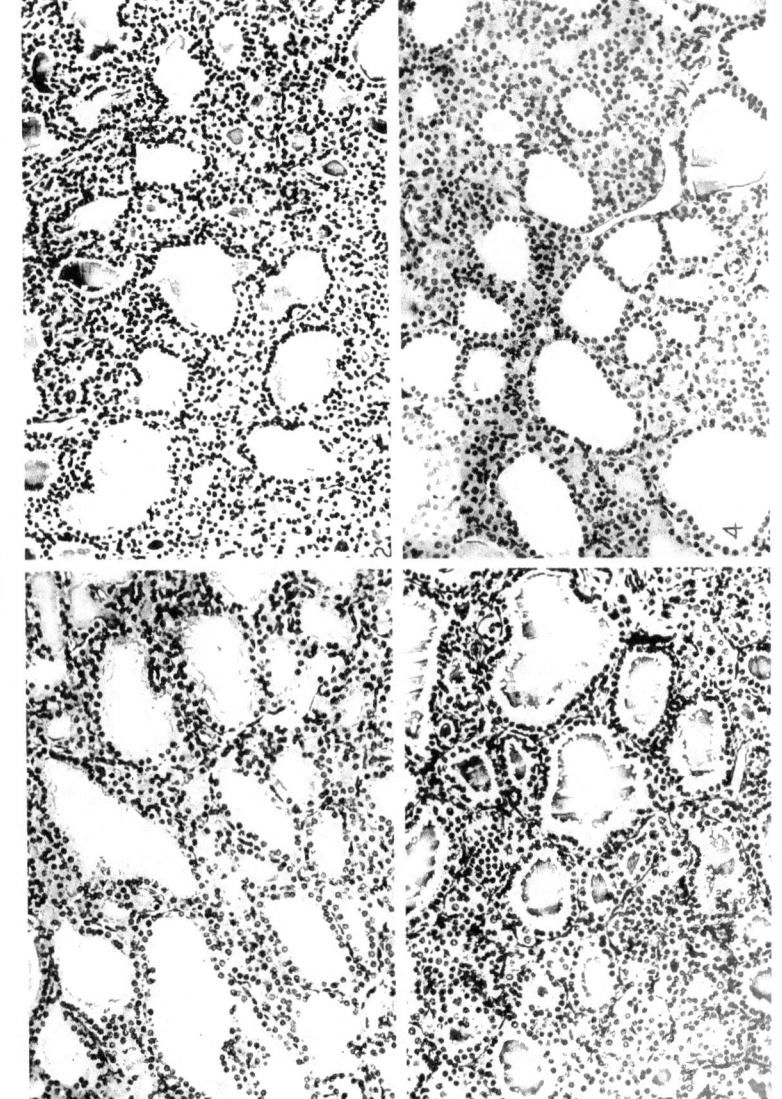

of the parafollicular epithelioid cells so typical of the Boston terrier gland. As we shall find beyond, this modified thyroid from an animal with deformed Boston terrier typed head is accompanied by an extremely distorted and cystic pituitary gland, illustrated by figure 2, plate 89.

These six sections of $F_2$ thyroid glands (pls. 85, 86 and 89), would lead one to believe that the histologic patterns of the thyroids in the dachshund and Boston terrier are definitely hereditary characters which, when the breeds are crossed, become redistributed among the $F_2$ hybrid individuals to form a series of intermediate conditions with the almost fully expressed parental types at opposite ends. The different histologic patterns of the thyroids appear to be closely associated with the structural characteristics of the parent stocks. The development of the Boston terrier bulldog head is definitely associated with the histologic pattern of the Boston terrier thyroid and we have the same association of physical type and gland histology in the dachshund.

Further evidence of this correlation between physical type and thyroid pattern is shown by the backcross hybrids resulting from mating the $F_1$ hybrid and the pure Boston terrier parent. In appearance these backcross hybrids, as shown in plates 43 and 44 (pp. 245 and 247), are of Boston terrier type, particularly in head form. The two photomicrographs in figures 3 and 4 of plate 86 are sections of the thyroids from 524 ♂ and 525 ♀, two backcross Boston terrier hybrids. These photomicrographs show exactly the same microscopic pattern as that of the pure Boston terrier (fig. 1, pls. 82 and 85). Four sections from different thyroids could scarcely show closer similarity. The pituitary glands accompanying these Boston terrier-like thyroids are seen in plate 90 (figs. 1 and 2); these are very cystic and abnormal.

The general correspondence between head type and the pattern of thyroid histology does not hold for all similar structural modifications in other parts, such, for example, as the screw-tail in the bulldog. Structural disharmonies such as dachshund head and upper jaw in association with the Boston terrier short mandible and dachshund legs are mosaic arrangements apparently due to genetic determination of localized growth reactions which break across endocrinic influences.

Very important questions arise as to the nature of the apparent correlation between the histologic structure of the thyroid and the physical type of the animal. Does the modified structure of the thyroid so alter the internal secretions as to bring about a distorted growth pattern? Or are both the disturbed histology of the thyroid and the modified form of the bulldog head due to an underlying common cause of which these are merely correlated symptoms? Or finally, if there is a common cause of endocrinic nature for both thyroid modification and skull distortion, might we logically suspect the pituitary gland, since there is much evidence to indicate its close interrelation with the thyroid and many investigators would suspect its influence on the growth distortions involved? Because of these questions, a survey of the microscopic structure and possible modifications of the pituitary glands in the Boston terrier-dachshund cross is desirable at this stage of our discussion, before proceeding with the consideration of other breed crosses.

## THE NATURE OF THE PITUITARY GLANDS IN THE BOSTON TERRIER-DACHSHUND CROSS AND THEIR POSSIBLE BEARING ON MODIFICATIONS OF THE THYROID AND GROSS STRUCTURAL DEFORMITY

The canine pituitary is a very unstable organ in both the details of its gross composition and its finer histologic arrangements, and this state of structural variation in the pituitary is probably connected in some way with the instabilities of physical form, type and size which, in the species *Canis familiaris*, give rise to the extremely diverse and numerous breeds. Among the mammals, as we have mentioned in an earlier section, only the human species approaches the dog in respect to this tendency to produce races and individuals of widely different types and sizes, and in man the disturbances of pituitary function are numerous and classical. On these accounts, it is highly desirable to learn the hereditary reactions in arrested, distorted and otherwise abnormal pituitary conditions in a manner similar to that which we have reviewed for the thyroid gland. The inheritance of pituitary modifications is of special importance in connection with the possible correlation of these modifications with thyroid, gonadal and other endocrinic disturbances. For such studies we again find among the dogs certain breeds in which the pituitary presents a fairly normal histology without symptoms of disfunction, and other breeds in which there is pronounced histopathology accompanied by both structural and functional symptoms commonly interpreted as resulting from pituitary distortions. By crossing breeds which present these apparently contrasted symptoms we hoped to gain information not only concerning the inheritance of pituitary abnormality but also information bearing on the correlation between pituitary defects and the physical and functional disturbances commonly attributed to them. The first such cross to be considered is between two breeds distinctly contrasted in the above respects: the dachshund and the Boston terrier.

In many cases the dachshund possesses one of the most typically normal pituitary glands to be found among the pure line dogs. Plate 87 shows photomicrographs of longitudinal sections of the pituitary glands from four prize typed dachshunds, but one may readily appreciate that all these are not completely normal. Figure 1, however, may be described as a perfectly normal example of the general arrangement and proportions in the dog pituitary. The anterior lobe or oral hypophysis surrounds the pars nervosa which is, in this specimen, relatively large. The saccular diverticulum from the third ventricle extends completely through the infundibular stalk and penetrates the nervosa, with cellular islands and cords passing from the saccular surface into the tissues of the pars nervosa. The residual lumen of the embryonic Rathke's pouch persists as a space separating the pars tuberalis and pars distalis from the pars intermedia. The pars intermedia closely envelops and fuses with the pars nervosa and its epithelial cells invade the nervosa to varying depths, forming follicles, cords and islands of cells. Various regions of the intermedia itself also give rise to follicles containing a colloid-like material closely resembling the small follicles of the thyroid. Several of these are seen at the distal end of the section in figure 1 (pl. 87).

A portion of the anterior pituitary extends along the infundibular stalk completely surrounding it and passing forward ventrally toward the optic chiasm. Tilney ('13) has very appropriately termed this part the pars tuberalis. Evaginations extend out from the residual lumen of Rathke's pouch as epithelial diverticula, particularly in this region of the pars tuberalis, as Atwell first pointed out ('18, '26). Alveoli, follicles or acini are more numerous and constant in the pars tuberalis than elsewhere. Also in this pars tuberalis region the remains of the epithelial stalk which connected the embryonic hypophysis with the buccal epithelium may persist in some breeds, although it has entirely disappeared in the dachshund and most other long muzzled types. However, this stalk frequently persists as an embryonic arrest in the short muzzled bulldog group and at times in the acromegalic giant breeds. The hypophyseal foramen through the basisphenoid may be patent, permitting direct connection between the pharyngeal lining and the glandular pituitary, as mentioned in an earlier section and illustrated in plate 53 (p. 285). The distal portion of the hypophyseal stalk and the diverticula from the residual lumen in the pars tuberalis region are frequently involved in extensive cystic formations within the anterior pituitary of many dog breeds.

The above details, quite typical of the dog pituitary, are clearly illustrated by the dachshund gland. But, as intimated, the glands from all dachshunds are not so nearly perfect as the one just described (fig. 1, pl. 87). Longitudinal sections from three other dachshund pituitary glands are shown in plate 87. None of these is exactly through the sagittal plane, as is figure 1, and on this account they fail to present entirely similar outlines. Nevertheless, so far as the dog pituitary is concerned, the several parts of the three glands can be very readily examined in these sections. In all three, the residual lumen of Rathke's pouch is clearly open between the pars distalis and pars intermedia, and diverticula lead away from it in the pars tuberalis region to form slender spaces extending among the glandular tissues. These are very extensive in figure 4. The pars intermedia intimately penetrates the nervosa to varying extents in these photomicrographs, and small colloidal follicles may be detected along this transitional zone.

The general distribution of acidophile and basophile, or alpha and beta cells in the pars anterior is not possible to estimate from examination of these low power photomicrographs which are primarily intended to give the histologic topography of the gland. However, the acidophiles are usually stained red, and their cytoplasm produces a darker shade in the photographs taken at higher magnifications. The two chromophilic types are distributed in the usual manner, and many countings indicate that they exist within the range of normal proportions. Rasmussen ('38) finds that in the human pituitary the acidophiles generally tend to concentrate in large areas posteriorly in each lateral half of the pars distalis, and therefore in anterior and marginal zones, as well as near the mid-sagittal plane, these cells are less numerous. Such areas are comparatively richer in chromophobes and basophiles. These general arrangements also apply to the distribution of the chromophilic types in the dog pituitary. Rasmussen's extensive counts of pituitary cells from male and female human beings ('29, '33, '38) show that the acidophiles constitute from about 20 to 60 per cent of the total cell number, while basophiles exist in much more variable and

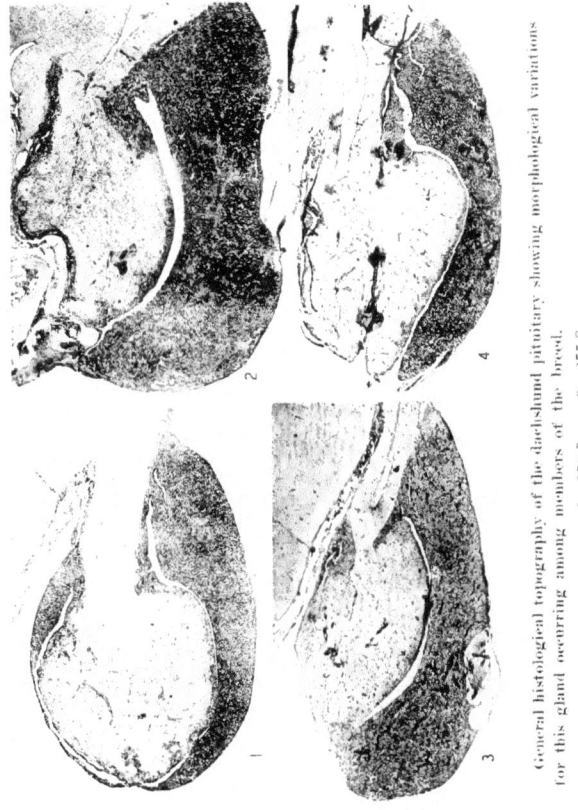

General histological topography of the dachshund pituitary showing morphological variations for this gland occurring among members of the breed.

1  253 ♀.   3  255 ♀.
2  85 ♀.    4  1178 ♀.

smaller proportions, composing from 5 to 27 per cent of the cell mass. The less differentiated neutrophiles or chromophobes make up from 34 to 66 per cent of all cells. We may express these estimates in other words and state that the percentage of acidophiles in man may range from four to twelve times higher than the low limit of basophile percentages, and that they range from only equal value to about double as high as the basophile upper limit. There is only slight intimation that the low percentage of acidophiles is necessarily accompanied by a rise in percentage of basophiles; the variations in relative percentages seem to be largely independent.

In the dog pituitary, the proportion of beta cells, or basophiles, to acidophiles is in general somewhat lower than the relative percentages given by Rasmussen for the human. We are indebted to Doctor S. R. Magruder for his assistance in making the counts of chromophilic types for the dog pituitaries over a period of 2 years. The method employed for counting the cells was as follows: The anterior pituitary lying ventral to the pars nervosa is conveniently divided into anterior, median and posterior thirds. Each of these thirds was then subdivided into zones A, B and C being, respectively, median, or adjacent to the residual lumen, intermediate and peripheral. A band of definite microscopic width passing through the three zones in the posterior ventral region was mapped, and the acidophiles and basophiles within each zone of this band counted and recorded. The same procedure was then followed for the medio-ventral and anterior ventral thirds of the pars distalis. This method of counting gives the relative distribution of acidophiles to basophiles from the posterior to the anterior end of the gland and from the zone adjacent to the pars intermedia to the periphery. The cells in from three to six longitudinal sections at various distances from the sagittal plane were counted for each pituitary, and the averages of these counts were used in estimating the relative proportion of one cell type to the other. The counts were made under high magnification only, and with the stains employed, hematoxylin and eosin and a modified Mallory stain, the acidophiles and basophiles can be quite definitely differentiated after a certain degree of practice. From experience with well stained specimens, one becomes familiar with the size, shape and general position of the basophiles as contrasted with acidophiles, and is enabled to distinguish them with considerable accuracy even in specimens not clearly stained. The acidophiles, as is well known, stain much more constantly and distinctly than the basophiles.

The nature of our study up to the present stage, as well as the wide variation in relative proportions of pituitary cell types in many pure breeds, has not warranted a minute cytological examination of the chromophobes in order to estimate their tendency towards one or the other chromophilic types, as Severinghaus ('38) has so beautifully demonstrated to be possible on the basis of the form and position of the Golgi apparatus in relation to the cell nucleus. The histopathology of these pituitaries seems to present sufficiently important deviations from the normal in such wide variety as to fully tax our present knowledge of endocrinic functions in attempting to unravel the consequences of these conditions.

The relative proportion of acidophiles to basophiles was eleven to one for the pituitary shown in sagittal section in figure 1, plate 87. The counts were made on three well spaced longitudinal sections. The basophiles are more abundant and exist in higher proportions through the mid-ventral region than elsewhere. The cytoplasm of some of the basophiles contains well stained rods or fibers rather than granules, although the fixation is good and the basophile nuclei are perfectly preserved.

The finer structure of the pars intermedia in this specimen is irregular, and there are many colloidal follicles of small but various sizes. The pars nervosa is extensive and fibrous in appearance. The entire pituitary may be classed in general as quite normal.

The three other photomicrographs of dachshund pituitaries given in plate 87 illustrate the morphologic variations which may occur in specimens from this breed. Figure 3 shows, in the mid-ventral portion of the pars distalis, a superficially placed epithelial cyst filled with mucoid substance. This cyst is lined by low non-ciliated cuboidal cells. As we shall see beyond, these anterior pituitary cysts are quite common in many of the dog breeds, and we have much evidence that they are definite embryonic arrests. In exaggerated cases, the cysts are lined with ciliated columnar epithelium and show types of mucous cells much like those of the early stomodeal lining from which they came. Tracing through serial sections, we find that the large cysts almost invariably extend toward the pars tuberalis in a peripheral direction, an indication of their early connection with the hypophyseal stalk. In other cases the proximal ends of the cysts become cord-like or almost completely lost, and the cyst itself may lie far from its early connections. Such cysts, however, are peripheral rather than central in position, and are lined with cells of less primitive embryonic type. The cyst in figure 3 is of this detached and rather benign nature, and this is also the case with the only two other small cysts which have been found in pituitaries from seven prize typed dachshunds. These cysts were all lined with low cuboidal non-ciliated epithelium. In contrast with many of the pituitary cysts found in other breeds, the quality of the dachshund pituitary cyst is interpreted to mean that the influences causing the embryonic arrest occurred rather early in the development of the pituitary and then ceased to act, thus not interfering with the later development and differentiation of the gland. The cysts, nevertheless, remain as evidence that there was a moment during pituitary development when differentiation was not progressing properly.

Other features of the photomicrograph (fig. 3) are quite normal except that the vessels are seen to be gorged with blood due to congestion at the time of death. The animal from which this gland was taken was a typical specimen of the breed and is shown from life as figure 1 in plate 29 (p.

127). As an adult bitch she whelped and reared a litter of five normal puppies.

Occasional longitudinal out-foldings of the pars intermedia may give indentations along the pars nervosa; this is indicated in part in figure 4 of plate 87. No significance for such peculiarities is known. Also occurring in the dog pituitary is a somewhat similar phenomenon in which the pars intermedia evaginates and grows into the distal end of the pars nervosa, carrying with it the space of the residual lumen. This also is partly illustrated in figure 4 (pl. 87), as well as figures 1 and 5 of plate 89.

Finally, figure 2 of plate 87 exhibits a most peculiar condition in an otherwise normal pituitary. The dachshund possessing this gland was a normal animal, as indicated by the fact that she was an unusually good matron bitch. At the distal end and in a dorsal position in this photomicrograph is a considerable formation of irregularly twisted plates of hyaline cartilage, in the folds of which lie perfectly developed red bone marrow. All types of developing blood cells are seen in the marrow, and many huge multinuclear giant cells or megakaryocytes are present. Such a marrow region is shown in the upper left corner of the photomicrograph. There was no calcification or truly bony structure present, as proof of which is the fact that the specimen cut smoothly on the microtome and there was no histological evidence of bone formation. The formation of cartilage and red bone marrow is in direct cellular continuation with the posterior tip of the pars distalis at its junction with the pars intermedia, the more extensive connection being with the pars intermedia. Although about 500 dog pituitaries were examined, such histologic formation in association with the pituitary was observed in this one case only.

The cellular nature of the glandular pituitary in this specimen is somewhat atypical. There is an excessive amount of connective tissue, and the basophiles show irregularities in granular reaction, some being completely filled with deeply staining coarse granules and others incompletely filled with pale, unevenly distributed granules. Some basophiles are unusually large, with large nuclei. The proportion of acidophiles to basophiles, as shown by counts made on six different sections of this gland, is eleven to one, which is toward high basophile distribution, the low specimens of the breed having ratios of twenty to one or even forty to one. From a relative point of view, the pars tuberalis and distalis are enormously large and wide. The nervosa is of usual size and is deeply invaded by the intermedia. It is somewhat irregular in form due to compression by the unusual cartilaginous invasion in the dorsal region.

The general shape of the dachshund pituitary is variable, as outlines of the four longitudinal sections indicate. Many glands are long and flattened dorso-ventrally with long infundibular stalks; others are short and somewhat spherical in shape.

We have entered into details in the discussion of these four dachshund pituitaries in order to present the general features of this gland in the dog, as well as to convey an idea of the morphologic differences which we are attempting to follow and interpret. In spite of the variations which have been shown in these dachshund glands, a thorough study of the conditions in pituitaries of other breeds would force one to class these as very close to normal in type.

The Boston terrier, for reasons which have been discussed in a foregoing section, is considered to be contrasted with the dachshund in many physical characters as well as functional reactions. We shall now attempt to determine whether the nature of its pituitary is also contrasted with what has been seen for the dachshund.

The pituitaries from six pedigreed Boston terriers have been studied, and in most of these the pars anterior contained one or more cysts, some of which were extremely extensive. The cells in both the pars tuberalis and pars distalis are frequently arranged in twisting cords and columns, with an excessive amount of connective tissue lying in trabeculate fashion among them. An exaggerated Boston terrier pituitary is shown in the photomicrograph from 436 ♀ in figure 1 of plate 88. An enormous cyst filled with mucoid substance is seen extending entirely across the anterior region of the pars distalis; two others lie at the periphery, only one of which shows in this section, and a smaller one lies in the margin of the tuberalis. These cysts are lined by columnar epithelium which is distinctly ciliated in places. The cord-like arrangement of the glandular cells is shown throughout the extent of the anterior pituitary. The pars intermedia contains numerous small colloidal follicles. The basophiles in this gland are in unusually low proportion to the acidophiles, and the entire gland gives the impression of being stained a bright red.

In spite of the extremely pathologic nature of this pituitary as compared with the normal dachshund gland (fig. 2), the Boston terrier bitch possessing it had produced two litters of three and four puppies, and successfully reared several of them. The size of these litters is comparatively small for dogs, and the bitch was somewhat abnormal in maternal reactions. Although appreciating these defects, it still seems surprising that an animal possessing so distorted a pituitary gland, with the associated modifications of the thyroid which have already been cited for the breed, could produce full term viable offspring and react to them in an even partially successful manner. This case at least suggests that some of the responsibility which has been attributed to the histopathology of human pituitaries in cases with diseases of growth and malfunction may not always be accurately placed.

It must be repeated that not every individual of the Boston terrier breed presents such gross distortions of the pituitary as those just described. This photomicrograph was selected to emphasize how very different the modifications in the Boston terrier gland are from those tendencies we have examined in the dachshund. Thus arises the point of interest as to whether the developmental arrests and defects of the

Boston terrier pituitary react as definite genetic characters in hybrids between these two breeds.

*The histopathology of the pituitary in the $F_1$ generation of Boston terrier-dachshund hybrids.* From the foregoing section one is forced to admit that in spite of the many variations concerned, the pituitary of the Boston terrier is far more pathologic in structure than is this gland in the dachshund. This can be said with even greater emphasis of the thyroid glands of the two breeds (cf. fig. 2, pl. 82 and fig. 3, pl. 84). Nevertheless, by crossing these pure breeds a well proportioned, vigorous $F_1$ hybrid is produced (see photographs from life in plate 29, p. 127). The hybrid is functionally normal and a prolific breeder. Four $F_1$ females have whelped sixty-five offspring from $F_1$ sires.

The pituitary glands from five $F_1$ hybrids were closely examined at autopsy and later studied histologically. All have cysts in the anterior pituitary, some of which could be seen at autopsy with the unaided eye as distinct blisters along the ventral surface. This fact is readily appreciated by referring to the photomicrograph of a sagittal section through the gland of $F_1$ 129♂, shown in plate 88 (fig. 5). This pituitary is riddled with enormous cysts which almost completely crowd out the pars tuberalis and much of the pars distalis. The arrested epithelial linings of these cysts greatly reduced the amount of normally differentiated pituitary tissue, yet the pituitary secreted sufficient quantities of the specific hormones to maintain normal functions in this dog until it was killed at almost 5 years of age. This animal sired four litters of four or five puppies each. The pituitary function in such an animal clearly shows that the full amount of glandular tissue in the pars anterior is not an item of importance, and that for normal life performances only a fraction of the usual amount is necessary as long as the quality of these secretions is normal.

Photomicrographs of longitudinal sections of four $F_1$ Boston terrier-dachshund pituitaries are shown in plate 88. All are rather long and flat in general shape, as is common for the

GENETIC TYPE AND THE ENDOCRINES 459

PLATE 88

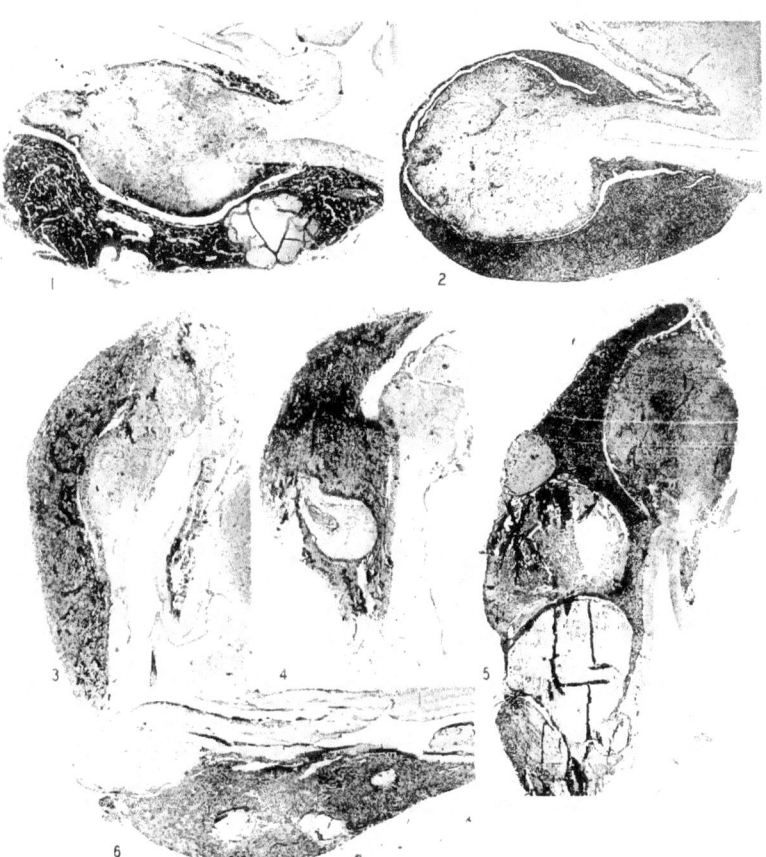

Boston terrier-dachshund cross. Histopathology of the pituitary in first generation hybrids.
1 Boston terrier 436 ♀.   3–6  $F_1$ hybrids.
2 Dachshund 253 ♀.        3  127 ♀.   5  129 ♂.
                          4  130 ♀.   6  128 ♂.

dachshund, and the ventricular sac passes through the infundibular stalk and far into the pars nervosa. The pars intermedia intimately infiltrates the nervosa around the periphery, and colloidal follicles of varying sizes are present in all its regions. Colloidal follicles and drops also occur in the pars distalis, as is seen in its posterior end in figure 6. The infundibular stalk is long and surrounded by the pars tuberalis, which is profusely and completely penetrated by diverticula from the residual lumen. These numerous diverticula are clearly seen in three of the $F_1$ sections in plate 88, and in figure 5 such diverticula from the original hypophyseal lumen appear to take part in the extensive cystic formations in the pars tuberalis area, leading back in many cases into the pars distalis. In most of the specimens, the glandular cells of the pars distalis exhibit a distinct tendency toward cord-like arrangements, such as are found in the Boston terrier gland, and there is more connective tissue than usual. The relative proportion of acidophiles to basophiles has a wide range, but averages about twenty to one, a relatively low basophile proportion.

The striking feature in these $F_1$ glands is the prevalence of large multiple cysts characterized by a lining of columnar epithelial cells of which many are ciliated and others filled with mucus to varying degrees, often attaining the typical goblet-cell form. The nature of these cysts as a whole is exactly similar to those in Boston terrier glands where the epithelium is high or columnar and frequently ciliated, exhibiting many features of the early stomodeal epithelium. Cysts are much rarer in the dachshund pituitary and differ from the above in that they are smaller and have linings of low cuboidal non-ciliated epithelium. Such characteristics indicate that in the dachshund much less extensive, less persistent and less frequent arrests are involved in the freeing of Rathke's pouch from its association with the stomodeal epithelium than in the Boston terrier and the $F_1$ hybrids.

The cystic condition in the $F_1$ pituitaries, as well as the cord-like arrangement of glandular cells in the pars distalis, indicate the dominance of the Boston terrier pituitary pattern over the more normal dachshund type. To test the validity of this indication, we studied pituitaries from thirty-three second generation hybrids, at the same time attempting to answer a question of even greater importance, that is, whether specific differences in physical characters among the individuals are closely linked and associated with definite deviations in the histopathology of the pituitaries.

*The possible relation of differences in pituitary structure to differences in physical type among the $F_2$ hybrids of the Boston terrier-dachshund cross.* The gross relative sizes of the pituitaries from thirty-three $F_2$ Boston terrier-dachshund hybrids range from a low of 8 milligrams per kilogram of body weight to a high of 26, the latter being more than three times that of the former. These pituitary proportions are shown in text-figure 82 (p. 415), which has been previously examined. The relative proportions for pituitary size shown in this chart are independent of possible sex influence, as is indicated by the fact that four of the five lowest as well as four of the five highest represent male pituitaries, and males and females are distributed irregularly throughout the series. Nor do cystic conditions seriously affect these relative sizes; when the cysts are large the amount of anterior pituitary tissue is diminished. Differences in relative amounts of total pituitary tissue are real, and on examining the $F_2$ series in the chart one might be led to admit the possibility of an irregular tendency for the long muzzled dachshund type to predominate at the high end of the series. But this type also occurs in almost the lowest recorded relative pituitary weight. As has already been concluded on the basis of other evidence, it is highly improbable that the relative amounts of total pituitary substance are of serious consequence in the determination of growth and structural characteristics in the mammalian body. This conclusion is entirely aside from the question of the important effects that may result from variations in the relative amounts of the several hormones emanating from the pituitary gland, and we should not be misunderstood as confusing the problems of tissue mass and hormone production.

The study of the microscopic structure of the $F_2$ pituitaries might supply evidence of qualitative differences in cellular composition, indicating differences in hormone production among these glands. Such differences might also be correlated with certain type differences in bodily form, as well as with modifications in both structural and functional qualities of the thyroid and other glands. More than thirty $F_2$ pituitaries were studied from these standpoints. Surprisingly wide histologic variations occur, these supplying material for analyzing the interrelations of pituitary deviations with the already discussed modifications in physical expression.

Among the $F_2$ Boston terrier-dachshund hybrids, we have already found that contrasted ancestral characters may be re-sorted in such ways as to give almost typical Boston terrier and dachshund individuals in the same litters, as well as specimens exhibiting various strange combinations of the breed characters, and still others showing many modifications and intergradations between them (see plates 30 and 39, pp. 129 and 236). We have just presented histologic evidence showing that the pituitary glands from the two breeds tend to differ very constantly and definitely in their microscopic constitutions, and our next step is to determine whether the $F_2$ hybrid approaching the Boston terrier in type will also possess a pituitary gland inclining towards the histopathology of that found in the pure Boston terrier stock, and, conversely if there is any correlation between dachshund body type and gland histology.

With the idea that any relation between pituitary histology and bodily type would be most easily recognizable in a comparison of glands from dogs showing completely contrasted characters, we selected in the first place two pituitaries, one from an almost perfect Boston terrier-like $F_2$ and the second from a well expressed dachshund typed $F_2$. Figures 1 and 2 in plate 89 illustrate the pituitaries from two such opposite typed $F_2$ Boston terrier-dachshund hybrids. Figure

PLATE 89

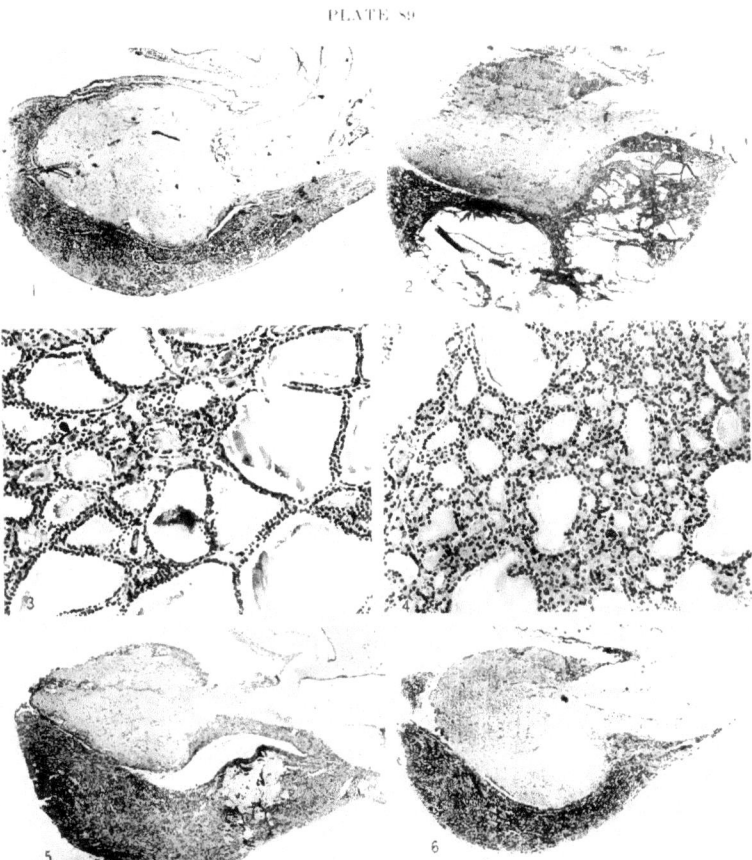

Boston terrier-dachshund cross. Differences in pituitary and thyroid structure in two strongly contrasted second generation hybrids, together with pituitary histological pattern in two second generation hybrids of intermediate type.

1  1523 ♂ pituitary.   3  1523 ♂ thyroid.   5  294 ♀ pituitary.
2  355 ♀ pituitary.    4  355 ♀ thyroid.    6  722 ♂ pituitary.

1 shows a longitudinal section very near the sagittal plane of the pituitary from 1523♂. The details of this photomicrograph resemble with fair constancy the same sections from the dachshund pituitaries shown in plate 87. The anterior pituitary is long and thin and completely surrounds the pars nervosa, being fused with it at the distal end through the pars intermedia. Also at the distal end of the gland the pars intermedia evaginates toward the nervosa, penetrating it and carrying in a portion of the residual lumen. A cleft lined by a thin layer of intermedia cells is thus formed in the posterior region of the pars nervosa. This, as shown in plate 87, is commonly seen in the dachshund pituitaries.

The pars nervosa in this pituitary is normal in appearance and not deeply invaded by intermedia cells. The pars intermedia is thin, and extends completely around the nervosa and partly onto the infundibular stalk, which is also a feature common in the dachshund. The intermedia contains numerous colloidal follicles throughout its extent.

The pars distalis of this $F_2$ pituitary completely surrounds the nervosa dorsally as well as ventrally, and like most dachshund pituitaries thus violates Tilney's apt likening of the relation of posterior to anterior pituitary in the dog to that of a ball lying in the depression of the catcher's glove. The "ball" in this case is completely encased, a condition which has not been observed in the Boston terrier or the bulldog glands. In removing the pituitary from the bulldog breeds at autopsy, one must exert care so as to avoid having the nervosa fall away from the pars anterior.

In our experience, the general form of the anterior pituitary in the dachshund inclines toward long and thin, permitting the nervosa to become encased within it. In the Boston terrier, however, the pars anterior is thicker and shorter and the nervosa is covered by only the thinnest layer of intermedia over its dorsal surface.

The cells of the pars distalis in 1523♂ are rather closely packed and with few spaces except in the ventro-peripheral zone; there is a slight tendency toward cord-like arrangements and also occasional small epithelial follicles. The average proportion of acidophiles to basophiles, as based on counts through three regions in five longitudinal sections, is about sixteen to one, and this relation is within the normal range for dogs.

A comparison may now be made between this pituitary and one from an $F_2$ hybrid of contrasted type (shown by photomicrograph of longitudinal section in figure 2 of plate 89). This gland was obtained from 355♀, an $F_2$ Boston terrier-dachshund which was killed when 3 years old. The animal had long legs and a Boston terrier head, with an undershot, prognathous mandible.

The general form of the pituitary in this animal is short and thick, and in the longitudinal section it will be seen that the wide and cystic pars distalis is too short to fold around the distal end of the nervosa and cover its dorsal surface. Tilney's simile of the ball in the catcher's glove is applicable to this case. The pars nervosa is more richly filled with nuclei and fusiform cells than in the dachshund-like section (fig. 1). The intermedia is thicker and its cells invade the nervosa more extensively, but it does not evaginate into the substance of the nervosa at its distal end as in the dachshund type. The cells of the intermedia show distinct cord-like and follicular arrangements. The tissues of the pars tuberalis and distalis are crowded out of normal position by the extensive and complex cystic formation. The cysts are lined in many places with ciliated columnar cells and mucous cells, some of which are of typical goblet form, which indicates the persistent retention of their early embryonic nature and the lack of a tendency toward differential development. Among these extensive cysts one sees outlying masses of fully differentiated pituitary epithelium consisting of the three well-expressed characteristic cell types. The acidophiles occur more abundantly toward the posterior end, and the basophiles, which vary in staining reactions, are quite plentiful in the middle region. The proportion of basophiles to acidophiles is low, and the total number of these chromophilic cells is obviously far below that contained in the $F_2$ gland at the left. It is difficult, in fact, to realize that this cystic pituitary can possess enough normally functioning tissue to supply the basic needs of the mammalian body. Yet one can scarcely doubt that it did, since this bitch lived a healthy kennel existence for 3 years, and although never used for breeding, expressed typical reactions of oestrus. Other individuals with apparently equally bad pituitaries have served as sires and dams in our experiments (see again photomicrographs of pituitaries from such animals, plate 88 (figs. 1 and 5)).

After an examination of these pituitaries from $F_2$ hybrids 1523 ♂ and 355 ♀, it is quite evident that the gland from the former closely resembles the dachshund histologic pattern, while the distorted structures of the second pituitary tend to be of the type commonly shown by the Boston terrier gland. Further, these glands in the $F_2$ hybrids differ as widely from one another as the glands of the dachshund differ from the Boston terrier. As intimated above, the $F_2$ Boston terrier-dachshund hybrids possessing these two quite dissimilar pituitaries also differed in bodily appearance and in general instinctive behavior in almost the same way as the dachshund and the Boston terrier. The general appearance of these two hybrid dogs and the histology of their pituitaries would make it seem that the dachshund body type and pituitary pattern are closely bound together; this likewise seems true for the Boston terrier typed body form and pituitary pattern. In line with this association of a given body type and a definite pattern of pituitary histology, a study of a considerable number of $F_2$ animals showing various mixtures and intergrades of the two types tends in large part to confirm the above probability, and one is led to suppose that the form of the head and body of the Boston terrier, as well as of the dachshund, may be impossible of attainment except in the presence of the given histopathology of the pituitary gland. These relations lead back to fundamental differences in genetic background, all of which indicate that a Boston terrier pituitary transplanted into a dachshund following the removal of its own pituitary would in no wise transform the dachshund into a Boston terrier. Also justified is the further inference that injections of identical pituitary hormones into the Boston terrier will induce responses somewhat different from those elicited in a dachshund, if it induced any at all. Evidence in substantiation of these inferences has been given in Section III where it was shown that in spite of the fact that the same endocrinic milieu prevails throughout the body, genetic constitution may determine distortions of growth in localized body parts while normal form is attained in other regions. The several structural disharmonies arising in hybrid combinations, as discussed in Section III, also add important evidence in support of the above statements, and still more direct facts relative to the varying effects of the same hormone on individuals of different types are already being accumulated in our experiments.

If the Boston terrier and dachshund types show probable correlation with certain histologic patterns of the pituitary, does this also apply in connection with other endocrine glands? Photomicrographs of sections of the thyroid glands from the two opposite typed $F_2$ hybrids supplying the pituitaries just discussed are shown in figures 3 and 4 of plate 89. Figure 3 is from 1523♂, seen from life as the right animal in figure 9 of plate 30. This dog had a long muzzle, long straight tail and short legs, and is a still better dachshund in type than his brother, shown less reduced as figure 7 in plate 30. The thyroid section shows the histologic pattern generally characteristic of long muzzled breeds and especially of the dachshund (see fig. 3, pl. 84 and fig. 1, pl. 85).

Figure 4 of plate 89 illustrates a thyroid histology clearly contrasted with figure 3 and is in every detail a striking example of the Boston terrier gland pattern (fig. 2, pls. 82 and 85). The $F_2$ bitch which supplied the short and rounded cystic pituitary and this thyroid with its small, irregular and numerous tiny follicles and nests of parafollicular cells lying among the follicles, also possessed, as we have said, Boston terrier-like head and an undershot lower jaw.

The striking contrast between the histologic patterns of the pituitaries and the thyroids from the dachshund typed $F_2$ and the Boston terrier typed $F_2$ in the dachshund-Boston terrier cross may be appreciated by comparing figures 1 and 3 with figures 2 and 4 in plate 89. More exaggerated differences in histologic patterns between endocrine glands would be difficult to find.

We have already seen from the consideration of thyroid histology among different dog breeds that some breeds present characteristic patterns which appear to be correlated with their physical types. The parathyroids, as we shall see later, also differ in their cellular arrangements, and here again developmental arrests play a rôle in the formation of cysts and tubular structures. For an understanding of the genetics of size differences and skeletal modifications in the mammals and man, these three endocrine glands—the thyroid, pituitary and parathyroids—must be carefully considered for their possible rôles as intermediaries between the genic mutations and the final structural modifications. Still further, since there is evidence of an association between structural types and behavioristic patterns, as examples of which are the proverbial giant and dwarf psychologies which have long been recognized, what rôle may the endocrinic complexes play in these expressions? If all these are genuine relationships, we may expect that when definite endocrinic modifications are accurately correlated with specific structural expressions these will indicate types of characteristic behavior. With such knowledge, an understanding of the influences of endocrinic diseases on instinctive and psychic reactions will be forthcoming.

Returning to the special consideration of pituitary histology in the $F_2$ dachshund-Boston terrier hybrids, it must be emphasized that all the glands from such animals are not such strong expressions of one or the other parent type as are the two cases just presented. As will be recalled, the great majority of these hybrids are intermediate in type, resembling the $F_1$ group, while a smaller number present various mixtures of characters from the two parent stocks. The pituitary glands in these $F_2$ type mixtures also present intermediate and mixed histologic patterns, not clearly directed towards either the extreme dachshund or the extreme Boston terrier histology. Figures 5 and 6 in plate 89 illustrate longitudinal sections through such pituitaries. Figure 5 is from $F_2$ 294 ♀, shown photographed from life in plate 39, figure 2 (p. 236). This bitch was killed as an adult of $2\frac{1}{2}$ years; her bones were heavy and well developed, and the skull was largely dachshund in type, with strong muzzle, while the legs were straight and long as in the Boston terrier. The pituitary presents peculiarities quite commonly found in both stocks. Boston terrier-like, the pars distalis does not fully encase the nervosa and a large irregular cyst with columnar epithelial lining extends through the anterior region of the pars distalis. The pars intermedia is thick and irregular in outline, deeply infiltrating the nervosa. On the other hand, the pars intermedia evaginates far into the distal end of the nervosa, with the space of the residual lumen following it; and the chromophilic cellular types are abundantly and normally expressed, the acidophiles predominating about eleven to one; all of these are dachshund-like qualities. This gland no doubt functioned quite normally.

Figure 6 in plate 89 is from $F_2$ 722 ♂, which had short legs and a partly modified Boston terrier head. The pituitary is short and thick with the general outline of the Boston terrier gland, but is entirely free of cystic formations.

In concluding this survey of the $F_2$ glands, we must repeat that neither all dachshund nor all Boston terrier pituitaries are of one definite pattern. The histology of this gland varies among the individuals of each dog breed. Yet in spite of this individual variability, the pituitaries from contrasted breeds present histologic patterns which are quite consistently different in detail.

Further evidence on the genetic nature of such pituitary patterns is furnished by the backcross hybrids from the two parental stocks.

*The histologic patterns of the pituitary glands in the backcrosses between $F_1$ hybrids and the two parental stocks.* In certain defective features, the histologic structure of the $F_1$ hybrid pituitary has been shown to approach more nearly the pattern of the Boston terrier than the dachshund. This fact would suggest that some of the arrested and modified tissues in these pituitaries may result from dominant mutations within the genes of the Boston terrier stock. Such a suggestion is largely supported by the correlations between head types and rather definite histologic patterns of the pituitaries among the $F_2$ hybrids, as was discussed in the previous section. In spite of the fact that a large amount of valuable material from this generation was available— sixty-five specimens were observed and measured during life and at autopsy, and the glands from thirty-three of these were studied histologically—the number of $F_2$ individuals has not been sufficiently large for an accurate genetic analysis of such intricate character complexes. However, we were fortunately able to supplement the study of these $F_2$ animals with evidence obtained from backcrossing the $F_1$ hybrids on the two parent stocks. In the analysis of a complex of modified characters resulting from polygenic mutations, as contrasted with the normal state, the chance of recovering more nearly complete combinations of parental genes is much greater in the backcross hybrids, of course, than it is in the $F_2$ generation.

Twenty-nine dogs have been produced from the backcross between the $F_1$ hybrid and the Boston terrier parent, and nine from the $F_1$ backcrossed with the dachshund. The pituitary glands from fourteen of the former and six of the latter have been studied histologically. The individuals among the backcross hybrids on the Boston terrier stock have equal chances of possessing either the Boston terrier pituitary pattern or that of the $F_1$ hybrid, and only these two patterns would result if the character depended upon a single gene-determinant, which is certainly not true in this case. Likewise, the backcross on the dachshund presents even chances for pituitary patterns of the $F_1$ hybrid or dachshund type.

Figures 1 and 2 in plate 90 illustrate longitudinal sections through the pituitaries from backcross Boston terriers, and figures 3 and 4 show similar sections from the backcross on the dachshund. The resemblance of these sections to those from the two parent stocks and to those of the $F_1$ hybrids may be estimated by a comparison with the photomicrographs in plates 87 and 88.

Figures 1 and 2 are from 524 ♂ and 525 ♀, brother and sister litter mates. Their dam was Boston terrier 435 ♀ and the sire was 128 ♂ $F_1$ hybrid. The brother and sister are shown from life in plate 44 (fig. 1) (p. 247). They are both brindle in color, with long legs and somewhat shortened, bent tail, indications of the Boston terrier stock. Their skull measurements fall between those of the $F_1$ hybrid and the Boston terrier parent, and they are not so strongly Boston terrier-headed as some backcross hybrids, as, for example, 635 ♂ (right in fig. 2, pl. 44).

Figure 1 in plate 90, from backcross Boston terrier 524 ♂, gives a picture that is strikingly similar to figure 5 in plate 88, a pituitary from an uncle, 129 ♂ $F_1$. The enormous cysts and the nature of their epithelial lining as shown in the pars tuberalis and anterior region of the pars distalis, as well as the cellular composition of the differentiated portion of the pars distalis, are closely similar in these two sections. The pars intermedia and nervosa in the backcross pituitary suggest the Boston terrier somewhat more closely than they do the corresponding parts of the $F_1$ gland. The reader will realize, however, that these comparisons of histologic deviations from the normal cannot be emphatically stated, since wide variations exist and the physiologic and type significance of such conditions are at present only partly understood. The point of real importance in the present

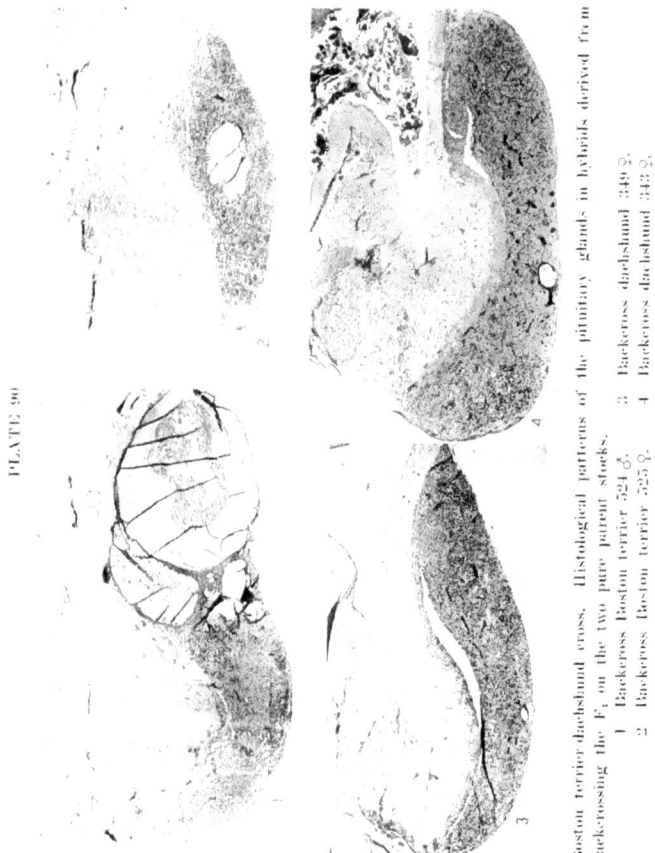

Boston terrier-dachshund cross. Histological patterns of the pituitary glands in hybrids derived from backcrossing the $F_1$ on the two pure parent stocks.
1 Backcross Boston terrier 524 ♂.   3 Backcross dachshund 349 ♀.
2 Backcross Boston terrier 525 ♀.   4 Backcross dachshund 343 ♀.

connection is the fact that the pituitaries from backcross Boston terrier hybrids are closely Boston terrier in pattern, and likewise that the backcross hybrid is an approach to the Boston terrier in type. In its complete detail, the thyroid of this backcross hybrid 524 ♂, is of the extreme Boston terrier pattern, as is well seen in figure 3 of plate 86. This thyroid is very different from the $F_1$ gland (fig. 3, pl. 85), and would seem to be more completely Boston terrier than is the pituitary, but this may be due to its much simpler microscopic pattern.

Again, figure 2 (pl. 90), from backcross Boston terrier 525 ♀, could very well pass as a defective Boston terrier pituitary. In this specimen the cord-like arrangement of the cells in the pars distalis, along with a high proportion of basophiles, resembles more closely certain of the pure Boston terrier glands than any of those from the $F_1$ hybrids. The thyroid in this animal is also of perfect Boston terrier quality (fig. 4, pl. 86).

Figures 3 and 4 in plate 90 are decidedly different from figures 1 and 2, both in general appearance and in detail, and these differences are comparable to those cited as distinguishing the pituitary of the Boston terrier from that of the dachshund. In figures 3 and 4, the pars distalis is long, and encases the pars nervosa in a manner similar to that common for the dachshund gland. In many of the backcross dachshund pituitaries no cysts are present, but in each of these two sections we find a single small cyst with the low inactive or degenerate epithelial lining occasionally found in the dachshund gland. These cysts are very unlike those of the Boston terrier and $F_1$ pituitaries. Figure 3 represents the pituitary from 349 ♀ backcross dachshund, which is shown from life in plate 45 (p. 248) and is seen to be almost exactly dachshund in character. Figure 4 (pl. 90) is from a sister, 343 ♀, who is also shown in plate 45. Both these sections of pituitary resemble more closely the glands from the dachshund stock (pl. 87) than the $F_1$ hybrid (pl. 88).

The backcross pituitaries supply strong evidence in favor of the deductions drawn from the $F_2$ glands above, that is, that the physical form and type of the individual is correlated with the histologic pattern and cellular nature of the pituitary gland, and that in line with the widely contrasted physical types of the Boston terrier and the dachshund there is a correspondingly strong divergence between the histologic patterns of the pituitary glands. Among the $F_2$ and backcross hybrids, a consistent relation between the specific types and the histologic qualities of the pituitary glands is expressed. We have also seen in a previous section that a similar correspondence is definitely maintained between the dachshund and Boston terrier body types and the microscopic patterns of the thyroid.

Linkage between a characteristic thyroid pattern and a given bodily type was not interpreted as a causal relationship. Are we then, from the foregoing evidence, justified in interpreting the relation of the pituitary quality to the physical types of the individual as being causal in nature? If the physical type of the dog is a developmental result of the pituitary quality, shall we also consider the characteristic pattern of the thyroid gland in a given type as simply another feature under the pituitary influence? Or, does the thyroid gland independently share, along with the pituitary, the responsibility for the characteristically modified body types? A satisfactory answer to these questions is still difficult, even on the basis of the extensive evidence already considered. An examination of the conditions in still another member of the endocrine series is therefore necessary if we are to find other possible clues to further interrelationships. And further, it is most essential that we survey these problems in other modified and contrasted breeds and their hybrids so as to secure comparisons for the dachshund-Boston terrier records just presented.

DEVELOPMENTAL ARRESTS AND THE QUALITY OF DIFFERENTIATION IN THE PARATHYROID GLANDS OF BOSTON TERRIER-DACHSHUND CROSSES

Modifications in bodily size, types of growth and quality of bone are known to result from thyroid deficiency through the experimental studies of Dye and Maughan ('29) on dogs, and of Todd, Wharton and Todd ('38) on sheep, as well as through numerous other contributions to this problem. Diseases of the pituitary gland have been known for many years to cause similar modifications in both size and shape of the skeletal framework of the body, and in many cases it is difficult to determine which of the two glands—thyroid or pituitary—is directly responsible for the growth modification. However, the weight of evidence at present attributes this influence largely to the pituitary gland, even in those cases where the initial conditions are thyroid deficiency or complete absence of thyroid, the result of which tends to reduce and disbalance pituitary functions. Numerous studies on rickets and the disturbances of calcium metabolism involved in the distortion of bone composition have pointed to the parathyroid glands as a serious factor for consideration in some growth abnormalities. Reports on the pathology of the parathyroid in cases of severe rickets, and the experimental studies of Nonidez and Goodale ('27) on the effects of ricket-inducing diets in birds have shown that the parathyroid glands undergo a primary hypertrophy with true hyperplasia followed by degeneration and complete obliteration of the normal secretory epithelial cells, thus suggesting that these glands must play an essential rôle in the growth and development of normal bone and body types.

In view of these facts, the modifications in size and pattern of the axial skeleton of the Boston terrier, and the appendicular skeleton, particularly the long bones of the extremities, in the dachshund forces us to investigate the quality of parathyroid glands in these breeds with the same interest as we have the thyroid and the pituitary and their relation to the peculiar types concerned. It will be recalled from previous chapters on skull types and leg lengths that the bone growth from endochondral and epiphyseal plate ossification may be much retarded in localized regions, as for example the basicranium and caudal vertebrae, while the increments in other regions with the same manner of growth, as well as growth from subperiosteal and membrane bone ossification, are little or not at all affected in an adverse manner, and may even be accelerated. Such differences in growth expression between localized regions of endochondral ossification in the same body have not been obtained by the experimental removal of endocrine glands, which gives general reactions that are equally evident in all the regions of the body where similar types of growth occur. These results from surgical methods have given rise to the widely accepted interpretation that modifications in form and quality of growth may result solely from endocrinic disturbance. However, the sharply localized distortions of endochondral and epiphyseal bone growth so decidedly expressed in several dog breeds do not lend themselves to this simple interpretation. In fact, in order to understand these localized reactions, we are forced to study not only the genetics of such characteristics, but also the different stages of susceptibility to developmental distortions and the possibility of temporary arrests and disturbances in early endocrinic functions which later may be completely repaired. The present consideration deals with the question of whether the histology of the parathyroid glands from adult Boston terrier-dachshund hybrids shows indications of such early developmental arrests and disturbances.

Before entering into the discussion of differences in microscopic structure among the parathyroids from the pure breeds and their hybrids, several general facts regarding them must be presented. To begin with, the number and size of the parathyroid bodies in the dog are quite variable. These bodies also vary in topographic relations and intimacy of contact with the thyroid gland. Usually two or more parathyroid bodies are found on each side, one closely attached to the mid-dorsal surface of the thyroid and the other located in the loose fascia at or near its anterior tip. Accessory parathyroids are frequently present in irregular positions. For convenience, those bodies lying about the thyroid may be designated as "external" parathyroids, since, in addition to these, one or more discreet masses of parathyroid tissue may lie within the connective tissue capsule or be completely buried within the tissues of the thyroid gland itself. These will be designated as "internal" parathyroids.

The parathyroid bodies are oval in outline and comparatively thin dorso-ventrally. They differ greatly in size, ranging from tiny particles of only one millimeter in length to fairly large masses almost one centimeter long. The external parathyroids are usually larger than those buried within the thyroid capsule, yet the internal parathyroids are often of considerable size. The size of parathyroid bodies varies in general with the size of the dog; they are very large in the St. Bernard and great Dane dogs and quite minute in the dwarf, midget and toy dogs. The parathyroid bodies in the bulldogs and St. Bernards are usually somewhat thicker dorso-ventrally, giving a plumper appearance than those in the long muzzled and more normal breeds. Since there are a number of distinct external and internal parathyroid bodies connected with the thyroid gland, it has not seemed practical to attempt estimates of the relative amounts of parathyroid tissue per unit of body weight for the different breeds, as was done for the thyroid and pituitary glands.

Histologically, the parathyroid is much more homogeneous than either the thyroid or the pituitary. In its normal state it is a uniform compact mass of epithelial cells that have a definite tendency toward irregular cord-like arrangements; the parathyroids are very vascular and have a sparse amount of connective tissue. Almost all the cells of the human parathyroid gland, and likewise of the dog parathyroid, are of the so-called principal cell type. Scattered irregularly among these are a few cells which are somewhat larger, granular and bluish staining.

The exact microscopic patterns of all parathyroid bodies from one individual are not necessarily the same. One parathyroid may show embryonic arrests with branchial epithelium and cystic formations, while others from the same thyroid may be fully differentiated with a typically normal histology. Nonidez and Goodale have found that in cases of experimental rickets in chickens one parathyroid body may be only slightly hypertrophied, while another shows advanced degeneration, and a third complete atrophy. From such facts it is quite obvious that modifications in the histology of one or more of the parathyroid bodies cannot very well be associated in a consistent manner with the special types and breeds of dogs. However, these glands are so definitely concerned with calcium metabolism, and through this with the growth and quality of bone in the mammalian body, that we are justified in seeking any possible clue which might relate them to either overgrowth of stature or dwarf tendencies, or possibly to the various distortions in form and type which result from chondrodystrophy and other skeletal growth disturbances.

The rôle of the parathyroid bodies in mineral metabolism, and particularly calcium metabolism, has been clearly established through studies of human and experimental tetany. The palliative and therapeutic effects of calcium on this condition were shown long ago by MacCallum and Voegtlin ('09), Luckhardt and Goldberg ('23) and many others. And finally, the hormone from the parathyroids was isolated by Collip from the glands of calves in 1925, and was shown to give direct relief in symptoms of tetany in man and to maintain a parathyroidless animal in a normal state.

The causal relation of the parathyroids to tetany is so complete, and tetany would seem to be so simple an expression, that one might suppose it an easy task to associate a definite histopathology of the glands with this condition.

Yet in spite of extensive investigations by able workers on this subject, the findings are very indefinite. The earlier studies recorded either fresh hemorrhage or residues of blood and pigment in the parathyroids, and associated this with the tetany. Yanase ('07) studied eighty-nine cases, out of which thirty-three showed either free blood or pigment in the parathyroids and only indefinite changes in the epithelium. It was thought that the hemorrhage not only interfered with the function of the tissue but that, through resorption of the blood, growth became inhibited in the newborn gland and tetany followed after a short time.

During the period when blood is being fully resorbed, hypoplasia and low function of the gland results. Nevertheless, there are cases of fatal tetany in which no bleeding or injury to the parathyroids could be found, and also cases of hemorrhage in which no symptoms of tetany appeared. Auerbach ('11) reported eight out of ten cases of tetany with bleeding in the parathyroid, but he also found eight cases of definite parathyroid hemorrhage among thirteen children with normal nerve reactions. Grosser and Betke ('10–'11) recorded similar findings from a study of more extensive material. There is, therefore, very indefinite evidence in the histologic picture of the parathyroid gland to indicate the cellular disturbance which gives rise to the calcium deficiency bringing about the violent nervous reactions of tetany.

For more than 30 years a group of diseases involving the bony skeleton has been directly attributed to disfunction of the parathyroid gland and disturbed calcium metabolism. These diseases involve the structural quality of bone and thus bear very closely on our immediate problems. One of the most typical of such disturbances is osteitis fibrosa cystica generalisata, commonly known as Recklinghausen's disease, which is a rarefying osteitis with fibrous degeneration and cystic formation. This disease is attributed to hyperfunction of the parathyroids. All cases show enlargement of the parathyroid bodies or organic hypertrophy and frequently distinct parathyroid tumors. F. Mandl in 1926 first conclusively demonstrated that the disease was due to overfunction of the parathyroids, since beneficial results followed the extirpation of parathyroid tumors. The pathogenetic connection between the disease and the overproduction of the parathyroid hormone was clearly demonstrated by the researches of Jaffé, Bodansky and Blair ('30) who showed that bone destruction similar to osteitis fibrosa in man could be induced in guinea pigs and dogs by excessive dosing with the Collip hormone.

A fact of particular interest in connection with osteitis fibrosa is that it occurs not only as a generalized disease but may also be quite sharply localized. The histologic structure of the diseased bone in both generalized and localized osteitis fibrosa is exactly the same. It has been suggested that trauma and mechanical effects of function in certain parts of the skeleton may cause these places to be more sensitive in their response to the parathyroid hormone, yet no direct evidence for such an explanation is available. It is significant that tumors of the parathyroids have not been found in localized osteitis fibrosa and that the blood calcium level is always normal. We thus have in the generalized state of this disease a reaction which may be definitely brought about by hormone overstimulation, while the same disease may appear in a localized region although no disturbance in hormone balance has occurred. There may be a genetic basis for the localized osteitis fibrosa reaction just as we have shown for the achondroplasic screw-tail in an animal with no further symptoms of chondrodystrophy. It is further suggested that generalized osteitis fibrosa resulting from disturbed calcium metabolism associated with parathyroid tumors and hypertrophy might be a definite genetic disease appearing during certain life periods only in those individuals carrying the mutation for parathyroid tumor and the associated disturbances.

The foregoing digression from our immediate subject is intended to emphasize the fact that the parathyroid glands are organs of importance in all considerations of growth and quality of osseous structures. We may now examine the histologic nature of the parathyroid glands from the Boston terrier-dachshund crosses.

The photomicrograph of a section through one of the parathyroid bodies from a 6 year old dachshund bitch, 255 ♀, is shown in plate 91 (fig. 1) together with a similar section from a 3 year old Boston terrier bitch 536 ♀ (fig. 2) for comparison. Both sections appear fairly normal. The epithelial cells are compactly arranged with clearly expressed patterns of straight and curved cord-like bands. Connective tissue is sparse and the vascular network is typical. Almost all the epithelial cells are of the principal cell type characteristic of the parathyroid, but at the mid-peripheral border in the dachshund section there is an accumulation of bluish granular cells seen as an irregular darker mass. This is not a constant characteristic in the dachshund, and there is no difference between the microscopic pictures of these two sections to which any significance can be attached. In this respect the parathyroid sections from the two breeds are out of accord with the histologic pictures of both the thyroid and pituitary glands, which differed quite definitely. However, a longer study of these glands might yield some differences in type, and other parathyroid sections showing arrests and histologic defects could no doubt be found in both these breeds.

Figure 3 illustrates the parathyroid from a Boston terrier-dachshund $F_1$ hybrid. This gland has a considerably stronger stroma of more abundant connective tissue than either section from the parent breeds. The pattern of epithelial arrangement is quite normal, and similar to that of the parent stocks, although the photomicrograph is from a section nearer the hilum and the larger vessels somewhat modify the picture. A number of parathyroids from $F_1$ hybrids have been studied, and all are fairly similar to figure 3. The differences between the glands from two individuals are little if at all greater than might occur among the separate parathyroid bodies from the same individual. We have not yet been able to consistently study all the parathyroid bodies from each individual, and the time and effort necessary to do so would scarcely seem worth while. It is felt that if the parathyroid glands play a type-determining rôle in differentiating the several contrasted breeds of dogs, a fair sample of the glands from any well expressed type should show indications of the modified function as well as any other sample or possibly even all the parathyroid bodies from the given individual.

Figures 4, 5 and 6 in plate 91 illustrate sections of the parathyroids from three second generation Boston terrier-dachshund hybrids. In this generation there is wide variation in general body form and type, and unique specimens may appear, the characteristics from the two parent stocks being strangely mixed and combined in one individual. As discussed previously, the thyroid and pituitary glands also differ very widely in their histologic patterns in these $F_2$ hybrids.

Figure 4 illustrates a section through a small parathyroid body lying within a compartment of the same connective tissue coat which surrounded a large cyst. This cyst was lined with embryonic branchial epithelium ciliated over most parts, and was filled with a lightly staining fluid containing sparsely scattered cells. There is no doubt that the lining of this cyst is a remnant of branchial epithelium which normally should have differentiated into parathyroid or thyroid tissue in this region. Smaller cysts of similar type are frequently found within the parathyroid bodies, and are indicative of arrests and inhibitions in the outgrowths of branchial epithelium designed to form the endocrine glands which arise from the branchial pouches of the embryo. We have already seen in the pure Boston terrier and these Boston terrier-dachshund hybrids that embryonic arrests in

PLATE 91

EXPLANATION OF FIGURES

Boston terrier-dachshund cross. Histologic nature of the parathyroid glands in the pure breeds and their first and second generation hybrids.

1  Dachshund 255 ♀.     3  $F_1$ 127 ♀.     5  $F_2$ 354 ♀.
2  Boston terrier 536 ♀.     4  $F_1$ 781 ♀.     6  $F_2$ 355 ♀.

PLATE 91

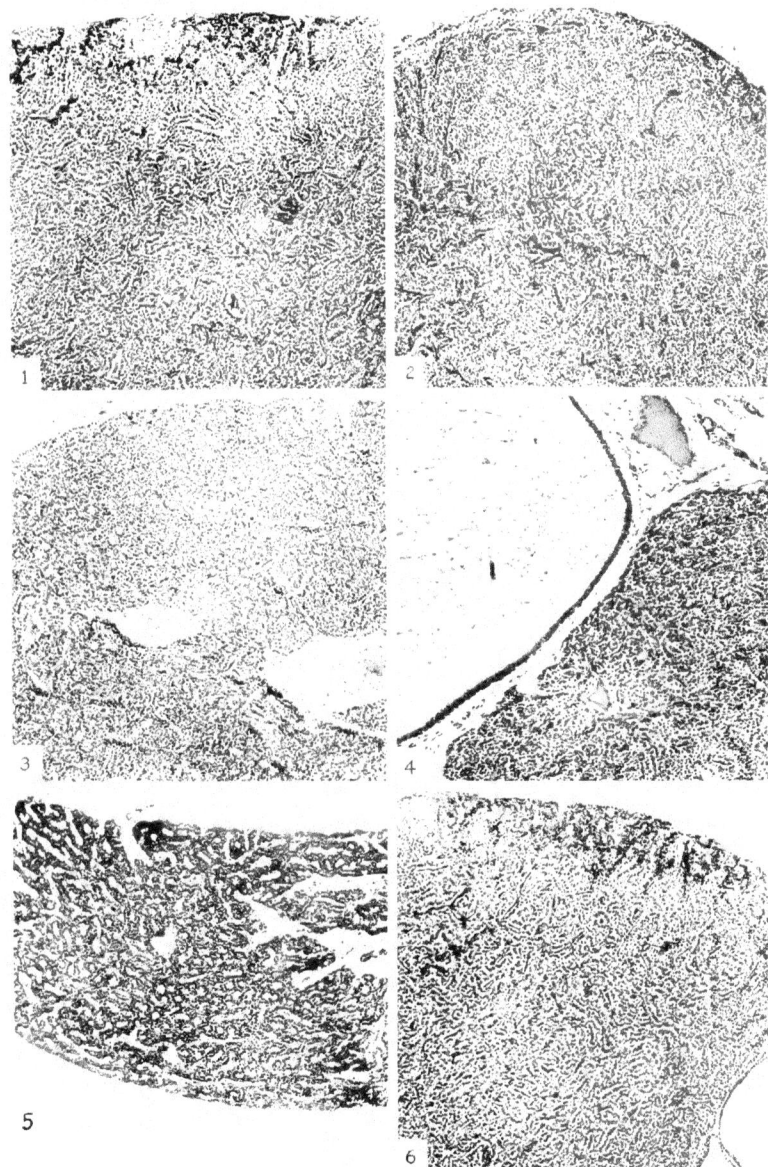

the origin and differentiation of the hypophysis from the stomodeal epithelium are not uncommon.

The parathyroid body and cyst just described were taken from $F_2$ 781 ♀, shown from life as figure 7 in plate 39 (p. 236). The other members of her litter are shown in plate 30 (figs. 1–5) (p. 129). The cranium and upper head of 781 ♀ is Boston terrier-like in type, and is associated with a weak and atypical muzzle. The life history of this animal was normal. The small parathyroid body shows the general cord-like arrangement of the principal cells, and at the periphery near the cyst there are irregular groups of bluish staining cells, darker in the photograph. These basophilic cells do not enter into the cord-like arrangement.

Figures 5 and 6 in plate 91 are parathyroid sections from $F_2$ litter sisters, 354 ♀ and 355 ♀, which are not illustrated from life although an extremely defective litter sister, 353 ♀, is shown in plate 39 (fig. 3). Figure 5, from 354 ♀ which was killed at 3 years of age, is extremely different in histologic appearance from the five other glands illustrated in plate 91. The tubules or cords formed by double rows of epithelial cells are strongly emphasized and facilitate a clearer understanding of the cord-like arrangements in the more normal parathyroids. All parathyroid cords are formed by two parallel rows of epithelial cells having their lateral surfaces in contact with the walls of sinusoidal blood capillaries. In this section the vascular walls are thickened, and an excessive amount of connective tissue has infiltrated the parathyroid, producing a trabecular-like pattern. The epithelial cells of the cords are smaller and more tightly packed than in the other glands. These conditions do not result from either postmortem changes or fixation shrinkage, since the animal was autopsied immediately after death and the gland was fixed at the same time and in the same manner as the parathyroid from the sister, 355 ♀ (fig. 6). The trabecular-like arrangement may possibly indicate an exhaustion of parathyroid secretion, since the amount of cytoplasm is extremely reduced. Localized areas showing this condition are frequently seen in parathyroids with otherwise usual structure. The bitch furnishing this gland had a dachshund typed head with a long muzzle, and was a fairly normal animal although she possessed a disproportionately large thyroid gland.

Figure 6, from 355 ♀, is quite similar to figures 1 and 2, from the two parent stocks. The double rows of cells form typical cords, and the cytoplasm is more abundant and less concentrated than in figure 5. The one peculiar feature of this section is the high concentration of the bluish staining cells in the peripheral region, which are shown by the darker masses at the top of the section. This animal was also 3 years old when killed and had a partial Boston terrier typed head with a prognathous undershot lower jaw. Sections from the pituitary and the thyroid glands of this bitch are illustrated in plate 89 (figs. 2 and 4). The pituitary is one of the most cystic specimens in our collection and has very little functional epithelium. The thyroid approaches in its peculiar pattern that of the Boston terrier and has medium and small sized irregular follicles as well as large numbers of very minute ones. Parafollicular cells are scattered in the interfollicular regions. These sections, in plates 89 and 91, from three endocrine glands of the $F_2$ Boston terrier-dachshund hybrid would indicate the highly pathologic state of her endocrinic system. The bitch was certainly not a normally vigorous animal, nor for that matter were many members of the $F_2$ generation of Boston terrier-dachshund hybrids. This may be seen by again referring to the mixed and distorted types illustrated in plate 39, and particularly by 353 ♀ (fig. 3), the extremely defective sister of the two bitches 354 ♀ and 355 ♀ supplying the glands just discussed.

Sections from two other $F_2$ Boston terrier-dachshund parathyroids are shown in figures 1 and 3 in plate 92. Figure 1 is from 779 ♂, a brother of 781 ♀ which supplied the cystic section in plate 91 (fig. 4). This dog, 779 ♂, was a definite midget in type, being much smaller than any of his litter mates, as shown in plate 30, figures 1–5 (p. 129). There are no cystic formations associated with his parathyroid as there are in the gland from his sister. The unusual conditon shown is again an accumulation of bluish staining cells along the outer peripheral border. These cells form irregular masses without the cord-like pattern typical of the principal cells. They are also somewhat larger than the principal cells, and their bluish staining cytoplasm gives a slightly granular appearance. At present there is no clue as to the significance of these basophilic cell masses in the hybrid parathyroids.

Figure 3 (pl. 92) illustrates a section of a parathyroid gland from $F_2$ Boston terrier-dachshund 620 ♂, shown from life in plates 39 (fig. 5) and 40 (fig. 1) (pp. 236 and 238). This animal was dachshund in type in all respects except that the lower jaw was of definite Boston terrier proportions and fell far short of proper association and dental occlusion with the upper jaw. A photomicrograph of a section from the thyroid of this animal, which was of typically dachshund pattern, is shown in plate 85 (fig. 4). This animal was killed when about 6 years old and the parathyroid gland shows a somewhat excessive amount of connective tissue. The principal cells show the typical double row cord-like arrangement, with frequent indications of a peculiar tendency to become separated at places giving the appearance of a single circle of cells enclosing small follicles. The tiny lumen of the apparent follicles may contain a drop of coagulum, and the wall consists of a single layer of parathyroid principal cell epithelium. A number of these small follicular-like arrangements may be seen in the left and the upper central regions of the photomicrograph.

The arrangement of principal cells in the double row cord-like pattern in the dog parathyroid might be mistaken for a potential tubular formation, but this arrangement is more

PLATE 92

EXPLANATION OF FIGURES

Boston terrier-dachshund cross. Parathyroid histological pattern in second generation and backcross Boston terrier hybrids.

1  $F_2$ 779 ♂.         3  $F_2$ 620 ♂.
2  Backcross Boston terrier 524 ♂.   4  Backcross Boston terrier 525 ♀.

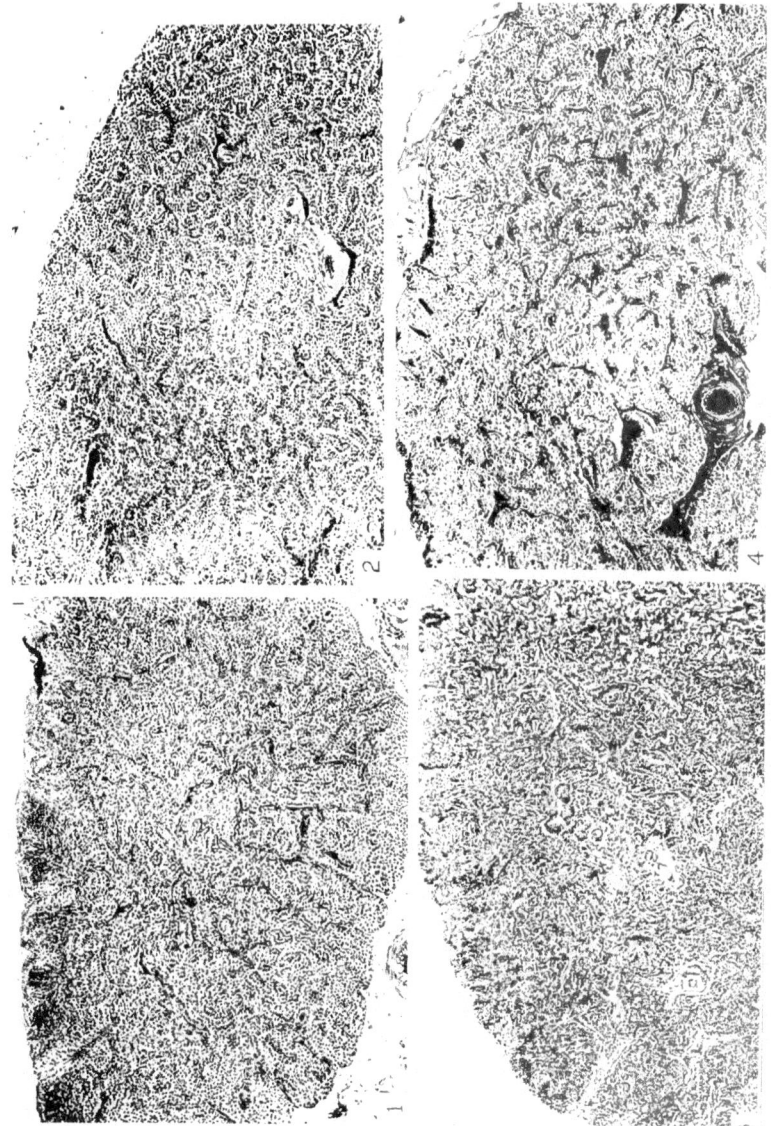

essentially due to the fact that only one side of the epithelial cell is in contact with a capillary; the other side is in contact with the accompanying cell (see again the emphasized cords in fig. 5, pl. 91). The early stages of the transition from the histologic pattern of parathyroid to the thyroid follicular arrangement, or vice versa, is not difficult to comprehend from the conditions present in these parathyroid sections.

Spots of the darker staining bluish cells are seen irregularly located near the periphery of the parathyroid from 620 ♂ and show chiefly in the left half of the photomicrograph. The parathyroid gland unquestionably presents histologic distortions, but whether these are related in a causal manner to defects in the structural constitution of the animal is at present impossible to state. The teeth of this dog were badly broken in places and undermined through degeneration and resorption of the alveolar bone, and this might possibly be associated with the parathyroid defects; but it is also possible that it is a direct result of mechanical irritation due to the extreme dental malocclusion which existed between the structurally disharmonious jaws. The general life history of the animal was normal except that it had difficulty in taking food in competition with other dogs and that the many attempts at breeding were unsuccessful.

Figures 2 and 4 in plate 92 illustrate sections of the parathyroids from 524 ♂ and 525 ♀. These animals were brother and sister litter mates from a backcross of the $F_1$ Boston terrier-dachshund with the Boston terrier parent. Photographs of the animals from life are shown in plate 44 (figs. 1 and 3) (p. 247). They resemble poor typed Boston terriers. Sections of the thyroid glands from these individuals have already been examined (figs. 3 and 4, pl. 86), and were described as presenting an almost complete histologic pattern of the thyroid distortion typical of the Boston terrier gland. The pituitary glands from these two dogs were seen to be cystic and abnormal (figs. 1 and 2, pl. 90), the gland from 524 ♂ being more distorted than that from the sister.

The sections of the parathyroids in plate 92 seem much less pathologic in structure than do either the thyroids or the pituitaries from the same animals. Figure 2, from 524 ♂, presents the typical double row cellular cords or tubule arrangements of the principal cell epithelium, and there are localized regions where the cytoplasm of the cell cords stains somewhat darker, as if more concentrated or in a different phase of activity. In some of these places the parallel alignment of the cells disappears and the cells appear to be of the bluish type. There is nothing in the histology of this parathyroid section that would lead one to anticipate the extreme histopathology shown by the accompanying pituitary and thyroid glands (pls. 86 and 90).

The photomicrograph of the parathyroid from the sister, 525 ♀ (fig. 4, pl. 92), shows congestion of the vessels near the hilum of the gland. This gland presents again a fairly normal histologic picture, and the general behavior of the animal gave no evidence of parathyroid disfunction.

## Summary and Deductions

The foregoing examination of the parathyroid glands completes the survey of the histologic qualities of the endocrine glands from the parental stocks and the hybrid generations of the Boston terrier-dachshund cross. Only three members of the endocrinic system have been included in this survey. The general functional quality of the gonadal secretions in these several generations is very well indicated by our rather extensive breeding records, but these will not be discussed at this time since the present consideration has been restricted to those glands more largely concerned with growth patterns and modified structural types. The discussion of the suprarenal glands in the different breed types is also reserved for a later report, since it is difficult to relate clearly their influences to the modifications of structural types and behaviors now being reviewed. Reference to the thymus is almost completely omitted; we merely record that the mass of thymic tissue differs greatly among the dog breeds as well as among the individuals of some hybrid generations. A number of cases of thymic death have occurred among hybrid puppies, in some instances being clearly due to acute edema of the thymic body. These findings will be reported in other places. There is little if any evidence at present to indicate that the thymus plays a significant rôle in the growth of structural types among dogs. However, there is the fact that the large St. Bernard typed $F_2$ bassethound-bulldog, as we shall show in the next chapter, has a large, meaty thymus accompanying a highly acidophilic pituitary, while litter mates of normal and smaller size are without highly acidophilic pituitaries and possess only small amounts of thymic tissue. Such relations between thymic quantity and acidophilic reaction in the pituitary may be involved in the precocious growth and development of thymic fed rats in the experiments of Rowntree and co-workers ('35).

The study of endocrines from the cross between the Boston terrier and the dachshund clearly indicates several general reactions of considerable importance. In the first place, a cross between two stocks, one of which clearly possesses a defective endocrine system accompanied by distorted physical type, may give rise to a first generation of hybrids with fairly well balanced physical types and vigorous functional reactions. Individuals of this generation may even be, in some respects, physically superior to either parent stock. In the second place, the offspring from these vigorous first generation hybrids are highly heterogeneous in type; scarcely two of them are closely alike and the great majority are defective in both their morphologic quality and functional reactions. Prenatal mortality among these $F_2$ hybrids is high; stillbirths are common and many are viable for only a short time after birth. Harelip, cleft palate, internal hydrocephalus and other developmental arrests and defects are not uncommon in this generation. Of the members surviving to adulthood, some tend to approach in type one or the other parental stock, while others present strange mixtures and combinations of ancestral characteristics which are in many cases incongruous and disharmonious in function. The majority of the viable members of the second hybrid generation are unstable and defective in behavior.

In the third place, it should be emphasized that on hybridizing mammals with contrasted features and characters, many of which are influenced in both their development and function by the state of their endocrinic balance, we are dealing with a far more complex genetic and developmental interaction than exists among lower invertebrate forms without specific endocrinic systems. The consequences of hybridization on human races and stocks can only be fully understood by experimental studies on higher mammalian forms in which the genetics of endocrinic differences and influences must follow paths closely similar to those in human beings. The study of the endocrines from the Boston terrier-dachshund generations definitely shows that the glands of the $F_2$ hybrids vary considerably. In size they range not only above and below the two parent stocks but far above the increased size in the $F_1$ animals. The histologic qualities of these $F_2$ endocrines are often more distorted and pathologic than those of either ancestral stock.

None of the results from the Boston terrier-dachshund cross offer encouragement to the indifferent attitude frequently expressed towards crossing and hybridizing the various human stocks. The attitude towards hybridizing the domestic breeds of animals is considerably more cautious, due, of course, to the serious economic consequences that would result from careless breeding.

## FURTHER TESTS ON THE SIGNIFICANCE OF ENDOCRINIC QUALITY IN RELATION TO PHYSICAL TYPE AS SUPPLIED BY BASSETHOUND-BULLDOG HYBRIDS

The results from only one cross between contrasted types would hardly be sufficient to indicate whether comparable disturbances might be expected among the hybrid progeny from other combinations, and for this reason these experiments were planned to include crosses between breeds of various constitutions. The cross just considered involves contrasted stocks of dwarf size, while the endocrine glands next to be examined are from a cross between two normal or full sized breeds with somewhat different character modifications.

The reader is already familiar with the highly modified head and body of the English bulldog, as well as with the distorted histologic pattern of its thyroid gland. The bassethound and its thyroid of rather low activity have also been described. There has been, up to now, no implication of a causal relation or direct connection between the physical types and thyroid patterns in these breeds; such interrelationships could be fairly discussed only after examining other members of the endocrine system. A further understanding should result from a study of the genetics of glandular modifications in the hybrid generations derived from crosses between these dogs of contrasted type.

## THE INHERITANCE OF CONTRASTED HISTOLOGIC QUALITIES OF THYROID GLANDS AND THEIR CORRELATION WITH PHYSICAL TYPES IN BASSETHOUND-BULLDOG HYBRIDS

The somewhat detailed treatment of the histology of the endocrine glands in the Boston terrier-dachshund cross presented in the previous chapter facilitates the discussion of the glands in the bassethound-bulldog cross, which will be given in as brief form as clarity permits.

Figure 1 in plate 93 illustrates a section of the thyroid gland from a prolific bassethound bitch, 277 ♀. Although at first glance this gland appears fairly active, it should be noted that the colloid is cracked and brittle and the follicular epithelium is low; both of these are characteristics of a

PLATE 93

EXPLANATION OF FIGURES

Bassethound-English bulldog cross. The inheritance of thyroid histological patterns in first and second generation hybrids.

1 Bassethound 277 ♀.   3 $F_1$ 739 ♂.   5 $F_2$ 1313 ♂.
2 English bulldog 120 ♂.   4 $F_1$ 741 ♂.   6 $F_2$ 1312 ♂.

PLATE 93

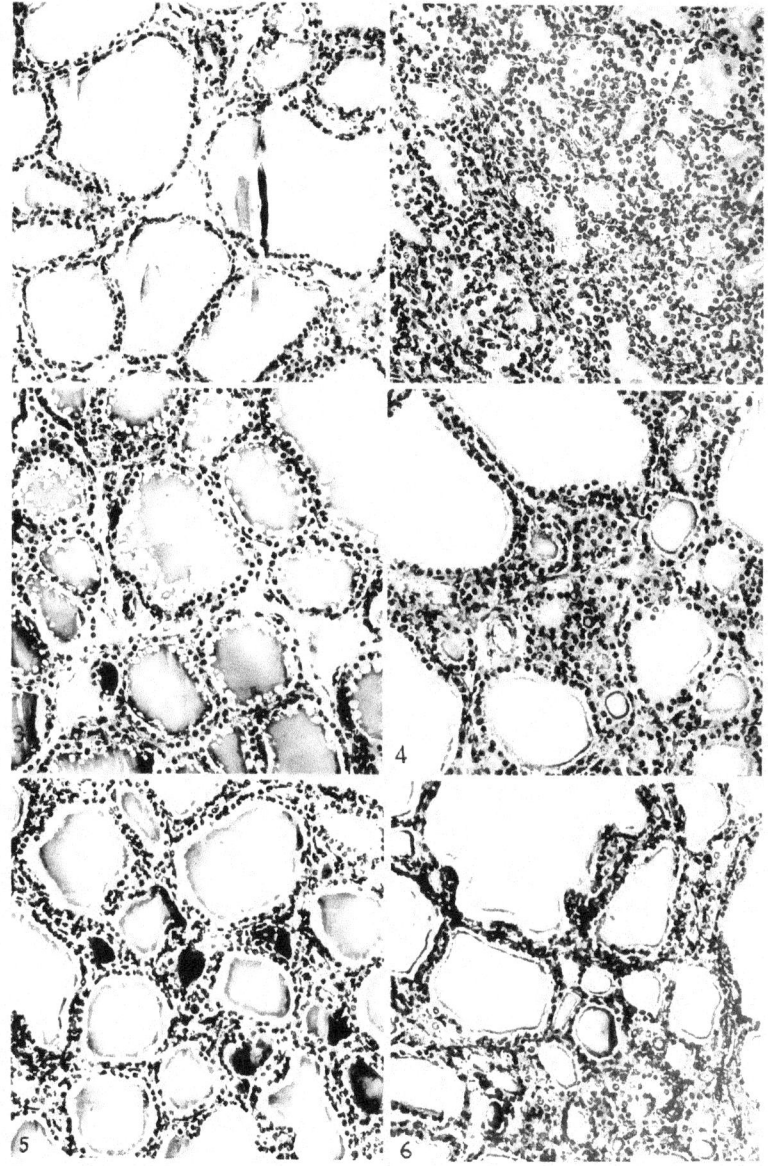

normal, low-functioning thyroid. Figure 2 shows a histologic section of the thyroid from a heavily typed male English bulldog, 120♂. The follicles are very small and contain little or no colloid, and the epithelium is high columnar. Much interfollicular tissue is present, and there are pathologic conditions in the gland other than simple hyperactivity. The histologic pictures of the bassethound and bulldog thyroids could scarcely be more completely contrasted.

The $F_1$ bassethound-bulldog hybrids show a thyroid histologic pattern which is quite consistent and differs from both parental stocks. These thyroids contain large and small follicles, many being as large as those of the hound and others as small as in the bulldog, although somewhat more regular in outline. The follicular epithelium in all these glands is high columnar and is more active than in the bassethound. Figures 3 and 4 (pl. 93) illustrate the histology of the thyroids from two $F_1$ brothers, 739♂ and 741♂, both of which were 3 years old when killed. The physical types of the parents and the $F_1$ animals are illustrated from life in plate 19 (p. 97).

Figures 5 and 6 illustrate the histological qualities of thyroids from two very dissimilar $F_2$ hybrid brothers, 1313♂ and 1312♂. These dogs were not quite 2 years old when killed. No. 1313♂ weighed 20 kilograms and was of about the usual size for such hybrids. The brother, 1312♂, was much larger and weighed 30 kilograms. These two animals are shown in front and side views in plate 22 (p. 102). No. 1313♂ has the size, shape and general appearance of the bassethound grandparent, while 1312♂ resembles neither the bassethound, as does 1313♂ (figs. 3 and 6), nor the bulldog, as does 1311♂ (figs. 1 and 4). His head, face and general bodily appearance and proportions are of the mastiff and the short haired St. Bernard type. This animal possessed a large and solid thymus body, while both the bassethound-like and bulldog-like brothers had only a small amount of loosely scattered thymic tissue.

Figure 5 in plate 93 shows a section of the thyroid from the bassethound-like $F_2$ hybrid. The epithelial pattern of this thyroid resembles somewhat more closely that of the bassethound than of the $F_1$ hybrid. The thyroid from the St. Bernard typed brother (fig. 6) does not clearly suggest either parental pattern, nor yet that of the $F_1$ hybrid. This gland has both large and very small follicles with flat, inactive epithelial walls, and there is no clear resemblance between it and the thyroid gland of the St. Bernard.

It is well recognized, of course, that the height of the follicular epithelium and the apparent thyroid activity as seen in the thyroid section depend upon the condition of the animal when killed. As far as was practical, all animals were killed at a time when they were in normal states of activity. Through close acquaintance with the living animals we do have a definite advantage in knowing the comparative active and inactive tendencies of the dogs concerned, and on this basis can predict with some degree of accuracy the functional symptoms to be found within the thyroid. However, the estimates of thyroid types must in all cases be based largely upon definite differences in histologic pattern, such as those we have pointed out between the bulldog types and the long muzzled breeds. Yet some importance must necessarily be attached to apparent differences in functional activity of the thyroids at the time of the animal's death.

Microscopic sections from five other thyroid glands of the $F_2$ hybrids are illustrated in plate 94 to show not only how completely the histologic patterns may revert to the bassethound and bulldog types but also the occurrence of new and unusual types. The upper left section, from 1055 ♀, presents the exact histologic picture of the thyroid gland from a bassethound; the follicles in limited regions are small, but in general are large with walls of low cuboidal epithelium, and the colloid is stale and brittle. As shown in plate 59 (fig. 3) (p. 324), the animal from which this specimen was taken is of general bassethound type although the head is somewhat short and heavy, partly bulldog-like. Figures 2 and 3 approach the distorted histology characteristic of the thyroids in the bulldog group. Figure 2 is from 1143♂, and shows follicles of irregular size and outline. The epithelial walls consist of actively secreting high columnar cells, and the colloid is soft. A large amount of interfollicular tissue is present. The entire picture brings to mind the thyroid of the bulldog. The animal supplying this thyroid, seen in plate 62 (fig. 1) (p. 331), is only slightly nearer the bulldog type than 1055♀ which supplied the hound-like thyroid (fig. 1). The overgrowth of skin and other distorted features are, however, more extremely expressed in 1143♂. The exaggerated amount of skin shown by a completely "stuffed" brother is well illustrated in plate 62.

Figure 3 (pl. 94) is one of the most striking pictures that can be presented by the thyroid. It represents a section of the gland from 1145♂, shown from life in plate 62 (fig. 2). This dog is a brother to the animal just discussed, and both were vigorous animals of 18 months when killed. No. 1145♂ has a clearly expressed, but poorly typed bulldog head. The thyroid section of this animal shows follicles that are medium or very small in size. The follicular walls are folded and irregular in outline and are not fully expanded. The follicular epithelium is high columnar and extremely active. The cell bodies are filled with granular cytoplasm, and the nuclei lie far away from the follicular lumen. Wide borders of confluent secretion droplets are seen around the periphery of the follicles, and small masses of fresh light staining colloid lie nearer the center. The thickness of the follicular walls is most remarkable. This gland clearly illustrates a state of extreme thyroid secretory activity, and the gland from the brother (fig. 2) is not far below in this respect.

PLATE 94
EXPLANATION OF FIGURES

Bassethound-English bulldog cross. Further illustrations of the variation in thyroid histological pattern to be found among second generation hybrids.

1  1055♀.  3  1145♂.  5  946♂.
2  1143♂.  4  902♀.

PLATE 94

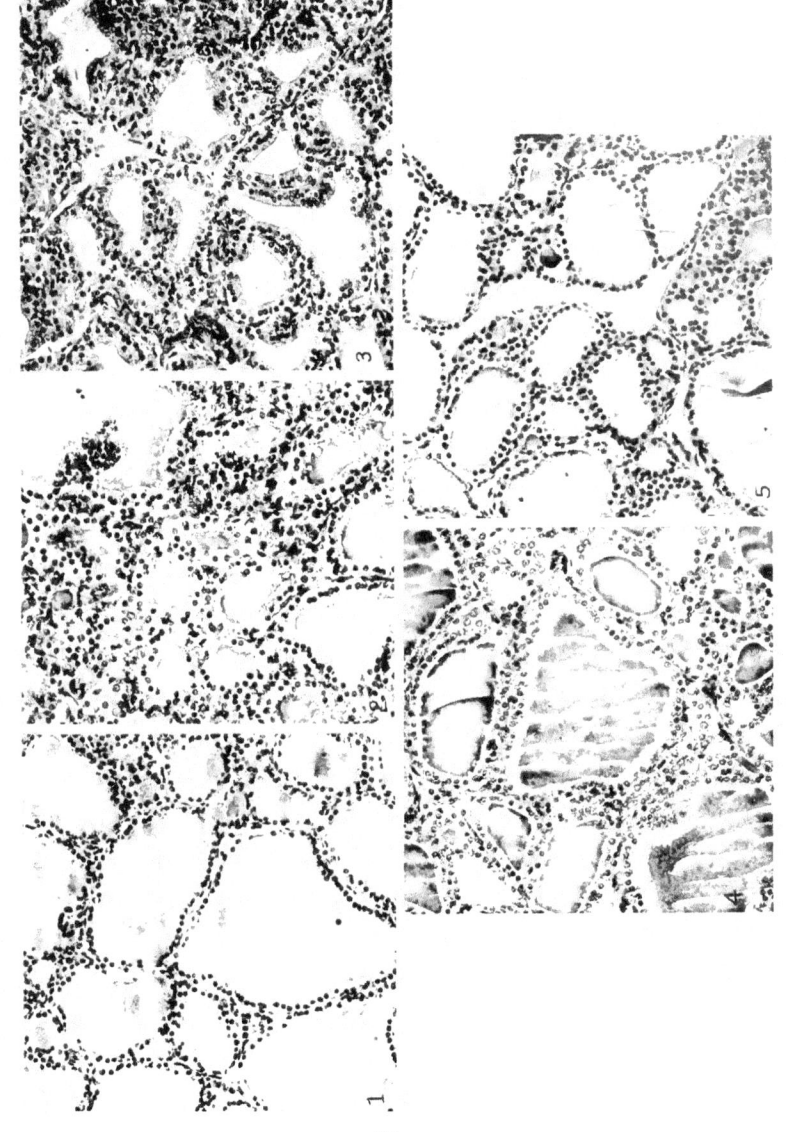

In spite of the evidently hyperactive condition of these peculiar thyroid glands, neither of the dogs showed any well known symptoms of so-called hyperthyroidism. On the contrary, they were fat and inactive, and although they had an inherited shyness, were not nervous nor restless. There was no tendency for exophthalmos, even when one discounts the excessively loose drooping skin which overhangs the eye and almost closes it from view, and in spite of the sagging of the lower lid which exposes the red conjunctiva at the median edge of the eyeball, the so-called haw well shown in the bloodhound eye.

Considerable evidence forces us to suspect that such thyroid glands, in association with rather typically modified pituitaries and probably other altered members of the endocrine system, do not secrete an amount of thyroid hormone in excess of the demand from the constitution concerned. We recognize that these thyroid pictures in differently constituted individuals might very readily be associated with symptoms of pathologic hyperthyroidism, but the fact remains that the animals described above are not so afflicted in spite of the high activity of their thyroids.

Figures 4 and 5 (pl. 94) illustrate rather unique and intermediate histologic patterns in the hybrid thyroids. Figure 4 shows a thyroid histology that is remarkably similar to that of the non-related Boston terrier gland. The follicular epithelium is cuboidal in form and moderately active. The follicles are irregular in size and the colloid is hard and slightly brittle. There is considerable interfollicular tissue as well as nests of parafollicular cells. The dog from which this gland was taken, 902 ♀, was killed when 18 months old. The head was partially bulldog in type, and the brain presented a moderate degree of internal hydrocephalus, a fairly common characteristic in the bulldog group.

Figure 5 shows a thyroid section from a 14 months old animal, 916 ♂. This $F_2$ bassethound-bulldog hybrid is shown from life in plate 19 (p. 97), and a photograph of his skeleton in plate 20 (p. 99). In body form, this hybrid approaches the bulldog in many respects but, as the skeleton shows, the bulldog proportions are modified by the influence of the hound. During life the head of the animal appeared more bulldog-like than does the skull. The skull shape is between that of the $F_1$ hybrid and the pure bulldog; it is not fully shortened, but the mandible is undershot and projects in front of the upper jaw. The thyroid section shows a histologic pattern which is clearly intermediate in its expression. The follicles are smaller than in the hound and more uniform in outline than in the bulldog. The follicular epithelium is cuboidal and of a higher type than that of the hound, but falls much lower than in the bulldog. After studying a great number of these hybrid thyroids one is surprised by the consistency with which differences in the histologic quality seem to follow definite variations in physical form, from the normal thyroid pattern and hound type through many intermediate and new conditions and on to the highly distorted thyroid picture associated with bulldog physical type. This correlation is so close that the histologic pattern of the thyroid may be fairly well predicted after a careful estimate of the type balance between the two breed stocks in the individual concerned.

The relations between histologic patterns of the thyroid and peculiar structural types as found in the hybrid generations of the bassethound-bulldog cross lend strong support to the comparable findings recorded for the Boston terrier-dachshund hybrids. The quality and degree of activity of the thyroid gland is intimately associated with the development and final expression of characteristic types. And as we shall report beyond, the peculiar morphologic types have limited and characteristic manners of behavior, and these functional reactions are also correlated with definite thyroid patterns. We shall still postpone any attempt to answer the question of whether the thyroid gland is the controlling element in determining structural types and behavior patterns; undoubtedly its secretion performs a most important function in these directions. Current opinion inclines toward the so-called thyrotropic hormone from the pituitary as the power behind all thyroid influences, but investigators studying more than one endocrine gland find it difficult to attribute the many variations in thyroid quality and function to the stimulating influences of this pituitary substance alone. It must be remembered that in some dogs the thyroid gland functions fairly well for some time after the pituitary has been completely destroyed.

Certain further evidence to aid in the solution of these problems may be derived from an examination of the pituitary glands in the bassethound-bulldog hybrids, and we shall now proceed to a discussion of this phase of our experiments.

## The Histologic Quality of the Pituitary Glands in the Bassethound-Bulldog Hybrids and the Possible Relations to Morphologic Distortions and Modifications in the Histologic Quality of the Thyroid

We may repeat the idea presented previously that the coordination of developmental processes among the different organs and parts of the newly forming individual is delicately and perfectly adjusted to bring about an harmoniously proportioned body complex. Any slight change in the environment during the development of a given organ, such as a momentary failure of the oxygen supply or circulation, would allow other body parts to gain material advantage over it, the seriousness of which would largely depend upon the developmental stage of the organ at the time the handicap occurred. These statements are fully substantiated by numerous studies in the field of experimental embryology. The pituitary gland, in its endocrinic predomination, is interrelated with so many other organs that should it be involved in developmental arrests or early handicaps, a number of parts would suffer consequent developmental disturbances, the symptoms of which would be structural distortions and modifications in type.

We have seen, in the Boston terrier and some of the Boston terrier-dachshund hybrids, all animals of dwarf size, that the pituitaries show symptoms of developmental arrests, with cystic formations surrounded by undifferentiated hypophyseal epithelium. In many such animals the normal canine type is altered, and bizarre modifications with a general tendency toward bulldog-like characters result. The features of the normal sized English bulldog are distorted far beyond the similar characteristics in the Boston terrier, and the thyroid glands in both these breeds deviate from the normal histologic pattern in characteristically different manners. At present we are to examine the nature of the pituitary in the bulldog and to determine its behavior in the bassethound-bulldog hybrids as compared with that of the thyroid, as well as to make general comparisons with what has been learned of the pituitary in the Boston terrier-dachshund crosses.

Photomicrographs of longitudinal sections of the pituitaries from the bulldog and the bassethound and their hybrid progeny are shown in plate 95. The general morphology of the pituitary of the bulldog differs somewhat from that of the long muzzled breeds. Figure 2 shows it to be short anteroposteriorly and thick dorsoventrally, being almost spherical in shape rather than oblong and flattened as in other breeds. The pars nervosa is particularly thick, and its dorsal surface is covered only by the thin roof of the hypophyseal sac which forms a double layer of pars intermedia and encloses a cleft of the residual lumen. The general interpretation of the development of such a condition in the adult might be as follows: the formation and upward growth of the hypophyseal sac from the stomodeal epithelium was such as to produce an unusually small area of the heavily thickened epithelium which gives rise to the future pars distalis and pars tuberalis; meanwhile, as the wall of the over-dilated hypophyseal lumen distended, the thin dorsal portion which forms the future pars intermedia was much increased in area. The contact with the infundibular process caused an over folding of this extensive thin roof in order to obliterate the exaggerated hypophyseal lumen. The small size of the future pars distalis area is only long enough to surround the ventrolateral part of the disproportionately large pars nervosa; its dorsal region is entirely free. The photomicrograph in plate 95 serves to illustrate these peculiarities.

In the human, the infundibular portion and the pars intermedia of the pituitary have been found to be larger in the male than in the female and, as pointed out by Rasmussen ('38), this relation probably holds for other mammals as well. At the same time, the pituitary as a whole is larger in women than it is in men, a condition due entirely to the larger pars distalis of the female gland. On the basis of such findings, the pituitary gland of the bulldog with its small pars distalis and disproportionately large pars intermedia and pars nervosa may be classed as strongly of the male type. It will be shown in later discussions on behavior that the female bulldog produces only small litters of puppies and displays definitely defective maternal instincts. This may be due in part to the masculine proportions of the pituitary gland. Yet there is also frequent histopathology in the tuberalis and distalis of the bulldog gland, as well as low basophile counts, and these conditions could account for such disturbances.

Figure 2 (pl. 95) illustrates an almost sagittal section of the pituitary from a bulldog of $2\frac{1}{2}$ years, 1083 ♀. The animal was a prize typed bulldog in spite of the fact that the localized achondroplasic condition in the basicranium had become somewhat generalized to involve the cervical vertebrae, causing ankylosis and a slight bend in the neck of the animal.

The pars nervosa of this pituitary is solid and almost spherical in shape. The third ventricle extends through the infundibular stalk only, and not into the nervosa, as is the case in some breeds. The distalis, as well as the intermedia, is intimately fused with the posterior pole of the nervosa, and cells from these portions invade the nervosa. Arrested

## PLATE 95

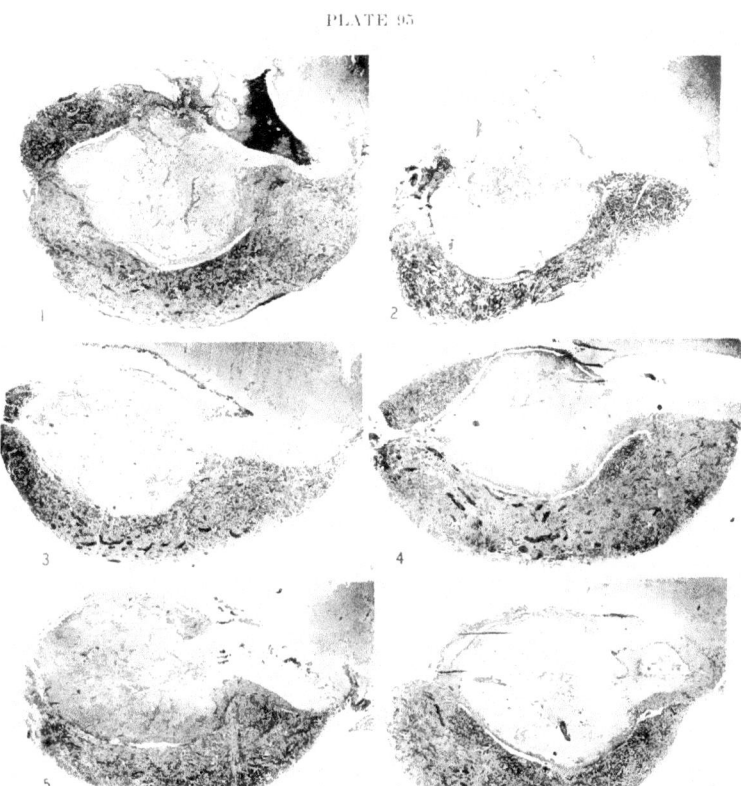

Bassethound-English bulldog cross. The inheritance of pituitary histological pattern in first and second generation hybrids.

1. Bassethound 218 ♂.
2. English bulldog 1083 ♀.
3. $F_1$ 742 ♂.
4. $F_1$ 739 ♂.
5. $F_2$ 1055 ♀.
6. $F_2$ 1583 ♀.

cystic formations occur at this point of fusion, and smaller cysts are present near the periphery in other parts of the distalis. The epithelial cells of the distalis show cord-like arrangements with excessive amounts of connective tissue separating them. All in all there is an abnormally small amount of secretory epithelium in the pars tuberalis and distalis. The alpha or acidophilic cells are bright staining and in high proportion, there being more than thirty acidophilic cells to one basophilic. The basophiles are frequently vacuolated, and signet typed castrate cells are seen. The relative proportion of acidophilic to basophilic cells is almost the reverse to that following operative castration and menopause, and yet the cytological quality of the basophiles is suggestive of the so-called castrate cells. As we have seen, the pituitary of the Boston terrier is in many ways not unlike that of the bulldog.

The pituitary glands from eight male and six female bulldogs have been studied microscopically, and while they are not uniformly alike in detail their general qualities are closely similar. The pars nervosa, intimately coated by the intermedia, is easily detached from the anterior lobe, and removal of the gland from the sella turcica must be performed with great care in order to preserve it intact. The pars tuberalis does not completely surround the short infundibular stalk, and the upper border of the cup-shaped pars distalis extends slightly above the equator of the nervosa. A common feature of the bulldog pituitary is the persistence of a membranous connection between the anterior lobe and a depression in the basisphenoid; in rarer cases, a complete foramen is present permitting the direct continuation between the glandular pituitary, Rathke's pouch, and the oral epithelium. All the above features vary among the fourteen glands in our series, yet they are constant enough to enable one to distinguish the bulldog pituitary from that of the long muzzled breeds. On the basis of this experience, one would not expect a flattened elongate pituitary with extensive pars distalis in the bulldog, and should a pituitary of apparently this type occur, care must be taken to establish with certainty the diagnosis for bulldog head and also the breed history of the animal. The chromophilic proportions of high acidophilic and low basophilic cells and the presence of undifferentiated cystic epithelium are also variable, but are in general characteristic of the bulldog gland.

In contrast to the bulldog, the bassethound pituitary adheres very closely to the normal canine pattern; this is shown by figure 1 (pl. 95). The pars nervosa is not disproportionately large and is completely encased by the pars distalis; the pars tuberalis surrounds the infundibular stalk, which in this specimen has been accidentally compressed and bent, distorting its elongate pattern. The two $F_1$ glands (figs. 3 and 4) serve as illustrations of the characteristic bassethound typed infundibular stalk. In most regions the intermedia intimately fuses with the nervosa, and its cells, particularly in the proximal regions, invade the nervosa deeply. The section illustrated in figure 1 is from the pituitary of a 7 months old immature dog, 218 ♂. The eosinophiles are bright staining and abundant, outnumbering the basophiles more than 50 to 1. A brother of this animal, killed at 7½ months or just about at sexual maturity, gave a relative count of acidophiles to basophiles of 12 to 1, showing within 19 days the sudden increase of the proportion of basophiles to over four times the number in the less mature animal. Another brother, which had been killed at the immature age of only 5 months, was rich in bright staining acidophiles and had a very low proportion of basophiles, about 260 to 1. Before puberty, the basophiles are not only scarce but show various incomplete stages in the process of granular formation. Some cells have so few basophile granules as to seem almost empty, while other cells are completely filled. The granules in young cells are frequently very coarse. These pituitaries from immature animals illustrate the early activity of the acidophiles and the later occurrence of the basophilic cells and their functions.

The pituitaries from first generation hybrids derived from crossing the bassethound and bulldog show the general topographic morphology of the bassethound gland, while the histologic pattern and cellular relations in the pars distalis are nearer those for the bulldog gland.

Figures 3 and 4 (pl. 95) illustrate longitudinal sections of $F_1$ hybrid pituitaries from animals 739♂ and 742♂. The rather normal and quite active thyroid gland from 739♂ has already been shown (fig. 3, pl. 93). Both figures 3 and 4 (pl. 94) would be considered fairly normal in their general morphology. Yet in 742♂ the pars intermedia is very unusual in its relation to the pars nervosa. The pars intermedia fails to intimately encapsulate and penetrate into the tissues of the nervosa. The looseness of fit is probably due to the over extensive area of intermedia during early stages of development. This might be considered a bulldog-like character, although the condition in 742♂, with its relatively smaller nervosa, is even more extreme than in the bulldog itself (cf. figs. 2 and 3). Diverticula from the residual lumen pass into the pars tuberalis, and the outline of the lumen itself is somewhat modified by foldings of the pars intermedia. The relative proportion of pars nervosa to pars distalis in the $F_1$ is similar to that in the hound and is not the distorted relation found in the bulldog. It should be recalled that the $F_1$ hybrids produce full sized litters and are successful mothers with well adjusted maternal reactions, in these respects resembling the bassethound and differing from the bulldog. The pars distalis contains more connective tissue than usual, and the cords and nests of epithelial cells are distinct and loosely packed, although this pattern is not so extreme as in the bulldog. Among the $F_1$ hybrids of adult age the general proportion of acidophiles to basophiles is very variable, and ranges from 15 to 1 in females to more than 80 to 1 in males. The over abundant acidophile cells are frequently of unusually small size and in some cases the chromophobes are quite large and resemble basophiles.

Longitudinal sections of six pituitaries from $F_2$ hybrids are shown in plates 95 (figs. 5 and 6) and 96 (figs. 1–4). Some of the pituitaries from the $F_2$ hybrids present morphologic patterns closely approaching those found in the two parent stocks. Figures 5 and 6 (pl. 95) are of two such specimens and should be compared with the bassethound and bulldog glands (figs. 1 and 2). Figure 5 is from 1055♀, shown from life, together with three litter brothers, in plate 59 (p. 324). The bitch was an almost perfect bassethound in type, while a brother, 1053♂, was the most completely bulldog typed animal among the 150 $F_2$ bassethound-bulldog hybrids. In the series of $F_2$ skulls in plate 57 (p. 321), his is first, at the bulldog end (fig. 8) and hers is at the bassethound end (fig. 15). The thyroid from 1055♀ is decidedly bassethound in pattern (see fig. 1, pl. 94). The pituitary resembles very closely that of the bassethound in figure 1, plate 95, and shows no resemblance to that of the bulldog (fig. 2). This $F_2$ animal, 1055♀, resembles the bassethound in general form, thyroid pattern, and microscopic anatomy of the pituitary gland.

Figure 6 (pl. 95) approaches the bulldog pituitary type, and is from a mature 16 months old $F_2$ hybrid 1583♀. The proportions and arrangements in this gland closely follow that of the bulldog (fig. 2). The pars intermedia is over extensive and folds back on itself to give two layers of tissue over the dorsal region of the pars nervosa. The pars distalis is correspondingly limited in area, and its discoidal form extends to the distal pole of the nervosa but fails to cover its dorsal surface; these are typical characters of the bulldog pituitary. No. 1583♀ had an extremely wide bulldog-like head with deep depression at the nasion, and a short but not fully bulldog muzzle. The thyroid gland of this bitch, not illustrated, approached the bulldog type. The finer histologic structure of the pars distalis shows a loose cord-like arrangement of its cells with an excess of connective tissue and small follicles with pale colloidal-like material at the posterior region. This $F_2$ hybrid illustrates the definite association of the bulldog typed head, the bulldog thyroid pattern and a pituitary closely following the microscopic anatomy for the bulldog gland.

Photomicrographs of pituitaries from three $F_2$ hybrid brothers are shown in plate 96 (figs. 1, 3 and 4). These pituitaries are of particular interest because of the differences in their relative proportions and histologic structures in association with the physical differences shown by the individual members of this litter.

Figure 1 gives a clearer picture of the general topography and relative proportions of parts as seen in the bulldog pituitary gland (fig. 2, pl. 95) than do either figures 3 or 4. The dog from which this gland was taken, 1145 ♂, was the most bulldog-like member in his litter, as can be seen by comparing figure 2 in plate 62 (p. 331) with others in the same plate. The skull from this dog is third from the bulldog end in the series of $F_2$ skulls in plate 57 (fig. 10). At the time of his death this animal was a mature adult of $1\frac{1}{2}$ years. A section of the very abnormal thyroid gland may be seen in plate 94 (fig. 3); the extreme activity of this thyroid has already been pointed out. The follicles are small and of irregular outline, and the cells in the walls of high columnar epithelium are loaded with granules and vacuoles and are in a most active state of secretion. However, the hyperactive thyroid functioning within the constitution of this dog induced no symptoms of hyperthyroidism unless one might interpret an hereditary shyness as symptomatic, against which we have much evidence to show that such shyness may be as fully expressed by an animal with a hypoactive and colloidal thyroid.

The pituitary of 1145 ♂ has a disproportionately large spheroidal pars nervosa, which is covered by the pars intermedia over its dorsal hemisphere only. The pars distalis is limited in area and discoidal in shape. The pars tuberalis does not completely surround the infundibular stalk and many diverticula from the residual lumen extend into this region. The groups and cords of cells in the pars distalis

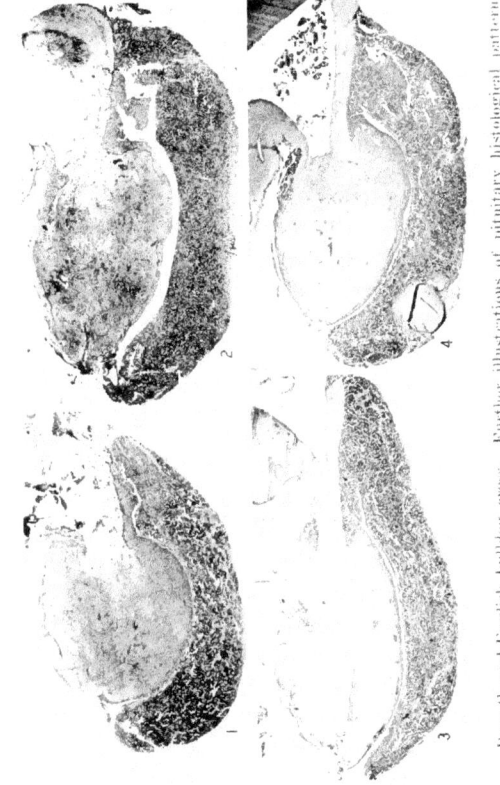

Bassethound English bulldog cross. Further illustrations of pituitary histological pattern in second generation hybrids.
1 1145 ♂   2 977 ♂   3 1146 ♂   4 1147 ♂

are separated by connective tissue, giving a loose rather than the usual compact appearance. The richly abundant and brightly staining acidophiles range in size from quite large to rather small. The basophiles are relatively few in number, there being only one to about fifty acidophiles.

The longitudinal section of the pituitary from 1146 ♂, a brother of the animal discussed above, is shown in figure 3. The shape and relative proportions of this gland differ from both figures 1 and 4. The entire gland is flattened dorsoventrally, and forms a long ovoid instead of being short, thick and rounded in shape as is the pituitary from 1145 ♂. The nervosa is relatively small and the infundibular lumen extends into its body. The pars intermedia deeply invades the nervosa along its dorsal surface and evaginates into it from the distal pole; this can be seen in the photomicrograph. The discoidal pars distalis again covers only the ventral half of the nervosa. The cells of the distalis are arranged in rows and cords and are separated by an excessive amount of connective tissue, which completely alters the usually compact appearance of this portion of the pituitary. The acidophiles are predominant and brilliantly stained, though distinct cytoplasmic granules are difficult to distinguish. Basophiles are very scarce, and the few present lie near the ventral surface of the gland; their cytoplasm is uniformly filled with medium sized granules. Although this animal was over 2 years old, acidophiles outnumber basophiles more than 100 to 1.

It is of interest to compare the head and body form of the dog from which this gland was taken with the physical characters associated with the pituitary of 1145 ♂, discussed just prior to 1146 ♂. No. 1146 ♂ had a head of mastiff rather than bulldog type, as is shown from life in figure 4 and by the carefully mounted specimen in figure 6 of plate 62. Figure 7 in the same plate illustrates the skeleton of this animal. The skull is clearly mastiff in type, with a slight prognathism of the mandible and small depression at the nasion, a far different pattern from the skull of 1145 ♂ with its deep depression at the nasion and extremely undershot jaw, illustrated in plate 57 (fig. 10). As previously pointed out, the acromegalic-like overgrowth of the skin was the most remarkable feature presented by this dog. The most excessive skin area was about the head and anterior regions of the body, and this was sufficient to cover an animal of twice this dog's size. Is the extreme acidophilic nature of the pars distalis related to the disharmonious growth distortion?

A longitudinal section of the pituitary from a third $F_2$ hybrid brother is shown in figure 4 (pl. 96). This gland is from 1147 ♂, an eccentric type among the $F_2$ bassethound-bulldog hybrids in that it resembled more nearly the acromegalic giant St. Bernard form than either parental stock. The skull of this dog is shown in plate 57 (fig. 19) and was closely similar in its indices to the skull of 991 ♂ (fig. 14). No. 991 ♂ is of a more pronounced St. Bernard type, as shown by photograph from life in plate 58 (fig. 1) (p. 323). The close similarity of the skulls from these two St. Bernard typed bassethound-bulldog hybrids to that of the pure St. Bernard acromegalic skull is clearly shown in plate 57.

The pituitary gland of the St. Bernard-like animal, 1147 ♂, differs in several respects from the gland of the bulldog-like 1145 ♂, and also from that of 1146 ♂ with its mastiff typed head. The pars nervosa is not of bulldog type and the pars intermedia differs from the other two specimens by showing many small follicles filled with colloid-like pink staining material, a character more common among the larger breeds than the smaller. The pars tuberalis is extensively invaded by diverticula from the residual lumen, which is a frequent characteristic of the St. Bernard hybrids, as we shall see beyond. A large branching cyst is present in the pars distalis and the cellular arrangements and proportions of this part exhibit most striking characteristics. The epithelial cells are in many regions more compact than in the glands of the bulldog and mastiff typed animals. At first glance, every epithelial cell seems to be an acidophile, there being very few chromophobes present. The acidophiles are somewhat smaller than is usual and stain a dull deep red, and the dark nuclei are filled with coarse chromatin granules. Basophiles are difficult to find and there is only one to about 600 acidophilic cells. The few basophiles are evenly filled with fine cytoplasmic granules.

The pars distalis presents an almost perfect histologic picture of the acidophilic adenomata or true hyperplasia of acidophiles associated with human acromegalic gigantism. As Cushing ('12) and Cushing and Davidoff ('27) have stated, no one today can have any reasonable doubt that the hormones or the substance provoking overgrowth are a product of these acidophilic cells. In the present case we have the first clear demonstration that acromegalic constitution may be brought about through strange combinations of qualities within the hybrid progeny derived from two non-acromegalic stocks.

Figure 2 in plate 96 illustrates a longitudinal section of the pituitary gland from another acromegalic-like $F_2$ hybrid. This dog, 977 ♂, is shown from life in plate 58 (fig. 5) where his short legs hide to some extent the strongly expressed short haired St. Bernard type. The skull of this animal is shown as figure 16 in plate 57. The head and body type, as well as the skull with its normal dental occlusion, all closely follow the St. Bernard in form and quality; the only dissenting feature is the short achondroplasic legs. The general morphology of the pituitary from this animal resembles more closely that of the St. Bernard than it does either the bassethound or bulldog. It is long, flat and oval in outline and in general shape resembles pituitaries from the hound-like group. The dorsal surface of the pars nervosa is not, however, covered by the distalis, and the pars intermedia folds and penetrates deeply into the body of the nervosa from its distal end; the latter feature is never seen in either the bassethound or the bulldog glands. The pars distalis is compact, its cells are arranged close together with only sparse intervening connective tissue, and the cord-like arrangements are indistinct. Again the acidophilic cells are the outstanding type, the chromophobes being less abundant and the basophiles very rare.

The three brothers and the St. Bernard-like $F_2$ male from which the pituitaries in plate 96 were taken, differed from one another in readily recognizable ways, and the histologic patterns of their pituitaries seem to show differences in close association with the differences in morphologic type. In other words, the pituitary of the strongly pronounced bulldog breed is rather characteristic in morphologic structure, and the same is true to a greater or lesser degree for the bassethound. In physical form, some individuals among the second generation hybrids between two such breeds tend to resemble one parent stock and some the other, and these resemblances are associated with the microscopic pattern of pituitary which is characteristic for the breed approached. Eccentric individuals also appear among the second generation hybrids. These may differ widely from the two parental stocks and present conditions foreign to both breeds. These strange growth reactions arising from new combinations of qualities may resemble distortions commonly known in other breeds or even again a well recognized pathologic state. In such cases the pituitary glands of these erratic individuals present histologic modifications well known to be closely associated with the specific physical deviations concerned. Many of these erratic combinations emphasize the dangers and disadvantages of breed hybridization from the standpoint of disbalance in endocrinic constitution.

Before making further comparisons between the endocrinic qualities found in the present cross with those of the Boston terrier-dachshund hybrids previously discussed, the parathyroid glands from the bassethound-bulldog generations will be examined.

## The Quality of Parathyroid Glands in the Bassethound-Bulldog Cross and the Possible Relations to Modifications in Skeletal Growth

The parathyroid glands in the bassethound and bulldog and in their hybrid progeny are very probably related in most important ways to the strange modifications in the shape and quality of the bony skeleton and the overgrowth of the skin. In spite of this probable relationship, it is extremely difficult to locate either histologic or cytologic modifications in the parathyroid epithelium which can be consistently associated with a definite skeletal distortion. The histologic nature of the parathyroid is very simple and homogeneous and, as mentioned before, the histopathology of so direct a disturbance as parathyroid tetany has not been clearly established, although the condition without doubt results from deficiency in the amount of parathyroid hormone. Other difficulties present themselves in any attempt to relate specific histologic defects of the parathyroid with definite modifications in growth. One of the most evident of these difficulties is due to the variable numbers of very small parathyroid bodies present in the animal, all of which may not present identical histologic conditions. It would be a most arduous task to examine microscopically every parathyroid body from each animal studied, even though one assumed that no small particle had been overlooked.

Yet in spite of these difficulties, it is essential in the present study to investigate as far as practical the nature of the parathyroids in the breed crosses showing such evident distortions in just those tissues with very high calcium requirements, such as the skeleton and skin. We recognize, of course, the close interrelation of parathyroid and pituitary functional activity, and from this it might be inferred that the definite modifications in the pituitary histologic patterns which accompany certain structural distortions in these hybrids may also be related to developmental arrests and histologic disturbances in the parathyroid bodies.

With these points in mind, the parathyroid glands of the bassethound-bulldog cross may now be examined.

The histological pictures of the parathyroids from all bassethounds are not exactly the same, yet they follow a somewhat common pattern. The epithelial arrangement gives a fairly normal picture of lines and cords, seen in sections as double rows of cells, and there are capillaries lying between the cords and very little connective tissue. Almost all the epithelium is of so-called principal cell type, with occasional small groups and irregular masses of cells stained a dull blue in color.

Figure 1 in plate 97 illustrates a section of parathyroid from the 6 year old bassethound bitch 277 ♀. Near the upper edge of the section a mass of sinusoidal capillaries is seen as greyish spaces filled with laked blood and with elongate endothelial nuclei at the borders. Lying among the sinusoids are dark, almost black, masses of cells. These are the blue stained cells which are frequently seen as dark streaks near the periphery of the parathyroid and are of interest in the present case in their intimate association with the complex of sinusoidal capillaries. This is a rather frequent arrangement. There are several small cysts with clear lumens in this section, and the principal cells in the lower region form numerous small circular arrangements which resemble follicles but are merely circular bends in the cell cords.

This parathyroid section is from a very prolific bitch which had produced and successfully reared several litters of puppies. The production and feeding of many puppies was no doubt a severe strain on the calcium metabolism in this animal, and the unusual degree of sinusoidal distention of the capillaries in the parathyroid may have been associated with this. It is interesting to note at this point that a forty-five pound bitch, as was 277 ♀, may whelp eight puppies, each weighing one pound. This means that during the 60 days of gestation she has produced animal substance weighing eight pounds, or 17 per cent of her own total body weight. After

PLATE 97

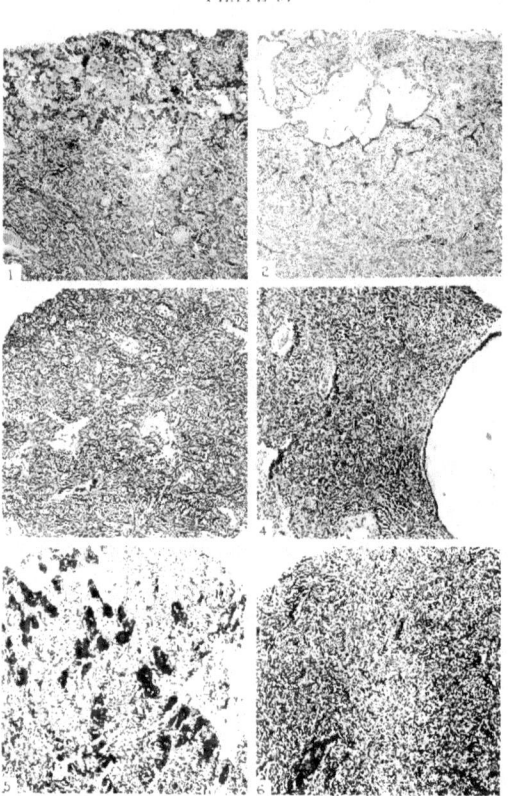

Bassethound-English bulldog cross. Histologic nature of the parathyroid glands in the pure breeds and their first and second generation hybrids.

1  Bassethound 277 ♀.   3  $F_1$ 603 ♀.   5  $F_2$ 1313 ♂.
2  English bulldog 152 ♀.   4  $F_1$ 741 ♂.   6  $F_2$ 1312 ♂.

birth the eight puppies increase at a rate of about one pound per day for almost 6 weeks, being nourished solely by the mother's milk. Translating this into terms of the production within 9 months of a 7 pound baby by a woman of 120 pounds, the performance of the bitch becomes astounding; on this production basis the baby would weigh about 80 pounds at birth. Undoubtedly the calcium metabolism of the pregnant and lactating bitch is very highly taxed.

The parathyroid of a bulldog is illustrated in figure 2 of plate 97. This section is from a 4 year old bitch, 152 ♀. The cytoplasm of the principal cells in this gland is vacuolar in appearance and so swollen that the cells are very large, and double rows of nuclei distinguishing the cord-like arrangements lie far apart. Marked differences in the size of the principal cells among the parathyroid glands may be the simple result of different states of functional activity at the time of fixation, and in this bulldog parathyroid the cell enlargement may be due either to high content of the secretory product or to a vacuolar degeneration. In the case of a Boston terrier-dachshund hybrid parathyroid previously discussed (fig. 5, pl. 91), the cytoplasmic content has been almost exhausted, and the principal cells are of minute size as compared with those in this bulldog section. Localized regions of such cells with diminished cytoplasm are seen in many parathyroids and may simply be those places from which the secretion had recently been discharged. There is, however, the strong probability that certain breeds do possess sluggish inactive parathyroids whose cells may be distended by accumulated secretory products; other types may be hyperactive with the cells discharging their secretion as promptly as it is formed. The thyroid gland furnishes a definite analogy in support of the latter interpretation, and the above parathyroid differences may be typical rather than due to periodic functional changes.

A large branching sinusoidal cavity is seen near the surface of the bulldog gland (fig. 2, pl. 97). This is filled with plasma and blood corpuscles. Numerous capillaries lying between the cords of cells lead directly into this large sinusoid. A faintly staining mass of bluish cells is seen at the top of the section above the sinusoid and immediately to the right of the mid-line. There is not the profuse arrangement of the bluish stained cells as was noted around the sinusoids in figure 1. The differences between these two parathyroid sections from the bassethound and the bulldog are as pronounced as the differences between their thyroids. Yet the parathyroid differences may not be equally expressed in a comparison of all parathyroid bodies of the two individuals; neither are they so consistent as the differences in histologic patterns of the two thyroid glands.

The parathyroid glands from two $F_1$ hybrids between the bassethound and bulldog are illustrated in figures 3 and 4. The size and general cord-like arrangements of the principal cells approach nearer the parathyroid picture of the bassethound than of the bulldog. In figure 3, from 603 ♀, a 6 year old brood-bitch, bluish cells are present in the upper left corner, and several large sinusoids lie among the cords of principal cells.

Figure 4 shows a very large parathyroid cyst lined by ciliated epithelium and filled with greyish granular cystic fluid. This might be interpreted as a definite persistence of embryonic branchial epithelium due to abnormal outgrowth during parathyroid development. In confirmation of this, the entire gland is lobulated, and loose loops of cell strings show failure to form the usually compact cord arrangements. Both large and small parathyroid cysts are not infrequent in these hybrids.

Figures 5 and 6 illustrate sections of the parathyroid glands from two $F_2$ brothers, 1313 ♂ and 1312 ♂. Figure 5, from 1313 ♂, shows a few clear sinusoidal spaces near the top and to the right. Conspicuous dark masses of different sizes are scattered throughout this section and careful examination shows these to be congested masses of cells with dull blue staining granular cytoplasm, a more pronounced expression of the streaks and masses of dull blue cells seen in other glands. The nuclei in these masses are closely packed in all directions, and while in thin sections only one or two levels of principal cell nuclei can be seen, several layers may be detected in these congested cell groups. A definite interpretation of such arrangements is difficult to offer. It is probable, but not entirely certain, that the cellular masses are to be classed as bluish staining rather than principal cell types. A study of the history and condition of the animal from which this section was derived does not furnish any valuable suggestions. This dog was killed as a young adult of 2 years, and the fresh glands were carefully fixed for sectioning at the same time as those from the brother, 1312 ♂, which furnished the parathyroid section in figure 6. The thyroids from these two animals, shown in plate 93 (figs. 5 and 6), were both fairly well fixed and are quite similar in pattern. Such dark bluish masses of cells in the parathyroid have been seen by other authors and are not to be dismissed simply as artefact due to the technique.

The $F_2$ hybrid 1313 ♂ was a short legged bassethound-like animal weighing 20 kilograms and with very little thymus glandular tissue. The brother, 1312 ♂, weighed more than 30 kilograms and was of St. Bernard type with long legs. In his case an unusually large mass of glandular thymic tissue was present. In these hybrids, an acidophilic condition of the pituitary is associated with an enlarged thymus. The parathyroids from these two hybrid brothers are very different, and yet it is impossible to satisfactorily associate their histologic pictures with the peculiar type differences between them.

Photomicrographs of three other $F_2$ bassethound-bulldog parathyroid glands at slightly higher magnification are shown in plate 98. These sections illustrate in a more pronounced manner several of the conditions mentioned above. Figure 1, from 918 ♀, shows the strong expression of circles and whorls formed by excessive twisting of the cellular cords about the capillaries. The more usual arrangement of serpentine cords of double rows of cells is less abundant. The adult animal from which this gland was taken is largely hound typed although it possessed the screw-tail of the bulldog, as seen in plates 19 and 20 (pp. 97 and 99). A parathyroid section from a litter brother, 916 ♂, is illustrated in figure 2. Here again circles and whorls of the principal cells are unusually marked, and irregular masses of bluish cells are indicated by the dark spots near the periphery. The cellular and vascular appearances in these two parathyroid sections are almost identical in detail, and yet the $F_2$ hybrid brother and sister from which they came were widely different in physical type. The brother, 916 ♂, was strongly bulldog in type with a heavy head and body and stocky, wide spread legs; this animal is shown from life in plate 19, and its skeleton in plate 20. The tall, hound-like, graceful body of the sister, 918 ♀, is widely contrasted with the bulldog-like brother. Certainly these particular differences in physical types have no perceptible indication in the closely identical histologic patterns presented by the parathyroid glands.

Figure 3 in plate 98 illustrates the probable embryonic nature of a large irregularly outlined cyst of branchial epithelium. A distinct connective tissue coat surrounds the epithelial wall, and the long more-or-less straight double row cords of principal cells definitely radiate from the wall of the cyst as if they were formed by columns of growth away from the branchial epithelial base. As the periphery is approached, toward the left part of the section, the cords are separated by sinusoidal dilations of the capillaries. Darkly stained bluish cells are shown in irregular groups in the vicinity of the sinusoids. This parathyroid gland was obtained from $F_2$ bassethound-bulldog hybrid 902 ♀ when a mature adult of 1½ years. The bitch had short bassethound legs and a slightly bulldog-like head with undershot lower jaw. There

PLATE 98
EXPLANATION OF FIGURES

Bassethound English bulldog cross. Further details of parathyroid histological pattern in second generation hybrids.

1 918 ♀.  2 916 ♂.  3 902 ♀.

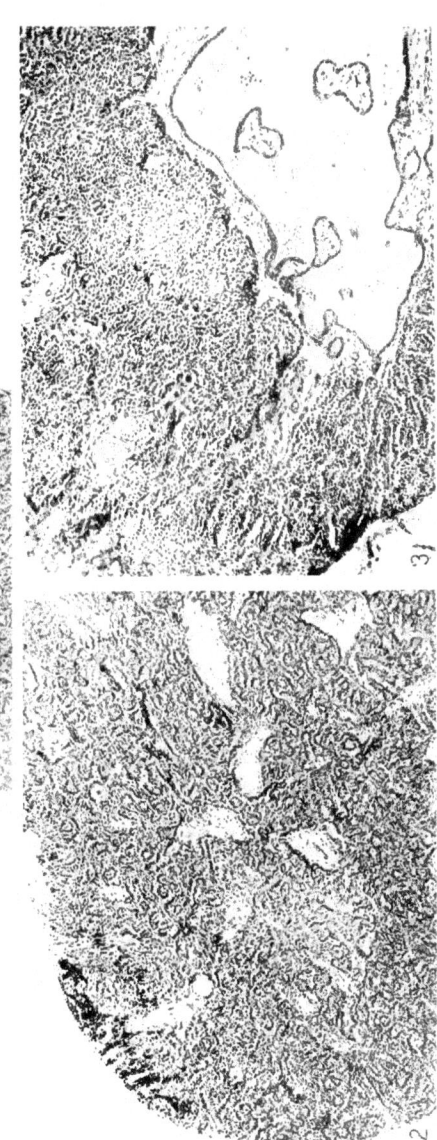

was moderate internal hydrocephalus which is frequent in those brains of the shape associated with the bulldog typed head.

The modified nature of the thyroid gland in this bitch, 902 ♀, is illustrated in plate 94 (fig. 4). Her pituitary gland presented an abnormal predominance of acidophilic cells, having a distorted ratio of about 100 acidophiles to one basophile.

If we compare the conditions just discussed in these basset-hound-bulldog parathyroids with those previously considered for the dwarf Boston terrier-dachshund hybrids (plates 91 and 92), surprisingly few histologic differences can be found. Probably the most definite difference between these two groups is the much less frequent presence of sinusoidal capillaries and spaces in the Boston terrier-dachshund parathyroids. The principal cells and their patterns of arrangement, as well as the occurrence and position of the bluish staining cells, are much the same in both breed crosses, and the cystic conditions and symptoms of arrested development are confined to neither group. The failure to discover more pronounced and consistent modifications in parathyroid histology among these highly distorted and widely different breed types merely indicates the difficulty of establishing a definite histopathology in a simple and rather homogeneous endocrine gland as contrasted with the striking differences in microscopic patterns presented by the thyroid and pituitary glands.

We have finally to proceed with the consideration of the histologic nature of the endocrine glands in the cross between the giant great Dane and the acromegalic typed giant St. Bernard in order to secure a final broad comparison among the giant, the normal sized and the dwarfed breed types. The necessarily opposite growth deviations from the normal in the production of giant and dwarf reactions should be readily associated with widely contrasted patterns of pituitary, thyroid and parathyroid glands if the secretions from these glands are to be considered the mechanisms through which the degree and type of growth are determined.

# SECTION VI

W. T. JAMES

# MORPHOLOGICAL FORM AND ITS RELATION TO BEHAVIOR

## A STUDY OF THE BEHAVIOR OF PURE BREED AND HYBRID DOGS BY CONDITIONED SALIVARY AND MOTOR REACTIONS

### INTRODUCTION

In the foregoing sections the significance of the genetic constitution and its relation to endocrine influences in the determination of development have been considered in different types of dogs. The organism has been treated as a developing entity, and the genetic and endocrine factors have been studied in their relation to the morphological form resulting from their integration. One of the most significant things about a living organism, however, is its activity, or responsiveness to external stimuli, and no study on constitution would be complete without a consideration of this phase of the problem.

The author wishes to express appreciation for the aid and advice of Dr. Charles R. Stockard during the course of these experiments. His continued encouragement and suggestions led to the classification of the complicated behavioral data presented here. It is hoped that the material reported will play some part in emphasizing the significance of treating behavior in relation to constitution.

The relationship between an organism and its environment after birth is dominated by the action of the nervous system, and this action is dependent on and related to the activity of every other part of the body. This means that a harmonious relationship must exist between the nervous system and bodily organs, including the endocrine glands, before an adequate adjustment can result from their integration.

The relationship between these factors begins long before the nervous system becomes the dominant influence in directing the actions of the body. The basis of the complicated network of nervous centers and connecting fibers is established early in the developing embryo. The refined differentiations within the nervous tissue, although they have a genetic basis, are dependent on the proper chemical balance of the blood. This has been demonstrated in many cases in which the endocrine glands have failed to react properly, resulting not only in a deficient bodily structure but also in deficient mental ability. A typical example of this is the retarded development of the cretin, which is due to insufficient thyroid secretion. If injections of thyroid material are given at an early stage of development, the organism will continue its growth processes, and normal bodily structure will result. The deficiency of other glands, the pituitary, parathyroid, testes, etc., also bring about physical deformities and behavior modifications.

Although typical deficiencies may be shown for a specific glandular abnormality, the normal action of the glands differs for different constitutions. The action of a gland is related to the genetic constitution of the particular organism, i.e., the glandular secretion does not affect every organism in the same manner. It has been shown that the patterning of the genetic factors affects the relationship between glands and form, and every other part of the organism is in turn related to the pattern of these factors. The behavior, which is dependent on nervous action in relation to every other part of the body, is one vital part of this complex. Since the organisms differ in form and glands, they should also have significant behavioral differences. In fact it has been recognized generally for centuries that the different physical types among humans have characteristic psychological qualities. It is due to this that so much attention has been given in recent years to the constitutional reactions of different types among humans.

In this consideration, three points of view have been prominent, depending on whether emphasis is placed on form, glands, or psychological qualities. Whatever the point of view, there has always been some recognition of the fact that each is related to, and integrated with, the others. In regard to the psychological qualities of different constitutions, it may be said that the work of Kretschmer ('25) has given the greatest impetus to experimental studies. Kretschmer's classification of human subjects into pyknics, asthenics, and athletics, with the psychological qualities and psychotic tendencies of each, led to many other studies on classification of normal and abnormal types. Such experiments have attempted to substantiate Kretschmer's theory, to arrive at a more definite method of isolating the types, or to contrast specific performances of the types which have been isolated among definite groups of individuals. A large variety of subjects has been employed, including hospital patients, criminals, college students, and children. We do not intend to give an extensive resumé of these works here; a brief review of such studies will impress one with the wide divergence in results.

There is disagreement not only in how the types differ, but also in the indices used to classify them. Wertheimer and Hesketh ('26) were able to separate hospital patients into two types, pyknics and asthenics, but found that most individuals are mixed types which distribute themselves on a graded series between the two extremes. In a study with college students, Klineberg, Asch and Block ('34), who used methods of classifying the types and applied many tests to each, could find no reliable qualitative differences among the types isolated. A number of tests were used to measure and compare specific behavioral patterns, but a criticism of the specific tests method is that it fails to determine the basic differences between the types. Aware of this criticism, Cabot ('38), who worked with adolescent boys, employed a variety of personality patterns in comparing the types as isolated by Kretschmer. He did not find the pyknosomes and leptosomes significantly different, but did find the athletosomes and leptosomes, classified together by Kretschmer, to be quite dissimilar. Cabot then studied the subjects which showed the widest physical differences and concluded that the athletic type had a distinct advantage in social adjustment. From this he postulates a theory of socio-biological advantage in terms of which socio-sthenic traits, or personality characteristics, are associated with a biologically good physique. In other words, as far as the personality traits investigated are concerned, those subjects with the best physiques were judged as having definite advantages over other members of a group.

All writers agree that there are differences among individuals, but there is great confusion as to the nature of these differences and how to determine them. The human subject is too complicated, too mixed genetically, and involves too many factors beyond control to be used in an analysis of the bases of such differences. Offering more promise of an understanding of the problem would be a study of psychological variations among animals, especially if the particular animal to be studied offered wide differences in both physique and behavior. The interdependence of morphological, neurophysiological, and psychological factors can be specifically determined only by experimental treatment and genetic control of the individual.

Since a good deal is known about the morphological and endocrinological side of constitution in the dog, it would be of special interest to investigate the psychological aspect. In this way, we may be able to isolate the significant organismal factor for psychological differentiation of types among the human, or at least to arrive at some understanding of the difficulties found in analyzing them.

Throughout the earlier sections of this book, references have been made to the general behavior differences among dogs. Close observation will contrast the active nature and overt movements of the German shepherd and Saluki with the inactive and sluggish nature of the bassethound. The two groups of dogs differ not only in general alertness, but also in mode of walking, orienting, and in voice. These dogs have been considered as normal physical types. Other types, however, have abnormal physical tendencies, as for example the giant St. Bernard and great Dane, which also have characteristic behaviors. Again there are midgets among the dog breeds, as among humans, and these likewise have definite behavioral tendencies. The active nervous nature and high voice of the Pomeranian poodle are suggestive of certain performances of human midgets. Some dogs are known for their friendly aggressiveness, and still others for their independence.

Just as the study of physical form and glandular conditions among the dogs was based on animals showing the widest differences in these characters, so a study of behavior can best be analyzed by using animals showing the widest differences in behavioral characteristics. It is among these types that the specific behavioral qualities are most easily differentiated.

*Method.* The program of research reported here involved a comparison of the performances of a large number of dogs whose reactions were observed in the same situation from day to day. Needless to say, the control of the situation and the method employed were of utmost importance. The experimental environment had to be the same for each dog, and the performance, considered as a sample of what the organism was doing, had to involve the same reaction systems. The conditioned reflex method, used throughout these experiments, offered an accurate control of these factors. In this method the performance of one effector, whether it be the salivary gland or a group of muscles, is the focus or center of the behavior under observation. This performance serves only as the basis of interpretation of what the organism is doing. It has already been shown in the experiments of Pavlov that this method emphasizes behavior differences among dogs. Although Pavlov ('27) indicated some of these differences, he placed no emphasis on their relationship to specific breeds, nor did he attempt to study their significance in relation to morphological characteristics of the animals.

The particular behavioral characteristics to be reported here involve the adjustment to food taking, in which the conditioned salivary response was recorded, and a definite conditioned avoiding reaction of the foreleg. The salivary reaction involves a more or less involuntary performance of the organism, while the motor reaction involves a wide range of neuromuscular patterns, and thus constitutes a voluntary action.

Within each reflex system there is some degree of quantification. Each one also has distinct qualitative aspects that are significant and will receive emphasis throughout the report. The latter is concerned with the manner in which a function runs its course, the changes throughout its progress, and the end result. The same environment does not affect all dogs in the same manner. There is a difference in the reaction to the stimulus and in the total organismal changes correlated with the reaction. There is, for example, great diversity in the degree of emotional disturbance shown by the dogs, and greater variability among some than among others. These variations, although difficult to measure, are very significant. The specific behaviors are used only as an indicator of the total behavioral complex. No one aspect of the salivary or motor reaction is more important than another. Pavlov analyzed the conditioned reflex phenomena. In the present experiments the interest is rather in how the reflex phenomena perform as a unified pattern, and how they differ among the dogs and in the total behavioral picture of each dog. It was considered of interest also to determine, if possible, whether those animals differing widely in behavior also had distinct physical peculiarities.

Although it was known that the dogs exhibited many different forms of behavior in the kennel, the experiments were started without a preconceived plan for their classification. Dogs of different breeds and physical types were trained under identical conditions, and they then classified themselves. By this plan a more natural means of segregation was evolved.

*The experimental situation and equipment.* The laboratory in which the experiments were conducted is relatively free from extraneous disturbance. It is situated in a basement with concrete walls, floor, and ceiling, and, as an added protection from accessory stimulation, the animal room was enclosed by a double celotex wall containing a dead air space between the partitions. Figure 1 of plate 99 shows the two rooms of the laboratory. An observation window of two plates of heavy glass was placed in the wall between the animal room and the experimental room. All communication between the rooms was made electrically or by means of quiet mechanical apparatus. The movements of the dogs were recorded by light strings running from the head and leg of the animal to recording levers on a kymograph. These recording strings passed from the animal room to the experimental room by means of small copper tubing.

During the experiments the animal was confined by a harness to the platform of a food table. On this table was a revolving aluminum disk 26 inches in diameter, and six pans were placed equal distances apart on the disk. As figure 2 (pl. 99) shows, the table is surrounded by a frame so that only one pan is visible to the dog at any one time. The disk is rotated by a pull on a rope around the axis and is stopped by a rubber cushioned brake which is released by a wire like the choke control on an automobile. One empty pan is before the dog at the beginning of the experiment, and five pans of food may be presented without entering the animal room.

The apparatus employed to measure the saliva is a modification of that used by Pavlov. The Lashley cup, consisting of two chambers, one for collecting saliva and the other for maintaining a negative pressure to hold the cup over the parotid fistula, has proved satisfactory. A small rubber tube runs from the inner or saliva chamber to a manometer in the experimental room. The manometer is a 1 millimeter tube graduated in hundredths of a cubic centimeter, and the

PLATE 99

1 Observation and animal room of the laboratory.   2 Animal platform and food table.

reading is based on an increase in air pressure in the closed system. After each reading, the manometer is returned to zero by releasing the pressure. A diagrammatic representation of the saliva recording arrangement is shown in text-figure 85 (fig. 1).

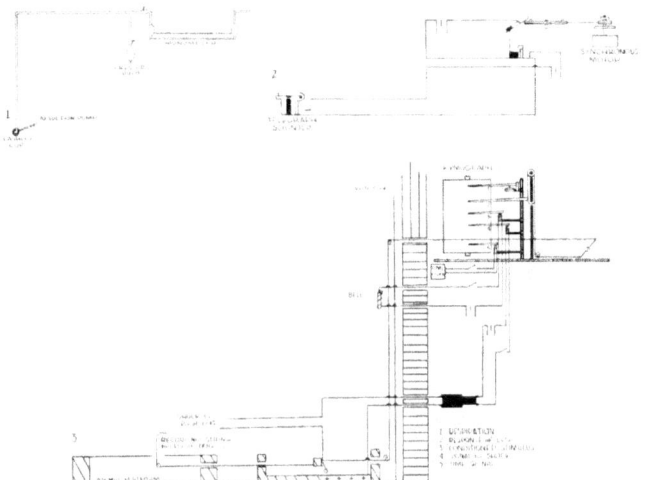

Text figure 85. (1) Diagram of the salivary recording apparatus. (2) Diagram of the apparatus used to produce clicking sounds of variable frequency. (3) Diagram of the shock avoiding apparatus. A string leading from the roller is fastened to the leg of the dog. As the leg is raised the roller is pulled left and breaks the electric circuit to the electrodes.

Since we were interested in the animals' general mode of behavior rather than in their ability to differentiate between stimuli, highly refined signals were not necessary. The most important factor was that the signal offer a satisfactory stimulus subject to simple control. A telegraph clicker was found to answer these needs. The positive signal in every case was a clicking rate of 120 beats per minute. The negative rates varied from 18 to 98 beats per minute, and in most cases a rate of 50 was used. The clicker sounds were made by a regular telegraph sounder activated by a controlled commutator from the experimental room (see text-fig. 85, fig. 2). The speed of the commutator could be varied by placing wheels of different diameters on the synchronous motor operating it. In addition to the clicker, other auditory signals, including a bell, buzzer and whistles, were used. All were of the regular commercial type with no form of refinement.

Tactile stimuli were presented by the same method as that used by Pavlov. A cup containing a small balloon studded with prickers (blunt metal points) was fastened to the skin of the dog. When the balloon was expanded, the prickers pressed against the skin. The mechanism was controlled from the experimental room by means of an atomizer bulb and tube.

Olfactory stimuli were used with some of the best balanced dogs. In most cases the odor of vanilla signalled the food. The vanilla was enclosed in a bottle with one tube leading from the bottle to the lower jaw of the animal, and another to the experimental room. By placing air pressure on the tube in the experimental room, the odor of vanilla was presented.

The specific motor response used in the experiments involved the avoiding movement of the foreleg to an electric shock. The electrodes were applied to the wrist. A Harvard inductorium was used and the strength of the shock evaluated in the units indicated on that apparatus. The complete avoiding method was employed, that is, the dog avoided the shock by breaking the circuit to the electrode when the leg was raised. The circuit was broken by a sliding contact switch activated by a string from the leg of the dog. A diagram of this apparatus is shown in figure 3, text-figure 85.

During the experiments, records of the reactions of each animal were made on a kymograph. The record includes the salivary and motor reactions, breathing changes, and head movements. Typical graphs of each dog were photographed for permanent records.[3]

[3] The photographs of the records were made before the paper was fixed by shellac. In this way all highlights were eliminated. Eastman process film was used and developed in the high contrast developer D9.

## ANALYSIS OF BEHAVIOR IN THE CONDITIONED FOOD TAKING SITUATION

These experiments were conducted to determine the range of behavior among the dogs in a food taking situation. From an observation of the animals under kennel conditions, wide differences in behavior were readily noted, and members of the first group selected for study were pure bred animals showing most obvious contrasts. Hybrid offspring of these dogs were also trained; and then others were chosen for a variety of reasons.

From the point of view of the observer, the conditioned food taking performance may be divided into definite patterns of action. The dog must first become acquainted with the experimenter and learn to lead on a leash. Next, it must become accustomed to the laboratory, the cup for recording saliva, the pneumograph, and the apparatus used to record postural movements. When the dog has become sufficiently familiar with the laboratory to take food, the conditioning signal is applied.

In the beginning, the signal is given simultaneously with the presentation of food. The performance at this time may be considered a series of excitatory and inhibitory phases and is represented graphically as follows:

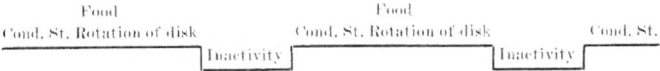

This procedure is repeated a number of times. When the food is then withheld for a few seconds after the signal is presented, the conditioned salivary reaction appears. In contrast to the above diagram this performance is represented as follows:

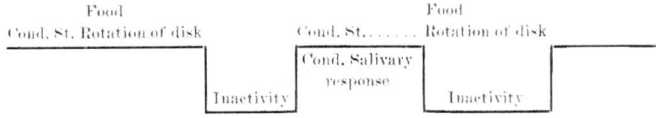

The conditioned salivary reaction seems, therefore, to be one observable factor of the total organismal reaction to food.

It is apparent that the behavior in this experimental condition is mainly one of restraint. As soon as the dog enters the room, activity is decreased, and the only real excitatory factor after the animal is placed in the harness is food. The animal responds to the signal only because it is presented with food. If the food is delayed each time, the food taking reaction and the conditioned saliva also develop along latent period in most dogs. From the biological point of view, food is the only significant part of the environment, and the salivary reaction alone is biologically of small import compared with other reaction systems. It may be for this reason that the response is so subject to inhibition. By presenting the signal and food together, however, and then occasionally delaying the food, we get an indication of the dog's nervous reactions. In this way the animal remains in the process of adjustment longer than would be the case were food delayed every time; and thus, as the experiment progresses, an opportunity is afforded to study the phases of excitation as indicated by the saliva and the inhibition of this reaction.

In most cases, the negative signal, or a second signal without food, was not presented until the nature of the positive reaction had been determined. The negative was introduced to indicate the intensity of the organismal setting for the food, and the ease or difficulty with which this functional system could be modified. In order to be certain that the same general behavioral pattern as in the response to the positive signal would be involved, the telegraph clicker was also used as the negative signal, but with a different frequency (positive 120; negative 50 or above). It had been determined by preliminary experiments that if the second signal differed widely from the first, the original behavioral pattern would not be involved, that is, the tendency would be toward orientation or escape rather than to the food pan.

The adjustment of the animal to the negative signal would, of course, require that it remain inactive during the sounding. This behavior is represented graphically as follows:

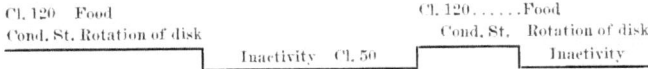

From four to six conditioning signals were given simultaneously with food every day. One signal of 30 seconds duration was applied to determine the value of the response for that period, and this value was measured in hundredths cubic centimeters by the manometer. It was found that as a general rule the response to the second signal of the day was the most vigorous, and this response therefore determined the value of the reaction. This procedure was varied from time to time so that the dog would not become accustomed to the order of the test signal. A typical daily procedure is shown in the record for animal 740 ♂, an English bulldog-bassethound $F_1$, dated May 3, 1933 (table 5).

TABLE 5
*Dog 740 ♂*

| STIMULUS | DURATION | LATENT PERIOD | VALUE OF RESPONSE |
|---|---|---|---|
| 75 cl. 120 | 3 sec. | .... | 0 reinforced with food |
| 76 cl. 120 | 30 sec. | 6 sec. | 4 reinforced with food |
| 77 cl. 120 | 3 sec. | .... | 0 reinforced with food |
| 18 cl. 50 | 30 sec. | .... | 0 not reinforced |
| 78 cl. 120 | 3 sec. | .... | 0 reinforced with food |

In this dog the only reactions of interest from the point of view of the conditioned salivary performance are the second and fourth, the former to the positive signal, and the latter to the negative. The response to the short signals are, of course, zero, since the salivary reaction did not have time to begin before food was presented. The experiments usually ended with a positive signal.

When the experiments were started it was thought that the value of the conditioned salivary reaction alone could be used as the criterion for behavioral type. Many difficulties appear, however, in dealing with this reaction, especially when a large number of dogs are studied. In the first place, many of the animals do not form the conditioned salivary response, yet observation of their behavior during the procedure gives some indication of their nature. In addition, variations in size among the dogs must be taken into consideration. Some small animals having many characteristics of the excitable dog, give comparatively less salivary reaction than would a larger animal of the same type, since the small animal consumes less food, resulting in a correspondingly weaker unconditioned salivary secretion.

Although the salivary reaction itself is significant in a classification of types, an additional important factor is the modification in behavior during the course of the performance, from the beginning to what may be termed the logical end. Thus, the elimination of unnecessary response, substitution and correlation of action, changes in the emotional aspect of the performance, etc., and all factors involved in habituation are significant modifications. Because of the novel situation in the laboratory, each dog begins the training above its normal outdoor level of excitability. As the adjustment progresses, numerous conditioned and unconditioned patterns of action appear, until finally a normal level of action is reached. When there is a minimum of change from day to day, the training may be said to have reached its logical end. The dogs differ when this point is reached, just as at the beginning of the training. In some cases, by the time 150 conditioning signals have been applied, the dog has completed his performance and reached a level of habituation and stereotyped performance. In others, it occurs in less than 100 applications of the signal. Other dogs never reach the point at which they react in a definite, habitual, and stereotyped manner even though over 300 conditioning signals have been applied. These differences did not take on a proper perspective until a large number of animals had been studied. Behavioral type is a relative matter, and can be determined only by comparing many dogs in the same situation.

In line with the studies of Pavlov, dogs have been classified as inhibitable or excitable, depending on their reaction under experimental conditions, and the terms excitation and inhibition have been used to apply specifically to action of the nervous system. Our observations are in agreement with the findings that dogs classify themselves into two widely different behavioral types, but the terms used to designate each group should refer to a general configuration of the total organism rather than to nervous action alone. The excitable dogs, as will become clear in the present work, not only have a more intense nervous action than the inhibited dogs, but there are indications that all their bodily processes are more intense in nature. An example of this is their higher metabolism. In the present experiments, therefore, the dogs will be designated as highly active and extremely lethargic types. For purposes of convenience and clearness, the lethargic class will be called group A, while the highly active will be classified as group B. The dogs falling between these polar types will be classified as intermediates and indicated as A-plus and B-minus, signifying that they are nearer the A or B polar group yet show certain differences which prevent them from being classified in these groups. At present our interest is in behavior rather than breed, and for this reason the types of behavior isolated will be discussed without emphasis on the breed of dog characteristic of each.

### Characteristics of the Lethargic Mode of Performance, Group A

A total of fifty-two animals have been studied in the experiments, and of this number thirty-nine were trained in the conditioned food taking situation. Of the thirty-nine trained, thirty-six were able to make a satisfactory adjustment. Eleven of these fall into the sluggish and inactive group, including the following: four bassethounds, 1426 ♂, 1427 ♀, 83 ♀, and 219 ♂; two dogs which were predominantly dachshund in inheritance, 335 ♀ and 148 ♀; two dachshund-Boston terrier $F_1$s,

127 ♀ and 128 ♂ ; one bassethound-German shepherd $F_2$, 863 ♂ ; and two bassethound-English bulldog $F_2$s, 979 ♂ and 980 ♂.

The animals of this group make friends with the experimenter in a short time. They learn to lead on a leash in 2 or 3 days, and in some cases on the first day. Although there is a tendency for all dogs to withdraw when first approached, this lethargic type does not become excited or hysterical.

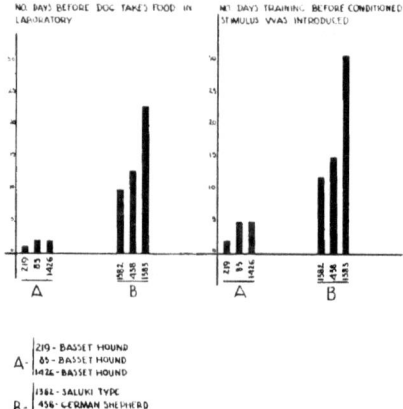

A - { 219 - BASSET HOUND
       65 - BASSET HOUND
       1426 - BASSET HOUND

B - { 1362 - SALUKI TYPE
       456 - GERMAN SHEPHERD
       1383 - SALUKI TYPE

Text-figure 86

After the training begins, they soon learn to run to the gate when the experimenter approaches, and readily become willing workers. The dogs of this group are not greatly disturbed when first brought into the conditioned reflex laboratory. There is no struggle against the harness and they appear able to restrain themselves in every way. The average dogs of the group take food after 2 day's training, and the conditioning signal may be applied in 5 days (text-fig. 86). When the training has progressed to the point where the conditioning signal is introduced, the animals go into the laboratory ahead of the trainer and voluntarily take their places before the food pan.

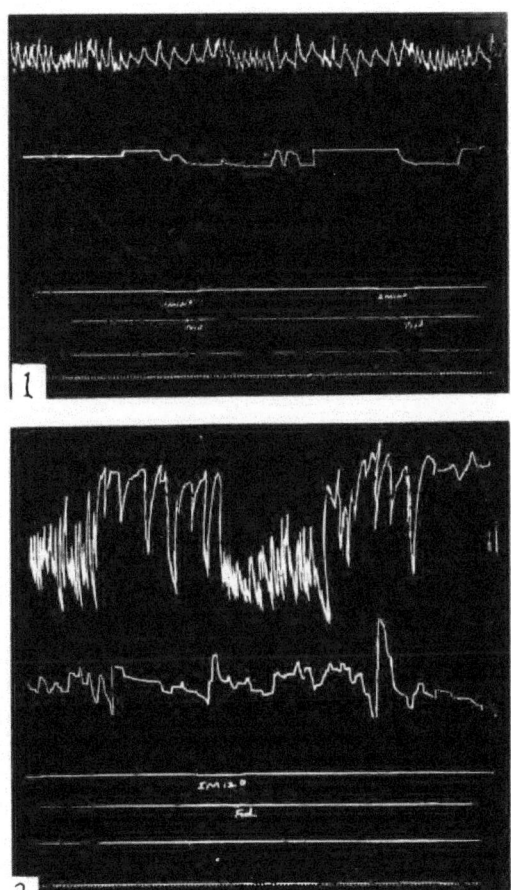

Text figure 87. — 1. Mild reaction of type A, the inactive group, to the first conditioning signal. 2. Record of the disturbing effect of the first conditioning signal on the animals of group B. There is a sudden orientation to the sound and a change in breathing.

At this stage of the experiment the animal stands quietly before the pan, holding the head in a fixed position. It is not disturbed by the first presentation of the mild clicker signal, and there is, in fact, little noticeable reaction (see text-fig. 87, fig. 1). After the initial presentation of food with the signal, however, increased activity accompanies subsequent signals. The first conditioned action is an orientation movement of the head to the pan. This movement is slow and deliberate. The next conditioned performance, or a further analysis of the total pattern of action, is the conditioned saliva. The conditioned postural reactions appear after ten to twenty applications of the signal, while the salivary response may appear after ten to forty applications (text-fig. 88).

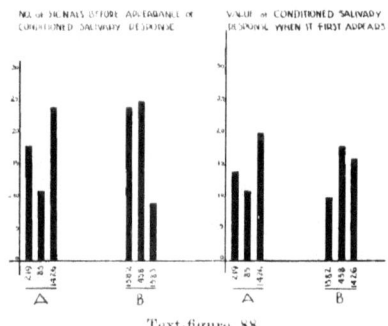

Text-figure 88

When the test signal is given, the dog places the head over the pan and holds it steadily until food is presented. The postural reactions are specific and directed. However, many changes occur as the experiments progress, and it is the direction and nature of these, together with the inert state which they reach, which differentiates the animals of A from those of B.

Although individuality is shown in the behavior of the dogs of group A, the course of the performance and the end products are the same in every case. The behavior charts of animals 83 ♀ and 219 ♂, both bassethounds, will indicate the common tendencies among the members of the group (text-figs. 89 and 90). The black lines show the value of the conditioned salivary reaction to the 30 second test signal for each experimental period. The negative signals are indicated by markings below the zero line. The blank spaces on the chart, which are not marked below the zero line, indicate that there was no salivary reaction to the positive signal.

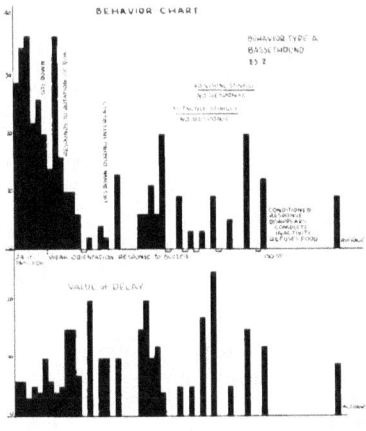

Text-figure 89

Only the reactions to the positive test signal and the negative are presented here. The lower chart indicates the delay, or the time between the presentation of the signal and the beginning of the flow of saliva. As we have pointed out above, four or five stimuli of short duration were given each day, but since they were not continued long enough before reinforcement for a conditioned reaction to occur, they are not included in the charts. At the lower left corner of each chart the number of signals given before the development of a conditioned reaction is shown. At the right of each chart the total number of clicker signals presented is indicated. This is important, since some dogs become completely inactive within a relatively short time, while others remain active indefinitely. Each chart indicates a course of performance which may be considered the result of interaction of the laboratory environment and the organism. The salivary reaction is the only factor considered quantitatively. Change

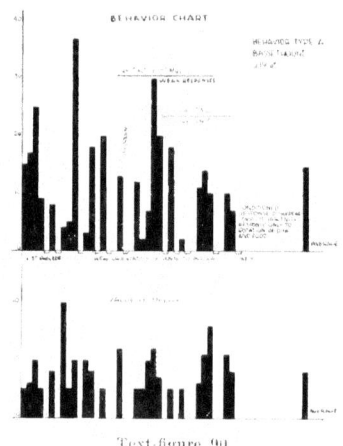

Text-figure 90

occurs not only in this reaction but also in the total performance. These modifications may be considered a progression of activity which takes place in the dog's adjustment to the food taking situation.

As indicated in the chart of animal 83 ♀ (text-fig. 89), in the beginning the reaction is relatively intense. The situation is new to the dog and the animal has not yet become adjusted to the laboratory. During this period the dog orients to the food pan when the conditioned signal starts; it is alert and remains in a standing position. As the chart clearly shows, the responses of this dog make a gradual descent, decreasing in intensity, becoming irregular, and finally dis-

# GENETIC TYPE AND THE ENDOCRINES

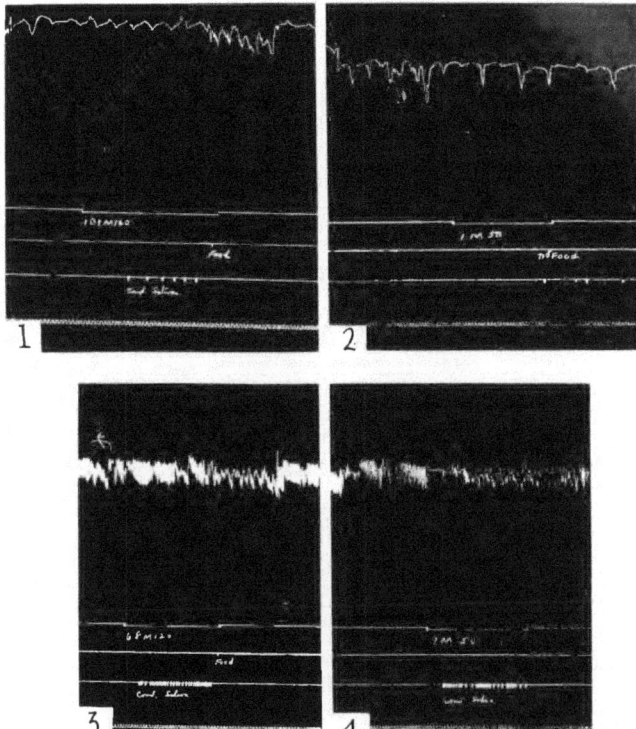

Text figure 91. (1) Characteristic record of the conditioned salivary reaction to the signal in the animals of group A before the onset of inhibition. (2) Absence of response in animals of group A to the first negative signal. Reading from top to bottom, lines indicate: breathing; presentation of signal; presentation of food; conditioned saliva; time in seconds. (3) Vigorous conditioned salivary reaction obtained in animals of group B. The response is characterized by a short latent period and vigorous secretion of saliva. (4) Response of the active group B to the first negative signal. As a rule this is as large as that given to the positive signal.

appearing altogether. As this decrease in intensity of the salivary response occurs, the reaction becomes longer delayed. A typical kymographic record of the reaction of this dog is shown in text-figures 91 (figs. 1 and 2), and 92 (fig. 1).

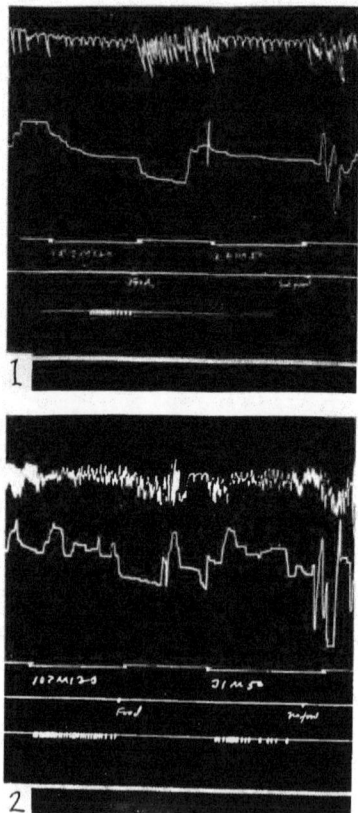

Text-figure 92. Graphic records of types A and B, including head movement (as indicated by second line from top) during the positive and negative signals. The movements of type A are deliberate and directed; those of type B are variable, alternating toward and away from the pan as the signal continues.

Finally the animal responds to the rotation of the disk and food rather than to the conditioning signal, and at this stage the dog sits down or sags against the harness and quietly waits. A typical example of the animal in this stage is shown in plate 100 (fig. 1). It seems that the organism is eliminating useless actions, making short cuts, and retaining only the movements essential for taking food. Spontaneous activity, which is low even in the beginning, is reduced to zero. By the time 150 conditioning signals, including thirty-eight test signals, had been given, the conditioned response disappeared altogether, and, unless the dog was starved, it would lie down and remain passive, as shown in plate 100 (fig. 2). The dog had now reached what may be termed the logical end of the performance. She fully comprehended the laboratory situation. She had learned that food comes with the rotation of the disk, and waited for this during both the test and short signals. Thus the dog no longer performed in a definite stimulus-response manner, even though the same experimental conditions were maintained. Even after the conditioned response disappears, however, the animal will go into the laboratory ahead of the trainer and remain alert while the apparatus is adjusted; then as soon as the experimenter leaves the room, the dog assumes her passive state.

At the beginning of the experiments, these dogs are in their most active phase and the variation in the performance is toward inactivity and sluggishness. Only when the bodily processes are functioning at their highest level can these dogs be aroused to conditioned action in a quiet environment.

*Reactions of the lethargic group to negative signals.* The records for animal 83 ♀ show that there was no response to the negative signals (text-fig. 91, fig. 2; text-fig. 92, fig. 1). These dogs became so passive under laboratory conditions that hardly had the negative been introduced when the inhibition advanced. Since they failed to respond to the clicker of fifty vibrations per minute, it was thought that they might be a good type to use in differentiation experiments. In the

PLATE 100

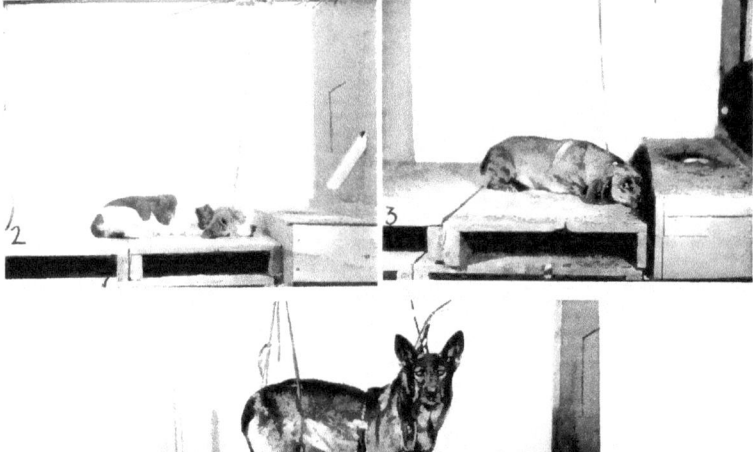

1  Position assumed by the animals of group A in the early stages of the experiments.
2  Position assumed by the animals of group A in later stages after the conditioned response has become inhibited.
3  The dachshund type, an animal of group A, which is entirely inhibited under laboratory conditions.
4  An animal of group B, German shepherd, alert and highly active. These dogs continue to give conditioned salivary responses for a long period of time, and become disturbed by repeated presentations of negative signals.

case of animal 83 ♀, however, by the time sixteen negatives had been applied, the positive had disappeared. Similar conditions occurred in all dogs of this group, even if the negative was not presented. Another bassethound, 1426 ♂, is a specific example. The negative signal was withheld in order to determine if the performance in this type of dog would then follow the same course as that of 83 ♀, which it did. It is extremely difficult to determine the limits of analytical ability in these dogs by this method of experimentation.

*Reactions of the lethargic group to intense auditory stimuli.* Since only a mild reaction to the clicker signal was elicited on the first presentation, a loud buzzer or bell was introduced after the performance had advanced to determine the inertia of the nervous actions of defense and orientation. The new signal caused little noticeable reaction and only a slight change in breathing (text-fig. 93, fig. 1). Here again, the dog's habitual mode of reaction in the laboratory is the important factor. By this time the animals are well acquainted with the laboratory, they have had only food in this environment, and they have made all the adjustments necessary. They are unprepared for any change and only a long series of accessory disturbances will arouse them to action. This seems to be based on a narrowing down or concentration of the neural patterns. The reaction in another situation, however, as for example in the outdoor environment, would undoubtedly be quite different.

*Reactions of the lethargic group to other signals.* After the adjustment to the auditory signal had been studied for a period, tactile and visual stimuli were introduced to determine if the reactions would follow the same general procedure. These signals were presented between the clicker signals. A black horizontal line on the charts (text-figs. 89, 90 and later) indicates the experimental periods in which these signals were introduced and the relative number of experimental periods during which they were continued. Animal 83 ♀ did not develop a conditioned reaction either to the tactile or visual signal, but one cannot conclude from this that the

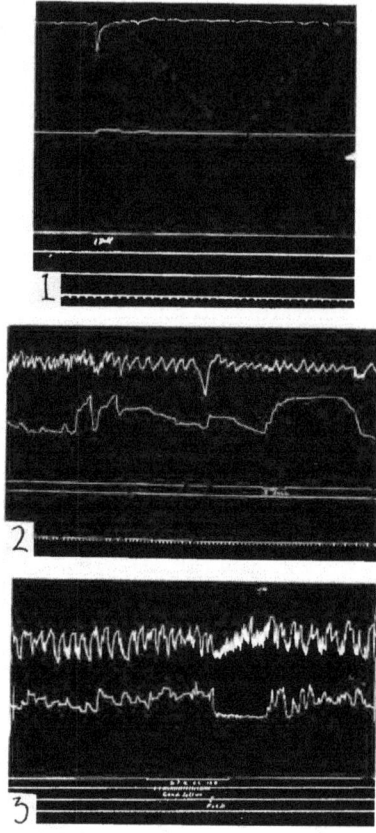

Text-figure 93. (1) Record showing the inertness among the dogs of group A after the period of training in the conditioned food taking situation. There is hardly any noticeable reaction to a bell introduced for the first time in the middle of an experimental period. (2) Record showing the alert and active nature maintained by the animals in group B in the conditioned food taking situation. There is a sudden orientation to a bell introduced for the first time in the middle of an experimental period. (3) A further example of the reactions of group B to the conditioning signal. Note the variable head movements, a short latent period of the conditioned reaction, and the great magnitude of the conditioned saliva.

animal is unable to form conditioned reactions to such stimuli. Under other conditions this animal is able to form both tactile and visual conditioned reactions. It must be remembered that these signals were not introduced until the animal had progressed in the performance of food taking, and had already begun to consider the rotation of the disk and the food as the significant factor. Since the same effector was employed with the tactile and visual stimuli as with the auditory signal, no further adjustment was required. Since no other effector was employed, the animal was not aroused to action but remained in a state of general inhibition. The dog did not become active when the new signals were introduced; this performance begins where the other ended.

A second dog of this group, 219 ♂, formed a weak conditioned reaction to tactile and visual stimuli. When the new stimuli were introduced, however, this animal had not reached the same stage of development in the situation as had animal 83 ♀. The general mode of performance and the end products are the same in both dogs although the exact course differs. With animal 83 ♀ the disappearance of the conditioned response and elimination of movement followed a gradual decrease in intensity. In the case of 219 ♂ the reaction was more abrupt.

Although the majority of the dogs classified in group A formed a conditioned salivary response, in some cases it was weak and continued for a short time only. Two of the dogs, however, reached a state of complete inactivity before forming the conditioned response. They developed a conditioned orientation reaction to the pan, but this reaction was suddenly eliminated, after which the animals attended only to the rotation of the disk. One of these dogs, 336 ♀, a three-quarters dachshund and one-fourth Brussels griffon, is shown in plate 100 (fig. 3). Within a short time they also refused to eat unless deprived of food for 3 days or more. It seemed that these animals were more lethargic in nature than the dogs which formed the conditioned response. The non-essential parts of the performance were eliminated earlier.

while many parts of the performance did not appear as observable reactions. The processes here are no different from those found in the other animals of group A; the difference is one of degree. This is a case in which the conditioned salivary reaction was not an observable factor in the adjustment. The end product, complete inaction, is the same, however, as in the others of group A.

It should be emphasized that the dogs of this group were not frightened into inactivity by the laboratory procedure. They entered the room without hesitation and took their places on the platform even after the response had disappeared. The behavior of these dogs would seem to approximate progressive relaxation in human experience.

In order to show that this was dependent partly on the absence of stimulation and partly on habituation of performance, some of these animals were trained in a salivary situation set up outdoors where they could hear other dogs, the sounds of passing automobiles, and the noises around the experimental station. The animals remained alert, and oriented to the pan when the signals were applied. In every case the conditioned salivary response returned. In this situation the organism was kept in a more excitable state because of the larger number of excitatory channels. This increased nervous excitation led to a heightened activity of all bodily processes, and, consequently, parts of the performance which were inhibited in the quiet room became active. The condition of the organism as affected by the environment is highly significant in interpreting the behavior of all animals.

As will be emphasized later, the dogs also perform in an inactive and inhibited manner when the motor reflexes are used as a basis for the behavioral classification. The quiet environment of the experimental situation, and the reduced stimulation are conducive to inaction, no matter which performance is studied.

*Summary.* The dogs of group A are easy to handle and train. Full cooperation is given, and little resistance is offered to any change that may be introduced. No apparent effort is needed for their adjustment to the laboratory and apparatus and they are content to remain in the room. Following this, the stimuli or signals cause no disturbance, and the dogs appear almost insensitive when the clicker is first applied. Since this signal accompanies food, the food taking reaction is elicited after a few applications, at which time there is a direct orientation movement to the pan as soon as the signal begins. There is a long delay between the beginning of the signal and the flow of saliva. After repeated presentation of the signal with food, the dog disregards the stimulus and waits rather for the rotation of the disk and the appearance of food. Postural movements are also elicited by the rotation of the food table. In reality this is a selection and elimination of patterns of action, and the process may occur gradually, as in the case of animal 83♀, or abruptly, as in the case of 1426♂. The response is not a widely generalized one, as emphasized by the failure to develop a reaction to other signals. After the dogs have reached what is termed the logical end of the adjustment, it is almost impossible to motivate them to further action in the laboratory environment. At this time they appear completely insensitive and show a tendency to remain inactive and unresponsive to variations in the laboratory.

## Characteristics of the Active Mode of Performance, Group B

Five dogs fall into this group, including the following: two bassethound-Saluki $F_2$s, 1382♀ and 1383♀, (these dogs were definitely of the Saluki type, showing no characteristics of the bassethound); two German shepherds, 1285♀ and 438♀; one bassethound-German shepherd $F_2$ 709♂ (with the physical form of the German shepherd).

In contrast to group A, the dogs of this group are slow to make friends with strangers. They have a tendency to become hysterical and must be approached with caution. Only after they are familiar with the trainer can the leash be employed or any effort made to handle them. When the leash is first used, the dogs struggle violently to release themselves. They jump, pull, bite, and whine as if in intense pain, and tremble and withdraw when touched. This intense syndrome is characterized by dilated pupils, rapid breathing, and accelerated heart beat. If the animals have recently been fed, the food is regurgitated. The extremes of the group require as much as 30 days' training before they will accept the leash without hesitation, and even then they must first be cornered in the run. When first taken to the laboratory it is necessary to force them into the room and on to the platform. The animals object to the harness and recording apparatus, and occasionally make hysterical efforts to release themselves. After a few days there is no longer any struggle, but the dogs refuse food until they have been starved for at least 2 or 3 days. It seems that they object to any attempt to fit them into a definite procedure.

A long pre-training period is necessary with the dogs of group B before the conditioning signal can be applied. This is shown in text-figure 86. An eager interest in the location of the sound is apparent when the signal is first introduced. Note the head movements of one of this group in text-figure 87, figure 2. A variety of orientation and investigatory reactions occurs, including head movements and bodily postures, and these continue until the animal is thoroughly familiar with the stimulus. At first the dog refuses food presented with the signal, but when once the food is accepted, a conditioned orientation to the pan soon appears. The number of applications of the signal before the development of the conditioned salivary response does not differ greatly from that found for the dogs of group A (text-fig. 88). When the signal begins, the dog moves the head over the pan quickly, and continues to move it back and forth as long as the signal sounds. This is illustrated in text-figure 93 (fig. 3) showing the typical reaction of one of the dogs of group B to the conditioning signal. At times these animals cock the head and fixate the pan. Tail wagging and other postural movements are correlated with the head movement. After the food is eaten they remain active and alert.

The behavior charts (text-figs. 94 and 95) of German shepherd 438 ♀ and a Saluki-bassethound F₂ 1382 ♀ are typical of this group. As the chart for 438 ♀ shows, the magnitude of the reaction at the beginning of the experiment is no greater than that of animal 83 ♀ (text-fig. 89). As a rule there was a short delay of the conditioned reaction, as shown

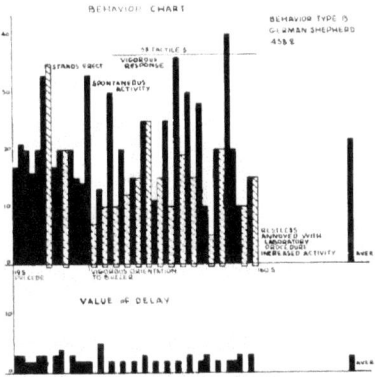

Text-figure 94

in text-figures 91 (fig. 3) and 92 (fig. 2). The response was intense, and did not dwindle and disappear but remained at its maximum value until an undue restlessness appeared in the animal. Since there is a continuation of the conditioned salivary reaction, the average of the response is larger than that of the animals of group A. Thus these animals retained a high level of activity. The short cuts made by the dogs of group A do not appear. The end product is also quite different in that the animals of group B do not settle down to a definite mode of performance. Spontaneous undirected movements occur at all times, and it is always necessary to use the harness lest the dogs leave the platform.

Plate 100 (fig. 4) shows a dog of this group whose alertness will be instantly noticed. They apparently have an excess of energy which must be released, either through directed movements to definite signals or undirected movements to non-specific signals. The significance of this will be more apparent when we compare the general activity of the two groups later in this study.

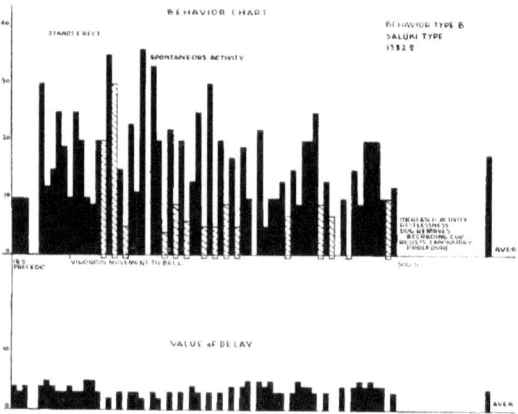

Text-figure 95

*Reactions of the active group to negative signals.* We have stated above that if the negative signal differs widely from the positive signal, there is no tendency for the food taking reaction to occur. It must be remembered also that thus far no other effector system has been employed. These two factors must be kept in mind in order to understand the behavior of the dogs.

Animal 438 ♀ and others of group B usually gave as large a salivary reaction to the negative as to the positive. The reaction to the negative is shown by the striped lines on the behavioral chart (text-fig. 94). This is illustrated also in the kymograph records of the reaction to the first negative in text-figure 91 (fig. 4). The nervous setting in the dogs of group B is more intense than for those of group A, and the nervous reactions in group B are released more quickly. Let us consider dog 438 ♀ in the experimental situation. The nervous setting for the food reaction is shown by her orientation to the food pan during the intervals. When the positive signal for food is applied, the dog quickly orients to the pan and looks for food. If a test signal is given, the dog goes through the same postural reactions, and, since food is delayed, there is a strong secretion of saliva during the sounding of the 30 second signal. The head moves right and left over the pan as though waiting for the food. Now the dog has the same nervous set when the first negative signal is applied as when the positive signal is given. Since the negative signal is the same in sound as the positive, the reaction is released just as quickly. As the experiments continue, the position of the negative is varied from time to time. Thus the dog does not develop a definite set for this signal but is always in a nervous attitude for positive signals and food. For this reason all initial reactions to both positive and negative signals are the same. As the signals are contrasted repeatedly, however, the dog seems to appreciate the difference between them; but since the initial setting is not changed, there is always some positive reaction. This is shown by the fact that as the signal continues and the difference in frequency is appreciated, the animal turns the head away from the pan until the signal stops, a definite negative movement but one which is superimposed on the first vigorous positive reaction. The salivary or glandular reaction cannot be cut off sharply, as can the neuromuscular actions, and there is, therefore, a flow of saliva even during these negative postural movements away from the pan.

The difference between the dogs of groups A and B is, then, one of nervous tension and setting for the specific reaction rather than of differentiation between the two sig-mals. If a different signal is used, or even if the negative is applied at the same place in each experimental period, the dog will develop a more stable negative reaction. It is this difference in nervous setting that is especially significant in emphasizing the types, and it is the repeated release of this action without reinforcement which probably contributes to the heightened excitability occurring in many of these dogs.

*Reactions of the active group to other signals.* A greater sensitivity and alertness was also exhibited by the dogs of group B when tactile stimuli were employed. The record of the reactions to these stimuli for dog 438 ♀ is similar to that of the auditory reactions. In the beginning the tactile signals elicited a variety of postural movements directed to the point of stimulation. As the experiments continued the postural movements were directed to the food pans. Although the reaction to tactile signals is weaker, the general course of the behavior is the same when tactile signals or auditory signals are given. The response continued in the case of 438 ♀ until the dog developed an increased restlessness.

*Response of the active group to intense auditory stimuli.* Because of the sensitive nature of these dogs, they were greatly disturbed when the loud buzzer was introduced (text-fig. 93, fig. 2). The signal caused vigorous orientation reactions and in some cases an escape behavior. Food presented with the signal was refused, indicating that although the animals were acquainted with the laboratory procedure they retained a low threshold of excitation. The postural reactions to the buzzer indicate a wide irradiation of excitation. Instead of a movement involving only the head, as with the animals of group A, these dogs reacted with total bodily movements, including head, tail, and legs. Further, the reactions continued for a longer time as an after discharge of excitation. Such behavior emphasizes the fact that these dogs are always subject to stimulation and never become inert and inactive in a habitual situation, as do the dogs of group A.

These dogs are disturbed when an attempt is made to develop a conditioned avoiding reaction to the shock. Once the signal for this reaction is introduced, the salivary response becomes completely inhibited, and remains so as long as the dog is in the laboratory. As we shall emphasize below, the conditioned motor response occurs repeatedly to the signal in those dogs without reinforcement, and extreme caution must be taken in order not to overexcite the animal.

Although in detail the behavior of 1382 ♀ is somewhat different from that of 438 ♀, these two dogs behaved in the same general manner. As text-figure 95 indicates, the reactions of animal 1382 ♀ continued for a longer period of training before she became unduly restless and offered an increased resistance to the laboratory procedure. In this case the training continued until 300 positive and 35 negative signals had been applied. After this time, on certain days there was a complete refusal of food. In this case the refusal of food was replaced by definite antagonism to the laboratory and a tendency to release herself, rather than complete passivity, as in the case of animals 83 ♀ and 219 ♂ above.

*Summary.* The dogs of group B are active and alert. They object to the experimental procedure and any change in the laboratory environment disturbs them greatly. Their behavior is characterized by extreme nervousness which is in danger of developing into hysteria. The conditioned salivary response is vigorous and continues so over a long period of time, and the delay of the response is short. Although in most cases these animals seem to recognize the difference between the positive and negative signals, even after a long period of training they repeatedly react to the negative almost as vigorously as to the positive. This is due to the intensity of the nervous setting for the performance and the suddenness with which their nervous energy is released. The dogs of this group never become habituated to the situation as do the dogs of group A. Most of them show a tendency toward increased activity and annoyance as the experiments progress. The contrast of positive and negative signals and varied stimulation is conducive to disturbance.

The logical conclusion of the training in these dogs is quite different from that found in group A. The dogs of B overact each time the signal is presented, that is, overact in the sense that most of the response has no connection at all with food getting. This overaction is the nature of the animal. Due to the inability to inhibit actions, these dogs become annoyed by the repeated presentation of the same signal, and especially by the introduction of negatives. The animals end the training with an understanding of the laboratory procedure, but are slightly disturbed by its repetition. This disturbance is evident by increased action to the signals and general restlessness.

### INTERMEDIATE GROUPS

Groups A and B represent the extremes in behavior, with the animals of each group standing out as separate and distinct behavioral types. Yet it is quite evident that in an animal as complicated as the dog, many individuals will fall between the two extremes, having, to a greater or lesser degree, the same general characteristics as the polar groups. These intermediate animals will be referred to as behavioral types A-plus and B-minus. The behavioral type A-plus includes those animals which, although of the lethargic type, do not reach the extreme of those in group A, and conversely, behavioral type B-minus includes animals of the active group not quite reaching the extremes of group B. Of the thirty-six animals trained, thirteen fall into the A-plus group while five are classified as B-minus. These two groups grade into each other and it is difficult in many cases to indicate whether a dog is nearer the A or the B group. The main point of emphasis here, however, is that the behavioral differences lie in the degree of excitability as expressed by the particular adjustment.

*Lethargic type A-plus.* Thirteen animals fall into this group, including the following: four bassethound-German shepherd $F_1$s, 251 ♂, 246 ♀, 1776 ♂ and 1780 ♀ ; two basset-hound-German shepherd $F_2$s, 1811 ♂ and 1812 ♂ ; one basset-hound-English bulldog $F_1$, 740 ♂ ; two bassethound-English bulldog $F_2$s, 1909 ♂ and 1310 ♀ ; four bassethound-German shepherd $F_2$s, 1297 ♂, 1298 ♂, 1300 ♀ and 1304 ♀.

The reactions of the dogs of this group to the preliminary training did not differ to any extent from those of the animals of group A, and the formation of the conditioned salivary reaction followed the same general course. As the experiments continued, however, it became evident that these animals were not of the extreme lethargic type, as are those of group

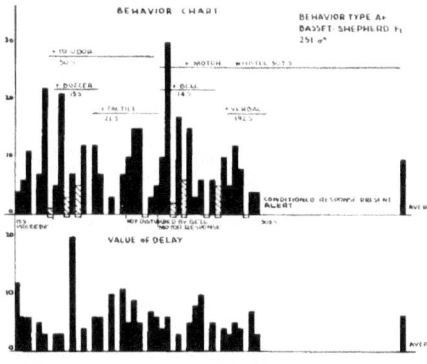

Text-figure 96

A. The conditioned response did not weaken after a period of training as it did in the dogs of group A, and there was no complete inactivity nor refusal of food. During the intervals between signals the animals might sit down and remain quiet, but the conditioning signal always aroused them to action.

A good example of a dog of this group is 251 ♂, a basset-hound-German shepherd $F_1$ (text-fig. 96). The training of this animal was continued over a period of 5 years, during which time conditioned salivary responses were formed to a clicking signal, the odor of vanilla, tactile stimulation on the right shoulder, a buzzer, and a bell. Motor reactions were formed to the clicker, verbal stimulus, and a whistle. Negative salivary reactions were formed to a clicking signal of sixty vibrations per minute and a second tactile signal on the right hip. The total behavioral study included 957 stimulations. The salivary reaction to the clicker signals and the motor reactions to the whistle and clicker signals were the only ones studied extensively. The mere fact that the animal could form the salivary and motor reaction to so many signals is significant when contrasted with the animals of group A, who become completely inactive, and with those of group B,

TABLE 6
*Dog 251 ♂*

| TIME | SIGNAL NO. AND NATURE | DURATION OF SIGNAL | LATENT PERIOD | RESPONSE |
|---|---|---|---|---|
| 3:00 | 92 clicker 120 | 10 sec. | .. | 0 |
| 3:04 | 93 clicker | 30 sec. | 6" | 30 (100 cc saliva) |
| 3:09 | 142 whistle (motor response) | 10 sec. | 2" | Raises leg to avoid shock |
| 3:11 | 94 clicker 120 | 30 sec. | 6" | 12 |
| 3:15 | 15 clicker 50 (−) | 30 sec. | 5" | 2 |
| 3:16 | 16 clicker | 30 sec. | .. | 0 |
| 3:18 | 95 clicker 120 | 5 sec. | .. | 0 |
| 3:20 | 96 clicker 120 | 5 sec. | .. | 0 |

who are greatly disturbed by a complicated patterning of the stimuli, especially if negatives are involved or if the motor reaction is employed. Animal 251 ♂ could give both the motor reactions and the salivary reactions in one experimental period, a task which is extremely difficult for most dogs. A typical record obtained during this period, dated October 2, 1933, is shown in table 6.

It is observed in this table that there was a vigorous conditioned salivary response on the second presentation of the signal. Immediately following this, the dog made an avoiding response of the right foreleg to the whistle, and 2 minutes after this signal the dog again gave a conditioned salivary reaction to the clicker. Another outstanding characteristic is the weak reaction to the negative, even though the signal for shock had been used in the experiment. A performance of this kind can be obtained only in the well balanced animals.

Animal 246♀, also a bassethound-German shepherd $F_1$, is another typical example of this group (text-fig. 97). The training in this case was not so extensive as that of 251♂, since the animal died before the experiments were terminated. The training was carried far enough, however, to indicate that she was of the same behavioral type. This dog formed

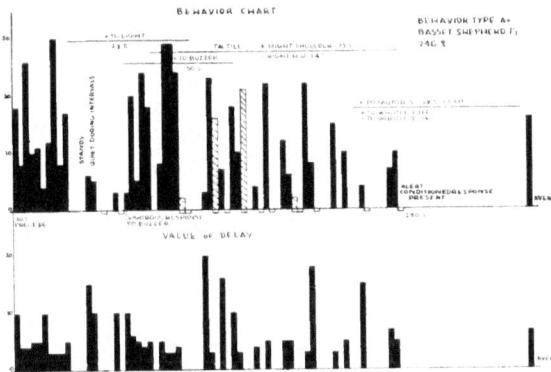

Text-figure 97

conditioned salivary reactions to a clicker rate of 120 vibrations per minute, a light hanging above the food pan, a buzzer, and a tactile stimulation on the right shoulder. Negative responses were developed to a clicking rate of sixty vibrations per minute, and to a second tactile stimulation of the right hip. The salivary reactions to the pricker were weaker than those to the clicker, but the development of the response and the course of the negative were the same as in the reaction to the clicker. Motor responses of the foreleg were formed to a whistle, and to a clicking rate of sixty vibrations per minute. A total of 182 signals for the motor reaction had been applied when the dog died, and the response at this time was a precise avoiding movement which occurred regularly. A negative motor reaction was formed to a second whistle. This dog would not give the conditioned salivary response in any period in which the motor signal was introduced, but she did differentiate between the two signals by turning to the food pan when the signal for food was given and by raising the foot when the signal for shock was applied. She was evidently slightly disturbed by the signal for shock, so that the salivary reaction was inhibited.

With the other dogs classified in this group so many different forms of stimuli were not used. The conditioned salivary reaction followed the same course, however, in all of them. All members of the group are characterized by the continued appearance of the salivary reaction without onset of inhibition, by a response to the first few negative signals, and by the ability to form a differential reaction after repetition of the signals. They are also characterized by their general alertness, although not greatly disturbed by the signal for shock, or sudden variations within the laboratory. The dogs were not disturbed, for example, if a stranger entered the laboratory during one of the experimental periods. A loud sound introduced for the first time would elicit a vigorous investigatory reaction, but the second and third time it was applied the dog was undisturbed unless it was accompanied either by food or by a shock on the foreleg. The total laboratory performance indicates a harmonious relationship between the excitatory and inhibitory processes and reaction systems which make for an adequate and quick adaptability.

*Active type B-minus.* If the dogs were studied as individuals and without relation to a large group, the significant differences between those of A-plus and B-minus would not be emphasized. The animals of B-minus are closely related to those of A-plus, yet they have characteristics of the animals of group B. Although alert and active they do not show the extreme restlessness of the latter group. There is less resistance to the training, and the laboratory and experimental procedure do not prove so disturbing.

Five dogs fall into this group, including the following: two bassethound-German shepherd $F_2$s, 1152 ♂ and 1528 ♀; one bassethound-English bulldog $F_1$, 579 ♀; one bassethound-German shepherd $F_1$, 308 ♂; one backcrossed bassethound-German shepherd $F_1$ on bassethound, 710 ♀.

The behavioral charts of 308 ♂ and 1152 ♂ (text-figs. 98 and 99) are typical of the group. As the chart for 308 ♂ shows, these dogs are capable of giving a positive salivary reaction to varied stimuli, without leading to a disturbance or the

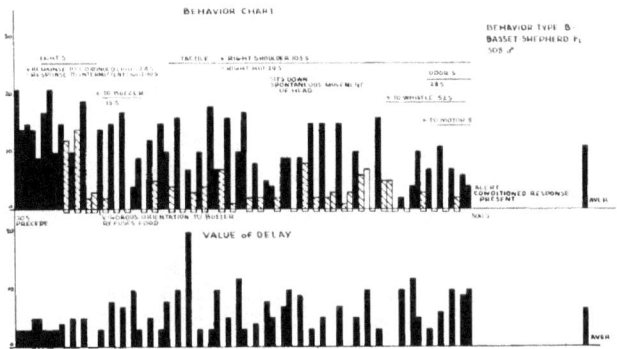

Text-figure 98

inhibition of the reaction. This dog formed positive reactions to a clicking sound of 120 vibrations per minute, a constant light, tactile stimulation of the right shoulder, odor of vanilla, a whistle, and a buzzer. Negative reactions were formed to a clicking sound of seventy-two vibrations per minute and intermittent light, and tactile stimulation of the right hip. The dog differs from those of A-plus in that the positive response to the signals retains its value, and in some cases increases slightly in value, as the experiments progress. Another characteristic is the instability of the negative reaction. On certain days the negative is weak, and the variation in the behavior is toward increased activity rather than decreased activity, as found in the dogs of A proper. The animals of B-minus are also more disturbed by a sudden change in the laboratory environment than the dogs of A-plus. The food taking reaction was inhibited by the first presentation of any signal. The response is also inhibited when a stranger enters the experimental chamber or any odd sound penetrates the room. These characteristics indicate the ease with which the dogs are excited. Another thing of importance is that although annoyed by the signal for the avoiding

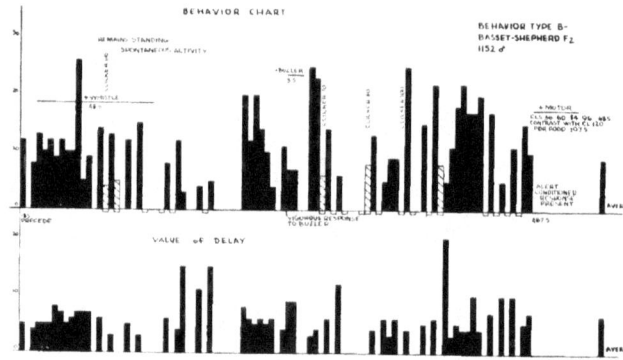

Text-figure 99

reaction, the best members of the group do form an avoiding response. The conditioned salivary reaction, however, and in most cases the food taking response, become inhibited after the signal for the motor response is introduced.

Another dog of this group is 1152 ♂, a bassethound-German shepherd F₂. As was the case with 308 ♂, this dog formed a positive conditioned salivary response to a clicking sound of 120 vibrations per minute, a whistle, and a buzzer, without showing signs of a disturbance or inhibition of the response. The first presentation of any of these signals did lead to vigorous investigatory reactions and the refusal of food. The fact that the dog retains a high level of activity is shown by the continuation of the response until the experiments were discontinued, and in this case the response had increased slightly in intensity. This dog was employed in the experiments over a period of 3 years, and during this time there were certain intervals when the animal was not used in the experiments. These intervals of rest did not affect the performance. When the experiments started again, the response was always as intense as it was when the last experiment ended.

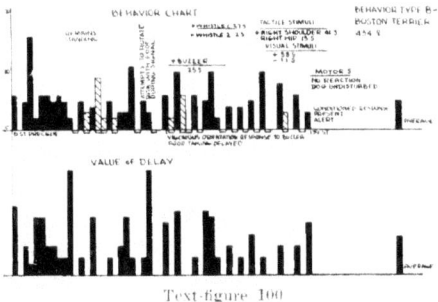

Text-figure 100.

As in the case of 308 ♂, this dog also refused food when the motor response was introduced. The animal did develop definite conditioned avoiding responses, however, and could differentiate between clicker rates of 84 and 120 vibrations per minute.

One dog of this group, Boston terrier 434 ♀, (text-fig. 100) had a relatively weak conditioned salivary reaction. This animal was smaller than the two discussed above, weighing less than 20 pounds, and could not be given as much food during the experiments as the larger dogs. Thus it necessarily follows that the conditioned reaction in this animal was much smaller. It is due to this difference in size that the value of the salivary reaction cannot be considered the sole criterion of excitability. The total performance of 434 ♀ was, however, the same as for the others of group B-minus. As we shall point out later, however, this animal varied from the others of the group when trained with the motor response, thus placing her in the mixed group instead of the pure B-minus group. Her reactions in the salivary performance conformed to the group, but that does not mean that all other performances will conform. The significance of this will become clear when we discuss pure and mixed behavioral types.

*Summary.* The dogs of the intermediate groups A-plus and B-minus approach the behavior of the polar groups A and B, but do not reach the extremes. Those of the A-plus type are quiet, but never become completely indifferent to the laboratory as do the animals of the A group. They remain alert and subject to stimulation over a long period of time. Some have difficulty in developing a stable negative response. A strong reaction to new and strange stimuli is given, but the animals are not greatly disturbed. Most of them are able to make adjustments to the signal for the motor reaction and the signal for food in the same experimental session. Although alert and active, the dogs of the B-minus group differ from those of the polar group in that they are better able to restrain themselves and form differentiation reactions, which are too confusing for the more excitable dogs of group B. They are slightly disturbed by the introduction of the motor reaction, since the food taking response becomes inhibited. They form good avoiding reactions, however, and are capable of differentiating between signals by this method.

In general, the animals of the intermediate types are more stable and better balanced than either of the polar types.

## Discussion

In the experiment just described, thirty-six dogs were observed as the adjustment to food taking under controlled conditions was made. The external factors, the stimuli, remained constant, but many variations in behavior among the dogs occurred in the course of the performance. These modifications in performance are due to a change in the relationship between the reflex systems as the behavior progresses. The development of this relationship between the extraneous forces and the reflex systems, and the change among the systems in the course of the adjustment, is based on excitatory and inhibitory processes. Each has a part in every modification. The performance of the organismal systems was limited to some extent by the experimental situation, but no attempt was made to restrict the performance to one aspect of the total behavioral pattern involved in this adjustment, or even to keep any part of it, as the conditioned saliva, at a definite magnitude. By following the same procedure with each animal, the differences in the course of the performance were emphasized. The conditioned saliva is the only aspect quantitatively observed, but this is not considered of any greater importance than the muscular components of the behavior. The significance of constitutional differences affecting behavior may be suggested by one part of the total behavior, but by using more than one aspect, together with the course of the adjustment, the interpretation is more evident. For example, if an animal is of a highly excitable nature, this is as evident in the performance of the muscular system as in the salivary reaction. In the same way, if an animal is of an inhibited type, this fact is evident in all factors of the performance. The course of the behavior must be considered, since a dog may have a relatively small conditioned salivary reaction yet be an excitable animal. This was noted particularly in the case of dog 434 ♀, a small animal.

The results of the experiments divide the performances of the animals into two outstanding types designated as lethargic (group A) and active (group B), the two poles of reaction. The performances of other dogs follow the same general behavior characteristics of the polar groups, but to a greater or lesser degree, and these dogs have been designated lethargic type A-plus and active type B-minus. There seems to be a continuous graded series in behavior from types A to B.

At the beginning of the experimental procedure, the dogs of group A are more excitable than under the usual conditions of the kennel, but they readily become adjusted to the laboratory and form conditioned postural and salivary reactions. Following this initial adjustment, the total behavioral pattern changes, and there is a gradual elimination of bodily movements not absolutely essential for food taking. The adjustment is directed toward an economical performance, and the animals soon cease to orient to the signals or even to the food pan, but hold the head just beside the pan until food is actually presented. In some instances during the intervals between signals, the head rests on the board beside the pan, and at times the animal may even go to sleep in this position. The specific negative signal cannot be introduced before the relationship between the positive signal and food has been established. As soon as this point is reached, the activity of the animal is gradually decreased. For this reason there is little reaction to the negative. This inactive stage is soon reached even though the negative is not introduced; thus it is not dependent on a specific negative signal. Following the disappearance of the conditioned saliva and bodily movements, most of the dogs refuse food under laboratory conditions. The quiet environment of the laboratory emphasizes their lethargic natures. It may be said that they passively accept the situation and make no effort to modify the procedure by their own actions. They never become impatient or try to leave the room, and after the first few week's training it is not even necessary to use the restraining harness. The dogs sit passively until food is presented, then slowly approach the pan to eat. The total perceptual situation, involving food as the center, is quite different in these dogs than it was found to be for the animals of group B. For the dogs of A, the laboratory becomes primarily a place in which food is obtained. If they are not hungry it is a place to sit until the experimenter leads them out. There is no definite urge on their part to leave if they are not hungry, nor to react to other signals in an environment which has taken on a specific meaning, e.g., a place where food is presented. It is possible that this relationship between the organism and its immediate environment is one of the most important in behavior. The training is considered ended when the animal reaches a point where there are no further changes in behavior from day to day.

The behavioral picture of the highly active group B is in direct contrast to that shown by the dogs of group A. These dogs never passively fit into the situation. They seem unwilling to enter into the training, but this is probably not so much unwillingness as difficulty in restraining themselves and a high degree of responsiveness to every change in the environment. These dogs never reach a level of stereotyped and predictable performance, as do those of the lethargic group. It is impossible to control the environment so definitely that their reactions fit into a groove. Whether the variation in action is due to excitation aroused by the external situation, or is the result of internal stimulation, cannot be determined on the basis of the present experiments. It is certain, however, that these animals do not reach a phase where they passively go through the performance. They remain active and alert at all times. They continue to orient to the food pan and are impatient of waiting. This may indicate that what has been termed the "attitude" or "set" as determined by the laboratory instruction is constantly released by the break-down of inhibition. This is similar to impatience in human behavior. It is this difference in "set" which accounts for the reaction to the negative. From the point of view of the observer, it may be said that these animals always expend energy, even though overtly it seems unnecessary. Such unnecessary movements as shifting the position, intermittent pawing with the foot, chewing on the harness, etc., are indicative of an inability to hold energy in reserve. They seem unable to dam up their energy, so to speak, as do the dogs of group A, but are forced to release it. The dogs of group B take an active part in the performance, and were they allowed to follow their own inclinations the end result would undoubtedly show wider differences than is the case in these experiments, in which an attempt is made to determine to some extent the course of action. The difference is not only one of energy but organization of neural processes as well.

The intermediate types are not dominantly lethargic or excitable. They are never too excited to enter into the performance, nor so sluggish as to lose all interest in the experiments; throughout the training, they remain active and motivated and are well able to restrain and adjust themselves. They are thus excellent subjects for general experiments in the salivary situation. The animals of the A-plus and B-minus groups are better balanced and more capable of making a wider variety of reactions in any situation than are the animals of either the A or B groups.

Pavlov also recognized two extreme behavioral types among dogs, with intermediates ranging between them. One of the extremes was considered highly excitable, while the other was inhibited and restrained. The intermediate dogs were considered better balanced, capable of making adjustments to a wider variety of stimulus situations than either of the extremes. Pavlov went further in his division of the types, however, and attempted to break them up into four groups and relate them to the traditional psychological temperaments of sanguine, melancholic, choleric and phlegmatic.

The sanguine type includes those dogs which are prone to inaction and inhibition under experimental conditions when single stimuli are employed. Pavlov states, however, that if many stimuli are used, eliciting both positive and negative reactions, they become more active. This is also true of group A, but if the two extreme types are compared in the same situation, there will always be the same relative differences between them. For example, the dogs of group A tend to become inactive under experimental conditions, but if a number of stimuli are introduced, and also more than one channel of reaction, they do become more active. On the other hand, if the dogs of B are studied under the same conditions, they will also be on a higher level of activity. If behavior is considered in this manner, referring always to differences under the same conditions, a specific designation as sanguine is difficult to understand.

The melancholic type seems to have some characteristics of group B, yet in many respects these dogs are similar to those of group A. Pavlov states that these dogs "... get used to the experimental surroundings and the associated manipulation very slowly, but when they become thoroughly familiar with the new conditions they make invaluable subjects of experimentation", and further "... such animals do not sleep in their stands when the experimental conditions remain more or less constant; on the contrary their conditioned reflexes, especially the inhibitory ones, remain extremely stable and regular" (p. 286). The first part of this description fits the dogs of group B, but the latter part would not. The animals of group B are slower in making adjustments to the laboratory situation, and retain a high level of activity. They require more time to make the laboratory adjustment and become acquainted with people because they are highly excitable and easily disturbed. But even after they do make this adjustment they remain on a higher level of excitation than those of group A. Their positive reactions remain at a greater magnitude and they have great difficulty in forming negative reactions, in most cases not forming any negative responses. The same thing may be said about the term melancholic as about sanguine — it has little significance when dogs are compared under the same conditions. The description of the melancholic type given above would seem to belong in what is termed a mixed behavioral group. The meaning of this term will be clarified later in the report.

The dogs of the intermediate group are just as difficult to relate to specific temperaments. Pavlov used the terms "choleric" and "phlegmatic" for the animals belonging to this group. The phlegmatic animal is quiet and restrained, tending toward inhibition under ordinary circumstances, but capable of high excitation under certain conditions, as for example, when the dog is frightened or hurt. This type would correspond more to the English bulldog, which is described in detail below, but which is a highly mixed behavioral type. This dog is quiet and restrained under ordinary conditions, but once a painful irritation is employed to elicit an avoiding reaction, intense excitement occurs. The animal has characteristics of both polar groups, yet it has characteristics not found in any other animal.

The term choleric would seem to refer to what we have called the B-minus group. These dogs are active and have difficulty in forming stable negative reactions.

Due to the complexity of the behavioral patterns of the dogs, and the differences found among them, it is best at present not to attempt to give them specific temperament designations. Each type should be studied in more variable controlled situations, and we should have a better understanding of their physiological processes before attempting to name the temperaments. The above terms may fit many of the dogs, but it seems that there are so many types and variations among dogs that a more diversified and finer differentiating method should be found. This will not come, however, until we have a better understanding of the types and the nervous disturbances each develops under difficult and restrained conditions.

It should be emphasized that the present experiments involved a wider variety of dogs than the experiments of Pavlov. This was necessary because of the difference in the object of the experiments. Pavlov was interested in determining the nature of the conditioned salivary response and something of the laws governing its action. For this reason animals were selected which would be of a more adjustable type. In the present experiments, a large group of different dogs was used in order to determine something of the variability of behavior among them, beginning of course with certain pure breeds which under kennel conditions were undoubtedly widely different in behavior. It may be due to the difference in materials studied that we have such difficulty in specifying the dogs with definite temperaments. Many of the dogs used by Pavlov were undoubtedly mongrels. In many cases these animals have behavioral characteristics of both polar groups, and thus there is great difficulty in understanding them. Unless one knows the genetic background of the animal for many generations, its behavior cannot be understood. Behavior is similar to physical form in this respect; a physical characteristic can be observed, but its significance cannot be understood unless the genetic background of the animal is known.

It will be of interest to observe the behavior of these animals under other conditions. The salivary response gives an indication of the reactions centering around the more or less "unconscious" or "volitionally uncontrolled" actions of a gland. For a further understanding of our problem, a behavior involving one of the more voluntary muscular types of performance will be of interest.

## ANALYSIS OF BEHAVIOR IN A CONDITIONED AVOIDING SITUATION

In order to obtain a true picture of motor performances, the reaction to be studied should have the characteristics of voluntary behavior yet enable the experimenter to control it as specifically as, or even more specifically, then the food taking behavior. Voluntary control in this case means that the performance may be dominated to a greater extent by higher nervous centers than the food taking processes. The withdrawal of the foreleg from a painful irritation has been used to advantage in many experiments, and this reflex system is employed in the present study. Animals from each of the four groups classified in the food taking experiments, and others, chosen for various reasons, were trained for this experiment.

The procedure in this experiment was to train the dog to raise the foreleg to a specific signal (bell, buzzer, or clicker) and thereby avoid an electric shock. The shock was applied by means of electrodes attached to the dog's right wrist;

the electrodes were connected to the secondary coil of a Harvard inductorium. Only one battery, which was renewed frequently, was connected to the primary coil. The break shock method was used, in which the painful irritation is avoided by means of a sliding contact switch which breaks the electric circuit to the electrodes when the leg is raised. A diagram of the apparatus is shown in text-figure 85 (fig. 3). The string operating the switch also moves the recording lever on the kymograph.

The break shock method is preferable to shocking the animal every time since the behavior reaction thus elicited approximates that which would be observed under natural conditions, for instance by the use of the water hose when the dogs become too noisy in the kennels. In such a case, the hose is turned on, accompanied by shouts of, "Get in the house", or, "Inside." The dogs run for shelter when the water is turned on them, and after a few repetitions of this procedure only the words are necessary to elicit the reaction. In many cases even the sight of the kennel man approaching the hose will quiet the dogs. This is a typical case of conditioned avoiding reaction. In this instance a movement is made to avoid an unpleasant wetting. The dogs might be trained to do the same thing by means of a shock or whip.

For the most part, the clicker, sounding at the rate of 120 per minute, was used as a positive signal. If this had been used in previous experiments, a whistle, buzzer, or bell

PLATE 101
EXPLANATION OF FIGURES

1 Characteristic posture of one of the well balanced animals giving the conditioned avoiding reaction. This animal is a bassethound German shepherd $F_2$.

2 Position assumed by the Saluki, a hyper-excitable animal, in the conditioned avoiding situation. The leg is held in a half flexed position during the interval between signals in what would seem to be a "set" in preparation for a quick avoiding response when the signal is applied.

3 and 4 Characteristic postures of excitable animals of group B avoiding the shock. The animal in figure 3 is a German shepherd; the animal in figure 4 is a Saluki.

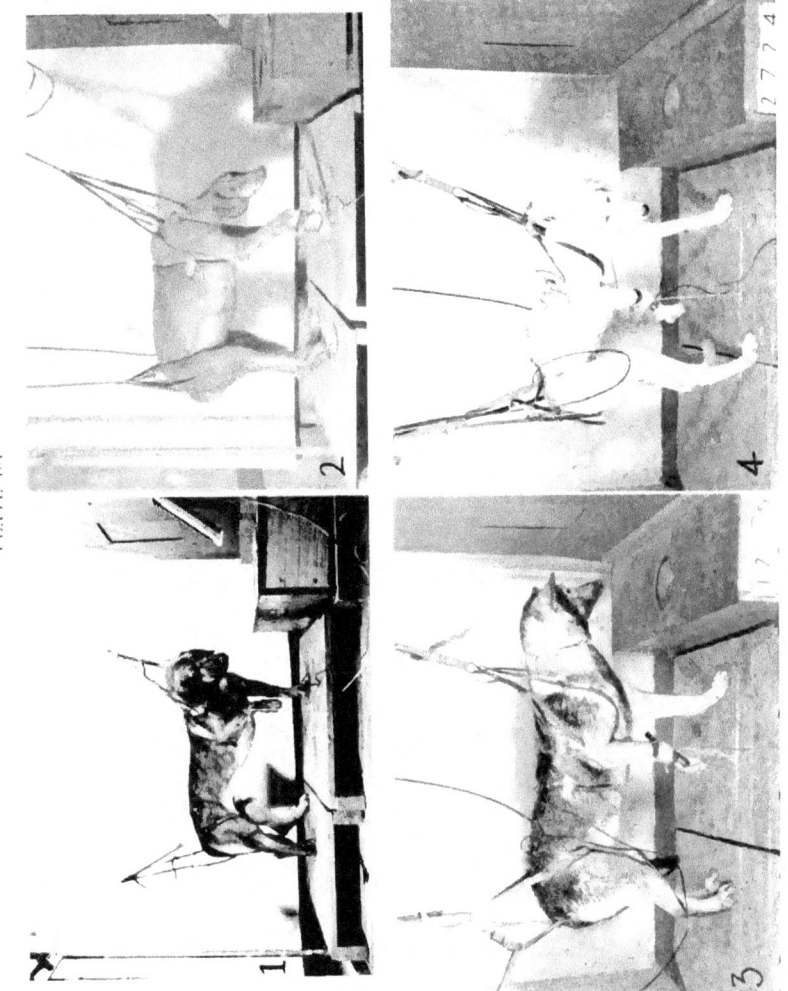

was employed as the conditioned stimulus. The conditioning signal preceded the shock for 5 seconds and then coincided with it for 5 seconds or longer. The animal was required to make a continued avoiding reaction, that is, the flexed leg must be sustained as long as the signal sounded. Each time the leg was lowered during the signal, the animal received the shock. The behavior may be understood better by reference to plate 101 (fig. 1) showing a dog holding the foot in the avoiding position while the clicker sounds. The kymographic record for this animal is shown in text-figure 101 (fig. 1).

Most of the dogs used in the development of the motor reflex had already been trained with the salivary reaction and were, therefore, accustomed to the laboratory. Straps under each leg confined the dog to the platform. In these experiments, as in the conditioned food taking reaction, every factor of the performance is important and must be considered in classifying the animals. The periods of inactivity, or intervals between the signals, are as significant as the leg movement and postural shift to the stimuli. Behavior differences among the animals were observed in every phase of the adjustment, including the following:

A. Initial laboratory adjustment.
B. Strength of shock to elicit the leg movement and nature of reaction to first shock.
C. The nature and course of the reaction.
    (a) time of making the adjustment.
    (b) true avoidance or simple flexion.
D. Reaction time.
E. Behavior during interval between signals.
F. Generalization, or reactions to other signals introduced.
G. Difference in excitatory-inhibitory ratio.

As in the previous section, the animals showing the greatest behavioral differences will be discussed first, and the groups will be designated again as lethargic group A, active group B, and intermediates, A-minus and B-plus. The results of the experiments are tabulated in table 7, with group A at

GENETIC TYPE AND THE ENDOCRINES 579

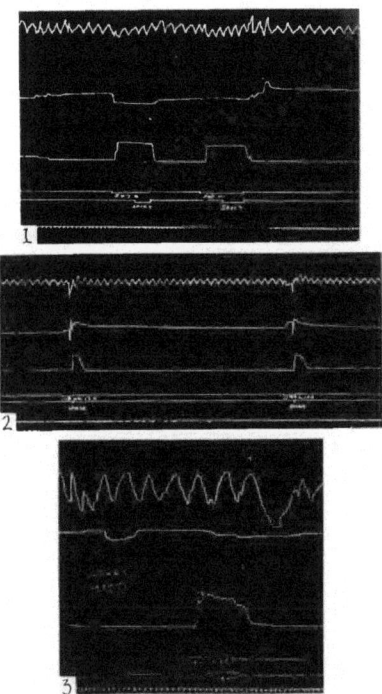

Text-figure 101. (1) A typical conditioned avoiding reaction of one of the mid-group animals. (The reaction of the leg is indicated by the third line from the top.) The leg is raised shortly after the signal begins and is held in the avoiding position until the signal ceases. Note that the signal precedes the shock for 5 seconds and is then coincident with shock for 5 seconds. (2) A typical reaction of the animals of group A to the conditioning signal and shock. After a short period of training, they respond only to the shock. Note the lack of movement on the part of the animal in the interval between signals. (3) Characteristic reaction of the active group B in the conditioned avoiding situation. The response is characterized by a short latent period and a variety of postural movements which are superimposed on the avoiding reaction.

TABLE 7

| | NUMBER DAYS IN LABORATORY BEFORE ANIMAL WAS SHOCKED | STRENGTH OF SHOCK REQUIRED TO ELICIT BRISK FLEXION OF LEG | DEGREE OF STRUGGLE ELICITED BY FIRST SHOCK | NUMBER OF SIGNALS BEFORE APPEARANCE OF CONDITIONED FLEXION OF LEG | NUMBER OF SIGNALS BEFORE APPEARANCE OF TRUE AVOIDING REACTION | AVERAGE DELAY OF LEG MOVEMENT FOLLOWING REACTION TIME IN SECONDS AND HUNDREDTHS OF SECONDS | BEHAVIOR DURING INTERVALS BETWEEN CONDITIONING SIGNALS | DEGREE OF GENERALIZATION | ANIMALS WHICH FORMED DISCRIMINATORY REACTIONS |
|---|---|---|---|---|---|---|---|---|---|
| 1504 Bas.Eng.Bull. F₁ Bas Shep. F₁ | 4 | 7 | — | .. | .. | 5 | Inactive | — | |
| 1427 Bassethound | 1 | 6 | — | 8 | .. | 5 | Inactive | — | |
| 1426 Bassethound | | 6 | — | 11 | .. | 5 | Inactive | — | |
| 336 Dachshund | | 6.5 | — | 4 | 30 | 1.28 | Inactive | — | |
| 348 Dachshund | | 6 | — | 9 | .. | 5 | Inactive | — | |
| 697 Bas. Eng.Bull. F₁ | | 6.5 | — | 9 | 24 | 1 | Inactive | — | |
| 863 Basset-Germ.Shep. F₂ | | 7 | — | 5 | 15 | 1.50 | Inactive | — | |
| 740 Bas. Eng.Bull. F₁ | | 7.5 | — | 11 | 47 | 1.90 | Inactive | — | |
| 246 Basset-Germ.Shep. F₁ | | 6 | — | 7 | 11 | 1.98 | Inactive | — | |
| 251 Basset-Germ.Shep. F₁ | | 6 | — | 23 | 52 | 2.34 | Inactive | — | |
| 2270 Basset-Germ.Shep. Bx | 7 | 7 | + | 19 | 46 | 1.32 | Inactive | + | |
| 1812 Basset-Germ.Shep. F₂ | 5 | 7 | + | 8 | 17 | 1.05 | Active Nervous | + | |
| 867 Basset-Germ.Shep. F₂ | 7 | 7.5 | + | 5 | 9 | .82 | Active Nervous | + | |
| 1811 Basset-Germ.Shep. F₂ | 4 | 7 | + | 10 | 15 | .84 | Active Nervous | + | |
| 819 Basset-Saluki F₂ | 10 | 7.5 | + | 5 | 9 | .82 | Nervous Whines | + | |
| 835 Saluki | 15 | 8 | + | 10 | 10 | .46 | Active | + | |
| 1152 Basset-Germ.Shep. F₂ | | 8.5 | + | 7 | 10 | 1.08 | Active Whines | | |
| 2224 Basset-Germ.Shep. F₂ | 10 | 7.5 | + | 4 | 4 | .775 | Active | + | |
| 1285 German Shepherd | | 8 | + | 12 | 12 | .76 | Active Whines | + | |

* These dogs had previously been trained with the salivary experiments and were already accustomed to the laboratory.

the top, group B at the bottom, and the intermediates distributed between the two polar groups.

*Initial adjustment to laboratory.* The initial behavior, or adjustment to the laboratory, has been discussed in the food taking situation. The dogs which had not been trained were taught to take food from the pan even though the conditioned salivary reaction was not specifically studied. In these cases, food acted only as an incentive. The shock, or unconditioned stimulus, was not applied until each dog was thoroughly acquainted with the laboratory and took food without hesitation. The difference in time required to make the adjustment to the laboratory is shown for all dogs in column 1 of table 7. The dogs of the active group B require from 10 to 15 days training before they will stand in the harness. The Saluki and German shepherd are typical of this group. In contrast to this, the bassethound, typical of the lethargic group A, remained quietly on the platform the first day and the initial reaction to the shock could be determined at once. Other dogs of the group fall between these two extremes. For example, one bassethound-German shepherd $F_2$ required 7 days' adjustment to the laboratory, another 5 days', and a third 4 days'. A bassethound-Saluki $F_2$ required 10 days for adjustment to the experimental room. These differences indicate the degree of sensitivity to environmental factors and are thus of significance in contrasting the types.

*Strength of shock necessary to elicit the flexion of the foreleg and the effect of the shock on the dog.* In the case of the Harvard inductorium, the secondary coil is supported by parallel bars in such a manner that this coil can be moved away from the primary coil, thus increasing the distance between them. The bars supporting the secondary coil are graduated in centimeters so the exact distance between the primary and secondary can easily be determined. At zero reading the secondary coil is directly over the primary and gives the maximum induced current. As the secondary coil is moved away from the primary, to 1, 2, 3, etc., centimeter readings, the induced current becomes weaker. In determining the shock strong enough to elicit the avoiding movement of the foreleg, the secondary coil was placed 10 centimeters away from the primary. The induced shock at this distance from the primary coil was found too weak to elicit the reaction in any of the animals. The secondary coil was then moved toward the primary in steps of ½ centimeter. At each step the shock was tried to determine whether it was intense enough to elicit the reaction. If the shock was strong enough, the leg was raised as soon as the shock was applied. The number of centimeters distance the secondary coil was from the primary when the shock was strong enough to elicit the reaction was considered the shock value for that animal. The shock used in determining this value was a continuous shock and not a single break or make shock. These values are shown in column 2 of table 7. As a rule, the dogs of group A required a slightly stronger shock to produce a brisk flexion of the foreleg than did the dogs of group B. For example, the German shepherd of group B gave a brisk movement when the secondary coil was 8 centimeters from the zero reading, while the bassethound of group A did not respond until the secondary coil was 6 centimeters from the zero reading. This is the lowest reading. A value of 8.5, made by a bassethound-German shepherd hybrid, 1152 ♂, was the highest reading (weakest shock). The other dogs responded to values of 7 and 7.5.

The reactions to the liminal shock showed significant differences. In the animals of group A even the initial reaction was limited to the distal leg segment, while in those of group B a more general reaction, involving all leg segments and postural systems of the head and neck, occurred. This would indicate a difference of irradiation of excitation throughout the nervous system, and also a different functional relationship between the various levels of neural organization. Furthermore, in group A the after-discharge of the excitation was weak, while in group B the activity was extensive and in many cases continued so long that it was necessary for the experimenter to enter the room to quiet the animal. This difference in degree of reaction to the first shock is indicated in column 3 of the table, one plus (+) sign indicating a more extensive reaction to the shock with wider postural performance than a minus sign.

*Nature and course of the reaction.* The course of the performance also differed in the two groups. As a rule, the dogs of group A developed a tolerance for the painful irritation and became less and less disturbed by it as the experiments continued. Thus the value of the shock had to be increased after the first few experimental periods. The animals of group B never developed a tolerance to the shock and continued to give vigorous general reactions until they learned to avoid the shock.

The sustained avoiding reaction of the foreleg to the conditioning signal usually followed the appearance of a conditioned flexion movement in which the leg was raised and lowered alternately as the signal and shock continued. Since the animal received a shock each time the leg was lowered, the signal was automatically reinforced. All animals which formed the conditioned flexion movement did so at about the same stage of the training. The continued avoiding movement, however, was not developed at the same time in all animals, as is shown in columns 4 and 5 of table 7. In most of the dogs of group B, the true avoiding reaction appeared at about the time the conditioned flexion developed. The excitatory value of the signal was so intense for these dogs, and the association between the shock and the clicker so well established, that the alternating reaction did not appear as an integral of the pattern.

The dogs of group A continued to give the alternating reaction for a long period of time and never developed a true sustained avoiding reaction. Furthermore, after the experiments continued for a time, most of these dogs lost the alternating response and only the actual shock would elicit the flexion of the leg; the signal was entirely disregarded. This is shown in text-figure 101 (fig. 2). The reaction to the shock was at this time a precise leg movement.

If the signal was continued, there might be a tendency to hold the leg in the avoiding position for a brief time, but as a rule alternate flexions and extensions of the leg were given.

In contrast to this, note the brisk response of an animal of group B in text-figure 101 (fig. 3). Although in this case the leg was held high enough to avoid the shock, the record shows movements of the leg while it is held in the avoiding position. These are due to the shifting of the body as the signal continued, which is superimposed on the avoiding movement. It may be assumed, on the basis of physiological experiments on muscular excitation, that excitation of a greater frequency is required to produce the sustained and continued avoidance than is required to produce the alternating or incomplete tetanus reaction. On this basis it must be concluded that the animals of group B are more excited during the conditioning signal than are those of group A. The greater irradiation of excitation is indicated by the sudden increase in breathing and the postural changes which accompany the avoiding reaction.

*Reaction time.* In addition to the differences in the development and form of the reactions, there are differences in the delay of the conditioned leg movement of the two groups of dogs. Throughout the experiments the conditioning signal preceded the shock for 5 seconds. In the animals of group B, which formed the true avoiding behavior, the reaction occurred shortly after the signal was introduced. The conditioned reaction time was measured in seconds and fractions of seconds by a Cornell chronoscope which is so arranged that the timer starts when the signal is cut on and automatically stops when the animal raises the leg. These readings were made when the reaction had become well established, and are not to be confused with reaction time in the usual sense. In this case, it is the average latent period of the conditioned avoiding movement to the signal which preceded the shock. This time is shorter in the dogs of group B. The readings are shown in column 6 of table 7. For example, the Saluki had the shortest time, of .46 seconds; that is, the leg was raised .46 seconds after the signal began, even though the shock was never applied before the fifth second. The dog responded repeatedly at about this time and was careful not to lower the leg so long as the signal continued. Another dog of group B responded .76 seconds after the signal began. After the experiments had progressed, the dogs of group A, as a rule, responded only to the shock after the 5 second interval; there was no conditioned withdrawal of the leg, and thus no conditioned reaction time. All other animals distributed themselves between these two extremes. For example, one bassethound-shepherd $F_1$ responded after a 1.98 second interval, another after a 2.34 second interval. One bassethound-shepherd $F_2$ had a delay of 1.05 seconds, another of only .82 seconds.

In the salivary experiments, if the duration of the conditioning stimulus was constant, the delay of the response tended to increase as the experiments continued. This was not true, however, in the motor experiments, even though the shock was always delayed for 5 seconds. The animals which formed the avoiding reaction always responded at about the same time after the presentation of the signal, although there were, of course, slight variations from day to day.

*Behavior during the interval between conditioning signals.* The behavior during the intervals between presentation of the conditioning signals is as significant in typing the dogs as the reaction to the signal. During this interval the animal should return to a normal level of activity. In the dogs of group A there was a quick return to normalcy after the shock. If the harness was used, they rested on it, or leaned their heads on the food table. If the harness was not used, many would lie down or lounge with the hind quarters flat on the platform. It was evident that they were in a condition of half sleep, or as Pavlov termed it, a state of almost complete inhibition. These animals did not struggle, whine, or move about during the intervals, as demonstrated by textfigure 101 (fig. 2).

On the other hand, the animals of group B remained active and alert, and there was a tendency to keep the leg or the whole body in motion (text-fig. 102, fig. 1). There was a tendency for some of these dogs to hold the foot in the avoiding position during the experiments and never place it on the floor. Others held the leg in a half flexed position suggesting a "set" to react when the signal was given. One

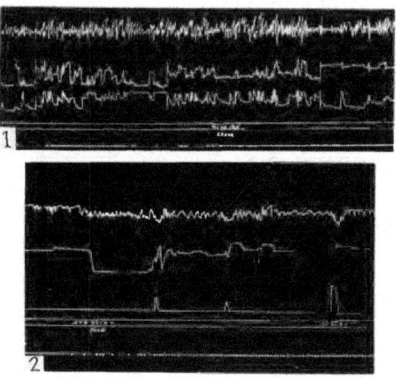

Text figure 102. (1) Record showing the excitable condition of many of the dogs of group B in the conditioned avoiding situation. The excitable nature is indicated by variable head movements and spontaneous movements of the foreleg. (2) Record of an animal of the mid-group differentiating between a sound with a frequency of 120 vibrations per minute and one of eighty-four vibrations per minute. The former is presented with food while the latter is accompanied by a shock on the foreleg. Only well balanced animals of the mid group can make such differentiations.

of these animals is shown in plate 101 (fig. 2). Occasionally these animals raised the leg, as if the nervous excitation had suddenly arisen releasing the avoiding movement. The animals which held the leg up all the time were those most severely disturbed by the shock when it was first applied. They retain this intense excitement later, even though they learn to avoid the shock. No. 819 ♂ avoided the shock but barked continually during the intervals as well as during the signals. This can only be indicative of a high state of excitement and emotional disturbance in the experimental situation.

*Generalization.* The term generalization is used here to designate the tendency to respond to signals other than the particular one used in training the animal. In the motor reflex, as in the salivary, the dogs of group A did not respond to all signals introduced. This is shown in column 8 of table 7, in which a plus sign indicates those dogs which reacted to all additional signals, while a minus sign designates those which did not. The dogs of group B responded to every signal presented, no matter how much it differed from the one used in the initial training. Kymographic records of the generalized responses of the extreme types to a bell are shown in text-figure 103 (figs. 1 and 2). Note that type A was not disturbed by the bell, while type B gave vigorous head movements as well as leg reactions.

Because of the wide generalization in the excitable animals, it was extremely difficult to develop a negative reaction, and in fact in most of them, impossible. Since the foreleg was raised in response to any signal given, it was evident that in order to form a negative it would be necessary to introduce a different reaction. This reaction had to be one which necessitated lowering the foreleg. In one method, food was presented with the negative signal. In order to take the food, the dog had to shift the whole posture, lower the foreleg, and step forward to the pan. This behavior, of course, would give a negative leg reaction, that is, negative in regard to its former positive avoiding position. It was thought that if this procedure was repeated often enough, the dog might learn to raise the leg when the signal for shock was given, but approach the pans for food when the second signal was given, and in this manner learn to differentiate between the two. Even with this plan, however, responses showing differentiation could be developed in very few dogs. Most dogs would refuse the food. And those dogs that did learn to respond to the two different signals in the desired manner were of neither the A nor B groups, but of the intermediates; they will be discussed below. In another method, the shock was applied to the left leg in contrast to the right. With this method also only the intermediates, or well balanced types, formed differential responses.

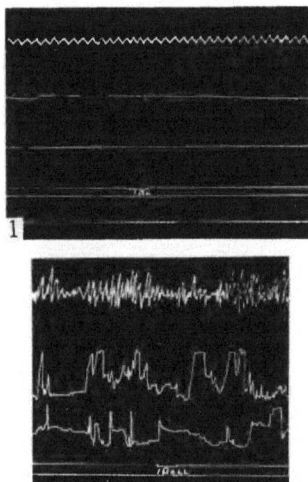

Text-figure 103. (1) Record showing the lack of generalization and inert nature in the dogs of group A. This record was obtained from a bassethound which had been trained in the motor situation. As the record shows, there was no leg response to the buzzer presented for the first time. (2) Generalization in the animals of group B, in this case a German shepherd. The dog had formed the conditioned avoiding reaction to a clicking signal. The record shows a vigorous avoiding response given to a bell introduced for the first time.

*Excitation-inhibition ratio.* It has been emphasized that some of the excitable dogs gave the conditioned response each time the signal was introduced, while the extremely inactive ones never gave a well developed avoiding reaction. Thus, in the former it was not necessary to reinforce the signal with the shock as often as in the latter. The frequency with which the reaction appears in the animals or the frequency with which they receive the shock after the response once occurs, serves as an indication of the degree of nervous excitability. The lethargic group received the shock more frequently than the active, tense group. In some active animals the signal appeared to be intense enough to elicit two or more avoiding movements before the association between the signal and the movement disappeared and the animal was shocked again. These ratios may be shown by indicating the number of true avoidance reactions to 100 signals. More than 400 signals were given to all the dogs, and in most cases more than 500. It was not necessary, however, to give this

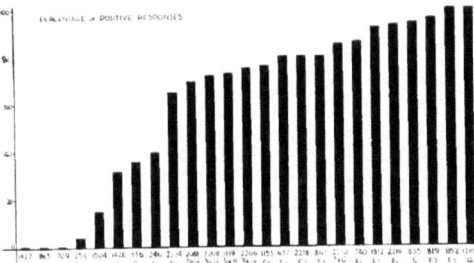

Text figure 104

number in order to arrive at an indication of the general degree of excitability of the dogs. If the animal is excitable, it is apparent as soon as the reaction is formed. The sluggish nature is also apparent from the beginning of the experiments, since these dogs are not greatly disturbed by the shock. The number of responses given to 100 signals is shown in text-figure 104.

The animals of group A, having a low response value, are on the left side of the chart. For example, 1427 ♀, 863 ♂, and 709 ♀ did not form a true conditioned avoiding reaction. Animal 251 ♂ gave a continued avoiding response in only two of the 100 applications of the signal. For the other

98 signals the dog gave either a series of flexions and extensions of the foreleg, a pumping reaction, or failed to respond at all. Animal 1504 ♀, next to 251 ♂, gave only eight continued avoiding responses in 100 signals. These two animals are low response types. In contrast to these, note the high response value of the German shepherd, 1285 ♀. This animal made a definite continued avoiding movement to every signal presented. Another excitable dog of group B, Saluki 835 ♀, responded to 97 of the 100 signals.

*Intermediate groups A-plus and B-minus.* Table 7 and text-figure 104 record the findings for the intermediate groups. These dogs gave a more balanced performance than either of the polar groups. They did not become hyper-excitable nor completely irresponsive, and, as a rule, formed a conditioned avoiding reaction. The frequency of the reaction varied, however; some gave a high ratio of responses to one reinforcement, and others gave a lower excitatory-inhibitory ratio. For example, for 100 positive signals, animal 1152 ♂ gave eighty reactions and failed to respond to twenty. Animal 246 ♀ responded to forty-four and failed to respond to fifty-six. In the latter case, one reinforcement is about equal to one avoiding reaction, while in 1152 ♂ the "effect" of the reinforcement is much greater.

Just as in the salivary reaction, these dogs were considered the best types for these experimental purposes, especially those of the B-minus group, in which the positive was formed and occurred regularly, and in which a negative reaction also could be developed. By contrasting food with one signal, and shock with another, one animal, 1152 ♂, was able to differentiate between a clicker rate of 96 and one of 120 vibrations per minute. Text-figure 102 (fig. 2) shows one of the differential responses. By contrasting right and left leg reactions, a bassethound-Saluki $F_2$, 929 ♂, formed a differentiation between 60 and 120 vibrations per minute.

*Summary and discussion.* In the motor reflex experiments, as in the salivary, twenty-three dogs were trained, and here, as in the previous experiments, the dogs gave two widely different types of performance, with many intermediates between the extremes.

The dogs classified as group A are unable to make a true continued avoiding adjustment. Some of them form the "alternating" or "pumping" reaction, that is, the dog raises and lowers the leg while the signal sounds. This definitely indicates the low excitatory value of the signal, since high excitation would lead to definite (and sustained) contraction. The inability of these dogs to make the avoiding adjustment again emphasizes their lethargic nature and the tendency to conserve energy. As in the salivary situation, they do not react unless it is necessary. The behavior of these dogs thus follows the same general pattern in the muscular performance and in the less controlled glandular behavior. When the signal is applied there is no perceptible increase in breathing or heart rate. Neither the signal nor the shock disturbs them. If the shock is increased beyond the liminal point, they give a short bark as it is applied, but there is no after-discharge of excitation and no further disturbance.

The dogs classified as B are the excitable animals. They formed the conditioned response readily, and it could be elicited frequently without reinforcement. This is expressed in terms of a high excitatory value for the signal. Even after the avoiding response is made, the signal does not lose its excitatory value. This is based not only on a delicate balance or association between the auditory centers and the neuro-muscular system of the leg, but also on a difference in ratio between nervous excitation and inhibition in the nervous system. An increase in the breathing rate is apparent when the signal is applied. Some of the dogs whine or bark during the signal, even though the painful irritation is avoided. All these reactions indicate a greater degree of irradiation of excitation throughout the correlated and associated reflex systems than that found in the dogs of group A. If these excitable dogs could not avoid the shock, they made violent efforts to escape from the laboratory and soon developed a nervous disturbance. This disturbance is evident by the dog's antagonism to the experimenter, and the laboratory situation. In most cases, as soon as they are led to the door of the laboratory they lie down and refuse to enter.

As in the salivary experiments, there are also intermediate types of behavior observed in the motor situation. The classification of the intermediate group of dogs is based on the excitation-inhibition ratio, and on the general behavior, made up of the reflex system correlated and integrated with the leg action. These animals were not consistent in their response to the signals. In some cases, a complete avoidance of the shock appeared to eliminate the excitatory effect of the following signal, and the animal received a reinforcement on the second signal. The ratio here is 50 positive to 50 negative responses. Other dogs responded with 2, 3, 4 or even 5 positive responses for one reinforcement. The phenomenon here is probably the same as the "effect" in trial and error learning. The significant thing is the difference in value of those constitutional factors determining the "effect." One of these is the difference in the ratio or predominance of excitation over inhibition, shown in the excitation-inhibition ratio. It is reasonable to suppose that in those animals in which the conditioned avoiding reaction occurred repeatedly after its formation without continued reinforcement, the excitation value of the signal is greater than in those which do not form the reaction. On the basis of our observations in these experiments, it is probable that as a larger number of animals are trained there will be a continuous gradation between the inactive and highly excitable types in terms of this excitation-inhibition ratio.

The dogs of group A become progressively less active as the experiments continue, until they finally lean against the harness and confine the reaction wholly to the foreleg segment. All movements of the head disappear. Generally the reaction is made to the shock rather than to the signal, and in every case there is an alternation of flexion and extension of the leg as the signal and shock continue. In the dogs of the B group, the postural systems are always active, and head and body movements are correlated with the leg reaction, indicating a wider involvement of neural processes and the inability to limit excitation to the one significant reflex system. The intermediates fall between the two extremes, the A-plus group showing less involvement of these centers as the experiments progress than the B-minus group. This again emphasizes the difference in degree of excitation and the involvement of correlated reflex systems.

One characteristic of the motor response places it in direct contrast to the salivary reflex. If food is always delayed for 30 seconds during the presentation of the signal, all dogs except the extremely excitable tend to delay the conditioned reaction. Pavlov calls this inhibition of delay. In the motor response, this did not occur even when the signal preceded reinforcement for 5 seconds in every case. The salivary and motor reactions are directly opposite in nature. The food taking performance involves a basic approach adjustment to a pleasant situation, while the motor defensive response is basically a withdrawal from a dangerous and painful object. Since the two systems involve different physiological backgrounds, and are directed toward different physiological adjustments, the laws of excitation and inhibition determining their action are not similar. The rules of conditioning refer not only to physiological drives, but to the external situation, and this should be taken into consideration in the interpretation of behavior.

Another factor of importance in the motor experiment, and one which shows the significance of the situational aspect, is generalization. In our experiments, all dogs forming the continued avoiding response had a tendency to give this response to every signal introduced. This was especially true for the highly active animals of group B. In a previous report (James, '33) the greater tendency of the dogs to generalize in the motor situation than in the salivary was emphasized, and the difficulty in forming differential reactions pointed out. In that report we suggested the possibility that dogs may make closer differentiations in situations involving danger. From the present experiments, however, this is doubtful. In the dogs of group B which responded to every signal introduced, it was almost impossible to form a negative response without the introduction of another reaction with the negative signal which would involve lowering the leg. This was attempted by presenting food with the signal. While this might be considered an incentive, it is really the involvement of another reflex system in the experimental situation, and an attempt to balance one against the other in terms of the excitation-inhibition ratio. When food is presented, the dog must shift the posture and approach the pan, and this reaction makes the leg segment negative, in contrast to its former positive movement to the signal. Another plan involves the employment of the other foreleg. If a second signal is accompanied by a shock on the left instead of the right foreleg, this, of course, will elicit a positive action of the left leg, and a negative action of the right leg. By contrasting the two signals and shocks on each leg, the dog may form a differentiation reaction. As a matter of fact, it is this type of balancing one system against another that involves the greater part of behavior, and for this reason it should be considered in reflex experiments. Even with such methods, however, "good" results were obtained only among the mid-group animals.

In the present investigation, no emphasis has been placed on the limits of differentiating ability. The interest was in the dog's natural tendency to react to every signal introduced and in the response itself. Close differentiation is concerned with cortical analysis; we were interested in how the wide variety of visceral systems affect the total response rather than in determining the analytical ability of each dog.

## UNTRAINABLE TYPES

The experiments just described show the range of behavior, or mode of adjustment, in two controlled situations. In this connection it would be logical to ask if all dogs can be conditioned to these situations and classified accordingly. Anyone acquainted with behavior, however, is aware that such is not possible. Some dogs cannot be trained, and it is impossible to elicit and direct a progression of behavior in them. These dogs are considered abnormal, in that they have special behavioral tendencies which limit their adjustment.

The first of these to be considered is the extreme "withdrawal" type; that is, an animal will occasionally show what has been termed an extremely passive defense behavior. This type is found particularly among some of the hybrids obtained by cross breeding the German shepherd and bassethound, and the condition is inherited from certain breeding bitches, although it is not a dominant factor. Three of the animals selected for training exhibited this extreme passive defense nature. It should be emphasized that this is different from the initial fear reaction shown by many animals when strangers approach, and which is overcome as they become accustomed to the situation. Such animals do not show the extreme passive nature. During the experiments three animals, two of which we shall describe, were handled constantly.

One case of the withdrawal type was particularly outstanding. This dog, 1301 ♀, was a member of a litter of five whose parents were three-quarters bassethound and one-quarter German shepherd, obtained by crossing an $F_1$ bassethound-shepherd on a pure bassethound. Neither of the parents exhibited the withdrawal nature. This litter was made the object of a special study because of the social order which formed among the five dogs and because of the peculiar nature of animal 1301 ♀. The other members of the litter, 1298 ♂, 1297 ♂, 1300 ♀, and 1304 ♀, were in the B-minus group in the salivary experiments and all four were as nearly equal in performance under laboratory conditions as any dogs we have studied. They were observed as a group in the kennel as well. The results of this study were reported in a previous publication (James, '36). A definite social order formed among the animals of this litter, with 1301 ♀ at the bottom of the hierarchy. This dog was easily dominated by her litter mates because of the extreme passive defense nature which could not be changed by training. The initial adjustment to the laboratory situation was never made, nor would she eat while in the experimental room. Plate 102 (figs. 1 and 2) shows the typical position she assumed in the laboratory. A characteristic behavior was also shown in the kennels. When anyone approached this dog, she moved to the background, while the other members of the litter came forward. It is difficult to believe that this reaction was conditioned, since the dogs had been together since birth and had been fed and handled by the same men.

Another dog with this peculiar withdrawal behavior, 1513 ♂, appeared in a litter of six produced by the same dam as the above group but with a different sire, a bassethound-shepherd $F_1$. A social order formed in this litter also, with 1513 ♂ at the bottom. This dog was so extremely inhibited by the presence of other dogs or of people that it could never be trained to walk on a leash. As in the case of 1301 ♀, he remained in the background when anyone approached. The animal was unable to make any new adjustment and was content only in the familiar environment of the kennel.

The question may be raised, whether this peculiar withdrawal attitude is based on a definite inherited neuromuscular pattern which involves definite neural pathways and relationships with the sympathetic system, which is activated by every change in the environment, or whether it is based on a general inhibition involving all neural processes. If the latter were true, all these "withdrawal" dogs would be the most extreme examples of group A. However, the dogs of group A all make some form of adjustment, that is, they enter the situation willingly from day to day and some modification in their behavior occurs. This does not happen

PLATE 102

EXPLANATION OF FIGURES

1 and 2 Characteristic postures assumed by the extremely submissive type under laboratory conditions. Such animals are untrainable.

3 Abnormal type whose behavior is characterized by hysteria to every great change in its environment. Dogs of this type are untrainable.

PLATE 102

with the withdrawal type. The withdrawal reflexes always remain dominant in these animals, making any form of refined adjustment impossible. The behavior seems to be based on inherited patterns of action which are elicited by every change in the environment.

Still another abnormal type, which occurs rarely, includes those dogs so disturbed by any change in their immediate environment that they exhibit a hysterical syndrome. This involves fear and the elicitation of a vigorous and total pattern of escape. Although every care is taken in handling these animals, they remain nervous from puppyhood. They will not walk on a leash and apparently cannot become accustomed to the experimenter. When anyone enters the run they pull away as far as possible or try to climb the fence. They are so disturbed by thunder and lightning and by incidental noises around the kennel that they must be chained. A picture of one of these animals, a three-quarters German shepherd and one-quarter bassethound, is shown in plate 102 (fig. 3). Note the crouching position and expression on the face of the animal. This dog has always exhibited this behavior which could not be unconditioned. In this case, then, an excitatory phase involving the total escape behavior is presented. Such behavior places the dog out of the range of the trainable types of groups A and B or the intermediates.

## BEHAVIORAL TYPE AND ITS RELATION TO PHYSICAL FORM

During the course of the experiments, certain behavior characteristics were observed which we believe point the way to an interpretation and understanding of the psychological qualities of different constitutions. There appear to be two widely different behavioral types, with intermediates forming a graded series between the two extremes. Most dogs were analyzed in the food (salivary) and motor (avoiding) situations, and in both the bassethound falls into the inactive or A group, and the Saluki and German shepherd into the active or B group. These breeds are also widely different in physical form.

The bassethound has an extreme degree of achondroplasia in the legs and disproportionately large feet, with toes tending to spread apart. No other region of the body, however, shows any noticeable trace of achondroplasia. The head is long and well developed, and characterized by long, drooping ears. The chest is rounded, and the abdomen full, and since there is a tendency to obesity, these animals present a stocky appearance.

In contrast to the bassethound, the German shepherd and Saluki have long, thin, straight legs. Like the bassethound, the head is long. The body is more thin and saggital shaped than round, and since as a rule the abdomen is not equally as deep as the chest, they have a thin "streamlined" appearance. The greatest depth of the arrow shaped chest occurs in the region of the seventh or eighth rib.

These two types of pure breeds differ so widely in physique and behavior as to suggest a possible relationship between morphological form and neurophysiological characteristics. This would mean that the animals inherited not only a definite physical form, but also a particular interorganismal structure, including nervous and glandular processes, which determine their modes of reaction. If such were the case, the question may be raised, whether the factors determining physical form and behavior may be dissociated, or whether a definite behavior nature would always occur with a certain form. Another question is whether the factors have a natural interdependence or have become linked by selective breeding. Further, why is there so little variation in the behavior of the members of each of these breeds while great variation is presented among other dogs? One approach to an answer for these questions would be a comparison of the behaviors and physical form of the first and second generation hybrids obtained by cross breeding the extreme types.

If the dogs are to be studied with reference to physical characteristics as well as behavior, some method of contrasting them must be determined. The indices used in contrasting human constitutions are of little value in studying dogs.[4] Most of them involve leg length, and since in the dog the leg length is a single genetic factor which may be completely dissociated from the body type of the hybrids, it is impractical to use this measurement. Indices based on bodily length, in conjunction with chest width and chest thickness, have not shown significant differences. The cephalic index was first considered as a means for contrasting the dogs, and then the cephalic index in conjunction with bodily length and thickness, but there is no appreciable difference in the cephalic indices among dogs. This is shown in detail in the measurements made by Johnson in Section III of this volume. The head shape varies more in the nasal region, the jaws and in length of ears, and width of zygomatic arches, than in the brain case. Absolute measurements of any one bodily factor are not satisfactory. They tell us a great deal about regional development, but little about the total morphological structure.

After a consideration of many possible measurements and indices, a relatively simple index, based on the thickness or leanness of the body, was used in this study, even though it was realized that this is not an adequate index for giving all the morphological characteristics of an animal. However, this region of the body is determined by a complex of genetic factors and its index has proved practical in contrasting the

---

[4] The adequacy of the indices used on the human has been discussed by Cabot ('38) and Wertheimer and Hesketh ('26).

Piget index: stature (cm)—chest circum. (cm) plus wt. (kg).

Wigert index: $\dfrac{\text{leg length}}{\text{chest trvs. dia.}}$ $\dfrac{10}{\text{chest sag. dia.}}$

Werthemer-Hesketh index: $\dfrac{\text{leg length}}{\text{trans. chest dia.}}$ $\dfrac{10}{\text{gas. chest dia.}}$ trunk ht.

K. A. P. index: $\dfrac{\text{standing ht.}}{\text{sitting ht.}}$ $\dfrac{\phantom{x}}{\text{wt.}}$

There is some agreement among investigators as to which factors are most significant, but the indices are not as yet definite enough to separate the human satisfactorily. If a number of individuals are compared by different indices an overlapping will be found between types.

types. The measurement for the indices involved, first, the greatest saggital length of the chest. This gives the largest vertical diameter of the chest. The measurement is made from the dorsum of the chest to a point on the ventral side which gives the greatest measurement. The region varies to some extent among the dogs, but it is as a rule around the eighth rib. The second is the greatest transverse measurement through the same area. By dividing the transverse measurement by the sagittal measurement and multiplying

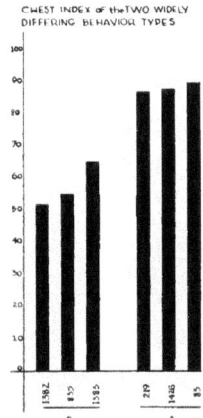

Text figure 105

the quotient by 100, an index is obtained which separates the dogs into round bodied and thin bodied types. As a rule, the round chested dogs are also thick in the abdominal region, and the thin chested dogs are thin in this region. Chest indices of three animals of each group are shown in text-figure 105, and photographs of each type appear in plates 100 (figs. 1, 2, 4) and 101 (figs. 2, 3, 4). The bodily indices of all animals trained are shown in text-figure 106, with the round bodied dogs at the right and the thin bodied animals at the left.

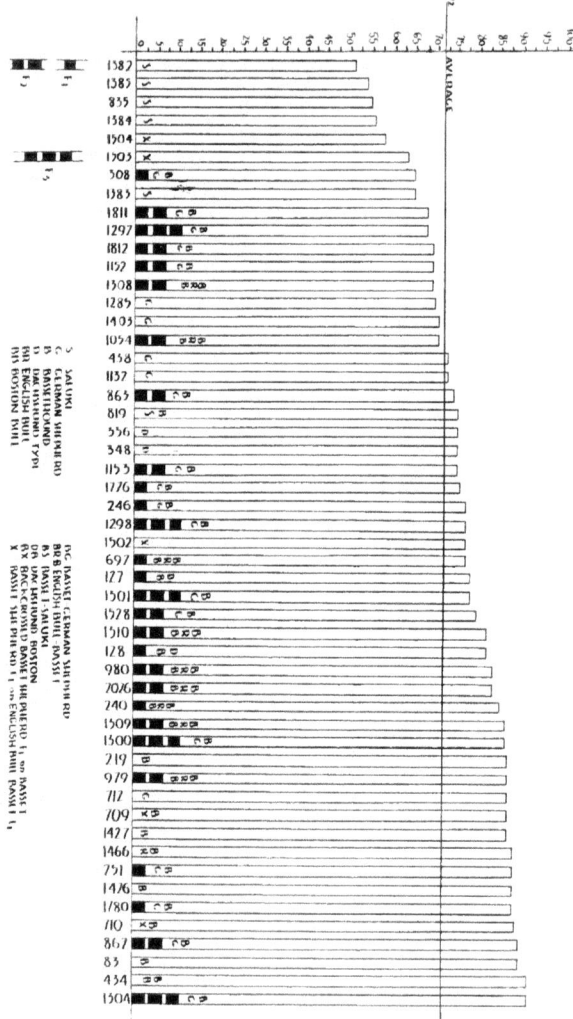

Text-figure 106

Since the bassethound and German shepherd differ so widely in behavior, and are entirely opposite in physical form, hybrids derived from crossing these two pure bred animals were analyzed to see how modification of the physical form by crossbreeding affected the behavior.

The criterion of the behavioral classifications has been treated fully in the previous sections, and the discussion to follow will be confined to a designation of the behavioral type of each animal and its relationship to physical form. As has already been pointed out, the bassethound falls into group A, or the inactive and inhibited group, under each experimental condition. The German shepherd, on the other hand, is highly active and excitable, and properly fits into group B. In any behavioral situation in which these two opposite types are studied, the contrast between them is marked. In the conditioned food taking situation, the reactions of the bassethound become sluggish, and the conditioned reactions are gradually inhibited; in the conditioned motor situation this animal again performs in a sluggish, irregular manner and tends to respond to the unconditioned signal rather than the conditioning one. The German shepherd, on the other hand, remains highly active and responsive in the conditioned food taking situation, giving vigorous conditioned salivary reactions, with short delays in the responses and without showing any tendency to develop complete inhibition. This animal forms positive responses to all signals with little difficulty, but has some difficulty in developing negative reactions. In the motor situations, the German shepherd is again highly responsive, somewhat disturbed, alert, tense, quick acting, and always careful to make the avoiding movement. The reactions of both the bassethound and the German shepherd are predictable in any situation in which they are studied — the bassethound will be among the inhibited dogs and the shepherd among the excitable.

*Bassethound-German shepherd $F_1$s.* Theoretically, the genetics of the animals obtained by crossing the bassethound and the German shepherd is relatively simple. Each $F_1$ should inherit the same factors from both parents, and for this reason should be similar in physical form, or have no greater variation than is found among the members of one breed. Thus, the bassethound-shepherd $F_1$s are similar in physical form, size, coat texture, and color, and all have short legs, although not so extreme as those of the bassethound parent. Each member of the group has the long, drooping ears of the bassethound. Although there is some variation among them, this is no greater than would be found among a large group of any pure breed (pl. 103, fig. 1).

The bodily indices of the bassethound-shepherd $F_1$s which were trained range from 65 to 88.

```
int.  308 ♂ — 65
int. 1776 ♂ — 77
int.  246 ♀ — 77
int.  251 ♂ — 88
int. 1780 ♀ — 88
```

Although 1776 ♂ and 1780 ♀ are litter mates, as are 246 ♀ and 251 ♂, the difference in bodily index between both pairs of sibs is 11 points. This is not, however, as wide a difference as is found between the bassethound and German shepherd parents. For example, the bassethound parent of 1776 ♂ and 1180 ♀ had an index of 90 and the German shepherd parent an index of 68, a difference of 22. This difference is much greater than will be found among a group of $F_1$s of one litter. It is noted that animal 308 ♂ had a chest index of 65, or 3 points less than the pure shepherd parent of 1776 ♂ and 1780 ♀. The shepherd sire of 308 ♂ died before these experiments were started and his bodily index could not, therefore, be obtained. If the shepherd parent of 308 ♂ had a lower index than the shepherd parent of 1776 ♂ and 1780 ♀, this $F_1$ with a thinner body than a pure shepherd would not be improbable. Since the $F_1$s are not exactly alike it would seem to indicate that the parents are not as pure genetically as they are thought to be, or that unexplainable interorganismal variations have occurred, due to mixing of genetic factors, which affects the development of each animal.

*Behavior classification of $F_1$s.* In the experiments on behavior, none of the animals was classified with the typical

PLATE 103

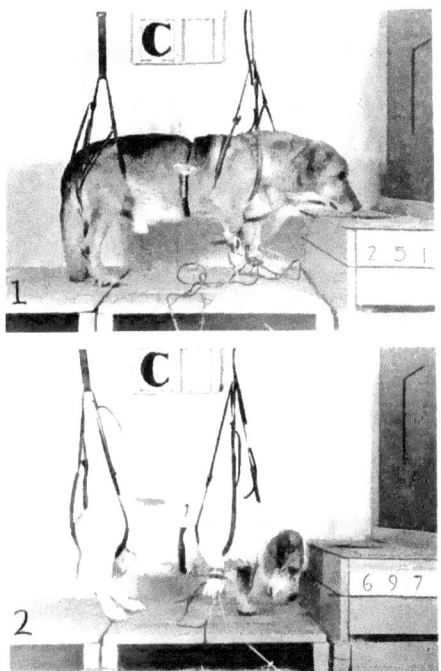

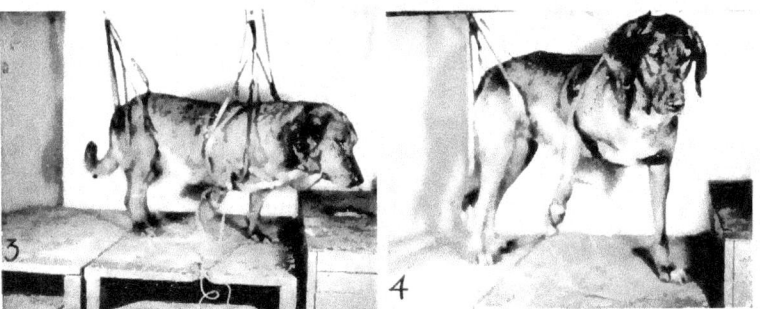

1 Bassethound-German shepherd $F_1$, a well balanced animal of the mid-group, holding the leg in the avoiding position as the conditioning signal sounds.
2 Bassethound-English bulldog $F_1$, a well balanced animal of the mid-group, holding the leg in the avoiding position as the conditioning signal sounds.
3 A short-legged, round bodied bassethound-German shepherd $F_2$ of group A, holding the leg in the avoiding position as the conditioning signal sounds.
4 A long-legged, round bodied bassethound-German shepherd $F_2$ of group B, holding the leg in the avoiding position as the conditioning signal sounds. The animals of figures 3 and 4 are sibs.

bassethound or German shepherd parents. The reactions of 246♀, 1776♂, 251♂, and 1780♀ were similar, and 246♀ and 251♂ have been discussed fully in the sections on the food taking reaction and the motor reaction. All four animals were placed in the A-plus intermediate group, or the well balanced type useful for general experimental purposes. The fifth $F_1$ studied, 308♂, was more excitable than others of this group, but still of the intermediate type; its rating is B-minus. This dog had greater difficulty in forming the negative reactions than did others of his generation. Although individual behavior differences are found among these $F_1$ animals, these are no wider than found for the bassethound and German shepherd parents. Another factor of importance is that there is no great variation in behavior when these dogs are studied in different situations. There is not only homogeneity among the members of a group, but also a rather harmonious blending of the behavioral determining factors in each dog as well as those determining physical form.

*Bassethound-shepherd $F_2s$.* When the short legged first generation hybrids are mated *inter se*, the second generation shows a clear cut redistribution of the contrasted grand-parental characters. Both the short, bent legs of the hound and the long straight thin legs of the shepherd reappear in the second generation in the expected Mendelian ratio of 3 to 1. The shortness of the leg differs among the members of the group; about one in three is as short as the bassethound while the other two resemble more closely the $F_1s$. The long legged animals of the $F_2$ generation are truly long, like the shepherd. There is also some variation in bodily form among these $F_2$ dogs. However, with the group used in these experiments, the variation is no wider than that found in the $F_1s$. The chest indices of the group are as follows:

```
      lg.  1811 ♂ — 68         lg.  1153 ♂ — 75
      int. 1152 ♂ — 69         int. 1528 ♂ — 80
      int. 1812 ♂ — 69         lg.  867 ♂ — 90
      sh.  863 ♂ — 74
```

When the members of one litter of $F_2$s are compared with each other, there is a wider range in bodily index than is found among a litter of $F_1$s. This can be demonstrated by two sibs, 867 ♂ and 863 ♂. The $F_1$ parents of these dogs, 247 ♀ and 308 ♂, had chest indices of 77 and 65, respectively, a difference of 12. The indices of 867 ♂ and 863 ♂ are 74 and 90, a difference of 16, giving them a greater variation than the parents and nearly as great as that between the pure bassethound, which is about 90, and the pure shepherd, which is 68. Animal 867 ♂ is shown in plate 103 (fig. 4), and animal 863 ♂ in the same plate (fig. 3).

The variations among the $F_2$s are further demonstrated by a litter of ten bassethound-shepherd hybrids of this generation, which were not trained in the experiments but which were offspring of two trained $F_1$s, 1776 ♂ and 1780 ♀. These dogs are shown in plate 104. The chest indices of this litter are as follows:

int. 2592 ♀ — 60        lg. 2586 ♀ — 70
lg. 2591 ♀ — 62         int. 2590 ♀ — 70
sh. 2587 ♂ — 63         int. 2588 ♀ — 70
lg. 2593 ♀ — 65         sh. 2594 ♀ — 79
int. 2585 ♀ — 68        sh. 2589 ♂ — 94

It will be observed that most of these dogs are as thin bodied as the shepherd, with indices below 70 and as low as 60; others are as round bodied as the bassethound, with the highest index reaching 94. Three dogs are short legged, like the bassethound grandparent; four are intermediate, like the $F_1$s; and three are long legged, like the shepherd grandparent. Two of the long legged animals, 2591 ♀ and 2593 ♀, have thin bodies, and thus are about the same in physical form as the shepherd grandparent. In addition, a thin body is found on one short legged dog, 2587 ♂. This animal had a more mixed physical form than the two long legged animals with thin bodies. Such variations in bodily structure give an odd appearance to many of these dogs. All dogs of this litter have the long, flopping bassethound ears.

PLATE 104

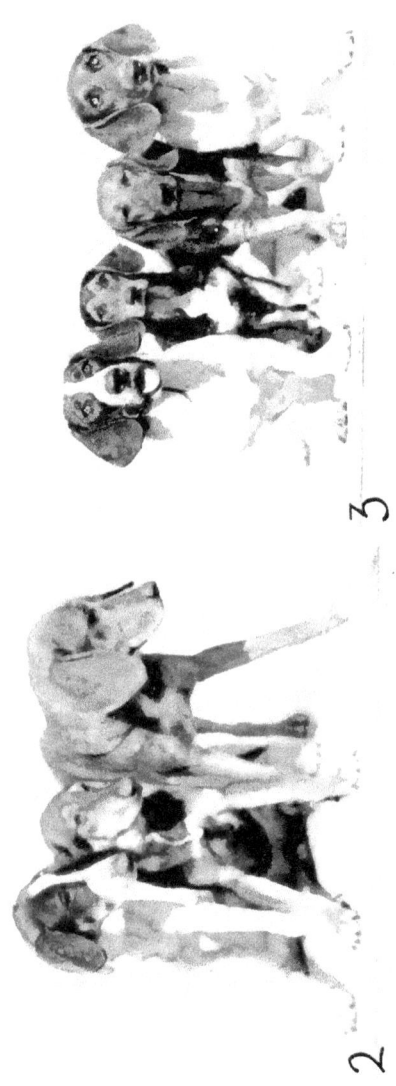

1, 2 and 3: Variation in physical form in a litter of bassethound-German shepherd F₂. There is also great variation in behavior among such dogs.

*Behavior classification of bassethound-shepherd $F_2s$.* If there are greater differences in physical form among the $F_2s$ than among the $F_1s$, and form and behavior are correlated or linked in any way, there should also be greater variety in behavioral characteristics among the $F_2s$. The behavioral classification, along with the bodily types, are shown in text-figure 107. Three of the $F_2$ animals are considered thin bodied and four round bodied. Animals 1811 ♂ and 1812 ♂ are classified as A-plus. They are similar in

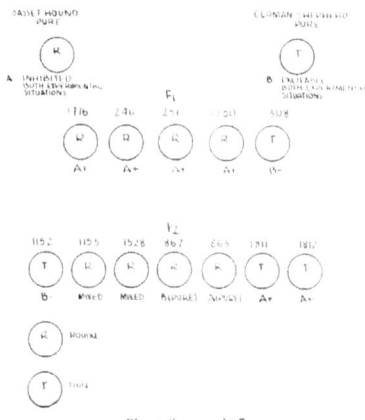

Text-figure 107

every respect to the $F_1s$ 246 ♀ and 251 ♂, the well balanced type referred to above. Animal 1152 ♂, a long legged dog below the average for bodily index and thus classified as thin bodied, falls into the B-minus group. This is the dog used so successfully in differentiation experiments and considered a well balanced type, although behaviorally more like the shepherd than the bassethound. In contrast to this animal, another long legged member of the group, 867 ♂, was round bodied, with a chest index of 90. This animal, therefore, is similar to the bassethound grandparent in bodily shape, yet behaviorally it falls with the shepherd into group B under each experimental situation. Therefore, the bodily form and behavioral relationship found in the bassethound grandparent would seem to be reversed in this case. One dog of the group, 863♂, a brother of 867♂, is not only round bodied like 867♂ but has the short legs of the bassethound. This dog looks very like a pure bassethound, as shown in plate 103 (fig. 3). It is also classified in the bassethound or A group in the experiments and is considered a pure A type. In this case, then, there is a body and behavior correlation similar to that found in the pure bassethound grandparent.

In the $F_2$s discussed thus far, 1811♂, 1812♂, 1152♂, 867♂, and 863♂, there has been no wide variation in the individual performances, that is, each animal gave about the same type of performance in the different experimental situations. Two dogs among the $F_2$s, however, 1153♂ and 1528♀, were unusual in this regard. Both performed well in the conditioned food taking situation and were classified as A-plus and B-minus, respectively. Yet when they were trained in the conditioned avoiding situation, they fell into a different classification. For example, when the attempt was made to develop the conditioned avoiding reaction in 1528♀, the animal became hyper-excitable. She could not restrain the escape reaction after the shock was introduced. In this case there is an exaggeration of the motor systems, and in contrast to the well balanced performance in the food taking situation, the motor situation causes hyper-excitability. This is in direct contrast to the bassethound grandparent, which is inactive under both conditions, and to the German shepherd grandparent, which is very active but trainable in all situations. For this reason, 1528♀ is considered a mixed behavioral type, in that she has behavioral characteristics similar to both, but with an exaggerated motor performance. Animal 1153♂ followed somewhat the same pattern as 1528♀.

This dog, however, was more inactive in the conditioned food taking situation, since the response was completely inhibited after a short time. In the motor experiments, however, 1153♂ was in the excitable or B group. Thus this dog is also classified as having a mixed behavioral nature.

*Bassethound-German shepherd $F_1$ backcrossed on bassethound.* Two hybrids, produced by mating a bassethound-shepherd $F_1$ to the parent bassethound, were studied in an attempt to determine if dogs theoretically more bassethound in inheritance would show the behavioral characteristics of the pure breed. All $F_1$ hybrids have legs of intermediate length and carry the factor for both long and short. When the $F_1$ is bred back to the pure bassethound, all offspring should be short legged (see p. 61, Stockard). In this case, however, the bassethound parent was 219♂, obtained by mating bassethound 83♀, referred to on page 50 (Stockard), to "Dilligence." Number 83♀ carried the genetic factor for long legs, since her line had been crossed with the foxhound. For this reason, one of the backcrosses used in the experiments, 710♀, was long legged while the other, 709♂, of the same litter, was short legged. Both dogs fall well within the bassethound group in bodily shape, however, with indices of 87 and 89 (text-fig. 108).

In the conditioned salivary situation, both dogs were classified with the thin group, 709♂ with a rating of B-minus and 710♀ with a rating of B. However, when 709♂ was trained with the motor experiments, it was found to fall into the A group with the bassethound. This dog never formed a satisfactory continued avoiding reaction and was not greatly disturbed by shock, an unexpected performance after the reactions to the salivary situation. Animal 710♀ was not trained with the motor response, but it is felt that one case is enough to indicate that the backcross of an $F_1$ on the bassethound parent will not necessarily give a type similar to the bassethound. The genetic factors determining behavior are too complicated to result in the pure type of performance when an $F_1$ is bred back to either parent type.

*Five offspring of the two above animals, 709 ♂ and 710 ♀.*
These dogs were included in the group to be trained and studied because they were predominantly bassethound in inheritance, and from general observations were very like the bassethound grandparent. The group included the following:

sh. 1297 ♂ — 67
sh. 1298 ♂ — 77
sh. 1301 ♀ — 79
sh. 1300 ♀ — 86
sh. 1304 ♀ — 92

A graphic representation of these indices is shown in text-figure 108. There is wide variety in bodily form among

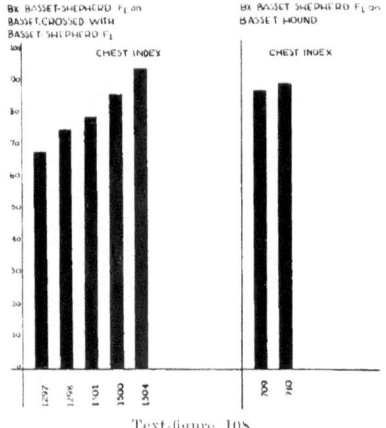

Text-figure 108

these dogs, although all have the short legs of the bassethound. Four animals are classed as round bodied types, while one falls into the extremely thin group. Thus we observe the thin body of the German shepherd inherited from the $F_1$ bassethound-shepherd grandparent.

In the behavior experiments, 1297 ♂, 1298 ♂, 1300 ♀, and 1304 ♀ formed the laboratory adjustment and developed vigorous conditioned salivary reactions. Among these four dogs there were no significant differences in behavior; all were classified as A-plus. However, one animal of this litter, 1301 ♀, was unable to make an adjustment to the laboratory and thus was classed with the extremely timid and inhibited group which was disturbed by every variation in the environment. She was discussed in detail in the section on abnormal types. Although this group of dogs is predominantly bassethound in inheritance, there is some variation in bodily form and also variations in behavior. The breeding together of two backcrossed $F_1$s on the bassethound, therefore, does not produce a homozygous type. The extremely timid behavior of 1301 ♀ would seem to be due to a highly mixed nature, since this peculiar reaction does not appear in the grandparents.

*General summary of the bassethound and shepherd crosses.* In the two polar types, A and B, there seems to be a definite correlation between bodily form and behavior. There is a harmonious relationship among the genetic factors for physical form, glandular conditions and behavior. When the two polar types are bred together, however, this relationship breaks up. There is more variation in behavior among the $F_2$s than among the $F_1$s. A dog may inherit the bodily form of the bassethound, yet behave like the excitable shepherd dog under experimental conditions. Others seem to have some characteristic physical qualities of each parent and the behavior qualities of both polar types. These are considered animals with mixed behavior patterns.

Consideration of the backcrossed bassethound-German shepherd $F_1$ on the bassethound, and offspring from two backcrossed animals, shows that among hybrids there may be great resemblance in bodily form yet a wide divergence in behavior. Once the physical form and behavior qualities of two pure types are mixed, it requires many selective breedings to isolate the two features again.

STUDY OF DOGS SHOWING EXAGGERATED DEVIATIONS IN
PHYSICAL FORM FROM THE MORE NORMAL TYPES

Under experimental conditions it was found that some animals could not be included within the range of normal behavior. These animals also have a mixed nature, in that they may conform to an inhibited type in one situation and to an excitable type in another. Most of these dogs are either hybrids obtained by crossing two widely different types, or pure breeds which have physical abnormalities, and they should not be overlooked in a study on constitution. The English bulldog in particular has this mixed and abnormal nature. Although this is considered a pure breed, there is great variation in physical form among the individual members.

*English bulldog.* The bassethound and German shepherd are considered normal types. There is no deviation in either physical form or behavior which would place them out of the range of the trainable animals. The peculiarities of each fit it for a particular job which is performed in a distinctive manner, but neither can be said to make better adjustments than the other; it can only be said that the form of the adjustment differs. The English bulldog, on the other hand, falls into a separate class. The extremities of the bulldog are stocky and straight, and the long bones of the legs show no evidence of chondrodystrophy. The bodily shape of the English bulldog is like the hound, with the full bodied chest and abdomen. There are, however, definite regional deformities on both ends of the axial skeleton. There is chondrodystrophy of the basal parts of the skull, which gives the dog the shortened snout, and also in the vertebrae of the tail, resulting in the twisted or "screw" tail. These regional deformities place the dog out of the range of the normal type in physical form.

*Behavior of the English bulldog.* The English bulldog also deviates from the normal type in general behavior. The hunting reaction in these dogs has been completely lost.

In many members, the maternal reaction is distorted. The puppies are often neglected after whelping, and in some cases there is a peculiar abnormal reaction during whelping, in that the bitch, instead of eating the amnion and biting it off at the proper place, chews it off too close to the body of the puppy, leading to hemorrhage or later infection. Besides these abnormal maternal reactions, the animal is noted for undue tenacity and ferocity during excitement and is, in fact, supposed to have been inbred to emphasize this tendency. It has been brought out in Section V that both the thyroid and pituitary of the English bulldog deviate from the normal types. As emphasized there, it is possible that the mixing of genetic types from different breeds and the modified glandular structure correlated with it has led to the distortion in both form and behavior in this dog.

Under the food taking situation, the English bulldog formed excellent salivary responses and the behavior was similar to the dogs of group B. There were characteristics, however, not found among these animals. A glance at the chart of the reactions of 1466 ♂ (text-fig. 109) shows that the response was vigorous. Yet it was not accompanied by all the bodily movements characteristic of the dogs of group B. The reactions were, in fact, so great that due to the limitations of the manometer, the total conditioned response could not be measured. The chart shows the values up to .50 cc. and in those cases in which the values were above .50, and over 1 cc. (the limit of the manometer), the columns in the chart are pointed at the top.

Another characteristic of the English bulldog was the frequent attempts to force the disk to rotate as soon as the signal began. This was an intense action, involving growling at the pan, pawing with the foot, and restless movements of the whole body. These reactions, together with the extreme salivary secretion, indicate a hyper-excitability and inability to limit the performance or to delay the reaction after the immediate signal was released. During the interval between signals, the animal would, as a rule, remain completely inactive, especially after the training had progressed for a long period, but a sudden and violent reaction occurred as soon as the signal was applied. This quick succession of extreme inhibition and high excitement was not observed in other dogs. Thus it seems that the amplitude of the phases of inhibition and excitation is greater in the bulldog. The bulldog is like the animals of group B in that it retains a vigorous reaction for a long period of time; it is like the

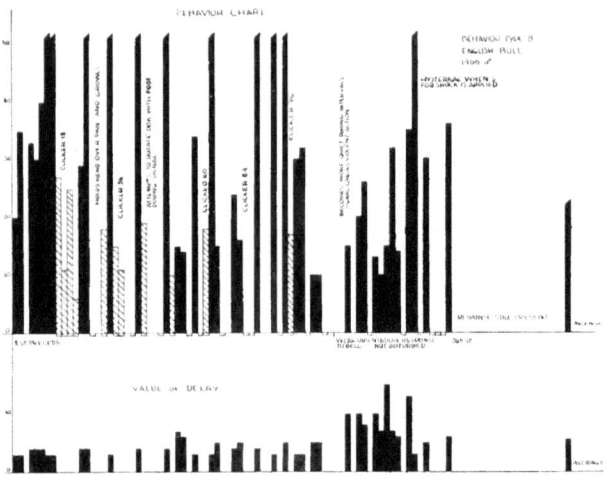

Text-figure 109

animals of A-plus in that although the negative is weak at first, it becomes stable after a period of training. In the latter part of the training the bulldog would not orient to the food pan during the negative signal (pl. 105, fig. 1). As soon as the positive signal for food was applied, however, the animal would go into violent action with quick orientation responses, growling, shifting of the front feet, and pawing at the food pan. Because of this wide behavioral pattern, which the dog was unable to limit to specific components, it

PLATE 105

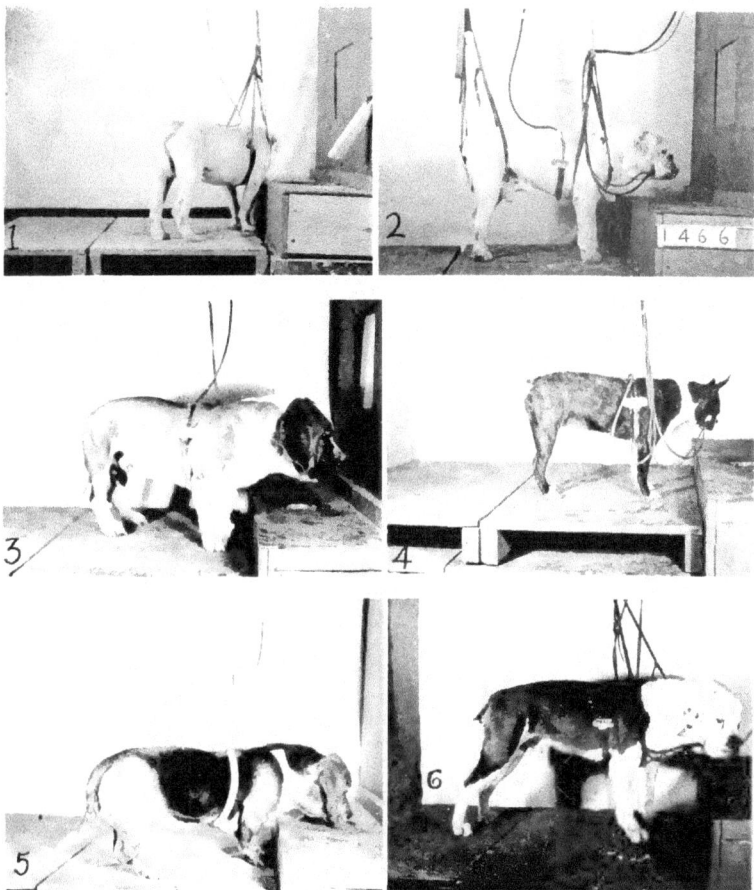

1 and 2. Characteristic postures of the English bulldog under laboratory conditions. In figure 1 the head is turned away from the pan during the negative signal; in figure 2 the animal holds the head over the pan during the positive signal and growls in anticipation of food as the conditioning signal continues.

3. Attitude assumed by a bassethound-English bulldog $F_1$ of the mid group during the signal for food.

4. Boston terrier orienting to the food pan during the signal for food. These dogs are relatively excitable but give a small conditioned salivary reaction to the signal.

5 and 6. Two types of bassethound-English bulldog $F_2$s. The animal in figure 5 is an extremely short legged hound type belonging to the mid group; the animal in figure 6 is long legged, with characteristic bulldog head. This animal made adjustment to the laboratory but did not form a conditioned salivary response. Such dogs have variable behavioral tendencies.

may be assumed that there is a high degree of irradiation, or a greater involvement of neural centers than that found in most dogs. We refer here to the lower postural centers.

As stated above, the English bulldog behaved like the animals of group A during the intervals between the conditioning signals, that is, in a state of almost complete inhibition. Especially was this the case after the experiments had progressed for a time, and the animal had become adjusted to the laboratory procedure. In order to determine the degree of inhibition during these intervals, a loud bell and a shock were applied during one of the periods. Neither stimulus produced any violent reaction at its first application. The dog turned its head slowly to the right when the bell sounded without making any involved movements of orientation. The first shock on the foreleg produced only a weak flexion. There was no struggle or other indication of disturbance. Both these weak reactions emphasize the unexcitable condition of the dog during the intervals. Since the dog was in a low or inhibited phase, similar to sleep, neither of these stimuli was disturbing. Upon the introduction of the signal for food, however, there was a sudden rise of excitation and violent action. It would appear that the dog had become specifically set for the clicker signal to the exclusion of all others.

Still another peculiarity of the English bulldog was shown when an attempt was made to develop the conditioned avoiding reaction. As pointed out above, the shock did not produce any intense response when introduced during one of the regular ''inhibited'' periods between signals for food. Repetition of the signal and shock, however, increased excitability, and the animal became so hysterical that it had to be removed from the room. If the signal for the shock was introduced in any experimental period thereafter, the animal would make violent hysterical attempts to escape, and these reactions continued until the experiments were terminated. This behavior occurred even though the shock was not applied. The dog continued to respond to the signal for food if the signal for shock was not given. Many efforts were made to develop the avoiding reaction without success.

As indicated previously, the dogs of group A did not form an adequate conditioned avoiding reaction; when the shock was given the leg was raised and as the shock continued the leg would be raised and lowered alternately. The animals of group B formed a good conditioned avoiding reaction, which appeared without reinforcement, and the whole level of excitability was raised to every signal. The English bulldog, however, was not disturbed until the signal for the shock was given, that is, the signal had to be more immediate or more closely related to the unconditioned stimulus, than was necessary with other dogs. The bulldog did not anticipate the shock by the situation, but if the immediate signal was given, a heightened excitatory phase, involving the total postural system, suddenly occurred. When the shock was applied, this animal was also more emotionally disturbed than the animals of groups A and B. It appeared that these dogs are unable to stand painful irritation and to make an adjustment to any situation in which a painful stimulus was used.

### Stable Types Produced by Crossing the English Bulldog with the Normal Bassethound

It has been pointed out above that the English bulldog has many physical abnormalities. The animal also has peculiar behavioral reactions, suggesting a mixed behavioral nature. Whether this is the case can be determined by cross breeding the animal with one of the more stable and predictable types, such as the bassethound. By these experiments we not only show the effect of cross breeding a mixed type with one of the more stable types, but also the result obtained when the mixed natures of the bulldog become further modified by bassethound characters among the $F_2$s.

*English bulldog-bassethound $F_1$s.* These dogs have the short legs, round body, and mild achondroplasia of the bassethound (pl. 103, fig. 2; pl. 105, fig. 3). The head shape is more normal than the parent bulldog, although, as a rule, the lower jaw is slightly undershot. The tail in these hybrids is long and straight, as in the bassethound.

Two dogs of this group, 740 ♂ and 697 ♀, were trained. The chest indices were 85 for 740 ♂ and 78 for 697 ♀, placing them both in the round bodied group.

*Behavior of English bulldog-bassethound $F_1s$.* Both 740 ♂ and 697 ♀ were classed with the intermediate group in behavior, although they were not alike. Each formed a good conditioned salivary response, but the positive was much more vigorous in 697 ♀ than in 740 ♂. Both developed inhibition of the positive reaction after a relatively small number of stimuli. The response disappeared in 740 ♂ after 133 stimuli; and in 697 ♀ after 130 stimuli. After disappearance of the salivary response, however, the reaction was elicited by the rotating disk. They did not become completely passive in the conditioned food taking situation, but did become sluggish and unresponsive to the mild tactile stimuli, as was shown for the dogs of group A. They differ from the bassethound in that a negative response is formed and they are able to give the positive and negative reaction for a short time before the positive becomes inhibited. Animal 697 ♀ had greater difficulty in forming a negative, and is therefore considered more excitable than 740 ♂. No. 697 ♀ was classified as B-minus while 740 ♂ was placed in the A-plus group.

In the motor reflex experiments, these dogs also conform to the mid-group type. They formed excellent avoiding reactions with an excitation-inhibition ratio similar to the mid-group dogs, as shown in the case of 697 ♀ and 740 ♂ of text-figure 104. The hyper-excitable nature of the English bulldog parent, as shown under similar conditions, was absent. Breeding the abnormal physical type, the English bulldog, to the homozygous bassethound of type A, results therefore in rather well balanced offspring.

Mixed Nature of the English Bulldog is Emphasized in the Second Generation Bulldog-Bassethound Hybrids

*English bulldog-bassethound $F_2$s.* As is the case with the bassethound-shepherd cross, there is wider variation in physical form among the bulldog-bassethound $F_2$s than among the $F_1$s. These differences are even more striking in the bulldog-bassethound cross, since there are modifications in nearly all bodily factors. For example, there are variations in leg length, tail, and in the degree of shortness of the skull. The variation in the skulls is treated fully in Section III and illustrated in plate 57 (p. 321). The heads in the $F_2$s differ in size, in the degree of undershot condition of the mandible and in the amount of shortening of the face (pl. 58, p. 323). There is also a difference in the degree of loose overgrowth of the skin, and a wide range of size and bodily form among the $F_2$s. The growth abnormalities are associated with a peculiar glandular condition and the constitutional complexes arising from the new combinations of factors among these hybrids. The mixed physical types in this group cause many of the dogs to be particularly odd and comic in form.

Among these $F_2$s there is less variation in bodily shape than in any other physical character. Most of the dogs inherit a round chest and full abdomen, although they are not all as round chested as the bassethound. The short legged dogs have the rounder chests, and the long legged dogs are slightly thinner, although never as thin as the shepherd. Plate 105 (figs. 5 and 6) shows two of these $F_2$s. The chest indices of the group are as follows:

```
    lg.  1308 ♀ — 69         int. 2026 ♂ — 83
    lg.  1054 ♂ — 71         int.  980 ♂ — 83
    lg.   991 ♂ — 71         sh.  1309 ♀ — 86
    int. 1310 ♂ — 82         sh.   979 ♂ — 87
```

*Behavior of English bulldog-bassethound $F_2$s.* All the dogs of this generation with short and intermediate legs — 979 ♂, 1309 ♀, 980 ♂, 1310 ♂, 2026 ♂ — fall into the inactive or A and A-plus groups in the food taking situation. Two of these, 980 ♂ and 2026 ♂, were also trained with the motor response, but in this situation they behaved like the grandparent English bulldog. They were unable to restrain themselves when the signal for the shock was introduced. The behavior and bodily type of this group is shown in text-figure 110.

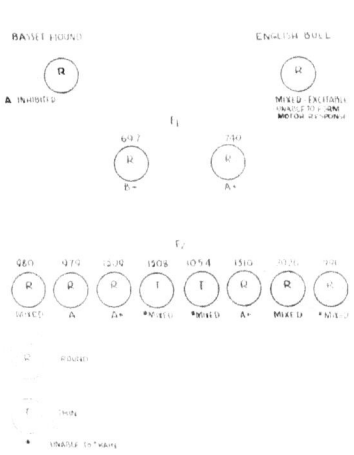

Text-figure 110

The long legged dogs, which are near the thin group in bodily form — 1054 ♂, 991 ♂, 1308 ♀ — also had highly mixed behavioral reactions. None developed a conditioned salivary response, and all were definitely untrainable in the motor situation. Two, 1308 ♀ and 1054 ♂, would remain quiet in the experimental situation and eat the food presented, but would not respond to the conditioning signal. After having eaten the food, these two animals continued to sniff the pan, waiting for more. Their failure to react to the signal would seem to indicate a low analytical ability, in that the food taking reaction could not be broken up into its separate and specific parts. Other relatively simple associations could not be formed. Their behavior seemed to be limited within the range of the kennel, and when removed from this environment they became highly disturbed.

*Summary.* The English bulldog has many physical abnormalities and behavioral tendencies not shown by the bassethound and German shepherd or the hybrids obtained by cross breeding these two dogs. The bulldog has some behavioral characteristics of both the bassethound and shepherd, yet in many situations is completely different from both. By mating the bulldog with the more normal bassethound, relatively normal hybrids are produced. The $F_1$s fall into the inactive group in behavior, but are more excitable than the pure bassethound. Among the $F_2$s, there is a wider variety of physical form as well as behavioral characteristics than is found for the bassethound-shepherd $F_2$s. This indicates that the parent bulldog is more mixed genetically than either the shepherd or the bassethound. The $F_2$s resembling the bassethound in appearance fall into the inhibited group in the salivary experiments, but none could be trained in the motor situation. The intense emotional nature shown in situations involving pain and danger is probably dependent on many factors, but since the bulldog has behavioral characteristics similar to the bassethound, these, together with the characteristics from the parent bassethound, dominate in the $F_1$s. Among the $F_2$s, however, in which the factors become separated, those determining this intense emotional nature are predominant. If a larger number of $F_2$s were trained, possibly some would be found which would behave like the bassethound in the motor experiments. The purposes of the present experiment had been completed, however, inasmuch as it was shown that where there is a greater variety in physical form and glandular conditions, there is also a greater variation in behavioral natures, and in this connection there was no need to train a larger number of animals.

*Bassethound-German shepherd $F_1$ by English bulldog-bassethound $F_1$.* Thus far we have dealt only with the first and second generation hybrids obtained by breeding the physical types A (bassethound) and B (German shepherd) together, and the mixed English bulldog and bassethound. A bassethound-shepherd $F_1$ and a bulldog-bassethound $F_1$, which had been employed in the above experiments, were crossed to determine the variability in behavioral patterns when all parent types are involved. Three dogs, theoretically one half bassethound, one quarter German shepherd, and one quarter English bulldog, resulted from this mating. One offspring, 1502 ♀, was short legged and round bodied with a chest index of 78. The other two, 1504 ♀ and 1503 ♀, were long legged and thin bodied with chest indices of 58 and 63, respectively. Animal 1502 ♀ was classed with the inactive group in behavior, but since she did not become completely passive under laboratory conditions, was considered A-plus rather than A. Animal 1504 ♀ was much more excitable and developed vigorous conditioned salivary reactions and a stable negative. The general course of its behavior was similar to that of the B-minus group. This dog was also trained with the motor reflex, and in this situation her behavior was precisely like that of the bassethound. She was unable to form a continued avoiding reaction, although more than 400 signals were applied and reinforced. She was never disturbed by the shock. This behavior was unexpected and could not have been anticipated on the basis of her performance in the salivary situation. The third dog of the group, 1503 ♀, was different from the other two. This animal was unable to make even the initial adjustment to the laboratory situation or the experimenter. She became hysterical and frightened by every change in the environment, and when anyone entered the kennel would attempt to jump the fence. It is possible that in this animal the excitable nature of the shepherd and the bulldog are dominant over the lethargic nature of the bassethound, although theoretically the bassethound is dominant in inheritance.

## THE SIGNIFICANCE OF SIZE AND ITS RELATION TO BEHAVIORAL TYPE

The question may be raised, whether the inactive nature exemplified by the bassethound, and the highly active nature as found in the German shepherd, occur in other breeds which differ in size and general appearance. In other words, does the behavioral nature, as isolated in the above experiments, bear any direct relation to the size of the animal, or is the significant factor the organization or patterning of the genetic factors? In order to answer this question, some of the smaller animals were studied in the same experimental situations discussed for the above breeds. There are other hound types, similar in general bodily form to the bassethound, which differ in size, as for example the dachshund, beagle hound, and bloodhound. Another bulldog type is the American bred Boston terrier which is smaller than the English bulldog but which has similar physical abnormalities. These animals differing in size yet with the same general morphological characteristics as those animals already discussed were not extensively studied. The dachshund, which shows many characteristics of the bassethound, was the first small dog to be considered.

*Dachshund.* The dachshund has a normal head, body and tail, resembling these characters in the bassethound; it also has pronounced achondroplasia in the much shortened extremities. Although these two animals are comparable in physical form, the dachshund is somewhat dwarfed, reaching only about half the size of the bassethound. The dachshund also tends to be round bodied, although it is not as extreme in this character as the bassethound.

Since no pure dachshunds were available for these experiments, two dogs which were predominantly dachshund in inheritance were trained. One of these, 336♀, with a chest index of 76, was a hybrid obtained by crossing a pure dachshund with a dachshund-Brussels griffon $F_1$. The other animal, 248♀, also with a chest index of 76, was obtained from a mating between a dachshund and a dachshund-Boston terrier

$F_1$. Both these animals were of the round bodied type. In the food taking experiments, animal 248 ♀ became completely inhibited after 50 signals had been applied with food, and a conditioned salivary reaction was never formed. The second animal, 336 ♀, developed a weak response, lasting for a short time only, and became completely inhibited after 100 signals had been applied with food (pl. 100, fig. 3). It was evident that in the salivary situation both dogs fell into the inactive group.

These two animals were also trained with the motor response. No. 248 ♀ failed to develop a conditioned avoiding reaction. Animal 336 ♀ formed a conditioned avoiding movement, but, as shown in text-figure 104, the percentage of responses was extremely low. This places the dogs in the round bodied group for the motor reaction as well as the salivary reaction. It is reasonable to assume, on the basis of the behavior of these two dogs, that the dachshund is like the bassethound in general behavior.

*Boston terrier.* The next type to be considered from this point of view was the Boston terrier. This breed has the same general physical abnormalities, including the undershot jaw, screw tail, round head, and very round body, as the English bulldog. The bodily index of the dog trained, 434 ♀, was 92 (pl. 105, fig. 4).

This Boston terrier was first trained with the food taking situation. In addition to the clicker signals, visual, tactile and other auditory stimuli were employed, and the animal developed good salivary responses to all (text-fig. 100). She appeared to be as excitable in these experiments as the English bulldog, but the conditioned salivary reaction was smaller. This is due to the fact that the Boston terrier is smaller in size and consequently has a smaller food intake. The total amount of food consumed by this dog in one experimental period is only a little more than that consumed by the English bulldog for two signals. Thus the value of the conditioned salivary reaction alone is misleading. The English bulldog has a larger mouth, as well as a larger salivary gland, and its reaction to the 30 second signal is greater, since more food is consumed. The size of the dog, then, must be considered in the salivary reaction, and for this reason we have emphasized the mode of the performance rather than the value of this reaction alone. The Boston terrier, like the bulldog, was disturbed by the delay of food during the 30 second test signals. During the sounding of the signal the dog would whine, jump up and down, and hold the head over the pan. At times the animal pawed at the disk with its foot. She continued to be highly active throughout the period of training, which extended over a period of more than 2 years. As in the case of the English bulldog, the Boston terrier formed negative reactions and settled down to almost complete inactivity during the interval between the signals. The general mode of performance was the same for both dogs.

The Boston terrier differed from the English bulldog when the shock and avoiding signal were introduced. The Boston terrier was not disturbed by the signal for shock and behaved similarly to the dogs of group A. This reaction was unexpected, after the experience with the English bulldog and in consideration of the behavior of the animal in the food taking situation. The animal was passive until the shock was applied. The leg movement was slow and deliberate. As the signal and shock continued, the dog made the alternate reactions typical of some of the animals of group A. In contrast to the English bulldog, the Boston terrier also lost the conditioned salivary response after the shock had been applied for a certain length of time. The application of the painful irritation had an inhibiting effect on all reactions, yet the signal for the shock did not elicit the avoiding movement.

These two dogs of bull type, which are considered pure breeds, do not fit into the behavior groupings of the large majority of the animals. They seem to have characteristics of both group A and B, and also behaviors which are not observed in either group. Their behavior cannot be predicted in the same manner as that of the pure types A and B.

*Dachshund-Boston terrier hybrids.* The hybrids obtained by crossing the dachshund with the Boston terrier show the same general variations in bodily form as found in the bassethound-English bulldog hybrids. The dachshund-Boston terrier $F_1$s are uniform in size and resemble each other closely. In cranial shape they more nearly approach the Boston terrier, but they have the shortened extremities, the long straight tail, and the flopping ears of the dachshund. Two of these dogs, 127 ♂ and 128 ♀, with chest indices of 79 and 80, respectively, and thus of the round bodied group, were trained in the salivary situation. Here they followed the same course of performance as the two dachshund types discussed above, placing them in the A classification. Animal 127 ♂ formed a conditioned response after sixteen signals had been applied; 128 ♀ formed the response after twelve signals. The conditioned response was weak in both cases. In the case of 128 ♀, by the time eighty-five signals had been applied the conditioned response had disappeared, after which the animal made no response at all or responded only to food. No. 127 ♂ behaved in the same manner, becoming completely inhibited after 100 signals.

The $F_2$s of this cross show a curious combination of the grandparental characters. The short legged condition again appears as a single factor dominant in conformity with the record for this character in the bassethound-shepherd $F_2$s. The Boston terrier head and tail are multiple factor expressions, entirely independent of the leg condition. There are dachshund-legged dogs with the Boston terrier head and long, bent or short screw tails. There are tall, long legged dogs with dachshund head and tail. The head is not altogether recessive; its full expression involves both dominant and recessive factors since all the $F_2$s show some resemblance for this feature to the Boston terrier.

None of the $F_2$ dachshund-Boston terriers was studied in the behavior experiments. On the basis of their general behavior in the kennel, and in comparison to the bassethound-

English bulldog $F_2$s, there are many reasons to believe that they have the same general behavior variations as found among the bassethound-English bulldog $F_2$s.

## MEMBER OF A PURE TYPE B WITH PHYSICAL ABNORMALITIES

It is well known that occasionally a member of a pure breed will deviate in physical form from the normal of that breed. In most cases this is due to a diseased condition, or to some abnormality in development, resulting, for example, from an unbalanced diet. A dog of this type was 712♀, a German shepherd, which was heavier than any other dog of this breed in our kennels. Ordinarily the German shepherd is thin bodied, but this animal had a chest index of 85, placing it in the round bodied group. In the conditioned salivary reflex situation, the behavior of this dog was similar to that of the bassethound. Complete inhibition was soon developed and the animal refused to react either to the signals or to food. When this dog was autopsied, the ovaries were found to be diseased and cystic, and the thyroids and pituitary abnormal. It is suggested that when a member of a breed deviates from the typical form for that breed in physique or behavior, specific glandular variations can be found. This further emphasizes the importance of glands on both behavior and morphological form, and is treated at length by Anderson in Section VII.

This case is an example of a pure bred German shepherd which does not conform to breed type either in physical form or behavior. It is not maintained that every German shepherd or bassethound will conform to the A or B classification. There are many factors which affect behavior even after the animal has matured and the body is formed. It is our contention, however, that when an abnormality in glands affects behavior, the bodily form will sooner or later reflect this condition. In every case of a deviation from the normal of the pure group, as the German shepherd just discussed, an abnormality will be found in the glands or some other bodily organ.

## CONTRAST OF THE BEHAVIOR OF THE PURE AND HYBRID DOGS UNDER KENNEL CONDITIONS

It was evident from our studies that under experimental conditions at least the pure bassethound differed in behavioral reactions from the pure German shepherd and Saluki, and that there were many variations in behavior among the hybrids obtained by crossing these types, most of the hybrids falling into the intermediate classes. Since this was so, it seemed of interest to determine whether differences would also be observed among the dogs in kennel surroundings, where there was less control over the behavior.

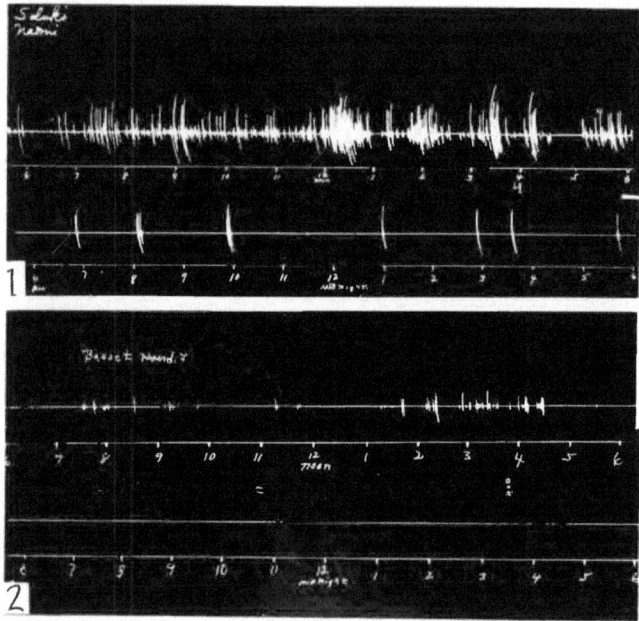

Text figure III. (1) Record showing the active nature of an animal of group B, in this case a Saluki, obtained by the vibrating platform. (2) The relatively inactive nature of the animals of group A, in this case a bassethound, on the vibrating platform.

General activity was the most obvious factor to consider, and two methods were employed in estimating this. In the first method, a pedometer was attached to the dog to record each step. Since all the pedometers were on the same adjustment and were alternated from dog to dog, a fairly accurate quantitative rating could be obtained for each animal. In the second method, the animal was placed in a specially constructed run in which the floor was mounted on springs. By the use of a bellows between the framework of the run and the vibrating floor, the dog's movements were transferred

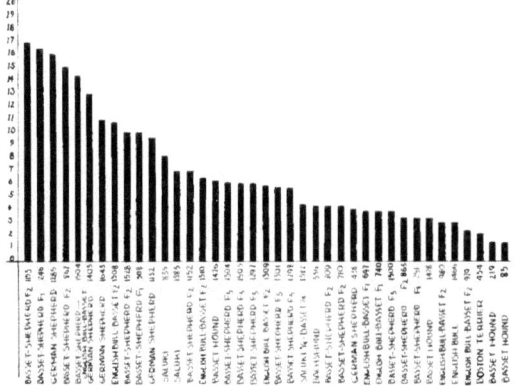

Text-figure 112. Differences in activity among all the dogs, obtained by attaching pedometers to the animals.

into air pressure variations which were recorded on a slowly revolving kymograph by means of a closed tube from the bellows to a Marey tabour and stylus. Characteristic records are shown in text-figure 111. A more comprehensive test of activity is shown by the pedometer records in text-figure 112.

These records clearly show the bassethound to be relatively inactive and the Saluki and German shepherd highly active. The hybrids distribute themselves between these two extremes, with some, as for example 246♀ and 1153♂ (an $F_1$

bassethound-German shepherd and an $F_2$ of the same cross) as active as the pure Saluki and shepherd types. As a rule, those animals which are excitable under laboratory conditions are also excitable in the kennels, but this is not true in every case. The animals of type A sleep or are inactive the greater part of the day. Some of the dogs of type B, on the other hand, move almost continuously. They run or walk back and forth, play and bark. They react to the animals in nearby kennels, to distant noises, to people passing by, or to wind variations. They are easily aroused from sleep, and are the first to give warning when anyone enters the kennel lot. It should be emphasized that age is a factor in activity. Naturally, the older animals are less active than the younger of each breed. It is for this reason, for example, that the German shepherd 438 ♀, and the bassethound 83 ♀ are less active than some of the other members of the group. The thing of importance, however, is that animals 438 ♀ and 83 ♀ are not of equal activity, although of about the same age.

## SUMMARY AND DISCUSSION OF BEHAVIOR AND ITS RELATION TO PHYSICAL TYPE

A study was made of the range of behavior found among the dogs under two experimental conditions, namely adjustment to food taking and the formation of a conditioned avoiding reaction. Of a total of fifty-two dogs used in this series of experiments, all but a few could be trained and given a definite classification. In those that could not be trained, a definite behavior pattern interfered with the formation of a satisfactory adjustment.

Under each experimental procedure, there are highly active, highly inactive, and intermediate types. Certain animals fall into either the active or inactive classification under any experimental condition, while others fall into the active group in one experimental situation, and into the inactive group in another. The dogs with the greatest variations in behavior were, as a rule, hybrid dogs. In this section the dogs were compared to determine the relationship between physical form, glands, and behavior among pure breed types and hybrids obtained by crossing these pure types.

Two pure physical types with opposite behavior classifications were determined — the lethargic and the active. The bassethound is found to be lethargic or inactive in all behavioral situations, and the Saluki and German shepherd fall into the active group. These types also differ widely in physical form. The bassethound is short legged, achondroplasic, has a round thorax and abdomen, and tends to become fat. The German shepherd and Saluki are lean and "streamlined" in appearance; they have long, thin legs, with thin thorax and abdominal regions, giving them a sagittal appearance.

It has been shown in Section V that the glands of the bassethound differ from those of the German shepherd, while the glands of the Saluki and shepherd are similar. The bassethound has a low active thyroid gland, giving the animal a low metabolism. This, in conjunction with the correspondingly low active nature of the other glands, is probably one factor responsible for the inexcitable nature of all the nervous processes. The German shepherd and Saluki have highly active thyroid glands, and this, and its influence on other active glands, undoubtedly contributes to their excitable nature. Within each breed there is a harmonious relationship between the genetic factors for physical form and the structure of the glands, and each breeds true for this relationship. These pure bred dogs also have characteristic behaviors. Thus the behavior factor has been integrated into a harmonious pattern with the glandular and physical factors. For this reason each breed is considered pure for both physical type and behavior, and since they fall into one of two opposite classifications behaviorally, they are considered normal extreme behavior types.

It has already been shown in Section V that there is great variation in form and glands among the $F_2$ bassethound-

German shepherd hybrids. Some inherit the bassethound form and glands, others the shepherd form and glands, and still others are mixed, having characteristics of both types. The questions asked regarding physical form and glands may also be asked regarding behavior. As the physical form varies, will the behavior type also vary? What is the possible explanation of the physical form-behavior relationship which exists in the bassethound and German shepherd? What will happen to the behavior characteristics when the two types are cross bred? In order to answer these questions, the behaviors of the pure breed and hybrid dogs have been compared in these experiments.

Since no one specific measurement would give a basis for contrasting the animals physically, a simple index based on two measurements of the thoracic region of the body was devised. This index has proved a convenient method for contrasting the dogs.

*Bassethound-German shepherd $F_1$s.* When the bassethound, a round type, is crossed with the thin German shepherd, the offspring have two dominant bassethound characters, the short legs and long ears. The texture and color of the coat are more like the shepherd than the bassethound. There is some variation in bodily form among the $F_1$s, but none is as thin as the shepherd nor as round as the bassethound.

When the $F_1$s are considered in the behavior situation, all fall within the same group, and none is so extremely sluggish as the bassethound nor so active as the shepherd. They are better balanced dogs and make a more satisfactory adjustment in any situation than either the bassethound or shepherd parent. This suggests that there is a blending of the behavior factors, as seems also to be the case in the head and body factors. Although these dogs show minor dissimilarities, there is no wide divergence among them.

*Bassethound-German shepherd $F_2$s.* When the short legged $F_1$s are crossed *inter se*, their offspring show a distribution of a number of the contrasted grandparental types. Both the short legs of the bassethound and the long straight thin legs of the shepherd reappear in the second generation in the Mendelian ratio of one short to three long. Head and body shape also vary among the $F_2$s. There is in no case a complete dominance of either the bassethound or shepherd bodily form.

Two striking observations were made regarding the behavior of these dogs. First, some dogs were as inactive as the bassethound grandparent and others as active as the German shepherd grandparent. Second, there was more variation in the behavior of the individual dogs in different situations. One dog of the group was round in bodily type and behaved like the bassethound in all experimental conditions; two were thin and very active. The others ranged between these extremes for both bodily type and behavior characteristics.

These observations on the $F_1$ and $F_2$ bassethound-German shepherd hybrids give some basis for an understanding and interpretation of quantitative variations among different constitutions. The bassethound and German shepherd may be considered pure constitutional types. Constitution, as used here, refers to the total organismal complex, including bones, glands, and nervous system, and in these two types a definite harmonious genetic complex determines these factors (see sections on inheritance of bones, glands, etc.). This purity refers also to behavior patterns and determiners, and in addition may be observed in regard to special aptitude. It is well known, for example, that the bassethound is easily trained for hunting. This ability is dependent not only on a highly sensitive olfactory center, but on the general nervous nature of the dog as well. An animal such as the bassethound is not easily diverted from the trail by accessory stimulation, as would be the case with an excitable dog. The general nervous nature and the special aptitude combine to form the basis of the hunting reaction. The two breeds, the bassethound and German shepherd, are each homozygous, not only for physical form, but, as shown in Section V, for glandular conditions; and, as we have shown here, each breed runs true to a form in behavior as well.

It has been shown for these $F_2$ bassethound-shepherds that the genetic relationship which determines physical form and behavior among the pure grandparents may be varied, since some of the dogs are thin bodied, yet behave like round bodied dogs. It was found that not only could the physical form and behavioral nature be modified, but that the same dog may behave like both the grandparental types under different conditions. These animals are considered as having a mixed constitution. Since the two behavioral types can be mixed by cross breeding the grandparent opposite types, and the results are quite different from either grandparent, it suggests that the homozygous relationship between the genetic factors determining the behavior and physical form which occurs in the pure grandparents is a result of a correlation by selective breeding. The pure breed has been selected and cross bred for generations on the basis of physical form. It is reasonable to suppose that in breeding out physical types the glandular and behavioral nature have also been determined. The dogs have a selected physical form, and in addition, a definite interorganismal structure and neurophysiological pattern which determines the performance, resulting in pure constitution. This is emphasized also by the data obtained on the inheritance of bones and glands.

Although selection has played a part in isolation of the pure types, this does not mean that it is responsible for the linkage between the physical form and behavioral factors. The linkage is natural, and can occur only if certain types are cross bred. There could never be a true bassethound with a German shepherd glandular system, for example. Unless some artificial selection had been made, the chances are that the pure types would never have become isolated. This would seem to be especially true after consideration of the influence of mutation and breeding among animals reared under natural conditions.

The production of mixed constitutional types by cross breeding opposite normal types gives us some basis for an understanding of the English bulldog. This dog has peculiarities not found among the normal types. It has behavioral characteristics of both polar groups as well as some not found in either group. Its physical form is also a mixture of opposite types. As Section III (Stockard on undershot jaws) emphasizes, physical disharmonies similar to that found in the head of the bulldog have been produced experimentally by crossing two widely different types. One such case was the cross of the short nosed Pekingese with the long nosed dachshund. Among the $F_1$s there was but little variation in the jaws, but in the $F_2$s many examples of abnormal jaw conditions are shown. It would seem that some of these $F_2$s inherit the short nose of the Pekingese and the long mandible of the dachshund, giving the same condition found in the bulldog. This suggests the possibility that the abnormal jaws of the bulldog came about by crossing a long nosed dog with a short nosed dog. Basically the bulldog seems to be a hound type. The bodily shape of the English bulldog is more like the round bodied or hound dog than any other breed, and the mandible of the bulldog is like that of the bassethound (Section III). Not enough of the history of the English bulldog is known to be certain that it did originate from a hound, but the above experiments with the dachshund and Pekingese indicate clearly how similar types can be produced.

In addition to the abnormal head, the bulldog has an abnormal condition of the vertebrae of the tail. This "screw" tail is a regional abnormality inherited as a recessive character (p. 387, Stockard). The bulldog, then, seems to have a round shaped body, with long legs and definite abnormalities at both ends of the axial skeleton. This suggests that the bulldog results from mixing different breeds, leading to an inharmonious blending of the physical characters. An analysis of the glands of this dog, reported in Section V, shows specifically that these also deviate widely from the normal hound and German shepherd types. Thus the bulldog is a mixed type in regard to physical characters, glandular factors, and behavior characteristics.

The mixed nature of the bulldog was further emphasized by crossing this animal with the stable and inactive bassethound. The offspring from this cross are rather well balanced hybrids, all of which are similar in physical form, with short legs, a long straight tail, and round stocky body; all also show a slight undershot condition of the mandible. Behaviorally, these dogs belong to the inactive group but are better balanced and capable of making a wider variety of adjustments than the bassethound.

Among the $F_2$s of this cross, however, many types of physique and behavior occur. The bulldog characters are dominant in most of the $F_2$s. The variations for the group are much wider than those found among the bassethound-shepherd hybrids since there are modifications not only in bodily form, but in the head and tail. There is apparently no linkage between the abnormal head condition and the screw tail, nor even the bodily shape, since all three characters vary in these hybrids. The heightened excitable nature of the bulldog in motor situations is shown by all the $F_2$s with abnormal head, long legs, and screw tail. Some of these are untrainable, and on autopsy all these untrainables have an extreme internal hydrocephalus. This would seem to indicate that there is a linkage between the factors determining form, behavior and glands, since the greatest divergence from normal is among those animals having the most extreme abnormal physical forms.

No further facts regarding the effect of crossing opposite physical types were brought out by a study of dogs whose inheritance involved more than two breeds. For example, when the bulldog-bassethound $F_1$ was crossed with the bassethound-shepherd $F_1$, the hybrids showed the same behavioral variations as were found among the bulldog-bassethound and bassethound-shepherd $F_2$s. The only factor of any importance was the wider variations shown by the members of such litters. The differences in behavior are not only greater among the members of the group, but the individual performances of each type tend to be more variable than either the bassethound-shepherd or the bulldog-bassethound.

It may be assumed that there are two basic factors influencing the constitutional complex. One is the combination and patterning of the genes which determine bone, glands and the nervous structures of the body, and the other is the action of mutations. The modifications brought about by these breeding experiments may be considered the result of recombinations of the genes involved. Only one of the many behavioral modifications which have occurred can possibly be attributed directly to a mutation. This is the extremely passive defense behavior which places the dogs possessing it in the abnormal group. In each of the three cases that have occurred, the animals were offspring of two pure types, a bassethound and a German shepherd, neither of which had the reaction. Since it is not typical of either breed it is either a recessive character from an ancestor not included among the dogs at the experimental station, or its occurrence is due to a mutation. Another possibility is that the behavior is based on a recombination of genetic factors, due to mixing widely different types, resulting in a character not observed in either grandparent type. In fact, one of the dogs, 1301 ♀, appeared in a litter with a highly mixed genetic background. The parents were offspring of a bassethound-shepherd $F_1$ bred back to the bassethound, making them theoretically three-quarters hound and one-quarter German shepherd. The other dog, 1513 ♂, appeared in a litter obtained by breeding two second generation hybrids. There have been only two extreme cases out of twenty-two related dogs, not enough to determine its genetic probability.

A consideration of the dogs which differ in size from the bassethound and English bulldog, yet which show similar behaviors, raises another important question. This involves the number of factors of the genetic complex that may be modified without leading to a different constitution. The dachshund has many of the physical features of the bassethound, although there is a great difference in size, due to a difference in bone length and thickness. The behavior of the dachshund is also similar to that of the bassethound. It must be concluded that bone length and thickness is not the basic linking factor of the constitutional behavioral type.

Originally the dachshund was probably of what is considered normal size for the dog, and the size modification was brought about by breeding to a midget type or by a mutation. The basis of the modification seems to have affected the bone size without altering the glandular complex, that is, the organization and patterning of the genetic factors have not been modified to result in a different type, as was the case with the bulldog.

According to the theory of constitution presented here, it is necessary to consider all possible behavioral tendencies before fully understanding any specific type. Two specifically controlled performances have been studied: an adjustment to food taking and an adjustment to a painful situation. Although each of these behavior systems involves extensive neurophysiological patterns, they do not present the total behavioral picture, and the general behavior of the animals under kennel conditions has been correlated with the experimental results. The dogs classified as a pure constitutional type fall into the same comparative rating under both situations.

At the present time, not enough is known about behavior, or even how to analyze behavior, to isolate every factor and study it experimentally. From the present experiments, however, an indication is given of what is meant by a constitutional type. It may be said that these experiments deal with two dimensions of a multiple dimension behavioral complex. The characteristics of the pure types and the possibilities for mixed behavioral types in these two behavioral systems may be indicated by text-figure 113. Lines AB and A'B' show the position of the two extreme polar types under each experimental situation. The vertical lines erected on each of these indicate the degrees of excitability under each experimental condition, ranging from the inactive animals of A and A' to the active animals of B and B'. This line is represented as a gradual rise because it is highly probable that if enough dogs were trained the differences in excitability would include many gradations between the two polar groups. The pure types fall at each end of the line under both experimental situations. Other animals fall near A in the food taking situation and near B' in the motor situation and vice versa. These are the animals with the mixed constitutional nature. There are possibilities for many forms of mixed types, dependent on the gradation between AB and A'B'.

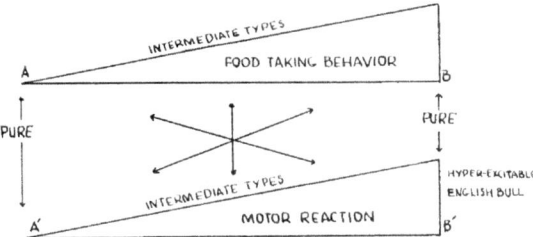

Text-figure 113

The cases represented on such a graph include only those animals which were trainable under any one experimental condition, that is, those dogs able to make an adequate adjustment.

It has been shown that within the specific reaction systems studied in the experiments there are differences in quality and degree of activity. It may be assumed that in the two pure behavioral types the genetics of each system is different, and the interaction between the genetic factors and the glandular processes also differs. Within the pure behavioral types there is a harmonious relationship between behavioral systems and the other bodily organs. This holds both for the inactive and the active types. Among the hybrids, however, in which there is mixed physical form, there is also disharmonious relationship between the bodily organs and the reaction systems. For example, one system may be easily excited, yet others may be extremely difficult to excite. The animal may be overly disturbed in situations involving pain, yet entirely undisturbed in another situation. Again the muscular systems of the limbs may be well developed, yet action limited because of a low energy factor. The factors which influence behavior become mixed and varied, just as do those which determine physical form. In the mixed types,

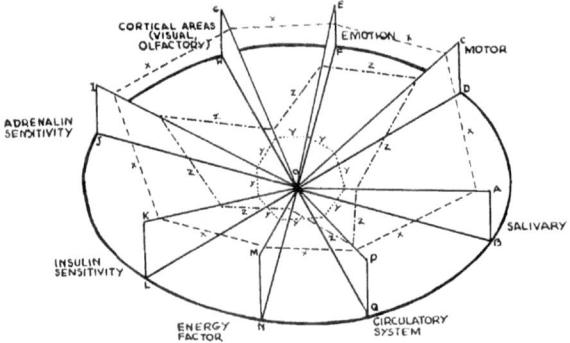

Text-figure 114

the harmonious relationship found within each pure behavioral type is broken up, and the result is a disharmony among the systems. We have diagrammed the variations found within two systems in text-figure 113. A diagram of the constitution is given in text-figure 114. In this case, each vertical plane erected on the circular plane and represented by abo; cdo; etc. indicates reaction systems and bodily process involved in activity. These are not given as the total picture, but to suggest the relationship of the various organismal parts in the pure and mixed types. Points on the line *ao* of plane abo represent the differences in degree of excitability of the salivary reaction systems and is similar to that in text-figure 113 above. In the same manner, points on line *co* of *edo* represent the differences in excitability of the motor reaction systems of the segments. The other vertical planes represent other systems of the organism, as for example, the emotional, *efo*; the sensory, *gho*; adrenal action, *lmo*; thyroid action, *npo*; etc. Within an organism the action of each system bears a relationship to the others, and this relationship differs for the pure and mixed type dogs. For example, a pure excitable type, in which there is a harmonious relationship between the parts, may be represented by line X joining systems of equal excitability and harmonious nature. On the other hand, the inactive type would be represented by line Y joining systems at the inactive end of the scale but of equal excitability and harmonious nature. A mixed type may be represented by line Z in which case the points representing excitability are not equally distant from the center *o*, but at unequal distances, which represents disharmony, that is, each part is not harmoniously related to the other. The possibilities for variation within any one of the systems of the body, and the degree of variation within any one system, or all systems, determine the degree of mixed behavioral type.

The representation of constitution given here is not complete. Other dimensions should be considered before a total picture of the pure lethargic constitutional type or the pure active type is obtained. However, these experiments do indicate what we believe to be the significant factors in constitutional differences and the approach to a further analysis of the problem.

# SECTION VII

## O. D. ANDERSON[5]

[5] Fellow of the Rockefeller Foundation.

# THE RÔLE OF THE GLANDS OF INTERNAL SECRETION IN THE PRODUCTION OF BEHAVIORAL TYPES IN THE DOG

BASED ON A STUDY OF BEHAVIOR BY THE CONDITIONED REFLEX METHOD

## THE PROBLEM

The present section deals with the influence of the internal secretions upon reflex action and behavior in the dog.

The author wishes to extend his thanks to Professor C. R. Stockard for supplying the valuable animals of known pedigree and morphologic type, since only with such material could these studies be fully dependable; for the benefit of his advice in planning and arranging the experiments; and for his constructive criticism and valuable suggestions during the progress of the work. The author wishes also to thank Professor Joshua Sweet, who not only performed all the more difficult surgical operations in this work, but who also gave freely of his time in discussions of the clinical and experimental significance of disturbances of the internal secretions.

The behavior of various dog breeds has been the subject of special investigation both at the Cornell Anatomy Farm and in the Department of Anatomy in New York City. James ('34) has made an extensive study of the conditioned reflexes in different pure breeds and their hybrids. And Anderson and James have studied the neuromuscular activity of the different morphological types employed in the general studies discussed in the foregoing chapters. Notable behavioral variations are found among the different breeds, and it has been demonstrated that these are associated with the breed differences. The mode of behavior thus depends in large part upon the influence of inherited constitutional factors associated with body conformation and build. Generally speaking, it was found that the tall, thin, narrow-chested dogs showed a great deal of muscular activity and were very alert to all stimuli. They tended to be "nervous" and flighty. The conditioned reflexes could be easily elicited, often by the slightest stimulation, and were very stable when once established. The general pattern is that of a restless and highly nervous animal. This behavior is typical, for example, of the German shepherd. On the other hand, the short-legged, stocky and wide chested dogs are not usually hyperactive and alert. The conditioned reflexes were elicited from them with difficulty, even by strong stimulation, and even then were very unstable. The behavior pattern is that of a calm or phlegmatic animal. The bassethound is a good example of this type.

What is the underlying nature of such fundamentally different modes of behavior? The earlier chapters in this volume have presented evidence which shows that body build is closely associated, through the operation of genetic principles, with the glands of internal secretion. For example, the thyroid and pituitary of the German shepherd are histologically different from the thyroid and pituitary of the English bulldog. Similarly, these glands are modified in characteristic manner in the bassethound and in the St. Bernard. Differences in the histology of the same gland in different breeds may be interpreted as signifying possible differences in the level or quality of the secretory activity of the gland. This suggests also that the characteristic types of behavior seen among the various breeds might be dependent upon differences in glandular quality and activity.

The present experiments were undertaken to study this question. We considered it desirable to study the effect of critical alterations in the internal secretions (administration of hormone substances and operative removal of glands) upon the behavior of a group of pedigreed dogs exhibiting the degree of behavioral reaction classified by James as intermediate or "mid-type." These dogs were neither highly nervous nor very phlegmatic, but were an almost intermediate blend of the two extreme types.

## THE METHOD

The classic conditioned reflex method was used. The procedure in general was to study the conditioned reflexes in a particular dog both before and after critical alteration of the internal secretions.

A group of pedigreed hybrid animals, the majority of which were second generation ($F_2$) from the cross between the German shepherd and the bassethound, were selected for the tests. These animals were more or less uniform in body build. The conditioned salivary reflex was formed in one group and the conditioned motor or defensive reflex in another. Before the disturbance or modification of the gland was induced, conditioned reflexes were stabilized in each animal for about 1 year in order to obtain as control a series of responses reasonably stable and uniform in character. The same kind of observations were continued after the disturbance for as long a time as feasible.

The conditioned reflex method is especially advantageous in experiments of this kind since not only can both the salivary and the motor conditioned responses be recorded graphically, but they can be measured for intensity with a high degree of accuracy. This technique is of special advantage in showing the most delicate and refined details of the behavioral pattern in animals whose glandular functions have been altered. However, we are also fully aware of the great importance of the simpler methods in observing animal behavior. Carefully "watching" what the animals are capable of doing has great value, and we have made it a practice to record descriptive notes of general behavior as a supplement to the data of the conditioned reflexes.

The general arrangements of the laboratory for the conditioned reflex studies are shown in plate 106. Two rooms were necessary, one for the investigator, from which the stimulations were applied and controlled and in which the conditioned reflexes were recorded and registered, and a completely separate but adjoining sound-deadened animal chamber. The dog's movements are easily observed from the apparatus room through a small reducing lens fitted into an opening in the wall between the rooms. The animal, however, is unable to see the experimenter. Figure 1 is a general view of the recording room, and figure 2 illustrates the animal chamber.

The conditioned salivary reflex was formed and recorded according to the method of Pavlov. The conditioning stimulus was the sound of a metronome beating at a rate of 120 beats per minute. This signal was usually presented for a period of 20 seconds and was immediately followed by the presentation of food. Each stimulation was of uniform duration for a given animal. The flow of saliva first elicited by the metronome stimulus and later by the food itself was registered separately by means of the well known pneumatic transmission system comprising a small suction cup placed over the parotid fistula and connected with a horizontal water manometer (shown on the left in fig. 1).

The conditioned motor defensive reflex was formed in a number of animals and recorded through the technique devised by Liddell, James and Anderson ('34). A particular procedure was adopted to obtain the reflex activity of a segment of the neuromuscular system, fairly comparable in energy quotient with that of the parotid gland. The motor reflex employed was the flexion movement of the right forelimb evoked by the application of a relatively weak single induction shock (the break shock alone) to the skin of the foot. The conditioned reflex was formed by the repeated

PLATE 106
EXPLANATION OF FIGURES

1 A general view of the apparatus room, showing in the background the horizontal manometer for recording the amount of salivary flow from the parotid fistula, and on the right the device for recording the reactions of the dogs in the salivary reflex and also in the motor reflex situation.

2 A view within the animal chamber. The platform upon which the animal stands facing toward the right and the revolving food dish are shown. *A* is the suction cup for the registration of saliva when fastened over the fistula in the animal's cheek. *B* represents the bracelet through which the electrical shock is delivered to the right forelimb of the animal. The graphic registration of the reacting limb is accomplished by attaching the leather bracelet *C* to the limb.

PLATE 106

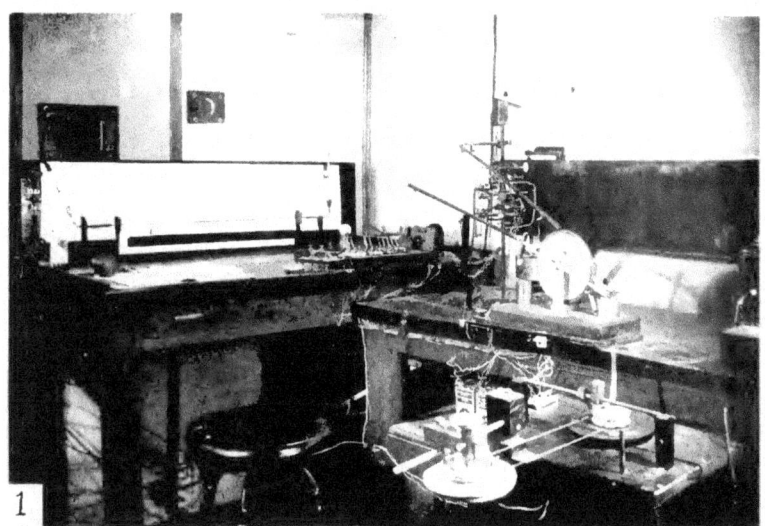

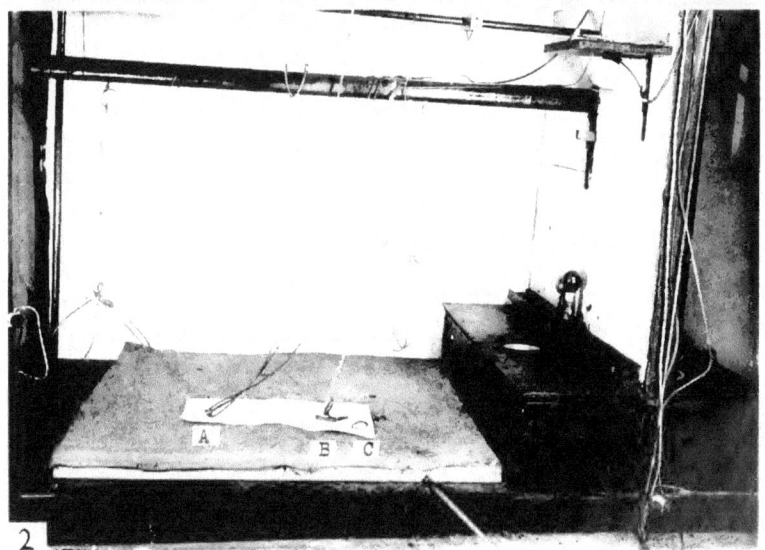

presentation of the metronome stimulus (beating 120 times per minute), followed at once by the shock. In the thoroughly trained animal the sounding of the metronome thus reinforced by the electrical stimulus constantly evoked vigorous defensive flexion movements of the reaction limb. The duration of the clicking metronome was always 10 seconds.

The technique of recording graphically the food-taking and the defensive reactions is best described by reference to photographic and graphic records of the typical actions shown by the animals in the two sets of circumstances (see figs. 1 and 2, pl. 107). Figure 1 shows the nature of the overt reaction of an animal to the metronome which had previously been followed many times by food; the photograph at the left shows the pose just before the stimulus is sounded, and at the right the reaction as soon as the clicks are heard. From the sitting posture, the dog rises to his feet, turns his head toward the place where food is presently to appear and remains in this posture until actually given the food. The conditioned salivary flow occurs while thus waiting. The dog often looks upward and listens to the sound, then lowers the head and gazes at the empty food pan in front of him. Such raising and lowering of the head may take place several times during the stimulation. When the food is presented, the animal lowers the head and eats in a vigorous fashion. Beneath these photographs is a kymographic record of the food-taking reaction. The third line from the bottom marks the conditioned metronome sound by means of an electromagnetic signal marker. The line below records by the same means the presentation of the food at the end of the metronome sound. The top line represents movements of the head; the upward and downward movements are shown in up and down strokes of the line. To obtain this record a thread is attached to the dog's head and connected with a reducing lever which marks vertical motion upon the moving paper. The line below records any gross or general movement of the body. This record is made by the movements upon the drum of a sensitive recording tambour connected with a

PLATE 107

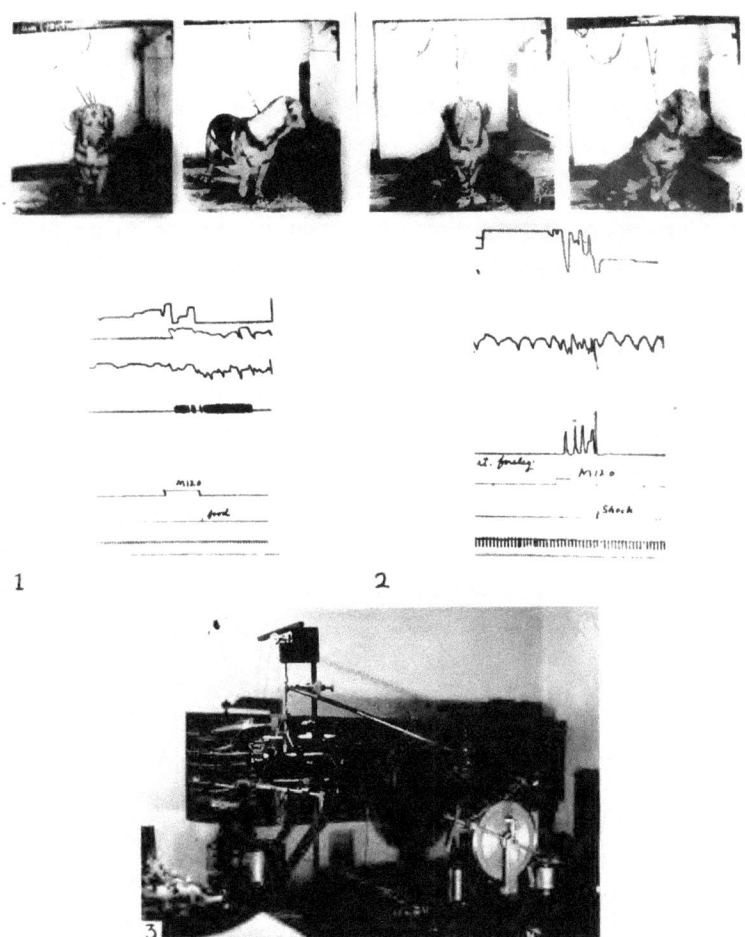

1. The reactions of the normal dog in the food taking salivary reflex situation. In the first picture, the animal is unstimulated. At the right a stimulus (Met. 120) is sounding. The stimulus in this case is to be followed by food. The graph below is a record of these reactions and shows the conditioned flow of saliva to the Met. 120. Top line indicates head movement; below, in order—general body movement, respiration, saliva in 1/100 cc., metronome signal, food, and time in seconds.

2. Reactions of a dog in the conditioned motor or defensive reflex situation; at the left, the animal in the unstimulated pose, and at the right, reacting by raising his right forelimb to the sound of the Met. 120 to be followed by the shock. The graph below is a record of these reactions. Top line, head movement; below in order—respiration, movements of right foreleg, metronome signal, shock, and time in seconds.

3. A view showing the details of the recording apparatus. The wheel at the right of the picture is the modified Fick work accumulator designed to register the magnitude of the conditioned motor reflex.

pneumatically cushioned platform upon which the animal stands. Such a platform consists simply of a light wooden floor over a framework resting upon a sealed rubber tube, the other end of which is connected to the tambour.[6]

Below the line representing the body movements is the record of the flow of saliva from the parotid duct. Each upward movement of the signal electro-magnet, which is manually operated by a telegraph key, represents a unit of 1/100 cc. The bottom line gives the time in seconds.

The record, considered as a whole, clearly shows the time relations of the various components of the total reaction. Note the oscillating head movement, the alert, tremulous body movement and pose, the hastened and altered respiratory rhythm and the ready and continuous flow of saliva while the metronome is beating. The saliva flows continuously when the animal is eating the food and ceases within a few seconds after the food has been consumed.

Figure 2 (pl. 107) shows the posture of another animal just before and during the sounding of the metronome signalling the approach of an electric shock. Note in the left picture the quiet and calm attitude of the animal before stimulation, in the right picture the anticipatory flexing movement of the limb as the clicking sound is heard. Below is shown the record of the total defense reaction. Again, the three lower lines show records of the conditioned stimulus, the unconditioned stimulus (the shock) and the time in seconds. Since the defense reaction involves movements of the head as well as the limb, these have also been recorded (top line), as in the salivary reflex.

At the beginning of the conditioned stimulus the dog lowers his head at once and assumes a crouching posture. The first flexion movement of the leg occurs in nearly every case at exactly this time. The head is soon raised and the foot again lowered to the floor. These two reactions, or integrated single reaction, occur repeatedly during the clicking signal. Note these facts by comparing the top line for head movement

[6] Used by Benedict in basal metabolism work on dogs.

with the third line from the top which records the flexions of the limb. The leg movements are recorded by means of a string attached to the foot and led over pulleys to a reducing lever in the instrument room where they are marked upon the moving smoked paper. When the metronome is stopped, the shock is applied by means of a small bracelet electrode placed about the wrist and connected with the secondary coil of a Harvard inductorium. The strength of the shock was that from a single dry cell in the primary circuit of the coil when the secondary was 2 cm distant from the primary; as the vibrator was short circuited, a single break shock was delivered. The shock was sufficiently mild to evoke only a single slight movement of the leg. The intensity of the shock is of great importance. The dog is apparently extremely sensitive to a strong shock and becomes quite wild and unmanageable when such is applied. Note in the record the brisk movement of the leg accompanied by an almost equally quick lowering of the head. The second line from the top is again the respiration. Here note the great hastening and disturbance of the normal rhythm during the clicking, and the sudden gasp at the shock.

Since the head and leg movements and respiratory changes were the principal components of the conditioned motor reflex in which we were interested, it was not considered essential to obtain the gross general movement of the body, except in cases where it was of obvious advantage. It is remarkable that in many cases the total defense reaction disappears (except in hyper-irritable dogs) within a few seconds after cessation of the stimulation.

In all following graphs, as in those of plate 107, the top line represents the head movement, the second line body movement (omitted in some cases), the third line respiration, the fourth line the C-R, the fifth line the conditioned stimulus, the sixth line the unconditioned stimulus, and the seventh line the time in seconds. The recording apparatus is shown in figure 3 (pl. 107).

In order to make the conditioned motor and the conditioned salivary reflexes quantitatively comparable, it was necessary that some measurement of the motor reflex be used. The height to which the forepaw was raised at each flexion of the limb was measured and summated automatically during the standard 10 second period of stimulation. During this interval, the limb to which the electrode was attached would, in some cases, be flexed three or four times, the foot being raised each time 5 or 6 inches from the platform. This type reaction we had previously termed "weak." In other cases, the limb would be flexed eight or ten times during the same period, the foot being raised 10 inches or more each time. This reaction was considered "strong." To bring these descriptions to numerical terms we used a modification of Fick's work accumulator, the ratchet wheel and pawl shown in figure 3 of plate 107. This device is so arranged that it registers in millimeters the reduced height of each flexion of the limb and thus gives the total value for the magnitude of successive flexions occurring during the standard time. The "weak" reaction may thus register only 100 mm, while the "strong" may have a magnitude of 300 mm or more. This method has been used over a period of 8 years for both the sheep and dog and has proved entirely accurate. It is of great value not only in providing means for comparing the values of the reflexes found in one animal with those found in another, but also in providing an accurate way of studying the comparative values of the reflexes in the same animal over long periods of time and during natural and experimental alterations of the animal's physiological state.

In order to provide further kinds of behavior before and after the critical procedure, most of the animals were tested for their ability to discriminate between two similar stimuli. The problem presented was that of distinguishing between a fast and a slow rate of the beating metronome. The rate of 120 beats per minute was *always* reinforced by food or by shock, as the case may be, while the rate of 28 beats (sometimes 42 beats) was *never* followed by the food or shock.

Discrimination was established when the dog reacted to the fast rate and gave no reaction to the slow. Both signals were presented during the same day's experiments.

The procedure in representative experiments was, in general, as follows: The day's testing of the salivary conditioned reflexes was begun by presenting the metronome 120 for 3 seconds followed at once by food. This short conditioned stimulus served to keep the animal alert for food as associated with the metronome. After an interval of 4 minutes, the following stimulations were always applied: metronome 120 sounded for 20 seconds, then food; pause of 4 minutes; metronome 28 sounded for 20 seconds, no food; pause 4 minutes; metronome 120 sounded for 20 seconds, then food; animal released. The testing of the motor conditioned reflexes was done similarly. In these tests the initial short stimulation was found unnecessary since the dogs were normally always alert in anticipating the shock. The following stimuli were applied: metronome 120 sounded for 10 seconds, then shock; pause of 5 minutes; metronome 28 sounded for 10 seconds, no shock; pause of 5 minutes; metronome 120 sounded for 10 seconds, then shock; animal released.

The metronome 120 followed by food or by shock, and the metronome 28 or 42 never followed by food or by shock, will henceforth be referred to as the *positive* and the *negative* conditioned stimulus, respectively.

Occasionally the order of presenting the various stimuli was altered to prevent the animals from forming a "position habit" (response to the *order* of the stimuli *per se*). At times the series began with the negative, metronome 28, no shock, and at other times the series ended with this stimulus. Such procedure disrupted any tendency to react in a certain way to a certain place in the series. Thus the dogs appeared to listen closely to the *rate* of the beating metronome.

A total of twenty-one trained dogs was used. The conditioned salivary reflex was formed in thirteen and the motor in eight. In the training experiments, seven normal dogs were employed for studying the effects on behavior of the gland extracts administered. Nineteen of the twenty-one dogs were operated upon in the final phase of the experiments. These operations were successful in thirteen cases. Four of the unsuccessful cases did not survive long enough to permit continuation of the behavior tests (two of the animals died after bilateral adrenalectomy and two after hypophysectomy). The experiments were begun in September 1932 and concluded in March 1936.

BEHAVIOR DURING THE TRAINING OR CONTROL PERIOD

It became evident early in the standardization period that the dogs presented more or less uniform behavioral types. Nearly all showed the well balanced type of nervous reaction for the "mid-group." They were all similar in body build, having the appearance of the $F_1$ bassethound-shepherd or $F_1$ bassethound-Saluki, and all behaved much alike.

The animals were kept in spacious new quarters on the top floor of the anatomy building in the Cornell Medical College. They were separated into congenial pairs. Each pair occupied a single compartment with about 80 square feet of exercising space. A solid door with a small glass window closed each compartment. The observer could thus watch the spontaneous behavior of the dogs without himself being seen.

The average trained dog is active and alert when among other dogs as well as when with the experimenter. The normal food-taking reaction, when a pan of palatable food is placed before him, is very vigorous and he is ready to eat at any time. When the daily feeding time approaches he runs about the compartment excitedly, barking and jumping upon the door at any sound of the pans. He may cease this from time to time to growl at his companion. To avoid fighting it is necessary to place the pans of food some distance apart in the pen.

At other than feeding times, the dogs run and romp with their companions. Occasionally they lie quietly sleeping but will respond quickly to the slightest stimulus. When the ex perimenter is seen at the door, the dogs become excited and run and jump about in a frenzy of motion and friendly barking. The same friendly overtures may be made to a complete stranger. When taken into the laboratory on the leash, the dog usually leads the way with erect head and wagging tail. He does not need to be dragged along. The leash may be removed when the laboratory is approached, and the dog will go at once and stand upon the platform in position, ready for the experiment. This is equally true whether food or shock are to be presented. During the experiment, the average dog salivates freely when the metronome to be followed by food is sounded, and the paw is vigorously raised at the clicking to be followed by the shock.

During the formation and stabilization of the reflex, two observations were made which indicate clearly the value of the conditioned reflex in studies of this sort. The C-R varied with subtle and delicate *natural* changes in the physiological states of the animal. The reflex is altered in a female in heat or while lactating. The magnitude of the salivary C-R was strikingly increased during the oestrus in an animal which normally gave a very weak response or none at all. A similar observation was made in Pavlov's laboratory by Kreps ('23).

Such conditions are illustrated by plate 108 and text-figure 115. Figure 1 (pl. 108) shows the absence of a conditioned salivation and the head and body movements when the dog was not in heat. Figure 2 (pl. 108) shows a typical strong salivary C-R accompanied by vigorous head reaction when the animal was at the height of the oestrus. In text-figure 115, the chart [7] shows the complete course of the C-R throughout a 4 month cycle, an inactive followed by an active phase.

[7] In all charts each bar represents the magnitude of the C-R evoked by a single application of the metronome. Only one trial out of a day's trials of positive-negative-positive stimuli was counted. It was the first positive conditioned stimulus (excepting the initial short, priming stimulus). This was selected as evoking the most characteristic response of the day's reactions, the one not being affected by "successive inhibition" from the preceding negative stimulus.

The magnitude of the selected response is expressed in 1/100 cc. for the salivary C-R and in mm. for the motor C-R. The ordinate shows these values. The duration of the experiment in months is shown on the abscissa.

The C-R began to increase within a few days after the vaginal bleeding ceased. The increased reflex persisted throughout the period of the congestion in the external genitalia and for some time afterward, in some cases as long as 10 days after all external signs of oestrus had disappeared.

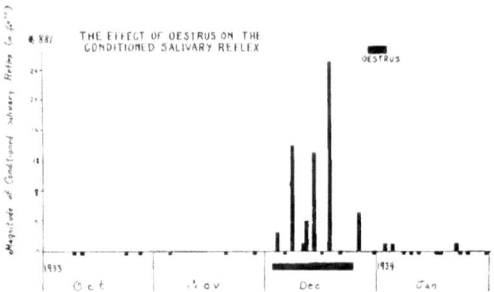

Text figure 115. Chart showing the effect of oestrus on the conditioned salivary reflex in dog S81. Each bar drawn on the abscissa represents the magnitude of the conditioned reflex (in 1/100 cc.) at a single presentation of the signal. Note the great enhancement of the conditioned reflex during oestrus.

PLATE 108

EXPLANATION OF FIGURES

1  A graphic record showing, in dog S81, the absence of the conditioned salivary reaction in the interval between oestral periods to the Met. 120 followed by food.

2  A graphic record showing the presence of a large and vigorous conditioned salivary reaction to the same stimulus in the same animal (dog S81) during the oestrus.

3  A graphic record showing the conditioned motor reflex in dog S69 during the last month of pregnancy. Note the small conditioned reaction (a single leg movement).

4  A graphic record of the conditioned motor reflex in the same animal (dog S69) during the period of lactation. Note the exaggerated motor reactions both of the head and of the reaction leg to the signal. The reactions continue even after the signal has ceased.

5  A graphic record showing in dog S66 the normal conditioned salivary response to Met. 120.

6  A graphic record from the same dog (S66) with the absence of the conditioned salivary reflex following thyroidectomy.

PLATE 108

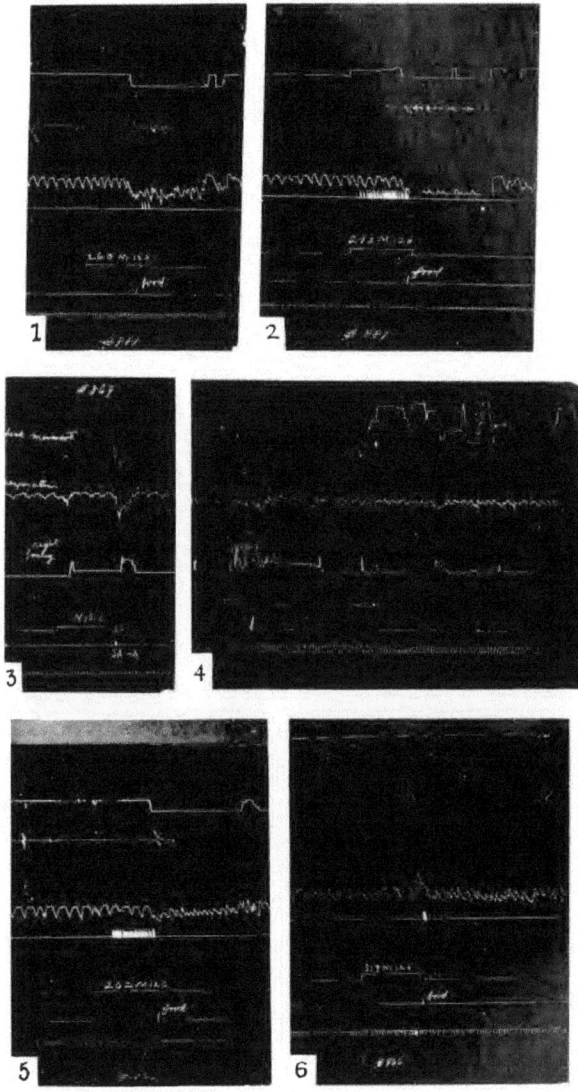

The increase in the salivary C-R is no doubt associated with the generally heightened excitability and increased neuromuscular activity of the bitch when the mating period is at its height. This heightened nervous irritability is probably closely associated with the underlying physiological glandular changes which presumably take place at the time, namely an acceleration in the secretory activity of the pituitary, the gonads and the thyroid. The effect upon the salivary C-R is strikingly similar to that seen when a hypothyroid dog is fed thyroid extract, as will be shown later.

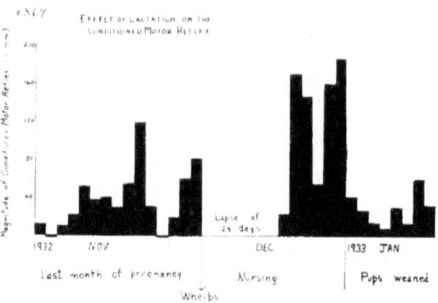

Text-figure 116. Chart showing the effect of lactation on the conditioned motor reflex in dog S69. Note the increase in the magnitude or vigor of the reflex during the nursing or lactation period and its diminution after the pups were weaned.

The conditioned motor reflex was greatly increased during the lactating period. Rosenthal ('22), an associate of Pavlov, found that the conditioned salivary reflex was positively affected when a bitch was lactating. Text-figure 116 shows graphically the effect of lactation. The defense reflex, tested during the last month of pregnancy, showed an average magnitude of 37 mm; but when tested about 3 weeks after whelping the puppies and at the height of the nursing period, the average value had risen to 124 mm, an increase of more than 200 per cent. After lactation ceased, the value dropped to 27 mm. These facts are interesting in view of the general behavior of dogs during pregnancy and the altered behavior during lactation. The pregnant bitch gives no behavioral sign to indicate an awareness of pregnancy until a day or so before whelping, when she will, if permitted, seek an appropriate nesting place. As soon as she whelps, her behavior changes. If she is normally docile and friendly, she may become hyperirritable and aggressive. This was true of the animal under study. A previously gentle animal, she now continually snarled and attempted to attack the experimenter or anyone approaching her and the puppies. She was also very restless. After the puppies were weaned she returned again to her docile behavior.

These changes in behavior are accounted for by the marked changes in the internal secretions of the lactating animal. The increase in thyroid activity may be largely responsible for the increase in nervous excitability, and the disturbance in body calcium may be linked with the excitement. There is abundant evidence for such views. One has only to recall the marked disturbance of central nervous function and neuromuscular coordination observed during parathyroidectomy, associated with changed balance in blood calcium. It is also well known that the nervous disturbance of lactating cows affected with so-called "milk fever" (convulsive seizures, lethargy, coma) is accompanied by a hypocalcaemia of the level usually found in parathyroid tetany.

## THE INFLUENCE OF THE THYROID AND THE PARATHYROIDS UPON THE REFLEX BEHAVIOR

The influence of the thyroid upon conditioned reflexes has been the subject of previous investigations. The effects of thyroid feeding upon the salivary C-R in the dog have been studied by several workers. Zawadowsky, Sacharow and Slotow ('29) reported that the C-R showed an initial depression and a subsequent stimulation. Crisler, Booher, Van Liere and Hall ('33) observed the opposite, namely, that the C-R showed an initial stimulation followed by depression. Kleitman and Titelbaum ('36), working with the defensive motor C-R in the dog, reported an improvement in the percentage of correct responses to the positive and negative conditioned stimuli during periods of thyroid feeding, and also an increase in the magnitude of conditioned as well as unconditioned responses.

The influence of thyroid deficiency upon conditioned reflexes has also been investigated. Valkov ('23), in Pavlov's laboratory, found that a thyroidectomized dog could form conditioned alimentary and conditioned motor (defensive) reflexes in as short a time as the normal control. The conditioned alimentary reflex in the operated animal was, however, quite unstable. The conditioned motor reflex, on the other hand, was stable.

Liddell ('27), in studies on the conditioned defensive motor reflex in the sheep and goat, was similarly unsuccessful in demonstrating a retarding effect of thyroidectomy on learning. The reflex was established and maintained as well in the thyroidless animals as in the normal controls. And differentiations were also as easily elaborated by the former as by the latter.

In the present study concerning the thyroid and parathyroid effects, nine dogs were used. Thyroid extract was administered to three and parathyroid extract to three in the normal state. Four were thyroidectomized and two were thyro-parathyroidectomized. The operated animals were treated from time to time with thyroid extract and with parathormone.

## THE EFFECT OF THYROID EXTRACT ADMINISTRATION IN THE NORMAL DOG

*Dog 814 ♂, bassethound × Saluki $F_2$.* The salivary C-R was used. The stimuli were Met. 120[*] (positive) and Met. 28 (negative). The dog was trained during a period of 14 months before the critical experiments were begun.

[*] We shall henceforth refer to the metronome beating at a rate of 120 times per minute (reinforced by the food or shock) as Met. 120, the metronome beating 42 and 28 times per minute (not reinforced) as Met. 42 and Met. 28, respectively.

This dog was quiet, obedient and docile, somewhat shy with strangers and sometimes slightly averse to the leash. Defending himself well from attacks by other dogs, he rarely took the offensive except when his food was approached by another dog.

Since experiments of this sort deal with the accomplishments and performances of the individual, *what the animal can do,* in terms of conditioned reflex action, it is important to present the detailed results of behavior with such concepts in mind. Thus we shall present for every animal the *efficiency* of his response, i.e., how often he responds in a correct and biologically appropriate manner in a given number of trials, together with the *magnitude* of the response. In this way one can best study the nervous system operating under normal conditions and under altered physiological states. We shall give the percentage of correct conditioned responses to both positive and negative stimuli and the average magnitude of the reactions to the positive stimulus.

The C-R in dog 814 ♂ was formed after fifteen trials and was fairly stable.

The animal was fed thyroid extract[a] 1 gm. daily for 23 days. Behavior was essentially unchanged during the thyroid feeding, the C-R remaining approximately as before.

Table 8 shows that the percentage of correct responses to Met. 120 remained exactly the same during the extract treatment but declined (82 per cent to 70 per cent) after the extract was withdrawn. The negative response increased in efficiency (60 per cent to 71 per cent) and afterward decreased slightly (66 per cent). The magnitude of the C-R was practically unchanged during the experiment. The dog's general behavior underwent no detectable change during or after the thyroid period.

[a] All gland extracts used in the present investigation (with two exceptions) were furnished by the research department of Eli Lilly and Company. The exceptions were an extract of the suprarenal cortex (eschatin—Parke-Davis) and a general extract of the anterior lobe of the pituitary (growth extract—Squibb).

TABLE 8

*Dog 814 ♂*

|  | TRAINING PERIOD | DURING EXTRACT | 1 MONTH AFTER EXTRACT WITHDRAWN |
|---|---|---|---|
| Correct responses to positive Met. 120 | 82% | 82% | 70% |
| Correct responses to negative Met. 28 [1] | 60% | 71% | 66% |
| Average magnitude of C-R to positive Met. 120 [2] | 13 | 14 | 16 |

[1] A correct response to a negative conditioned stimulus was counted as such only when there was no response at all.
[2] Hundredths cubic centimeter of saliva.

*Dog 868 ♂, bassethound × shepherd $F_2$.* The motor C-R was used and the stimuli for this were Met. 120 (positive) and Met. 28 (negative). The dog was trained for 14 months before this experiment.

This animal exhibited a well-balanced behavior and was alert, playful, energetic, quite friendly with people, somewhat aggressive with dogs, and showed little evidence of shyness. When brought to the laboratory he always trotted into the room ahead of the experimenter, and when placed in the loose straps on the platform would, when not being stimulated, sit quite still for periods often exceeding 1 hour in length. He sometimes fell asleep on the experimental platform. This calm behavior is remarkable in view of the fact that an electric shock was applied during the experiments.

The defensive C-R was developed in the animal in eleven combinations of Met. 120 and shock. The response was thereafter highly efficient.

The dog was fed thyroid extract, 1 gm. daily for 39 days, and the C-R and the general behavior were definitely affected by the treatment. The magnitude of the response was augmented, and the animal became at this time quite nervous and restless. The efficiency of the C-R was, however, not materially altered. The effects tended to disappear on withdrawal of the extract.

As can be seen from table 9, the percentage of correct responses to Met. 120 was not materially affected during

TABLE 9

Dog 868 ♂

|  | TRAINING PERIOD | DURING EXTRACT | 1 MONTH AFTER EXTRACT WITHDRAWN |
|---|---|---|---|
| Correct responses to positive Met. 120 | 94% | 91% | 75% |
| Correct responses to negative Met. 28 | 61% | 73% | 100% |
| Average magnitude of C-R to positive Met. 120 | 12 | 18 | 9 |

the administration of the extract (94 per cent to 91 per cent). The percentage showed a sharp drop, however, after the substance was stopped (91 per cent to 75 per cent). The percentage of correct negative responses increased somewhat (61 per cent to 73 per cent) and increased further in the after period (100 per cent).

The average magnitude of the C-R to Met. 120 increased considerably during the administration of the substance (twelve to eighteen) and fell after it was discontinued (to nine).

These percentages and averages obviously show only certain trends. The magnitude of the effect of the thyroid substance upon the responses is masked to a considerable extent by the statistical treatment. It is readily seen that since the effect of the extract is not revealed immediately after the first treatment but is apparent only after a lapse of a week or 10 days, and since the effect outlasts the administration period by as long as 2 weeks or more, the statistical records confined exactly to the administration period, or to a succeeding period when no extract was given, cannot present the exact history of the effect within the periods themselves. For these reasons it is of advantage to illustrate graphically the entire course of the C-R during the experiment. We shall accordingly present charts as well as the tables for each experiment in which the facts can thus be better presented.

Text-figure 117 is such a chart. The reflex showed a noticeable increase on the sixth day after the extract was begun, and this reached a maximum on the twenty-eighth day. The reflex values were slightly higher than normal for 8 days after the treatment was discontinued, and then showed a marked decrease.

After the injections were started the dog became definitely more nervous, showing restlessness and general hyper-irritability as he was being prepared for the day's testing. When led upon the platform he would crouch and tremble, lower his ears and suddenly turn his head about in all directions. After the straps were loosely placed about the forelimbs, and

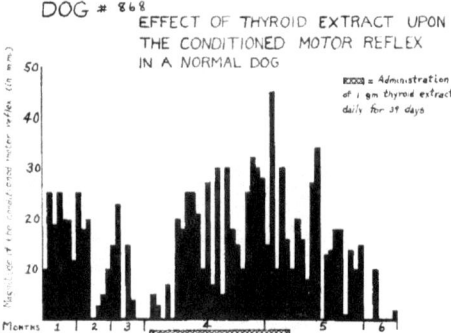

Text figure 117. The effect of thyroid extract on the conditioned motor reflex of dog 868. Note the increase in the magnitude of the reflex during the administration of the extract and its subsequent diminution after the extract was withdrawn.

the experimenter turned to leave, the dog attempted to extricate himself, first by trying to step out of the straps, then by lunging against them. The straps had to be securely fastened. The restlessness during the interval between one stimulation and the next showed definite characteristic form. Being confined within a narrow area, the animal did not struggle as violently as during the preparation period, but continually raised the reaction leg in small, jerky movements. Sometimes the leg movements were directed toward shifting the body position slightly forward, or back, or to the side, and others were quick flexions of the leg or incipient flexions (twitching of the flexor musculature).

The head was also moved in a jerky fashion. At times the animal raised its head suddenly and stared wildly about at the slightest sound, such as a faint scratching sound made by scraping the finger nail on the wall of the adjoining room.

The head and limb movements were in every case more frequent and vigorous in the interval just before the presentation of the negative conditioned stimulus than in the interval following it. During the former interval one would expect the more marked evidence of nervousness since the approaching negative stimulus was to be differentiated from the preceding (a problem which the animal must solve). In the interval following the negative stimulus, no problem is, of course, anticipated, and the dog relaxes.

The development and course of the nervous symptoms may be seen in text-figure 118. To contrast clearly the increases and decreases in nervousness, the total sum of the reaction leg movements was registered in millimeters by the modified work accumulator during the first 5 minute interval between the positive and negative stimuli. The total readings during each interval bore a definite relation to the total number of nervous movements within the interval; the higher the reading, the greater the number and *vice versa*. In the figure, each bar represents the total reading for the first interval in each day's experiment. It is seen at once that the readings increased tremendously during the administration of the extract and dropped back to normal shortly after the substance was withheld. The increase was noticed on the ninth day after treatment began (the initial increase in the C-R occurred on the eighth day) and reached a maximum on the twenty-eighth day (the same day when the C-R was maximal). The increase was still present on the sixth day after withdrawal of the substance, but then returned to the normal level. This relationship between the nervous movements and the magnitude of the C-R suggests that restlessness and hyper-irritability are closely associated. We shall discuss this association in another connection.

One may compare records of typical reactions during the normal period and during the period in which the extract was given in the two figures of text-figure 119. Figure 1 shows the conditioned motor reflex to the Met. 120 and to the shock, but no reaction to the negative Met. 36 during the normal condition of the animal. The recording drum is

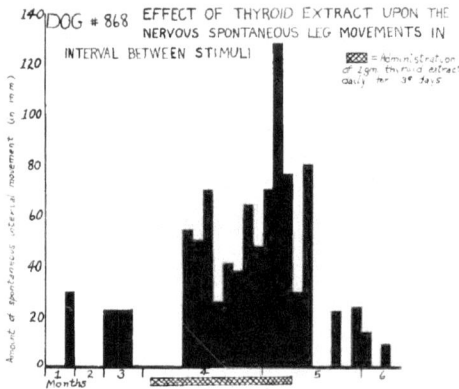

Text-figure 118. The effect of thyroid extract upon the nervous spontaneous leg movements during the 5 minute intervals between stimuli in dog 868. The nervous leg movements increase in amount during administration of thyroid and decrease after its withdrawal.

allowed to run throughout the entire interval between the stimuli, its speed being slowed during a portion of the period in order not to produce a record of too great a length. Note the slow and relatively infrequent movements of the head, the almost entire absence of movements to shift the body posture, the normal respiratory curve and the brisk conditioned and unconditioned reactions. Figure 2 shows a record obtained in exactly the same way from the animal during the administration of the thyroid substance. Note the frequent, quick, jerky movements of the head in the upper line,

GENETIC TYPE AND THE ENDOCRINES 671

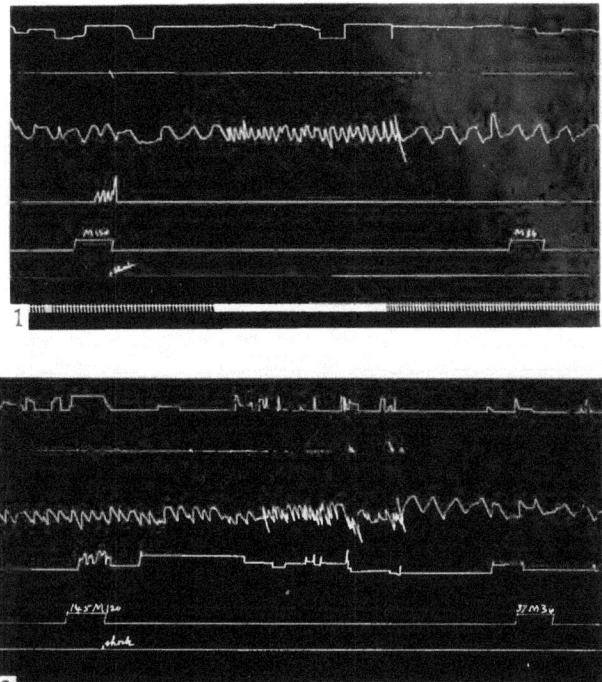

Text-figure 119. (1) Kymographic record showing the motor reactions of dog 868 in the period prior to the administration of thyroid extract. Note the conditioned leg reaction (fourth line from top) to the Met. 120 and shock and the lack of reaction to the Met. 36 (negative). Note that the animal stands quietly in the interval between the two stimuli. (2) Graphic record showing the reactions of dog 868 during the administration of thyroid extract. Contrast the exaggerated motor reactions with those shown in figure 1. Here the reaction is evoked not only by Met. 120 but also by the negative Met. 36. Notice also that the animal constantly moves the right foreleg in small, jerky movements. The movement of the head and irregularity in respiration, together with these spontaneous leg movements, suggest the picture of the highly nervous or neurotic animal.

the frequent, slight body movements, second line, the hastened and markedly irregular breathing, and the vigorous, quick reactions of the leg. Note that these latter reactions are evoked not only by the positive Met. 120, but also by the negative Met. 36, and that brief, jerky movements of the leg occur frequently during the quiet interval between the two stimulations.

The interesting fact should be noted that the behavior picture shown in figure 2 (text-fig. 119) is an almost exact duplicate of the behavior picture obtained in the "experimental neurosis" in the sheep, observed by Anderson and Liddell ('35). It is not claimed, however, that this dog was neurotic. The symptoms here observed were transitory, associated directly with and limited to the period of thyroid administration, while the symptoms of the "experimental neurosis" were permanent. It is significant that the characteristic signs of the nervous disturbance can be exactly reproduced in the normally calm and almost phlegmatic dog during thyroid administration. This fact brings to mind the difficulty encountered by the clinician in making a clear-cut differential diagnosis between the neurotic and the slightly hyperthyroid individual.

*Dog 881 ♀, bassethound* × *Saluki F$_2$.* In this animal, the conditioned salivary reflex was studied and the conditioned stimuli were Met. 120 (positive) and Met. 28 (negative). The dog was trained for 14 months before the critical experiments.

After several months' training it was discovered that this bitch's behavior in the kennel and in the laboratory was quite different from that of the other animals employed in the investigation. During the early part of the training period only slight differences in normal behavior were noticed. The dog often ran to avoid having the leash placed about her neck to take her to the laboratory. She was also shy with strange persons and with dogs placed in her pen, and frequently allowed the companion dog to eat her food while she stood trembling in a corner. A sudden scraping of the foot on the floor almost always startled this animal.

The C-R in this dog was formed easily in sixteen trials. The reaction, though weak, was considered normal during a period of 9 months. During this time the formation of a discrimination between Met. 120 and Met. 42 was attempted. The animal failed almost completely in this. After repeated attempts during 3 months to force her to discriminate between the two rates, the general behavior gradually became abnormal. The C-R slowly diminished in magnitude until finally, at almost every trial, no flow of saliva was evoked by the Met. 120. This dog previously had stood quite still during the intervals between stimuli but now moved restlessly about and constantly attempted to back off the experimental platform. The head was moved about in alert poses. The restlessness almost always became much more pronounced the moment the negative Met. 42 was started. All the slight signs of nervousness and shyness noted earlier now became greatly exaggerated until she was almost unmanageable. At this point we concluded that all the typical signs of the experimental neurosis as in Pavlov's classical experiments ('27) were evident. Realizing that symptoms of this disturbance in the dog often manifest themselves coincidently with the continued presentation of a problem too difficult for the animal to solve, an easier problem was presented. The Met. 42 was changed to Met. 28. Although some discrimination was evident with this slower metronome, the animal still remained as disturbed as before.

The C-R in this bitch, although entirely absent most of the time after the "experimental neurosis," did appear with considerable frequency and strength every time she came into heat (see plate 108 and text-figure 115). As pointed out earlier, there appears to be an association between the reappearance of the C-R and the heightened glandular activity presumably occurring during the oestrus. This animal provided a means of testing one aspect of this question, namely, whether it would be possible to cause a reappearance of the

C-R during the silent inter-oestrous period by the continuous administration of thyroid extract, since the magnitude of the motor C-R increased when this substance was fed to a normal male dog (868).

As a preliminary experiment the animal was fed thyroid extract 1 gm. daily for 7 days during the inter-oestrous period. The C-R was definitely not stimulated by the treatment. The percentage of correct responses decreased and the signs of nervousness were greatly intensified. Nervous movements while on the platform became so violent on the seventh day after the extract was begun that the equipment attached to the dog was torn off and the leather straps and rubber tubes were chewed apart. The experiment was then abandoned for 2 weeks, then resumed. When tested after a lapse of 3 months, the dog was calmer. She was then given 4 months' rest from the experiments. When work was resumed, the dog was about as quiet as in the early training period. However, after 2 weeks of testing the signs of the nervous disturbance reappeared.

Thyroid extract was tried again during the inter-oestrous period with the same test in mind. The daily amount of the substance was increased and the period of treatment was lengthened. She was fed 2 gm. daily for 21 days.

The C-R was, as before, unaffected, and again the general nervousness was increased. Her escape reactions became extremely violent, this time on the sixth day after the treatment was begun. The C-R trials were discontinued for 1 week, but when resumed her reactions were still violent. The dog was somewhat calmer 1 month after the extract was withdrawn.

Table 10 shows a marked decrease in the percentage of correct responses to Met. 120 from the early training period (68 per cent) to the period after the signs of the neurosis appeared (30 per cent). A further marked diminution occurred during the first thyroid experiment (30 per cent to 17 per cent) and the value was still below the initial level for 3 months after the thyroid extract was withheld (12 per cent).

A still further slight diminution in the percentage occurred during the second thyroid treatment (9 per cent). The percentage of correct responses to the negative Met. 28 increased from 92 per cent to 100 per cent during the first experiment and from 93 per cent to 100 per cent during the second. The average was quite unchanged.

Viewed as a whole, the values represent a gradual deterioration of the positive conditioned response (68 per cent—30 per cent—17 per cent—12 per cent—9 per cent) associated in some way with the advancing stages of the "experimental neurosis."

TABLE 10
*Dog 881 ♀*

|  | EARLY TRAINING PERIOD | "EXPERIMENTAL NEUROSIS" PERIOD ||||
|---|---|---|---|---|---|
|  |  | No extract | During first thyroid extract | Afterward | During second thyroid extract |
| Correct responses to positive Met. 120 | 68% | 30% | 17% | 12% | 9% |
| Correct responses to negative Met. 42 | 50% |  |  |  |  |
| Correct responses to negative Met. 28 |  | 92% | 100% | 93% | 100% |
| Average magnitude of C-R to positive Met. 120 | 3 | -1 | -1 | -1 | -1 |

*Summary of the thyroid effects.* It is clearly apparent that in dog 814 there was little or no effect on the C-R that could be attributed directly to the thyroid extract. Since the slight increase in correctness of the negative continued after withdrawal of the extract, it was probably due to training rather than to the extract.

In dog 868 (motor C-R), the extract had a decided effect on behavior. The dog became generally more excitable, and this excitability diminished when the extract was no longer given. The total behavior picture indicates clearly a rise in the general level of nervous excitability. The C-R was augmented and the animal was more restless between experiments. As in dog 814, the increase in efficiency of the negative reaction was probably due in large part to the further training, since this efficiency continued to increase after the experiment.

Dog 881 offers a special case, since this animal was a "neurotic." The extract increased motor activity enormously during the experiment, but curiously enough diminished the values of the salivary C-R. This lessened salivary C-R value is undoubtedly linked with the experimental neurosis since there was a definite gradual loss of the conditioned reaction with the passage of time, apart from the extract. This "inhibitory" tendency in experimental neurosis has been noted in the dog by Pavlov and his co-workers, and also in the sheep, reported by Anderson and Liddell.

The increase in the magnitude of the motor C-R observed in dog 868 is in essential agreement with the observation of Zawadowsky and his associates, and also with that of Kleitman and Titelbaum, although the observation of the former, that the C-R shows an initial depression, was not confirmed.

The fact that the conditioned salivary C-R decreased in one animal, 881, during the extract treatment, is not a real disagreement since the result cannot reasonably be attributed to the substance. On the other hand, the heightened nervousness in this dog and in dog 868 (clear cases of heightened excitability), tends to confirm the findings of all these workers.

Finally, then, we have tested the salivary C-R in two and the motor C-R in one normal dog. Each animal was fed thyroid extract for a specific length of time. The *efficiency* (percentage of correct responses) of the *positive salivary* C-R was somewhat diminished by thyroid treatment in one dog but was not affected in the other. The efficiency of the motor C-R was also not affected in the third dog. The percentage of correct responses to the *negative* stimuli was, however, noticeably increased in each animal.

The magnitude of the motor C-R was appreciably increased while that of the salivary C-R was unaffected. In the former case, as the motor C-R became more vigorous the animal became extremely nervous.

In the case in which the efficiency of the salivary C-R was decreased, the animal, a "neurotic" dog, exhibited general reactions of a most violent sort during the administration of the extract.

### The Effect of Thyroidectomy

*Dog 866 ♂, bassethound × shepherd $F_2$.* The conditioned stimuli were Met. 120 (positive) and Met. 42 and Met. 28 (negative). The C-R was standardized for 13 months before the operation.

This dog represented the well-behaved type. He was gentle, friendly, and cooperative, being obedient to gesture; in addition, he was lively and active but somewhat aggressive with other dogs. He showed no evidence of shyness under any circumstances.

A relatively constant salivary C-R was formed in seventeen trials. The dog was then completely thyroidectomized without removing the external parathyroids. Behavior was studied for 6 months after the operation.[19]

The C-R vanished almost completely after the operation. It was revived by the continued administration of thyroid extract. When the extract was withdrawn the C-R again disappeared.

The typical general behavior of the hypothyroid individual was presented. As the neuro-muscular lethargy set in, a considerable decrease in the animal's general activity was noticed. He was less alert than before in his reactions to both the experimenter and to the dogs. He slept during much of each day, and often could not be aroused by calling him by name. He paid little attention to the other dogs about him, never barking, playing or fighting with them as had formerly been his wont. He was, however, almost normally

[19] The C-R tests were never resumed immediately after the operation; to allow recovery from post-operative trauma at least 5 days elapsed before again starting them.

reactive to strong stimulation, such as an electric shock applied to his toe pad.

Behavior was studied for 2 months while the dog was in this condition. At this point, in order to check the experiment and determine definitely that the behavioral effects were due to deficiency in the thyroid secretion, the animal was given thyroid extract subcutaneously, 1 gm. daily for 32 days. The salivary C-R tests were continued. The treatment produced great improvement in the C-R and in behavior generally (table 11).

TABLE 11
*Dog 866 ♂*

| | TRAINING PERIOD | AFTER THYROID-ECTOMY | DURING THYROID EXTRACT | AFTER THYROID EXTRACT WITHDRAWN |
|---|---|---|---|---|
| Correct responses to positive Met. 120 | 85% | 9% | 58% | 30% |
| Correct responses to negative Met. 42 | 39% | | | 100% |
| Correct responses to negative Met. 28 | 44% | 100% | 100% | |
| Average magnitude of C-R to positive Met. 120 | 8 | 1− | 5 | 2 |

The efficiency of the salivary C-R to the Met. 120 was reduced after the operation (85 per cent to 9 per cent), enhanced during the extract treatments (to 58 per cent) and again reduced when the substance was withdrawn (to 30 per cent). The efficiency of the responses to the negative Met. 42 and Met. 28 was at the same time increased (39 per cent to 100 per cent and 44 per cent to 100 per cent, respectively). This increase remained unchanged during the injection of extracts.

The average magnitude of the C-R was affected. The response to the Met. 120 was reduced (from 8 to 1-) after thyroidectomy, was enhanced (to 5) during the extract, and was again decreased (to 2) afterward.

The effect upon the positive C-R may be viewed to best advantage graphically. Plate 108 (figs. 5 and 6) shows graphic records of the effect of the thyroid deficiency on the reflex. Figure 5, taken before the operation, shows a record of head and body movements, respiration and strong reflex flow of saliva during the Met. 120. Figure 6, after the operation, shows the absence of head and body movements, the slow, regular breathing, and the absence of the flow of saliva during the same stimulation. In both records the reactions to food itself are normal.

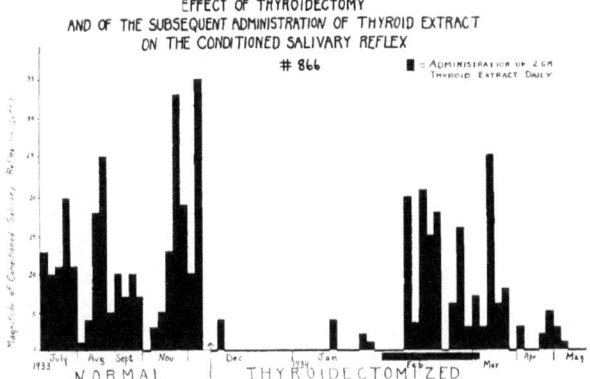

Text-figure 120. Chart showing the effect of thyroidectomy and of subsequent administration of thyroid extract on the conditioned salivary reflex in dog 866. Note the almost complete collapse of the reflex following the thyroidectomy and its subsequent revival, almost to normal magnitude, by thyroid extract. When the extract is withdrawn, the reaction tends to diminish and disappears completely within 2 months after withdrawal.

In text-figure 120 the magnitude of the positive salivary C-R is shown during all the phases of the experiment. The almost complete disappearance of the response after thyroidectomy is followed by an enhancement of the C-R within 10 days after the thyroid treatment was begun. This enhancement continued throughout the treatment and for nearly a month after it was stopped, then the C-R again collapsed.

The length of the latent period of the C-R indicates the degree of alertness. In this thyroidless dog, the enormously lengthened latent period indicates the retardation of higher central nervous activity. Although the response in the postoperative period was absent in the great majority of cases, when it did appear it was remarkably retarded. Normally the saliva begins to flow briskly within 4 seconds after the stimulus is started. Following operation, the saliva began slowly to flow only after 12 seconds (a retardation of 200 per cent).

The dog's appetite did not seem to be appreciably affected throughout the greater part of the experiment. No loss of weight occurred. Appetite did wane, however, during the terminal phase of the deficiency. The C-R experiments, since they involved the salivary food-taking response, were then abandoned. Twenty days before the dog died tetanic convulsions were seen. *This was 6 months after the operation.* The convulsions occurred almost daily and were alleviated temporarily by parathormone (Collip) 25 units, and intravenous calcium lactate given during the seizure. Just before an attack the dog was in a state of stupor. He showed no response when his name was called or when he was patted. He was also apathetic to a moderate electric shock on the foreleg and to pinching by forceps.

The autopsy showed an absence of parathyroid tissue. Apparently there occurred a gradual absorption of the external parathyroids left intact at the operation, but the deficiency in parathyroid secretion was not evident until 6 months after the operation. It is therefore reasonably certain that the effects of the operation upon the C-R were due to a deficiency of thyroid rather than parathyroid secretion.

*Dog 869 ♀, bassethound × shepherd $F_2$.* Since the results in the previous case were based on the salivary reflex, the motor reflex was used in dog 869. The conditioned stimuli were Met. 120 (positive) and Met. 42 and Met. 28 (negative). The standardization period was 13 months in length.

This animal was most active and alert in all reactions. She was what is known as a good watch dog, running about and barking violently at the slightest unusual sound, although when approached by a stranger she often ran away to hide. She represented the all-around, well balanced behavior type.

The motor C-R appeared initially at the second combination of the metronome and shock and thereafter it occurred in 116 cases out of 120.

In the previous experiment, the weakened reflex was revived by thyroid injections. To test whether a small bit of thyroid tissue left behind at operation would, after a time and through regeneration, restore the reflex, the present dog was partially thyroidectomized. The upper portion of each thyroid lobe was removed, leaving behind portions about the size of a pea. The external parathyroid bodies were not removed.

The results were striking. The strong motor C-R declined to 0 after the operation. Within 3 months, however, the response was gradually built up to almost normal without the aid of thyroid injections. At this point, the site of the operation was reopened and the bit of thyroid tissue on each side was found to be greatly hypertrophied (about doubled). Complete thyroidectomy was then performed. The results of this latter phase of the experiment will be reported under another heading.

TABLE 12

*Dog 865 ♀*

|  | TRAINING PERIOD | AFTER PARTIAL THYROIDECTOMY |
|---|---|---|
| Correct responses to positive Met. 120 | 97% | 82% |
| Correct responses to negative Met. 42 | 17% | 45% |
| Correct responses to negative Met. 28 | 100% | 100% |
| Average magnitude of C-R to positive Met. 120 | 46 | 23 |

As shown by table 12, the efficiency of the positive C-R declined (97 per cent to 82 per cent) while that of the negative C-R to Met. 42 rose (17 per cent to 45 per cent). Negative responses to Met. 28 were unchanged. The magnitude of the positive reflex decreased (46 to 23).

The results are shown graphically in text-figure 121 and 122. Text-figure 121 (fig. 1) is a record of the positive con-

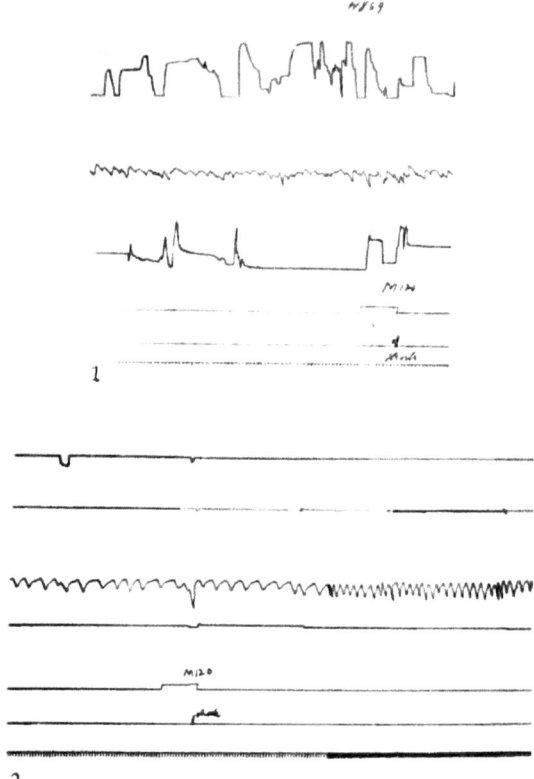

Text figure 121. 1. Graphic record of the normal vigorous reactions of dog 869 to Met. 120 followed by shock. Note the frequency of the head movements (top line) and reaction leg movements (third line). 2. Graphic record of the reactions of the same animal immediately following partial removal of the thyroid. Note here the almost complete absence of head and leg movements under exactly the same stimulation conditions.

ditioned reflex in the pre-operative period. Note the frequent, alert head movements, the rapid, slightly irregular breathing hastened by the stimulus, and the movements of the reacting leg before the metronome was sounded. These latter movements were also evoked by the sound of the kymograph in the next room. The metronome sound itself evoked the usual brisk defensive leg movements. Figure 2 shows the striking post-operative behavior of this animal. Note the almost total lack of head movement and general body movement, the slower and more regular breathing curve, and the almost complete absence of movements of the reacting leg. Met. 120 evoked only a single weak leg movement. The usual quick unconditioned response to the shock was almost suppressed. As the dog became less and less alert following the operation, the latent period of the motor C-R increased proportionally. The average latent period was 3 seconds in the pre-operative period and 7 seconds in the post-operative period, an increase of more than 100 per cent.

The course of the change in the magnitude of the positive response may be seen in text-figure 122. Note the complete temporary disappearance of the C-R following the operation and the subsequent gradual increase in the magnitude toward the normal during the 3 months of thyroid regeneration. The return toward normal is not complete but the enhancement is clearly seen.

During the height of the deficiency the only change in behavior outside the laboratory was the appearance of signs of muscular lethargy and a certain lack of responsiveness, but the dog was to all appearances normal at the end of the 3 months' period.

*Dog 864 ♂, bassethound × shepherd $F_2$.* An experiment similar to the previous one was now carried out with another dog in which the salivary instead of the motor conditioned reflex was employed. The conditioned stimuli were Met. 120 (positive) and Met. 42 and Met. 28 (negative), and the animal was trained for 1 year prior to the operation.

This dog was a brother of 869, used in the preceding experiment, and the behavior of the two animals was strikingly similar. No. 864 was very active and muscularly powerful. He was friendly and alert, and showed no trace of shyness under any circumstances.

The salivary C-R was formed at the sixteenth trial and was relatively constant.

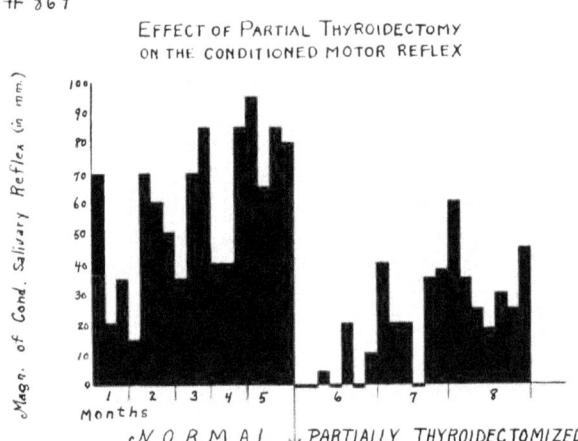

Text-figure 122. Chart showing the effect of partial thyroidectomy on the conditioned motor reflex in dog 869. Note the complete collapse of the reflex following the operation and the gradual return of the reflex during the three ensuing months. This return may be associated with the regeneration of the remaining portion of the gland.

As in the previous case, a partial thyroidectomy was performed. A minute piece of thyroid tissue of the left lobe remained, together with the corresponding external parathyroid.

When the tests of the salivary C-R were resumed, following the operation, it was found that this reflex had disappeared, as had the motor C-R in 869. Again, within almost exactly the same time (3 months) the response gradually regained its normal value. One year after the operation the thyroid region was again exposed surgically. The left thyroid lobe had hypertrophied enormously (approximately 20 times). The lobe was then completely removed, leaving behind only the parathyroid body. When the C-R was again tested it was found absent in almost every trial and did not revive during 5 months of testing. The autopsy showed complete absence of thyroid tissue. The parathyroid body was present.

At the stage of maximal thyroid deficiency, the general behavior picture was typical for the condition. Although general activity was impaired for a time, the dog suffered no loss of appetite.

TABLE 13

*Dog 864 ♂*

|  | TRAINING PERIOD | AFTER PARTIAL THYROID-ECTOMY | AFTER COMPLETE THYROID-ECTOMY |
|---|---|---|---|
| Correct responses to positive Met. 120 | 88% | 54% | 30% |
| Correct responses to negative Met. 42 | 5% | 77% | 80% |
| Correct responses to negative Met. 28 | 30% | 85% |  |
| Average magnitude of C-R to positive Met. 120 | 9 | 3 | 1 |

The results presented in table 13 are almost the exact duplicate of those in the previous experiment. The efficiency of the positive C-R very noticeably decreased (88 per cent to 54 per cent) after the first operation and decreased further after the second (54 per cent to 30 per cent). From a very low percentage, the correct responses to the negative Met. 42 increased enormously (5 per cent to 77 per cent) and this increase was maintained after the second operation (80 per cent). This was largely due to a lack of response to any stimulus rather than to an "appreciation" of the negative metronome. The negative C-R to Met. 28 was also increased (30 per cent to 85 per cent).

The magnitude of the positive C-R dropped after the first operation (9 to 3) and showed a further decrease after the second (to 1).

Text-figure 123 shows the effect upon the positive response. Note the sharp decline of the C-R value after the partial thyroidectomy, the gradual enhancement with time and its disappearance again after complete thyroidectomy. As the positive responses declined in efficiency and magnitude there was a decline in alertness, as is shown by the notable increase in the average latent period of the C-R. The latent period increased from 5 seconds to 13 seconds.

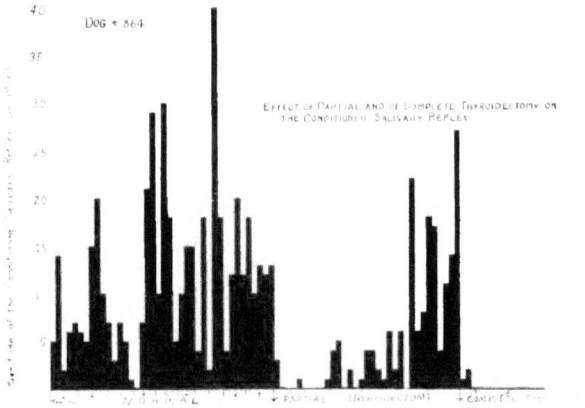

Text-figure 123. The effect of partial and of complete thyroidectomy on the conditioned salivary reflex of dog 864. Note here the complete collapse of the reflex value following the operation and its subsequent return to normal within 3 months. As was the case in dog 869, so in this case the gradual return may be associated with thyroid regeneration. Note the complete disappearance of the reflex after the thyroid was totally removed.

During the entire training period, this dog gave an exceedingly poor showing in the differentiation tests. In view of this it is remarkable that when the tests were resumed during the post-operative period, there should be evidence of marked improvement. As the positive C-R began to revive after the first operation, and before it had recovered its full strength, we tried not only the usual negative differential stimuli Met. 28 and Met. 42, but entirely new ones in relation to Met. 120 (positive). The rate of the negative metronome was then increased to 60 beats per minute and presented after a positive C-R of fair strength (8-100 cc. of saliva). Met. 60 evoked no response. This was tried under the same conditions once each day for several days, with the same result. The rate was further increased from 60 to 78 beats, by the above procedure, with complete success. When the rate was advanced to 96, however, it evoked at every application a positive flow of saliva. The limit had been reached. We shall discuss this result later.

*Dog 1030 ♂, bassethound × Saluki $F_2$.* The salivary conditioned reflex was used. The conditioned stimuli were all positive Met. 120; no negative differential stimuli were employed. The aim of the experiment was to study the effect of complete thyroidectomy upon the formation of the C-R, and the effect of the subsequent administration of thyroid extract upon the stability of the response.

This animal was selected because it was evident that, under normal conditions, the salivary C-R could be formed with comparative ease. The dog exhibited an exceedingly strong general food-taking reaction and was quite manageable in the laboratory, showing little or no evidence of being uneasy or afraid.

In general this animal was normally playful and alert and was fairly friendly, even with strange people. All reactions towards other dogs were also normal.

Thyroidectomy was performed, the parathyroids being left intact. Behavior was studied for 1 year and 9 months afterward. A period of 3 months without tests was allowed after the operation during which time characteristic symptoms of thyroid deficiency appeared. After the general behavioral reactions were clearly affected (without any evidences of loss of appetite or body weight), the conditioned reflex experiments were begun.

The results were clear. No conditioned salivary reflex could be developed. The procedure used successfully with other dogs was carefully followed. The animal, when taken to the laboratory and lifted upon the platform (he was too weak and stiff to climb upon it), simply did nothing at all when the food was presented. He stood perfectly still with his head held low. At times, when attempts were not being made to stimulate him, he lay upon the platform and slept. When awake, he made no responses to stimuli such as the Met. 120, the sound of a door buzzer or a flashing light. Light touch stimulation applied to the flank by the Krasnogorski skin stimulator (pneumatically actuated) evoked only the shaking reflex of that region of the skin. Sniffing reactions were evoked by a strong odor of oil of cloves.

The results were the same during 41 days of behavior testing in the laboratory. The dog ate food readily enough at the regular daily feeding time in the kennel.

At this point, the animal was fed thyroid extract, 1 gm. daily for 57 days. The results during this time were also definite and striking. Five days after the beginning of the extract therapy the dog began to eat the food presented in the laboratory. After 1 month, when the unconditioned food reflex was considered to be normal, the trials were begun to develop the C-R to Met. 120. The response was formed well within the normal time in twenty-one trials, and it was maintained at a normal level during the first 25 days after the extract was withdrawn. After this the reflex failed completely.

The continued administration of thyroid substance to this dog was tried on two other occasions with exactly the same result. On one occasion, 2 gms. of the extract daily were given subcutaneously for 41 days; and on another, 3 gms. daily were given in the same way for 25 days. During each period the C-R reappeared soon after the treatment was initiated and was maintained normally throughout the period and for a considerable time afterward.

Table 14 shows the fluctuations of the conditioned reflex during the alternate periods of thyroid sufficiency and deficiency. The efficiency of the response was fairly high during the first period of administration of the extract (63 per cent), but this declined after the extract was withdrawn (to 13 per cent). It increased again during the second thyroid period (to 58 per cent) and again declined afterward (to 39 per cent). During the third thyroid period it was again enhanced (to 62 per cent), and when the substance was withheld it dropped enormously (to 0 per cent).

The magnitude of the C-R followed the same course almost exactly. During the first thyroid period the average response was of medium strength (3). In the next period the value dropped markedly (to less than 1); in the next, during which double the amount of thyroid substance was given daily (2 gms. instead of 1 gm.), the value became more than double that of the first period (7). After this the average declined

TABLE 11

Dog 1030 ♂

|  | DURING FIRST THYROID EXTRACT PERIOD | AFTER-WARD | DURING SECOND THYROID EXTRACT PERIOD | AFTER-WARD | DURING THIRD THYROID EXTRACT PERIOD | AFTER-WARD |
|---|---|---|---|---|---|---|
| Correct responses to positive Met. 120 | 63% | 13% | 58% | 39% | 62% | 0% |
| Average magnitude of C-R to positive Met. 120 | 3 | 1— | 7 | 5 | 7 | 0 |

(to 5). It was increased again during thyroid injection (to 7) but this was not proportional to the further increase in the amount of the extract given (3 gms. daily). In the final phase, when no extract was given, the magnitude decreased greatly (to 0).

The animal's general condition appeared to be considerably worse with each succeeding period of thyroid deprivation. In the second period, trophic disturbances of the skin, myxoedema associated with mange, developed in addition to the neuro-muscular symptoms. The skin was greatly wrinkled, puffy, dry, scaly and nearly hairless. In the last period the skeletal muscle reflexes were exceedingly slow. It was very interesting to note the retardation, for example, in the reaction of shaking the body. The normal dog, when his coat is wet or when something tickles or irritates the skin, will begin first to shake his head, flopping his ears vigorously from side to side, then his body, and lastly his rump and tail, and this reaction may be repeated time after time. This complex reaction was rather abortive in the thyroidless dog. It usually consisted of only a single, slow twist of the head, sometimes two twists, accompanied by a slight, awkward shifting of the body weight from one foreleg to the other. The reaction ceased with this. Such a reflex obviously did not serve its purpose, since the shaking movements were not of sufficient vigor even to dislodge a small block of wood placed between the shoulder blades. This curious abortive reaction was noticed in another thyroidless dog, 866. These skin and motor disturbances responded almost at once to the thyroid treatments.

Plate 109 illustrates by photographs and graphic records the behavior of this typical thyroidectomized dog in the conditioned reflex laboratory. Figure 1 shows the posture of the enfeebled animal just before stimulation and the posture during stimulation with the metronome followed by food. There is no observable response. Below the photographs is a typical graphic record showing the absence of all components of the *conditioned* reflex (reading from top line down: absence of head movements, body movements, respiratory alteration and conditioned saliva). These reactions were all evoked by the presentation of the food itself. In figure

PLATE 109

EXPLANATION OF FIGURES

1 The photographs at the top show the absence of any reaction during the Met. 120 signalling food after animal 1030 was thyroidectomized. The graphic record below shows the absence of the reflex actions. When food is given, it evokes movement of the head, general body movement, some disturbance in respiration, and a flow of saliva.

2 The photographs at the top show, in dog 1030, the normal conditioned reaction to the Met. 120 after thyroid extract was administered for 5 weeks to this deficient animal. The tracing below shows the vigor of these reactions. The metronome evoked reactions of the head, body, respiration, and a vigorous flow of saliva.

PLATE 109

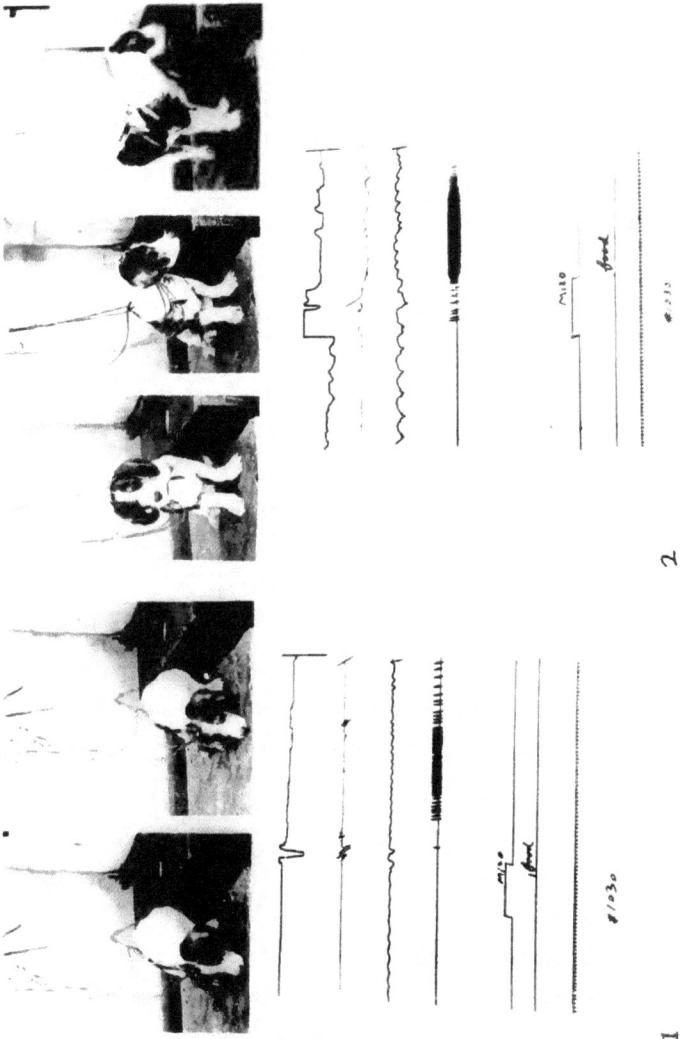

2 the three photographs show the postures of the same dog after 5 weeks of daily administration of 2 gms. of thyroid extract. The first of these (left) illustrates the typically alert pose of the animal just before the stimulation was applied, the next shows the posture at the moment the metronome began, and the last shows the reaction during the course of the stimulation. Below these, a graphic record of the behavior during this phase shows (from top line down)

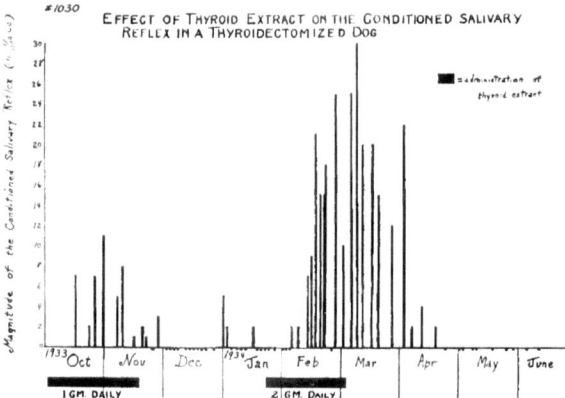

Text-figure 124. Chart showing the effect of thyroid extract on the conditioned salivary reflex in the thyroidectomized dog (1030). Note the increase in the values of the reflex when the amount of extract administered was doubled.

the quick movement of the head at the beginning of stimulation, the movement of the body as the dog gets to his feet, the alteration in respiration and the ready flow of saliva beginning almost immediately after the metronome began to click.

In text-figure 124 the influences of two periods of thyroid administration on the C-R are shown. In the first period, a stable and fairly strong response was maintained with 1 gm. daily, but, as is shown, it disappeared completely 12 days after discontinuing the treatment. Two months later the extract was again administered in doses of 2 gms. daily. Within about 20 days a definite effect on the reaction could be observed, and this effect thereafter increased enormously. The magnitude of the maximal response was more than four times that of the maximal response of the preceding thyroid deficient period. The response increased still further for a time after the thyroid was withheld and was strong for 29 days afterward. A weak reaction was elicitable even after this time but disappeared entirely within about 20 days more. As the conditioned reflex improved on each occasion during the thyroid treatment, the average latent period of the response was shortened. The latent period was decreased in length from 8 seconds in the deficient intervals to 5 seconds in the treatment intervals. This fact illustrates in a quantitative way the great increase in alertness brought about by the administration of the extract.

In the last stage of the experiment, when no extract was being administered, the study of the salivary conditioned reflex was discontinued. With the animal in a low condition, attempts were made to establish the conditioned *motor* reflex to a tone of 256 cycles. The attempts were only partially successful. A conditioned response did not appear until the fourteenth trial, when a slight twitch of the reaction leg muscles was seen. The paw was not lifted from the floor. This rate of formation of the reflex is exceedingly slow. From this point on, the slight twitch of the limb was observed only twice in twenty-five consecutive trials. The shock always evoked an equally slight leg tremor.

We may conclude from the above cases that the efficiency of the positive C-R (both salivary and motor) *decreases* after thyroidectomy. Simultaneously, the negative C-R increases. To interpret the increased efficiency of the negative as "discrimination" or "differentiation" on the part of the thyroidless animal would be an absurdity which is entirely inconsistent with observation on cretinous individuals. It is also inconsistent with our own observations on the behavior of operated animals under positive stimulation. The latent period is lengthened and alertness is lost. Therefore, the 100 per cent efficiency viewed as a reaction to a negative stimulus really means no reaction at all, or, in other words, apathy.

It has been pointed out above that the *increased* positive efficiency resulting from injecting the normal dog with thyroid extract is due to a heightened excitability of the nervous system. In the present section, we have found that efficiency of the positive C-R *decreases* after removal of the gland. This is interpreted as due to a state of lessened excitability. Under the thyroidless state we have the negative C-R *increasing* in efficiency! This negative increase, then, (frequently going up to 100 per cent), is actually a lowering of sensitivity or excitability to the stimulus.

The results do not agree in all respects with the findings of Valkov. In his experiment, the salivary C-R was unstable, and in the present work the salivary reflex is aroused by the usual stimuli only with great difficulty, and in the great majority of cases it cannot be aroused at all. Our results are in definite disagreement with his concerning the formation of the conditioned reflexes. Valkov points out that both the motor and salivary C-R could be established as well in the thyroidless dog as in the normal one, the motor reflex being normally maintained after its establishment. We were quite unable to form the salivary C-R in such an operated dog, and could develop only the weakest sort of motor C-R, which was maintained only very poorly.

The results are also different from those obtained by Liddell in the sheep and goat.[11] The thyroidectomized animals formed and maintained the motor conditioned reflex equally as well as the normal controls. They could also form conditioned differentiations equally well. The disagreement between these results and those of the present experiment may be apparent rather than real. The two investigations are not comparable in a fundamental respect, namely in the use of two widely different animal forms, the sheep and goat on one hand and the dog on the other. One would naturally expect the behavior

[11] The present author worked with some of the animals in Liddell's experiments.

of such different animals to be different in some fundamental way. Such a divergence may have to do with a difference in the fragility of the C-R. Since the dog has a far more delicately poised central nervous system than the sheep or goat it is probable that the C-R is also far more fragile and sensitive to disturbances in physiological functions. The recent work of Liddell, James and Anderson ('34) also establishes the fact that the conditioned reflexes in the sheep and goat are not disturbed or destroyed so easily as in the dog. The C-R in the former animals was, for example, unaffected in any noticeable way by the action of stimuli intended to distract, but in the case of the dog, as clearly shown by Pavlov and confirmed many times in the present experiments, the C-R tends to be easily destroyed by any one of a great variety of distracting sounds, sights or odors ("external inhibition"). Exact and detailed analysis of such fundamental differences in behavior from the comparative point of view offers a field for further profitable investigation.

It must be pointed out that the criterion or standard by which the effects of thyroid deprivation are judged is not the same in the experiments of Valkov and of Liddell as in the present study. Both workers compared the behavior of a normal control animal with that of an operated animal but in the present investigation each animal has served as his own control. Behavior in the pre-operative period was directly compared with behavior in the post-operative period in one and the same animal. In conditioned reflex experiments on higher animals the former procedure often leads to some confusion in the interpretation of the results. The conditioned reflex method deals specifically with the *individual organism* and its *individual performances* and *achievements*. It is becoming increasingly apparent that the common idea of a "control" must be reinterpreted when one deals with the physiology of individual achievement. The behavioral performances and achievements of one animal obviously cannot be fully compared with that of another as a control. Experience shows that the behavior of one animal may not only differ in many notable ways from that of another at a given moment of comparison, but that each animal may pursue a strikingly divergent course during different periods of time. Thus the characteristic behavior of a sheep, or a dog, or a person, undergoes a continual reorganization. It responds sensitively to a changing system of stimulations from the environment, both internal (change in internal body chemistry) and external (changes in the patterns of sound, sight, odor, or touch). Alterations in response to environmental change are a consequence of education or conditioning. Thus, in experiments of this kind, the aim of which is to determine the effect upon the C-R of thyroidectomy or of other physiological alterations, it is unquestionably of advantage to study the reactions in one and the same animal in the period prior to and following the operation. The animal is thus his own best control.

Neither Valkov nor Liddell employed a means of quantitatively estimating the vigor or magnitude of the conditioned *motor* reflex. A method of numerically designating whether a reaction was strong, or medium, or weak, might conceivably have been helpful in the analysis of the consequences of thyroidectomy on the response. Further experiments using the modified Fick work accumulator under their exact conditions would, of course, be a way of testing this.

Finally we may state that the effects of thyroidectomy on the salivary C-R in three dogs and the motor C-R in one dog were briefly as follows. Both the salivary and motor positive responses in all the animals were greatly decreased in efficiency and in magnitude after the operation. Efficiency and magnitude tended to return to the normal level following the chronic administration of thyroid extract in two dogs and following the natural regeneration of thyroid tissue in two others. Decrease in general alertness was shown in all the animals by lengthening of the latent period of the C-R. This was shortened by thyroid administration.

In all cases the percentage of correct responses to the negative conditioned stimuli increased after thyroidectomy.

The results are interpreted to mean that a decrease in, or an absence of the thyroid secretion results in a lowering of the general level of excitability. This lowering also accounts for the apparent improvement in the discriminating ability of the animals, as explained above.

### The Effect on Behavior of the Administration of Parathyroid Extract to the Normal Dog

*Dog C-1 ♀, bassethound × shepherd $F_3$.* The salivary C-R was used. The conditioned stimuli were Met. 120 (positive) and Met. 28 (negative). The dog was trained for 6 months before the critical tests.

The general behavior picture of this dog was that of the well balanced type, friendly and cooperative, and with no trace of shyness. She had been born and reared in the laboratory and handled a great deal, and proved to be an intelligent and extremely versatile animal.

The C-R was formed very rapidly, in five trials, and thereafter appeared with a high degree of regularity. The magnitude of the response was remarkably uniform from one test period to another. For these reasons, the animal was used not only in this experiment but also in others, in which the effects of the administration of anterior lobe pituitary extract and of adrenalin on the normal dog were studied; and in a later experiment, this dog was used to study the effect of hypophysectomy.

Parathormone (Collip), 5 units daily, was administered for 20 days. The C-R tests were carried out each day, 4 hours after the injection. The positive C-R was altered appreciably. Both the efficiency and the magnitude of the response increased.

Table 15 shows that the percentage of correct responses to Met. 120 increased slightly during administration of the extract (86 per cent to 88 per cent), and increased afterward to better than normal (to 100 per cent). The negative response became somewhat less efficient (33 per cent to 25 per cent) and afterward continued to decrease (to 0 per cent).

The average magnitude of the C-R rose considerably during the extract period (9 to 14) and decreased afterward to exactly the former level (9).

The animal became noticeably more restless in the laboratory during the intervals between one stimulus and another throughout the period of the administration of the substance. She looked about with quick, jerky movements, and shifted from one place to another on the platform as though she was not "satisfied" in any position. Such restlessness was in contrast to her previously calm behavior under the same stimulation conditions. No change could be detected in her general behavior outside the laboratory.

TABLE 15

Dog C-1 ♀

|  | TRAINING PERIOD | DURING PARATHYROID EXTRACT | AFTER EXTRACT WITHDRAWN |
|---|---|---|---|
| Correct responses to positive Met. 120 | 86% | 88% | 100% |
| Correct responses to negative Met. 28 | 33% | 25% | 0% |
| Average magnitude of CR to positive Met. 120 | 9 | 14 | 9 |

*Dog 814 ♂, bassethound × Saluki $F_2$.* Since this animal was used in an experiment already described, i.e., the effect of thyroid extract administration upon the normal dog, the details of his training period need not be repeated here.

Parathormone (Collip), 5 units daily, was administered subcutaneously for 10 days. As in dog C-1, the behavior tests were carried out each day 4 hours after the injection.

The C-R was altered during the 10 day period. As in the previous case, both the efficiency and magnitude of the response were increased to some extent.

As shown in table 16, the percentage of correct positive responses showed a slight increase (82 per cent to 87 per cent) and the percentage of correct negative responses to Met. 42 a marked increase (28 per cent to 75 per cent). The average magnitude of the positive response increased slightly (13 to 17), and that of the negative response decreased sharply (6 to −1). No change in general behavior was noted either in or outside the laboratory.

These results indicate that the level of excitability is slightly raised during the administration of small doses of parathyroid extract. Positive efficiency shows a percentage increase, while the negative shows a slight decrease in one case and a considerable increase in the other. The magnitude of the reflex is of significance here.

TABLE 16

*Dog 814 ♂*

|  | TRAINING PERIOD | DURING PARATHYROID EXTRACT |
|---|---|---|
| Correct responses to positive Met. 120 | 82% | 87% |
| Correct responses to negative Met. 42 | 28% | 75% |
| Average magnitude of C-R to positive Met. 120 | 13 | 17 |

In brief, it may be stated that in both animals the efficiency and magnitude of the *positive* C-R were slightly increased. In one, the efficiency of the *negative* C-R diminished somewhat, its magnitude remaining about the same. In the other the efficiency of this response increased considerably, while its magnitude definitely decreased. The former animal became more restless in the experiment, while the latter showed no change in general behavior.

## The Effect of Complete Thyro-Parathyroidectomy

*Dog 869 ♀, bassethound × shepherd $F_2$.* An account of the training period and the period following partial thyroidectomy in this dog has been discussed above in connection with the thyroid effects. It will be recalled that the positive motor C-R decreased sharply after the removal of the greater part of the thyroid and that the response gradually improved accompanying the natural regeneration of the small portion of thyroid tissue left behind along with the parathyroids. At this stage of the experiment thyro-parathyroidectomy was performed. Subsequent autopsy showed the complete absence of the thyroids and parathyroids.

700    O. D. ANDERSON

Since maintenance of the dog in a chronically low state of parathyroid deficiency was not practicable, the next best procedure was to administer parathormone and calcium lactate when signs of a tetanic seizure were observed. In this way, periods of deficiency alternated with periods of sufficiency, and the post-operative behavior of the dog could be studied over a longer period of time.

Parathormone (Collip), 15 units at a single injection, was given subcutaneously during an attack of tetany which occurred 3 days after the operation. After the attack had been relieved, the dog was given 15 gms. of calcium lactate by mouth. The same procedure and dosages were carried out at intervals thereafter of 4, 7, 6, 9 and 4 days.

TABLE 17
Dog 869 ♀

|  | TRAINING PERIOD | AFTER PARTIAL THYROIDECTOMY | AFTER COMPLETE THYRO-PARATHYROIDECTOMY | |
|---|---|---|---|---|
|  |  |  | Before tetany | After treatment |
| Correct responses to positive Met. 120 | 97% | 82% | 40% | 55% |
| Correct responses to negative Met. 42 | 17% | 45% | 67% | 86% |
| Average magnitude of C-R to positive Met. 120 | 46 | 23 | 8 | 10 |
| Average amount of nervous movements in first interval between stimuli (in mm) |  |  | 142 | 45 |

The tests of behavior during the periods of deficiency were all made on the same days on which attacks of tetany occurred. The experiment was always carried out immediately after the first sign of an approaching attack and the tests were usually made 4 or 5 hours before the actual seizure. The behavior tests during the periods of sufficiency were all made on days immediately following the seizures and therapy, at which time the animal showed marked improvement. The dog often appeared almost normal on these days.

The results during the two periods are considered separately in table 17. The C-R was greatly reduced as to efficiency and magnitude during the parathyroid deficient period. The animal was very restless in the intervals between stimulation. The C-R was noticeably augmented, however, after the administration of the parathormone and calcium lactate. The animal was calm in the experiments. Restlessness or calmness were registered in the interval between the first and second stimuli in each experiment by the Fick work accumulator, as in the case of animal 868.

Comparative results of the training period and of the period after partial thyroidectomy have already been discussed.

It is apparent from table 17 that the percentage of correct responses to the positive Met. 120 was *further* decreased on the tetany days (82 per cent to 40 per cent) but after treatment there was a noticeable increase toward the normal percentage (to 55 per cent). At the same time the percentage of correct negative responses (to Met. 42) showed a steady increase in each period (45 per cent to 67 per cent to 86 per cent).

The effect upon the average magnitude of the C-R was remarkable. The positive response fell at once during the deficient period (23 to 8) but was revived to a slight extent during the administration of the extract (10).

In the first 5 minute interval between the positive and negative stimuli in the experiments just before tetany and before treatment, the dog moved about incessantly. She would rise from the sitting posture and move from one side of the platform to the other, moaning softly at almost every expiration and pressing her head against the wall or against a portion of the food box before her; after this she would lie down on the platform and rub her nose and forehead with the forepaws as though suffering from headache. After a short interval she would spontaneously rise to her feet and repeat the same behavior. In the period after treatment the restlessness was superseded by calm. This result is shown quantitatively in the table. On the tetany days the amount of spontaneous interval movement (in mm) was high (142), and on the days following, the amount dropped strikingly (to 45).

As would be expected, the dog's general behavior outside the laboratory was very noticeably altered after the operation and before the treatments. The legs were somewhat rigid and the walking gait was slow and uncoordinated, the body swaying from side to side as though the dog were intoxicated with alcohol. An occasional twitching of the temporal muscles was seen. Mourning sounds were frequently heard.

*Dog 856 ♂, bassethound × Saluki $F_2$.* The motor C-R was used in this dog. The conditioned stimuli were Met. 120 (positive) and Met. 42 (negative), and the C-R was standardized for 8 months before the operation.

This dog was somewhat nervous in general reactions. He was of a thin build and his skeletal movements were quick and jerky. Motor reactions could be aroused with the slightest stimulus. He was continually running about the pen and barking in a frenzied fashion at the other dogs, and was always slightly shy of people. The defensive motor C-R was formed quickly in five trials, and was absolutely stable throughout the normal period. The dog showed some degree of restlessness in the laboratory during the experiments. This was characterized by movements in the intervals between stimulations and was especially noticeable after attempts were made to form differentiations.

The procedure with this dog was somewhat different from that with animal 869 in the preceding experiment. It was thought that a chronic state of *partial* parathyroid deficiency might be brought about if at the operation a minute portion of parathyroid tissue was left behind as a transplant. Accordingly, the thyroid and parathyroids were removed and a small portion of one of the parathyroid bodies dissected away from the thyroid lobe and transplanted into the fascia near the thyroid region on the right side.

Parathormone (Collip), 10 to 20 units daily, was given subcutaneously just before and for 3 days after the operation, along with 10 gms. daily of calcium lactate by mouth. This was simply a precautionary measure carried out until the transplant should "take."

The behavior tests were resumed 15 days after the operation. The C-R was noted to be much weaker than in the normal period, and signs of parathyroid deficiency became apparent at about this time. For 2 days marked anorexia and vomiting, accompanied by coarse twitching of the temporal muscles and by disturbances of locomotion, were noted. Parathormone, 10 units on alternate days, was then given subcutaneously during a period of 45 days.

The vigor of the reactions returned to some extent during the first portion of this period, but during the latter portion, in spite of the extract, the responses again deteriorated. No tetanic seizures were observed during the administration of

TABLE 18
Dog 856 ♂

| | TRAINING PERIOD | AFTER THYRO-PARATHYROIDECTOMY | | |
|---|---|---|---|---|
| | | No parathormone | During administration of parathormone | Terminal phase; no parathormone |
| Correct responses to positive Met. 120 | 100% | 75% | 100% | 66% |
| Correct responses to negative Met. 42 | 38% | 50% | 20% | 44% |
| Average magnitude of C-R to positive Met. 120 | 45 | 8 | 24 | 6 |

the substance. The C-R remained weak for 6 weeks after the withdrawal of the extract; again no tetany was observed. The positive reaction now disappeared completely. Three determinations of the blood serum calcium were made on 3 consecutive days, with the calcium values 5.4 mg., 8.1 mg., and 6.1 mg., respectively. These are below the normal values. Eight days after these determinations were made, typical attacks of tetany began to appear and the dog died in tetany a few days later.

At autopsy, histological examination of the transplanted parathyroid tissue revealed the presence of a few apparently functional parathyroid cells.

Table 18 summarizes these results. The efficiency of the positive C-R dropped at once after the operation (100 per cent to 75 per cent) but was returned completely to normal during the administration of parathormone (100 per cent). The efficiency of the response dropped back to about the pre-injection level after the extract was withdrawn (66 per cent). The percentage of correctness of the negative C-R increased after the operation (38 per cent to 50 per cent), decreased during the extract period (to 20 per cent) and increased in the after period to about the previous level (44 per cent).

The average magnitude of the C-R was changed enormously after the operation, being reduced more than five times (45 to 8). This was increased notably during the administration of the extract (to 24) although the normal level was not attained. After the substance was withheld, the value dropped to approximately the same level (6) as before the parathormone was given.

The detailed data are presented in graphic form in plate 110 (figs. 1–4) and text-figure 125. In plate 110 graphic records of the motor reactions of this dog during the normal control period are shown. The graphs are described begin-

PLATE 110

EXPLANATION OF FIGURES

1 The fairly calm and deliberate reactions of animal 856 before attempts to form a differentiation between positive and negative stimuli.

2 and 3 The extreme state of nervousness produced in this dog (856) following attempts to form discrimination between Met. 120 and Met. 42. The animal not only reacts to both positive and negative stimuli, but also reacts when not being stimulated at all. The head and body movements, respiration, and leg movements illustrate the extent of the nervousness.

4 The effects of removing the thyroid and parathyroids on the nervous behavior and conditioned reflexes in animal 856. Note the greatly diminished reaction of the right forelimb to the Met. 120 and to the shock. Note also that interval movements of head, body and reaction leg have practically disappeared.

5 Graphic record of the conditioned salivary reflex in dog 492 prior to hypophysectomy. Note the alert head movement and vigorous conditioned salivary flow to the Met. 120 followed by food.

6 Graphic record showing the absence of the conditioned salivary reflex in the same dog (492) following complete hypophysectomy. Food itself evoked vigorous reactions of the head, body, respiration and salivation.

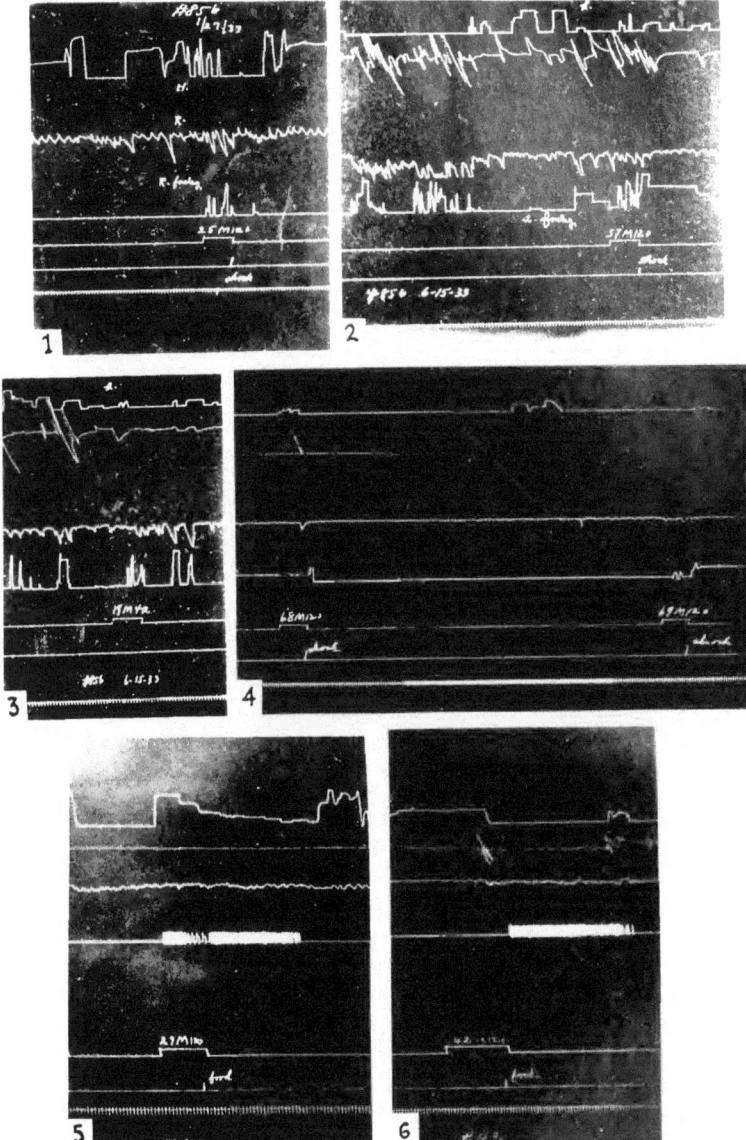

ning with the top line and proceeding downward. Figure 1 shows a typical record of the responses before the introduction of the differentiation problem (the negative stimulus Met. 42). Note the quick movements of the head, before, during and after the Met. 120 stimulation, the irregular respiration, and the brisk flexion movements of the reaction leg during the stimulus and at the end when the shock was applied. The animal stood fairly quiet before the sound was presented. In figures 2 and 3, characteristic records after the introduction of the differentiation problem are shown. In figure 3, the negative Met. 42 was presented, and in figure 2 the positive Met. 120. In both note the increase in the frequency of the spontaneous head movements, the numerous shiftings of the body posture, the noticeably more disturbed respiratory rhythm, and the appearance of restless, spontaneous movements of the reaction leg. Notice especially that the conditioned leg movement response is nearly as vigorous to the negative stimulus as to the positive.

In figure 4, typical reactions of the same dog are shown during the post-operative period after the parathyroid extract had been discontinued. Contrast this record with those of figures 1, 2 and 3. The record shows a complete 5 minute period between two positive stimuli. Note the weak, slow and infrequent head movements, the almost complete absence of body movements, the undisturbed respiration which is hardly affected even during the conditioned leg reaction to the first stimulus, an excessively weak response to the second stimulus, and no spontaneous leg movements at all. As the motor C-R weakened, its latent period was lengthened twofold. In the normal period, the average latent period of the response was 2 seconds, while in the post-operative period it was 5 seconds. This was in accord with the observation that the dog was less alert in the latter period.

The C-R in all phases of the experiment is represented in text-figure 125. Note the sharp drop in the magnitude of the C-R following the operation, the revival of the response for a short time during the administration of the parathormone, the decline during the continued administration of the substance, and the weak state in the period after withdrawal of the extract, followed by disappearance in the terminal period.

During the 4 months in which the dog was studied after operation, general behavior outside the laboratory was also

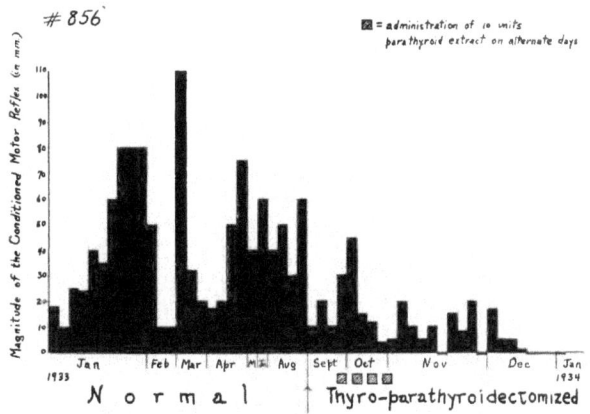

Text-figure 125. A chart showing effect of thyro-parathyroidectomy and of the subsequent administration of parathyroid extract on the conditioned motor reflex in dog 856. Note diminution of the conditioned reflex after the operation and the slight enhancing effect of the extract. The value of the reflex is reduced to zero in the fourth month after the operation.

affected. The limbs were stiff, and movements were poorly coordinated in walking. The gait was peculiar, the body swaying from side to side, and the course being on a zig-zag line. Each step was jumpy. Occasional twitching of the temporal muscles was observed. The animal slept a great deal and was very unresponsive to various natural stimulations in the kennel. It is also interesting to note that on no occasion after the operation was this dog known to bark. The appetite was poor at times, but there was no loss in body weight.

Due to the inherent difficulty in separating the function of the parathyroid from that of the thyroid, one cannot definitely say that these results are due to disturbance of the parathyroid alone. But since the administration of parathyroid extract (in both dogs) had a restorative effect on the responses, it is reasonable to suppose that this restoration, though not complete, was due in part to the presence of the parathyroid substance. As a result of the operation the level of excitation was lowered in the same way as in the absence of the thyroid. In the one case (parathyroid) the disturbance in calcium may be the chief factor in producing the alteration in nervous irritability, and in the other case (thyroid) the alteration in excitability is unquestionably associated with the lowering of the rate of general metabolism.

As after thyroidectomy, the efficiency of the negative reactions increased after the parathyroid operation. Also as with the thyroid, this increased efficiency of the negative after the operation is associated with the general lowered responsiveness or excitability. Not only is the responsiveness to the C-R below par, but the dog is also unresponsive to stimulation in general. As was pointed out, the animal failed to respond even to a shock applied to his leg or when pinched by a steel forceps.

It is interesting that there is an obvious lowering of the level of excitability in a dog just before going into tetany. At first consideration, such results may be considered inconsistent. It must be remembered, however, that prior to the attack the animal's responsiveness is externally aroused (by stimulation), whereas in the tetanic attack external stimulation is not being tested. The hyper-irritability in tetany is expressed as an incoordination of the neuro-muscular system, which is due to a disturbance in the function of the motor cortex. The unresponsiveness before tetany and the tetany itself are related to the same disturbance in internal chemistry, the lowering of blood calcium, since blood calcium is about as low before tetany as during the seizure.

This relationship is borne out by the further observations that parathormone, which is known to raise the level of blood calcium, also makes the animal more responsive to stimulation before the seizure, and alleviates tetany if given during an attack.

In brief, then, removal of the parathyroid and thyroid glands from two dogs was followed by a marked decrease in the efficiency and in the magnitude of the conditioned motor reflex. The negative reactions were improved. Both the magnitude and the efficiency of the conditioned reflex were increased considerably during parathormone administration.

## THE INFLUENCE OF THE PITUITARY UPON BEHAVIOR

### THE EFFECT OF THE ADMINISTRATION OF A GENERAL EXTRACT OF THE ANTERIOR LOBE IN THE NORMAL DOG [12]

*Dog C-1 ♀, bassethound × shepherd $F_3$.* This quiet dog was selected for this experiment because of her remarkable stability in the C-R observed during the training experiments. Negative stimulation was not used in this experiment.

Since the behavior of the dog in the normal training period has already been described in detail we may repeat only as much of the data as is necessary to a clear exposition of the results in the present experiment.

General anterior lobe extract, 10 units daily, was administered subcutaneously for 12 days. The C-R test continued uninterrupted. The salivary C-R was somewhat enhanced as to efficiency and magnitude during the administration of the substance.

Table 19 shows that the percentage of correct responses to the positive stimulus increased slightly (86 per cent to 90 per cent) and declined in the after period to below the

[12] Growth extract—Squibb.

normal level of performance (80 per cent). The average magnitude showed a very definite increase (9 to 17) and this value also declined after withdrawal of the extract (to 12).

A slight rise in the magnitude of the C-R was observed on the fifth day after administration of the extract was begun. The maximal increase was not observed till the twelfth day, the last day of the treatment. Two days after the substance was withdrawn, the reading was still slightly above normal, and subsequent values were within normal range. No behavioral change outside the laboratory was detected.

TABLE 19
*Dog C-1 ♀*

|  | TRAINING PERIOD | DURING ANTERIOR PITUITARY EXTRACT | AFTER EXTRACT WITHDRAWN |
|---|---|---|---|
| Correct responses to positive Met. 120 | 86% | 90% | 80% |
| Average magnitude of C-R to positive Met. 120 | 9 | 17 | 12 |

It is interesting to note that an effect upon the C-R was detectable following the administration of anterior pituitary extract. To attempt an explanation of such effect, based on observations on one animal only, would presume too much. The result, however, furnishes a basis for further work.

### THE EFFECT OF HYPOPHYSECTOMY

*Dog 492 ♂, bassethound × shepherd—bx bassethound.* Both the salivary and the motor C-R were formed and studied in this dog prior to the operation. The former was established to Met. 120, while the latter was established to a tone of 256 cycles. It was found best, however, to study one reflex at a time. Thus the salivary reflex was observed for a few weeks, then the motor reflex for a similar period, and so on. Negative differential stimuli were not used. The duration of the training period was 3 months.

This dog had been reared as a pet and was therefore accustomed to handling. He was a gentle animal, showing no evidence of shyness, and his calm, even phlegmatic disposition made it possible to form the two different types of conditioned reflex. The shock did not destroy the food reaction even when the two reactions were studied during the same day.

Complete hypophysectomy was performed, and the conditioned reflex tests carried on for 2 months afterward.

The results are clear cut. After the operation, the salivary C-R disappeared entirely and the stronger motor C-R almost entirely. Behavioral reactions outside the laboratory, including reactions to food and to a shock, were not affected in any observable way until a week or 10 days before the dog's death from pituitary insufficiency. To all appearances the animal was perfectly normal up until the terminal phase.

After the operation, and during a period in which the conditioned motor reflex alone was being observed, extracts of the anterior and of the posterior pituitary lobes were administered as a check on the results. General anterior lobe extract (growth extract—Squibb), 2 cc. daily, was given subcutaneously for 6 days, and following this the dose was combined with posterior lobe extract (pituitrin) $^3/_4$ cc. daily for 3 days (also given subcutaneously). The motor C-R alone was tested at this time. Little, if any effect on behavior was noticed during the administration of the extracts.

Table 20 shows the post-operative changes in the two conditioned reflexes. The efficiency of the salivary C-R dropped from a high level (84 per cent) to zero, and the magnitude of the response naturally decreased to zero (5 to 0).

The efficiency of the motor C-R was also enormously decreased (100 per cent to 19 per cent) in the period just after the operation. This was not improved very noticeably during the administration of the anterior lobe extract, and an obvious decrease was evident when the anterior and posterior lobe substances were given together. In the terminal phase of the experiment the motor reflex could not be elicited at all (0 per cent).

The magnitude of the motor C-R followed a similar course. It declined strikingly in the first post-operative period (28 to 3). The values were not enhanced during the anterior lobe extract; rather they showed a further decrease (to 1), and were unchanged when both substances were given (1). The magnitude in the terminal phase was, of course, zero.

The results are shown graphically in plates 110 and 111 and text-figures 126 and 127. Figure 5 (pl. 110) shows a typical conditioned salivary reflex in the animal in the normal period. Note the sudden, alert raising of the head (top line) as the Met. 120 was started and its lowering as the time for the food approached, the absence of body movement, the

TABLE 20

*Dog 1924 ♂*

Conditioned salivary reflex

|  | Training period | No extract | After hypophysectomy ||| 
|---|---|---|---|---|---|
|  |  |  | During anterior lobe extract | During ant. and post. lobe extract | After extract withdrawn |
| Correct responses to positive Met. 120 | 84% | 0% |  |  |  |
| Average magnitude of CR to positive Met. 120 | 5 | 0 |  |  |  |
| Conditioned motor reflex ||||||
| Correct responses to positive tone 256 cycles | 100% | 19% | 25% | 11% | 0% |
| Average magnitude of CR to positive tone 256 cycles | 28 | 3 | 1 | 1 | 0 |

slight respiratory change and the ready flow of the conditioned saliva. Figure 6 (pl. 110) gives a representative record of the effect of the operation. Notice the absence of the alert head movement during the conditioned stimulation, and the absence of body movement, respiratory change, and flow of conditioned saliva. Note especially that all these components do appear when the food itself is presented. As soon as the dog sees the food the head is lowered into the pan and the animal begins to eat; while eating, the dog shifts the weight of the body from one foot to another, the breathing is irregular, and the saliva flows freely.

Text-figure 126 shows the course of the effect of hypophysectomy upon the salivary C-R. It will be seen that the response, normally vigorous and regular in appearance during 3 months, was completely absent in every test after the gland was removed.

Figures 1 and 2 in plate 111 show the records of the motor C-R before and after the operation. In figure 1 before the operation, note the vigor of the head movements, the change in respiration and the quick defensive raising of the paw when the tone of 256 cycles was sounded. In figure 2, for the post-operative period, note the slow lowering of the head,

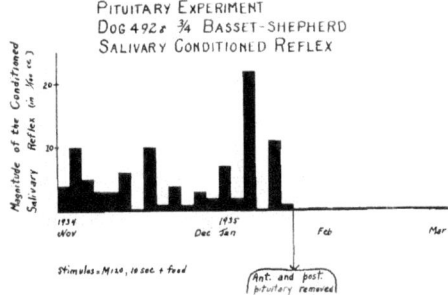

Text figure 126. A chart of the effect of complete hypophysectomy on the conditioned salivary reflex in dog 492. The response to the Met. 120 disappeared completely.

slight alteration in breathing, and the absence of the conditioned leg movement. In this animal, even the shock failed to evoke a movement of the leg.

The detailed course of the motor C-R throughout the several phases of the experiment can be seen from text-figure 127. This chart indicates the disappearance of the response almost immediately following the operation; there was no reappearance except on one occasion, when no gland material was being administered. During the last month of the experiment, attempts to restore the response by extracts were only partially successful. A slight enhancement of the magni-

PLATE III

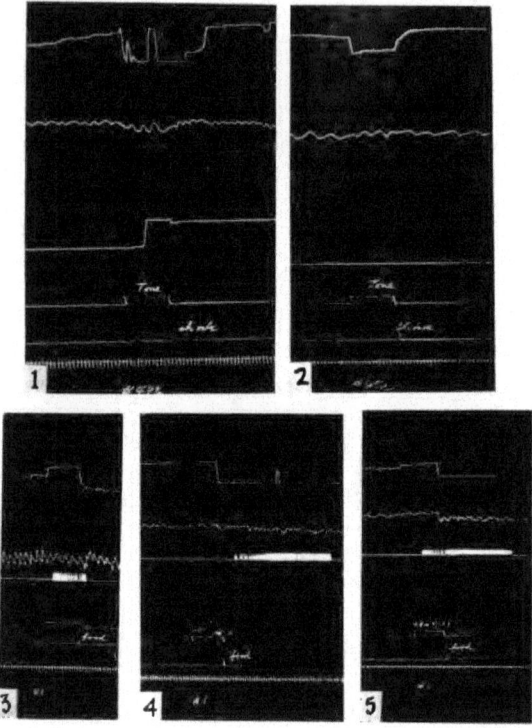

1  A graphic record showing the conditioned motor reflex in dog 492 prior to hypophysectomy. The response involves vigorous head, respiratory and reaction leg movements to a pure tone followed by a shock.

2  A graphic record showing the absence of the reaction leg component of the conditioned motor reflex in the same dog (492) following complete hypophysectomy. Note that although the leg movement disappeared, the conditioned head and respiratory effects remain.

3  A graphic record showing the conditioned salivary reflex in dog C-1 prior to complete hypophysectomy. The head, respiratory and salivary reactions to Met. 120 are vigorous.

4  Graphic record showing the absence of the entire salivary reaction complex in the same animal (C-1) following complete hypophysectomy.

5  Graphic record showing the return of the salivary reaction complex in dog C-1 after the administration of thyroid extract.

tude of the C-R was observed on the second day after the injection of anterior lobe extract was begun, but this effect diminished as the therapy was continued, and soon disappeared altogether. The reflex was aroused slightly during the administration of the two extracts simultaneously, but this again was quite transient. After the cessation of the treatment the response disappeared completely.

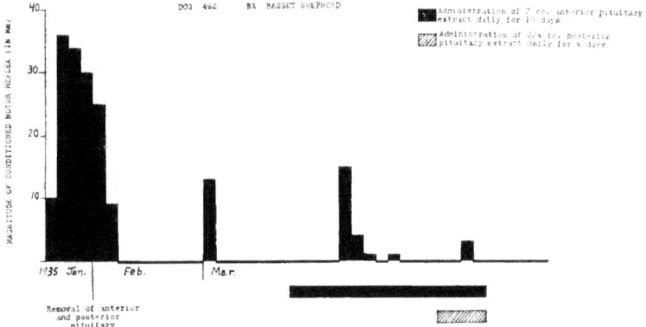

Text-figure 127. Chart showing the effect of complete hypophysectomy and of the subsequent administration of anterior pituitary extract and posterior pituitary extract on the conditioned motor reflex in dog 492. Note the almost complete cessation of the formerly vigorous conditioned defensive reaction following the operation. Neither gland substance had any pronounced effect on the dormant reaction.

It is important that although the two different types of conditioned reaction deteriorated to a marked degree after the operation, the animal's behavior in the kennel, towards both food and punishment, did not appear to be affected. When a pan of food was held for the dog to see and smell, he showed every sign of being hungry, that is, stared fixedly at the food and licked his chops. When the pan was placed upon the floor he advanced quickly to it and began to bolt the food. Evidence of the anticipation of punishment was equally clear, as illustrated by the fact that the animal always crouched and crawled slowly toward the attendant at a sharply spoken word of command or at the sudden clapping of the hands. Such food-taking and defensive reactions have been referred to by Pavlov as "natural" conditioned reflexes and are to be distinguished from what is ordinarily understood by the term "conditioned reflex." During the terminal phase of the gland disturbance, however, such responses could be aroused only rarely.

The dog became gradually less active, and the movements in walking, although coordinated, were slow.

The autopsy showed no trace of pituitary tissue.

*Dog C-1* ♀, *bassethound* × *shepherd* $F_3$. This dog was selected for a more exhaustive analysis of the effect of hypophysectomy on the C-R for the reason, mentioned before, that the salivary response could be elicited with machine-like precision in a relatively uniform and regular manner. The control period thus offered an excellent standard for comparison (a high level of performance) with the post-operative period.

Description of the behavior of dog C-1 during the training period has already been given. The total length of the training period, including experiments on the administration of parathormone, anterior pituitary extract and later adrenalin, was 17 months. The C-R was completely standardized before the operation was performed.

A complete hypophysectomy was performed in this animal. To obviate any possible effect of post-operative trauma, the behavior tests were not resumed until after a lapse of 41 days, when it was found that the formerly efficient and vigorous conditioned salivary reaction had disappeared completely.

General anterior lobe pituitary extract (growth hormone— Squibb), 20 units daily, was given subcutaneously for 19 days to determine whether the C-R could be revived, and if so, to what extent. The response reappeared with almost normal magnitude, but soon diminished and finally disappeared again even though administration of the extract was continued.

Since the thyroid frequently shows evidences of atrophy after hypophysectomy, it was thought that the absence of the C-R might be accounted for in part by the resulting low thyroid condition. To test this hypothesis, the dog was given thyroid extract, 2 gms. daily, subcutaneously, for 24 days. The result of this procedure was instructive. The response reappeared and gained considerably in magnitude, although it never attained the normal level, and continued fairly brisk for some time after the substance was withdrawn, when it completely disappeared. This stage was approximately 5 months after the operation.

The dog's behavior outside the laboratory was at first only slightly affected. The most noticeable sign was a certain slowness in general body movement. The gait in walking was normal. Appetite was unaffected. As time went on, the effects became more pronounced. At the end of the fifth month the dog had become extremely fat; the body had a decidedly barrel-shaped appearance, and the head seemed much too small in proportion. The fat hung in folds about the neck and trunk. The muscles were flabby. The skin was in fair condition but was noticeably dry and scaly. All skeletal movements were exceedingly slow. The gait in walking was now very much affected. It was a definitely staggering, stiff-legged walk in which the head bobbed about in an uncertain, tremulous and uncoordinated manner. When attempt was made to have her run, the gait was a series of curious bowing movements which carried her from one side of the long run to the other. She occasionally ran against the fence as though unable to see it. When at the water pail for a drink, she did not seem able to locate the surface of the water accurately. She would stand over the pail, head bobbing aimlessly about, and her nose frequently went under the surface almost to the bottom of the full bucket. Muscular action was weak, as illustrated by the fact that she could be easily pushed over.

At this stage pituitary transplants were tried. The fresh, whole pituitary taken from a dog at autopsy was directly transferred under aseptic conditions to a "pocket" in the pectoralis major muscle. Such a transplant was made three times during the ensuing period of 10 months. Marked improvement in general behavior was noted about 10 days or 2 weeks after each transplant, an improvement so striking that the dog appeared almost normal. This lasted about 1 month, after which a noticeable decline set in, and approximately 3 months after the transplant the dog was again in a lowered condition, but not so low as before this form of treatment was tried. At this time another transplant was given and the cycle was repeated.

To facilitate tabulation of the results in table 21, the 10 month period, during which the three transplants were tried, is treated as a single unit.

TABLE 21

Dog C-1 ♀

|  | TRAINING PERIOD | AFTER HYPOPHYSECTOMY | | | |
| --- | --- | --- | --- | --- | --- |
|  |  | No extract | During anterior pituitary extract | During thyroid extract | During period of pituitary transplants |
| Correct responses to positive Met. 120 | 86% | 20% | 40% | 58% | 25% |
| Correct responses to negative Met. 28 | 33% | 80% | 80% | 100% |  |
| Average magnitude of C-R to positive Met. 120 | 9 | 1 | 3 | 3 | 2 |

It can be seen from table 21 that the normally stable C-R was greatly diminished in efficiency after the operation (86 per cent to 20 per cent), was increased during the anterior pituitary extract (to 40 per cent), was further increased during thyroid administration (to 58 per cent), but diminished on the whole and was maintained at a diminished level during the period of pituitary transplants (25 per cent). The efficiency of response to the negative Met. 28 was considerably increased after the operation (33 per cent to 80 per cent), remained at that level during the anterior pituitary extract, but was augmented during the administration of thyroid substance (100 per cent). Tests of the negative response were discontinued during the transplant period.

The average magnitude of the C-R was tremendously changed after the hypophysectomy. It dropped at once (9 to 1-), was augmented considerably during the anterior lobe extract (to 3), and was maintained during the thyroid extract period (3). During the period of the transplants, the response declined to a new level (to 2), yet this was a great deal above the level in the period when no treatment at all was given (1-). The results are graphically presented in plate 111 and text-figure 128.

Plate 111 shows records of the typical conditioned food-taking reactions of dog C-1 in the normal period (fig. 3), in the period after hypophysectomy (fig. 4), and in the period during the administration of the anterior lobe extract (fig. 5). Notice in figure 3 the normal head movements, alterations of respiratory rate, and copious salivary flow during the Met. 120. Note in figure 4 the absence of all three components of the reaction. In figure 5 notice that the stimulus evoked an alert head movement, a change in respiration and a strong flow of saliva closely similar to the normal. It can be seen that the normal responses evoked by the food itself remained unaltered.

The chart, text-figure 128, shows the course of the experiment in detail with the exception of the period of the transplants. It is clearly shown that the C-R disappeared almost altogether following the operation and remained so for about 1 month. It increased noticeably on the fifth day after the injection of anterior lobe extract was begun, but this gain was lost as the C-R dropped to zero during the continued therapy. On the fourth day after thyroid extract was injected the response began to return, and on the twenty-third day it was maximal. The C-R fell rapidly after the extract was withdrawn, and in 20 days its value was zero.

The autopsy at the end of the experiment showed the pituitary to be entirely absent. The transplants in the pectoral muscles had been completely resorbed.

*Dog C-2 ♀ , bassethound × shepherd $F_3$*. The effects of hypophysectomy in dogs 492 and C-1 were considered a result of the absence of the anterior rather than the posterior lobe of the gland. The experiments did not, however, offer proof that such was the case, and it was considered of interest to carry out an additional experiment, in the nature of a control, in which the posterior lobe alone was removed, the anterior portion being left essentially undisturbed. This was successfully done in dog C-2.

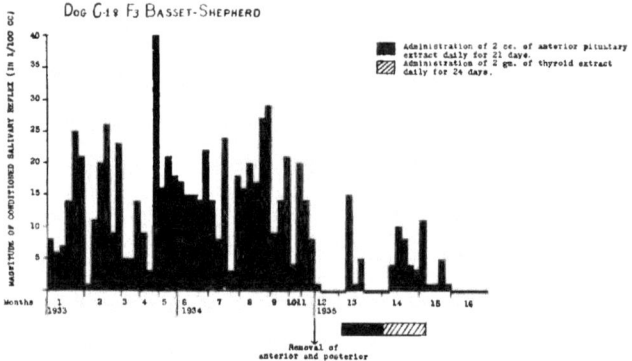

Text-figure 128. Chart showing the effect of complete hypophysectomy and of the subsequent administration of anterior pituitary extract and thyroid extract on the conditioned salivary reflex in dog C-1. As in the case of thyroidectomy, note that the reaction here also collapses post operatively. It is revived transitorily by the anterior pituitary extract but the effect disappears during a continuation of the therapy. Thyroid extract was then given and produced a noticeable return of the reaction, which subsided after withdrawal of therapy.

The operation was performed prior to any behavior studies when this animal was only 3 months of age. Salivary conditioned reflex trials were begun 4 months later, and were continued for 1 year and 8 months. During this entire time it was clear that the operation had had no effect whatever upon the behavior of the animal. The general reactions outside the laboratory were those of any normal, lively, friendly dog. She was a pet and had been born and reared in the laboratory. There were no signs of shyness, and her general health was good.

A strong C-R was established in eight trials, which is about the usual rate at which the salivary response is formed in dogs. And the reaction thereafter appeared with undiminished strength and with a relatively high degree of efficiency. A differentiation was then normally established and maintained.

When the conditioned reflexes of this dog are compared with those of normal, unoperated dogs, on the basis of efficiency and magnitude, it is at once apparent that her behavior was quite normal. Table 22 gives the values in dog C-2 as compared with the average values of eight normal dogs, trained in exactly the same way as C-2.

TABLE 22
Dog C-2 ♀

| | AFTER REMOVAL OF POSTERIOR LOBE OF PITUITARY | AVERAGE VALUES FOR 8 NORMAL DOGS |
|---|---|---|
| Correct responses to positive Met. 120 | 87% | 85% |
| Correct responses to negative Met. 28 | 76% | 47% |
| Average magnitude of C-R to positive Met. 120 | 7 | 8 |

Autopsy on this animal showed that the pars posterior of the pituitary had apparently at the time of the operation been "squeezed out" of the surrounding hypophyseal tissue and removed. In addition, a minute portion of the pars anterior, on the left posterior aspect, had been removed. This gave a slightly asymmetrical shape to the pars anterior. Otherwise the tissue appeared normal.

We may conclude in general that, as in the case of dogs after thyroidectomy and parathyroidectomy, hypophysectomy increases the efficiency of the negative reflex and decreases the efficiency of the positive reflex, all of which is due to a general lowering of excitability. It is reasonable to expect that as general metabolic activity is diminished there would be a concomitant diminution of the functional activities of the central nervous system.

Such effects as were observed after pituitary removal may well be associated in some way, at present poorly understood, with the lowering of general metabolism occurring at the time, and which may be due to an impairment of thyroid function. To test how far such a view is tenable we tried restoring the weakened C-R by administering thyroid extract and were partially successful. Previous observations by many workers in the field of endocrinology had indicated that removal of the pituitary is followed by atrophy of the thyroid, and that this in time brought about a lowering in general metabolism.

Assuming that the lessened efficiency and magnitude of the conditioned reflex in a hypophysectomized dog is due alone to absence of the anterior lobe, we were able to build a reflex in an animal from which the posterior lobe had previously been removed. Since the posterior lobe was removed while this animal was young, and since there was no difference between his performance in the C-R tests and those of normal dogs in the training period, we conclude that the tremendous reductions in C-R values after complete pituitary removal resulted from the absence of the secretion of the anterior rather than the posterior lobe.

In summary, the tests were as follows. Two dogs were completely hypophysectomized and from a third dog only the posterior lobe of the gland was removed. One of the first two dogs was tested with both salivary and motor reflexes, the other was trained in the salivary C-R only. In both types of reflexes the efficiency and magnitude of the C-R were reduced to zero. The administration of extract of the anterior lobe revived the reflexes to some extent but this effect was transitory. The subsequent administration of both anterior and posterior pituitary extract together had practically no restorative effect. In one of the dogs, administration of thyroid extract raised the efficiency of the reflex to a value above that which resulted from the anterior pituitary extract, and almost to normal level. Finally, in this same animal, a succession of pituitary transplants were made. Following each transplant the efficiency and the magnitude of the reflex did not rise as high as under the thyroid administration, but the level was raised above that prevailing during the time after hypophysectomy. The third dog, which had only the posterior lobe removed, showed C-R values (efficiency and magnitude) typical for normal dogs.

## THE INFLUENCE OF THE SUPRARENALS UPON THE BEHAVIORAL REACTIONS

### THE EFFECT OF ADMINISTRATION OF ADRENALIN ON BEHAVIOR IN THE NORMAL DOG

*Dog 868 ♂, bassethound × Saluki $F_2$.* The effect of a single massive dose of adrenalin upon the motor C-R was observed in this dog. The animal's training period has already been described.

Control tests of the positive response alone were carried out, the negative differential stimulus being omitted. Adrenalin, 1 cc. of 1:1000 solution, was given intravenously. The same positive response tests were resumed a few minutes after the injection.

The C-R showed an increase shortly after the injection, but this was followed by a marked decrease. As the values decreased it was noticed that the dog became somewhat restless and nervous, as shown by an increase in the amount of spontaneous movement of the reaction leg in the intervals between stimuli. The effect disappeared $4\frac{1}{2}$ hours after the injection. Statistical treatment of the results failed to show this, since the effect is diphasic and the increase masks the decrease in the averages. However, for the purposes of comparison with preceding tabulations, the results are given in table 23.

TABLE 23

*Dog 868 ♂*

| | TRAINING PERIOD | AFTER ADRENALIN 1:1000 |
|---|---|---|
| Correct responses to positive Met. 120 | 94% | 90% |
| Average magnitude of C-R to positive Met. 120 | 12 | 12 |

In order to show the details of the effect, the entire protocol of the experiment is given in table 24. The C-R magnitude increased (20 to 40) in 20 minutes after the injection. No increase in the leg movements between stimulations appeared at this time. At the end of 2 hours and 16 minutes, the response to the stimulation was reduced to zero, and during the interval between stimuli the spontaneous movements (nervousness) were enormously augmented (55 to 170 mm.). As the tests

TABLE 24
*The effect of a single, massive dose of adrenalin upon the conditioned motor reflex in the dog*

*Dog 868 ♂*
*Experiment of Sept. 18, 1933*

| TIME | CONDITIONED STIMULUS | DURATION OF CONDITIONED STIMULUS | C-R IN MM TO POSITIVE CONDITIONED STIMULUS MET. 120 | AMOUNT OF NERVOUS LEG MOVEMENT IN MM IN 5' INTERVAL BETWEEN STIMULI | REMARKS |
|---|---|---|---|---|---|
| 11:07 A.M. | Met. 120 | 10 sec. | 20 | | |
| 11:12 | Met. 120 | 10 sec. | 15 | 55 | dog alert but quiet |
| 11:21 | 1 cc adrenalin 1:1000 intravenously | | | 21 | |
| 11:36 | Met. 120 | 10 sec. | 10 | | |
| 11:41 | Met. 120 | 10 sec. | 40 | 60 | dog alert but quiet |
| 11:46 | Met. 120 | 10 sec. | 10 | 35 | |
| 1:32 P.M. | Met. 120 | 10 sec. | 10 | | |
| 1:37 | Met. 120 | 10 sec. | 0 | 170 | nervous |
| 1:48 | Met. 120 | 10 sec. | 10 | | |
| 1:53 | Met. 120 | 10 sec. | 20 | 135 | nervous |
| 1:58 | Met. 120 | 10 sec. | 10 | 140 | nervous |
| 3:59 | Met. 120 | 10 sec. | 10 | | |
| 4:04 | Met. 120 | 10 sec. | 4 | 24 | dopey |
| 4:09 | Met. 120 | 10 sec. | 12 | 0 | dopey |

continued the C-R gradually gained in magnitude while the amount of spontaneous movement diminished. At the end of $4\frac{1}{2}$ hours the response was about normal while the movement had diminished to zero.

*Dog 742 ♂, bassethound × English bulldog $F_1$.* The motor C-R was used. Only the response to the positive Met. 120 was studied. The aim of this experiment was to determine the effect of successive injections of adrenalin upon an especially weak conditioned motor reflex.

This dog was a remarkably quiet animal, exhibiting certain signs of shyness. His disposition seemed, curiously enough, partly shy and partly phlegmatic. He seemed afraid of other dogs and of people yet lay around dozing at intervals throughout the day. The training period was 9 months, during which time only a weak motor C-R, formed in five trials, could be established. Adrenalin, 1 cc. of 1:25,000 solution, was given intravenously on 3 successive days, and the C-R was definitely affected in the period after each injection. The efficiency of the response was diminished somewhat on all 3 days, while its magnitude during the same period showed an increase followed by a marked progressive decrease. The dog was observably restless on the second day.

TABLE 25
Dog 742 ♂

|  | TRAINING PERIOD | AFTER ADRENALIN | | |
|---|---|---|---|---|
|  |  | 1st day | 2nd day | 3rd day |
| Correct responses to positive Met. 120 | 94% | 80% | 80% | 83% |
| Average magnitude of C-R to positive Met. 120 | 16 | 18 | 13 | 4 |

It can be seen from table 25 that the efficiency of the reaction was lowered noticeably on the first day (94 per cent to 80 per cent) and remained through the critical tests at about the same level. The average magnitude showed a slight increase on the first day (16 to 18), a decrease on the second day (to 13) and a further notable decrease on the third day (to 4). The experiment is presented in exact detail in table 26.

On the first day, a slight increase in the value of the C-R was noticed immediately upon resuming the tests after the injection (15 to 25 within 18 minutes). The value continued to rise gradually, and the magnitude was maximal 39 minutes after the injection. Thereafter it gradually decreased and after 5 hours and 19 minutes was reduced to zero.

On the second day the reflex did not increase appreciably over the maximal reading just before the injection (24 to 25). The most striking result was the reduction of the value

TABLE 26

*The effect of the continuous administration of adrenalin upon the conditioned motor reflex in the dog*

*Dog 742 ♂*

Experiment of Sept. 26, 1933

| TIME | CONDITIONED STIMULUS | DURATION OF CONDITIONED STIMULUS | C R IN MM. TO POSITIVE CONDITIONED STIMULI: MET. 120 | REMARKS |
|---|---|---|---|---|
| 11:12 A.M. | Met. 120 | 10 sec. | 8 | |
| 11:16 | Met. 120 | 10 sec. | 15 | quiet |
| 11:30 | 1 cc adrenalin 1:25000 intravenously | | | |
| 11:48 | Met. 120 | 10 sec. | 25 | " |
| 12:00 | Met. 120 | 10 sec. | 20 | " |
| 12:04 P.M. | Met. 120 | 10 sec. | 30 | " |
| 12:09 | Met. 120 | 10 sec. | 15 | " |
| 12:11 | Met. 120 | 10 sec. | 35 | " |
| 4:35 | Met. 120 | 10 sec. | 10 | " |
| 4:40 | Met. 120 | 10 sec. | 10 | " |
| 4:45 | Met. 120 | 10 sec. | 12 | " |
| 4:49 | Met. 120 | 10 sec. | 0 | " |
| 4:53 | Met. 120 | 10 sec. | 0 | " |

Experiment of Sept. 27, 1933

| TIME | CONDITIONED STIMULUS | DURATION | CR | REMARKS |
|---|---|---|---|---|
| 2:58 P.M. | Met. 120 | 10 sec. | 0 | " |
| 3:03 | Met. 120 | 10 sec. | 2 | " |
| 3:07 | Met. 120 | 10 sec. | 15 | " |
| 3:12 | Met. 120 | 10 sec. | 20 | " |
| 3:15 | Met. 120 | 10 sec. | 10 | " |
| 3:20 | Met. 120 | 10 sec. | 24 | " |
| 3:40 | 1 cc adrenalin 1:25000 intravenously | | | |
| 3:58 | Met. 120 | 10 sec. | 25 | " |
| 4:03 | Met. 120 | 10 sec. | 23 | " |
| 4:07 | Met. 120 | 10 sec. | 15 | somewhat restless |
| 4:13 | Met. 120 | 10 sec. | 5 | " " |
| 4:19 | Met. 120 | 10 sec. | 0 | " " |

Experiment of Sept. 28, 1933

| TIME | CONDITIONED STIMULUS | DURATION | CR | REMARKS |
|---|---|---|---|---|
| 3:38 P.M. | Met. 120 | 10 sec. | 0 | quiet |
| 3:44 | Met. 120 | 10 sec. | 0 | " |
| 3:47 | Met. 120 | 10 sec. | 5 | " |
| 4:10 | Met. 120 | 10 sec. | 3 | " |
| 4:12 | Met. 120 | 10 sec. | 7 | " |
| 4:15 | Met. 120 | 10 sec. | 0 | " |
| 4:18 | 1 cc adrenalin 1:25000 intravenously | | | |
| 4:36 | Met. 120 | 10 sec. | 4 | very still |
| 4:41 | Met. 120 | 10 sec. | 5 | " " |
| 4:45 | Met. 120 | 10 sec. | 7 | " " |
| 4:49 | Met. 120 | 10 sec. | 5 | " " |
| 4:54 | Met. 120 | 10 sec. | 0 | " " |
| 4:59 | Met. 120 | 10 sec. | 4 | " " |

to zero in a much shorter time than on the preceding day (in 39 minutes instead of 5 hours and 19 minutes after the injection). The dog showed the first signs of restlessness 27 minutes after the adrenalin.

On the third day the responses, both before and after the injection, were exceedingly low in value. As on the preceding day, the value did not increase above the maximal reading before the adrenalin (7). There were, however, more correct responses after the injection than before (5 out of 6 against 3 out of 6). The reaction was zero within 36 minutes after the adrenalin.

The motor C-R was quite normal when tests were made 10 days after the experiment.

The behavior of the dog in the kennel was not observably affected during these experiments.

*Dog C-1 ♀, bassethound × shepherd $F_3$.* The aim of this experiment was to test the effect of adrenalin upon the salivary C-R in a normal dog. The negative differential stimulus was not used.

In dog C-1 adrenalin was administered continuously during three separate periods, the dose being increased in strength at each period. Throughout each experiment the injections were made subcutaneously, 1 hour before the behavior tests were begun. In the first period, adrenalin, 1 cc. of a 1:50,000 solution, was given daily for 5 days. After a lapse of 16 days the second period was begun, in which adrenalin, 1 cc. of a 1:25,000 solution, was given daily for 4 days. After a lapse of 39 days the third period was begun, with adrenalin, 1 cc. of a 1:1000 solution, given daily for 3 days.

Behavior was quite appreciably affected in each period. In the first and second periods the C-R showed an initial increase followed by a decrease; in the third it showed a decrease. The average magnitude of the C-R was increased slightly during the mild dosage and very noticeably during the stronger dosage, but when the dosage was very strong, the value, instead of showing a further increase, declined far below normal.

The extent of the changes in efficiency and magnitude of the C-R are shown in table 27. The increase in efficiency was not large (86 per cent to 100 per cent). The slight increase in the magnitude of the C-R during the first adrenalin period is shown (9 to 12), followed by a further rise in the second period when the stronger doses were given (to 19), followed in turn by the enormous decrease in the last period (to 3).

TABLE 27

*Dog C-1 ♀*

|  | TRAINING PERIOD | DURING ADRENALIN 1:50,000 | DURING ADRENALIN 1:25,000 | DURING ADRENALIN 1:1,000 |
|---|---|---|---|---|
| Correct responses to positive Met. 120 | 86% | 100% | 100% | 100% |
| Average magnitude of C-R to positive Met. 120 | 9 | 12 | 19 | 3 |

Table 28 shows the entire protocol of the three injection periods in dog C-1. In the first period, note the rise of the reaction value during the first day (11 to 19) and its fall to below the normal level on the third day (to 7). Note the similar result in the next period, the increase on the first day (12 to 28) followed by the decrease on the third day (to 12). And in the last period note the amount of the decrement from the minimal response in the preceding control period to the minimal response in the critical period (16 to 1).

The efficiency of the C-R showed an apparent small increase when the three critical periods were compared with the training period.

It is of interest to note that several hours after a massive dose of adrenalin, the motor C-R declined to zero, and that simultaneously the amount of spontaneous activity in the intervals between stimulations was greatly augmented. The lowered value of the salivary C-R occurring on the third day of injection is strikingly similar to the result found in the sheep by Liddell, Anderson, Kotyuka and Hartman ('35). In this study, on both normal and neurotic sheep, the conditioned motor reflex was lowered on the third day after the

TABLE 28

*The effect of the continuous administration of adrenalin on the conditioned salivary reflex in the dog*

*Dog C-1 ♀*

| DATE OF EACH DAY'S TESTING | CR IN 1/100 CC. TO THE POSITIVE MET. 120" | REMARKS |
|---|---|---|
| 3-2 | 11 | quiet |
| 3-8 | 9 | " |
| 3-12 | 9 | " |

1 cc adrenalin 1:50000 given subcutaneously 1 hr. before each day's testing

| | | |
|---|---|---|
| 3-19 | 19 | quiet |
| 3-20 | 16 | " |
| 3-21 | 7 | " |
| 3-22 | 11 | " |
| 3-23 | 11 | " |

no adrenalin

| | | |
|---|---|---|
| 3-26 | 11 | " |
| 3-27 | 12 | " |
| 4-3 | 8 | " |

1 cc adrenalin 1:25000 given subcutaneously 1 hr. before each day's testing

| | | |
|---|---|---|
| 4-9 | 28 | quiet |
| 4-10 | 18 | " |
| 4-11 | 12 | " |
| 4-12 | 18 | " |

no adrenalin

| | | |
|---|---|---|
| 4-30 | 18 | " |
| 5-3 | 16 | " |
| 5-8 | 20 | " |
| 5-15 | 17 | " |

1 cc adrenalin 1:1000 given subcutaneously 1 hr. before each day's testing

| | | |
|---|---|---|
| 5-22 | 7 | quiet |
| 5-23 | 1 | trembling, dopey, slow movements |
| 5-24 | 1 | trembling, dopey, slow movements |

no adrenalin

| | | |
|---|---|---|
| 5-25 | 1 | trembling |
| 5-27 | 27 | quiet |
| 5-29 | 29 | " |

* The figures given in this column represent the average magnitude of the *two* positive responses in each day's tests.

administration of adrenalin. Further, in the neurotic sheep the amount of nervousness increased to an enormous extent on the third day. Thus the present work on the dog corroborates the phenomena observed previously on a widely different mammal, the sheep.

The present results are briefly as follows. Injections of adrenalin were given to three dogs previously trained for conditioned reflexes. The motor reflex was used on two, and in the third the salivary reflex. In the first dog, to which a massive dose of adrenalin was given, the motor C-R showed an initial increase followed by a marked decrease. The efficiency of the response in the second dog to which adrenalin was administered on 3 successive days increased and then decreased on each day, the increase followed by the decrease being less on each succeeding day; finally the conditioned reactions were almost entirely obliterated. The efficiency was slightly decreased. In the third dog, adrenalin was given continuously in three isolated periods from 3 to 5 days in length. The dosage was increased in each period. In the first and second periods, in which mild and medium doses respectively were given (1:50,000 and 1:25,000), the salivary C-R showed an initial increase followed by a decrease, which was maximal on the third day. In the third period, in which a very strong dose was given (1:1000), the C-R was enormously decreased. The efficiency of the C-R in this dog was somewhat increased.

In general the increases and the decreases in the C-R values, together with the appearance of general restlessness, are interpreted as alterations in the level of general excitability.

## The Effect of Bilateral Adrenalectomy

*Dog 1398* ♂, *bassethound* × *Saluki* $F_2$. The positive motor C-R alone was used, the stimulus being Met. 120.

This dog was an exception among those used in the study in that he was, under normal circumstances and from the very beginning, extremely active and excitable. He was also not very cooperative in the C-R laboratory, which made it difficult to record and register the motor reactions.

The behavior of this animal merits the following detailed description. He ran incessantly in the pen with tongue lolling, and barked frenziedly. When the observer came to the door he growled and barked, slowly backing away, and when the pen was entered he ran quickly into the cage or into a dark corner. He crouched, trembled and urinated when the leash was put about his neck, and dashed this way and that in attempting to escape. But he always wagged his tail when patted. He was very watchful and alert towards everything about him. When put into the straps for experiment and left alone, he would immediately plunge forward or suddenly back up, and struggle violently to free himself, frequently getting tangled in the straps. In the fits of violent struggling he would bite at the recording string, the electrodes and the restraining straps. On two occasions he snapped at the observer's hands when being calmed. His motor responses to the metronome followed by the shock were extremely vigorous, diffuse and often violent, and were always quite prolonged. Such responses often began when he heard the drum starting.

The dog was trained for 3 months before the critical experiment. The C-R was established with remarkable rapidity in 3 trials and thereafter readily appeared at every trial.

The adrenalectomy was performed in two stages. The gland on the right side was removed at the first stage and, after 2 weeks, during which time the animal seemed to recover completely, the left adrenal was removed. In order to protect the animal against the consequences of the second operation, an extract of the suprarenal cortex, Eschatin, 21 cc., was administered subcutaneously just prior to the operation.

When the C-R tests were taken up again 10 days after the operation, behavior was not affected in any observable way, and no effect was noticed for a period of 11 days. At the end of this period, and 21 days after the operation, behavior generally became very noticeably disturbed. The reactions during this period also merit detailed description and should be compared with the foregoing description in order that the magnitude of the changes both in the kennel as well as in the laboratory may be realized.

Usually the dog would be lying asleep when the room was entered and would come slowly out of his bed to stand wagging his tail. He did not retreat or move when patted or when the leash was now put on, but walked slowly and quite readily beside the attendant. There was no crouching or urinating. When taken to the laboratory and led to the platform, he stood perfectly still, head held low, and when left alone in the room sat down calmly, and after a few minutes lay down. In the majority of cases, no conditioned reaction was observed when the Met. 120 was sounded. In a few cases there was an abortive response. At the stimulus he raised his head, looked to the side and rose to his feet. There was no further reaction. Even when the shock was applied there was often no reaction.

TABLE 29
Dog 1398 ♂

| | TRAINING PERIOD | AFTER BILATERAL ADRENALECTOMY | | |
|---|---|---|---|---|
| | | First period | Second period | Third period — Eschatin |
| Correct responses to positive Met. 120 | 100% | 100% | 38% | 100% |
| Average magnitude of C-R to post. Met. 120 | 75 | 82 | 9 | 35 |

The behavior was studied for 2 days with the dog in this condition. The animal was then given Eschatin subcutaneously, 21 cc. daily in two 10.5 cc. doses morning and afternoon, for 3 days. Great improvement in behavior in general was noticed almost at once and both the efficiency and the magnitude of the C-R were improved to a very noticeable extent.

As indicated in table 29, the efficiency of the response was unaffected in the first post-operative period (100 per cent) but in the second, 21 days after the operation, it was greatly lowered (100 per cent to 38 per cent). In the third period during the Eschatin therapy the level was restored to normal (100 per cent).

The average magnitude of the reflex was essentially unaffected in the first period (75 to 82) but was enormously weakened in the second (to 9), and during the therapy the vigor of the response was restored to about half the normal (35).

The graphic records in plate 112 show the motor responses in three phases of the experiment; the normal period (fig. 1), the period of the deterioration of the response after the adrenalectomy (fig. 2) and the period of its partial restoration during the cortical extract (fig. 3). Notice in figure 1 the enormous vigor of the head movements, the body movements, the tremendously disturbed respiration and the exaggerated, diffused struggling evoked at once by the Met. 120 and continuing long after the stimulus and shock had ceased. The records in figure 2 contrast strikingly with those of figure 1. In figure 2 two stimuli are shown together with the 5 minute interval between them. The first Met. 120 and shock evoked no motor reaction. The animal stood immobile during the interval, and the second stimulus and shock evoked only weak and retarded reactions of the head, the respiration and the foreleg. Note the absence of the after discharge in the leg response. Figure 3 shows revival of the reactions during the Eschatin. Notice that the head and body movements, the respiration disturbance and the leg movements are almost as vigorous and prolonged as normal.

In spite of the administration of the extract of the suprarenal cortex, the general reactions became weaker and more retarded on the third day. Every gross body movement was exceedingly slow in execution. All food was refused. The dog walked about but little in the pen and was found lying down most of the time. At this time, pinching the legs with forceps or pricking between the toes with a needle (a very tender spot in the dog) or applying a moderate shock to the toe pad evoked no observable reaction in most cases, but in very few there was a noticeable twitch of the flexor muscles of the limb. On the next day no extract was given and the animal sank rapidly. He lay upon his side and did not raise the head or otherwise react either when called or when the above stimuli were tried again. The conditioned reflex tests were, of course, abandoned, due to the depth of the stupor and prostration. The dog died on the day following and the autopsy showed a complete absence of suprarenal tissue.

Just as the injection of parathyroid substance in an animal which had been thyro-parathyroidectomized raised the values of the C-R, so in the present experiment the injection of suprarenal cortical extract partially restored the reflex in an animal with the adrenals removed. The incomplete restoration points to a lack of medullary substance, adrenalin. We interpret the decline in the responsiveness of the animal to stimulation following adrenalectomy to a decline in the level of general excitability for these reasons: An active, excitable dog with a well established motor conditioned reflex when bilaterally adrenalectomized shows deterioration of the reflex as well as general activity, and is changed from super-active to sluggish and apathetic. Injection of suprarenal cortical extract restores the efficiency of the reflex to its former level and partially restores its magnitude and also gives improvement in the general behavior.

PLATE 112

EXPLANATION OF FIGURES

1 Vigorous motor (defensive) reactions of dog 1398 prior to adrenalectomy. The defensive head, body, respiratory and leg reactions were initiated by the Met. 120 followed by the shock. Note that the responses were so violent that they continued even after the stimulus was withdrawn.

2 The effect of bilateral adrenalectomy on the motor reactions in dog 1398. Notice that the first application of the metronome and shock evoked no response whatever, while the second evoked a very weak reaction of the head, respiration and limb.

3 The return of the vigorous defensive behavior in dog 1398 after the administration of an extract of the suprarenal cortex (eschatin). The head, body, respiratory and leg reactions are almost as vigorous as before the operation.

PLATE 112

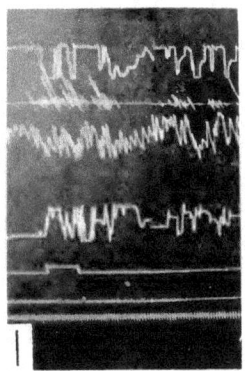

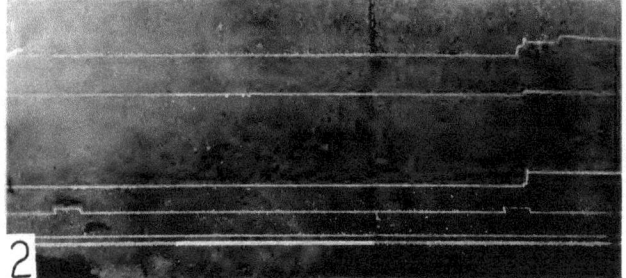

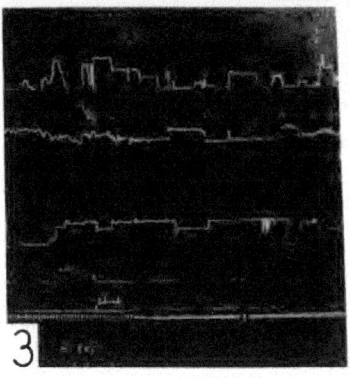

## THE INFLUENCE OF THE GONADS UPON THE BEHAVIOR REACTIONS

Since really potent whole testicular and ovarian extracts were not immediately available at the time of this experiment, study of the influence of these substances upon the reactions of the normal male and female dog were not attempted. The experiment, therefore, is concerned only with observations of the conditioned reflex following castration and ovariectomy. Three dogs were used, two males and one female.

### THE EFFECT OF CASTRATION IN THE MALE

*Dog C-6 ♂, bassethound × shepherd $F_3$.* The conditioned salivary reflex was used, the stimuli to which were Met. 120 (positive) and Met. 28 (negative).

In this dog the aim was to study the effect of *early* castration on the formation, maintenance and differentiation of the C-R. The animal was therefore castrated when a small puppy, at the age of 2 months, this being of course prior to any special observations of behavior. Four months after the operation, when the puppy was 6 months of age, the C-R tests were begun. They were carried out over a period of 1 year and 11 months.

The results are interesting. The C-R was established in about what may be called the "usual" time, namely, in seven combinations of Met. 120 and food, but the reflex was far weaker and more erratic than was observed in the "usual run" of dogs in this study and in that by James ('34). Both the efficiency and the magnitude of the response were far below par.

As indicated in table 30, the efficiency of the positive response was 39 per cent below that of eight normal dogs (46 per cent as compared with 85 per cent) and that of the negative was 21 per cent higher than the normals (68 per cent compared with 47 per cent). The responses of the castrate were only one-fourth as large and vigorous as those of the normal group (2 compared with 8).

The dog showed no loss of appetite in the kennel or in the experiment. When the food was presented following the Met. 120 the dog always ate in a greedy and hungry manner, salivating copiously.

Except for sexual activities, the animal's behavior in general differed little from that of the normal dogs. The dog was considered by several persons, unaware that he was a castrate, to be rather phlegmatic. Evidence of this was especially noticeable in the laboratory, since he frequently "nodded" or slept through many of the intervals between the stimuli. In the kennel he always trotted about in an awkward, clumsy manner, moving his limbs as though they were "weighted." Indeed, the clumsiness of the gait was very suggestive of that of a long-legged young puppy.

TABLE 30

Dog C-6 ♂

| | AFTER CASTRATION | AVERAGE VALUES FOR 8 NORMAL DOGS |
|---|---|---|
| Correct responses to positive Met. 120 | 46% | 85% |
| Correct responses to negative Met. 28 | 68% | 47% |
| Average magnitude of C-R to positive Met. 120 | 2 | 8 |

*Dog 1150 ♂, bassethound × shepherd $F_2$.* The salivary C-R was used, the conditioned stimulus being Met. 120. No negative differential stimulus was tried.

In this animal, the usual procedure in this investigation was employed, that is, behavior was observed before and after the operation. The length of the standardization period was 2 months. The dog was a typical representative of the "mid-group" with respect to general behavioral reactions. He was active, alert, obedient and exceedingly affectionate. The C-R was easily established in twelve trials and was extremely constant and regular afterward.

Castration was performed when the dog was a fully grown adult, 2 years of age. The C-R was studied for 4 months afterward. The behavior effects were similar to those observed in the preceding experiment with dog C-6. The C-R became definitely weaker.

As shown by table 31, the efficiency of the response remained quite unaffected (100 per cent to 100 per cent). The average magnitude, on the other hand, dropped more than 100 per cent (9 to 4). No other behavioral changes were noticed. The dog suffered absolutely no loss of appetite in the laboratory or in the kennel, and he was no more phlegmatic after the castration than before.

TABLE 31

Dog 1159 ♂

| | TRAINING PERIOD | AFTER CASTRATION |
|---|---|---|
| Correct responses to positive Met. 120 | 100% | 100% |
| Average magnitude of C-R to positive Met. 120 | 9 | 4 |

## The Effect of Ovariectomy

*Dog C-4 ♀, bassethound × shepherd F_3.* The salivary C-R was used, the stimuli being Met. 120 (positive) and Met. 28 (negative). The dog was trained for 6 months before the operation. In general, the behavior in the kennel and in the laboratory was that of any quiet, obedient dog. She was normally alert and active in the runs and readily defended her pan of food from the encroachment of her companion dog. The C-R was formed in six trials and regularly appeared afterward.

The dog was ovariectomized when fully grown, at the age of 1-year and 2 months. The C-R tests were continued for 1-year and 3 months afterward. The effects upon the C-R were slight. Behavior reactions in general became slightly phlegmatic.

TABLE 32

Dog C-4 ♀

| | TRAINING PERIOD | AFTER OVARIECTOMY |
|---|---|---|
| Correct responses to positive Met. 120 | 92% | 87% |
| Correct responses to negative Met. 28 | 10% | 47% |
| Average magnitude of C-R to positive Met. 120 | 8 | 7 |

Table 32 shows that the reflexes were but slightly affected following the operation. The efficiency of the positive response declined somewhat (92 per cent to 87 per cent). The efficiency of the negative reflex, however, increased considerably (10 per cent to 47 per cent). The average magnitude of the C-R showed a very slight decline which may or may not be significant (8 to 7).

The positive conditioned responses were, on the whole, retarded, as the average latent period showed an increase from 3 to 5 seconds.

At the end of about a year after the operation the dog presented the characteristic appearance and reactions of the spayed bitch. She was extremely fat, having a somewhat barrel-shaped body, and the head appeared far too small in proportion. The body shape was very similar to that of the hypophysectomized dog C-1. The animal seemed somewhat less energetic than before. She seemed to prefer to lie down rather than run about as her companion dog did. However, she appeared quite alert and responsive to the various natural stimulations about her. The apparent lack of desire to exercise may be related in some way to the extreme obesity.

Although with these castrates there were no experiments on restoration of the reflexes by hormone injection, the striking result is that in all three dogs (one early male castrate, one male castrated in maturity, and one female ovariectomized in maturity) the changes in the C-R were all in a common direction—towards deterioration. In other words, the reflex was weaker. The two dogs operated on during maturity showed less of this deterioration than did the individual castrated while young. This parallels common observation on the physical changes in castrates. The animal operated upon at an early age shows, in maturity, more change in general body form than does the animal operated upon when fully grown.

The efficiency of the negative C-R was enhanced in one dog after the operation. As we have heretofore interpreted it, such an increase means a lower level of excitability. Consistent with this observation is the fact that the percentage of efficiency of the negative in the early castrate, also, is much higher than the average figure for normal animals. This fact is another way of illustrating the lowered level of excitability. The diminished C-R was accompanied in two dogs by a lowered degree of activity in general responsiveness.

## DISCUSSION

### Comparison and Correlation of the Results

The results of the various phases of this investigation lead to the general conclusion that the endocrine glands play an important rôle in the nervous responsiveness of dogs. Administration of gland extracts to normal dogs raised the threshold of excitation so that the fundamental nervous responses were to some extent easier to arouse, while on the other hand, the removal of a gland resulted in a lowering of excitation and the reactions were more difficult to arouse. The administration of extracts of the thyroid, the parathyroids, the anterior pituitary and the adrenal medulla all resulted in an increased excitability towards controlled external stimulation given under exact laboratory conditions. Extirpation of the thyroid, the thyroid and parathyroids, the pars anterior of the pituitary, the suprarenals and the gonads results in a marked lowering of the nervous responsiveness under the same conditions.

That the post-operative diminution in responsiveness was due in some way to a deficiency of the hormone elaborated by the gland in question was directly indicated in the case of the thyroid, parathyroids, the anterior pituitary and the suprarenals by the fact that the weakened C-R was definitely strengthened through the introduction of an extract containing the active principle of the gland—thyroid substance, parathormone, anterior pituitary extract and extract of the adrenal cortex. The fact that the reaction was not fully restored to the previous or normal level was probably due in part to the imperfection of the available gland extracts, and further to the fact that these materials cannot be supplied to the body in the normal physiological amounts or manner.

The alteration in responsiveness is not necessarily due *directly* and *primarily* to the absence or excess of the secretory principle of the gland in question. The observed effect may well be secondary to some primary disturbance induced by the gland modification which the experimenter induced. The experiment in which the salivary C-R was obliterated following hypophysectomy and later more completely revived by thyroid than by anterior pituitary extract bears upon this point. The diminution in response in such a case may have been due more directly to regressive changes in the thyroid and its secretion following the hypophysectomy than primarily to the loss of anterior pituitary secretion itself.

The constancy and the magnitudes of the positive conditioned reflexes were impaired to various degrees following endocrine ablations, most complete after hypophysectomy and least following removal of the gonads. The several operations are listed in table 33 in the direct order of the magnitudes of the ensuing effects. The figures represent the average values from the two or more animals concerned in each operation, except for adrenalectomy, where only one dog is recorded.

TABLE 33

*Percentage of decrease in the positive C-R following operations*

| | CONDITIONED REFLEX | |
|---|---|---|
| | Constancy decrease | Magnitude decrease |
| Hypophysectomy | 65% | 900%+ |
| Thyroidectomy | 67% | 750% |
| Adrenalectomy | 62% | 900% |
| Thyro-parathyroidectomy | 45% | 600% |
| Castration (male and female) | 2.5% | 56% |

Almost the same degree of impairment resulted in the case of the first three operations. The figures for the thyro-parathyroidectomy indicate a somewhat lesser effect because of the fact that the deficiency of the parathyroid was not allowed to progress, since it was feared that the animals might succumb. Many of the C-R tests were made when the animal was in a state of medium parathyroid deficiency, so to speak. It will be recalled that when dogs were allowed to present symptoms of very marked deficiency of parathyroid hormone, the conditioned and other responses were entirely obliterated. The decrease in the constancy and the magnitude of the C-R following castration was small when compared with the enormous decreases following the other operations.

In the majority of cases in which a negative differential stimulus was tried, the number of correct (zero) responses in the post-operative periods increased as the number of correct positive responses decreased. The percentage of the increase in the negative reactions for each operation are tabulated in table 34.

TABLE 34

*Percentage of the increase in the constancy of the negative C-R following the operations*

| | |
|---|---|
| Thyroidectomy | 53% |
| Hypophysectomy | 47% |
| Ovariectomy | 37% |
| Thyro-parathyroidectomy | 6% |

The increase in the constancy of the negative C-R was quite considerable in the case of the first three operations listed, but was very slight following thyro-parathyroidectomy; indeed, one of the dogs, 869, showed a 50 per cent decrease in the constancy of the negative following the latter operation. The negative C-R was not used with the adrenalectomized dog.

The results obtained by administering the different gland substances to normal dogs were not so striking as those following the removal of the glands. This, of course, was to be expected, since imbalance of the internal chemistry is undoubtedly far less extensive and critical following the administration of secretory material than as a consequence of removal of part of the glandular mechanism. The enhancement of the C-R following the administration of various extracts was in almost every case greater when the extract was given to a dog from which the gland had been removed than when given to a normal, unoperated dog. The greater the physiological need for the substance, the greater its effectiveness when introduced.

All extracts used exerted approximately the same kind of influence upon the positive C-R. They were uniformly followed by an increase in the magnitude of the response. This enhancement was greater after injection of some extracts than others. The greatest increase in magnitude of the reflex followed anterior lobe pituitary extract and the least followed adrenalin. The poor record for adrenalin is due to the fact that it produces an increase followed by a decrease, and in the average the two phases almost completely counter-balance one another. The constancy of the reflex was only slightly affected by any of the extracts. The extracts are listed in table 35 in the order of their effects. Each figure represents the average values for two dogs, except for the anterior pituitary extract, which represents one dog.

TABLE 35

*Changes in the positive C-R following the administration of extracts in the unoperated dog*

| SUBSTANCE | CONDITIONED REFLEX | | |
|---|---|---|---|
| | Constancy | | Magnitude increase |
| | Increase | Decrease | |
| Anterior pituitary | 14% | | 47% |
| Parathormone | | 3% | 29% |
| Thyroid | | 3% | 20% |
| Adrenalin | 0% | | 18% |

Anterior pituitary extract increased the constancy of the response somewhat (14 per cent), while the other substances had almost no effect upon the constancy of reaction. The negative stimuli were not used in many cases during the experiments on the administration of extracts for the reason that the substances were given early in the training period, prior to the attempts to form differentiations between positive and negative signals. This stimulus was used, however, in three dogs following the administration of anterior pituitary, parathyroid and thyroid extracts, respectively. Both thyroid and parathyroid extracts were given to two dogs while anterior pituitary material was given to only one dog. The constancy of the negative C-R increased following the parathyroid and thyroid substance by averages of 32 per cent and 11 per cent, respectively, and it decreased 33 per cent during the administration of the anterior lobe extract to the one animal.

As the constancy and the magnitude of the *positive* C-R *decrease* following the ablations, the constancy of the *negative* C-R *increases*. There were occasions in the post-operative periods when the positive Met. 120 served to evoke a weak positive response, and during the same time the negative Met. 28 gave no response at all. According to the usually accepted criterion of differentiation in conditioned reflex experiments, this record would constitute a differentiation. It will be recalled that with one post-operative dog, 864, the negative metronome rate was advanced on successive days to 42, to 60 and to 78 beats per minute. The Met. 120 evoked the reflex response and the other rates did not. The response appeared when the negative rate was advanced to 96. This observation was on a dog *after thyroidectomy*. Before the operation, this dog, during 8 months of differential tests (Met. 120 against Met. 28), gave no evidence whatever of distinguishing between the two rates. In the same way, after thyroidectomy, thyro-parathyroidectomy, complete hypophysectomy, castration, and ovariectomy, there was evidence of discrimination between the positive and negative stimuli, which was better *after* the operation than *before*. Little is known, from either clinical or experimental observation, concerning the relation of the parathyroids, the pituitary, the testes and the ovaries to the higher nervous activities (mental processes) in the human subject or the lower animals. But a great mass of information has been collected concerning the retardation of the psychical processes in hypothyroid conditions. The intellectual sluggishness and apathy of the human cretin is proverbial. It would therefore be entirely unreasonable to interpret the above facts to mean that the dog is capable of better auditory discrimination under the condition of thyroid deficiency than in the normal state. An increase in the number of times the animal fails to respond to the negative stimulus because of a subnormal condition cannot signify an increase in discriminating and differentiating ability.

According to the theory of Pavlov, these results may be interpreted as showing a strengthening of the inhibitory process to a point where inhibition is almost completely predominant over excitation. In this interpretation both excitation and inhibition are viewed as dynamic processes. Accordingly, the diminution in the values of the positive C-R, together with an increase in the number of negative reactions following the operations, would mean that inhibition had arisen from the deficiency in the gland secretions and was thus predominant over excitation. Such a concept concerning inhibition in the interpretation of these results is not only unnecessary, but erroneous. We are concerned with an alteration or lowering of the degree of excitation rather than with a shift in the balance between the opposing forces of excitation and inhibition viewed dynamically.

The level of excitation varies inversely with the threshold of stimulation; the higher the level of excitation, the lower the threshold of stimulation and *vice versa*. The response to a positive conditioned stimulus, and the response to a negative, differ not in kind but in degree. When the animal is rendered ill or otherwise disturbed, the level of excitation is lowered and both responses are less easy to arouse than before. Thus we see that the positive and the negative responses have a constant relation to one another and to the level of excitation.

These animals, before operation, showed evidence of a relatively high level of excitation. The positive conditioning stimulus evoked a strong response in nearly every case, and the negative stimulus in many cases evoked a response almost equally strong. This indicated the relatively low threshold of stimulation. After the operations, the same positive stimulus was not capable of evoking its former strong positive response but gave only a weak response or none at all. The negative stimulus now evoked no observable reactions. Both types of stimulation fall below the threshold, but the negative further below than the positive.

The increase in responsiveness in the animals following the administration of the various extracts can similarly be interpreted as due to a rise in the level of excitation.

We may inquire as to the way in which the disturbance of the gland produces alterations in the level of nervous excitability. The explanation of this probably concerns the chemistry of the nerve cell and its surrounding medium. Disturbance of the internal secretions results, of course, in a general disturbance of the chemical equilibrium of all body fluids. A change in the metabolism of the salts of the metallic elements, for example, may modify nervous function, and such changes are probably closely related to changes in the endocrine secretions. The ablation of a gland of internal secretion may alter the juices surrounding the nerve cell in such a way as to bring about a fall in the level of excitability.

### The Probable Rôle of the Glands in the Production of Behavioral Types in the Dog

The differences between the behavioral types observed by James may be thought of as definitely bound up with fundamental differences in nerve function, which in turn are associated in some way with congenital and inheritable differences in the internal secretions. The excitable, the inhibitive, and the intermediate types possess respectively high, low and intermediate levels of excitation. In the present experiments, the behavior of the intermediate type was caused to vary in the direction of either extreme. The excitability level was raised by thyroid extract and by adrenalin, so that the behavior for a time was suggestive of the excitable type.

Conversely, the excitability level was lowered by removal of the thyroid, thyroid and parathyroids, pituitary, suprarenals and gonads, so that the behavior was suggestive of that of the phlegmatic type.

The differences in the general behavior of different individuals may be due, at least in part, to inherent differences in the amount and degree of activity of an endocrine gland or group of glands. It may be possible that the *activity pattern of the gland* is of importance in determining the individual's *pattern of behavior*.

The inherited pattern of the internal secretions may differ but slightly between one "normal" individual and another and, consequently, behavior may deviate but little from one to the other. But when the pattern is a markedly distorted one, the individual's behavior may show correspondingly great deviation from the normal. The glands may thus be found to play a significant role, not only in the production of the various "normal" types or patterns of behavior, but also in the production of the abnormal types. Consequently, the present investigations bear not only upon the problems confronting the psycho-physiologist, but upon those of the psychiatrist as well.

## LITERATURE CITED

PAGE

ALLEN, G. M. 1920 Dogs of the American aborigines. Bull. Mus. Compar. Zool. (Harvard Univ.), vol. 63, pp. 431–517. ................ 28

ANDERSON, O. D., AND H. S. LIDDELL 1935 Observations on experimental neurosis in sheep. Arch. Neurol. & Psychiat., vol. 34, pp. 330–354. 672

ATWELL, W. J. 1918 The development of the hypophysis cerebri of the rabbit (Lepus cuniculus L.). Am. J. Anat., vol. 24, pp. 271–337. 449

——— 1926 The development of the hypophysis cerebri in man, with special reference to the pars tuberalis. Am. J. Anat., vol. 37, pp. 159–193. ............................................................ 449

AUERBACH, P. 1911 Epithelkörperchenblutung und ihre Beziehungen zur Tetanie der Kinder. Jahrbuch f. Kinderh., n.F., Bd. 73, Ergänzungsband, S. 193–221. .................................. 479

BREUIL, ABBÉ H. 1912 Les subdivisions du paléolithique superieur et leur signification. Cong. Internat. Anthrop. et Archéol. Prehist., 14th sess., Genéve, Compt. Rend., pp. 165–238. ................ 28

# LITERATURE

|  | PAGE |
|---|---|

BROWN, WADE H. 1929 Constitutional variation and susceptibility to disease. Arch. Int. Med., vol. 44, pp. 625–662. .......... 402, 419

CABOT, P. S. DEQ. 1938 The relationship between characteristics of personality and physique in adolescents. Genet. Psychol. Monogr., vol. 20, pp. 3–120. .......................................... 527

COLLIP, J. B. 1925 Extraction of a parathyroid hormone which will prevent or control parathyroid tetany and which regulates level of blood calcium. J. Biol. Chem., vol. 63, pp. 395–438. ............ 478

CREW, F. A. E. 1923 The significance of an achondroplasia-like condition met with in cattle. Proc. Roy. Soc., London, s.B., vol. 95, pp. 228–255. ............................................ 3–5, 20

CRISLER, G., W. T. BOOHER, E. J. VANLIERE, AND J. C. HALL 1933 Effect of feeding thyroid on salivary conditioned reflex induced by morphine. Am. J. Physiol., vol. 103, pp. 68–72. .......... 663

CUSHING, H. 1912 The pituitary body and its disorders. J. B. Lippincott Co., Philadelphia. ........................................ 512

CUSHING, H., AND L. M. DAVIDOFF 1927 The pathological findings in four autopsied cases of acromegaly with a discussion of their significance. Rockefeller Inst. Med. Res. Monogr. 22. .............. 512

DAHL, L. EVV., AND THORDAR QUELPRUD 1937 Die Vererbung der Haarfarbe beim deutschen Boxer. Ztschr. f. Züchtung., Reihe B, Bd. 37, S. 159–177. ...................................... 7

DARLING, FRASER F. 1932 Color inheritance in bull terriers. Chapter IV "Coloured and Colour Breeding." A. Walker and Son, Galashiels, Scotland. ............................................... 7

DARLING, FRASER F., AND P. GARDNER 1933 A note on the inheritance of the brindle character in the coloration of Irish Wolfhounds. J. Genetics, vol. 27, pp. 377–378. ......................... 7

DARWIN, CHARLES 1896 The variation of animals and plants under domestication. 2nd edit., 2 vols., D. Appleton and Co., New York. ................................................. 21, 29–35

DOBZHANSKY, THEODOSIUS 1937 Genetics and the origin of species. Columbia University Press, New York. .................... 143

DYE, JOSEPH A., AND GEORGE H. MAUGHAN 1929 Further studies of the thyroid gland. V. The thyroid gland as a growth-promoting and form determining factor in the development of the animal body. Am. J. Anat., vol. 44, pp. 331–379. ..................... 360, 475

ELLIOT, G. F. S. 1925 Prehistoric man and his story; a sketch of the history of mankind from the earliest times. 3rd edit., J. B. Lippincott Co., Philadelphia. ................................... 28

FREY, MARTIN 1934 Morphologische und histologische Untersuchungen an der Hypophyse und Schilddrüse verschiedener Hunderassen in Beziehung auf die einzelnen Konstitutionstypen. Endokrinologie, Bd. 14, S. 116–128. ..................................... 422

GREENE, HARRY S. N., C. K. HU, AND WADE H. BROWN 1934 A lethal dwarf mutation in the rabbit with stigmata of endocrine abnormality. Science, vol. 79, pp. 487–488. .................. 22

GROSSER, P., AND R. BETKE 1910–1911 Epithelkörperchen-Untersuchungen mit besonderer Berücksichtigung der Tetania infantum. Ztschr. f. Kinderh., Bd. 1, S. 458–486. .................................... 479

JAFFÉ, H. L., A. BODANSKY, AND J. E. BLAIR 1930 Erzeugung von Ostitis fibrosa (Osteodystrophia fibrosa) durch Epithelkörperchen-Extrakt. Klin. Wchnschr., Bd. 9, S. 1717–1719. ................ 480

JAMES, W. T. 1933 The effect of reward on the response to painful experience in the conditioned reflex. Am. J. Physiol., vol. 106, pp. 71–79. ................................................. 593

——— 1934 Morphological form and its relation to reflex action. Chapter in "The Biology of the Individual," A. Research Nerv. & Ment. Dis., pp. 28–54, Williams and Wilkins Co., Baltimore. 647, 736

——— 1936 The effect of the presence of a second individual on the conditioned salivary response in dogs of different constitutional types. J. Genet. Psychol., vol. 49, pp. 437–449. ................ 595

JANSEN, MURK 1912 Achondroplasia: its nature and its cause. Baillière, Tindall and Cox, London. ................................... 16

KAMPMEIER, O. F. 1937 Origin and development of mediastinal and aortic thyroids and the periaortic fat bodies. Illinois Med. & Dent. Monogr., Univ. of Illinois, vol. 2. ........................... 401

KEITH, SIR ARTHUR 1928 The evolution of the human races. (Huxley Memorial Lecture, 1928.) J. Roy. Anthrop. Inst., Great Britain & Ireland, vol. 58, pp. 305–321. ............................. 28

KLEITMAN, N., AND S. TITELBAUM 1936 Effect of thyroid administration upon differentiating ability of dogs. Am. J. Physiol., vol. 115, pp. 162–167. ............................................... 663

KLINEBERG, O., S. E. ASCH AND H. BLOCK 1934 An experimental study of constitutional types. Genet. Psychol. Monogr., vol. 16, pp. 140–221. 527

KNÖTZKE, FRITZ 1929 Bemerkungen zur Wirbelsäure des Chondrodystrophen. Beitr. z. path. Anat. u. z. allg. Path., Bd. 81, S. 547–567. ........................................... 16, 45, 282

KREPS, E. M. 1923 Conditioned reflexes of a dog in heat. Report Fiziol. Bes. (in Russian). ........................................ 659

KRETSCHMER, E. 1925 Physique and character. (English translation). Harcourt Brace, New York. ................................... 527

LANDAUER, WALTER 1931 Untersuchungen über das Krüperhuhn. II. Morphologie und histologie des Skelets, insbesondere des Skelets der langen Extremitätenknochen. Ztschr. f. mikr.-anat. Forsch., Bd. 25, S. 115–180. ...................................... 3–5, 16

——— 1932 Studies on the creeper fowl. III. The early development and lethal expression of homozygous creeper embryos. J. Genetics, vol. 25, pp. 367–394. .................................. 3–5, 16, 21

——— 1933 Untersuchungen über das Krüperhuhn. IV. Die Missbildungen homozygoter Krüperembryonen auf späteren Entwicklungsstadien. Ztschr. f. mikr.-anat. Forsch., Bd. 32, S. 359–412. 3–5, 16, 21

LANDAUER, WALTER, AND L. C. DUNN 1930 Studies on the creeper fowl. I. Genetics. J. Genetics, vol. 23, pp. 397–413. ............... 3–5, 16

| | PAGE |
|---|---|
| LANG, A. 1910 Über alternative Vererbung bei Hunden. Ztschr. f. indukt. Abstammungs-u. Vererbungsl., Bd. 3, S. 1–3. | 7, 8 |
| LIDDELL, H. S. 1927 Higher nervous activity in the thyroidectomized sheep and goat. Quart. J. Exper. Physiol., vol. 17, pp. 41–51. | 664 |
| LIDDELL, H. S., O. D. ANDERSON, E. KOTYUKA, AND F. A. HARTMAN 1935 Effect of extract of adrenal cortex on experimental neurosis in sheep. Arch. Neurol. & Psychiat., vol. 34, pp. 973–993. | 728 |
| LIDDELL, H. S., W. T. JAMES, AND O. D. ANDERSON 1934 The comparative physiology of the conditioned motor reflex. Comp. Psychol. Monogr., vol. 11, pp. 1–89. | 650, 695 |
| LITTLE, C. C., AND E. E. JONES 1919 The inheritance of coat color in great Danes. J. Hered., vol. 10, pp. 309–320. | 7 |
| LUCKHARDT, A. B., AND B. GOLDBERG 1923 Preservation of life of completely parathyroidectomized dogs. J. A. M. A., vol. 80, pp. 79–80. | 478 |
| LYONS, MALCOLM, AND W. M. INSKO, JR. 1937 Chondrodystrophy in the chick embryo produced by a mineral deficiency in the diet of the hen. Science, vol. 86, p. 328. | 297 |
| MACCALLUM, W. G., AND C. VOEGTLIN 1909 On the relation of tetany to the parathyroid glands and to calcium metabolism. J. Exper. Med., vol. 11, pp. 118–151. | 478 |
| MANDL, FELIX 1926 Klinisches und Experimentelles zur Frage der lokalisierten und generalisierten Ostitis fibrosa. Arch. f. klin. Chir., Bd. 143, S. 1–46. | 479, 480 |
| MARIE, PIERRE 1889 Acromegaly. Brain, vol. 12, pp. 59–81. | 13 |
| MOHR, OTTO L. 1926 Über Letalfaktoren, mit Berücksichtigung ihres Verhaltens bei Haustieren und beim Menschen. Referat. V. Jahresv. Deutsch. Ges. Vererbwiss., Hamburg 1925. Ztschr. f. indukt. Abstammungs.-u. Vererbungsl., Bd. 41, S. 59–109. | 4, 20 |
| ——— 1929 Letalfaktoren bei Haustieren. Ztschr. Züchtung., Bd. 4, S. 105–125. | 4, 20 |
| MOHR, OTTO L., AND CHR. WRIEDT 1930 Short spine, a new recessive lethal in cattle; with a comparison of the skeletal deformities in short-spine and in amputated calves. J. Genetics, vol. 22, pp. 279–297. | 4, 20 |
| NONIDEZ, JOSÉ F. 1932 a The origin of the "parafollicular" cell, a second epithelial component of the thyroid gland of the dog. Am. J. Anat., vol. 49, pp. 479–505. | 426 |
| ——— 1932 b Further observations on the parafollicular cells of the mammalian thyroid. Anat. Rec., vol. 53, pp. 339–353. | 426 |
| ——— 1933 The "parenchymatous" cells of Baber, the "protoplasmareichen Zellen" of Huerthle, and the "parafollicular" cells of the mammalian thyroid. Anat. Rec., vol. 56, pp. 131–141. | 426 |
| NONIDEZ, JOSÉ F., AND H. D. GOODALE 1927 Histological studies on the endocrines of chickens deprived of ultraviolet light. I. Parathyroids. Am. J. Anat., vol. 38, pp. 319–347. | 475, 478 |
| OSBORN, H. F. 1915 Men of the old stone age; their environment, life and art. Scribner Co., New York. | 28 |

| | PAGE |
|---|---|
| PAVLOV, I. P. 1927 Conditioned reflexes. Oxford University Press, London. | 529, 530, 673 |
| PLATE, L. 1930 Über Nackthunde und Kreuzungen von Ceylon-Nackthund und Dachel. Jenaische Ztschr. f. Natur., Bd. 64, S. 227–282. | 7 |
| RASMUSSEN, A. T. 1929 The percentage of the different types of cells in male adult human hypophysis. Am. J. Path., vol. 5, pp. 263–274. | 450 |
| ———— 1933 The percentage of the different types of cells in anterior lobe of hypophysis in adult human female. Am. J. Path., vol. 9, pp. 459–471. | 450 |
| ———— 1938 The proportions of the various subdivisions of the normal adult human hypophysis cerebri and the relative number of the different types of cells in pars distalis, with biometric evaluation of age and sex differences and special consideration of basophilic invasion into the infundibular process. Proc. A. Research Nerv. & Ment. Dis., vol. 17, pp. 118–150. | 416, 450, 502 |
| ROSENTHAL, I. S. 1922 The effect of pregnancy and lactation on conditioned reflexes. Russian J. Physiol., vol. V. | 662 |
| ROWNTREE, L. G., J. H. CLARK, AND A. M. HANSON 1935 Biologic effects of thymus extract (Hanson); accruing acceleration in growth and development in five successive generations of rats under continuous treatment with thymus extract. Arch. Int. Med., vol. 56, pp. 1–29. | 490 |
| ROWNTREE, L. G., J. H. CLARK, A. STEINBERG, A. M. HANSON, N. H. EINHORN, AND W. A. SHANNON 1935 Further studies on the thymus and pineal glands. Ann. Int. Med., vol. 9, pp. 359–375. | 490 |
| SEVERINGHAUS, AURA E. 1938 The cytology of the pituitary gland. Chapter in "The Pituitary Gland." A. Research Nerv. & Ment. Dis., Williams and Wilkins Co., Baltimore. | 453 |
| SMITH, PHILIP E., AND EDWIN C. MACDOWELL 1930 An hereditary anterior-pituitary deficiency in the mouse. Anat. Rec., vol. 46, pp. 249–257. | 3–5 |
| ———— 1931 The differential effect of hereditary mouse dwarfism on the anterior pituitary hormones. Anat. Rec., vol. 50, pp. 85–92. | 3–5 |
| STOCKARD, CHARLES R. 1907 A peculiar legless sheep. Biol. Bull., vol. 13, pp. 288–291. | 22 |
| ———— 1921 Developmental rate and structural expression; an experimental study of twins, "double monsters" and single deformities, and the interaction among embryonic organs during their origin and development. Am. J. Anat., vol. 28, pp. 115–277. | 6 |
| ———— 1923 a The significance of modifications in body structure. The Harvey Society Lectures, J. B. Lippincott Co., Philadelphia. | 3, 6 |
| ———— 1923 b Human types and growth reactions. Am. J. Anat., vol. 31, pp. 261–288. | 3 |
| ———— 1926 Constitution and type in relation to disease. Medicine, vol. 5, pp. 105–119. | 3, 421 |
| ———— 1927 a Constitutional types in relation to disease. Johns Hopkins University, DeLamar Lectures, pp. 154–169. Williams and Wilkins Co., Baltimore. | 3, 421 |

LITERATURE

PAGE

STOCKARD, CHARLES R. 1927 b Hormones and structural development. The Beaumont Foundation Lectures, series 6. Williams and Wilkins Co., Baltimore. ................................................... 3

——— 1928 Inheritance of localized dwarfism and achondroplasia in dogs. Anat. Rec., vol. 38, p. 29. ................................ 3, 421

——— 1930 The presence of a factorial basis for characters lost in evolution; The atavistic reappearance of digits in mammals. Am. J. Anat., vol. 45, pp. 345–377. ................................. 3

——— 1931 The physical basis of personality. W. W. Norton and Co., New York. ............................................. 3, 8, 421

——— 1932 a Heredity and development of skull type and leg form. Anat. Rec., vol. 52 (suppl.), p. 37. ............................... 3

——— 1932 b The genetics of body form and type in breed crosses among dogs. Proc. 6th Internat. Cong. Genetics, vol. 2, p. 244. ... 3

——— 1932 c The genetics of modified endocrine secretions and associated form and pattern among dog breeds. Proc. 6th Internat. Cong. Genetics, vol. 2, pp. 193–195. ............................ 3

——— 1934 Internal constitution and genetic factors in growth determination. Cold Spring Harbor Symp. Quant. Biol., vol. 2, pp. 118–127. ................................................. 3, 421

——— 1935 Giant skin growth on mammals of normal size. Science, vol. 82, pp. 538–539. ......................................... 3, 421

——— 1936 a An hereditary lethal for localized motor and preganglionic neurones with a resulting paralysis in the dog. Am. J. Anat., vol. 59, pp. 1–53. .................................... 3, 24

——— 1936 b Defective endocrine glands associated with structural disharmonies and lethal reactions. Anat. Rec., vol. 64 (suppl. 3), pp. 47–48. ................................................. 3, 421

——— 1936 c Constitutional and genetic reactions associated with modifications in the pituitary gland. Proc. A. Research Nerv. & Ment. Dis., vol. 17, pp. 616–633. ............................. 3, 421

——— 1937 The mechanisms of heredity. Chapter II "Milestones in Medicine," pp. 39–79, D. Appleton Century Co., New York. ..... 3

——— 1938 a Interactions of endocrine glands and nervous system. Joseph Collins Lectures. Diplomate, vol. 10, pp. 44–51. ........ 3

——— 1938 b Structural disharmony: The genetic and developmental independence of the upper and lower jaws. Anat. Rec., vol. 70 (suppl. 3), p. 75. ............................................. 3

STUDER, T. 1901 Die prähistorischen Hunde in ihrer Beziehung zu den gegenwärtig lebenden Rassen. Abhandl. Schweiz. Paläontol. Gesell., Bd. 28, S. 1–137. ..................................... 28

——— 1905 Étude sur un nouveau chien préhistorique de la russe. Anthropologie, vol. 16, pp. 269–285. ........................... 28

SUMMERS, DOUGLAS, AND G. H. WALLACE 1913 Observations on the pathological changes in the thyroid gland in a cretinistic variety of chondrodystrophia foetalis. Arch. Int. Med., vol. 12, pp. 37–48. 273

| | PAGE |
|---|---|
| TILNEY, F. 1913 An analysis of the juxtaneural epithelial portion of the hypophysis cerebri with an embryological and histological account of a hitherto undescribed part of the organ. Internat. Monatschr. f. Anat. u. Physiol., Leipzig, Bd. 30, S. 258–293. | 449 |
| TODD, T. WINGATE, AND RALPH E. WHARTON 1934 The effect of thyroid deficiency upon skull growth in the sheep. Am. J. Anat., vol. 55, pp. 97–115. | 360 |
| TODD, T. WINGATE, RALPH E. WHARTON, AND ARTHUR W. TODD 1938 The effect of thyroid deficiency upon bodily growth and skeletal maturation in the sheep. Am. J. Anat., vol. 63, pp. 37–78. | 475 |
| VALKOV, A. V. 1923 Experimental study of higher nervous activity of thyroidectomized puppies. Publications from Pavlov's Laboratory (in Russian). | 664 |
| WARREN, D. C. 1927 Coat color inheritance in greyhounds. J. Hered., vol. 18, pp. 513–522. | 7 |
| WERTHEIMER, F. I., AND F. E. HESKETH 1926 The significance of physical constitution in mental disease. Williams and Wilkins Co., Baltimore. | 527 |
| YANASE, J. 1907 Über Epithelkörperbefunde bei galvanischer Übererregbarkeit der Kinder. Wien Klin. Wchnschr., Bd. 20, S. 1157–1160. | 479 |
| ZAWADOWSKY, B. M., W. R. SACHAROW, AND M. S. SLOTOW 1929 Über den Einfluss der Schilddrüse auf die höheren Nervenfunktionen der Hunde. Pflüger's Arch. f. d. ges. Physiol., Bd. 223, S. 548–560. | 663 |

# SUBJECT INDEX

Page numbers in **bold faced** type are those on which illustrations occur.

## A

Achondroplasia, of axial skeleton, 91, 126
  embryology of, 45–46
  general considerations of, 13–17, 25, 45–46, 119, 125, 297
  of leg, description of, 45–46, 105–106, **107**, 131
    expression of, in homozygous or heterozygous state, 50–54, 64–69, 87–88, 89, 98–101, **107**, 116–118, **117**, **121**, **133**, 145–146
      bone constitution as factor in, 52, 62–63, 75–89, 77, 96–101, **102**, 106–123, **107**, **112**, **115**, **121**, **123**, 145–146
    genetic considerations of, 49–50, 53–54, 57, 61–62, 67, 87–88, 125, 128, 140–145, **141**
    inheritance of, in hybrids. (see leg inheritance)
    summary of, 145–146
    test for absence of, in bulldog, 91–92, 93
  in man, 13–17, 45
  of pectoral and pelvic girdles, 92
  of skull, (see skull, bulldog typed)
Acromegaly, general considerations, 13–16
  in man, 12–13
  tendency toward, in bassethound-English bulldog hybrids, 119–122, **321**, 322–325, **323**, **324**
  in bassethound-Saluki hybrid, 76, 84
Activity of dogs, in experiments, 579, 585–586, **586**
  in kennel, 630, 631, **631**
Albinism, in dachshund-Pekingese hybrid, 350, 351, 352
Amelia, in lambs, 22

## B

Bassethound, behavior of, 640
  in conditioned avoiding situation, 578–590, **588**
  in conditioned salivary situation, 543–547, **543**, **544**, **545**, **546**
  behavioral types in, 539–553
  general characteristics of, 17, 41, 47–48, 51, 63, 73, 83, 93, 97, 295–296, 633, 640
  leg characteristics of, 9–10, 45–46, 51, 55, 63, 73, 83, 93, 97, 99, 100, 105–106, **107**
  origin of, 46–47
  parathyroid of, 515, **516**
  pituitary of, **417**, 503, **505**
  skeleton of, 55, 99, 100
  skull of, general characteristics in, 299–301, **321**, 329, 356, 368, 369
    indices and measurements in, 208, 299–301, 316, 318, 319
  thyroid of, 404–406, **405**, **408**, **425**, 428–429, 492–494, **493**

756    SUBJECT INDEX

Bassethound-dachshund cross, to determine location of genes for achondroplasia, 142–143
  leg inheritance in hybrids of, 142–143
  size inheritance in hybrids of, 327–328, 329
  skull characteristics in hybrids of, 329

Bassethound-English bulldog hybrids, behavioral types in, 617, 620, 622–623
  general characteristics of, 93, 95, 97, 102, 323, 324, 331, 333, 619
    and parathyroid pattern, 518–522
    and pituitary pattern, 505–513
    and thyroid pattern, 494–500
  leg inheritance in, 93, 94–101, 97, 99, 100, 102, 106–111, 107, 118–123, 121, 123
  parathyroid of, 516, 518–522, 521
  pituitary of, 417, 419–420, 503, 505–513, 509
  size variations in, 118–122, 321, 322–325, 323, 324
  skeleton of, 98, 99, 100
  skin overgrowth in, 328–335, 331, 333
  skull of, general characteristics in, 285, 301–325, 321, 323, 324, 326, 356
    indices and measurements in, 300–325, 305, 308, 310, 311, 316, 318, 319
    nasal bones in, congenital absence of, 321, 322
    size variations in, 321, 322–325
  tail inheritance in, 388–396, 390, 393, 395
  thymus of, 419, 490
  thyroid of, 405, 412–413, 493, 494–500, 497

Bassethound-German shepherd hybrids, behavioral types in, 604–606, 605, 609, 609
  general characteristics of, 51, 52–57, 56, 59, 61, 63, 68, 603, 604, 606, 608
  leg inheritance in, 49–64, 51, 55, 59, 60, 63, 67, 68, 106–113, 107, 112
  physical characteristics and behavior in, blending of, 634
    inheritance of, 634–635, 638
    mixed types of, 609, 610, 636
  skeleton of, 55, 60

Bassethound-German shepherd-foxhound hybrids, general characteristics of, 65
  leg inheritance in, 65, 66

Bassethound-Saluki hybrids, acromegalic tendency in, 81
  general characteristics of, 72–76, 73, 76, 77, 79–86, 79, 83, 85
  jaw disharmony in, 367–370, 369, 371
  leg inheritance in, 73, 74–89, 76, 77, 79, 83, 85, 86, 89, 106–111, 107, 113–118, 115, 117, 120–123, 123
  skull characteristics of, 285, 367–370, 369, 371

Behavior, (see also conditioned reflexes)
  activity of dogs, 630, 631, 631
  as affected by, adrenalectomy, 730–734, 735
    and suprarenal cortical extract, 732–734, 735
    adrenalin, 723–730

castration, 736-740
   hypophysectomy, total, 705, 710-720, 713, 714, 715, 720
      and pituitary transplants, 717-720
      and thyroid extract, 714, 716-719, 720
   of posterior lobe, 719-721
   ovariectomy, 738-739
   parathyroid extract, 697-699
   thyroid feeding, 664-677, 668, 670, 671, 691
   thyroidectomy, 661, 677-697, 679, 682, 684, 686, 691, 692
before gland ablations, 658-663, 661, 679, 682, 684, 686, 705, 707, 714, 720, 735
maternal instincts and reactions among dogs, 11, 289-291
mating instincts among dogs, 70
and skull type, possible correlation of, 151, 273
whelping reactions, abnormal, 289-291

Behavioral types, abnormal, effect of crossbreeding on, 637
   English bulldog as an, 614, 616
   cases of, 629
   nature of, 614
   summary of, 623
difficulties using salivary response in classification of, 539
discussion of, in salivary experiments, 568-575
   in motor experiments, 578-594
excitable, discussion of, 571, 591
   reaction of, to conditioned avoiding situation, 577, 578-590, 579, 586, 588, 605
      to conditioned salivary situation, 540, 541, 542, 545, 546, 548, 550, 553-560, 555, 556
   summary of, 632
intermediate, in bassethound-German shepherd hybrids, 605, 606, 609, 609
   reaction of, to conditioned avoiding situation, 577, 579, 586, 589, 590-594, 605
      to conditioned salivary situation, 560-568, 561, 563, 565, 566, 567, 617
lethargic, discussion of, 570, 591
   reaction of, to conditioned avoiding situation, 578-590, 579, 588, 605
      to conditioned salivary situation, 539-553, 540, 541, 542, 543, 544, 545, 546, 548, 550
   summary of, 632, 640
mixed, effect of hybridization on production of, 636-637
   nature of, 610
   systemic variation in, 642, 642
   rôle of glands in production of, 746-747

Birds, 27, 475

Bloodhound, 13

Body form, (see also growth, structural deviations)
   as affected by castration, 19
   and parathyroid pattern, 481-488, 518-522

and pituitary pattern, 458-474, 506-513
and pituitary weight, 420
and thyroid pattern, 441-446, 494-500
and thyroid proportional size, **403**, 404, 408-414

Bodily index, differences in, among dogs, 601, 602, 602
in classification of dogs, 600
variations of, in bassethound-German shepherd hybrids, 604, **605**, 606-607, 609, 612

Bone, formation of, and parathyroids, 475, 478-480, 514
marrow, in dachshund pituitary, **451**, 455
metacarpal, abnormality in, 132, 133

Bone constitution, as factor in expression of leg achondroplasia, 52, 62-63, 75-89, 77, 96-101, **102**, 106-123, **107**, **112**, **115**, **121**, **123**, 145-146
in legs of dog hybrids, (see leg inheritance)
deformation of, in achondroplasia, 45-46

Boston terrier, achondroplasia in, 126
behavioral characteristics of, 567, 617, 626-627
general characteristics of, 17, 41, 126-128, **127**, 245, 626-627
jaw growth in, 229, 357
leg characteristics of, 126, **127**, 131
parathyroid of, 481, 483
pituitary of, **415**, 456-458, 459
skull of, general characteristics in, 226-232, 229, 231, 233, 239, 245, 276
indices and measurements in, 208, 215-217, **216**, **221**, 227, **251**, **254**, **257**, 258
skeleton of, 128, 131
thyroid of, 402, **403**, 408, 429-430, 431, 434, 441, **443**

Boston terrier-dachshund hybrids, (see dachshund-Boston terrier hybrids)

Brain size, in relation to cranium size, 167

Breed purity, F₁s as proof of, 53, 72

Brussels griffon, general characteristics of, 17, 41, 135, **136**, 336, **338**, 435-436
jaw growth in, 357
leg characteristics of, 135, **136**
origin of, 336
skull of, general characteristics in, 135, 274-276, **275**, 336, **338**, 435
indices and measurements in, 208, 210-211
thyroid of, 435-436, **437**

Brussels griffon-dachshund hybrids, (see dachshund-Brussels griffon hybrids)

Bulldog, deformities in non-related breeds, 335-367
typed skulls, (see under skull)
types, in man, 273, 276-284

Bull terriers, 7

# C

Calcium metabolism, disturbance of, in dachshund-Brussels griffon hybrids, 339–342
 and parathyroids, 475, 478–480, 514

Cartilage defects, in girdles of bulldog, 92
 underlying achondroplasia, 16, 45

Castration, effect on, body form, 19
 behavior, 736–740

Cattle, 3, 4, 5, 19, 20

Cell, distribution in pituitary, 450–453
 parafollicular, general considerations of, 426–427

Chihuahua, 9, 14

Chow, 9, 10, 39, 208

Chromosomes, number of, in dog, 140

Coat, shedding of, 10
 variations in, among dogs, 10

Cocker spaniel, 208, 438

Color inheritance in dogs, studies on, 7

Conditioned avoiding situation, (see conditioned reflexes, motor)

Conditioned reflexes, (see also behavior)
 as affected by partial thyroidectomy and thyroid regeneration, 680–687, 684, 686
 changes in, during lactation, 661, 662–663, 662
  during oestrus, 659–662, 660, 661
 method of, 649–658, 651, 653
 motor, as affected by, adrenalectomy, 730–735, 735
  and suprarenal cortical extract, 732–735, 735
  adrenalin, 723–730
  hypophysectomy, 710–716, 714
  and anterior lobe extract, 711–716, 715
  thyroid extract, 662–672, 668, 670, 671
  thyroidectomy, partial, 680–684, 682, 684
  thyro-parathyroidectomy, 699–709, 705, 707
 behavior between signals in, 585, 586
 behavior in, summary of, 590–594
 behavioral classification in, 578–590
 delay of, among types, 584
  nature of, 593
 generalization of, among types, 587, 588
 kennel behavior compared with, 576
 reaction to negative signals in, 587, 590
 type of, used in experiments, 533, 575

salivary, as affected by, adrenalin, 727–729
    castration, 736–738
      hypophysectomy, total, 705, 710–720, 713, 714
        and anterior lobe extract, 711–717, 720
        and thyroid extract, 714, 716–720, 720
      of posterior lobe, 719–721
      ovariectomy, 738–739
      parathyroid extract, 697–699
      pituitary anterior lobe extract, 709–710
      thyroid extract, 664–666, 672–675
      thyroidectomy, 661, 677–680, 679, 683–694, 686
    behavior between signals in, 547, 548, 554
    delay of, 546, 555
    establishment of, as affected by thyroidectomy and thyroid feeding, 687–693, 691, 692
    generalization of, 547, 549, 556, 558
    kind of, used as criterion of excitability, 537
    limitations of, 529–530, 537
    procedure used in development of, 533, 535–539
    reaction to negative signal in, 545, 547, 555, 556, 565–566
  salivary and motor, description of, 649–658
    procedure in, before and after gland alterations, 649–658

Constitution, basic factors influencing, 639
  definition of, 635
  meaning of, 640–643, 641
  significance of, in growth response, 109–123

Cranium size, in relation to brain size, 167

Creeper fowl, 3, 5, 21

Cretin, 4, 5

# D

Dachshund, endocrines of, Frey's study on, 422
  general characteristics of, 17, 41, 125–126, 127, 136, 245, 261, 338, 345, 625, 640
  leg characteristics of, 9–10, 45, 127, 128, 131, 136
  origin of, 46–47
  parathyroid of, 481, 483
  pituitary of, 415, 448–456, 451, 459
    red bone marrow in, 451, 455
  skeleton of, 128, 131
  skull of, general characteristics in, 226–232, 229, 231, 239, 245, 261, 265, 329, 338, 345, 346, 347, 355
    indices and measurements in, 208, 214–215, 214, 251, 254, 257, 258, 267, 268, 270, 271
    mandibular condyle peculiarity in, and its inheritance, 241, 242, 243
  thyroid of, 402–404, 403, 408, 436–438, 437, 441, 443

SUBJECT INDEX 761

Dachshund-bassethound hybrids, (see bassethound-dachshund hybrids)

Dachshund-Boston terrier hybrids, endocrines of, summary of, 489-494
  general characteristics of, 127, 129, 234, 236, 238, 239, 244, 247, 248, 628
    and parathyroid pattern, 481-488
    and pituitary pattern, 458-474
    and thyroid pattern, 441-447, 467-468
  jaw inheritance in, 234-244, 236, 238
  leg of, inheritance in, 126-134, 127, 129, 131, 133
    metacarpal bone abnormality in, 132, 133
  parathyroid of, 481-488, 483, 487
  pituitary of, 415, 419-420, 458-474, 459, 463, 472
  skeleton of, 128, 131
  skull of, general characteristics in, 229, 231, 232-249, 236, 238, 239, 245, 247, 248
    indices and measurements in, 227, 249-259, 251, 254, 257, 258
    mandibular condyle inheritance in, 241, 242, 243
    mandibular rami divergence in, inheritance of, 241, 244
  thyroid of, 403, 409-412, 441-447, 443, 445, 463, 467-468

Dachshund-Brussels griffon hybrids, calcium disturbance in, 339-342
  general characteristics of, 136, 337-343, 338, 340, 341
  leg of, inheritance in, 135, 136
    disproportion in, 334, 340
  mange infection in, 339-342
  rickets in, 339-342
  skull characteristics of, 337-343, 338, 340, 341

Dachshund-French bulldog hybrids, general characteristics of, 259-272, 261, 263, 264
  leg inheritance in, 134-135, 261, 263
  skeleton of, 263
  skull of, general characteristics in, 259-263, 261, 263, 264, 265
    indices and measurements in, 266-272, 268, 270, 271

Dachshund-Pekingese cross, to determine location of genes for achondroplasia, 143-144

Dachshund-Pekingese hybrids, albino member among, 350, 351, 352
  behavioral type in, 637
  general characteristics of, 345, 346-354, 350
  jaw inheritance in, 351-354, 352, 355
  leg inheritance in, 143-144, 345, 350
  skull characteristics of, 345, 347, 348-354, 350, 352, 355

Dachshund-hairless Ceylon dog cross, Plate's study on, 7

Dachshund-St. Bernard cross, Lang's study on, 7-8

Dental defects, in distorted skulls, 229, 232, 233, 234-235, 262, 265, 278

Dental occlusion, establishment of, 372–376, 375
  in man and dogs, comparison of, 370–372, 371
  skull indices related to, 376–382, 377, 378, 379, 380, 381, 383
Dentition, in various dog breeds, 149–150
Development, (see growth)
Discriminating ability, in dogs, 693–694, 744–746
Disease, and endocrine gland modifications, 399–400, 420–421
Dog, (all index entries in this study refer to dogs unless otherwise stated)
  association of, with man, 11, 28–29, 70–71
  breeds, ancient, 29–35
    resemblance of, to modern, 31
    establishment and perpetuation of, 6–7, 36
    general differences in, 9–15
    imported, degeneration of, 34–35
    number of, 9
    origin of, 28–36
    purity of, $F_1$ hybrids as proof of, 53, 72
    survey of, to determine normal ancestral type, 39–41
    value of, in growth studies, 6–7, 12, 22, 37
  chromosomes in, number of, 140
  domestication of, 28–29, 31–32
  genetics of, contributions to, 7–8
  hairless, 10
  intelligence vs interest in, 71
  web toes in, 27
  wolves, crossed with, 32
  wolves and jackals, similarity to, 32
Domestication of dog, 28–29, 31–32
*Drosophila*, 124, 143
Dwarfism, in dogs and man, 13–15
  and leg achondroplasia, possible linkage of, 119
  in mice, 3–5
  tendency toward, in bassethound English bulldog hybrids, 119–122, 321, 322–325, 323, 324

## E

Embryonic growth, (see growth)

Endocrine glands, (see also parathyroid, pituitary, suprarenal, thymus, thyroid)
  and behavior, relation of, 526, 633, 637 (see also behavior and conditioned reflexes)
  Frey's study on, 422
  and genetic constitution, rôle of, in growth expression, 3–6, 11–12, 17–19, 24, 26–27, 37, 45–46, 224–225, 296–297, 332–335, 360–361, 399–400, 475–476

histological technique for, 422-423
interactions of, 420-421
modifications of, and disease, 399-400, 420-421
peculiarities of, among dogs, 11, 399-400, 421

English bulldog, behavioral types in, 614-619, **616, 617**, 637-638
achondroplasia in, 91-92
general characteristics of, 9-10, **41**, 90-94, **93**, **97**, 290, 296, 427, 428, 614
jaw growth in, 357
leg of, characteristics in, 9, 91, **93**, 96, **97**, 99, 100, 104-105, **107**
bone constitution in, susceptibility of, to achondroplasia, 120-122, **123**
test for absence of achondroplasia in, 91-92, **93**
origin of, 36, 90
parathyroid of, **477**, **516**, 517-518
pituitary of, **417**, 501-505, **503**
shoulder and hip dislocation in, 92-94
skeleton of, **99**, **100**
skull of, general characteristics in, 273-274, **275**, 290, 302, 321, 356
indices and measurements in, 208, 215-220, **216**, **219**, **221**, 299-301, 305, 308, 310, 311, 316, 318, 319
thyroid of, 404, **405**, 408, 425, 426-429, **493**, **494**
Frey's study on, 422

English bulldog-bassethound hybrids, (see bassethound-English bulldog hybrids)

English bulldog-German shepherd hybrids, general characteristics of, 92, **93**, 289-294, 290, 293
jaw disharmony in, 370, **371**
leg inheritance in, 91-92, **93**
maternal reactions, abnormal, in, 289-294
skull characteristics of, 289-295, 290, 293, **371**

Environment, changed, effect of, on dog breeds, 34-35

Evolution, structural changes and, 24-28

Excitation, levels of, before and after gland alterations, 697, 708, 730, 745-746

## F

Facial features, in puppies, 285, 373

Facial skeleton, measurements of, (see skull measurements)

Fecundity in dogs, 11, 399-400

Fish, 22-23

Fowl, 21, 297, 478

Foxhound, general characteristics of, 9, **41**
skull indices and measurements of, 212, 213
thyroid of, **425**, 426, 428-429

French bulldog, general characteristics of, 14–15, 41, 134, 259, **261**
  jaw growth in, 357
  skull of, general characteristics in, 259, **261**, 265
    indices and measurements in, 208, 215–217, 216, 267, **268**, **270**, **271**
  thyroid of, **425**, 428
French bulldog-dachshund hybrids, (see dachshund-French bulldog hybrids)

## G

Generalization, (see conditioned reflexes)
Genes, allelic association of, influence on one another in, 64–66, **65**
  controlling achondroplasia, determining location of, 142–143
  dominance of, as affected by breed constitution, 108–123
  expression of, in homozygous and heterozygous state, 50–54, 64–69, 87–88, 89, 98–101, **107**, 116–118, **117**, **121**, **133**, 145–146
  mutations of, and evolution, 24–28
  nature of, in breeds with similar growth distortions, 140–145
Genetic constitution and endocrines, interrelations of, contributions to problems of, 3–5
  rôle of, in structural expression, 3–6, 11–12, 17–19, 24, 26–27, 37, 45–46, 224–225, 296–297, 332–335, 360–361, 399–400, 475–476
Genetics, (see also various characters concerned)
  of bulldog screwtail, 388–396, **390**
  of dog, studies on, 7–8
  of leg achondroplasia, (see achondroplasia)
German boxer, 7
German shepherd, behavior of, 540, 548, 553–556, **555**
  in conditioned avoiding situation, 577, 578–590
  and endocrine glands, 633
  bodily index of, 601, **602**
  general characteristics of, 9–10, 40–42, 41, 48, 51, 59, 61, 65, 93, 290
    in relation to ancestral dog type, 40–42
  leg characteristics of, 9, 51, 55, 59, 65, 71, 93, 104, **107**, **112**
  skeleton of, 55
  skull of, general characteristics in, 153, 273–274, **275**, 290, 302
    indices and measurements in, 155, 208, 210–211, **212**, **213**, 217–220, **219**, **221**
  thyroid of, 426, 430–432, **431**, **433**
German shepherd-bassethound hybrids, (see bassethound-German shepherd hybrids)
German shepherd-English bulldog hybrids, (see English bulldog-German shepherd hybrids)
Gigantism, in man and dog, 12–13
  tendency toward, in bassethound-English bulldog hybrids, 118–119, 321, 322–325, **323**, **324**
  in bassethound-Saluki hybrid, 84

SUBJECT INDEX 765

Goat, 22

Great Dane, general characteristics of, 7, 9, 12, **41**
  parathyroid of, 477
  pituitary of, **418**, 419
  skull of, indices and measurements in, 208, 214–215, 214
  thyroid of, 406–408, **407**, **437**, 438

Great Dane-St. Bernard hybrids, (see St. Bernard-great Dane hybrids)

Greyhound, 7, 9, 10

Growth and development, determining factors in, 297
  deviations in, (see structural deviations)
  distortions in, localized, 17–18
    analysis of, 359–361
  in man and dog, similarity of, 12–19
    value of dog in study of, 6–7, 12, 22, 37
  embryonic, modifications of, 5
    temporary disturbance in, 18, 500
      possible relation of, to achondroplasia, 46
  failure in, due to hereditary defects, 4
  mechanisms of, 5, 325–327
  rôle of endocrines and genetic constitution in, 3–6, 11–12, 17–19, 24, 26–27, 37, 45–46, 224–225, 296–297, 332–335, 360–361, 399–400, 475–476
  significance of individual constitution in, 109–123

## H

Hair, shedding of, in dogs, 10

Head characteristics, (see skull)

Hip joint, dislocation of, in bulldog, 92–94

Horse, 20

Hound, 39, 422

Hunting instincts among dogs, 11

Hybridization, experiments in, importance of, 37
  racial, 37–38, 122, 358, 491

Hyperirritability, adrenalin and, 724–730
  thyroid extract and, 668–677
  training and, 662–663

Hysterical types, nature of, 598

## I

Inheritance, (see headings under behavior, endocrine glands, legs, skulls, and tail; scattered notes on inheritance of coat, eye, ear, and other characters will be found in discussions of hybrids)

Intelligence, differences in, among dogs, 10
  vs interest, in dogs, 71

Instincts, differences in, among dogs, 9-11

Irish wolfhound, 7, 9, 12

## J

Jackal, 32

Jaws, (for inheritance, measurements, etc., see skull)
  deformed, dental defects in, 229, 232, 233, 234-235
  differences in, among dogs, 10
  embryonic origin of, 354-357, 367
  growth of, disharmonies in, 235-237, 236, 349-357, 355, 356, 358, 361, 367-372, 369, 371
    period of, 373-376, 375
    mutations affecting, 357
  independent expression of upper and lower, 235, 367-372
  mandible of, condyle peculiarity and its inheritance in, 241, 242, 243
    rami divergence and its inheritance in, 241, 244
  in puppies, 373
  size of, in relation to tooth size, 177-178
  structural arrangements in, 228-232

## K

King Charles spaniel, 17, 149

## L

Labrador huskie, 9, 10, 39, 70, 208

Laboratory, adjustment of dog to, 581
  description of, 531, 532
  outdoor, reactions in, 552

Lactation, effect of, on behavior, 661, 662-663, 662

Legs, (see also achondroplasia)
  characteristics of, in bassethound, 9-10, 45-46, 51, 55, 63, 73, 83, 93, 97, 99, 100, 105-106, 107
    in Boston terrier, 126, 127, 131
    in Brussels griffon, 135, 136
    in dachshund, 9-10, 45, 127, 128, 131, 136
    differences in, among dogs, 9-10
    in English bulldog, 9, 91, 93, 96, 97, 99, 100, 104-105, 107
    in German shepherd, 9, 51, 55, 59, 65, 71, 93, 104, 107, 112
    in Pekingese, 139
    in puppies, newborn, 95-96
    in Saluki, 71, 73, 83, 104, 107, 139
  disproportion of, in dachshund Brussels griffon hybrids, 334, 340

SUBJECT INDEX    767

  inheritance of, in dog hybrids, bassethound-dachshund, 142–143
    bassethound-English bulldog, 93, 94–101, 97, 99, 100, 102, 106–111, 107, 118–123, 121, 123
    bassethound-German shepherd, 49–64, 51, 55, 59, 60, 63, 67, 68, 106–113, 107, 112
    bassethound-German shepherd-foxhound, 65, 66
    bassethound-Saluki, 73, 74–89, 76, 77, 79, 83, 85, 86, 89, 106–111, 107, 113–118, 115, 117, 120–123, 123
    dachshund-Boston terrier, 126–134, 127, 129, 131, 133
    dachshund-Brussels griffon, 135, 136, 334, 340
    dachshund-French bulldog, 134–135, 261, 263
    dachshund-Pekingese, 143–144, 345, 350
    English bulldog-German shepherd, 91–92, 93
    Saluki-Pekingese, 137–138, 139
Linkage, of characters in dogs, 54, 140

## M

Maltese poodle, skull characteristics of, 208, 435
  thyroid of, 436, 437
Mammals, aquatic, 25, 27
Man, achondroplasia in, 13–17, 45
  acromegaly in, 12–13
  association of dog with, 11, 28–29, 70–71
  community averages for, inadequacy of, 317
  facial disharmonies in, 358, 370–372, 371
  growth distortions in, similar to dog, 12–19
  hybridization of, 37–38, 122, 358, 491
  pituitary of, 416–419, 450–452, 502
  skull characteristics of, 150, 273, 276–284, 277, 279, 283, 285, 358
Mange, in dachshund-Brussels griffon hybrids, 339–342
Maternal, instincts and reactions among dogs, 11, 289–291
  influence, in cross breedings, lack of, 57, 62, 126–128, 259
Mating instincts in dogs, 70
Metabolism, differences in, among dogs, 633
Metacarpal bone abnormality, in dachshund-Boston terrier hybrid, 132, 133
Mice, dwarf, 3–5
Midget types, (see dwarfism)
Motor, neurones, of spine, loss of, 25–27
  reflex, (see under conditioned reflexes)
Muscle degeneration, due to loss of motor neurones, 26–27

Mutation, dog breed establishment through, 36
and evolution, 24–28
growth distortions due to, 124–125
possible effect of, on behavior, 639

## N

Neurosis, experimental, thyroid feeding and, 670–672, **671**
training and, 672–675
Newfoundland dog, 13

## O

Oestrus, effect of, on behavior, 659–662, **660, 661**
Osteitis fibrosa cystica, 479–480
Ovariectomy, effect of, on behavior, 738–739

## P

Palate, formation of, 182–183
relation of, to skull type, 184–186, **185**
Paralysis, hereditary, of thigh muscles, in dog, 25–27
Parathyroid, and bone formation, 475, 478–480, 514
and calcium formation, 475, 478–480, 514
characteristics of, in bassethound, 515, **516**
and body form, 481–488, 518–522
in Boston terrier, 481, 483
in dachshund, 481, 483
in English bulldog, 477, 516, 517–518
in great Dane, 477
in St. Bernard, 477
extract of, effect of, on behavior, 697–699
general discussion of, 475–481, 514
histological technique for, 423
inheritance of, in bassethound-English bulldog hybrids, 516, 518–522, **521**
in dachshund-Boston terrier hybrids, 481–488, **483, 487**
and osteitis fibrosa cystica, 479–480
and rickets, 475, 478
size of, 477
and tetany, 478–479
thyro-parathyroidectomy, effect of, on behavior, 699–709, **705, 707**
Pavlov, behavioral types of, discussion of, 572–575
Pekingese, general characteristics of, 9, 10, 14–15, **41, 137, 139, 336, 343–344, 345, 362, 429**
jaw growth in, 357
leg characteristics of, **139**

SUBJECT INDEX 769

origin and antiquity of, 36, 47, 125, 336, 343–344
skull of, general characteristics in, 336, 343–348, 345, 347, 355, 359, 363, 364
  indices and measurements in, 208, 210–211
thyroid of, 429, 431, 434

Pekingese-Saluki hybrids, (see Saluki-Pekingese hybrids)

Pekingese, sleeve, 9

Physical abnormalities, significance of, among types, 629

Piget index, 600

Pincher, 9, 14

Pituitary, bone marrow in, 451, 455
cell distribution in, 450–453
characteristics of, in bassethound, 417, 503, 505
  and body form, 458–474, 506–513
  in Boston terrier, 415, 456–458, 459
  in dachshund, 415, 448–456, 451, 459
  in English bulldog, 417, 501–505, 503
  in great Dane, 418, 419
  in man, 416–419, 450–452, 502
  in St. Bernard, 418, 419
cysts in, 454
extract of anterior lobe of, effect of, on behavior, 709–710
general discussion of, 448–456, 500–504
hereditary deficiency of, 4
histological technique for, 423
hypophysectomy, total, effect of, on behavior, 705, 710–720, 713, 714, 715, 720
  and pituitary transplants, effect of, on behavior, 717–719
  and thyroid extract, effect of, on behavior, 714, 716–719, 720
  of posterior lobe, effect of, on behavior, 719–721
inheritance of, in bassethound-English bulldog hybrids, 417, 419, 420, 503, 505–513, 509
  in dachshund-Boston terrier hybrids, 415, 419–420, 458–474, 459, 463, 472
  in St. Bernard-great Dane hybrids, 418, 419–420
removal of, method of, at autopsy, 414
rôle of, in growth, 4–5, 13, 16, 25, 27, 325–327, 332–335
size of, proportional, in pure breeds and hybrids, 414–420, 415, 417, 418
  related to thyroid size, 416
weight of, in man, 416–419
  method of determining, 414
  relation of, to body size, 419–420
  variability of, 419

Pointer, 9, 36, 39, 208

Pomeranian, 9, 14

Puberty, 19

Pug, 9, 10, 39

## R

Rabbit, 22

Racial hybridization, 37–38, 122, 358, 491

Ram, ancon, 22

Reactions, negative, (see conditioned reflexes)

Reptiles, 23

Restlessness in dog, adrenalin and, 724, 726
  training and, 672–675

Rickets, 339–342, 475, 478

## S

St. Bernard, general characteristics of, 9, 13, **41**
  parathyroid of, 477
  pituitary of, **418**, 419
  skull of, general characteristics in, 326
    indices and measurements in, 208, 214–215, **214**
  thyroid of, 406–408, **407**, 430–434, **431**, **433**, 438

St. Bernard-great Dane hybrids, dental occlusion in, establishment of, 373–376, **375**
  jaw growth in, 373–376, **375**
  pituitary of, **418**, 419–420
  thyroid of, **407**, 443

Saluki, association of, with man, 70–71
  behavior of, in conditioned avoiding situation, 577, 578–590
    in conditioned salivary situation, 553–560, **556**
    and endocrine glands, 633
  general characteristics of, 9, 10, 31, 39, **41**, 69–72, 73, 83, 137, 139, 362, 599
  leg characteristics of, 71, **73**, 83, 104, **107**, 139
  origin and antiquity of, 31, 69–70
  skull of, general characteristics in, 233, 363, **364**, 367–368, **369**
    indices and measurements in, 208, 210–211, **212**, 213

Saluki-bassethound hybrids, (see bassethound-Saluki hybrids)

Saluki-Pekingese hybrids, general characteristics of, 139, 362, **365**, 367
  jaw inheritance in, 361–367
  leg inheritance in, 137, 138, 139
  skull characteristics of, 361–367, 363, **364**, **365**

Sensory differences among dogs, 10

Setter, 9, 36, 39

Sex, differences in skull type, 207
  pituitary weight and, 416–419
  ratios, unusual, in bassethound-Saluki litters, 74–75
  thyroid size and, 404

SUBJECT INDEX 771

Sheep, 22, 360

Sheep dog, 10

Shock, method of evaluating, 581
 reaction of behavioral types to, 581

Shoulder joint, dislocation of, in bulldog, 92-94

Size, behavior and, relation of, 625-629, 639
 differences in, among dogs, 9-10
 effect of, on conditioned salivary response, 558-569
 inheritance of, in bassethound-dachshund hybrids, 327-328, 329
 pituitary weight and, 449
 variations in, in hybrids of normal sized parents, 118-122, 321, 322-325, 323, 324

Skin overgrowth, in bassethound-English bulldog hybrids, 328-335, 331, 333

Skull, (see also jaws)
 bulldog typed, 205-217, 216, 272-295, 285, 313-314
   in man, 276-284, 277, 279
 characteristics of, in bassethound, 208, 299-304, 316, 318, 319, 321, 329, 356, 368, 369
 and behavior, relation of, 151, 273
 in Boston terrier, 208, 215-217, 216, 221, 226-232, 227, 229, 231, 233, 239, 245, 251, 254, 257, 258, 276
 in Brussels griffon, 9, 135, 208, 210-211, 274-276, 275, 336, 338, 435
 in Chow, 208
 in Cocker spaniel, 208
 complexity of, 149-152, 224-226, 294-295, 339, 359
 in dachshund, 208, 214-215, 214, 226-232, 229, 231, 239, 245, 251, 254, 257, 258, 261, 265, 267, 268, 270, 271, 329, 338, 345, 346, 347, 355
 in English bulldog, 208, 215-220, 216, 219, 221, 273-274, 275, 290, 299-301, 302, 305, 308-310, 311, 316, 318, 319, 321, 356
 in foxhound, 212, 213
 in French bulldog, 208, 215-217, 216, 259, 261, 265, 268, 270, 271
 in German shepherd, 153, 155, 208, 210-211, 212, 213, 217-220, 219, 221, 273-274, 275, 290, 302
 in great Dane, 208, 214-215, 214
 in King Charles spaniel, 449
 in Labrador huskie, 208
 in long and short types, 215-224, 221, 273-276, 275
 in Maltese poodle, 208, 435
 in man, 150, 273, 276-284, 277, 279, 283, 285, 358, 370-372, 371
 in Pekingese, 208, 210-211, 336, 343-348, 345, 347, 355, 359, 363, 364
 in pointer, 208
 in puppies, 283, 284-287, 285, 373
 in St. Bernard, 208, 214-215, 214, 326

in Saluki, 208, 210–211, 212, 213, 233, 363, 364, 367–368, 369
    sex differences in, 207
growth of, in man, 280–284
    in puppies, 284–287, 283
indices of, (see also skull characteristics of pure breeds and skull inheritance
        in hybrids)
    and dental occlusion, relation of, 376–382, 377, 378, 379, 380, 381, 383
    method of determining, 154, 207
inheritance of, in dog hybrids, bassethound-dachshund, 329
    bassethound-English bulldog, 285, 304–325, 305, 308, 310, 311, 316, 318, 319,
        321, 323, 324, 326, 356
    bassethound-Saluki, 285, 367–370, 369, 371
    dachshund-Boston terrier, 227, 229, 231, 232–259, 236, 238, 239, 245, 247, 248,
        251, 254, 257, 258
    dachshund-Brussels griffon, 337–343, 338, 340, 341
    dachshund-French bulldog, 260–272, 261, 263, 264, 265, 268, 270, 271
    dachshund-Pekingese, 345, 347, 348–354, 350, 352, 355
    English bulldog-German shepherd, 289–295, 290, 293, 371
    St. Bernard-great Dane, 285, 373–376, 375
    Saluki-Pekingese, 361–367, 363, 364, 365
measurements of, auditory meatus to bregma, 186, 187
    auditory meatus to internasal suture, 187–189, 189, 193–196, 194, 197
    auditory meatus to nasion, 187–188, 188, 193, 193
    auditory meatus to superior dental alveolus, 190, 191, 193–199, 195, 198
    auditory meatus to supraoccipital spine, 190–192, 192
    bregma to nasion, 199, 200
    bregma to supraoccipital spine, 202–203, 203
    cranial height, 167, 168
    cranial width, 157–158, 158, 163, 164
    infraorbital foramen to incisal alveolus, 172, 172
    internasal suture to superior dental alveolus, 201–203, 202
    interorbital width, 158, 159, 165–166, 165, 166
    least frontal width, 158, 159, 163–164, 164, 166–167, 166, 168, 169, 169
    mandibular canine tips, distance between, 161–162, 161
    mandibular length, 173–175, 174, 179, 180
    mandibular premolar region, 180, 181
    mandibular premolar tooth size, 178, 178, 180, 181, 181
    mandibular thickness, 180, 180
    maxillary canine tips, distance between, 161–162, 161
    maxillary incisal alveolus width, 162, 162
    maxillary premolar region, 175, 175
    maxillary premolar tooth size, 176–178, 176, 177, 205, 205
    method of determining, 153–156, 154, 186
    nares, anterior floor of, 199, 201–202
    nasal length, 172–173, 173
    nasal width, 159, 160
    nasion to internasal suture, 200–203, 201

# SUBJECT INDEX

  palate length, 174, **171**
  palate length related to skull length, 182, **182**
    related to skull type, 184–186, **185**
  palate process related to total palate, 182–184, **183**
  palate width, 160, **160**
  skull length, 169, **170**, 203–204, **204**
    related to maxillary premolar tooth size, 203–205
  zygomatic width, 156–157, **157**
  modifications of, underlying factors in, 359–360
    and dental defects, **229**, 232–235, **233**, **262**, **265**, 278, 370–372, **371**
  nasal bones of, congenital absence of, **321**, **322**
  normal type, 152–155
  occipital crest in, 190
  premolar carrying interval of, 230
  size variations of, in bassethound English bulldog hybrids, **321**, 322–325
  type differentiation of, value of indices and measurements in, 184–186, 190, 206, 210–211, 220–224, 305–306
    and distortions, analysis of problems concerning, 225–226
  variety of, among dogs, 9, 151–152, 210–211

Species, origin of, 24, 35

Spinal motor neurones, loss of, 25–27

Stimuli, auditory, nature of, 534
    response to, 549, 558
  olfactory, nature of, 536
  tactile, nature of, 534
    response to, 549, 558, 562
  visual, response to, 549, 563

Structural changes, in evolution of species, 24–28

Structural deviations, (see also growth)
  among different species, 9–11, 19–26

Suprarenal, adrenalectomy, effect of, on behavior, 730–735, **735**
    and suprarenal cortical extract, effect of, on behavior, 730–735, **735**
  adrenalin, effect of, on behavior, 723–730
  deficiency of, and disease, 421
  histological technique for, 423

Swine, 21

## T

Tail, differences in, among dogs, 9–10
  inheritance of screwtail in bassethound English bulldog hybrids, 388–396, **390**, **393**, **395**

Teeth, (see also dental defects, dental occlusion, dentition)
  differences in, among dogs, 10
  premolar, size of, 176–178, **176**, **177**, **178**, 180–181, **181**, 205, **205**
  size of, as related to jaw size, 177–178

SUBJECT INDEX

Terrier, 10

Testes, castration, effect of, on behavior, 736–738

Tetany, 478–479

Thymus, 119, 489–490

Thyroid, and behavior, 633
  characteristics of, in bassethound, 404–406, 405, 408, 425, 428–429, 492–494, 493
    and body form, 441–446, 467–468, 494–500
    in Boston terrier, 402, 403, 408, 429–430, 431, 434, 441, 443
    in Brussels griffon, 435–436, 437
    in Cocker spaniel, 438
    in dachshund, 402–404, 403, 408, 436–438, 437, 441, 443
    in English bulldog, 404, 405, 408, 425, 426–429, 493, 494
    in foxhound, 425, 426, 428–429
    in French bulldog, 425, 428
    in German shepherd, 426, 430–432, 431, 433
    in great Dane, 406–408, 407, 437, 438
    in long and short muzzled breeds, 423–440
    in Maltese poodle, 436, 437
    in Pekingese, 429, 431, 434
    in St. Bernard, 406–408, 407, 430–434, 431, 433, 438
  extract of, effect of, on conditioned motor reflex, 666–671, 668, 670, 671
    effect of, on conditioned salivary reflex, 664–666, 672–675
  general discussion of, 401–402, 423–424
  histological technique for, 422–423
  inheritance of, in bassethound-English bulldog hybrids, 405, 412–413, 493, 494–500, 497
    in dachshund-Boston terrier hybrids, 403, 409–412, 441–447, 443, 445, 463, 467–468
    in St. Bernard-great Dane hybrids, 407, 413
  material, in dog, 401
  parafollicular cells of, 426, 427
  secretions of, growth response to, 4–5
  size of, proportional, in pure breeds and hybrids, 401–414, 403, 405, 407
    and body size, 404, 408–414
    and pituitary size, 416
    sex differences in, 404
  thyroidectomy, effect of, on behavior, 661, 677–697, 679, 686
    and thyroid feeding, effect of, on behavior, 679, 687–693, 691, 692
    partial, effect of, on behavior, 680–687, 682, 684, 686
      regeneration after and effect of, on behavior, 680–687, 684, 686
  thyro-parathyroidectomy, effect of, on behavior, 699–709, 705, 707
  volume, method of calculating, 401–402

## U

Untrainable dogs, extreme passivity in, nature of, 595-596, 597
  form of hysterical behavior in, 597, 598
  resistance of, to laboratory, 594

## W

Web toes, 27
Wolf, 32

www.ingramcontent.com/pod-product-compliance
Ingram Content Group UK Ltd.
Pitfield, Milton Keynes, MK11 3LW, UK
UKHW041404060326
11116UKWH00022B/1663